S0-AFX-899

Microcosm
AND Mediator

*The Theological Anthropology
of Maximus the Confessor*

Second Edition

Lars Thunberg

Foreword by A. M. Allchin

Open Court
Chicago and La Salle, Illinois

To order books from Open Court, call toll free 1-800-815-2280.

Cover illustration by Duccio di Buoninsegna, Italian (Sienese), active 1278–1319, *The Raising of Lazarus,* c. 1308–11, egg tempera and gold on wood, 17⅛ × 18¼ in. Photograph by Michael Bodycomb provided by the Kimbell Art Museum, Fort Worth, Texas.

Open Court Publishing Company is a division of Carus Publishing Company.

This book has been reproduced in a print-on-demand format from the 1995 Open Court printing.

© 1995 by Open Court Publishing Company

SECOND EDITION

First printing 1995

All rights reserved. No part of this publication may be reproduced, stored in a retrieval system, or transmitted, in any form or by any means, electronic, mechanical, photocopying, recording, or otherwise, without the prior written permission of the publisher, Open Court Publishing Company, 315 Fifth Street, P.O. Box 599, Peru, Illinois 61354-0599.

Printed and bound in the United States of America.

Library of Congress Cataloging-in-Publication Data

Thunberg, Lars, 1928–
    Microcosm and mediator : the theological anthropology of Maximus the Confessor / Lars Thunberg ; foreword by A.M. Allchin.—2nd ed.
      p.   cm.
    Includes bibliographical references and index.
    ISBN 0-8126-9211-X (pbk.)
    1. Maximus, Confessor, Saint, ca. 580–662. 2. Man (Christian theology) I. Allchin, A. M. II. Title.
BR65.M416T5 1995
233'.092—dc20
                                    95-16644
                                        CIP

TO THE MEMORY OF MY PARENTS

CONTENTS

FOREWORD

The republication of this book almost thirty years after its first appearance is in itself a remarkable tribute to the continuing value of Thunberg's pioneering work in this field. It is also an event of no little importance in the world of theological scholarship as a whole, for the thinker to whom it is dedicated is a man of towering significance. Maximus the Confessor needs to be seen not only in the context of the Eastern Christian tradition but in the context of the whole of historic Christianity. He is one of the outstanding figures of the Orthodox East who expresses with unrivalled authority the full balance and integrity of Byzantine thought, a writer whose name deserves to stand beside the greatest representatives of the Christian West.

When this book was in the process of being written, the theology of Maximus was much less known in the English-speaking world than it is today. The work of scholars such as John Meyendorff and Jaroslav Pelikan has done much to bring to public notice the crucial place of this thinker in the Eastern tradition, "the real Father of Byzantine theology," as Meyendorff calls him in his study *Byzantine Theology* (1974). It is significant that in the second volume of his history of the development of Christian doctrine, *The Spirit of Eastern Christendom (600–1700)*, published that same year, Pelikan should devote the whole of his opening chapter to Maximus. That chapter marks something of a turning point.

The same decade also saw the publication of a number of substantial studies in French by writers such as Garrigues, von Schönborn, Léthel, and Riou, which have advanced our appreciation of the many dimensions of the Confessor's work. All this is gain, but much remains to be done. Thunberg's work, admirable alike for the precision of its analysis and the thoroughness of its historical investigation, remains an indispensible tool for anyone who wishes to come to grips with the thought of this great but still-neglected writer.

For if it is true that Maximus is better known than he was, no one who cares about his work can feel that it has received the attention it deserves. This is at least in part due to the fact that it is not altogether easy of access. As Thunberg himself remarks, Maximus "loved clarity, and for that reason he always looked for distinct formulations. His definitions and aphorisms are admirable. But he also knew the complexities of Christian theological reflection. He often constructed his sentences like Chinese boxes which have to be opened slowly and with undisturbed attention, to reach the precious final truth he wanted to communicate to his readers." Although more of Maximus' work is now available in English, for instance in the *Classics of Western Spirituality* series and in the second volume of the ongoing English translation of *The Philokalia,* some of the most important texts remain tantalizingly inaccessible to the general reader.

Those who come to know the theology of Maximus through this study of his anthropology will surely want to turn back to Thunberg's other, briefer work, *Man and the Cosmos.* This book has as its subtitle *The Vision of Saint Maximus the Confessor.* The key word here is *vision.* For as Thunberg points out, through all its complexity there is an extraordinary unity and coherence in the thought of this theologian. "His theology was not one of different entities . . . Maximus was aware of the dangers of fragmentation. His system of theology was in fact a spiritual vision." This is a vision at once universal and all-embracing, eschatological and ultimately transcendent. Yet at the same time it touches us at every point in our ordinary daily anxieties and achievements. As Thunberg remarks at the end of the same book, what is of capital importance for Maximus is "that through the vision which we achieve for ourselves through our practical efforts and our actual experiences," we can receive from God strength and encouragement, gifts which assure us that we are on our way towards the kingdom of eternity.

It is fitting that the life of the scholar whose academic work began with this study of a Byzantine saint should have been in large part devoted, in a great variety of ways, to work for Christian unity in his own native Scandinavia, and that in the international sphere he should have made a particular contribution towards the progress of Lutheran/

Catholic dialogue. The work of theological scholarship, when it is carried on with an appropriate degree of openness to others and fidelity to the tradition, has of itself vital ecumenical implications; and to study a writer such as Maximus is to come into contact with a person whose work will hardly leave one unchanged in this regard.

A. M. ALLCHIN

PREFACE TO
THE SECOND EDITION

When I was invited to prepare a second edition of my doctoral thesis from 1965 on Saint Maximus the Confessor, for many years now not available, I realised immediately that it had to be revised due to the great amount of research devoted to Maximus in recent years. On the other hand, it was also obvious that this revision could not be but a very slight one. Otherwise, I should have had to rewrite the whole book.

Still, the anthropology of Maximus, and a strictly theological one indeed, has not been treated extensively by any other scholar thus far, so I feel confident that a new edition of my work is not out of place. I have inserted references to new research; however, this does not mean that I have felt obliged to take all smaller studies into consideration. I have further regarded it a duty to refer to those critical editions of Maximus which have appeared since 1965. I have also noted—in my bibliography —what has been published in the way of translations into different languages in recent years (as far as I am aware of them). On both these fields, very valuable and studious work has been done by Maximus scholars of different nationalities.

In this context it should be noted that generally the Migne text, on which I built my dissertation almost entirely (with the exception of the *Centuries on Charity,* where in the end I had access to A. Ceresa-Gastaldo's lifelong work on a very great number of manuscripts), seems to be fairly reliable. A necessary renumbering of the *Quaestiones et dubia,* though, was undertaken by J. H. Declerck in his critical edition; I have taken notice of that in my footnotes.

In 1985 Saint Vladimir's Seminary Press published a second book by me on Saint Maximus, entitled *Man and the Cosmos: The Theological Vision of St. Maximus the Confessor.* Twenty years had then passed since my first study, and I had had the opportunity of attending the first scholarly congress ever held on Maximus, in Fribourg, Switzerland, in 1980. I had also been invited to lead a seminar on Maximus in the Benedictine monastery of La Pierre-Qui-Vire in middle France (where monks and nuns from a wide vicinity were invited to take part); on the preparations for that course I based my book. Both these occasions manifested the considerable interest in Saint Maximus as a most outstanding Christian theologian and spiritual master, interest which had come to the fore since I first wrote about him. Such a refreshing insight has also comforted me in trying to adjust my dissertation for a reading public which might not yet be acquainted with Maximus.

There are three persons whom I want to mention at the end of this preface. The first of them is the late professor Paul Eudokimov of the Saint Sergius Theological Academy in Paris, my first Orthodox mentor and adviser, who originally called my attentioin to Saint Maximus back in 1954. The second is the late professor Father John Meyendorff of Saint Vladimir's Theological Seminary and Fordham University, who furthered my second book to print and took the initiative to recommend this revised version of my first book. Father John supported me amiably through the years, and though we never met physically, he remains in my memory as a very close friend; his regretted early departure from this world left a pain in me as in so many others. The third person I want to mention is my very old friend Father A. M. Allchin, doctor and professor h.c. He revised the English of my dissertation and wrote the foreword to the second book. (He has checked my English through the years in different contexts.) Father Donald, an outstanding representative of ecumenical Anglicanism, has conceded to write another foreword to this revised version of *Microcosm and Mediator.*

A note of gratitude thus predominates when the difficult work of a "slight" revision is now brought to an end.

Ebeltof, Denmark, in the season of Trinity 1993

Lars Thunberg

Introduction

1. Life of the Saint

Maximus the Confessor, or as he is sometimes called Maximus of Chrysopolis, was born around A.D. 580 in Constantinople and died a martyr's death in exile in Lazica on the south-east shore of the Black Sea in 662. Between these two dates there lies a life, engaged in imperial service, the pursuit of the monastic life and Church politics, equally full both of deep theological penetration and dramatic events. For our particular purpose in this thesis it is obvious that all the details of Maximus' biography are not of the same interest. We shall then only describe the general development of the Saint's life in a brief summary.

According to his ancient biographer, an unknown admirer, evidently of a date only slightly later than that of his subject,[1] Maximus was of noble descent and enjoyed a devout home life.[2] According to the same biographer he received a very good education, to which he devoted himself with deep interest and zeal, specifically engaging in the study of philosophy.[3] At this point, at least, all readers of Maximus will testify to the accuracy of his biographer, since the writings of the Saint show that his rhetorical and philosophical education must have been at the very highest level of his times.[4] According to the biography, however, his

---

[1] See R. DEVREESSE, La vie de S. Maxime le Confesseur et ses recensions, AB 46 (1928), p. 44, which dates the first redaction of this *Vita* at about the time of the VIth ecumenical council (680–81).

[2] PG 90, 69 A. This biography, *Vita ac certamen,* which, although partly mutilated, was printed already by COMBÉFIS in his edition and reprinted by MIGNE (PG 90, 68 A–109 B), is in fact, as DEVREESSE, *art. cit.,* pp. 5–49, has shown, based to a great extent on other documents belonging to the *Acta.* In addition it contains details about Maximus' youth and earlier years which cannot be confirmed by other documents and which are at such a distance from the biographer, that their source value must not be taken for granted.

[3] PG 90, 69 C.

[4] On the basis of contemporary research P. SHERWOOD has pointed out that when the biographer says, that Maximus received the ἐγκύκλιος παίδευσις, this would mean, that his training lasted from about his sixth or seventh year till his twenty-first, and contained grammar, classical literature, rhetoric and philosophy (including arithmetic, music, geometry, astronomy, logic, ethics, dogmatics and metaphysics), and also that it must have

progress in virtue was as admirable as his philosophical understanding,[5] and his good reputation in different respects finally attracted the attention of the Emperor Heraclius, who made him his first secretary.[6]

After a comparatively short time, however, Maximus left the palace and entered a monastery in Chrysopolis on the Asian shore just opposite Constantinople. There his zeal for an ascetic life was highly rewarded and aroused new admiration among his fellow monks.[7] This must have taken place about 613—14.[8] This date is of importance for the question of his motivation for leaving the court and becoming a monk. For if this date is correct—and the scholars seem to be in agreement on it, at present—it can hardly be correct that Maximus decided to enter the monastery on account of the growth of monothelitism, the motivation suggested by the biographer.[9] Even if monothelitism—in the form of monenergism—may be traced back as far as before 619,[10] it cannot have had any important impact by the time Maximus became a monk, according to our chronology. Thus, if this dating is correct, Maximus must have had another motivation. In fact his biographer indicates it, as

---

included his first contact with Aristotle and the Neo-Platonists (through the commentaries of Proclus and Iamblichus). See SHERWOOD, Notes on Maximus the Confessor, *Amer. Benedictine Review I* (1950), p. 347 f. and IDEM, *An Annotated Date-list of the Works of Maximus the Confessor*, (SA 30) Rome 1952, p. 1 f. This influence is reflected throughout Maximus' writings.

[5] PG 90, 72 A.

[6] PG 90, 72 C. The biographer goes on to tell us, that Maximus was very gifted in realizing the demands of the situation, able to give good advice and well prepared to express his opinion without delay. Thus both the emperor and the court rejoiced in his presence and were deeply impressed by the man.

[7] PG 90, 72 D–73 A. The biographer tells that he maltreated his body, not only through fasting and other exercises, but also by standing upright in prayer all the night through.

[8] An older chronology, constructed by E. MONTMASSON (La Chronologie de la vie de Saint Maxime le Confesseur, EO 13 (1910), pp. 149–54) placed his entry into the monastery as late as 630, but was convincingly refuted by V. GRUMEL, (Notes d'histoire et de chronologie sur la vie de Saint Maxime le Confesseur, EO 26 (1927), pp. 24–32). The latter has established that *Relatio motionis*, one of the *Acta*, included in the first Migne volume, written by Maximus' disciple Anastasius and presenting the narrative of Maximus' first trial before the tribunal of the imperial palace (see for this source also DEVREESSE, AB 46, 1928, p. 8), shows that the disciple Anastasius at this time, in 655, had been with his master for 37 years, i.e. since 618. If we allow for some time in the monastery before Maximus was joined by his disciple, we thus arrive at about 613–14 (PG 90, 128 C and GRUMEL, *art. cit.,* p. 25). This has been accepted by later scholars. Cf. H. URS VON BALTHASAR, *Kosmische Liturgie*[1], *Maximus der Bekenner: Höhe und Krisis des griechischen Weltbildes,* Freiburg i. Br. 1941, p. 35 f. and n. 48, and e.g. SHERWOOD, *Amer. Ben. Rev.* I (1950), p. 349.

[9] PG 90, 72 C: monothelite doctrine distorted the Church.

[10] Cf. M. JUGIE, *art.* Monothélisme, DTC 10: 2, Paris 1929, col. 2316.

Sherwood has pointed out.[11] He had been longing for a life of ἡσυχία.[12] We may conclude that there may have been circumstances in Constantinople which strengthened this inclination, though there seems to have been no change in his good relations with the court, as is clearly shown by his frequent and very friendly letters to John the Chamberlain.

In this context it would also seem to be of some importance that the biographer, in describing Maximus' life in the monastery, does not at all stress his supposed fight against heresy, but rather his remarkable advancement in ascetic practices and his devotional life.[13] In the biography this leads up to an account of how his fellow monks, deeply impressed by his religious zeal, ardently tried to make him their hegoumen and finally succeeded in persuading him to accept charge over them, though with some reservations on his part. This story seems however to be inaccurate.[14]

One of the reasons for being sceptical in relation to the biographer's note about Maximus' hegoumenate is the fact that—to judge from other evidence—we find that this period of his life must have contained an outstanding literary activity, which such an administrative, or at least pastoral, charge in his own monastery, would hardly have permitted; though, on the other hand, it must be said that he shows in his writing a considerable insight into the pastoral problems of a monastic community.

How long he stayed in his monastery we do not exactly know, nor whether he moved from his first monastery to another. Here it may therefore be sufficient to point out that we find him at least in 632 in Africa (Carthage) as a final result of his forced departure from his

---

[11] SHERWOOD, *An Annotated Date-list*, p. 2.

[12] SHERWOOD, *Amer. Ben. Rev.* I (1950), p. 348, has given the expression καθ᾽ ἡσυχίαν a somewhat too definite interpretation in translating it "the Hesychast life" and commenting upon it, that although this may seem to "crystallize into a doctrine what was as yet only a tendency", to speak of the "solitary" or monastic life would miss all the overtones, (n. 10). He has later—perhaps—modified his statement by writing "life of solitude (the hesychast life)", *An Annotated Date-list*, p. 2.

[13] PG 90, 72 D–73 A.

[14] As a whole it is very doubtful, whether Maximus ever held any office or was other than an ordinary, if venerable monk. The other tradition may be a fruit of pious imagination, built on the fact that Maximus is known to have been called "abbas" Maximus. GRUMEL, EO 26 (1927), p. 32 has pointed out that in many instances Maximus is presented simply as a monk; so in Pyrrh: εὐλαβέστατος μοναχός (PG 91, 288 A); among the 37 signatures of a petition that the acts of the Lateran council be available in Greek: *Maximus monachus* (at the age of about 70); in the *Acta* of Maximus, in relation to his being brought to Rhegion (PG 90, 160 C); in the inscription of most of his works. VON BALTHASAR, on his part, has been so convinced by this argumentation, that—already in KL¹—he simply states: "Abt ist er nicht gewesen" (p. 36).

monastery on account of the invasions of the Persians, who in 626 had reached Constantinople.[15] He may have arrived there some time earlier. The part of his curriculum which covers the years 626–32 is rather difficult to reconstruct, but Sherwood may be right in assuming, that Maximus stayed for a time in Crete and perhaps even in Cyprus.[16] In Carthage he probably stayed in a monastery called Euchratas which had as its abbot Sophronius, who in 634 was elected patriarch of Jerusalem and was the first to fight the monothelite heresy.[17] Maximus seems to have dwelt with Sophronius in this monastery for some time, before the latter left for Alexandria to participate in the discussions which took place there on the Tome of Union in 633.[18]

From about 634[19] Maximus himself was, however, deeply involved in

[15] Concerning the time of Maximus' establishment in Africa MONTMASSON, EO 13 (1910), p. 153 had the impression that he left his convent temporarily for Alexandria in 633 and definitely for Africa in 640. GRUMEL, EO 26 (1927), pp. 24–32, is not quite sure about the date but thinks about 633. The question was, however, definitely settled by DEVREESSE, (La fin inédite d'une lettre de Saint Maxime: Un baptême forcé des Juifs et des Samaritains à Carthage en 632, RSRUS 17 (1937), pp. 25–35) who published the unedited final paragraphs of Maximus' Ep 8, from which he was able to conclude that Maximus was referring to the forced baptism of Jews and Samaritans which took place at Pentecost 632 in Africa as a result of a decision by emperor Heraclius, and thus to prove that Maximus must have been in Africa at least by that time. For the invasion of the Persians as the reason of his flight from the monastery, see the arguments put forward by GRUMEL, *art. cit.*, p. 26; cf. IDEM, Maxime le Confesseur, DTC 10: 1, Paris 1928, col. 449, and DEVREESSE, *art. cit.*, p. 32, n. 1. The information given by the ancient biographer, that Maximus left his monastery for Africa for the same reason, for which he had entered it: monothelitism, does not deserve serious consideration (PG 90, 76 A). The Saint himself indicates another situation in his letters 28, 29 and 31 to bishop John of Cyzicus (?). (See PG 91, 620–621, 621–624 and 624–625 and for the question of their correspondent SHERWOOD, *An Annotated Date-list*, p. 27.)

[16] In ThPol 3; PG 91, 49 C Maximus tells us that once he had had a dispute with Severian bishops in Crete, and a stop in Cyprus might be inferred from the correspondence which the Saint had with the Cypriot Marinus, see SHERWOOD, *An Annotated Date-list*, p. 5.

[17] SHERWOOD has established with considerable evidence this early relationship with Sophronius and seems to have shown that the absence of Sophronius, who had gone to take part in the affair of the Pact of Union in Alexandria, is the reason for Maximus' renewed interest in being brought back to his former monastery, expressed in Ep 8 (PG 91, 440 C–445 B), which is, then, not addressed to Sophronius but to John of Cyzicus, as two manuscripts seem to indicate. See SHERWOOD, *An Annotated Date-list*, p. 28 ff. VON BALTHASAR, KL², p. 67 f., takes a somewhat unclear position on this matter, when he accepts the general position of SHERWOOD but—without comment—preserves the traditional idea of Ep 8 as being addressed to Sophronius. On a possible Palestinian provenience, see S. BROCK, An Early Syriac Life of Maximus Confessor, AB 91 (1973), pp. 299–346. See also J. STARR, St. Maximos and the Forced Baptism at Carthage in 632, BNJ 16(1940), pp. 192–196. On Sophronius, see Chr. VON SCHÖNBORN, *Sophrone de Jérusalem*, Paris 1972.

[18] See MANSI, XI, coll. 564–568; cf. C. J. HEFELE, *Conciliengeschichte* 3, Freiburg i Br. 1858, p. 126 ff.

[19] Cf. VON BALTHASAR, KL², p. 71.

the monothelite controversies, and the rest of his life was to be entirely shaped by the clarity and rigidity of his dyothelite position. As his theological importance in this field and the development of his thinking in regard to monothelitism will be treated to some extent in the second section of this introductory chapter, it may, at this particular stage of our presentation, be sufficient just to sketch in the main facts of this involvement and the most important events of his life which resulted from it.

Maximus must have stayed in Africa as a monk for quite a long time. We have no indications to suggest that he left his monastery there for some years. He had good and close relations with the imperial governors of Africa, such as Peter the Illustrious and George, covering the time from about 634[20] to about 642/3.[21]

The Emperor Heraclius had died in 641, and his successor Constans tried to settle the monothelite controversy by editing a *Typos,* written by the patriarch of Constantinople, Paul II, in 647;[22] but before that in 645 Maximus—probably in Carthage—held his successful dispute with Pyrrhus, the predecessor of Paul, who was then in exile. This dispute resulted in Pyrrhus' return to orthodoxy and his recognition as patriarch by the Roman See, although Pyrrhus already in 646 again changed his mind.[23] From the *Relatio motionis* we also know that Maximus was in Rome in 646 together with Pyrrhus.[24] Another result of the dispute may have been the fact that several African councils in the summer of 646 took their standpoint against monothelitism.[25] The imperial *Typos,* however, changed the situation definitely. The policy of Constantinople had become, more clearly than before, not only unfavourable but dangerous to Maximus' position. On the side of Rome he had now to fight for orthodoxy, as he saw it.

Maximus stayed in Rome. Pope Theodore excommunicated Pyrrhus

---

[20] Ep 13, PG 91, 509 B–533 A; cf. SHERWOOD, *An Annotated Date-list,* p. 39 f.

[21] According to SHERWOOD, *op. cit.,* p. 52 the excerpts of a letter to Peter, given in ThPol 12; PG 91, 141 A–146 A, can be dated to 643/4 and the letter itself to 642/3; while e.g. in a letter to John the Chamberlain from the winter of 642, Ep 44; PG 91, 641 D–648 C, Maximus deplores the recent departure from Africa of its beloved eparch George; cf. SHERWOOD, *op. cit.,* p. 49 f.

[22] For this date, see W. M. PEITZ, Martin I. und Maximus Confessor, HJG 38 (1917), p. 219, and DEVREESSE, AB 46 (1928), p. 44.

[23] See PEITZ, *art. cit.,* p. 213 ff. VON BALTHASAR, KL², p. 71 agrees that the dispute took place in Carthage. SHERWOOD, *An Annotated Date-list,* p. 18, n. 81, however, underlines that, although this is true, to take the interlocutors of Maximus in *Relatio motionis* (PG 90, 120 C) literally, one would have to assume that their discussions took place in Rome as well.

[24] PG 90, 112 C; cf. SHERWOOD, *op. cit.,* p. 18.

[25] See MANSI, X, col. 761/2 ff. and PEITZ, *art. cit.,* p. 215 f.

when he changed his mind again, but in Constantinople the latter was later (in 652) reintroduced as patriarch. The complete break between Rome and Constantinople was a fact.[26]

The new pope, Martin I, went even further than Theodore and, inspired by Maximus, called a Lateran Council together in 649, at which Maximus was probably present as a simple monk and an old man.[27] This council condemned the monothelite heresy, and punishment was promised to those adhering to it. The decisions were sent around the whole Christian world.[28] The emperor Constans reacted at once, but the exarch, who had been sent to Rome, joined the papal party, and so the Pope (and probably Maximus) was not arrested until 653. They were both brought to Constantinople, where the trial of the Pope took place in 654. The latter was sent in exile to Cherson in 655, and died in September of the same year.[29]

The trial of Maximus—together with his disciple Anastasius—however, did not take place until May 655. The exact date of his arrival in Constantinople is thus not quite clear.[30] It seems even, as though the authorities had tried to fix political crimes upon him rather than heresies[31]—an attitude quite in line with the imperial attempt to favour "watery unions". These efforts failed completely; as did efforts to present Maximus' refusal to communicate with the See of Constantinople on account of the *Typos* as a decisive crime, for which he ought to repent. Maximus was sent for a temporary exile to Bizya in Thrace.[32] A new attempt to persuade him to a more conciliatory attitude was made as early as 656, at Bizya itself, by a court bishop, Theodosius, who had been sent by Peter, the new patriarch of Constantinople. But Maximus did not change his mind.[33] On the 8th of September (according to the *Acta*) Maximus was called to the monastery of St. Theodore at Rhegion, where he was again tempted to surrender to the will of the Emperor, but

---

[26] Cf. DEVREESSE, AB 46 (1928), p. 17.

[27] MANSI, X, col. 910. On the Synod, see R. RIEDINGER, Die Latheransynode . . . , in HEINZER-SCHÖNBORN, *Maximus Confessor . . .* , pp. 111–121.

[28] MANSI, X, coll. 863–1170; cf. PEITZ, *art. cit.,* p. 220 f.

[29] See PEITZ, *art. cit.,* p. 225 f. and DEVREESSE, *art. cit.,* p. 23, n. 1. On the theological implications of this whole process of conflict, see LÉTHEL, *Théologie de l'agonie du Christ . . .* , pp. 103–121.

[30] See PEITZ, *art. cit.,* p. 226 ff.

[31] Cf. L. BRÉHIER in A. FLICHE & V. MARTIN (ed.), *Histoire de l'Église* 5, Paris 1938, p. 173 (cf. p. 171).

[32] The trial is related in *Relatio motionis* (PG 90, 109 C–129 C) and shows indirectly not only the firmness of Maximus' convictions but also his influence and position. For the content and tradition of this account, see also DEVREESSE, *art. cit.* pp. 27–33.

[33] This dispute is related in the second tome of the *Acta* (PG 90, 136 D–172 B).

refused.[34] He was then sent into exile a second time to another place in Thrace, Perberis, where he remained for six years.[35]

Accompanied by Anastasius the apocrisiarios and Anastasius the monk, Maximus was, however, brought back to Constantinople in 662, where a council was held. There he and his disciples were anathematised and condemned to a new exile.[36] The council was now clearly monothelite.[37] The tongues and the right hands of the condemned were probably amputated and they were sent to Lazica on the south east shore of the Black Sea, where Maximus broken by ill treatment and age, died on the 13th of August of the same year (662). His victory was soon to be won but he himself could no longer take part in it.[38]

2. *Maximus' historical and theological importance*

The general evaluation of Maximus' contribution to the history of Christian thinking has to a very great extent followed the intentions of the *Vita:* Maximus is seen as the defender of the Chalcedonian faith in relation to the problem of the wills of Christ, laying the foundations of the decisions of the sixth ecumenical council (680). He is the classical enemy of monothelitism. Even in modern patristic presentations this generalizing picture has not quite disappeared.[39]

---

[34] PG 90, 160 D ff.; cf. DEVREESSE, *art. cit.,* p. 35 f.

[35] See e.g. SHERWOOD, *An Annotated Date-list,* p. 21 f.

[36] For the procedure of this council, see the fragment published in MANSI, XI, coll. 73–76, and the account of Macarius to be read in MANSI, XI, col. 357.

[37] See the judgment by SHERWOOD, *op. cit.,* p. 22.

[38] The death of the Saint is related in the letter by Anastasius the apocrisiarios to the presbyter Theodosius (PG 90, 174 AB) and in the *Hypomnesticon* 5, DEVREESSE, AB 53 (1935), p. 75, 20 ff.

[39] An evaluation of Maximus based mainly on his fight for dyothelitism is recognizable in older works of patristic theology or Ancient Church history. As late as in O. BARDENHEWER, *Geschichte der altkirchlichen Literatur* 5, Freiburg-i.-Br., 1932, we read the following words: "Er hat sein ganzes Können, glänzende Geistesgaben und unverwüstliche Ausdauer und schliesslich auch sein Leben dem Dyotheletismus geweiht" (p. 28). Another manner of understanding Maximus in relation to his controversy with the monothelites is expressed in Harnack's idea, that for the sake of scholasticism Maximus did not want to abandon the complicated formulas about the two natures and the two wills in the *one* Person, into the depths of which he had penetrated (A. HARNACK, *Dogmengeschichte* 2⁴, Tübingen 1909, p. 431). It may also be added that R. SEEBERG, when stating in *Lehrbuch der Dogmengeschichte* 2, Erlangen-Leipzig 1923, p. 295, that Maximus has a Christology which is close to that of the Antiochenes and thus is of a particular importance, bases his opinion almost entirely on *Disp. c. Pyrrh.,* a first hand document from the monothelite controversy.

On the other hand, this tendency in older patristic literature does not, of course, exclude a wider evaluation. A good example of this is to be found in E. PREUSCHEN—O. KRÜGER, *Handbuch der Kirchengeschichte* I², Tübingen 1923, where Maximus is treated under the headline "Dyotheletische Schriftsteller" but where we also learn that the

Confessor enriched Christian exegesis and ascetics and widely influenced the theology and mysticism of a later time (p. 249). Far more interesting, however, is the article by J. A. WAGENMANN (finished after his death by SEEBERG), Maximus Konfessor, RE 12, Leipzig 1903, p. 470, where Maximus is characterized by e.g. the following words: "einer der achtungswürdigsten und grössten christlichen Denker und Dulder aller Zeiten", though JOHN CHAPMAN, Maximus of Constantinople, CE 10, London-New York 1911, p. 78 is probably more representative of the older evaluation of Maximus, when expressed in its most generous way. Chapman summarizes: ". . . one of the chief names in the Monothelite controversy, one of the chief doctors of the theology of the Incarnation and of ascetic mysticism, and remarkable as a witness to the respect for the papacy held by the Greek Church in his day." From the articles, now mentioned, we may conclude that in older patristic literature Maximus is evaluated mainly from what were at that time regarded as three well-established facts: Maximus' contribution to Christological theology is best expressed in his dyothelite writings, while his scholies to Ps.-Denis show his interpretation of mystical theology, and his ascetic contributions are mainly to be drawn from the Centuries. (To these three the Roman Catholics added Maximus' relation to the Pope in Rome.) All these three "established facts" have, however, been seriously affected by later research (see the last section of this chapter), while at the same time more detailed studies of other works of the Confessor have shown the far wider range of his importance and position. This has, of course, also influenced the general opinions, expressed in modern patristic surveys.

    Above all, a change of accent takes place. We note it clearly even in the careful formulations of H.-G. BECK in RGG³, 4, Tübingen 1960, col. 814, where we read that Maximus is one of the most important Byzantine theologians, and this importance refers equally to the fate of Monothelitism, to exegesis and to the development of ascetic mysticism.

    The title of J. HEINTJES' introductory article in StC 11 (1935), pp. 175–200: "Een onbekende leeraar van ascese en mystiek: Sint Maximus Confessor" is characteristic of the situation at this time. The attitude to the Saint, which was here presented, was felt as something revolutionary and new. Thus, it is hardly surprising that a somewhat polemical tone may be recognized in the statements of K. FRIZ, Maximus Confessor, EvKL 2, Göttingen 1958, col. 1275, where we learn that Maximus' primary importance does not lie in the field of the monothelite controversy but in the "Fruchtbarmachung der Lehre von der *Vergottung des Kosmos* in Mystik und Liturgie" (with a reference to the 5th ed. of HARNACK's *Lehrbuch der Dogmengeschichte,* p. 450 ff.). This new evaluation is also presented in K. BIHLMEYER—H. TÜCHLE, *Kirchengeschichte* I¹⁶, Paderborn 1958, p. 432, where Maximus is characterized as a scholar, a dialectician and a mystic, to some extent the creator of a dogmatically founded Byzantine mysticism and a forerunner of the later scholastics of the Middle Ages. And in LThK² 7, Freiburg 1962, A. CERESA-GASTALDO, who is an expert on the manuscript tradition of Maximus' works, expresses the conviction that the Confessor is the most important Greek theologian of the 7th century, without laying any particular stress on his struggle with monothelitism.

    To underline this change in the scholarly evaluation of Maximus is, however, not to say that a complete revolution had taken place. GRUMEL's studies in monothelitism (Recherches sur l'histoire du monothélisme, EO 27, 1928–29, 1930) pointed to the problems of a doctrinal development in the works of Maximus, and VON BALTHASAR's discussion of the reasons behind this development still show a certain tendency to regard the problem of monothelitism as a necessary point of entrance into the complexity of Maximus' theology. Though we are not going to deny this absolutely, we think nonetheless that the fact, that this is as it were taken for granted by many scholars, shows the continued influence of the older evaluation. B. ALTANER, in his *Patrologie* (5th revised edition), is a good example of this tendency; he characterizes Maximus as the most outstanding Greek theologian of the 7th Century and the scholarly refuter of monothelitism. Maximus' works also reveal him as a

In our presentation, the fact of this particular position of Maximus will, of course, not be underestimated, but it is our intention to add further evidence to support the conviction that other aspects of Maximus' theology and contribution—or better the wider context of his thinking—have been somewhat overshadowed by this concentration of attention on his dispute with monothelitism. It is rather in virtue of his work of synthesizing and correcting the teaching of the earlier theological tradition, that he was capable of establishing the orthodox solution of the monothelite question which was not officially proclaimed until after his death.

Related to our basic attitude there is, however, also a certain scepticism about all attempts to demonstrate any change of a profound or revolutionary character in Maximus' theology. In our conviction Maximus' theology reveals rather a natural and logical development on the basis of a general Chalcedonian conviction, which is never seriously doubted or shaken. Our intention is thus, among other things, to make clear that this is no less true in relation to the monothelite propositions, however indifferent or uncertain Maximus may seem to have been about them in the first instance.

Such a statement involves a certain criticism of positions taken by scholars like Grumel and von Balthasar (in KL[1]), who have elaborated various theories of a crisis or readjustment on the part of Maximus. For our purpose in this introduction it may perhaps be sufficient to indicate the main lines of their discussions, since the solution of this problem affects our general picture of the theological significance and personality of the Confessor.

First of all, V. Grumel[40] has correctly shown, that Maximus in his first known reactions to monothelitism (or better: at that time monenergism), i.e. in his Letter to Pyrrhus,[41] seems to be favourable to the later heretic and at least refuses to take a firm standpoint for or against one or two energies in Christ. But he has also shown that this was to some extent true even of Sophronius—monk and patriarch, later regarded as the first promotor of dyothelitism—in his synodal letter of 634, because both seem to respect the *Psephos* of Sergius, patriarch of Constantinople, forbidding any mentioning of one or two wills.[42]

---

penetrating dogmatician and a deep-sighted mystic, who also devoted his time to exegetical and liturgical questions. He underlines that Maximus' struggle did not concern monothelitism until after 642, but it seems to be presupposed, that Maximus' theological endeavour had its inner culmination in the fight against this doctrine (see p. 484).

[40] See esp. his third article on the history of monothelitism in EO 28 (1929), pp. 19–34.
[41] Ep 19; PG 91, 589–597.
[42] See the summarizing statement in GRUMEL, *art. cit.*, p. 34.

So far there is in itself no problem. But Grumel also underlines the fact that in Maximus' letter the human will is completely left in the background, and that he speaks only of the divine will in this connection. For it is to him the divine will which is predominant, and—to him as to Sophronius—it is a *moral* oneness which should be professed. Thus in this connection one gets the impression that the existence of two wills in Christ is not yet of any interest to Maximus, and that he is not yet clear about his own position in regard to monothelitism. This at least is a conclusion which has been drawn by some scholars, based on the results of Grumel's work.[43]

But against this tendency to mark a difference of weight and interest in Maximus' theology between an earlier and a later time it should be argued, that the two wills of Christ in fact played a far more important role already in Maximus' earlier writings (such as e.g. Ep 2), though they are in a way regarded as self-evident. Put in the wider context of his general theology of man's sanctification and deification Maximus' view on this point can be made clear already from the beginning. It is his terminology which is later more clearly defined and not his theology. The stress which Grumel puts on the hesitation of Maximus before entering the discussion, has undoubtedly, to some extent, coloured the general picture of Maximus' position in later writing.[44]

This is remarkable, and it remains one of the aims of this study to show—as Sherwood has to some extent already done—that there is a very considerable degree of consistency in Maximus' theology from the

---

[43] So HEINTJES, *art. cit.*, p. 177, where it is said that Maximus around 633–34 is not yet quite involved in the matter of dispute. He was said to have given a vague answer to the questions of Pyrrhus, and not until 640 to have found his clear direction, and only then to have broken entirely with Pyrrhus. Besides, GRUMEL, DTC 10: 1, col. 449, has himself to some extent confirmed this impression in his article on Maximus, since he underlines that Maximus in his letter to Pyrrhus praises Sergius the patriarch, and adds that this shows that Maximus had not yet entered the fight against the new doctrine. Until 640–41 he thus fights only against monophysitism (col. 449).

[44] Already E. CASPAR, Die Lateransynode von 649, ZKG 51 (1932), p. 102, n. 61, however criticized Grumel's tendency—in relation to Honorius this time—to minimize the crucial character of the positions taken already at an early stage of the debate, and he also showed, that Maximus' decisive distinction between ἐνέργεια and ἐνέργημα in this context may be traced back through his writings, and is at least anticipated in his letter to Pyrrhus, see *art. cit.*, p. 96, n. 49. Cf. too SHERWOOD, in ACW, who also criticizes Grumel's position and says that the later *Ambigua* and the letter to Pyrrhus, which are both not much later than the year 634, are the first clear indications of Maximus' non-acceptance of monenergism (p. 14 f.), while ThPol 20 (by 640) is the first datable antimonothelite document by Maximus—and not the letter to Peter about Pyrrhus from 643, as Grumel had suggested (p. 21). Sherwood underlines at the same time the very close connection—in the theology both of the epoch and of Maximus—between dogmatic and ascetic viewpoints.

first ascetic writings onwards, even though Maximus develops his terminology and concentrates his attention on the problem of the will in the course of the Christological dispute, in which he plays such an important rôle.

H. Urs von Balthasar brought up the problem of a possible crisis in the life and thinking of Maximus in relation to his study of the two so called *Gnostic Centuries,* which he proved to be correctly attributed to Maximus.[45] According to von Balthasar, in the first part of his monastic life Maximus underwent such a strong Origenistic influence, reflected in the Centuries, that we must speak of a crisis.[46] Against this hypothesis Sherwood has provided the strongest argument by showing that already the earlier *Ambigua,* which he dates to about 634, but which he thinks were conceived earlier during Maximus' stay at Cyzicus, contain a very strong and conscious refutation of Origenism.[47] This gives him the courage to conclude, that the first ten sentences of the *Gnostic centuries,* which even von Balthasar characterizes as ‚Gegenmotive' to the rest of the work, are to be regarded as a summary of Maximus' position against Origenism and at the same time as giving the framework, in which the rest, with all its reminiscences of Evagrius and Origen, is meant to be understood.[48] Here Sherwood has in fact led the way to a new evaluation, and it is our intention to continue on this line. It should be noted, further, that von Balthasar himself, in the second edition of his *Kosmische Liturgie,* has accepted Sherwood's position—though somewhat minimizing the change, which it implies—and allowed the idea of a crisis to disappear in the development of Maximus' life and thinking. Maximus' history can, in fact, hardly be dramatized in this way.

On the contrary, it may be one of the correct tendencies of the *Vita,* that it knows of no theological changes in Maximus' position. In fact, the Saint seems to have had his line of thought very clearly fixed from the beginning. This fact is perhaps not so astonishing, if we remember that he had an outstanding synthesizing faculty, and—above all—that he shared the viewpoint of most of the Fathers, that their primary duty was not one of creating original theological systems but of reproducing and

---

[45] See VON BALTHASAR, *Die 'Gnostischen Centurien' des Maximus Confessor,* Freiburg i. Br. 1941, after revision reprinted in *Kosmische Liturgie²,* Einsiedeln 1961, pp. 482–643.

[46] The idea is very sharply put forward in the first edition of VON BALTHASAR's book *Kosmische Liturgie,* Freiburg-München 1941, esp. pp. 27–35, but also indirectly p. 35 ff. J. GARRIGUES has later discussed this whole problem and tried to divide Maximus' life into different, precise periods; see *Maxime Le Confesseur . . . ,* Paris 1976, pp. 35–75.

[47] See SHERWOOD, *The Earlier Ambigua of St. Maximus the Confessor* (SA 36), Rome 1955.

[48] See SHERWOOD, *An Annotated Date-list,* p. 3 f. and 35, and in ACW, p. 8 f.

manifesting the faith and convictions of their predecessors, i.e. of the tradition of the Church.

3. Other research and the purpose of the thesis

Scholarly works devoted to the theology and position of Maximus the Confessor can be divided into different categories and different epochs. For the background of this thesis, a chronological distinction seems, however, to be most relevant, even though it may leave certain studies, devoted to technical or other problems of different kinds, out of focus. Our main attention is given to the development of a theological evaluation of the work of Maximus, while problems related to e.g. text criticism or Maximus' direct or indirect influence in later times are of interest only in so far as they throw light on his theological position and contribute to such an evaluation.

Chronologically Maximian research may be roughly divided into *five periods*. The *first* of these brings us up till about 1930. It is a period of systematic studies in the doctrine of the Confessor and into some technical and historical problems. In the first category the works by Weser,[49] Straubinger[50] and Schönfeld[51] should be mentioned, but also articles of Steitz and Lampen on Maximus' doctrine of the Eucharist[52] and of Montmasson on the concept of $\dot{\alpha}\pi\dot{\alpha}\theta\epsilon\iota\alpha$[53] or Michaud on the problem of *apocatastasis*.[54] In the second category may be placed Soppa's critical work on the *Diversa capita*,[55] the Moscow material presented by Epifanovitch,[56] and the considerations about the life of Maximus made by Montmasson,[57] as well as articles on Maximus' relationship to other writers and his later influence by Stiglmayr and Draeseke.[58]

Around 1930 a *second* period begins, characterized to some extent by

---

[49] H. WESER, *S. Maximi Confessoris praecepta de incarnatione Dei et deificatione hominis exponuntur et examinantur,* Diss., Halle—Berlin 1869.

[50] H. STRAUBINGER, *Die Christologie des hl. Maximus Confessor,* Bonn 1906.

[51] G. SCHÖNFELD, *Die Psychologie des Maximus Confessor,* Diss., Breslau 1918 (unprinted, not available to the writer).

[52] C. G. STEITZ, Die Abendmahlslehre des Maximus Confessor, *Jahrb. f. deutsche Theol.* 11 (1866), pp. 229–238 and W. LAMPEN, De Eucharistieleer van S. Maximus Confessor, StC 2 (1926), pp. 33–54.

[53] E. MONTMASSON, La doctrine de l'apatheia d'après s. Maxime, EO 14 (1911), pp. 36–41.

[54] E. MICHAUD, Saint Maxime le Confesseur et l'apocatastase, *Rev. Intern. de Théol.* 10 (1902), pp. 257–272.

[55] W. SOPPA, *Die Diversa capita unter den Schriften des hl. Maximus Confessor in deutscher Bearbeitung und quellenkritischer Beleuchtung,* Diss., Dresden 1922.

[56] S. L. EPIFANOVITCH, *Materials to serve in the study of the life and works of St. Maximus the Confessor* (in russian), Kiev 1917.

[57] MONTMASSON, EO 13 (1910), pp. 149–154.

[58] J. STIGLMAYR, Maximus Confessor und die beiden Anastasius, *Katholik* 88 (1908),

a critical attitude to Maximus' works or the originality of his thinking. Most representative of the critical attitude is M. Viller, who in an article in 1930 tried to prove Maximus' complete dependence on Evagrius Ponticus, at least in his primary ascetic work, the *Centuries on Charity*.[59] Working on a similar line, we also find Grumel, on the one hand reconstructing the chronology of the Confessor and thus arguing the irrelevance of the *Vita,* and on the other hand demonstrating at least Maximus' hesitation in regard to monothelitism, when it first appeared.[60] It should perhaps also be noted, that Grumel devoted a whole article to the problem of Maximus' possible dependence on Leontius of Byzantium,[61] in relation to a subject where E. Stéphanou, a few years later, showed the orthodoxy of Maximus.[62] Also characteristic of the situation during this period is the fact that Pegon, in editing the Centuries in French, though showing in his notes essential differences between Evagrius and Maximus, was not yet in the position to draw all the positive conclusions from them.[63] It was also during the end of this period that von Balthasar wrote his important article proving that the majority of the scholies to Ps.-Denis had been falsely attributed to Maximus and were in fact probably the work of John of Skythopolis.[64]

In 1941, however, clear signs of a new and positive re-evaluation of Maximus appeared; this was a somewhat hesitant attitude at first, but later it becomes more and more convinced. This *third* period continued into the 1970s, and this present thesis was intended originally to widen this evaluation to cover some of the aspects which had to that time not been sufficiently treated.

It is very significant that in 1941 three works devoted to Maximus appeared. First of all there was a fairly scholastic but effectively systematized and very helpful study of Maximus' doctrine of sanctification and deification, written by the late jesuit J. Loosen.[65] It starts from

---

pp. 39–45, and J. DRAESEKE, Maximus Confessor und Johannes Scotus Erigena, ThStKr 84 (1911), pp. 20–60 and 204–229.

[59] M. VILLER, Aux sources de la spiritualité de saint Maxime. Les œuvres d'Evagre le Pontique, RAM 11 (1930), pp. 156–184, 239–268.

[60] See GRUMEL, EO 26 (1927), pp. 24–32 and 28 (1929), pp. 31–34.

[61] GRUMEL, La comparaison de l'âme et du corps et l'union hypostatique chez Léonce de Byzance et S. Maxime le Confesseur, EO 25 (1926), pp. 393–406.

[62] E. STÉPHANOU, La coexistence initial du corps et de l'âme d'après saint Grégoire de Nysse et saint Maxime l'Homologète, EO 31 (1932), pp. 304–315.

[63] *Maxime le confesseur, Centuries sur la charité,* Introduction and translation by J. PEGON (SCH 9), Paris—Lyon 1945.

[64] VON BALTHASAR, Das Scholienwerk des Johannes von Skythopolis, Schol 15 (1940), pp. 16–38, reprinted in IDEM, *Kosmische Liturgie*[2], pp. 644–672.

[65] J. LOOSEN, *Logos und Pneuma im begnadeten Menschen bei Maximus Confessor* (MBTh 24), Münster (Westf.) 1941.

the presupposition that Maximus' thinking is of central importance at the end of the patristic period and, within its restricted sphere, shows clearly the consistency of the Confessor's theology, even though it is marked by a certain tendency to over-systematize. Secondly, von Balthasar continued his study, and in his work on the so called Gnostic centuries presented evidence in favour of their Maximian origin,[66] though in accepting them he felt forced to regard them as partly Origenistic and thus to make room for "an Origenistic crisis" in the life of the Confessor. This theory became in its turn an integral part of von Balthasar's great work of 1941, *Kosmische Liturgie.*[67] This, however, cannot at all take away from the fact that this ambitious and gener-ous work for the first time brought Maximus the Confessor into the foreground of interest as one of the most important Church Fathers, the relevance of whom was further underlined by frequent refer-ences to modern theology and speculation. This book is one of the great and early testimonies of the modern revival of patristic studies, as is also shown by the fact that a French translation was published already in 1947.[68]

Another example of a new positive evaluation was provided by J. Heintjes, who had, however, as early as 1935 published an article presenting Maximus as an unknown teacher of the Church,[69] but in 1942 and 1943 completed his studies in two articles on Maximus' doctrine of deification and sanctification, which bring together a lot of valuable material.[70] They are comparable with the work of Loosen but less scholarly, extensive and exhaustive.

In the 1950s this tendency of positive re-evaluation of Maximus was deepened and strengthened by the works of Sherwood, Dalmais and Hausherr. In 1952 Sherwood published his chronology of Maximus' life and works, and introduced his denial of the idea brought forward by von Balthasar of an Origenistic crisis in the Confessor's life.[71] The same year

---

[66] H. Von Balthasar, *Die 'Gnostischen Centurien' des Maximus Confessor,* Freiburg i. Br. 1941.

[67] References to this work will be found here with the abbreviation KL[1], and to its second edition with KL[2].

[68] Von Balthasar, *Liturgie Cosmique, Maxime le Confesseur,* Transl. by L. L'Haumet and H.-A. Prentout, Paris 1947.

[69] Heintjes, Een onbekende leeraar van ascese on mystiek: Sint Maximus Confessor, in StC 11 (1935), pp. 175–200.

[70] Heintjes, De opgang van den menschelijken geest tot God volgens Sint Maximus Confessor, BiNJ 5 (1942), pp. 260–302; 6 (1943), pp. 64–123. (Heintjes' dissertation *Sancti Maximi Confessoris de cognitione humanae doctrina* of 1937 has remained unpublished, and has not been available to me.)

[71] Sherwood, *An Annotated Date-list of the Works of Maximus the Confessor* (SA 30), Rome 1952.

I. Hausherr published his very personal but important study on self-love in relation to Maximus,[72] and I.-H. Dalmais, who had in 1948 published a translation of Ep 2 with a short introduction, wrote two basic articles, one an introduction into the spiritual thinking of Maximus, and the other a presentation of the very important doctrine of the 'logoi'.[73] In 1953 Dalmais wrote again two valuable introductions, one on Maximus' commentary to the Lord's Prayer[74] and one on his *Liber asceticus*.[75] Sherwood continued his work and published in 1955 both his study of the *Ambigua*, where—against the hypothesis of von Balthasar —he proved that Maximus had in fact early refuted Origenism,[76] and the Maximus volume of the series *Ancient Christian Writers*, where he gave a very extensive general introduction to Maximus' thinking as well as detailed notes to the *Liber asceticus* and *The Centuries on Charity*.[77]

The second edition of von Balthasar's *Kosmische Liturgie* (1961) summarizes excellently these efforts of the third period, to which should be added not only e.g. Dalmais' chapter on Maximus in *Théologie de la vie monastique* of the same year,[78] or his succinct summary of Maximus' position and theology in the Canadian magazine *Sciences Ecclésiastiques*,[79] but also E. von Ivánka's informed contributions to the understanding of Maximus against the background of the philosophical attitude of Origenism,[80] as well as W. Völker's articles on Maximus'

---

[72] I. HAUSHERR, *Philautie. De la tendresse pour soi à la charité, selon Saint Maxime le Confesseur* (Orientalia Christiana Analecta 137), Rome 1952.

[73] See I.-H. DALMAIS, S. Maxime le Confesseur, Docteur de la Charité, VS (1948), pp. 296–303; L'œuvre spirituelle de s. Maxime le Confesseur, VS Suppl. 21 (1952), pp. 216–226 and La théorie des "Logoi" des créatures chez s. Maxime le Confesseur, RSPT 36 (1952), pp. 244–249.

[74] DALMAIS, Un traité de théologie contemplative: Le commentaire du Pater Noster de s. Maxime le Confesseur, RAM 29 (1953), pp. 123–159.

[75] DALMAIS, La doctrine ascétique de s. Maxime le Confesseur d'après le *Liber asceticus*, Irénikon 26 (1953), pp. 17–39. It should be added that the magazine Irénikon had published as early as in 1936–1938 a translation of Maximus' explanation of the Liturgy, *Mystagogia*, with an introduction by the late Mme M. LOT-BORODINE, Irénikon 13 (1936), pp. 466–472, 595–597, 717–720; 14 (1937), pp. 66–69, 182–185, 282–284, 444–448; 15 (1938), pp. 71–74, 185–186, 276–278, 390–391, 488–492.

[76] SHERWOOD, *The Earlier Ambigua of St. Maximus the Confessor* (SA 36), Rome 1955.

[77] *St. Maximus the Confessor, The Ascetic Life, The Four Centuries on Charity.* Intr. by P. SHERWOOD. (ACW 21). Westminster—London 1955. (References to this work will be found here with the abbreviation ACW.)

[78] DALMAIS, Saint Maxime le Confesseur et la crise de l'origénisme monastique, in *Théologie de la vie monastique*, Paris 1961, pp. 411–421.

[79] DALMAIS, La fonction unificatrice du Verbe Incarné dans les œuvres spirituelles de Saint Maxime le Confesseur, *Sciences Ecclésiastiques* 14 (1962), pp. 445–459.

[80] E. VON IVÁNKA, Der Philosophische Ertrag der Auseinandersetzung Maximos des Bekenners mit dem Origenismus, JÖBG 7 (1958), pp. 23–49 (cf. IDEM, Korreferat zu P.

relationship to Ps.-Denis in the honorary tributes to A. Stohr and E. Klostermann.[81]

This last contribution also announced a new monograph on Maximus by Völker, who had already devoted a number of scholarly works to the doctrine of sanctification and spiritual perfection in such writers as Philo, Clement of Alexandria, Origen, Gregory of Nyssa and Ps.-Denis.[82] Maximus certainly affords a logical culmination to this admirable series. Völker's *magnum opus* on Maximus appeared in 1965: *Maximus Confessor als Meister des geistlichen Lebens.* Two specified theses, later reported, should even be mentioned in this context: by M. Wallace on Maximus' affirmative and negative theology[83] and by J. D. Zizioulas on his Christology. Other studies were also announced.[84] Maximus the Confessor obviously has attracted an increasing number of scholars of different nationalities and confessional background.

A *fourth* phase of Maximus studies commenced in the 1970s and is constituted by the number of monographs which have emanated from the "school" of the Dominican M.-J. Le Guillou, who has written a foreword to all of them. First of these studies was A. Riou, *Le monde et l'église selon Maxime le Confesseur,* which contains a development of Maximus' cosmology which goes much further than my indications, and which also makes clear that Maximus himself already regarded the λόγοι as divine energies. More biased is J. M. Garrigues, *Maxime le Confesseur. La charité, avenir divin de l'homme,* published in 1976. The tendency of the "school" to interpret Maximus in terms of the later Western theological tradition is here apparent. Maximus is obviously a

---

Sherwood, Maximus and Origenism, in *Berichte zum XI. Internationalen Byzantinisten-Kongress, München 1958,* Munich 1958 [2 pp.]) and IDEM, Einleitung, in MAXIMOS DER BEKENNER, *All-Eins in Christus,* Einsiedeln 1961, pp. 5–14.

[81] W. VÖLKER Der Einfluss Pseudo-Dionysius Areopagita auf Maximus Confessor, in A. STOHR, *Universitas,* I, Mainz 1960, pp. 243–54, and in *Studien zum Neuen Testament und zur Patristik* (TU 77), Berlin 1961, pp. 331–350. V. CROCE's study of Maximus' theological method should also be mentioned here with appreciation; see *Tradizione e ricerca . . . ,* Milan 1974.—Maximus' roots in Cappadocian theology are obvious. On this theme, see G. C. BERTHOLD, The Cappadocian Roots . . . , in HEINZER-SCHÖNBORN, *Maximus Confessor,* Fribourg 1982, pp. 51–59.

[82] See VÖLKER, *Fortschritt und Vollendung bei Philo von Alexandrien,* Leipzig 1938; IDEM, *Der wahre Gnostiker nach Clemens Alexandrinus* (TU 57), Leipzig 1952; IDEM, *Das Vollkommenheitsideal des Origenes* (BHTh 7), Tübingen 1931; IDEM, *Gregor von Nyssa als Mystiker,* Wiesbaden 1955; and IDEM, *Kontemplation und Ekstase bei Pseudo-Dionysius Areopagita,* Wiesbaden 1958.

[83] M. WALLACE, *Affirmation and Negation in the Theology of St. Maximus the Confessor* (in typescript), Pontif. Inst. S. Anselmi, Rome 1960.

[84] See SHERWOOD, Survey of recent work on St. Maximus the Confessor, *Traditio* 20 (1964), p. 436. This article also contains Sherwood's evaluation of modern Maximus research. For further details about books mentioned on pp. 17–18 below, see Bibliography.

person who cannot be interpreted as a Byzantine scholastic entirely. There are many elements in his theological thinking which indicate that he is both "Western" and "Eastern" (the appreciation of the papacy and the preparation for a positive appraisal of a "filioque" clause, e.g.). However, to make him a "Thomist" is to push it too far!

The third study in this series is restricted in theme but convincing. It was published in 1979 by F.-M. Lethel and entitled *Théologie de l'agonie du Christ. La liberté humaine du Fils de Dieu et son importance sotériologique mises en lumière par Maxime le Confesseur.* This study proves that the struggle about the two wills in Christ was not an occasional or theoretical business for Maximus but one of central Christological importance. Its anthropological implications cannot be denied. For my own part, I must admit that I had not quite realised how Maximus' description of the Gethsemane incident constitutes a basic affirmation of the status of man (in Christ) as basically free in existential choice.

The culmination of this impressive series of studies is represented by P. Piret and his book from 1983 *Le Christ et la Trinité. Selon Maxime le Confesseur.* Also here we have some valuable translations. The study deepens the analysis of Maximus' understanding of the problem of the two wills in Christ but relates it as well to his Trinitarian basis (which I have not developed enough here but have extended in *Man and the Cosmos*).

A parallel study of great importance from this period is F. Heinzer's dissertation *Gottes Sohn als Mensch. Die Struktur des Menschseins Christi bei Maximus Confessor* from 1980. This is a very balanced analysis of the anthropological side of Maximus' Christology, where not least the concept of περιχώρησις plays an important role.

A kind of culmination of this period of Maximus research is represented by the symposium volume of 1982, edited by F. Heinzer and Chr. Schönborn under the title *Maximus Confessor. Actes du Symposium sur Maxime le Confesseur Fribourg, 2–5 septembre 1980.* At the same time single contributions to this volume indicate new areas of Maximus research.

Thus, the last and *fifth* period is indicated. I regard my own book *Man and the Cosmos* as belonging to this period, although it more summarizes reflections than breaks new ground. The most impressive work from this period, however, is P. M. Blowers penetrating study of Maximus' method of exegesis in *Quaestiones ad Thalassium: Exegesis and Spiritual Pedagogy in Maximus the Confessor* (1991). The presupposition of this work is C. Laga's and C. Steel's critical edition of the text.

Mention from this last period should also be made of J. P. Farrell's continuing study of Maximus' concept of free will (bringing the earlier works to a kind of summary, although not always quite convincing), *Free Choice in St. Maximus the Confessor* from 1989. Farrell has also made an important translation of the *Disputation with Pyrrhus.* A number of smaller contributions could be mentioned in this context. It seems as if the present state of Maximus studies is characterised by more detailed pieces of research. As Blowers has pointed out, there is also a lot to do in this field. Maximus' texts have been more used for systematic summaries than for their own intrinsic specialties.

In all this, anthropology has been touched upon, especially within the context of Christology, but no study has been devoted entirely to Maximus' anthropology since mine. Closest to my concern comes the most recent monograph on Maxiums, written by the French philosopher and theologian J.-C. Larchet, *La divinisation de l'homme selon saint Maxime le Confesseur,* presented as a doctoral dissertation to the Faculty of Protestant Theology, Strasbourg in 1994 (and about to be published as a printed book). This admirable study, which I have hardly been able to take into consideration here, however, does not cover the whole field of my own. Therefore, this new edition seems, after all, well-motivated.

Anthropological aspects are, of course, treated in the major works of von Balthasar and Sherwood (as well as by others from a later time), but since von Balthasar's study *Kosmische Liturgie* keeps the viewpoint of cosmology particularly in focus, and since Sherwood's work on the earlier *Ambigua* and other contributions have Maximus' refutation of Origenism as centre of interest, these aspects serve as elements of another vision or another argumentation than one which is purely anthropological.[85] Dalmais, on the other hand, has from the beginning shown a particular interest in anthropological viewpoints, especially in their relationship to the ascetic and mystical theology of Maximus,[86] and he has more recently contributed other expressions of this interest in articles on the spiritual anthropology of the Confessor,[87] but this excellent expert on Maximus' thinking has never had the opportunity to bring

---

[85] This is also true of SHERWOOD's contribution to the international congress of Byzantinists in Munich 1958, though to a large extent it deals with anthropological statements by Maximus; see IDEM, Maximus and Origenism. APXH KAI TEΛOΣ, in *Berichte zum XI. Internationalen Byzantinisten-Kongress* (27 pp.).

[86] The same is true also of HAUSHERR.

[87] DALMAIS, L'anthropologie spirituelle de saint Maxime le Confesseur, *Recherches et Débats* 36 (1961), pp. 202–211 and La manifestation du Logos dans l'homme et dans l'Eglise, in HEINZER-SCHÖNBORN, *Maximus Confessor,* pp. 13–25.—In this connection one should also mention K.-H. UTHEMANN, Das anthropologische Modell der hypostatischen Union bei Maximus Confessor, *ibid.,* pp. 223–233.

all his material together into a single more extensive study. There is, thus, still a certain need for a monograph, which regards Maximus' theology and spirituality primarily from his understanding of man.

The present thesis was an attempt to respond to this need. It has been written with the clear conviction that Maximus' anthropology holds the key to his theology as a whole, and that this anthropology, in its turn, is a fruit of the Confessor's personal reflection on the Christological convictions of the Council of Chalcedon, as they were further demonstrated and explained through the Council of Constantinople in 553. Maximus' doctrinal and personal positions—as well as his remarkable eclecticism—are motivated by his vision of man as the centre of God's creation and a particular object of His providence, man as both microcosm and mediator. Christian spirituality implies for him the restitution of this microcosm and the fulfilment of this mediating function. All is, therefore, orientated from the Incarnation of Christ, through which this restitution and fulfilment is already a fact, open to man. A unity which does not violate the differences constitutes the mystery of this incarnation, but it is, thereby, also the mystery of man and of the world. Love alone as a unifying factor is for Maximus capable of combining these elements into one divine-human activity, since it includes all and respects the freedom of all.

In the following chapters we shall try to work out the different aspects of this anthropological vision of Maximus the Confessor from his Christology, through his cosmology and into the details of his doctrine of spiritual perfection. For obvious reasons—e.g. Maximus' clear indebtedness to a long tradition of earlier Christian thinking and the far-reaching eclecticism which characterizes his relationship to his predecessors (such as Evagrius, Ps.-Denis, the Cappadocians, Nemesius of Emesa etc.)—this presentation will inevitably include sections of comparative study. These sections will be enlarged at points of particular interest, where systematic presentations of such comparative material are lacking or insufficient, or where a detailed knowledge of Maximus' background seems necessary for the understanding of his position, as well as for the argument of the thesis itself. At other instances, though a similar presentation of comparative material may in itself be equally interesting, but being of less importance for the argument and general purpose of the thesis, it has had to be left out.

Our concentration on Maximus' anthropology and on aspects of it which are particularly apt to show the originality and consistency of his theological position, makes it further necessary to leave out elements of his thinking which are of great importance but are less central to our

theme. Such elements are Maximus' ecclesiology and his doctrine of the
sacraments, his exegetical principles, his practical knowledge of spiritual
exercises etc. Here should also be mentioned Maximus' doctrine of the
Holy Spirit and the role of the Spirit at different levels of spiritual
development, to which we shall return at various occasions but to which
we shall not be able to devote any particular section. The reason for this
last omission is mainly the fact that we wish to concentrate our attention
on points where the influence of Maximus' Christological convictions as
the core of his whole thinking may be seen most clearly, while the
pneumatological convictions which he shares with his Eastern tradition
in general are of less interest in our context.[88]

Our viewpoint is properly theological. For this reason aspects which
rather belong to the field of history and phenomenology of religion have
unfortunately to be neglected. Strictly philosophical viewpoints are also
introduced only in so far as they belong to the necessary background of
Maximus' thinking, or provide a framework for the understanding of the
particular stress or aspect of his argument.

---

[88] Loosen, *Logos und Pneuma*, pp. 87–126, gives a systematic presentation of
Maximus' understanding of πνεῦμα, and particularly of its rôle in man's spiritual
development and perfection. It summarizes well the most important aspects of this theme,
but shows at the same time clearly—even through its very formal character and rather
restricted length—that Maximus' doctrine at this point is not original, nor interesting to an
extent which is comparable with his doctrine on the Logos and the λόγοι.

CHAPTER ONE
The Christological Background

A. The Chalcedonian Heritage and Maximus' Theology of the Incarnation

There is a general agreement among scholars that the doctrine of Christ and the theology of the Incarnation form the very centre of Maximus' thinking. It may be sufficient to refer to Sherwood's statements at this point. According to him Maximus' theological system forms an integrated whole, a synthesis, and the core of this synthesis is "the mystery of Christ",[1] which is at the same time "the mystery of love".[2] Other experts on Maximus have made similar generalizations.[3] Any student of Maximus' writings is capable of seeing for himself the truth of these opinions.

It is, however, equally apparent that the type of Christology with which we have to deal in this case is very closely linked with the formulations of the Council of Chalcedon. The Incarnation to Maximus means precisely the hypostatic union of divine and human nature. The Chalcedonian key terms are found everywhere in Maximus' writings; indeed, one may even argue, that these frequent allusions to Chalcedon indicate the main direction of his thought, and go far beyond what belongs to a theology of the Incarnation in a more restricted sense.[4]

---

[1] See SHERWOOD, in ACW, p. 29.

[2] SHERWOOD, op. cit., p. 91.

[3] See e.g. LOOSEN, Logos und Pneuma, p. 50; HEINTJES, StC 11 (1935), p. 194 and IDEM, BiNJ 6 (1943), p. 78 f.; DALMAIS, Irénikon 26 (1953), p. 21; HAUSHERR, Philautie, pp. 151–154, and not least VON BALTHASAR, KL², pp. 62 f., 66 and 204 ff.

[4] As such a key term we find e.g. ἀδιαίρετος in Ep 15; PG 91, 560 D; ἀδιαιρέτως in Ep 13; PG 91, 524 D; Amb 5; PG 91, 1052 B; Amb 7; 1097 B; Amb 10; 1136 B; Amb 41; 1312 C (together with ἀδιαίρετος). Cf. VON BALTHASAR, KL², pp. 37, 55, 232. More frequently used are, however, ἀσύγχυτος and ἀσυγχύτως; see e.g. Ep 12; PG 91, 469 AC; Ep 15; 557 D; Amb 3; PG 91, 1040 C; Amb 4; 1044 D; Amb 7; 1077 C; Amb 10; 1176 C; Amb 27; 1269 B (ἀσύγχυτος); and ThPol 15; PG 91, 169 B; Pyrrh; PG 91, 296 D; Amb 5; 1052 B; 1053 B; 1057 D; Amb 7; 1077 C; 1097 B and Amb 42; 1320 B (ἀσυγχύτως). Cf. VON BALTHASAR, KL², pp. 37, 54 f., 57, 150, 158, 204, 230, 250 and 330. Also ἀτρέπτως is used, e.g. in Thal

We may however go further and claim that Maximus' dependence upon Chalcedon and its theology does not find its most prominent expression in an intentional repetition of the Council's formulas, but in a theological reflection upon its Christological content, which thus proves to be decisive in a variety of theological contexts. And it is particularly Maximus' thinking around the question of the *communicatio idiomatum* of the two natures, which deserves our attention, for at this point he seems to some extent to have made a pioneering contribution, not least because in this thinking he has also provided a well thought-out foundation for his theology of deification and spiritual perfection.

Neither the *communicatio idiomatum* idea as such, nor its central position, is, of course, an innovation on Maximus' part. The idea had acquired a central position already. Even before Chalcedon obviously— with a more or less definite purpose—one started to use it, and after Chalcedon—as all through the 6th century—it seems to have become very popular to apply divine attributes to Christ as man and human attributes to Christ as God in a more or less mechanical way. Different circles and parties simply developed the idea in different ways. It has, quite correctly, been pointed out that the Marian attribute θεοτόκος presupposes a form of *communicatio idiomatum,* and that the so-called theopaschite formula, used in 'monophysite' circles: *unus ex Trinitate passus est* exemplifies a particular application of the same idea.[5]

The idea of a *communicatio idiomatum* is found as early as in Irenaeus and not least in Origen; it is already further developed in the early Church,[6] even though it was particularly actualised in the 5th century, and acquired a more precise function after the Council of Chalcedon. In Apollinaris the idea is given a prominent position,[7] while the Antiochenes, on the other side, regarded a too frequent use of *communicatio* formulations as dangerous. The positive evaluation of it by Apollinaris provoked in Nestorius a corresponding negative limitation. According to his modification of the idea, the *communicatio idiomatum* may only be applied to the *person* of the union, Christ. But in relation to the divine Logos and to human nature as such its application is prohibited.[8] Such a restrictive attitude towards the idea was, however,

---

22; CCSG 7, p. 137; Ep 15; PG 91, 556 D and Amb 42; PG 91, 1320 C (cf. also ἀναλλοιώτως, Thal 22; CCSG 7, p. 137). ἀχωρίστως is even rather frequently used by Maximus; see e.g. Amb 4; PG 91, 1044 D; Amb 5; 1049 C and 1052 C.

[5] See E. AMANN, *art.* Théopaschite, DTC 15, col. 505 ff.

[6] See A. MICHEL, *art.* Idiomes, DTC 7: 1, col. 596 ff.

[7] See A. GRILLMEIER, Die theologische und sprachliche Vorbereitung der christologischen Formel von Chalkedon, Chalk I, p. 112.

[8] See MICHEL, *art. cit.,* col. 597.

known already from an earlier time,[9] and was later also found among the orthodox. Thus, the pope Gelasius, at the end of the 5th century, certainly teaches the *communicatio idiomatum,* but is at the same time very eager to emphasize that it does not at all affect the natures.[10] It was in a way easier for the monophysites to use the idea without reservation.[11] As a matter of fact, it came in later monophysitism—e.g. in Severus—to play a very important role. However this did not prevent a man like Sahdona, who stood in a close relationship to the Nestorians, from teaching a real *communicatio idiomatum.*[12]

Maximus' personal contribution at this point is, thus, to be sought in another direction. As we shall see later, an unlimited and irresponsible use of the *communicatio* idea in a more formal sense is, as a matter of fact, entirely foreign to Maximus. His contribution to the theological development in this field is, consequently, less related to the idea of *communicatio idiomatum* as such, than to an elaboration of the idea of a mutual permeation, *perichoresis.* This last idea acquires in Maximus a central position, and is developed in such a way that it modifies and qualifies the *communicatio* idea.

The importance of Maximus' achievement is best illustrated by the fact that the term *perichoresis*—as an expression of the kind of *communicatio* relationship which exists between divine and human natures in Christ—seems to have been used for the first time precisely by Maximus.[13] In Ps.-Cyril's *De sacrosancta Trinitate* we find this term used with a similar intention,[14] but this treatise can hardly be dated to a time before Maximus. It seems rather to have been influenced by Maximus' ideas in a way which reminds us of John of Damascus.[15]

What then does this *perichoresis* imply to Maximus? The answer to this question is of the first importance, primarily because it may help us decisively to define the character of Maximus' Chalcedonian position. If Maximus understands *perichoresis* more or less exclusively as a divine permeation into the human nature, then the original hesitation over

---

[9] Such an attitude was taken e.g. both by the anti-Arian Eustathius of Antioch and by the Arian Eusebius of Emesa; see Grillmeier, *art. cit.,* pp. 128 and 134.

[10] See F. Hofmann, Der Kampf der Päpste um Konzil und Dogma von Chalkedon von Leo dem Grossen bis Hormisdas, Chalk 2, p. 63 f.

[11] See e.g. J. Lebon, La christologie du monophysisme sévérien, Chalk I, p. 568 and n. 98.

[12] See W. de Vries, Die syrisch-nestorianische Haltung zu Chalkedon, Chalk I, p. 634.

[13] See G. L. Prestige, *God in Patristic Thought²,* London 1952, p. 291.

[14] Ps.-Cyril, *De sacrosancta Trinitate,* 22; PG 77, 1164 A; 24; 1165 C; 27; 1172 D.

[15] As a matter of fact it is incorporated into John's *De fide orthodoxa* (though not ch. 22), and it has been argued, that it might even be a work of John. See J. M. Hoeck, *art.* Joh. von Damaskus, LThK², 5 (1960), col. 1024.

against the beginnings of monothelitism which some scholars have found in Maximus' earlier writings,[16] might be confirmed, since this one-sided view of *communicatio idiomatum* was common in 'monophysite' circles. On the other hand, if Maximus uses the concept of *perichoresis* only with strong reservations in all respects, then an Antiochene tendency would be noticeable.

The question is further complicated by the fact that partly contradictory opinions have been put forward by scholars, who have been particularly interested in this aspect of Maximus' theology.[17] About the general presupposition, that Maximus' concern for the *communicatio* idea is closely linked with his interest in Christ's activities, there is general agreement,[18] but about the nature of this concern opinion has been divided. An older systematic scholar like H. Weser noticed already the central position of the term *perichoresis* in Maximus' theology, but he defined it rather vaguely, when pointing out that the two natures of the hypostasis rotate in a mystical way and move within each other like the wheels of the four creatures of Ezek. I: 16, and "post personalem unionem et actiones et qualitates secum commutant".[19]

But Weser goes further and arrives at the fairly definite conclusion that the divine will exerts an overwhelming dominion over the human will within this process.[20] From this point of view permeation must be understood primarily as a divine activity. A similar opinion is also to be found in G. L. Prestige, who otherwise ascribes to Maximus a very important position, as far as the further development of the *communicatio* idea is concerned. Prestige starts from the sense in which the word *perichoresis* is used by Anaxagoras, "rotation",[21] and translates it in Maximus—in a particular, non-Christological context—as "completion of a cycle".[22] In the Christological context, however, he recognizes a basic sense of "reciprocity of action",[23] but defines it later—

---

[16] See Introduction, p. 10 above.

[17] That it has been quite neglected by Loosen, *Logos und Pneuma*, where the term *perichoresis* is not even mentioned, is surprising.

[18] Von Balthasar, KL[2], p. 253 emphasizes even that already the term ἀντίδοσις (*communicatio*) has an active sense in Maximus. This term is, in fact, a kind of equivalent of περιχώρησις.

[19] Weser, *S. Maximi Confessoris praecepta de incarnatione*, p. 15.

[20] See Weser, *op. cit.*, p. 16: "Apparet etiam hoc loco humanitatem privilegia sua non satis conservare". However, Maximus also develops a soteriology, which is based on the cooperation between nature and grace; see B. Studer, Zur Soteriologie des Maximus, in Heinzer-Schönborn, *Maximus Confessor*, pp. 239–246.

[21] See Liddell & Scott, *Greek-English Lexicon* II, the word περιχώρησις.

[22] Thal 59; CCSG 7, p. 53.

[23] Prestige, *op. cit.*, p. 293.

referring to the original sense of the term—as "rotation from a fixed point back to that point again". He underlines that we find in Maximus always a *perichoresis* "to" (εἰς or πρός) but never "in" or "through" each other. By using the term Maximus aims at showing, Prestige emphasizes, not the unity of Christ as such but the unified activity of the two natures.[24] Prestige then goes on to analyse how the term *perichoresis* is used in Ps.-Cyril, a use which he regards as a further development of Maximus' intentions, and he comes in the end to the characteristic conclusion that the process is after all one-sided, and that the metaphor with which we are concerned is not particularly illuminating or fit for its purpose. Prestige regards its use as more or less a form of play upon words.[25]

Against such an opinion H. A. Wolfson has, however, reacted rather strongly and with the full support of the texts themselves. Wolfson thus emphasizes that Maximus and Ps.-Cyril do not hesitate at all to talk of a penetration "through" the other nature, and also that the process expressed through the concept of *perichoresis* is not regarded as one-sided but mutual. But Wolfson restricts the importance of this statement to some extent by underlining at the same time, that the reason for this courageous attitude from the side of these ancient Christian writers is the fact that whether the "humanation" of the divine nature or the penetration of the human nature into the divine is concerned, the actual reference is simply to the *Incarnation*.[26] Wolfson has here hinted at the secret of Maximus' use of the concept of *perichoresis*, though without indicating the complexity and richness of his theology of the Incarnation, and without providing much more than a formal criticism of the position which we have found in Weser and Prestige. More insight into the theology of Maximus is, in fact, found in V. Lossky, who indicates that the impression of one-sidedness which one may get from the texts is linked with the fact that the process of *perichoresis* is self-evidently regarded as starting from the side of God—and thus from the divine nature—because *perichoresis* is part of the economy of salvation, but that when the Incarnation is a fact it implies, both for Maximus and John of Damascus, that the human nature is really made capable of penetrating into the divine.[27]

---

[24] See *ibid.*, p. 294.
[25] See *ibid.*, p. 294 f.
[26] H. A. WOLFSON, *The Philosophy of the Church Fathers*, Cambridge, Mass. 1956, p. 424 f.
[27] V. LOSSKY, *The Mystical Theology of the Eastern Church*, London 1957, p. 145 f. That Lossky combines this fact with the doctrine of the divine "energies" is another problem, which cannot be treated here.

The discussion among scholars regarding the *perichoresis* idea in Maximus obviously calls for further clarification. It motivates first of all a closer analysis of the texts where this idea is most explicitly expressed. We shall see that such an analysis will give us a clearer impression of Maximus' personal contribution to Christological theology, as well as of his basic faithfulness towards Chalcedon.

If Maximus is the first Christian writer who has given to the term *perichoresis* a central position within orthodox Christology, it is not very difficult to discover *where* he found his starting-point. Indirectly he has indicated it himself. In the Scholies to Ps.-Denis there is a reference in one place,[28] apparently by Maximus himself,[29] to Gregory Nazianzen's *Ep.* 101, where Gregory speaks, in reference to Eph. 3: 17, about the inhabitation of Christ and about a certain "mixture" (κρᾶσις) of the two natures and their attributes. Gregory goes on to state: ". . . and penetrating (περιχωρῶν) into each other on account of their mutual adhesion" (συμφυΐα).[30] It seems in the context as if the mutual application of attributes is seen more as a consequence of the *perichoresis* than as its cause. And it is exactly this tendency which might have attracted Maximus, who is far more interested in *perichoresis* as an expression of activity than in the mutual application of the divine attributes as such. Starting from Gregory's use of the verb περιχωρεῖν Maximus thus probably developed his own conception of *perichoresis*.[31]

In Maximus this concept appears in fact to be very rich, particularly when one adds to texts, where we find the term *perichoresis* as such, other texts where identical or similar ideas are developed, though without an explicit use of the noun περιχώρησις or the verb περιχωρεῖν. For the sake of clarity we shall here try to systematize Maximus' different aspects of the idea.

a. First of all we recognize, of course—as Weser and Prestige have underlined—a primary stress on the divine penetration into the human level. Already in its most fundamental sense the Incarnation may be regarded as a *perichoresis*.[32] It is, however, difficult to prove that

---

[28] PG 4, 533 C.

[29] According to von Balthasar, KL², p. 255, n. 11 this passage should obviously be attributed to Maximus, though the majority of the scholies are attributed to John of Skythopolis (see KL², pp. 644–672).

[30] Gregory Nazianzen, *Ep.* 101; PG 37, 181 C. This letter is quoted also elsewhere in Maximus, see Amb 42; PG 91, 1336 A. On this background and Maximus' use of the concept, see further P. Piret, *Le Christ et la Trinité*, p. 349 ff.

[31] For the Gregorian use of the term in a non-Christological context, see e.g. *Or.* 18; PG 35, 1041 A and 22: 4; 1136 B.

[32] That Maximus develops at the same time a theology of the Incarnation, the scope of which is far wider, must here be left out of view.

Maximus regards the initial act of the divine Incarnation as the most characteristic element of the idea of *perichoresis*. For it is only in relation to deification—and the reciprocal relationship between human and divine within the process of deification, itself the gift of grace—that the term *perichoresis* is frequently used. The clearest example of a use of the term which refers to the divine penetration into the human world as such, is a passage which contains a chain of definitions in Thal 59,[33] where we read—and even here with reference to the incarnation which takes place in an individual believer—that the true revelation of the object of faith is the ineffable penetration ($\pi\epsilon\rho\iota\chi\dot{\omega}\rho\eta\sigma\iota s$) of this 'object' in accordance with the amount of faith present in the believer.[34] This *perichoresis* is, however, itself defined as an ascent ($\dot{\epsilon}\pi\dot{\alpha}\nu o\delta os$) of the believers to their Cause and End.[35] Scholars like Weser and Prestige seem, therefore, to have overstressed the first and underestimated the second aspect of the process of *perichoresis*.[36] A clear parallel—though not in a Christological context—is provided for example in Myst 2 where, though the term *perichoresis* is not used, Maximus speaks about a relationship of transference between the intelligible and the sensible levels of the created order. For there too Maximus emphasizes a certain reciprocity, within which the different elements remain unconfused ($\dot{\alpha}\sigma\nu\gamma\chi\dot{\nu}\tau\omega s$) in relation to each other.[37]

b. The particularly characteristic element of Maximus' thought on this point is, in fact, not introduced into the picture until we arrive at the second aspect of the *perichoresis* idea, i.e. the human penetration into the

---

[33] CCSG 22, p. 51 ff.

[34] CCSG 22, p. 53: $\dot{\eta}$ $\kappa\alpha\tau\dot{\alpha}$ $\dot{\alpha}\nu\alpha\lambda o\gamma\dot{\iota}\alpha\nu$ $\tau\dot{\eta}s$ $\dot{\epsilon}\nu$ $\dot{\epsilon}\kappa\dot{\alpha}\sigma\tau\omega$ $\pi\dot{\iota}\sigma\tau\epsilon\omega s$ $\dot{\alpha}\rho\rho\eta\tau os$ $\tau o\hat{\nu}$ $\pi\epsilon\pi\iota\sigma\tau\epsilon\nu\mu\dot{\epsilon}\nu o\nu$ $\pi\epsilon\rho\iota\chi\dot{\omega}\rho\eta\sigma\iota s$. Notice, however, in this text already the active role of human faith ($\pi\epsilon\pi\iota\sigma\tau\epsilon\nu\mu\dot{\epsilon}\nu o\nu$) in relation to this revelation ($\dot{\alpha}\pi o\kappa\dot{\alpha}\lambda\nu\psi\iota s$). The expression $\kappa\alpha\tau\dot{\alpha}$ $\dot{\alpha}\nu\alpha\lambda o\gamma\dot{\iota}\alpha\nu$ is important in this context. It ought to be compared with the *tantum quantum* formula, which will be treated in paragraph d. below.

[35] CCSG 22, p. 53. The term $\dot{\epsilon}\pi\dot{\alpha}\nu o\delta os$ should not necessarily be translated "return".

[36] It should be noted, however, that exactly this last text was regarded by Prestige as supporting his opinion, that there is no reciprocal permeation of the two natures, in the true sense of the word, but only a circular movement from one fixed point back to that point again; see PRESTIGE, *op. cit.*, p. 293. But thereby Prestige had failed to observe the important fact that the human *perichoresis*, about which Maximus speaks as often as about the divine, is hardly regarded by him simply as a return to a fixed starting-point. Prestige's interpretation of *perichoresis* as a one way movement does not do justice to the texts. The passage we have cited speaks rather in favour of Wolfson's opinion, that the incarnation of the Divine and the deification of the human are more or less the same process. It should also be noted that Prestige's supposition that Thal 59 is "a neutral instance, having no bearing on theology" hardly makes his own interpretation more reliable!

[37] PG 91, 669 BC. The parallel is also worked out here in regard to the Church on earth in its relationship to the world above, and in that context, at least, the word $\pi\rho o\sigma\chi\omega\rho\epsilon\hat{\iota}\nu$ is used; see *loc. cit.*

realm of the divine. A good example of this aspect is found in Amb 5
where the penetration (Maximus uses the verb περιχωρεῖν) of human
nature into the *totality* of divine nature is said to be the fruit of that
union without confusion (ἀσυγχύτως) with divine nature which has
taken place in Christ. In this way, says Maximus, absolutely nothing of
what is human is separated from the divine, with which it is hypostatically united.[38] This text shows clearly that the term *perichoresis* is not just an
expression of the predominance of the divine over the human, but rather
regarded as an appropriate expression of a union without confusion in its
consequences of full reciprocity. Human *perichoresis* is in Maximus'
opinion real and not illusory. Wolfson has quite correctly referred to this
text in his criticism of Prestige.[39]

c. What the term *perichoresis* is intended to express in Maximus'
writings is, first of all, precisely the aspect of *reciprocity* within a
divine-human relationship as understood in a Chalcedonian way. This
reciprocity, therefore, must be introduced here as our third aspect. For in
most places, where Maximus refers to the *perichoresis* idea, he also
speaks of *a double penetration*. The background of his position may quite
naturally be found in the aspect of reciprocity (notice the expression εἰς
ἀλλήλας) which we have noticed already in Gregory Nazianzen.[40] The
union of the two natures in Christ may, as we have seen in Gregory, be
expressed as a kind of "mixture" (κρᾶσις)—in the Stoic sense of this
word[41]—and therefore one must quite naturally expect that the words
περιχωρεῖν, περιχώρησις as a further elaboration of the Stoic concept of
χωρεῖν, should be used, in connection with the explanation of the term
"mixture", as a kind of synonym for ἀντιπαρεκτείνω, in which case it
means the interpenetration of mixed bodies.[42]

Wolfson has emphasized that when the Fathers used the term
perichoresis in order to explain the meaning of *communicatio
idiomatum*, it implied an attempt to explain the relationship by means of
the analogy offered by the Stoic concept of "mixture" (κρᾶσις).[43] But
then the aspect of reciprocity is also self-evident and cannot be excluded

[38] PG 91, 1053 B.
[39] See Wolfson, *op. cit.,* p. 425, where we also find the following commentary by way of summary: ". . . there is mention only of one kind of penetration, and that is the penetration of the human nature though the divine nature, and this penetration is said to have taken place in virtue of the union of the human nature with the divine nature." Heinzer, *Gottes Sohn als Mensch,* fully supports this idea of mutual penetration; see pp. 122–125.
[40] *Ep.* 101; PG 37, 181 C.
[41] See e.g. Wolfson, *op. cit.,* p. 380.
[42] See *ibid.,* p. 419 f.
[43] *Ibid.,* p. 420.

by the fact that—to take a classical example, also cited by Wolfson—it is the wine which is poured into the water and not the water into the wine. As soon as the union has taken place, the *perichoresis* is mutual.[44] Von Balthasar too, as a matter of course, has underlined the reciprocal aspect of the concept of *perichoresis* as linked with Stoic physics. For in both cases, he emphasizes, the presupposition is that the bodies may penetrate into each other without being damaged.[45] It is, thus, rather characteristic when Maximus, in a general cosmological context, speaks, on the one hand, of "the penetration of the opposites into each other in virtue of their mixture" (κατὰ τὴν κρᾶσιν εἰς ἄλληλα περιχώρησις) and defines this process, on the other hand, as "an undamageing advancement through each other" (χωρεῖν δι' ἀλλήλων ἀλυμάντως).[46] If one further understands the term *communicatio* (ἀντίδοσις) as expressing an activity and to a certain extent being a synonym for *perichoresis,* the aspect of reciprocity is even more strengthened. In *Disp. c. Pyrrh.* Maximus' terminology has obviously grown into a formula. It is then all the more remarkable that the words εἰς ἀλλήλας there form an integrated part of the whole.[47]

That it is an *active* reciprocity which the term *perichoresis* is intended to express, is made particularly clear in texts where this term is used together with another word, which expresses the more static aspect of the union of the two natures. Already in Gregory Nazianzen—in the very text where Maximus probably found his starting-point for the development of his concept of *perichoresis*—such a static term is to be found. For there we learn that the natures penetrate into each other "in virtue of their mutual adhesion" (τῷ λόγῳ τῆς συμφυΐας). This adhesion is the presupposition for an active *perichoresis.*[48] Exactly the same way of thinking is found in Maximus, as we may gather from two sections of *Op. theol. et pol.,* written a few years earlier than *Disp. c. Pyrrh.*[49]

In the first of these sections Maximus speaks of the two energies of Christ: the divine energy which in accordance with the economy of

[44] For the example of wine and water, see further WOLFSON, *op. cit.,* p. 420 f.

[45] VON BALTHASAR, KL[2], p. 231.

[46] Amb 17; PG 91, 1228 C. What we have now said must, of course, not be understood to imply that Maximus was exclusively bound to a Stoic terminology in this context. His frequent use of the Aristotelian term *synthesis* for example (also found in the context just quoted), is, among other things, a warning against such a hasty conclusion. Here as elsewhere Maximus is, in fact, very eclectic.

[47] See PG 91, 345 D: τῷ ἀπορρήτῳ τρόπῳ τῆς εἰς ἀλλήλας τῶν Χριστοῦ φύσεων περιχωρήσεως.

[48] See *Ep.* 101; PG 37, 181 C.

[49] ThPol 7 and 20. For their dating, see SHERWOOD, *An Annotated Date-list,* pp. 51 and 41 f.

then contents after would tell why

salvation is clearly presented as taking the initiative, and the human which, according to this divine plan, is entirely (δι' ὅλου) united with the divine "through their mutual adhesion and penetration" (τῇ πρὸς ἀλλήλας συμφυΐᾳ καὶ περιχωρήσει).[50] Since the context shows that Maximus is here dealing primarily with the activity of Christ, the idea that the two terms "adhesion" and "penetration" are synonymous seems to be excluded. The first word denotes rather the relationship established between the two natures through the Incarnation, while the second term denotes—as a consequence of this relationship—their mutual penetration. The second section seems to confirm this interpretation. For there we learn that one and the same activity proceeds from Christ in a joined and united manner (συμφυῶς καὶ ἡνωμένως), i.e. as from two subjects united into one, though with the clear reservation: "according to the unitary interpenetration in them" (κατὰ τὴν ἐν τούτοις ἑνιαίαν περιχώρησιν).[51] Through *perichoresis*, which is an activity of the natures towards each other, a common activity and a unified direction of intention is effected.

The purpose of Maximus' stress on reciprocity is, thus, first of all to underline the unified activity, which it expresses and of which it is an expression. However, according to Maximus it belongs to the character of this unity, that it is in all respects "unconfused" (ἀσύγχυτος).[52] Therefore it is, of course, never "of nature" (κατὰ φύσιν).[53] There is "a newness of modes" (τῶν τρόπων καινότης) but never "an alteration of *logos*" (κατὰ τὸν λόγον ἀλλοίωσις).[54] It is a union which can be best characterized as similar to that between fire and iron. Iron glows in the fire but remains what it is in itself. In one and the same hypostasis iron and fire are found together, but the piece of iron effects exactly that which is in accordance with its own nature—as well as that which belongs to both—i.e. it glows, but in a way which is proper to iron alone.[55] "Bona profecto integritas!", Weser exclaims in front of such a one-sided predominance of the divine,[56] but evidently for Maximus the question appeared in a very different light. We are dealing here certainly with a kind of adoption of the human into the sphere of the divine, but human nature itself tends towards this adoption, and, therefore, (as in the case of iron and fire) develops within this union always what is inherent in itself

[50] ThPol 7; PG 91, 85 D–88 A.
[51] ThPol 20; PG 91, 232 A.
[52] A favourite Chalcedonian term in Maximus.
[53] See ThPol 8; PG 91, 108 C.
[54] See Amb 5; PG 91, 1053 B.
[55] See ThPol 16; PG 91, 189 C–192 A.
[56] WESER, *op. cit.*, p. 16.

and proper to itself. The glowing sword cuts and burns at the same time.[57] In this last case too there is a *perichoresis* and a *communicatio* for the perfection of both (διὰ τὴν ἄκραν τούτων), as Maximus says,[58] and through it is manifested "the mode of communication which is in accordance with their ineffable union".[59] As e.g. Lossky has emphasized, Maximus (and John of Damascus) certainly speak of a humanity which is made divine, but this deification—without change of what is proper to each nature—is in full accordance with *human* nature as such.[60]

d. Thus Maximus remains faithful to Chalcedon in its attempt to express the redemptive unity of human and divine in Christ. The degree and the character of this faithfulness is most clearly manifested, however, through what we might call the fourth aspect of the *perichoresis* idea. Everywhere Maximus wishes to underline both the "newness" of this redemptive union *and* the fact that it implies precisely a true development of what is peculiar to human nature.[61] But in accordance with this double purpose Maximus makes his most important contribution, not only by emphasizing the continuing difference between the two natures as well as the unity of the hypostasis, but above all by making the one aspect directly related to and dependent on the other. The union of the two natures is based on a certain *polarity* between them in virtue of the very fact that they are human and divine. Maximus obviously regards such a positive polarity as being the decisive insight of the Council of Chalcedon, and for Maximus the primary instrument with which to express this polarity is what von Balthasar has appropriately called the great "Entsprechungsformel" (*tantum—quantum* with its synonyms).[62] The examples of the use of this *formula of reciprocity* in connection with the *perichoresis* idea are numerous. Only a short analysis of a few texts can be given here.

[57] See Amb 5; PG 91, 1060 A, where the same imagery is developed.

[58] ThPol 16; PG 91, 189 D.

[59] Amb 5; PG 91, 1057 D. Maximus works here with his characteristic dialectic between an immutable principle of nature (λόγος φύσεως) on the one hand, and a unified mode of existence (τρόπος ὑπάρξεως) on the other.

[60] See LOSSKY, *op. cit.*, p. 146, where the author likewise underlines, that the image of iron and fire is frequent among the Fathers as an expression of the status of deified human nature. One can add that deification within this patristic context implies exactly this blessed, unconfused but active *status* of 'hypostatic' and 'perichoretic' union with God in Christ.

[61] Cf. VON BALTHASAR, KL[2], p. 254, who has stressed the important fact that the great word of Chalcedon is σώζειν, and that this "salvation" means the preservation of the peculiarity of both natures.

[62] See VON BALTHASAR, KL[2], p. 277. It is one of von Balthasar's great merits to have discovered the theological weight of this formula.

2 Natures "DIVINE" and Human

We may find a suitable starting-point in a passage of Amb 10 (in spite of the fact that the term *perichoresis* itself is lacking there). Here Maximus points out that God and man are regarded as exemplars (παραδείγματα) one of another, i.e. they stand in relation to each other in a particular polarity, a relationship which finds its classical expression in the idea of the *imago Dei*. Having stated this Maximus goes on, using the characteristic formula of reciprocity which we have referred to: ". . . and that God makes himself man for the sake of love for man (διὰ φιλανθρωπίαν, a characteristic expression among the Greek Fathers of the benevolence of God which leads to the Incarnation), *so far as* man, enabled by God, has deified himself"—and, *mutatis mutandis,* "that man is rapt up by God in mind to the unknowable, *so far as* man has manifested through virtues the God who is by nature invisible".[63]

If we start from the evident presupposition that this statement about deification has the process of union in Christ as its paradigm, we realize immediately that it is also relevant to an analysis of Maximus' Christology, and we are further allowed to draw the conclusion that according to Maximus there exists thus such a relationship of polarity between God and man, that the incarnation of God and the deification of man condition each other mutually. It is, in fact, it seems, a reciprocity of this kind which the term *perichoresis,* developed on the basis of the formulations of Chalcedon, is intended to express. Man becomes god as it were, in proportion to God's becoming man, and he is elevated for God's sake to the extent to which God has emptied himself, without change, and accepted human nature.[64]

Consequently Maximus can—in quite paradoxical terms—speak of a "blessed inversion" (καλὴ ἀντιστροφή), an active polarity, which makes God become man thanks to the deification of man, and makes man become god thanks to God's becoming man.[65] In the same way man's *kenosis* in relation to his passions is proportioned to God's *kenosis* in his becoming man,[66] and the contraction (συστολή), through which God, for his own sake, holds man to himself, corresponds to the expansion (διαστολή), through which he has come down to this world for man's sake.[67]

---

[63] Amb 10; PG 91, 1113 BC. For the translation, see SHERWOOD, *The Earlier Ambigua,* p. 144.—This passage will be interpreted from other aspects in ch. III: A, 4 (see p. 126 f.) and in ch. VI: 10 and 11 (see pp. 426 and 431 f. below).

[64] Amb 60; PG 91, 1385 BC. This is really no form of docetism but a broadly elaborated Chalcedonian theology.

[65] Amb 7; PG 91, 1084 C.

[66] OrDom; CCSG 23, p. 32 f.

[67] Amb 33; PG 91, 1288 A.

Against what we have said so far one might object, that we have dealt with statements about deification, i.e. with the appropriation of the divine work of salvation by the believer, when we have tried to prove the general, and Christological, importance of the formulas of reciprocity. The close relationship between these statements and Christology is certainly quite evident in itself, but if the polarity which is expressed through "the formula of reciprocity" is really intended to be a further elaboration of Chalcedonian Christology, we should have expected this formula to have been used also to express the preservation of the individuality of each of the natures. In fact, we do not find that this is so.

To this objection we may answer, however, that there are in Maximus' writings, in fact, other expressions than the *tantum-quantum* formula which are related to this polarity between human and divine.[68] A very characteristic synonym is for example provided by the expression ἕως-μέχρι, as it is used in Th Pol 8, and that in a context of the kind we are looking for.[69] For there we read, in reference to the *Tome of Leo*, that the unity between divine and human is safeguarded precisely through the preservation of the difference between them. We learn that the union of the two opposites is a fact, only so long as (ἕως-μέχρι) their natural difference (διαφορά) is preserved (σώζεται).[70] Their unity is thus not threatened by the fact that there is neither confusion nor change; on the contrary, precisely the fact that each nature preserves its own character and develops its activity in accordance with it guarantees their inseparable and indivisible union. The Christological insights of Chalcedon could not have been more strongly expressed in a single formula than by this ἕως-μέχρι. And at the same time the close relationship between this expression and the more well-known Maximian "formula of reciprocity" has become evident.[71]

But then there is no reason either to suppose that this faithful attitude

---

[68] Within the theology of deification one should refer to the expression κατὰ ἀναλογίαν in Thal 59; CCSG 22, p. 53.

[69] PG 91, 97 A. The importance of this passage within the context of Chalcedonian theology has been recognized by von Balthasar (KL², p. 254), who has also underlined the striking character of the formula itself (KL², p. 259). He has, however, not drawn the wider consequences which we are invited to draw, when we see this expression as a synonym of the *tantum quantum* formula. The originality which Maximus manifests at this point has been brought forward in a far stronger way by J. Ternus, Das Seelen- und Bewusstseinsleben Jesu. Problemgeschichtlich-systematische Untersuchung, Chalk 3, p. 107.

[70] PG 91, 96 D–97 A.

[71] Cf. also Ep 15; PG 91, 560 A: ὅπερ καθ' ὅσον μὲν διαφέρει τοῖς ἀφορίζουσιν αὐτὸ (sc. τὸ συντιθέμενον) τῶν κατ' οὐσίαν ὁμογενῶν ἰδιώμασι, τοσοῦτον τῷ συγχειμένῳ καθ' ὑπόστασιν ἑνίζεται ταὐτιζόμενον.

→ to the extent to which God has emptied himself without change and accepted human Nature

to Chalcedon disappears, when Maximus in some texts is more concerned with the aspect of unity than with that of difference. We have, in fact, seen that to him unity presupposes the preservation of the characteristics of each nature, indeed, that the unity with which he is concerned is precisely that unity which exists only when this requirement is fulfilled. As a matter of fact, such characteristic Maximian terms as *theandric* (θεανδρικός) and *identity* (ταυτότης), ambiguous in themselves, acquire their richness and importance precisely through this personal Chalcedonian interpretation. We shall give just a few indications to demonstrate this fact.

As regards the term *theandric*, the most interesting text is to be found in Amb 5. There Maximus discusses in detail Ps.-Denis' *Ep.* 4, to Gaius,[72] and not least its much debated expression "new theandric energy" (ἡ καινὴ θεανδρικὴ ἐνέργεια),[73] falsely and tendentiously changed by Cyrus into "*one* theandric energy" (μία . . . ἐνέργεια),[74] a falsification, however, which Maximus does not even mention in Amb 5.[75] In Amb 5—as in Th Pol 7—Maximus argues that Ps.-Denis' expression should be interpreted as divine and human energy in co-operation, and not as a mixed form of both.[76] For this reason Ps.-Denis does not in fact speak of one energy but of a new energy. This "newness" expresses the aspect of unity, but the unity with which we are concerned at this point is not a matter of arithmetic, Maximus makes clear.[77]

In accordance with this interpretation Maximus also shows in this whole section of Amb 5 that he is particularly concerned to emphasize both the duality of the unity and the aspect of unity in relation to the duality of Christ's activity. A number of clear and striking expressions may be noticed here:[78] 1) that Christ is in virtue of the hypostatic union a "man above man" (ὑπὲρ ἄνθρωπον ἄνθρωπος) (the same expression is found also in Ps.-Denis); 2) that there is a difference between the *logoi*

---

[72] PG 3, 1072 A–C.

[73] PG 3, 1072 C.

[74] See Sherwood, *The Earlier Ambigua,* p. 113, n. 17. Sergius tried for some time to make this expression, in its falsified form, a basis for union (so in the Alexandrian Union of 633); cf. W. Elert, *Der Ausgang der altkirchlichen Christologie,* Berlin 1957, pp. 228 f. and 231.

[75] That he knew of the falsification becomes indirectly apparent from what he says in ThPol 7; PG 91, 85 A, where the same text is discussed. Cf. also the Scholia to Ps.-Denis; PG 4, 533 BC.

[76] PG 91, 1056 B. On the theandric dimension generally, see my study *Man and the Cosmos,* pp. 71–91.

[77] ThPol 7; PG 91, 85 A. This problem has been analysed by A. Riou, *Le monde . . . ,* pp. 73–121. On the relationship between Maximus and Ps.-Denis, see also E. Bellini, Maxime interprète . . . , in Heinzer-Schönborn, *Maximus Confessor,* pp. 37–49.

[78] See PG 91, 1056 A–C.

according to nature (οἱ κατὰ φύσιν λόγοι), implying the preservation of the natures and their characteristics, and the 'supernatural' modes (οἱ ὑπὲρ φύσιν τρόποι), implying that the natures, from the point of view of their activity, in virtue of their union transcend, as it were, their own boundaries; 3) that the aspect of reciprocity implies that the sufferings of Christ take place "in a divine mode" (θεϊκῶς), since they are freely accepted, while, on the other hand, the divine acts of Christ are made "in a human mode" (ἀνθρωπικῶς), since they are made in flesh; 4) that the hypostatic union, for this reason, implies that there is no longer a "mere man" (ψιλὸς ἄνθρωπος) or a "naked God" (γυμνὸς Θεός); 5) that the divine energy is, therefore, "humanized" (ἀνδρωθεῖσα); 6) and, finally, that the theandric process implies that the divine and the human energy effect together, in a manner which is at the same time both divine and human (θεϊκῶς ἅμα καὶ ἀνδρικῶς), that which belongs to human and divine nature as such.

It seems self-evident, precisely in this context, that what is really important to Maximus is to apply the attributes of both natures in relation to their common unity, though, of course, always without change or confusion. In other words, it is only against this background that the application of the idea of *communicatio idiomatum* becomes meaningful to him. Now he is free to say, without causing any misunderstanding, that God may also be called passible (παθητός). Th Pol 9 is a text which provides very good examples of this mutual application of attributes,[79] and there we learn too—in reference to Gregory Nazianzen—that what belongs to man is in Christ not effected "according to man" (κατὰ ἄνθρωπον) and what belongs to God not "according to god" (κατὰ θεόν)—a negative equivalent, as we see, of what is formulated in positive terms in Amb 5.[80] And in another text Maximus professes, in a similar and characteristic way, that what is unlimited (the divine) is co-limited with that which is limited (the human), while that which is limited (the human) is developed according to the measurements of infinity.[81]

This is, thus, the "ineffable *mode* of mutual adhesion" with which Maximus is so intensely concerned.[82] It is, however, itself paradoxical, a mystery, which it manifests through its power to transcend the boundaries of the unified elements while keeping them entirely intact.[83] This mystery of hypostatic union—on the basis of the polarity and reciprocal

---

[79] PG 91, 120 B: παθητόν—ἀπαθῆ; ἄκτιστον—κτιστόν; περιγραπτόν—ἀπερίγραπτον; ἐπίγειον—οὐράνιον; ὁρώμενον—νοούμενον and χωρητόν—ἀχώρητον.
[80] PG 91, 120 A.
[81] See Ep 21; PG 91, 604 B.
[82] See Amb 5; PG 91, 1056 D–1057 A.
[83] Cf. von BALTHASAR, KL², p. 211.

relationship between human and divine—Maximus now calls "identity" (ταυτότης), a word which can be easily misunderstood, if it is separated from the context which we have now indicated, and which, therefore, one should avoid translating simply as "identity" (though this is the original sense of the word)—as von Balthasar has correctly argued—but perhaps as "unified preservation" or by a similar expression.[84] For this term is qualified by Maximus as "an entirely unchangeable identity" (ἀπαράλλακτος ἐν ὅλοις ταυτότης).[85] One has thus to conclude that this is an "identity", which implies precisely that the elements preserve and develop their own identity in virtue of their unity. In accordance with this understanding Maximus also defines ταυτότης as "unchangeableness" (ἀπαραλλαξία), i.e. within its own unity.

Thus here again we find a reference back to Chalcedonian theology, which clearly shows where Maximus stands in relation to the latter in his own speculation about *perichoresis* and *communicatio idiomatum*. Maximus' faithfulness to the Chalcedonian insights implies that he develops the content of its formulations to a point where their inner tensions are reconciled in the acknowledgement of a Christological mystery of unity in diversity.

B. Maximus and the Neo-Chalcedonian Position

Hans Urs von Balthasar, in the second edition of his important study of Maximus, *Kosmische Liturgie,* emphasizes, among other things, that Maximus' relationship to Neo-Chalcedonian theology has not yet been studied by scholars, though, as he points out, it would now be possible to do so, since the hypothesis put forward by Loofs regarding the connection between the different writers called Leontius has been effectively disposed of.[86] Since we have tried in the first part of this chapter to analyse some aspects of Maximus' Christology which clearly show the character of his dependence upon the formulas and the theological insights of the Council of Chalcedon, it is obviously also of importance that we should try, if possible, to find out in what direction the investigations which von Balthasar suggests could perhaps lead us. We shall not be able here to do more than give a few indications concerning Maximus' relationship to Neo-Chalcedonian theology; we hope, howev-

---

[84] On the ambiguity of the word ταυτότης, see VON BALTHASAR, KL², p. 231 f.

[85] Amb 10; PG 91, 1189 A (here used as a more general cosmic law).

[86] See VON BALTHASAR, KL², p. 13.

er, to show that he was aware of this relationship, not only because of his faithfulness to the *Council of Constantinople,* where this theology was victorious, but also as a result of a theological reflection on the problems raised by the positions of the Neo-Chalcedonian theologians themselves.

The concept of a Neo-Chalcedonian theology has only fairly recently been introduced into the historical surveys of 6th century Christian doctrine. It would, however, take us too far afield to give a detailed account of the scholarly discussion which eventually led to the establishment of this concept. In fact, a general summary of this discussion has already been presented in a Bonn dissertation, published by S. Helmer in 1962.[87] Let us then simply indicate some essential elements of the thought of this school of theology—which in part are also to be found in the formulations of Constantinople in 553—by which Maximus' own relationship to it may be judged.

The concept of Neo-Chalcedonianism was originally suggested by J. Lebon, who used it in his book on Severian monophysitism to denote a particular group of Chalcedonian theologians, in whom he had noticed two characteristic features: first, they referred widely to the writings of Cyril of Alexandria, whose ambiguous Christological formulations they tried to harmonize with those of Chalcedon, and secondly, they used philosophy of an Aristotelian variety in order to construct a scientific theology of the Incarnation.[88] Lebon's suggestions were further developed especially by Ch. Moeller, who tried to trace the Neo-Chalcedonian stream of thinking so far back (till before Chalcedon), that the concept itself threatened to lose its meaning.[89]

---

[87] S. HELMER, *Der Neuchalkedonismus.* Diss. Bonn 1962.

[88] LEBON, *Le monophysisme sévérien.* Diss. Louvain 1909. For the summary of Lebon's position, cf. M. RICHARD, Le Néo-chalcédonisme, MSR 3 (1946), p. 157.—A more precise definition was presented by Lebon five years later, when he stated that Neo-Chalcedonianism is a theological position in the beginning of the 6th century which tries to unite and reconcile the seemingly irreconcilable formulas of Cyril and Chalcedon in their original sense; see LEBON, Ephrem d'Amid, patriarche d'Antioche (526–44), *Mél. d'Hist. offerts à Ch. Moeller* I (1914), p. 213 f.; see also IDEM, Restitutions à Theodoret de Cyr, RHE 26 (1930), p. 535.

[89] CH. MOELLER, Un représentant de la christologie néo-chalcédonienne au début du VIᵉsiècle en Orient, Nephalius d'Alexandrie, RHE 40 (1944–45); pp. 73–140; cf. IDEM, Le chalcédonisme et le néo-chalcédonisme en Orient de 451 à la fin du VIᵉ siècle, Chalk I, pp. 637–720.—Independently of Moeller R. V. SELLERS, *The Council of Chalcedon,* London 1953, especially pp. 302–350, arrived at a similar result.—A negative attitude to the new concept has been expressed particularly by H. M. DIEPEN, *Les Trois Chapitres au Concile de Chalcédoine,* Oosterhaut 1953, and by J.-M. ALONSO, En torno al 'neocalcedonismo', *XV Semana Española de teologia,* 1956, pp. 329–366.—An inclusive critical evaluation of the discussion is given, not only in Helmer's thesis (see note 86), but also by GRILLMEIER, Der Neu-Chalkedonismus. Um die Berechtigung eines Neuen Kapitels in der Dogmengeschichte, HJG 77 (1958), pp. 151–166.

At this point, however, M. Richard felt obliged to react and tried to effect a critical evaluation and a more precise definition of the concept. Richard thus resolved that the decisive difference between a Neo-Chalcedonian and a strictly Chalcedonian position is the fact that the former accepts both the formula "the one incarnate nature of the God Logos" (μιὰ φύσις τοῦ θεοῦ λόγου σεσαρκωμένη)[90] and the so called theopaschite formula, which was derived from Cyril's 12th anathematism,[91] while the latter rejects them.[92] Moeller later accepted this position, and in his article in "Das Konzil von Chalkedon" provided an even sharper distinction: for a Neo-Chalcedonian position is it not sufficient merely to quote these formulas—for this may be done also by those outside this group—, but the Christological formulations "one nature" and "two natures" must be held together and both be regarded as essential for a correct presentation of Christian doctrine.[93] A further characteristic of Neo-Chalcedonian theology is, according to Moeller, that it tries—as we may observe in the case of Leontius of Jerusalem—to preserve Basil's trinitarian concept of hypostasis and use it in a Christological context, in which "hypostasis" is understood as "notae individuantes" and the empirical qualities of human nature consequently disappear into the hypostasis of the Logos.[94] For this reason, Moeller concludes, the possibility cannot be excluded that the roots of monenergism and monothelitism are to be found in Neo-Chalcedonianism rather than in Severian monophysitism.[95] It should further be mentioned that Neo-Chalcedonian theology understood hypostatic union as "synthetic" union (ἕνωσις κατὰ σύνθεσιν), and that it stressed that this union is *ex duabus naturis* as much as it is *in duabus naturis*.[96]

Among the representatives of this theological position, which in Constantinople in 553 became to a great extent the official position of the Church, have been counted such names as Nephalius, John Grammaticus, Ephrem of Antioch, Leontius of Jerusalem (who is to be distinguished from Leontius of Byzantium), the emperor Justinian, Theodore of Raïthu, Eulogius of Alexandria and Ps.-Pamphilus.[97] In this

---

[90] See Cyril, *Ep.* 46; PG 77, 241.

[91] Cyril, *Ep.* 17; PG 77, 121 D.

[92] See RICHARD, *art. cit.*, p. 159.

[93] See MOELLER, Chalk I, p. 666.

[94] See MOELLER, Textes 'monophysites' de Léonce de Jérusalem, ETL 27 (1951), p. 471 ff.

[95] See MOELLER, Chalk I, p. 695, n. 167 and p. 720.

[96] Cf. e.g. P. GALTIER, L'Occident et le néo-chalcédonisme, Greg 40 (1959), p. 55 and also von BALTHASAR, KL², p. 242, n. 4.

[97] See GRILLMEIER, HJG 77 (1958), p. 161.

group should also be included John of Skythopolis, the scholiast of Ps.-Denis, and Theodore of Pharan, who is, however, according to W. Elert to be identified with Theodore of Raïthu.[98]

Through its victory in 553 Neo-Chalcedonianism has been of the greatest importance for the later development of orthodox theology. A study of Maximus' relationship to it is, therefore, in itself of great interest, and if it is true to say that monenergism and monothelitism both have their roots in it, such a study becomes even more important. For if Moeller, who has emphasized that this is the background of the two 7th century heresies with which Maximus had to fight, is right, it is difficult to understand how Maximus could combine faithfulness to the Council of Constantinople with an active resistance to these heresies. Knowing Maximus' later position and pre-supposing the consistency of his think-ing, one would rather expect him to follow the line of a stricter Chalcedonian theology and to be restrictive in his attitude towards Neo-Chalcedonianism. On the other hand, if it could be sufficiently demonstrated that Maximus accepted Neo-Chalcedonianism in an un-critical way, one would at least have to admit that Maximus' primary hesitation in relation to monenergism and monothelitism, emphasized by Grumel and other scholars, had a natural motivation: a common theological starting-point. It might further be claimed that there is a certain parallelism to be recognized between the emperor Justinian's attempts at the unification of the different parties in the 6th century, for which a similar theology provided the intellectual presuppositions, and the corresponding attempts made by the patriarch Sergius in the 7th century. The problem which interests us in this section may thus also be able to throw some light upon Maximus' theological methods in that complicated historical situation, in which his contribution was made.

As we shall see later, however, it would be unfair to say that Maximus' relationship to Neo-Chalcedonianism could be demonstrated merely by showing the character of his faithfulness to the Council of Constantino-ple. For, as a matter of fact, the Council of Constantinople did not explicitly treat all the questions which had been discussed by the Neo-Chalcedonian theologians, nor did it express all the convictions which scholars have found to be characteristic of Neo-Chalcedonianism as a whole. And Maximus, on the other hand, did not restrict his interest in Neo-Chalcedonian formulas and positions to those, which were

---

[98] See ELERT, *op. cit.* pp. 203–212; cf. also MOELLER, in Chalk I, p. 695, n. 167. Elert sees in Theodore of Pharan the theological adviser behind the Alexandrian union of 633, who tried for the first time to effect the synthesis between Cyril and Chalcedon by means of the Areopagite (see *op. cit.*, p. 228 f.).

explicitly treated in Constantinople. In order to give some ideas of Maximus' relationship to this stream of thinking as a whole we must, therefore, study his position in regard to the most characteristic elements of Neo-Chalcedonianism, whether or not expressed in Constantinople. At the same time, however, we shall not try to deal here with his relationship to the different Neo-Chalcedonian theologians individually, which is another, wider and more complicated problem. Let us, thus, use some of the characteristic elements in Neo-Chalcedonian theology, pointed out by scholars, as a kind of criterion by which to judge Maximus' relationship to this stream of thinking in general.

1. The position of Cyril of Alexandria in Maximus' writings

As an authority Cyril of Alexandria plays a rather outstanding role in Maximus' writings. This fact, however, is not in itself of any decisive importance. For already in the 6th century Cyril was frequently cited and referred to as an authoritative source of orthodox theology, and his position as a cited authority had certainly been strengthened by the references to him in *Constantinopolitanum II* with its anathemas against "the three chapters". In a time when monenergism and monothelitism threatened to overrun the Church, unqualified reference to Cyril ought, however, to have been more difficult to make. Yet, we can find no hesitation on the part of Maximus in this respect. Quotations from Cyril, used in 'monophysite' and monothelite circles, are also used by Maximus, though interpreted by him in an orthodox way. (Even other passages from Cyril are quoted to some extent or referred to.) One might argue that Maximus was more or less forced to discuss these passages, since they were all closely related to the arguments for or against monophysitism and monothelitism, but it is at least striking that the passages from Cyril which Maximus deals with are given an energetic and definite interpretation based on what Maximus claims to be Cyril's own intentions. It is, therefore, not altogether easy to understand Dalmais' supposition that Maximus' knowledge of Cyril was defective.[99]

By this period it is, indeed, always uncertain whether a particular writer quotes Cyril directly, or uses one of the numerous florilegia, which were circulating, but it is nevertheless striking that Maximus claims to interpret Cyril in accordance with the latter's own intentions, while at the

---

[99] See DALMAIS, RAM 29 (1953), p. 133.

same time he is aware that those against whom he is fighting also refer to Cyril as their authority.[100] Besides, Maximus himself constructed florilegia, in which there are quotations from Cyril, though their number is very restricted. In Th Pol 15, which is the most extensive of Maximus' florilegia, we find two such quotations,[101] and in Th Pol 27, which is a florilegium dealing with the problem of the two energies, there are also two quotations from Cyril.[102] It is further to be noticed that Cyril's statements are not only defended and interpreted by Maximus against those circles, where Cyril's words were, in Maximus' opinion, misused, but they seem also to have been retained as part of a definite theological programme.

Maximus' attachment to Cyril is, finally, most remarkable at a number of points which had been actualised by Neo-Chalcedonian theology, as we shall see in the following paragraphs.

2. Positive evaluation of Cyril's expression "one incarnate nature of the God Logos"

This widely debated formulation is discussed by Maximus on several occasions. Maximus continues the older fight against monophysitism in clear relation to it. He refers directly—particularly in Ep 12 (addressed to John the Chamberlain and dated to November-December 641)[103]—to this formula, as we find it in Cyril's *Ep. 2 ad Succensum* and in his *Ep. ad Eulogium*,[104] and interprets it in a way which harmonizes with an orthodox standpoint. Thus according to Maximus Cyril never intended to abolish the difference between the natures in Christ after their union (ἔνωσις),[105] as Apollinaris, Eutyches and Severus wished to do,[106] a fact which Cyril himself had also quite clearly pointed out.[107] In numerous passages in Cyril, Maximus says, it is made clear that he never intended to prevent anyone from speaking of two natures also after their union, nor wished to do away with the difference between them.[108] The expression which Cyril uses in his letter to Succensus must be understood from

---

[100] See Ep 12; PG 91, 472 A.
[101] PG 91, 176 BC.
[102] PG 91, 281 C and 284 C ff.
[103] See SHERWOOD, *An Annotated Date-list*, p. 45.
[104] PG 77, 241 and 225 B.
[105] PG 91, 496 B.
[106] PG 91, 501 D.
[107] PG 91, 472 A and C.
[108] PG 91, 477 D–480 A.

the point of view of the fact that this letter was directed against the Nestorians.[109]

Also in other places, and earlier, Maximus emphasizes that the two natures in Christ are "unconfused" even after their union.[110] For one is obliged to interpret Cyril's statements about one nature in Christ in accordance with what he says elsewhere and analyse the ambiguous formula in the light of the latter. And then it becomes evident, Maximus shows, that human nature is also regarded by Cyril as intact and perfect even after the union.[111] With the expression "incarnate" ($\sigma\epsilon\sigma\alpha\rho\kappa\omega\mu\acute{\epsilon}\nu\eta$) Cyril has in fact denoted human nature, for man consists of flesh ($\sigma\acute{\alpha}\rho\xi$) and an intelligible soul ($\psi\upsilon\chi\grave{\eta}$ $\nu o\epsilon\rho\acute{\alpha}$).[112] According to Cyril, Maximus argues, the Incarnation is the union between the Logos and a flesh which possesses an intelligible and reasonable soul ($\nu o\epsilon\rho\grave{\alpha}$ $\tau\epsilon$ $\kappa\alpha\grave{\iota}$ $\lambda o\gamma\iota\kappa\grave{\eta}$ $\psi\upsilon\chi\acute{\eta}$), and thus the word "incarnate" in the formula simply denotes "the substance of our nature" ($\acute{\eta}$ $\tau\hat{\eta}\varsigma$ $\kappa\alpha\theta$ $\acute{\eta}\mu\hat{\alpha}\varsigma$ $\varphi\acute{\upsilon}\sigma\epsilon\omega\varsigma$ $o\grave{\upsilon}\sigma\acute{\iota}\alpha$).[113] This is an interpretation of Cyril which is obviously also intended to be in harmony with the text of the 4th anathema of the Council of Constantinople.[114] The same conviction is further expressed by Maximus in the important Ep 12, where we learn that "humanity" ($\grave{\alpha}\nu\theta\rho\omega\pi\acute{o}\tau\eta\varsigma$) according to Cyril is "flesh intelligibly inanimated" ($\sigma\acute{\alpha}\rho\xi$ $\grave{\epsilon}\psi\upsilon\chi\omega\mu\acute{\epsilon}\nu\eta$ $\lambda o\gamma\iota\kappa\hat{\omega}\varsigma$), and thus in the expression "one incarnate nature of the God Logos" both natures are denoted through "name" ($\check{o}\nu o\mu\alpha$) and "limiting definition" ($\check{o}\rho o\varsigma$). $\check{o}\nu o\mu\alpha$ is indicated through the words "the one nature of the Logos", for through them Cyril mentions both that which is common to the substance and that which is individual in relation to the hypostasis, and $\check{o}\rho o\varsigma$ is indicated through the word "incarnate", for the latter denotes human nature.[115]

It is, thus, obvious that this much discussed formula in Cyril is, in Maximus' mind, so resistant to a monophysite interpretation, that it provides rather a perfect description of the relationship in Christ between two natures which remain intact. A Neo-Chalcedonian interest, that of preserving Cyril's expression as an alternative formula, therefore receives here in a way which is characteristic of Maximus, a precise interpretation which is at the same time strictly Chalcedonian. And at the same time, $\mu\acute{\iota}\alpha$, formally related to $\varphi\acute{\upsilon}\sigma\iota\varsigma$, seems to be identified by

---

[109] PG 91, 481 B.
[110] See Ep 15; PG 91, 565 C. For the dating of this letter, see SHERWOOD, *op. cit.*, p. 40.
[111] Ep 12; PG 91, 496 C.
[112] *Ibid.*
[113] Ep 13; PG 91, 525 A.
[114] See *Concil. Oecumen, Decr.*, p. 91.
[115] PG 91, 501 BC.

Maximus—in a way which reminds us of Cyril himself—with μία ὑπόστασις.

3. The expressions "one nature" and "two natures", correctly understood, are complementary to each other

This position also, characteristic of Neo-Chalcedonianism, is found in Maximus, though not very often. In this context there are two texts, particularly, which call for our attention. Thus Maximus emphasizes in Ep 12 that the expression "two natures" is used when one wishes to point out that there is a difference between the natures even after their union, but speaks about one incarnate nature, when reference is given to the ineffable way in which the mystery of their union in Christ is realized.[116] And in Ep 18 we recognize a dialectic which seems to be very much influenced by Neo-Chalcedonianism in general, and is also clearly attached to the Council of Constantinople. We learn in this letter that just as one who does *not* profess that Christ is *one* incarnate nature of the God Logos on the basis of the hypostatic union, provided that it is correctly understood in Cyril's own way, does *not* believe that this *union* has really taken place, so likewise one who does *not* confess *two* natures after their union, two natures of which Christ now is, can*not* really make clear that the *difference* (sc. between the two natures) is preserved.[117] As we see, Maximus establishes here too a very characteristic relationship between the two aspects, in that he says not only that they are acceptable or necessary alternatives but also that they are mutually dependent.

4. Hypostatic and "synthetic" union

In the formulations of Chalcedon the expression "hypostatic union" (ἕνωσις καθ᾽ ὑπόστασιν) was missing, but in Constantinople it was accepted in Cyril's version, introduced into the 4th anathema and there identified with "synthetic" union (ἕνωσις κατὰ σύνθεσιν).[118] Maximus is faithful to this understanding. Thus he underlines e.g. in Ep 12 that the union of human and divine in Christ is καθ᾽ ὑπόστασιν,[119] and in Ep 18 the formula ἕνωσις καθ᾽ ὑπόστασιν is obviously taken for granted.[120] This fact is, of course, in no sense surprising, but we also find that he

---

[116] PG 91, 477 B.
[117] PG 91, 588 B.
[118] *Concil. Oecumen. Decr.*, p. 91; cf. *Anath.* 8, *ibid.*, p. 93 f.
[119] PG 91, 481 D f.
[120] PG 91, 588 B.

understands both the unity of body and soul in man and the union of
divine and human in Christ as a σύνθεσις.[121] This last term is at the same
⅄ time free from any associations with the concept of mixture in the sense
of confusion. For it is, according to Maximus, characteristic of every
kind of "synthesis" that it is a unity which, though inseparable, allows
for a true fulfillment of the individuality of its elements.[122] We may, thus,
once more conclude that Maximus uses what may be called a Neo-
Chalcedonian terminology with a certain (Chalcedonian) strictness in its
application. In the same direction it is obvious also that his interpretation of Cyril is to be found.

5.   Christ is said to be not only "in duabus naturis" but also "ex duabus naturis"

It was important to Neo-Chalcedonianism to underline that the Incarnation in Christ implied the rise of a new unity. For that reason they were
particularly eager to emphasize the expression "ex duabus naturis" in
this context. Maximus is acquainted with this tendency also, though he
seems more hesitant here to accept the Neo-Chalcedonian position than
at the other points we have mentioned. This hesitation may to some
extent be due to the formulations of the Council of Chalcedon where
both expressions were avoided.[123] Maximus has obviously no difficulties
in using the expression σύνθεσις ἐκ,[124] but he is at the same time very
careful not to emphasize the unity at the expense of the importance of the
elements. In Ep 13 he manifests once more his dialectical capacity in
precisely this context, when he underlines that in the same way as one
professes that Christ is "*of* two natures" (ἐκ δύο φύσεων) as the whole is
"of its parts" (ἐκ μερῶν), so likewise one believes, when one says that
Christ even after the union of the two natures is "*in* two natures" (ἐν δύο
φύσεσιν), that he is "in divinity and humanity" (ἐν θεότητι καὶ
ἀνθρωπότητι) as the whole is present in its parts.[125] Maximus' eagerness

---

[121] See Ep 12; PG 91, 496 A. See further on Maximus' use of this analogy ch. III: A, 1;
pp. 99–104 below. To this whole problem and its background, see HEINZER, *op.cit.,* pp.
94–108. Cf. also K.-H. UTHEMANN, Das anthropologische Modell . . . , in HEINZER-
SCHÖNBORN, *Maximus Confessor,* pp. 223–233.

[122] See Ep 13; PG 91, 521 C and VON BALTHASAR's summarizing treatment of the
concept in KL², pp. 57–66.

[123] Cf. SELLERS, *The Council of Chalcedon,* p. 344, n. 4.

[124] We find it e.g. in Ep 12; PG 91, 496 A.

[125] PG 91, 524 D–525 A. For a general discussion of the doctrine of the two natures in
Christ, see PIRET, *op.cit.,* pp. 203–239. Cf. also PIRET, Christologie et théologie
trinitaire . . . , in HEINZER-SCHÖNBORN, *Maximus Confessor,* pp. 215–222.

not to stress the concept of "ex duabus naturis" to such an extent as to diminish the importance of "in duabus naturis" is rather characteristic of his whole attitude. For to him, as we have seen, the emphasis on the unity between the elements in Christ is intimately connected with, and even dependent on, an equal emphasis on the preservation of these elements. If Sherwood is right in dating Ep 13 to a comparatively early period in Maximus' life, it is obvious that Maximus' interest in and use of Neo-Chalcedonian formulations does not imply any inclination to be favourable to the possible "heretical" consequences of this theological tendency, for which they are an expression. The unity which exists in Christ is to him a mystery, the mysterious character of which can be upheld only if the emphasis on this unity is not allowed to violate the integrity of its constituent elements. The formula "ex duabus naturis" thus to him expresses this unity as a new, overwhelming fact, while "in duabus naturis" expresses precisely the mystic character of this union.

6.   *"One energy"*

The kind of interpretation of Cyril which Maximus uses in regard to texts quoted by 'monophysite' circles, he also uses *mutatis mutandis* in relation to Cyril's statements concerning *one energy* (μία ἐνέργεια). The most important monothelite quotation from Cyril was the expression "one connatural energy in (or through) duality" (μία τε καὶ συγγενὴς δι' ἀμφοῖν ἐνέργεια),[126] which was frequently referred to together with Ps.-Denis' expression "the new (falsified to "one") theandric energy".[127] Both these formulas are treated in detail by Maximus and are given an orthodox interpretation. For a study of his relationship to Neo-Chalcedonian tendencies it is, however, sufficient to analyse his treatment of Cyril's text.

Maximus uses a method, according to which he derives the true interpretation of Cyril's words from his understanding of "substance" (οὐσία) and "nature" (φύσις). Thus, Maximus refers in Th Pol 7 to a passage in Cyril, which is supposed to show that the expression "one will" could be used by Cyril only in reference to one and the same substance.[128] In his florilegium Th Pol 27 Maximus further provides a

---

[126] *In Ioann.* 4; PG 73, 577 CD; cf. also HEFELE, *Conciliengeschichte* 3, p. 115.

[127] See p. 34 above; cf. also HEFELE, *op. cit.,* p. 116 f.

[128] PG 91, 81 A. The quotation is from Cyril, *In Ioann.* 10 and belongs to those texts which are only preserved in a fragmentary form. It reads: Μιᾶς γὰρ οὐσίας, ἕν δὴ καὶ τὸ θέλημα. This formulation was referred to also at the 6th ecumenical Council, see *Actio* 10, MANSI, 11, ch. 416.

longer quotation from Cyril, where the latter combines the concepts of nature and substance with that of energy.[129] On the basis of this conviction it is relatively easy for Maximus to claim that Cyril has in fact taught the "coexistence" (συμφυΐα) and "union" (ἕνωσις) of energies each of which related to its own nature. For on the one hand God has become flesh, and the energy which is linked with flesh is thereby made "divine" without ceasing to be what it is in itself, and on the other hand it should also be said that the Logos has become man and performs his divine work in a human manner.[130] It is, thus, according to Maximus no mixed energy which Cyril wished to affirm but simply a *perichoresis* between divine and human energy. Each energy remains what it is, at the same time as it so to speak transcends itself.

It follows from this that Maximus in the disputation with Pyrrhus is able to press his interpretation of Cyril's words about the one energy still one degree further. By "one energy", Maximus says here, Cyril had not wished to maintain that the divinity and humanity of Christ should possess one single common energy. What Cyril had wished to emphasize was the unity and identity of the divine will itself, with or without the flesh. The Father works "in an unembodied way" (ἀσωμάτως), but the incarnate Son has carried out his divine acts "in the body" (σωματικῶς), i.e. through his connection with his own flesh. In spite of this connection there is only one and the same divine energy at work, but at the same time, according to Cyril, Christ's works are done δι' ἀμφοῖν.[131] Once again, therefore, we meet the question of *perichoresis*. This implies that the divine energy, without losing its identity, can work σωματικῶς.[132] This is the sense in which one can speak of one energy. But the human energy becomes, as we have seen, "divine", i.e. it can work "in a divine manner" (θεἵκῶς), and for this reason one must *also* speak of two energies. Thus just as in the question of the two natures Maximus can say—in a Neo-Chalcedonian way—that both expressions are appropriate and complementary to each other, but this does not imply, on Maximus' part, any monenergetic or monothelite consequences, nor even any hesitation in regard to them.

The expression "one energy" is, therefore, for Maximus just as little objectionable in itself, as "one nature", when rightly explained. Cyril,

---

[129] PG 91, 284 C–285 A. Among the formulations of this text we also find the following one: Τὰ γὰρ τῆς αὐτῆς ἐνεργείας ὄντα, καὶ τῆς αὐτῆς οὐσίας ὁμολόγηται. Cf. also the reference to the same view of Cyril given in ThPol 9; PG 91, 125 A and 25; PG 91, 273 A.

[130] ThPol 8; PG 91, 101 AB.

[131] Pyrrh; PG 91, 344 BC.

[132] Cf. the same argument in ThPol 9; 125 AB.

Maximus points out, by his expression συγγενὴς καὶ δι' ἀμφοῖν ἐπιδεδειγμένη μία ἐνέργεια[133] did not wish to abolish the substantial difference between the energies which are united to their natures, i.e. the natures "of" which and "in" which the one Christ exists, but only to maintain "the constitutive conjunction" (σύστασις) which consists in the union in Christ of the energies to the utmost point.[134]

7. The concept of hypostasis

In its determination to maintain the Cappadocian concept of hypostasis Neo-Chalcedonianism among other things came to define *hypostasis* as *notae individuantes*. This had the consequence that the concrete characteristics of human nature threatened to be swallowed up in, or mixed with, the divine hypostasis.[135] What was Maximus' reaction to this tendency? This question is one of those which must be posed if we are to shed light on his relation to Neo-Chalcedonianism. Von Balthasar has shown clearly that Maximus in his use of the concept of hypostasis has in large measure gone further than his predecessors in general.[136] On the one hand Maximus can certainly (in a Cappadocian way) define hypostasis as a substance with its individual characteristics (οὐσία μετὰ ἰδιωμάτων),[137] but on the other hand he speaks of a *synthetic hypostasis*—in itself a Neo-Chalcedonian concept—in such a way that, in the case of Christ, it can include full humanity, not only the universal human nature but also its individual qualities.[138] The Logos has assumed the flesh in its hypostatic "identity" (ταυτότης),[139] but this fact does not imply that the qualities of the human nature are swallowed up by those of the divine nature. The hypostasis unites not only two natures but also two modes of existence (τρόποι ὑπάρξεως).[140] The hypostasis of Christ, however, is unique, and human nature can therefore find its fulfilment precisely in relation to this hypostasis. Human nature with its energy and will is maintained and confirmed in synthetic union with the divine nature in

---

[133] Maximus quotes Cyril's text in a slightly different way at different places.

[134] ThPol 7; PG 91, 85 C. The term σύστασις is neutral in this context, and Maximus likes to use it to emphasize a bringing together of different or opposite qualities, as e.g. form and matter in Char 3. 30; CSC p. 158. On the importance of ThPol 7 in relation to the struggle about the wills of Christ, see LÉTHEL, *op.cit.*, pp. 65–74.

[135] See MOELLER, ETL 27 (1951), p. 469 and 473.

[136] VON BALTHASAR, KL[2], especially pp. 227, 243 and 247–253.

[137] See Ep 15; PG 91, 557 D.

[138] Cf. VON BALTHASAR, KL[2], p. 227.

[139] Amb 3; PG 91, 1040 C.

[140] Cf. VON BALTHASAR, KL[2], p. 242.

Christ and is enhypostasized there.[141] Precisely the fact that this hypostasis is one and synthetic is thus so far from threatening to swallow up what
is naturally human, that the latter is fully realized only there. The further
development of this line of thinking is, however, closely linked with
Maximus' concept of freedom, which cannot be dealt with here.

As a general summary of what we have found, we may thus conclude
that Maximus, already in the earlier period of his activity, consistently
combines his acceptance of Neo-Chalcedonian formulations and
positions—whether they are affirmed by the Council of Constantinople
or not—with a more strict Chalcedonian dialectic, which he develops
even further at particular points.[142] Thus no hesitation in relation to
monenergism or monothelitism is at this point demonstrable in
Maximus, in spite of the fact that both these heresies seem to have their
roots in Neo-Chalcedonian positions. Maximus' openness to Neo-
Chalcedonian theology and his faithfulness to the Council of Constantinople are, as we have seen, in fact combined with a deepened understanding of the Chalcedonian Christological insights which seems in itself to
exclude any serious hesitation of this kind.

---

[141] See Ep 13; PG 91, 532 B and ThPol 4; PG 91, 61 B; cf. von BALTHASAR, KL², p.
243.—On this scheme in general, cf. the clarifying analysis in PIRET, *op.cit.*, pp. 157–185.

[142] The so-called Theopaschite formula, *unus ex Trinitate passus est,* seems to be the
only Neo-Chalcedonian area of interest, which cannot be traced in Maximus' writings.

CHAPTER TWO

The Cosmological Context

It may seem strange to deal with Maximus' cosmology after his Christology. Behind this arrangement, however, lies the conviction that Christological insights, particularly as they had been expressed in the general councils of the Church, are of primary importance to Maximus in the development of his theology of creation of which his anthropology, in its turn, is the most important part. As we hope to show in this chapter, his view of creation is in fact best understood in relation to the central dogma of Chalcedonian Christology: the definition of the union of the two natures in Christ as without confusion, change, division and separation but in mutual communication. This implies that the Christological combination of inseparable unity and preserved identity is, in Maximus' view, equally characteristic both of the relationship of God to creation and of the different entities of creation in relation to one another, though of course, there are other elements of Maximus' cosmology which do not immediately enter into this perspective.

A succinct summary of the basic elements of Maximus' cosmology is not easily found in his own writings. The first section of Char 4 may, however, serve this purpose to some extent. For this reason we intend to use its content as a suitable outline for this chapter. Additional aspects will be brought in from elsewhere.

In this section of Char 4 at least 8 elements of cosmology may be distinguished, which can be more or less elaborated in different directions in order to give a more complete picture of Maximus' theology of creation. Arranged in a different order than that of Maximus these elements (on which Maximus does not dwell very long in the text itself) are: 1) *creatio ex nihilo,* with a particular stress on the aspects of distance and difference, which distinguish Creator and creation (4. 1); 2) creation because of God's will (4. 3, 4); 3) creation because of God's benevolence (4.3); 4) creation by the Word (4.3); 5) creation because of God's prudence (4.1); 6) creation as divine condescension introducing an element of motion (4.1, 2, 6); 7) every creature composite of substance and accident (4.9); 8) creation, not of qualities but of qualified substances, which are, however, in need of divine providence (4. 6, 9, 14). In the following subsections we shall deal with them one after the other.[1]

1. The creatio ex nihilo idea and other expressions of the aspect of differentiation within creation

That God created the world out of nothing is a conviction affirmed throughout orthodox Christian tradition. It expresses the superiority of God over against man and all other created beings. God is not in need of any pre-existent material in order to create. It expresses the conviction that God is the creator of all that is, and is himself in no sense subordinated to or dependent on anything else. In this aspect the doctrine of *creatio ex nihilo* is closely related to negative theology, and to the conviction that no human categories are capable of expressing the mystery of God.[2]

Maximus refers several times explicitly to this doctrine. In Char 4.1 he praises God that He has brought that which is into existence from nothing,[3] and in Amb 7 he not only takes it for granted that God has brought things into existence from that which is not,[4] but also expresses the conviction that God has established visible and invisible creation out of non-being.[5] It should further be noted that in another passage of the same Amb Maximus gives a definition of τέλος as "that for the sake of which all things are, though itself for the sake of nothing",[6] and in combination with the affirmation, given later in the same text,[7] that this end is in God alone, these statements show that for Maximus arguments of causality and teleology may serve together to underline the absolute superiority of God in relation to all else.

This absolute distance between God and his creation is of the utmost

---

[1] See CSC, pp. 194–200.—A ninth element ought to have been added here: creation takes place within time. It would have given us an opportunity to discuss Maximus' understanding of the created category of time as related to eternity. But since this subject would lead us beyond the scope of this chapter, we have decided to leave it out.

[2] For testimonies to the idea of *creatio ex nihilo* in the early Church, see e.g. Theophilus of Antioch, *Ad Autolyc.* I, 4; PG 6, 1029 B; 2, 10; 1064 B; Irenaeus, *Adv. haeres.* 2. 10, 4; PG 7, 736 B; cf. 3. 8, 3; 868 AB; Origen, *De princ., praef.* 4; GCS Orig. 5, p. 9, 14; Chrysostom, *In Gen. hom.* 2, 2; PG 53, 28 and Augustine, *In Io., tract.* 42, 10; PL 35, 1703; *Conf.* 11, 5; CSEL 33, 285 and 12, 7; CSEL 33, 314.

[3] CSC, p. 194.

[4] PG 91, 1077 C.

[5] PG 91, 1080 A. The same conviction is implied in the very beginning of the same text; 1069 B.

[6] PG 91, 1072 C.

[7] PG 91, 1073 B.

importance in Maximus' cosmology. The idea of *creatio ex nihilo* is only the most basic expression of it. It corresponds rather closely to the role which the concepts of "non-confusion" and "non-change" play in Maximus' Christology, and for this reason we shall dwell for some time upon some other expressions of the same conception.

The basic gulf

Maximus recognizes in principle a basic *gulf* ($\chi\acute{\alpha}\sigma\mu\alpha$) between created and uncreated nature,[8] which only the creative will of God can overbridge.[9] Thus not only the economy of salvation, instituted in favour of fallen man, but also the primary act of creation is to be seen as an expression of God's loving-kindness. For in creation God places over against himself a world which is utterly distinct and which he yet intends to bring into union with himself without annihilating the difference. On the one hand, God must always be recognized as a sovereign God, but on the other, the biblical evaluation of creation in its multiplicity as essentially good must not be denied. From these presuppositions Maximus is bound to rule out the Origenist myth of a prehistoric fall, which caused God to create the empirical world, and at the same time to preserve all the apophatic terminology of the Areopagite. A sharp distinction and a positive relationship between earthly creation and its creator must go together, a double prerequisite which is thus for Maximus cosmological as well as Christological. And the work of unification, of overcoming the distance without letting it disappear, is to him God's alone, for only God's nature can remain unaffected by such a concern.

This basic conviction is, as we have said, expressed not only through the idea of *creatio ex nihilo* or of the fundamental gulf between created and uncreated, but also in a number of terms, which, as we shall see, are to a surprisingly large extent primarily or at least secondarily Christological.

$\Delta\iota\alpha\phi\text{o}\rho\acute{\alpha}$, difference

seems to be the most general of these terms. It had been used e.g. in the Christological conflicts, not least by Cyril of Alexandria, who had admitted a $\delta\iota\alpha\phi\text{o}\rho\acute{\alpha}$ but no $\delta\iota\alpha\acute{\iota}\rho\varepsilon\sigma\iota\varsigma$ in Christ,[10] and had also been

---

[8] Cf. von Balthasar, KL[2], pp. 89 and 161.

[9] Cf. *ibid.*, p. 111.

[10] *Scholia de incarn.;* PG 75, 1385 C; cf. also *Adv. Nestor.* 2, 6; PG 76, 85 B.

quoted in the creed of Chalcedon in its affirmation of the remaining διαφορά of the two natures in Christ after their hypostatic union.[11] But on the other hand, Ps.-Denis seems to have used the word in a wider cosmological sense, speaking of διαφοραί as characteristic of all things in mutual relationship to one another within a whole,[12] and also about a general difference of being (τὸ τῆς οὐσίας διάφορον).[13]

This general sense of the word, however, actualizes the way in which Leontius of Byzantium had made use of the concept of διαφορά. Building chiefly, it seems, on Porphyry—for whom the word denoted not only all differences between things but also the difference between various species, and who had divided the latter type of διαφοραί into συστατικαί (those which concern characteristics as coming together into one particular species) and διαιρετικαί (those characteristics into which a particular species may be differentiated)—Leontius likewise used the concept to denote all kinds of difference in the world of things,[14] and also in reference to the characteristic marks of one particular species. He even knows the term συστατικαὶ διαφοραί.[15]

All these predecessors have probably had a certain influence on Maximus in relation to this term. Maximus himself speaks of at least two kinds of διαφορά: a difference of substance or nature (διαφορὰ οὐσιώδης),[16] which remains for ever, and a difference of will among men which is called to disappear in a harmony of will,[17] the first, thus, being of an ontological and the second of a moral character.[18]

The *first* Maximian type of διαφορά is, of course, first of all used in his Christology. Thus Maximus, like Cyril, makes a clear-cut distinction between διαφορά and διαίρεσις[19]—a distinction which shows that Porphyry's διαφορὰ διαιρετική could no longer have been used in a positive sense—and affirms with Cyril and Chalcedon that the διαφορά between the two natures in Christ is preserved (σώζεσθαι, notice the

---

[11] See *Concil. Oecumen. Decr.*, p. 62, 35 ff.; cf. Cyril, *Ep. 4 ad Nestor.*; PG 77, 45 C.

[12] *De div. nom.* 8, 9; PG 3, 897 C; cf. 12, 4; 972 B.

[13] *De eccles. hier.* 4. 3, 1; PG 3, 473 C; cf. *De div. nom.* 5, 8; 824 B; his use of the term, however, is less fixed than VON BALTHASAR seems to suggest; see KL², (GLDG 8,3), p. 40 f.

[14] *Epilysis;* PG 86: 2; 1921 C.

[15] See *Trig. cap.* 23; PG 86: 2; 1909 A; cf. J. P. JUNGLAS, *Leontius von Byzanz* (FLDG 8.3), Paderborn 1908, p. 70 f.

[16] ThPol 14; PG 91, 149 D.

[17] Thal 2; CCSG 7, p. 51.

[18] To these may be added a third kind: a difference of persons (διαφορὰ προσωπική), used in the Trinitarian context, see Ep 15; PG 91, 553 D.—διαφορά of the persons of the Holy Trinity is also used by e.g. Basil, see *Adv. Eun.* 1, 19; PG 29, 556 B; cf. Ps.-Cyril, *De sacros. Trin.* 10; PG 77, 1144 A.

[19] Ep 12; PG 91, 469 AB.

double sense of this word, "save" and "preserve", frequently used in later Christology) even after they have been united into one hypostasis.[20] This διαφορά is thus κάτα φύσιν[21] or κατ᾽ οὐσίαν.[22] In Chalcedonian terms it is also called an ἀσύγχυτος διαφορά[23]—and as such it denotes the preservation of each nature in Christ[24]—though it is no more a naked difference, ψιλὴ διαφορά, because there is a living relationship established between human and divine nature in Christ.[25]

From there Maximus, however, goes on, it seems, to use this concept of διαφορά of nature in a more general, cosmological or anthropological, sense. In fact, one does not always know from the beginning whether Maximus intends a Christological statement or not, for he speaks frequently in quite general terms about these subjects. Thus he defines διαφορὰ οὐσιώδης, which is the opposite of ἕνωσις οὐσιώδης, but is an equivalent of διαφορά as it was understood by Porphyry and Leontius, as a principle (λόγος) according to which οὐσία or φύσις remain altogether undiminished and unchanged (ἄτρεπτος), unconfused and unmixed (ἀσύγχυτος),[26] or as a principle according to which diversity in relation to others (ἑτερότης) is preserved. It may be used both in relation to God and the divine, and between different kinds of created beings. As in the case of Christ it may also, in this context, be said of a deified Christian, that the διαφορά between human and divine remains ἀσύγχυτος.[27]

About this διαφορά, which is a general characteristic of the created world in comparison with the divine and uncreated, Maximus states that it is constitutive (συστατική) and distinctive (ἀφοριστική), which is not only to say that it will never disappear, but also—and more important— that it has a positive sense, in so far as it is an expression of God's purpose.[28] This immutability of nature and essence Maximus contrasts

[20] See e.g. *ibid.;* 91, 472 D.

[21] Ep 15; PG 91, 556 A.

[22] *Ibid.;* 561 AB.

[23] Ep 13; PG 91, 521 C.

[24] Ep 15; PG 91, 556 B.

[25] Ep 12; PG 91, 473 A; cf. ThPol 2; PG 91, 41 AB. As von Balthasar, KL², p. 255, has pointed out, this fact is a presupposition of Maximus' development of the περιχώρησις idea (see also ch. I above).

[26] ThPol 14; PG 91, 149 D.

[27] See e.g. ThPol 20; PG 91, 233 C and 236 B. On the Christological importance of this *opuscula,* see further Léthel, *op. cit.,* pp. 74–77.

[28] See ThPol 21; PG 91, 249 C; cf. Amb 67; PG 91, 1400 C. ἀφοριστική seems here to be the Maximian equivalent of Porphyry's διαιρετική; for this aspect Leontius, however— possibly for reasons of Christology—*also* uses the term συστατική (*Trig. cap.* 13; PG 86:2; 1909 A).—Von Balthasar (who does not refer to Leontius at this point) has dwelt considerably upon this positive sense, which to him is one of the most characteristic features of Maximus' theology, see KL², pp. 63 f. and 117; cf. pp. 153, 258 and 327.

with ἰδιότης, which is the individualizing element and thus not general
but partial (μερική).[29]

We see clearly, how the aspects of unity and differentiation are
carefully kept together by Maximus at all levels, in Christology and
cosmology alike: the concept of difference (διαφορά) unifies in fact all
created beings, though they are individually differentiated. God alone is
supremely elevated above all διαφορά and διάκρισις, and yet as Creator
of all he permits rational beings to be partakers of him.[30] This double
implication of a difference characteristic of creation—which comes very
close to the Christological formulas—Maximus develops at length in
various texts. Thus we learn in Myst 2 that creation, which consists of
visible and invisible beings,[31] is *one* and not as such divided together with
its different parts. The very difference (διαφορά) of its parts according to
their natural ἰδιότης is circumscribed by its relation (ἀναφορά) to its own
unity.[32] And in Amb 7 Maximus emphasizes that difference (διαφορά)
and diversity (ποικιλία) are characteristic of the world of created beings,
but manifest themselves in such a way that the one Logos is recognized as
many λόγοι in the indivisible difference (ἀδιαίρετος διαφορά) of creation,
because of the unconfused individuality (ἀσύγχυτος ἰδιότης) of all
beings—though, on the other hand, the different λόγοι may be seen as
the one Logos thanks to the relationship (ἀναφορά), which exists between
him and all that is unconfused (ἀσύγχυτον).[33]

Thus, according to Maximus, in God's creation difference conditions
unity and unity difference, just as they do in Christ.[34] The same
theological principle is, finally, very well illustrated in section 41 of Amb
10, where the relationship of unities to parts, and of parts to one another
is described with the same complicated dialectic, including Christological terms. There is, Maximus says, a convergence (σύννευσις) of the parts
towards the unities and a corresponding unity (ἕνωσις) of the unities
in relation to the parts, and in the mutual relationship of the parts to
one another there is noticeable not only an unmixed differentiation
(διάκρισις) according to the individualizing difference (διαφορά) of each
of them, but also an unconfused unity (ἀσύγχυτος ἕνωσις) according to
their immutable identity (ταυτότης) in general.[35]

---

[29] ThPol 21; PG 91, 249 C.
[30] Amb 7; PG 91, 1080 AB.
[31] Myst 2; PG 91, 668 C.
[32] PG 91, 669 B.
[33] Amb 7; PG 91, 1077 C.
[34] Cf. the same kind of polarity between τὰ καθόλου and τὰ μερικά in Amb 10; PG 91,
1169 C.
[35] Amb 10; PG 91, 1188 C–1189 A. Cf. also ch. VI, 9; pp. 398–404 below.

διαφορά in God's creation is thus an established order, safeguarding both variations and unity within a creation, distinct from its Creator.[36] It is finally a matter of divine providence and reveals a judgment, according to which God is manifest as a wise distributor of appropriate λόγοι.[37]

The *second* type of difference, that of will and mind (διαφορὰ γνωμική) is less treated by Maximus—there are other terms which express this kind of differentiation in a better way. It is clear, however, that it mostly denotes a lack of harmony, e.g. between parts and their universals, i.e. a situation where only the differentiation but not the unity is manifested and the double aspect has disappeared.[38] However, to such a difference between individuals, which is relative to their different "lives and behaviour, minds and decisions, desires, understanding, needs, habits and ideas", there also corresponds wisely a multiform, divine providence.[39] Thus even here a positive principle of unity in diversity finally enters into the picture.

Διαίρεσις, division

Our next key-term is the negative equivalent of the concept of difference, for difference of nature or substance does not necessarily imply division. It is not a constitutive element of creation and is thus not positively related to the doctrine of *creatio ex nihilo*. We have chosen to mention it here, however, just to point out how it is contrasted with the positive concept of difference. διαίρεσις is ruled out, when separate natures or entities are positively related to one another. This is again a conviction based on Christology: the unity of human and divine in Christ, in the words of Chalcedon, is acknowledged "without division", ἀδιαιρέτας. (At the council of Constantinople in 553 διαίρεσις in Christ was expressly rejected.) As a non-constitutive element of fallen creation, division should thus not be confused with difference, but rather be abolished through man's restoration and deification in Christ.

This understanding of διαίρεσις (in contrast to διαφορά) had in fact been worked out within orthodox Christology, but the monophysites do not seem to have accepted it. Already Gregory Nazianzen had been eager to stress that there is in Christ no διαίρεσις in the Arian sense, and that διαίρεσες in Christ does not imply estrangement (ἀλλοτρίωσις).[40] And

---

[36] This order is, of course, also to be regarded as a preparation for its confirmation in Christ.

[37] Amb 10; PG 91, 1133 CD.

[38] See Thal 2; CCSG 7, p. 51.

[39] Amb 10; PG 91, 1192 D–1193 A.

[40] *Or.* 39, 11; PG 36, 348 A.

more important, Cyril of Alexandria in relation to Christ, had not only rejected a φυσικὴ διαίρεσις,[41] but also distinguished between an acceptable διαφορά[42] and a rejectable διαίρεσις.[43] Maximus, in a characteristic way, uses this traditional thinking also in his general cosmological and anthropological understanding.

διαίρεσις is thus to Maximus never constitutive of creation. Before he enters into its Christological consequences he may e.g. make a strictly terminological definition of διαίρεσις in contrast with διαφορά. That which is subject to διαφορά is just distinguished and determined by it, for it shows how things are constituted, but that which is subject to διαίρεσις is cut in pieces, and things are separated from one another by it.[44] In his Christology Maximus is in complete harmony with his tradition, accusing Nestorius of having introduced a διαίρεσις in relation to Christ,[45] and affirming that Cyril accepted διαφορά but never introduced thereby διαίρεσις.[46]

With Gregory Nazianzen, to whom he refers, Maximus also professes that number (ἀριθμός) is related to quantity,[47] and with Leontius of Byzantium, who further developed the same idea,[48] that it does not therefore introduce διαίρεσις among things.[49] Every number manifests a certain διαφορά but no διαίρεσις, he affirms.[50] Neither unity nor separation is introduced by it.[51] Thus in Christ two natures, and two wills, do not cause division, but the same is equally true in relation to things, which are always subject to the category of number.

Maximus also knows, however, another use of the word διαίρεσις, which seems at first sight more difficult to understand against the background of what we have said. Within the context of general cosmology and anthropology—though with reference to Christology—Maximus thus distinguishes (in Amb 41) between five different διαιρέσεις, which include differences usually called διαφοραί: 1) separa-

---

[41] *Ep. 40 ad Acac. Melit.;* PG 77, 196 A.
[42] *Scholia de incarn.;* PG 75, 1385 C.
[43] See *Adv. Nestor.* 2, 6; PG 76, 85 B.
[44] Ep 12; PG 91, 469 B.
[45] ThPol 2; PG 91, 41 AB.
[46] ThPol 7; PG 91, 88 AB.
[47] *Or.* 31 (*Theol.* 5), 18; MASON, p. 166. Notice that Maximus reads διαίρεσις, not φύσις, which makes it easier for him to use the text, since it had originally served a Trinitarian, not a Christological purpose.
[48] *Epilysis;* PG 86: 2; 1920 A–C.
[49] Ep 12; PG 91, 473 C.
[50] PG 91, 477 A.
[51] Ep 13; PG 91, 513 A.

tion between uncreated nature and the whole of creation;[52] 2) separation in creation between intelligible and sensible; 3) separation of heaven and earth within the sensible world; 4) separation of the earth into paradise and the inhabited earth; 5) separation in humanity between man and woman.[53] Man is, however, at the same time regarded as originally intended to reconcile these divisions, a reconciliation which has in fact taken place through Christ, and thus the word διαίρεσις has not lost its negative sense. The point of emphasis lies in the idea that all these differences should be overcome by man as mediator.

But his function in this respect is still understandable, only if one keeps in mind that διαφορά and διαίρεσις to Maximus are two completely different concepts. For man as mediator is called to annihilate divisions as διαιρέσεις on the moral level, but not as διαφοραί on the ontological level. In the latter sense they are to be preserved but kept together by him.

Διάστασις-διάστημα, distance and separation

are more ambiguous terms. They are neither wholly negative, nor entirely positive.

διάστασις does not usually have a Christological connotation in the early Church, though Eusebius denies it of the Son in relation to the Father, and Cyril of Alexandria uses it, in a Christological context, as an equivalent of διαφορά.[54] διάστημα, which is primarily understood as a temporal or spatial expression, is in the former sense said to have been used by Arians in their Christological argumentation.[55] For Maximus, however—who uses διάστημα also in a strictly spatial sense[56]—the generalized, partly metaphorical sense in which Gregory of Nyssa used the term seems to have been more influential. To Gregory διάστημα—distance in time and space—is a characteristic of creation as a whole, by which God alone remains unaffected.[57]

As such the term is thus another expression of the abyss which separates God from creation. Maximus obviously starts from this latter understanding of διάστημα, as von Balthasar has most convincingly shown, but he seems to arrive at a somewhat different appreciation of the

---

[52] PG 91, 1304 D.

[53] PG 91, 1305 AB.—Maximus' presentation of these five "divisions" will serve as our principle of systematization in ch. VI below.

[54] See Eusebius, *Demonstr. evang.* 4, 3; PG 22, 257 B and Cyril, *Adv. Nestor.* 2, 6; PG 76, 85 A.

[55] See e.g. Alexander Alex., *Ep.* 6; PG 18, 557 A.

[56] See e.g. Ep 2; PG 91, 393 A.

[57] *In Eccles., hom.* 7; JAEGER 5, p. 412, 14.

concept in the end, symbolised perhaps by his preference of διάστασις to διάστημα.[58] E.g. in Ep 2, we can see how spatial διάστημα between men may be overcome by spiritual communication,[59] and how διάστασις from God and fellow men may disappear.[60] Not that Maximus would deny the basic διάστημα of which Gregory speaks, but his point of emphasis is different.

Maximus may very well start from the idea of Gregory—and he sometimes even uses the term διάστημα in exactly this sense. In such a case he affirms that all beings, which naturally have a beginning because they exist, also have a διάστημα because they are moved. In the first case they are "under nature", and in the second "under time".[61] Thus διάστημα in its cosmological use, based on its temporal sense, is intimately connected for Maximus with motion, and this last aspect is predominant in his use of the term. διάστημα-διάστασις is first of all a positive starting-point for the natural movement of created beings, which he constantly professes in clear refutation of Origenism, for which movement was a consequence of the fall. This may be illustrated from other passages. In Gnost 1.5[62] Maximus says that time has a beginning, a middle phase and an end.[63] For time itself, which has an apportioned movement, is distinguished by number, and even aeon, which is found within the category of "when", suffers διάστασις, because it has a beginning. As we see, διάστασις here denotes the fact that by establishing history God has marked out a distance to himself. This distance is, however, a positive presupposition for a God-ward movement. Maximus' use of the term thus comes close to Gregory's, but the aspect of time and action dominates. As Sherwood has correctly pointed out in relation to this problem, the "Maximian emphasis falls on motion".[64]

This is, however, also to say that for Maximus διάστασις stands, first of all, in a particular relationship to στάσις, rest. Becoming means to him not only existence but also movement under the category of time, a situation expressed by the term διάστημα-διάστασις, and this movement

---

[58] See von Balthasar, KL², pp. 132 f. and 601; cf. Sherwood, *The Earlier Ambigua*, p. 109.

[59] PG 91, 393 A.

[60] *Ibid.;* 396 C.

[61] Amb 67; PG 91, 1397 B.

[62] PG 90, 1085 A.

[63] We recognize the usual triad ἀρχή, μεσότης, τέλος.

[64] Sherwood, *The Earlier Ambigua*, p. 109, in a criticism of von Balthasar, *Die 'Gnostischen Centurien'*, Freiburg i. Br. 1941, p. 109. The latter who had somewhat minimized the difference between Gregory and Maximus at this point, has later slightly modified his position in the second edition of his work on the *Gnostic Centuries*, KL², p. 601.

is intended to lead to its τέλος, which is God.[65] When this is accomplished man is in the stage of στάσις (a reason why Maximus prefers διάστασις to διάστημα ?). Seen from the point of view of the starting-point, there is thus no διάστασις any more, though the basic natural διάστημα in relation to God, of which Gregory was thinking, remains.

But more important, what takes place in this rest is deification, a term which is always to be understood on the basis of *communicatio idiomatum* and *perichoresis:* man becomes god, while God becomes man; man's deification is from another point of view God's continuing incarnation.[66] That is the reason why Maximus may say that διάστασις disappears (in στάσις). Living in Christ, in whom the hypostatic union overbridges any difference and distance, man experiences this. Thus Maximus affirms that through the Incarnation God will finally be without any spatial διάστασις in relation to "those who are worthy", and refers in the same text to deification and to Christ as the head of the body.[67] Similarly in Gnost 2.77—78 διάστημα in Gregory's sense is seen, first of all, as a positive starting-point of, or an advancement in, γνῶσις which includes the virtues, seen as an incarnation of the Logos in man, and which leads in the end to a mystical communion with God.[68]

From this point of view it is not surprising that Maximus states *both* that there is no separation and διάστασις τῶν ἄκρων (i.e. of the distinct natures and their qualities) in Christ, though there are two energies in his person,[69] *and* that Christ keeps this τῶν ἄκρων διάστασις together.[70]

Having reached the very limit of his natural capacities, moved by God, man in this στάσις shares with Christ the non-distanced character of his hypostatic union of distinguished but not separated natures, energies and wills. He does not penetrate into the mysteries of God, as He is in himself, but he partakes of the divine. There is an infinity, in which there is—as it were—no διάστημα and where every natural movement reposes,[71] which is not to say that it is not moved any longer, for motion belongs to the condition of created being. Thus the στάσις of

---

[65] See under 6. below, pp. 81 ff.

[66] Cf. ch. VI:11; pp. 429–432 below

[67] Gnost 2. 25; PG 90, 1136 BC.

[68] PG 90, 1161 A–C. This order of spiritual development will be treated in ch. VI below.

[69] ThPol 20; PG 91, 232 D.

[70] Ep 15; PG 91, 556 A. The same aspect is relevant also when Maximus in Ep 18 speaks of disunity in the Church as a τομὴ καὶ διάστασις from the body of Christ; PG 91, 589 B.

[71] Amb 15; PG 91, 1217 C.

man—in the paradox of Maximus—is ever-moving rest (ἀεικίνητος στάσις).[72]

Διαστολή, distinction, expansion,

is a term with both positive and negative connotations in Maximus' writings. It has, however, to be seen within the same context of a dialectic between unity and differentiation, based on Christological presuppositions, which we have already found to be characteristic of Maximus' cosmology. The term has its counterpart in συστολή and both are necessary aspects of creation. Von Balthasar has emphasized that for Maximus this interplay of διαστολή-συστολή is a cosmic law, which reaches its culmination in its Christological consequences,[73] but we could talk with equal right about a Christological conviction worked out in Maximus' cosmology, and then also developed further in his Christology.

Maximus' purpose, here too, seems to be to safeguard a unity which does not violate the difference of its parts, but rather gets its strength and persistence through these parts.[74] Both συστολή and διαστολή are characteristic of οὐσία, says Maximus. Thus, the whole of creation—all that partakes of created being—moves (because movement belongs to the conditions of creation) according to a double principle and mode of διαστολή and συστολή, expansion and contraction. The movement of διαστολή goes from the most general to the more differentiated species, and the movement of συστολή in the opposite direction. In both cases, however, the movement comes to a limit, drawn by the character of created being itself: there is nothing more particular than that which is made particular by the Creator, and nothing more universal pertains to creation than the fact that all is created.[75]

Thus, the unity of creation extends to all that which has a particular existence, and the particularities preserve their identity within their common share in created being. Outside these conditions there is the gulf, which cannot be overbridged under the conditions of creation itself, but only through God who is the Creator. We may thus easily conclude that in Maximus' view the movement of διαστολή, of differentiation, as the movement of God's condescension in creation, comes very close to the incarnation, and the movement of συστολή, consequently, comes

---

[72] Thal 59; CCSG 22, p. 53; 65; CCSG 22, p. 285. and Amb 67; 91, 1401 A; cf. ἀεικινησία, Ep 6; PG 91, 432 B.

[73] KL², p. 278; cf. pp. 157 and 163.

[74] Ep 15; PG 91, 564 AB.

[75] Amb 10; PG 91, 1177 BC.

close to deification. In fact, there is not only a Christological inspiration behind Maximus' cosmic view at this point; it is also further developed on the Christological level. For Maximus affirms himself, using the *tantum-quantum* formula (which testifies to the same idea of a double movement without violation), that God effects a συστολή of the believers for his own sake into union with Himself to the same extent in which He had expanded Himself for their sake according to the principle of condescension.[76]

In its right context the concept of διαστολή has, thus, to Maximus a positive sense. In the Christological discussions, however, Maximus probably also felt bound to distinguish between this positive aspect and a negative one. There are, in fact, he states, two kinds of διαστολή: a) that which is κατ' ἐναντίωσιν, i.e. a distinction between contraries which do not exclude one another, e.g. between body and soul; and b) that which is κατὰ τὸ ἀντικεῖσθαι, i.e. a distinction between mutually exclusive contradictories, e.g. life and death. The first kind is characteristic of substances or natures, which cannot be contradictories, because they participate in created being; the second kind concerns particular qualities of natures and may thus be mutually exclusive.[77] Contradictory qualities are, however, in themselves results of the fall and do not affect the positive view of creation. A διαστολή which has a positive relationship to a συστολή is indeed a sign of the limitation of creation, but has a positive sense within the purpose of God, as the latter is revealed in Christ. But isolated from the principle of unity, διαστολή, even in relation to Christ, has no positive function,[78] for it is the unity of natures, as well as of their particularities, which safeguards communion with God, who is essentially unique and simple.

Other terms

There are, of course, a number of other terms and concepts in Maximus' writings which supply other aspects of the natural limitations and distinctions of created being, but we have no reason to dwell too long upon these. Let us only mention some of them and indicate their function.[79]

As creation is characterized by "immense difference and multiplici-

---

[76] Amb 33; PG 91, 1288 A: τοσοῦτον ἡμᾶς δι᾽ ἑαυτὸν πρὸς ἕνωσιν ἑαυτοῦ συστείλας, ὅσον αὐτὸς δι᾽ ἡμᾶς ἑαυτὸν συγκαταβάσεως λόγῳ διέστειλεν.

[77] ThPol 17; PG 91, 212 CD.

[78] See ThPol 19; PG 91, 221 BC.

[79] They are, of course, also more or less self-evident in their context, and we mention them just to show the richness and complexity of Maximus' view.

ty" (ἄπειρος διαφορὰ καὶ ποικιλία)[80]—and difference and multiplicity belong together[81]—one should of course mention first of all number (ἀριθμός) and its correlative, quantity (ποσότης).[82]

Ἀριθμός, *number*, though in Maximus' opinion itself neither quality nor quantity, is nevertheless closely related to quantity,[83] for every difference (διαφορά) reveals a certain quantity, which brings number with it.[84] Number denotes quantity and not quality.[85] And yet, it is related also to quality, in so far as number and quantity are always based on an existing difference which is that of quality.[86] What is excluded in relation to number is, however, διαίρεσις,[87] for every number is in fact ἀδιαίρετος.[88] In itself it is affected neither by changing movement, which is characteristic of quality, nor by διαστολή and συστολή, which are characteristic of being, nor by increase or decrease which belong to quantity.[89] Number is thus a neutral term, dependent on the difference and multiplicity of creation, but not qualifying those concepts. The numbers in their multiplicity are, however, as von Balthasar has pointed out, at the same time seen as a synthesis of the unity of being, which has its ground in God, who is above both numbers and oneness.[90]

Another concept, related to creation as relative, is that of *motion* (κίνησις)—see below under 6.—positively based on distance (διάστημα) of *space* (τόπος) and *time* (χρόνος). Maximus states that space and time pertain to everything,[91] and that χρόνος, αἰών and τόπος are characteristic of this world.[92]

But God has also established the categories of τάξις, *order,* and θέσις, *position,* institution—both are frequent in Ps.-Denis[93]—, which denote not only difference in relation to God but, first of all, God's active care

---

[80] Amb 7; PG 91, 1077 C.
[81] Amb 22; PG 91, 1256 D.
[82] The historical background of Maximus' thinking is summarized by VON BALTHASAR, KL², pp. 100–103.
[83] Ep 15; PG 91, 564 D; cf. e.g. Ep 13; 513 A; cf. also VON BALTHASAR, KL², p. 104.
[84] Ep 12; PG 91, 477 A.
[85] *Ibid.;* 476 C.
[86] *Ibid.;* 477 A. Maximus talks also about a quality of essence, ποιότης οὐσιώδης; see ThPol 21; PG 91, 248 C; cf. Cyril of Alexandria: ποιότης φυσική, *Ep.* 40; PG 77, 193 B.
[87] See e.g. Ep 12; PG 91, 477 A and 13; 513 A.
[88] Ep 15; PG 91, 564 A.
[89] Ep 12; PG 91, 477 AB.
[90] See VON BALTHASAR, KL², pp. 107–109; the references are, however, to the scholies to Ps.-Denis, the authenticity of which is doubtful, not least to von Balthasar himself.
[91] Amb 10; PG 91, 1180 BC.
[92] *Ibid.;* 1153 B.
[93] For their rôle in Ps.-Denis, cf. e.g. VÖLKER, *Kontemplation und Ekstase,* p. 121.

for his creation.[94] The meaning of τάξις, which in Ps.-Denis denotes the established hierarchical order,[95] is not worked out in detail by Maximus —nor is it a key-term in his writings—but seems to be similar to that in Ps.-Denis. θέσις is in more frequent and more distinctive use in Maximus. It denotes all things, characterized also by distinction and movement. Thus all thinking is said to be a quality (or accidence) but to have its fixity of position (θέσις) in the substance,[96] and lines drawn from the centre of a circle to its periphery have an undifferentiated position in the centre itself.[97] θέσις is in fact a willed fixity of created things which does not exclude motion[98] or their unity in God.[99] It denotes a sovereign divine act, but true θέσις in relation to God—as experienced by the mystic—is found only as an affirmation within negation.[100] From the same point of view deification is regarded as a θέσις, exclusively established by God's grace, and is no consequence either of man's nature, or of his natural relationship to God.[101] As a whole the terms τάξις and θέσις thus confirm Maximus' belief in creation as a result of a positive act of God, including as its purpose unity without violation.

Finally, in this context we should also notice how Maximus, in a characteristic way, in Amb 41—a text to which we have referred already—clearly expresses the combination of differentiation and unity, which to him is a constant reflexion of God's purpose for his creation. He thus states that only in one respect are created things separated from one another, for in another sense they are fully identical. Different individuals of a γένος are united by the nature of this γένος, shared by them all. And so are the higher forms of the γένη and the particular categories in relation to the universals, etc. Finally, all created beings are identical in the sense that they all may be naturally summarized within the category of γένος. And Maximus concludes, that all differentiated things are united through this universality of category and species.[102]

This last example reveals once more what is obviously the dominating aspect of Maximus' cosmology: that what differentiates in God's creation (e.g. the category of γένος) also unites, and what unites (e.g. the created

---

[94] Among terms generally characterizing creation they appear together, e.g. in Amb 10; PG 91, 1176 B and 1188 D.

[95] See e.g. *De coel. hier.* 10, 2; PG 3, 273 AB.

[96] Gnost 2. 3; PG 90, 1125 D.

[97] Gnost 2. 4.; PG 90, 1125 D–1128 A.

[98] Cf. Amb 10; PG 91, 1136 B.

[99] Cf. in Ps.-Denis the use of θέσις, see e.g. in *De coel. hier.* 13, 3; PG 3, 301 D and of θεσμός, see e.g. *ibid.* 10, 1; 273 A; cf. R. ROQUES, *L'univers dionysien*, Paris 1954, p. 83 f.

[100] See Thal 25; CCSG 7, p. 165.

[101] Amb 20; PG 91, 1237 AB.

[102] See Amb 41; PG 91, 1312 B–1313 A.

character of all that thus exists) also maintains its individuality. And it is this aspect of unity in diversity which, on the basis of the idea of a *creatio ex nihilo* and a gulf between God and his creation, at the same time combines his cosmology with his Christology in such a way that a unified vision of God's purpose and activity is gained.

2.   *Creation because of God's will*

This second aspect of Maximus' cosmology is closely related to his idea of the great gulf between God and created being, and thus also to the *creatio ex nihilo* idea. For there is, according to this view, no other factor but God's sovereign will, counsel and decision which may cause Him to create the world.[103]

In Char 4 Maximus emphasizes twice that God created the world, when He willed.[104] His primary interest in doing so is, thus, to assert the sovereignty of God. The Creator is bound by no necessary obligation and all laws and categories are created by Him, for a purpose which He has established.[105] Through a decision of God's will alone, visible and invisible creation are brought into being.[106] That is also why Maximus — in a much discussed reference to Pantaenus[107] — affirms that God knows the very things which are, as His own wills (ὡς ἴδια θελήματα) because He has created all by will (θελήματι).[108]

This last statement, however, immediately actualizes another complex of Maximus' thinking: his theology of the λόγοι, the principles of differentiated creation, pre-existent in God. For these λόγοι are in fact regarded by him as divine wills or intentions.[109] Since a more detailed

---

[103] Because of his good will God established the world out of nothing, Maximus affirms in Amb 7; PG 91, 1080 A.

[104] 4. 3 and 4; CSC, p. 194; cf. Amb 42; PG 91, 1328 C.

[105] Thus also the category of *time,* which is particularly emphasized in the citations from Char 4. From this point of view creation by God's will alone implies a *transcendence* of the sphere of eternity, which is God's, to that of temporality, characteristic of finite existence; cf. von Balthasar, KL², p. 121, where this absence of confusion of categories in Maximus is stressed.

[106] Thal 22; CCSG 7, p. 137. This is in complete accordance with Cappadocian theology, see e.g. Gregory of Nyssa, *De anima et resurr.;* PG 46, 121 B.

[107] See O. Stählin in GCS Clemens 3, p. lxv; cf. von Balthasar, KL², p. 114, notes 4 and 5; cf. also Sherwood, *The Earlier Ambigua,* p. 175, n. 70.

[108] Amb 7; PG 91, 1085 B.

[109] How far this theology of intentional λόγοι is directly related to the later idea of uncreated energies, as developed in Palamite theology, as Lossky, *The Mystical Theology,* p. 99 suggests, is a particular problem, which cannot possibly be sufficiently dealt with in this thesis. Cf., however, Sherwood, *The Earlier Ambigua,* p. 179 f. and Idem, Survey of recent Work, *Traditio* 20 (1964), p. 435 f.

treatment of Maximus' doctrine of the λόγοι will be given under 4 below, it may be sufficient here simply to underline the close relationship between this doctrine and the doctrine of creation by God's will. The λόγοι represent in Maximus not only a defining and unifying factor, but a divine purpose, summarized in the Logos, where all partial λόγοι are held together.

In developing this idea of the λόγοι of creation Maximus builds upon Alexandrian theology, completed, and partly corrected, by Ps.-Denis. For as Sherwood has pointed out the Logos doctrine, as it is developed e.g. in Amb 7, completes Maximus' refutation of Origenism,[110] and has as the basis for its dynamic aspect the work carried out by Ps.-Denis.[111] In fact Ps.-Denis had already emphasized the intentional character of the λόγοι of creation.[112] In *De div. nom.* 5, 8, he identifies παραδείγματα and pre-existent λόγοι, and defines them as "divine and good wills".[113] To Maximus this definition has become more or less self-evident.[114] For he does not only say that these λόγοι were pre-existent in God in His good counsel and that, according to them, God brought creation into existence,[115] nor does he simply refer to the Areopagite as an authority,[116] but he also sees this particular character of the λόγοι as a manifestation of a general law, formulated in the following way: *always and in all God's Word and God wills to effect the mystery of His embodiment* (ἐνσωμάτωσις).[117] Further he stresses that the λόγοι, known through creation, also reveal a divine purpose (σκοπός),[118] of which we know that it pertains primarily to human beings.[119]

Thus we see that the doctrine of the λόγοι of creation as divine intentions both safeguards a positive evaluation of a diversified created existence *and* expresses a unifying factor and a common divine purpose.[120] The Ps.-Dionysian dynamism of the emanations of divine grace

---

[110] SHERWOOD, *The Earlier Ambigua*, p. 167.
[111] Cf. SHERWOOD, *op. cit.*, p. 175 f.
[112] Cf. DALMAIS, La théorie des "Logoi", RSPT 36 (1952), p. 244.
[113] PG 3, 824 C.
[114] He states that it is the custom of the "divine men" to call the λόγοι good wills (Thal 13; CCSG 7, p. 95).
[115] Amb 7; PG 91, 1080 A.
[116] *Ibid.;* 1085 A.
[117] *Ibid.;* 1084 CD.
[118] Thal 13; CCSG 7, p. 95.
[119] It is characteristic that the third petition of the Lord's Prayer is referred by Maximus to a right use of the rational power (ἡ λογικὴ δύναμις) of man's soul, which is said to bring rational beings (λογικοί) to their first principle (λόγος), see OrDom; CCSG 23, p. 57 f.
[120] The λόγοι κατ' εὐδοκίαν and the λόγοι κατ' οἰκονομίαν are closely related, as we can see also in Ep 2 (PG 91, 393 C).

has been combined with a strong emphasis on unity in unviolated diversification, based on Christological convictions. For the embodiment of the Logos, which is the core of the λόγοι doctrine—in creation as well as in incarnation—, is an act of both.

3.   *Creation because of God's benevolence. The concept of providence and judgment*

The doctrine of creation by God's will alone in Maximus not only safeguards the sovereignty of God over against all created being but also the relative independence of creation. For it indicates, that separate beings in their differentiated existence are not in any sense as such a result of a primitive fall—as they were for the Origenists—but are an expression of a purpose: they are to find in freedom their own fulfilment in communion with God, and their unity only in relation to their common principle of being.

Empirical creation is, as we have seen, supplied with a purpose (σκοπός), to which differentiated existence stands in a positive relationship, though, of course, this purpose at the same time has to be worked out in a world, also immediately marked by sinful separation.

This same understanding is expressed by the idea of creation because of God's benevolence, which we have chosen as our third aspect of Maximus' cosmology. For here we see, that the purpose of creation goes, in Maximus' view, beyond mere reunion of what has been torn asunder by sin. It is an original divine intention, which has been interrupted by the fall of man.[121] Thus when Maximus says, in Char 4. 3, that God created the world because of his infinite goodness,[122] we may understand him as referring to this purpose, even as it is realized in Christ's act both of salvation and deification.[123]

This, however, immediately brings Maximus' doctrine of divine *providence* (πρόνοια)—and the related concept of *judgment* (κρίσις)—

---

[121] SHERWOOD, *The Earlier Ambigua*, p. 29, has noticed that, though in *Liber asceticus* the divine σκοπός means almost exclusively salvation, at least in Amb 7 it refers to deification.

[122] CSC, p. 194.

[123] SHERWOOD, in ACW, p. 263, n. 191, sees e.g. in Char 4. 3 an allusion to the doctrine of the good as naturally diffusive of itself, which for him creates a problem unsolved by Maximus, at least in *Cent. de Char*. But is it not possible to see in the discussion of time in 4. 3–4 simply a reference to the economy of salvation and deification as manifestations of the goodness and benevolence of God? If the good of God the Creator is self-diffusive, it is manifest as such only within this economy and its providential action, but it does not *have* to be so, for God is sovereign in himself (cf. SHERWOOD'S comment on diffusive goodness and intra-Trinitarian relations, in ACW, p. 43).

into the picture. For even if it is the purpose (σκοπός) of providence, in a more restricted sense, to unite what evil has divided, providence as such is more or less identical with divine charity, which has, indeed, a wider aim.[124] And providence to Maximus implies at the same time preservation of the finite world in its differentiation.[125]

In fact—as von Balthasar has most clearly shown[126]—Maximus provides in the end a radical re-evaluation of the Evagrian and Origenist double concept of providence and judgment, and this gives both to creation and human perfection a sense far beyond the scope of mere restitution of an original unity, though it is clear that this theological emancipation on Maximus' part had not been easy, as some ambiguous formulations, particularly in *Cent. gnost.*, manifest.[127] In the Origenist conception, the terms providence and judgment were closely linked with the myth of a prehistoric fall of rational beings and a subsequent, second, creation of the material world. For Evagrius κρίσις thus means the judgment implied in this (second) creation, and πρόνοια the divine restitution of an original spiritual unity.[128] Maximus uses this conception as his starting-point but develops it in a quite different direction.

At first sight, the relationship to Evagrius may actually seem very close. For Maximus recognizes among three different kinds of providence, not only one which is preserving (συντηρητική) but also those which are convertive (ἐπιστρεπτική) and educative (παιδευτική) or punitive,[129] though the latter may, of course, be understood entirely within an orthodox conception of the economy of salvation. Further, Maximus uses a triad of μονάς, πρόνοια, κρίσις which is in itself entirely Origenistic, though he affirms at the same time that the λόγοι of the latter "go together with" the λόγος of the former,[130] or compares the λόγος of a

---

[124] See Char 4. 17; CSC, p. 200.

[125] See the πρόνοια συντηρητική of QuDub 17; CCSG 10, p. 15; cf. VON BALTHASAR, KL², p. 607.

[126] For a summary, see particularly VON BALTHASAR, KL², p. 131.

[127] To Evagrius providence and judgment belong to the objects of *five modes of contemplation* (see e.g. *Cent. gnost.* 1. 27; in PO 28, 1958, p. 29) and already VILLER, RAM 11 (1930), p. 243 ff., showed the similarity between Maximus and Evagrius at this point (see e.g. Char 1. 78; CSC, p. 80). See further ch. VI: 3, pp. 343–355.

[128] See e.g. VON BALTHASAR, Die Hiera des Evagrius, ZkTh 63 (1939), p. 95 and KL², p. 131.

[129] QuDub 17; CCSG 10, p. 15.

[130] Gnost 2. 16; PG 90, 1132 B.—The three elements of the triad are here related to the three tabernacles which Peter wanted to build on the mount of Transfiguration, and to the three forms of salvation which Elijah, Moses and Christ symbolize: the Monad is related to Christ and θεολογία, providence to Moses and γνῶσις, and finally judgment to Elijah and virtue (*vita practica*). Thus, we see that the whole triad may be regarded within a Christological context—with reference to the divine simplicity as manifest in Christ the

slightly different triad of judgment, providence and divinity with the body, blood and invisible bones of the Logos.[131] Finally, he speaks of providence in relation to reunion of what has been scattered through evil,[132] and we can add that he establishes a similar relationship between providence, judgment and human pain,[133] which altogether brings him very close to Origenist interpretations, though it is at the same time clearly stated that this suffering is caused by lack of knowledge of the λόγος of providence and judgment itself, and thus not an integral part of it. Whatever the balance of these passages we may at least conclude, that in them the real sense of Maximus' use of the terms is somewhat ambiguous.

We have, however, in Amb 10 another passage[134] which is as clear as these other texts may seem ambiguous, and consequently all that Maximus has to say at this particular point should be compared with what he says there.[135] And there he obviously refutes the Evagrian understanding of providence and judgment and introduces his own.[136]

Maximus refers, first of all, to a series of five modes of contemplation, different from the five modes of Evagrius.[137] Natural contemplation, he affirms, thus concerns the following five objects: substance (οὐσία), motion (κίνησις), difference (διαφορά), mixture (κρᾶσις) and position (θέσις).[138] Of these the first three give a certain knowledge of God, though

---

Logos—and this fact shows that one must be very careful even here to establish the real correspondence between Evagrius and Maximus.

This becomes even more obvious in relation to a parallel text in Amb 10, where a similar triadic arrangement is used in relation to the NT pericope on the Transfiguration. For there that which concerns providence and judgment is qualified as affirmative theology ('economy'), in contrast to the negative theology of Monad and Triad. For the latter the face of the Transfigured serves as an image, for providence and judgment his shining clothes (PG 91, 1168 AB) but also Moses and Elijah, who both symbolize moral aspects (Elijah still virtue), and not at all ontological considerations (1168 CD). Maximus is apparently more careful in Amb 10 than in the other text but, at the same time, it is difficult to deny the consistency of his thinking on this ground alone.

[131] Thal 35; CCSG 7, p. 241. This interpretation obviously goes back to Evagrius, who in practical virtues sees the flesh of Christ, in natural contemplation the blood of Christ and in knowledge of God the heart of Christ (*Mirror for Monks,* no. 118–120; GRESSMANN, p. 163).

[132] Char 4. 17; CSC, p. 200.

[133] Thal 64; CCSG 22, p. 239.

[134] PG 91, 1133 A–1136 B.

[135] Cf. VON BALTHASAR, KL², p. 532.

[136] This text has been commented upon by VON BALTHASAR, KL², p. 532, and several times by SHERWOOD (see *The Earlier Ambigua,* pp. 36 f. and 144 ff. and in ACW, pp. 38–40).

[137] Cf. p. 67, n. 127 above.

[138] 1133 A.

only in his relationship to creation,[139] namely as Creator, Provider and Judge, while the last two give education about man in his life of virtues and his relationship to God.[140]

Developing the different elements of this system Maximus not only gives us his alternative to the Evagrian concept of providence and judgment but also some indications of his cosmology in general. Thus, analysing more in detail what he has to say, we find that the first category of creation, *substance*, is here said to be a teacher of *theologia*, which, however, does not in this context refer to a contemplation of God as He is in Himself, but is merely an indication of God the Creator as Cause of all that is caused. It shows *that* God is, but not *what* he is, Maximus is eager to underline.[141]

The second category, *motion*, is said to indicate the providence which is related to created beings.[142] This naked statement refers clearly to the Evagrian and Origenist understanding of πρόνοια—for to the latter, providence is related to the movement of restoration through which fallen beings return from their primitive diversity to an original unity—but the development of the idea is Maximus' own. He makes clear that he refers to the natural movements of each being (in an Aristotelian sense)[143]—remaining immutable in their own species and standing therefore in a particular identity of substance—that is to say not to their return but to their positive self-realization. And coupled with this aspect is what Maximus has to say about the opposite category of *difference,* which indicates divine judgment. Here again the starting-point looks similar to that of Evagrius—by whom differentiated existence of rational

---

[139] Notice that there is no direct contemplation of the Trinity—or of God as he is in himself—at the level of these five modes, as there seems to be in Evagrius (see Evagrius, *Cent. gnost.* 1. 27; PO 28, p. 29).

[140] 1133 B.

[141] 1133 C. This is an important point, for it shows that, as e.g. SHERWOOD, in ACW, p. 34 f., has emphasized, the mystery of the Trinity as such is referred by Maximus to the sphere of negative theology (cf. ch. VI: 10 below).—This restrictive understanding of *theologia* must be kept in mind also in relation to Gnost 2. 16 (PG 90; 1132 BC), where we can see that *theologia,* used in relation to μονάς, obviously requires explicit revelation and is different from natural contemplation. We may conclude, that for Maximus natural contemplation leads direct to *theologia* only in a restricted sense—it indicates that there is a primary Cause but not the nature of that Cause—while *theologia* in a wider and more proper sense requires active revelation. Cosmology (with natural contemplation) and theology are in this respect in principle kept apart. This kind of distinction was not upheld by Evagrius, for whom contemplation of the Holy Trinity remained virtually a γνῶσις οὐσιώδης, though the only real one (see e.g. *Cent. gnost.* 2. 47; PO 28, p. 79; cf. *Letters* 29; FRANKENBERG, pp. 586–87). See further our treatment of this problem in ch. VI below, particularly pp. 355 ff. and 366 ff.

[142] PG 91, 1133 C.

[143] See further under 6. below.

beings in earthly creation was, indeed, regarded as a judgment, since
it was caused by the fall. But Maximus develops his idea in an entirely opposite direction. To him—as Sherwood has underlined[144]—
Origen and Evagrius had obviously made a false mixture of ontological and moral considerations in relation to the concepts of providence and judgment. These two aspects should be radically kept apart.
Providence and judgment in the cosmological sense refer to different aspects of the order of creation; convertive providence and punitive judgment have to be restricted to the moral level. Thus, Maximus
explains that by difference in creation we are educated to learn
that God is a wise distributor of individual purposes ($\lambda \acute{o} \gamma o \iota$), in
relation to the natural power of each being, proportioned accord-
ing to the subject of each substance.[145] Divine judgment is thus
regarded as a wise preparation for providential motion; and individuality and unifying relationship to God as Creator are closely kept together.

To Maximus differentiated existence is a good arrangement by God,
serving a purpose indicated by the individual capacities for motion. He
feels obliged, however, to make this view still more clear, and thus he
goes on to repeat what kinds of providence and judgment he can accept
or has to reject in the *cosmological* field. In this context he cannot accept
convertive ($\dot{\epsilon} \pi \iota \sigma \tau \rho \epsilon \pi \tau \iota \kappa \acute{\eta}$) providence, he says, for this term should be
restricted to a kind of "economic" providence related to the return of
beings from what is not necessary to what is necessary, but he accepts an
all-embracing and preserving ($\sigma \upsilon \nu \tau \eta \rho \eta \tau \iota \kappa \acute{\eta}$) providence. Nor does he
accept an educative ($\pi \alpha \iota \delta \epsilon \upsilon \tau \iota \kappa \acute{\eta}$) or punitive judgment on sinners on the
ontological level, but rather a saving and defining distribution of
beings,[146] expressing what the Creator, from the beginning, judged and
constituted concerning being, substance, mode and quality.[147] The refutation of the Evagrian and Origenist ideas could hardly be more distinctly
expressed, or a positive evaluation of creation in individualized diversity
more openly affirmed.

Maximus adds, however, that he does not thereby deny the existence
of a *moral* providence and judgment as well—related to "the volitional
desires" of men. Nor does he pretend, that the latter are *another*
providence and judgment. They are one and the same in relation to their
power, but are different and differentiated when they pertain to the moral

---

[144] See SHERWOOD, *The Earlier Ambigua*, p. 36 f. and in ACW, p. 39.
[145] 1133 CD.
[146] 1133 D.
[147] 1136 A

decisions of men.[148] We might add, that in one sense they *have* to be the same—in Maximus' opinion—because all are related to the common purpose of God's creation and salvation: living relationship to God.

The ontological and moral aspects are not always as strictly kept apart as here, even in texts where there is no ambiguity as such, over against the Evagrian understanding. But then the moral aspect—in Maximus' sense—is more or less restricted to the concept of judgment in so far as the latter is related to virtuous life. Thus e.g. in Amb 32 we find substance combined with wisdom (God as always the same), knowledge with providence (God as the ground of the whole of creation) and virtue with judgment (God as Saviour).[149] In the last element Maximus passes, as we see, from a cosmological to a soteriological point of view.[150] This shows, however, not a Maximus haunted by Origenist temptations, but a Maximus for whom the idea of a general purpose of creation, and of Christ as the centre of understanding, is of primary importance.

This fact also makes it easier to understand a number of texts on providence and judgment in which these are interpreted entirely from within a Christological context, and which thus have a mediating position between the clear statement of Amb 10 and those passages, which we have called ambiguous.[151] Christ alone as the centre of understanding, has affinity with all aspects of Maximus' speculation. Thus, in Thal 53 we learn that judgment and providence are the eyes of the Logos, with which, even when he suffers, he keeps oversight over the universe,[152] and in Thal 54 that providence and judgment are the wings, on which the Logos comes flying, unknown, to that which is—though, at the same time Maximus seems to relate providence rather with the λόγοι of wisdom (the ontological aspect) and judgment with the modes (τρόποι) of education (the moral, ascetical aspect).[153] Finally, in Thal 63 Maximus

---

[148] *Loc. cit.*

[149] See PG 91; 1281 D–1284 A.

[150] Cf. Amb 37; PG 91, 1297 A, where λόγος προνοίας is related to "natural philosophy" and λόγος κρίσεως to "practical philosophy", and Amb, *Prol.;* PG 91, 1032 A, where wisdom is said to be related equally to γνῶσις and πρᾶξις, and thus also to ὁ τῆς προνοίας καὶ κρίσεως λόγος.

[151] Among the latter we have already referred to Thal 35 (CCSG 7, p. 241), where λόγοι of judgment, providence and divinity are compared with the body, blood and bones of the Logos.

[152] CCSG 7, p. 431.

[153] CCSG 7, p. 457. This last tendency to distinguish between different aspects in relation to the two concepts is, as we have seen, found elsewhere in Maximus. Here, however, the soteriological context seems clear, and one must ask whether both terms are, in fact, not taken in their "economic" sense.—To the image of the two wings in this connection, cf. Ps.-Origen (Evagrius?), *Sel. in Psalm.*, LOMMATZSCH, 12, 405, where the wings of Ps. 67: 13 are interpreted as a reference to πρᾶξις and θεωρία, and 12, 362, where

refers providence to the hypostatic union in Christ and judgment to the life-giving sufferings of the incarnate God. In the first instance, this might also seem open to an Evagrian interpretation. But we must notice, that the more restricted soteriological aspect is here clearly dominant—with the direct references to the economy of salvation—and since the hypostatic union is never said by Maximus to do away with natural difference, the idea of an ontological restitution is, of course, entirely excluded.[154]

It has thus again become clear that Maximus' thinking is marked by a consistent dialectic, which allows an interplay of unity and individual freedom. The Evagrian pairing providence—judgment is used by him to express this double attitude: judgment, with the principle of purposeful differentiation, has a positive rôle to play within the context of divine providence, along with the principle of unification without violation.

4. Creation by the Word

The constitution of beings is, however, a work not only of the Father but of all the persons of the Holy Trinity.[155] Therefore, Maximus also affirms that God, the eternal Creator, when He wills and acts because of infinite goodness, creates by His consubstantial Word and Spirit.[156] If we bear in mind that, according to Maximus, the concrete world in which human beings are living is brought into existence in accordance with pre-existent λόγοι which are identical with God's purposes for this world, we realize that this statement actualizes, first of all, the relationship between the Logos and these λόγοι, and between Christ and creation.

Considering this aspect, we shall find, however, once again the two most characteristic features of Maximian theology: the double principle of differentiation and unification and the close relationship between

the wings of the dove are interpreted as ἡ θεωρία τῶν σωμάτων καὶ ἀσωμάτων through which the mind ascends and finds its rest in knowledge of the Trinity. (For the Evagrian authorship of *Sel. in Psalm.*, see VON BALTHASAR, ZkTh 63, 1939, pp. 90–106 and 181–189, confirmed by M.-J. RONDEAU, Le Commentaire sur les Psaumes d'Evagre le Pontique, OCP 26, 1960, pp. 307–348.)

[154] See Thal 63; CCSG 22, p. 169. What remains, is the 'negative' interpretation of judgment; but within a moral and soteriological understanding this is to be expected. The sufferings of Christ are motivated by sin, and not by differentiated creation as such. On the other hand, this and other Christological texts reveal Maximus' interest in relating his cosmological and soteriological, ontological and moral terms to one another.

[155] See Thal 28; CCSG 7, p. 207.

[156] Char 4. 3; CSC, p. 194. We are not going to deal here with the idea of creation by the Spirit (cf. the Introduction, p. 20 above). It is hardly placed in the foreground by Maximus himself. What he wants to underline in Char 4 is that creation is a Trinitarian act.

cosmology and economy of salvation. Let us thus make a short study of these two points.

The λόγοι of a differentiated creation reflect together the purpose of the Creator

The ancient Christian idea of λόγοι of creation—related to the Logos-Christ—seems to have been developed much further, and in a more systematic way, by Maximus than by any of his predecessors.[157] In him it

---

[157] On the basis, probably, of the Stoic idea of the λόγος σπερματικός, combined with early Christian Logos speculation (see further M. SPANNEUT, *Le stoïcisme des Pères de l'Église,* Paris 1957, p. 324 f.), Origen was the first thinker of the Church—though preceded by Philo (who, however, regards the λόγοι as a kind of angels; see further J. DANIÉLOU, *Philon d'Alexandrie,* pp. 163–172)—who presented a noticeable theology of the λόγοι of creation. He regarded them as ideas present in Christ as Wisdom (*In Io.* I, 34; GCS Orig. 4, p. 43, 21; cf. *De princ.* I, 2, 2; GCS Orig. 5, p. 30), where—understood in a Platonic way—they together form the intelligible world (cf. *In Io.* I, 38; GCS Orig. 4, p. 50), a model of the world of the senses (cf. *In Io.* I, 19; GCS Orig. 4, p. 23 f.), and represent the original "goodness" of created things (*In Io.* 13, 42; GCS Orig. 4, p. 268, 23 ff.). This line of thinking may to some extent be followed in Athanasius, who affirms that God, as he saw that a creation differentiated according to its individual λόγοι, would be a divided world, created the world in accordance with his own Logos (*Or. contra gentes* 41; PG 25, 84 A), and is reflected in Augustine, who uses the word *rationes* to denote λόγοι, which he regards as immutable and eternal principles (*De div. quaest. 83,* 46, 2; PL 40, 30 and *De civ. Dei* 11, 29; CSEL 40: 1, p. 537), and conceives of ideas as contained in the Logos (see *In Io., tract.* 1, 9; PL 35, 1383 f.; cf. WOLFSON, *The Philosophy of the Church Fathers,* pp. 280–285). The dominant influence upon Maximus in this respect was, however, obviously exerted by Evagrius and especially by Ps.-Denis, who introduced the dynamic and intentional understanding of λόγοι. For Evagrius the concept of λόγοι of creation in Origen's sense is more or less taken for granted, but the idea is hardly developed any further (see e.g. *Cent. gnost.* 1. 20; PO 28, p. 25; cf. FRANKENBERG, pp. 62–63; 1. 23; PO 28, p. 27; cf. FRANKENBERG, pp. 64–67; 2. 35–36; PO 28, p. 75 f.; cf. FRANKENBERG, pp. 154–155 ff.,; 2. 45; PO 28, p. 79; cf. FRANKENBERG, pp. 160–161; 5. 40; PO 28, p. 193; cf. FRANKENBERG, pp. 334–335; 5.54; PO 28, p. 201; cf. FRANKENBERG, p. 340–341; 6. 54; PO 28, p. 239; cf. FRANKENBERG, pp. 394–395; 6.72; PO 28, p. 247; cf. FRANKENBERG, pp. 404–405; *Liber gnost.* 104 and 107; FRANKENBERG, pp. 546–547; 125; FRANKENBERG, pp. 548–559; cf. DALMAIS, in RSPT 36, 1952, p. 244 with n. 2). We may, however, notice the characteristic Evagrian stress on the λόγοι of providence and judgment (see e.g. *Cent. gnost.* 5. 16; PO 28, p. 183; cf. FRANKENBERG, pp. 324–325; 5. 23–24; PO 28, p. 187; cf. FRANKENBERG, pp. 326–329) and the idea of a final "spiritual contemplation", in which the λόγοι are seen in mystical communion with God (see *Cent. gnost.* 5. 40; PO 28, p. 193; cf. FRANKENBERG, pp. 334–335).

This last aspect brings the Evagrian dismissal of material and bodily existence into the picture. In the end only that which is known through the intellect will remain, for the rest is accidental (see *Cent. gnost.* 1. 20; PO 28, p. 25).—From Ps.-Denis Maximus has received a more positive influence. For—as we have pointed out under 2) already—Ps.-Denis—and his commentator John of Skythopolis—seems to have provided the dynamic aspect, and the understanding of λόγοι as divine wills, which Maximus took for granted (cf. e.g. DALMAIS, *art. cit.,* p. 244; VON BALTHASAR, KL², p. 110 ff.; cf. also *ibid.,* p. 496). VON BALTHASAR (KL², p. 113) has, however, drawn the important conclusion that Maximus shows his independence from all his predecessors in that he does not understand the λόγοι as identical either with the essence of God or with the worldly existence of things. The former

is deeply integrated into a personal, general vision of the mysterious and deifying presence of Christ the Logos in the world.

Maximus uses different expressions to describe or define the λόγοι of creation. The most general term is λόγος τοῦ εἶναι, which is primarily related to God as Cause. Thus it denotes the created existence of a thing as founded in God's will that it should be, it is the principle of its coming to be and implies a participation in God as being. As such it should, however, be distinguished—though the two λόγοι are intimately connected—from the λόγος τοῦ εὖ εἶναι, which expresses participation in God as good and is the principle of motion in each being, i.e. λόγος as regulating moral action and will.[158]

Thinking more of the aspect of differentiation Maximus uses other terms, such as λόγοι τῶν γεγονότων,[159] or λόγοι τῶν ὄντων.[160] His favourite expression, however, is λόγος φύσεως.[161] Sometimes he also uses the term φυσικὸς λόγος.[162] Now what is characteristic of these λόγοι is that they define not only the essence (οὐσία), but also the coming into existence (γένεσις) of things, thus revealing both Maximus' anti-Origenist understanding of the λόγοι and, once again, his positive evaluation of the differentiated world of beings.[163]

For, on the other hand, the differentiated λόγοι pre-exist in God, who keeps them together.[164] This pre-existence of the λόγοι in God implies, first of all, that they are fixed in Him.[165] There are λόγοι for all things which exist or will exist, and they are firmly fixed and pre-existent in God. According to them all things are and have been brought into existence and abide; which, on the other hand, is not to say that things or beings themselves are fixed, for there is always an element of freedom and motion in the created world as well, and this element has to be made

---

alternative would have been an Evagrian tendency, and the latter a Ps.-Dionysian 'danger'. See also J. PRADO, *Voluntad y naturaleza,* pp. 154–157.

[158] Amb 7; PG 91, 1084 B. Beside these two there is also a third, 'supernatural' λόγος, that of ἀεὶ εἶναι. As can easily be noticed, the whole understanding of the λόγοι, as it is most frequently developed, is anthropological at its centre.—On the three forms of being and their λόγοι, see further ch. VI: 5 below. See also my study *Man and the Cosmos,* pp. 132, 137.

[159] See e.g. Thal 2; CCSG 7, p. 51.

[160] See e.g. Char 4.45; CSC, p. 212.

[161] See e.g. OrDom; CCSG 23, p. 65; Ep 2; PG 91, 404 B; Amb 31; PG 91, 1280 A; 42; 1341 C and D (definition of man).

[162] See Thal 35; CCSG 7, p. 239 Char 1. 99; CSC, p. 88.

[163] See Amb 7; PG 91, 1081 B.

[164] Thus they may be called "divine" (see Thal 46; CCSG 7, p. 309), which is, however, not to say that any created nature possesses the λόγοι of 'supernatural' qualities (see Thal 59; CCSG 22, p. 55).

[165] Amb 7; PG 91, 1081A; 42, 1329 A.

active in their drawing nearer to their λόγος (i.e. as λόγος τοῦ εἶναι), according to God's purpose for that particular being as well as for the whole created world. Thus beings may be in or out of harmony with their λόγος, but at least if they are in harmony with it, they will also move according to a fixed purpose of God (πρόθεσις).[166]

We see immediately, that the pre-existence of all λόγοι in God safeguards their unity in Him, but that their differentiation and the mobility of created beings, also ordered by God, safeguard at the same time their independence and individual existence. With God is the truth of all λόγοι, says Maximus on the one hand,[167] but on the other affirms that things are seen as limited, because existing according to their own, individual ideas, through which—as through those of adjacent beings—they are defined and altogether circumscribed.[168] Or we hear, on the one hand, that the one Logos is many λόγοι,[169] but on the other, that all the λόγοι subsist eternally in God's good counsel,[170] and pre-exist monadically in God.[171] Therefore, Christian contemplation (θεωρία) may see the Logos in the λόγοι,[172] but on the other hand, the eternal presence of the Logos in the λόγοι is one which in this world of time and space is to be perceived by faith and in a strictly Christological perspective; only in the end, from an eschatological point of view, will it also be existentially (ὑπαρκτικῶς)[173] realized.

The λόγοι, pre-existent in God, are held together by the Logos

We have seen how the principles of differentiation and unity are inseparable in Maximus' theology of the λόγοι. This is apparent, also when we study the relationship between the Logos and the λόγοι. For while on the one hand they are summarized in the Logos, it belongs to the very nature of the Logos, on the other hand, that he wills to become flesh, to be incarnate, which is also to say, in some way differentiated. We may indeed, in this context, speak with I.-H. Dalmais, of a "mystique du Logos",[174] because the secret of this theology is that the Logos is the place

---

[166] See Amb 42; PG 91, 1329 A.
[167] Amb 7; PG 91, 1081 A.
[168] *Ibid.;* 1081 B.
[169] *Ibid.;* 1077 C.
[170] *Ibid.;* 1080 A.
[171] Thal 60; CCSG 22, p. 81.
[172] Cf. Loosen, *Logos und Pneuma*, p. 76.
[173] See this term in Maximus' criticism of the Origenists, Amb 7; PG 91, 1089 B. Cf. Sherwood, *The Earlier Ambigua*, p. 191.
[174] Dalmais, Un traité de théologie contemplative, RAM 29 (1953), p. 143.

of all the λόγοι.[175] For, as von Balthasar has pointed out, the orthodox counterpart of the Origenist doctrine of the primitive henad of λογικοί is for Maximus this unity of the λόγοι in the Logos.[176] This in fact, however, is also to say that the refutation of Origenism at this point could hardly be more central in Maximus' theology. For it is in their differentiation that the λόγοι are held together in the Logos.

Consequently, Maximus makes a double affirmation. A person who regards the multiplicity of things in wisdom, he says, will see both the one Logos as many λόγοι and the many λόγοι as the one Logos, for in Him, he adds with reference to Col. 1: 16, i.e. in Christ the Logos, all has been created.[177] This is, however, not to say that the Logos as mediator is deprived of his super-essential character. He is all the time regarded as a person in the mysterious Godhead, for whom the principles of apophatic theology remain relevant. But nevertheless it is equally true, that the many λόγοι are one Logos, and the one Logos is many λόγοι.[178]

One should perhaps add, that, according to the general structure of Maximus' thinking, the relation between the Logos and the λόγοι can hardly be one of a simple identification, since unity and differentiation are equally important, first of all, because the presence of the Logos in the λόγοι is always seen as a kind of incarnation—a parallel to the incarnation in the historical Jesus—and thus as an act of divine condescension. On the other hand, the pre-existent unity of the λόγοι in the Logos is ideal and only in an eschatological perspective will their unity be existential (ὑπαρκτικῶς).[179]

Thus only Christian contemplation (θεωρία) is able to see the Logos in the λόγοι.[180] But then there is to Maximus no doubt, that—seen from the point of view of unifying contemplation—the λόγοι are seated like birds on the branches of the great Logos tree,[181] which has grown from the mustard seed of the Gospel, while—from the other point of view, that of the incarnation and differentiation of the Logos—the λόγοι of intelli-

---

[175] Cf. DALMAIS, La fonction unificatrice, *Sc. Ecclés.* 14 (1962), p. 452. This idea has been further developed by RIOU, *op.cit.,* 54–63.

[176] See VON BALTHASAR, KL², p. 126. For a more recent discussion of this problem, see P. FARRELL, *Free Choice . . .* , pp. 133–142.

[177] Amb 7; PG 91, 1077 C.

[178] *Ibid.;* 1081 BC; cf. SHERWOOD, *The Earlier Ambigua,* p. 179 f., where the relationship between these two aspects leads to a problem requiring a specific study: are the λόγοι situated in the divine essence or only in the divine energies? Cf. p. 64, n. 109 above.

[179] Cf. SHERWOOD, *op. cit.,* p. 191. For a more recent discussion of this theme and its relation to Palamism, see my study *Man and the Cosmos,* pp. 137–143.

[180] Cf. LOOSEN, *op. cit.,* p. 76.

[181] See Gnost 2. 10; PG 90, 1129 A; cf. VON BALTHASAR, KL², p. 547 f.

gible beings may be understood as the blood of the Logos, and the λόγοι
of sensible things as the flesh of the Logos, through which those who are
worthy are allowed to have spiritual communion with God.[182] Thus the
λόγοι are to Maximus not identical either with the essence of God or with
the existence of the things in the created world.[183] In fact an apophatic
tendency is combined in Maximus with an anti-pantheistic tendency. For
the created world is attributed a positively independent existence,
without interfering with the sovereignty of God above and in the world.
This is effected, above all, thanks to the understanding of the λόγοι as
decisions of God's will.[184]

**The λόγοι of creation are intimately connected with the λόγοι of the economy
of salvation and of Christ's Incarnation in the flesh**

The cosmological (ontological), the providential and the historical Logos
are not separate elements in Maximus' theology, but consciously depicted as one and the same: Christ, the Son of God the Father, and the
Lord of the Church. He is the centre of the universe in the same manner
as he is the centre of the economy of salvation. This fact is particularly
made evident in a passage in Amb 33, where Maximus indicates a
three-fold embodiment of the Logos, not only in His coming in the flesh
(παρουσία ἔνσαρκος), but also already in the λόγοι of created beings
(λόγοι τῶν ὄντων) and in the letters and sounds of Scripture.[185] This
three-fold embodiment seems to be closely linked with Maximus' idea of
three general laws in the world: natural law, written law and the law of
grace.[186] Thus in Maximus' view, the Logos, on account of his general will
to incarnate himself, holds together not only the λόγοι of creation but
also the three aspects of creation, revelation (illumination) and salvation.[187]

---

[182] Thal 35; CCSG 7, p. 239.

[183] Cf. VON BALTHASAR, KL², p. 113.

[184] Cf. *ibid.*, p. 114 f. One can, in fact, hardly agree with HEINTJES, De opgang van den
menschelijken geest, BiNJ 5 (1942), p. 299, who says explicitly that the λόγοι are reflections
of God's essence; cf. also HEINTJES, Een onbekende leraar, StC 11 (1935), p. 181. Generally,
see DALMAIS, La théorie des 'logoi' . . . .

[185] Amb 33; PG 91, 1285 C–1288 A; cf. DALMAIS, RSPT 36 (1952), p. 249 and IDEM, La
manifestation du Logos . . . , pp. 13–25.

[186] VON BALTHASAR, KL², p. 289 f., has emphasized this connection and the fundamental importance of the text, while SHERWOOD, *The Earlier Ambigua*, p. 52, systematizes the
passage in a different way. On the three-fold 'incarnation', see also BLOWERS, *op.cit.*, p. 119
and p. 168, n. 114.

[187] Notice the *tantum-quantum* formula used in Maximus' summary of the effect of this
three-fold action of Christ, in *ibid.*, 1288 A.

Consequently, contemplation of the λόγοι in creation (θεωρία φυσική) belongs to the work of the Spirit in man's sanctification and deification. This intellectual process is not separated from spiritual growth but is an integral part of it. The outward impressions suggest the λόγοι of things to an attentive soul, so that they—and the Logos in them—may be spiritually contemplated.[188] The reasonable part of the human soul may gain an analytical knowledge of things through the λόγοι.[189] But this knowledge of the λόγοι is as such a divine gift.[190]

A similar relationship to the powers of salvation is, of course, presupposed also in relation to the λόγοι of Scripture. Incarnate in the words and sounds of Scripture, the living Lord must also illuminate their deepest sense, as he did once in his earthly career, revealing the secrets of the OT.[191] And this holds true not only of the spiritual contemplation of the mysteries of Scripture, but also of its ethical teaching, that is to say the λόγοι of the commandments, an expression found already in Evagrius.[192] For in the latter there is also a true knowledge[193] (though its primary implications are for the *vita practica*), and the Logos is really present in his own commandments.[194] He is, however, hidden in them, and has thus to be revealed through practical obedience to them. And here the dialectic of incarnation and unification is at play again: in the *vita practica,* thanks to his presence in the λόγοι of the commandments, the Logos becomes incarnate, but this incarnation is a counterpart to the opposite movement of human ascent towards the divine simplicity, which takes place in the *vita contemplativa* and in true *gnosis.*[195] Maximus says that in the first movement, that of condescension, the Logos becomes "thick", while in the second he becomes "thin", as he was in the beginning.[196] It is this incarnation of the Logos in the virtues which is so eloquently described for instance in Ep 2,[197] where this process is not simply regarded as a preparation for a necessary higher stage of natural contemplation but may, as in the case of a layman living in the world,

---

[188] See e.g. Amb 10; PG 91, 1113 A and 1116 A and Amb 21; 1248 B.

[189] Amb 10; PG 91, 1113 A.

[190] See Thal 63; CCSG 22, p. 159. On θεωρία φυσική and its relationship to the λόγοι of creation, see further ch. VI: 3; p. 349 ff. below.

[191] Cf. DALMAIS, RAM 29 (1953), p. 124.

[192] Evagrius, *Cent. gnost.* 4. 55; PO 28, p. 161; cf. FRANKENBERG, p. 294 f.

[193] See Thal 36; CCSG 7, p. 243.

[194] Gnost 2. 71; PG 90, 1156 D.

[195] QuDub 142; CCSG 10, p. 101.

[196] Gnost 2. 37–38; PG 90, 1141 CD. The idea goes back to Origen; see on the general background of Maximus' thinking here VON BALTHASAR, KL[2], p. 518 ff.

[197] See particularly PG 91, 401 AB.

lead directly to deification. The two aspects are in fact held together in one purpose of communion with God, through Christ the Logos. The Lord Christ is to Maximus also the substance of all the virtues, and thus everyone who partakes consistently of virtue, partakes of God himself.[198] The Logos holds all together, as he is the embodiment both of being and of true existence.[199]

This unification without annihilation is thus indeed the divine purpose itself. It has been prepared in creation by the diversification of the Logos—itself a primary incarnation and a presupposition for the historical incarnation in the flesh—and it has been brought to a victorious conclusion by Christ's unification, not only of what had been torn asunder by sin, but also of that which was naturally differentiated. Of these two kinds the former is, however, an annihilation of unnatural divisions, but the latter a unification characterized by a preservation of differentiation in immutable unity. In the life of Christian believers this process is fulfilled in a will to unity, which destroys unnatural divisions in opinions and on the social level, and is deemed worthy to receive illumination through the multiplicity of the world by the one Logos, present in all.

This dominant concern for the preservation in unity is well illustrated by a passage in Amb 10, where we learn that the shining clothes of the transfigured Christ symbolize the fact that, when God, the Sun of righteousness, appears to the mind, then all the true λόγοι of intelligible and sensible things will also appear together with him.[200] And the providential aspect of Maximus' whole theology of the λόγοι of creation is equally well illustrated by another passage, in Amb 41, where we learn that in the Incarnation God united in himself both the natural diversifications of the universal nature, and the λόγοι of that which is produced partially, λόγοι thanks to which, however, even this unification had been made possible.[201]

Creation by the Word thus implies to Maximus not only a positive evaluation of creation but the inclusion of the latter in a purpose of universal unification, on the basis of the Incarnation by grace of the Logos, in which all the λόγοι of things abide.

---

[198] Amb 7; PG 91, 1081 CD.—On the incarnation of the Logos in the virtues, see further ch. V: B, 5 and on the relationship between the *vita practica* and the *vita contemplativa* in this context, see particularly ch. VI: 2 (p. 339 ff.) below.

[199] Notice the close relationship between λόγοι and τρόποι in the field of ethics; see Thal 22, CCSG 7, p. 143; cf. von Balthasar, KL², p. 638.

[200] PG 91, 1156 AB.

[201] PG 91, 1308 D.

5. Creation on the basis of God's prudence

There is for Maximus no sense in trying to penetrate into the reason of God's creation. His apophatic theology implies resignation at this point on the part of man. Man has simply to trust in God's prudence (φρόνησις), which has marvellously brought the world into its complex being.[202]

One should notice, however, that the word used here is φρόνησις. Aristotle for instance had distinguished between prudence and wisdom (σοφία)[203] and given to the former a practical and to the latter a theoretical function. For Maximus this distinction is equally relevant. φρόνησις implies to him a practical understanding, and is related to active life, being a function of the λόγος rather than of the νοῦς to which wisdom (σοφία) is related.[204] Maximus at this point too comes very close to Evagrius, who expresses the same duality of prudence—wisdom,[205] and who says that φρόνησις contemplates the powers but not the λόγοι, which are revealed through σοφία.[206] Maximus also sometimes contrasts φρόνησις, as expression of a right use of the irascible and the concupiscible elements in man, with knowledge (γνῶσις),[207] and says that it is a capacity for discernment between virtue and vice.[208] Thus, by using the word prudence in relation to God's creation Maximus obviously underlines once more the apophatic understanding of God. Though God must be supposed to have contemplated the λόγοι of creation and so to have created the world,[209] the rational background in God of the concrete world—which is an expression of His practical reason—remains still "unsearchable".[210]

---

[202] See Char 4. 1; CSC, p. 194.

[203] See e.g. *Eth. Nicom.* 6, 7, 3; 1141 a.

[204] Amb 10; PG 91, 1109 B. This distinction is also found in *Capita alia,* a work probably by Elias Ecdicus; see M.-Th. DISDIER, Elie l'Ecdicos et les hetera Kephalaia attribués à S. Maxime le Confesseur et à Jean de Carpathos, EO 31 (1932), p. 34.

[205] See e.g. *Pract.* 1. 45; PG 40, 1232 D and *Mirror for Monks* 126 and 131, GRESSMANN, p. 164; cf. no. 133, where the same duality of functions is presupposed.

[206] *Liber gnost.* 146; see Socrates, *Hist. eccl.* 4, 23; PG 67, 520 AB and FRANKENBERG, p. 552 f.; cf. also PG 40, 1285 B. This text seems to have been partly misunderstood by VILLER, RAM 11 (1930), p. 171, n. 69, who renders λόγοι "paroles". Cf. for Evagrius also *Pract.* 1. 60; PG 40, 1236 A, which shows clearly that φρόνησις is related to ethical judgments, and 1. 61; 1236 B, where σύνεσις is introduced in a list of virtues between φρόνησις and σοφία.

[207] See Char 3. 3; CSC, p. 144.

[208] Char 2. 26; CSC, p. 102.

[209] See Char 4. 4; CSC, p. 194; cf. SHERWOOD, in ACW, p. 263.

[210] Char 4. 1; CSC, p. 194.

6. Creation—an act of divine condescension, which introduces the element of motion

We have seen how Maximus regards even the practical and creative prudence of God as unsearchable. Nevertheless he is equally certain that creation is in itself good, because it has a good Cause. We have also seen how already in the initial act of creation, God bridges the gulf between the created order and Himself by intention introducing a relationship to creation, which is particularly apparent as that between the λόγοι of beings and the Logos, who is at the same time a person in the Godhead. Now these λόγοι are the divine intentions for creation, and thus the whole act of God's creation is seen to be an act of intentional condescension from the side of God, and the presence of the Logos in the λόγοι may e.g. be understood as a primary divine incarnation. God is thus boundless and unsearchable, and yet at the same time he is active goodness revealed through his creative acts.

God may, therefore, be said to be like an abyss or an ocean (πέλαγος), not only in his unsearchableness,[211] but also in his creative goodness.[212] God is the immense source of all. Thus, no matter pre-existed its coming to be,[213] and spiritual or rational nature is created in the same sense as matter is created. No created things have existed eternally with God, but all are wholly brought into existence by him in time and space.[214]

Consequently Maximus entirely rejects—as we have indicated—the Origenist idea of a primitive henad of rational beings, coexisting with God and from which, by surfeit, they have afterwards fallen.[215] Sherwood has shown how fundamental and radical this refutation of the Origenist myth and its theological consequences was.[216] A detailed presentation of his results need, of course, not be given here.[217] Let us only underline that

---

[211] *Ibid.*

[212] Char 4.2; CSC, p. 194. Also the utterings of the Holy Spirit may be called an infinite ocean, see Thal, *Prol.;* CCSG 7, p. 19.

[213] Char 4.2; CSC, p. 194.

[214] See Char 4. 6; CSC, p. 196.

[215] SHERWOOD has counted the term 'henad' six times in all in Maximus, four times in Amb 7 and twice in Amb 15; see *The Earlier Ambigua*, pp. 85–92.

[216] This is the main theme of SHERWOOD, *The Earlier Ambigua*, see particularly pp. 92–102. It should be noted, however, that VON BALTHASAR already in 1941 (in KL¹, p. 97 ff.) pointed out that Maximus criticizes the Origenist idea of an original stability (στάσις) of all created spirits in God, and establishes an anti-Origenist triad of becoming (γένεσις)—motion (κίνησις)—rest (στάσις).

[217] SHERWOOD makes clear, however, that Maximus sets out to refute specifically *the primitive henad of rational beings,* a term which may go back to Origen himself (see SHERWOOD, *op. cit.,* p. 73) and is at least found in Justinian's anti-Origenist documents (see SHERWOOD, *op. cit.,* p. 85 f.). Maximus does this by changing the (in his mind wrong) Origenist triad μονή, κίνησις, γένεσις (see Amb 7; PG 91, 1069 A) into his own: γένεσις,

this refutation implies, first of all, a positive evaluation of the concept of motion in relation to the created world. Maximus, who adheres to an Aristotelian understanding of motion,[218] thus regards the movement of rational beings towards God, not as a return to a primitive unity, but as a

κίνησις, στάσις (see e.g. Amb 15; PG 91, 1217 D), probably using as his point of departure "the Plotinian use of *stasis,* as indicating the final end of all motion and desire" (SHERWOOD, *op. cit.,* p. 96). Maximus thus breaks the spell of the Hellenic circle by way of its own logic, and there is no longer any idea of successive falls and endless generations, nor of any satiety in the stage of στάσις. For Maximus στάσις "belongs to the realm beyond" (SHERWOOD, *op. cit.,* p. 94), and is reached only when man has moved to the point where for him the ultimate desirable is (see Amb 7; PG 91, 1069 B).—A word should be added on the relations to Evagrius at this point. That Evagrius was included in the anathemas of 553 has long been evident; in fact his texts were directly quoted in some of them (see e.g. SHERWOOD, *op. cit.,* p. 85 and note 30). It may also be taken for granted that Evagrius actually taught the primitive henad in the sense indicated, though explicit statements are difficult to provide (see VON BALTHASAR in his commentary on the *Gnostic centuries,* KL², p. 531; cf. also W. BOUSSET, *Apophthegmata,* Tübingen 1923, pp. 294–300, esp. p. 229 about the fall as κίνησις). At least one may now conclude—since A. GUILLAUMONT has restored the reliable (Syriac) text of Evagrius' *Gnostic centuries* (see PO 28, 1958, fasc. 1)—that it must have been quite possible to deduce the Origenist triad which Maximus rejected in the *Ambigua* from Evagrius himself. See esp. *Cent. gnost.* 6. 20, PO 28, p. 225, where the primitive movement of beings is described as a fall away from God, after which God—who was from the beginning the creator of non-corporeal beings—also became creator of bodies and judge etc.; and further *Cent. gnost.* 6. 75; PO 28, p. 249, where a triad of ἡ πρώτη γνῶσις of the λογικοί (which is "contemplation of the Holy Trinity")—ἡ τοῦ αὐτεξουσίου κίνησις (followed by πρόνοια)—κρίσις (followed by an opposite movement and providence and judgment) can be discovered (for the Greek terms, see W. FRANKENBERG, *Euagrius Ponticus,* Berlin 1912, p. 411, where the distorted Syriac text is retranslated). This last triad is in fact very similar to that which is transformed and corrected by Maximus, for there the original contemplation of rational beings presupposes an existing unity in God, and κρίσις (in the first sense) is, as we have seen, for Evagrius also an equivalent of creation in diversity, second creation (on the concept of double creation, see further ch. III: B, 1, p. 147 ff. below; cf. VON BALTHASAR, KL², p. 531; on the idea of a double creation as judgment in Evagrius, cf. also *Cent. gnost.* 3. 38; PO 28, p. 113 and 4. 4; p. 137, commented upon by A. and C. GUILLAUMONT themselves in RHR 142, 1952, p. 187 ff.). Since Evagrius also knew a redemptive triad of κίνησις, πρόνοια and κρίσις, Maximus may very well have found his positive starting-point there, too.

   That the complicated process of Maximus' refutation of Origenism is part and parcel of the intricate process of his assimilation and rejection of Evagrian thinking has at least become more credible in recent years, since the findings of GUILLAUMONT have helped us considerably to rediscover Evagrius as a primary source of the anti-Origenist anathemas of 553 (for the discussion of this problem in relation to the text of the *Gnostic centuries* of Evagrius, see the important study by A. GUILLAUMONT: *Les "Kephalaia gnostica" d' Évagre le Pontique,* Paris 1962; cf. the earlier indications by F. REFOULÉ, La christologie d'Évagre, OCP 27, 1961, pp. 221–266).—Thus when Maximus, e.g. in Ep 2 (PG 91, 396 C), underlines that love alone brings man to the true στάσις, this is to be seen in the light of the corrected triad, and the idea is in fact non-Evagrian. For love has this power because it is divine, and not because it gathers together things which have had their στάσις in God already.

   [218] Cf. SHERWOOD, *op. cit.,* p. 99.—See also the concept of "moving rest" as analysed by P. PLASS, 'Moving Rest' in Maximus the Confessor, pp. 177–190.

development in the direction of a unifying end, fixed by God in his creation. This movement is conceived as a growth which presupposes a willed establishment of a created world with its own identity, by nature separated from, but at the same time orientated towards God, its Creator.

Creation as an act of divine condescension thus introduces a movement of fulfilment, so that God himself, though immovable, might be said to have realized his creative power in motion.[219] For motion towards God as end presupposes—not a fall from a primitive henad, as for the Origenists, but—a condescending 'motion' from the side of God as Creator and Provider.

7. *Every creature is composite of substance and accident*

The decisive difference between Creator and creatures is to Maximus the fact that God, from one point of view, is pure substance, simple and unqualified, while creatures have qualified substances, and are composite and mutable.[220] In the cosmological context of the present chapter this plain and obvious statement requires, however, at least a short study of Maximus' understanding of the key concepts of substance and nature.

The concept of substance

Von Balthasar has noticed that Maximus uses the word *substance* (οὐσία) in two different senses, a duality which recalls the two ways in which the concept was used by Leontius of Byzantium.[221] The duality as such, however, probably goes back in both cases to the Aristotelian concepts of *prima* and *secunda substantia*. For there already an individual aspect of the term, related to *substantia prima,* and a conceptual aspect, related to *substantia secunda,* are balanced against each other. For Leontius too, though differing from the original Aristotelian understanding, there is a first sense, in which substance is regarded as that which exists for itself, but of which all beings then partake, including God, and something like a second sense, in which substance is more or less identical with "form" or "nature".[222] And in the same manner Maximus distinguishes between οὐσία as a supreme ontological category, which includes all beings—with

---

[219] This idea seems to be implicit in Char 4. 2; CSC, p. 194. Cf. our discussion of the Ps.-Dionysian concept of divine ecstasy in Maximus in ch. VI: 10, p. 423 ff.

[220] See Char 4. 9; CSC, p. 198.

[221] See VON BALTHASAR, KL², pp. 213 ff.

[222] See JUNGLAS, *Leontius von Byzanz,* p. 72 f.

the exclusion of God, of course—and another substance, οὐσία καθ᾽ ἕκαστον, which is almost identical with "nature".[223]

We see, however, immediately that for both Leontius and Maximus, Aristotle's *substantia prima* has more or less disappeared—οὐσία in the first sense comes very close to a general concept of being, or idea of being—and thus the element of individuality is no longer safe-guarded by the term in any of its senses. At the same time Maximus, by elevating God above οὐσία—as Ps.-Denis particularly, on the basis of his mainly Neo-Platonist philosophy, had already done—has opened up the possibility of considering elements in creation which are not identical with substance and yet not merely accidental, and the possibility of a created existence which is more than participation in *general* being. This other aspect—which is that of freedom, movement, individuality in a positive sense—though instigated by the Aristotelian philosophical tradition, so influential in Maximus' whole thinking, would certainly not have been developed to such a considerable extent, had it not been integrated with a post-Chalcedonian Christology which made the hypostatic mysteries the very core of Christian thinking.

In relation to the concept of substance (οὐσία) the dynamic element just indicated may be observed at a few definite points.

a) οὐσία itself, as we know it, is a category of creation. God, though being, is above οὐσία,[224] and created οὐσία is not eternal as "the Greeks" presume.[225] In a first sense οὐσία is thus a general category of created being, for which the principle of being (λόγος τοῦ εἶναι) is the unifying norm, and which includes all families of creation.[226] As a created element—though a totality including even the universals—it is, however, characterized by limitations, which belong to all creation. Thus it is not without a *contrary,* since non-being is its contrary;[227] it is not simple but stands in a certain *duality* because related to accident, and is present in things, characterized by *difference* (διαφορά).[228]

---

[223] VON BALTHASAR, KL², p. 214 f. See further on "nature" p. 87 ff.

[224] See on God as ὑπερούσιος e.g. Amb 1; PG 91, 1036 B; 7; 1081 B; 17; 1224 B. Cf. Gnost 1. 2; PG 90, 1084 A. Maximus builds here chiefly on Ps.-Denis (see *De div. nom.* I, 1; PG 3, 588 AB and particularly *De div. nom.* 5, 2; 816 C), though already Gregory of Nyssa had regarded God's οὐσία as transcendent in an absolute sense; cf. DANIÉLOU, *Platonisme et théologie mystique²*, Paris 1954, p. 300 f.

[225] Char 3. 28; CSC, p. 156. This idea was of pagan neo-Platonist origin and had been attacked by John Philoponus and Zacharias; cf. VON BALTHASAR, KL², p. 148.

[226] Thal 48; CCSG 7, p. 343 f. VON BALTHASAR, KL², p. 214, emphasizes correctly, that as such it should however be distinguished from Aristotle's *substantia secunda.*

[227] Char 3. 28; CSC, p. 156. God's substance alone has no contrary, while created substance depends on the will of the Creator. Cf. 3. 29; CSC, p. 156 ff.

[228] Amb 67; PG 91, 1400 C. Maximus says here that all created things are dual: sensible

b) οὐσία and εἶναι are not quite identical. Von Balthasar has made clear that, though the two concepts are more or less identical, the term εἶναι seems to include and underline the aspect of being as existence.[229] He has particularly drawn attention to Ep 12, where Maximus tends to contrast "the principle of substance" (similar to "the principle of nature") against the wider or higher concept of "the principle of being".[230] Another indication of this tendency is, of course, the fact that οὐσία in the precise (second) sense is more or less identified with "nature" (φύσις), while εἶναι is introduced into a triadic scale of "being—well-being—ever-being".[231]

c) οὐσία needs to be realized in an act of self-fulfilment.[232] In rational creatures, this leads to well-being, and from natural potentiality to effective actuality.[233] This is made clear by Maximus especially in Amb 65, where we learn that being as such possesses no more than the potentiality of its realization, which is effected through the intentional activity of rational beings, and which implies the natural transcendence from mere being to well-being. There is, however, a mutual dependence between the elements of substance and intention, in so far as the latter, in order to function, must also be carried by the former.[234] We also learn, in the same passage, that the first stage is one of substantial potentiality (δύναμις) and the second one of intentional ἐνέργεια. For human beings there is finally the third stage of ever-being, which is reached only through the active grace of God.[235] Being as created life is at the same time at every stage only a participation in what God gives to his creation out of his own being, goodness, wisdom and life.[236] Thus substance exists on account of God's will as Creator; natural self-realization of substance is effected on account of God's will as creator of good things and the source of all good; but the transcendence of substance is made available to human beings thanks to God's 'economy' which relates 'independent' creation to the Creator in positive communication.

---

things consist of matter and form, intelligible things of substance and accident.

[229] VON BALTHASAR, KL², p. 215 f.

[230] PG 91, 488 BC.

[231] See further ch. VI: 5 below.

[232] Motion is characteristic of οὐσία as of all created life; see Amb 10; PG 91, 1177 B.

[233] The third stage, ever-being, intended for human beings, i.e. the stage of eternal bliss in deification, is a divine gift, which as such properly transcends the boundaries of οὐσία (cf. ch. VI: 5, p. 368 ff. below).

[234] PG 91, 1392 AB. This is an indication that Maximus still moves in the Aristotelian line of thinking; cf. on Ps.-Denis as his predecessor at this point, VON BALTHASAR, KL², p. 40.

[235] Cf. Amb 7; PG 91, 1073 C.

[236] The λόγοι of the three modes of being are pre-existent in God; see Amb 7; PG 91, 1084 BC; cf. Char 3. 27; CSC, p. 156.

d) οὐσία in the second sense is integrated into a dynamic relationship between the different aspects of generalization. Since *substantia prima* in the Aristotelian sense tends to disappear in Maximus,[237] the element of individuality and particularity has had to be related to substance in the second sense, but the latter concept of substance is not able to give proper place to this element of individuality. Therefore, οὐσία as related to universals, families or species—and as almost identical with φύσις[238]—cannot be identified with such concepts as hypostasis or existence (ὕπαρξις), which are apt to include the realization of the element of freedom, movement and will. οὐσία in the second sense may imply a successive scale of particularity[239]—from universals to families and from families to species[240]—but it remains a fact, that all φύσις is general and all οὐσία (in the second sense) concerns an entire species.[241] And thus—though every individual substance moves and is moved[242]—the personal element in the realization of the potentiality of the substance is not included in the concept of substance itself.

And so Maximus has had to work with an idea of *individual subsistence,* which is not identical with his concept of particular substance, though he does not develop it in full.[243] But then we may also conclude that Christological requirements are met by now in a way,[244] which is also able to transcend the limitations of older ontological considerations. The aspects of unity and true self-realization have—for soteriological reasons—had to be interrelated in such a way that a proper balance and perfect harmony are equally safeguarded.

---

[237] That Maximus is aware of Aristotle's concept is, however, quite clear. In ThPol 23 Maximus agrees with Clement of Alexandria (in the lost writing *De provid.;* GCS Clem. 3, p. 219) in defining first substance as that which subsists for itself, and distinguishing in all four kinds of substances, exemplified as follows: first substance, by a stone; second substance, by the plant; third substance, by the horse; and fourth substance, by man (PG 91, 265 D–268 A). But in ThPol 26 he refers almost with disdain to an Aristotelian definition of οὐσία (αὐθυπόστατον πρᾶγμα) as to that of "the philosophers" (as such he could have found it also in Leontius, see JUNGLAS, *Leontius von Byzanz,* p. 72 f.) and contrasts it with that of "the Fathers", who regard οὐσία as ὀντότης φυσική (PG 91, 276 A). A criticism of this latter understanding has been made by PRESTIGE, *God in Patristic Thought,* p. 279.

[238] In ThPol 14; PG 90, 149 B, Maximus states expressly that οὐσία and φύσις are the same thing.

[239] This means no degradation. A species is of no less worth than substance, Maximus affirms in Amb 10; PG 91, 1181 C.

[240] See e.g. Amb 41; PG 91, 1312 B–D; 10; 1169 C and 17; 1228 D.

[241] Cf. VON BALTHASAR, KL[2], p. 215.

[242] Gnost 1. 3; PG 90, 1084 AB.

[243] Cf. VON BALTHASAR, KL[2], *loc. cit.*

[244] See Maximus' discussion of the problem in Ep 13; PG 91, 517 D–520 C.

The concept of "nature"

The concept of *nature* (φύσις) is strictly reduced to the sphere of universals. The Christological struggles had worked out a clear distinction between nature and hypostasis, which to Maximus with his Chalcedonian orthodoxy was, of course, beyond discussion. Aristotle had understood φύσις in a more concrete, though also general and varied sense, but such philosophical theologians as Leontius of Byzantium had made a definite mark on its Christian meaning. Thus, to Maximus also φύσις is related to universals, families and species. It denotes what is common to all individual beings belonging to each of them and is as such identical with οὐσία in what we called its second sense.[245] The term 'nature' pertains to the principle of being as it is common to many, while hypostasis is related also to the principle of individual being, as Maximus affirms in complete accordance with Leontius.[246] φύσις is strictly reduced to the species (εἶδος) and expresses—not to the philosophers but to the Fathers, he says—the qualified existence of a whole.[247]

The term thus has a limited scope and is primarily related to a differentiation which is characteristic of all creation, without containing the transcending character of the hypostasis. But on the other hand, within its limits φύσις keeps individuals together, and the λόγοι of creation—which are primarily related to the different natures—are the basis of unification within each species. For this reason, it is on the basis of φύσις and its λόγος, that unity between human beings may also be acquired.

But this is not all that is to be said about the category of nature in Maximus. For to him the dynamic element in creation is also related to nature. Though Maximus does not base himself exclusively or perhaps even deliberately on pagan philosophers, it seems quite clear that Aristotle's understanding of φύσις as the source of movement and rest[248] serves as his undisputed starting-point. The only difference is that this dynamic element of nature is also seen as created by God and intended by him to be its qualification.

From his Aristotelian point of view Maximus is thus free to regard the movement of each nature as decisive for it—and so to reject the negative

---

[245] ThPol 23; PG 91, 264 AB–265 C, and Ep 15; PG 91, 545 A.

[246] ThPol 23; PG 91, 264 AB, where we find direct quotations from Leontius of Byzantium, *Lib. tres;* PG 86; 1, 1280 A; cf. *Epilysis;* PG 86: 2, 1924 A.

[247] ThPol 23; 265 C and 26; 276 A; cf. with the latter text what Leontius says about οὐσία in *Epilysis;* PG 86: 2, 1921 C.

[248] ἀρχὴ κινήσεως καὶ ἠρεμίας, see DIELS, *Doxographi graeci*, Berlin 1879, p. 274; cf. Aristotle, *Phys.* 2.1; 192 b; cf. 3.1; 200 b and 8.3; 253 b.

attitude to movement which was characteristic of the Origenists—safeguarding at the same time its relative freedom, its dependence upon a general divine purpose and the absolute distinction between created nature and divine immutable substance.[249] Motion and nature are closely knit together by Maximus, in a characteristic way, which allows both a purposeful general drive towards indissoluble unity with its end, God the Creator, and at the same time a strict observance of the individuality of species and individuals in the created world. The concept of nature here represents the aspect of limitation and relativity, while the concept of hypostasis opens up the perspective of a wider expansion outside these limitations, in spite of their strict preservation.

The dynamic potentiality of nature itself is manifest in Maximus' affirmation that a nature is defined through the principle of its ἐνέργεια,[250] which is to say that a nature is not made manifest until its potentiality is realized in actuality. The active dynamism of a nature is thus the element which reveals a species as what it is.[251] The concept of φύσις is not static, and yet its character as that of a limited species—i.e. its character as created substance—is preserved. Thus we see clearly, how Maximus arrives logically at his dyo-energetic position.[252] If a nature is defined by its dynamic element, then, consequently, each nature can have only one natural energy and can permit of no differentiation in its natural existence,[253] while two natures are bound to have two different energies, since they are defined in their differentiation by these very energies. This is also why Maximus comes to the conclusion that all virtues are simply realizations of nature,[254] and why Maximus is also bound to regard sin as, in a way, leading naturally to its own punishment.[255]

In his definitions of natural energy Maximus thus underlines the qualifying character of this energy, and its necessary relationship to a particular nature or substance, within the limitations of which it,

---

[249] Here, however, he could hardly have got any support from Leontius of Byzantium on whose definitions of nature and substance he had to a great extent relied. For Leontius seems to have had Origenist leanings himself (on this hypothesis, see RICHARD, Léonce de Byzance, était-il origéniste?, REB 5, 1947, pp. 31–36). Maximus' attitude to Leontius is typical of an eclecticism motivated at a deeper level by his preference for theology to philosophy.

[250] See Amb 5; PG 91, 1057 B.

[251] Cf. Amb 7; PG 91, 1073 AB.

[252] He claims to have clear support in Cyril of Alexandria; see ThPol 27; PG 91, 284 C–285 A.

[253] ThPol 16; PG 91, 201 C.

[254] See Pyrrh; PG 91, 309 B.

[255] See Amb 10; PG 91, 1164 C; cf. VON BALTHASAR, KL², p. 143.

consequently, has an unconfused character.[256] And in relation to will he likewise refers to those who regard it as a natural element, and sees it as bound to its particular substance, nature or species.[257]

And yet, there is more to be said about this dynamic element in relation to nature. For, as in the case of οὐσία, also in the case of φύσις there is a certain perspective which leads outside the realm of mere nature. Existence includes more than being, but *hypostasis* too as the principle of *personal* being, related particularly to the aspect of the realization of what belongs to nature, is a reality which seems to transcend the strict limits of nature.[258] This is not to say that there is anything within the sphere of hypostasis that is contrary to nature, but it is to assert the fact that for all differentiated creation there is a divine purpose which co-ordinates all natural dynamism. In fact, this transcendence is indicated by nature itself. For, according to Maximus' Aristotelian principles, all movement moves towards an end (τέλος), but created things cannot be an end in themselves (only God is αὐτοτελές), and thus the end of the natural movement of creation must be outside nature itself. And the ultimate end of the whole of creation must be that for which all things are, and which itself is caused by nothing, that which is its own end, i.e. God.[259] Now this aspect of transcendence cannot be grasped by any automatism of nature as such; rather it is an expression of personal existence,[260] of decisive freedom. Here man's "gnomic will" comes into the picture as that which may be persuaded to be positively related to the powers and purpose of human nature.[261] The realization of these powers remains entirely natural—the limitations of natural existence are preserved—but in relationship to the end man may experience the aspect of transcendence, a transcendence, in preservation of nature, effected for man in Christ as hypostasis of two natures, each with its own will and energy.

We must conclude with von Balthasar, that a new perspective is

---

[256] ThPol 27; PG 91, 280 CD.

[257] See e.g. ThPol 1; PG 91, 12 C; 14; 153 A; 26; 280 A.

[258] Here, of course, we touch the sphere of anthropology rather than that of pure cosmology, but this makes no real difference, for, all the time in Maximus, it is only through anthropology that the Christological insights have repercussions in general cosmological principles.

[259] See Amb 7; PG 91, 1072 BC.

[260] Not only is the hypostasis existent in a substance (ἐνούσιος), but also the substance has to be enhypostasized, says Maximus in ThPol 16; PG 91, 205 B. See further VON BALTHASAR's study of the term *hypostasis* etc. in KL², pp. 219–232.

[261] On Maximus' view of different aspects of man's voluntary activity, see ch. IV:B below.

opened up,[262] where personal existence and the mystery of union in infinity are brought together on the basis of Christological insights into what was felt as the deepest secrets of created life.

8. *Creation, not only of qualities but of qualified substances, which are, however, in need of divine Providence*

When Maximus affirms that God created not only qualities but qualified substance,[263] he does so not only in rejection of pagan philosophers, who had assumed the eternal existence of substances and thus also their lack of contrariety,[264] but also in order to underline that the qualifying element in creation is not of a secondary value. Substances and qualities are created together, while at the same time both are merely created, separated by nature from God's ever-being and by his act of creation from non-being, and thus entirely dependent on condescending divine grace for their subsistence.

This fact, however, brings the dynamic aspect into the foreground once more, and invites us to deal, for a short while, with the duality in Maximus' system between nature, together with the *principle of nature* (λόγος φύσεως), and existence, together with the *mode of existence* (τρόπος ὑπάρξεως). We have already seen, how the qualifying element in nature is that which pertains to it as being moved and moving; and now the term τρόπος represents, in relation to the differentiated world, in Maximus' thinking, this element of energetic qualification, since it is through the τρόπος that the powers of nature are transferred to the level of existence. Originally used by the Cappadocians and by Amphilochius of Iconium, but also occasionally by e.g. Leontius of Byzantium, the concept of "mode of existence", as counterpart to "principle of nature", plays in fact a very important rôle in Maximus' Christology and in his whole understanding of the dynamism of God's created world.[265] And according to this view the principle of nature is to a certain extent contrasted with the mode of existence. For the former is immutable, in so

---

[262] VON BALTHASAR, KL[2], p. 148 f.

[263] Char 3. 28; CSC, p. 156; 4. 6; p. 196.

[264] COMBÉFIS refers in the note of the Migne edition (PG 90, 1025) to Aristotle's opinion, that there is no contrariety in substance, and VON BALTHASAR, KL[2], pp. 148 and 452 f., n. 2, recalls the fact that Zacharias the Rhetor and John Philoponus had had to refute Ammonius of Alexandria's idea of the eternal co-existence of God and the substances.

[265] Starting from the work of K. HOLL, *Amphilochius von Ikonium in seinem Verhältnis zu den grossen Kappadoziern,* Tübingen 1904, which he criticizes, SHERWOOD, *The Earlier Ambigua,* pp. 155–168, has made a most valuable study of the history of this concept and of its use in Maximus, on which we have relied to a great extent in this paragraph.

far as it expresses the fixed divine intention for a particular nature, while the mode of existence is variable.

To the λόγος belongs the fixity of a "law", while the τρόπος implies the possibility of degrees of realization of the natural powers.[266] This should not be understood, however, as if the τρόποι were indifferent in relation to the λόγοι.[267]

Maximus, consequently, draws the conclusion that any innovation— the paradigm is, of course, the innovation brought about by Christ— pertains to the τρόπος and not to the λόγος. For innovation in the λόγος would imply corruption and change of nature, but innovation in the τρόπος simply calls forth the inherent powers of nature itself.[268] This rule obviously has a Christological purpose first of all, but its use is not restricted to the field of Christology. In relation to cosmology it is for example used in a passage of Amb 15, where we learn that in the whole of creation there is the sphere of an immutable substance with its principle and another sphere of "economy" with a principle of movement.[269]

In Christ this innovation is a newness of quality (ποιότης), which has nothing to do with quantity (ποσότης), i.e. with the continuing fact that there are two natures.[270] In the Incarnation an immutable relationship between two natures is combined with a theandric newness of quality and existence, which implies, as we saw in ch. I, an ongoing communication of attributes between the natures.[271] Not because there is just one energy or will but because the fruits of the two energies and wills come together in the sphere of this newness of existence.

The concept of "mode of existence" thus opens up the same perspective of self-transcendence, which we have studied in relation to the concepts of being and hypostasis. This becomes quite clear in a number of passages. In Thal 22 we read e.g., that there are certain, more or less fixed, "modes of virtues", precisely corresponding to an intellectual understanding of the principles of the commandments, but Maximus then goes on to say that it is through these modes that God always wills to

---

[266] Cf. VON BALTHASAR, KL², p. 121.

[267] As a matter of fact there is a certain fixity also in the τρόπος, for to each nature belongs a true mode of existence, which may or may not be manifested; cf. VON BALTHASAR, KL², p. 638.

[268] Amb 42; PG 91, 1341 D.

[269] PG 91, 1217 A. Though the word τρόπος is lacking in this passage and λόγος is used in both senses, it is evident that the basis of the statement is the same kind of duality as between λόγος and τρόπος in the field of Christology and anthropology. Cf. Amb 5; PG 91, 1052 B, where the reference is to Christ but the formulation is of a generalizing character.

[270] Amb 5; PG 91, 1057 AB.

[271] See p. 34 ff. above.

become man in those who are worthy.[272] Here Maximus thus refers to an incarnation in the virtues of the believers which is the consequence, in the field of sanctification, of the *communicatio idiomatum* and *perichoresis* which take place in Christ. It does not interfere with nature, but calls forth the natural powers of human nature, so that the boundaries of the latter are reached and the human person may experience, by grace, the transcendence which is properly called deification. This leads, finally, to consequences in the understanding of the freedom of the individual. Thus Maximus can also say, that as man in general, everyone operates principally, but as someone, Peter or Paul, he "gives form to the mode of action".[273] Consequently, persons are developing and variable in their modes, though their natural operation is immutable in accordance with the immutability of the principle of their nature.

This form-giving function of the individual thus makes the development of the energies of nature into something which transcends in freedom any merely ontological necessity, though without changing in any sense the character and quality which is due to nature. But then, at the same time, the whole of creation, in all its differentiation—though not evil in its substance or in its natural movement[274]—is in need of divine Providence with its power of unification, in order to fulfil the true manifestation of what is given in nature and substance.[275] For divine Providence provides the inspiration to a right movement of all that is moved.

Summarizing very shortly, what our previous notes on Maximus' cosmology have shown, we must emphasize that Maximus is, on the one hand, eager to stress the preservation, under all circumstances, of the ontological distinction between what is divine and what is created, as well as all the other distinctions which are necessarily linked with a differentiated creation, regarded as positive manifestations of the divine intentions. But on the other hand, he includes in his system an element of dynamic transcendence, in relation to all these distinctions, which is connected with his high evaluation of motion, based, first of all, on the idea of a providential purpose setting before the whole of creation a unifying τέλος which lies outside these limitations—and yet does not violate the given fixity of substances, natures and species. We have also seen that these two aspects are mutually dependent and interrelated

---

[272] CCSG 7, p. 143.
[273] ThPol 10; PG 91, 137 A.
[274] See Char 4. 14; CSC, p. 198; Thal 27, CCSG 7, p. 193.
[275] Char 4. 9; CSC, p. 198; Thal 13; CCSG 7, p. 95.

through a reciprocity, understood in terms of the Christology of Chalcedon and Constantinople. In developing this system Maximus relies considerably on his predecessors within different traditions (such as Origen, Evagrius, Ps.-Denis and Leontius of Byzantium)—as well as on Platonic, Neo-Platonist and Aristotelian philosophical presuppositions —but by insisting on and developing this idea of reciprocity he has also made his own personal and characteristic contribution.

CHAPTER THREE

Maximus' Anthropology in General

A. The Constitution and Position of Man

1. The unity of body and soul

Maximus' positive evaluation of the created world of substance and accident inevitably ought to include a positive evaluation of the empirical man as such. That it, in fact, does so Maximus shows first of all at three particular points: a) the co-existence in principle of body and soul; b) the idea of man as a composite nature and a complete species; and c) the conscious analogy between the natural unity of body and soul in man and the hypostatic unity of human and divine in Christ.

Co-existence of body and soul

Maximus affirms this co-existence in two ways: as both an initial and a continuing co-existence. The assertion of the initial co-existence of body and soul is in the first place for Maximus part of his refutation of Origenism, in which the pre-existence of the soul was a predominant element; at the same time it also implies a denial at this point of the position of Nemesius of Emesa, who seems to have agreed with Origen in relation to at least some pre-existence of souls, though attacking him in other respects.[1]

In Origenism the doctrine of the pre-existence of the soul was from the very beginning one of the most well known characteristics. Origen himself, in whom this idea is closely linked with his notion of a double creation, first of souls and, as a consequence of sin, also of bodies, obviously held this doctrine,[2] but a primary source of equal importance

---

[1] Nemesius, *De nat. hom.* 2; PG 40, 572 B; ef. the commentary by W. TELFER in *Cyril of Jerusalem and Nemesius of Emesa* (LCC 4), London—Philadelphia 1955, p. 282 f., n. 8. It should be noted here that in the little florilegium of ThPol 26; PG 91, 277 C—and elsewhere—Maximus refers to and quotes this work of Nemesius.

[2] Cf. the evaluation of Origen's texts in this respect, made by H. CROUZEL, *Théologie de l'image de Dieu chez Origène*, Paris 1956, p. 148 ff.

judging by the reference to it in all the attacks on Origenism[3] was probably, as Guillaumont has shown, not Origen but Evagrius. For Evagrius clearly professed the doctrine of a double creation[4] and of the pre-existence—if not of souls in a proper sense—at least of pure intellects, which had fallen and for which the material world of bodies had been created, thanks to God's providential judgment.[5]

When refuting the idea of the pre-existence of souls—together with that of the pre-existence of bodies—and stating an initial co-existence of both, Maximus probably built to a great extent on Gregory of Nyssa and followed very closely his conclusion which was to avoid both the extremes.[6] Stéphanou has, in fact, made a valuable analysis of the positions of both, though in the end most of his interest is centred on the problem of creationism versus traducianism, which is of less interest for our purpose.[7] The most important conclusion to be drawn from his study is, however, that the point of emphasis is different in the two writers. The main interest behind Maximus' argument is to safeguard the sovereignty of God and his positive purpose for the empirical psychophysical creation, as we know it; and this interest is not one which was predominant in Gregory.

Gregory of Nyssa's argument in favour of an initial co-existence of body and soul is chiefly found in *De hom. opif.*, and that of Maximus in Amb 42, with the addition of some shorter statements in Amb 7. If we now compare these two types of argument in relation to the idea of a pre-existence of souls, which is our primary interest—because in both cases it is directed against Origenism, and because the arguments against the idea of a pre-existence of bodies seem to be put forward mainly for the sake of the exposure of *two* extremes, both leading to unacceptable

---

[3] The pre-existence of souls was mentioned in the IVth century both in the *Panarion* of Epiphanius (GCS Epiphanius 2; p. 411, 1–5) and in Jerome's treatise against John of Jerusalem (7; PL 23, 360 B). In the anathemas against Origenism of the edict of Justinian in 543 (see ACO 3, p. 213) and of the Council of Constantinople in 553 (see Mansi 9, p. 396) it was quoted as the first point of refutation.

[4] See e.g. *Cent. gnost.* 2. 64; PO 28, p. 87 (cf. for the Greek text Barsanuphius, PG 86:1, 893 AB) and 6. 20; PO 28, p. 225.

[5] See e.g. *Cent. gnost.* 3.38, PO 28, p. 113 and 6.75; 249; cf. Guillaumont, *Les "Kephalaia gnostica"*, pp. 103–113.

[6] Later e.g. Ennaeus of Gaza had energetically refuted the idea of the pre-existence of the soul, see *Theoph.;* PG 85, 948 B–949 A, but his argumentation differs more from that of Maximus.

[7] See Stéphanou, La coexistence initiale, EO 31 (1932), pp. 304–315. Here we leave aside the specific problems of creationism and traducianism, since it is more interesting for us to follow the problem of pre-existence. Stéphanou thinks that Gregory is traducianist and Maximus creationist, though both agree on the co-existence of body and soul, see *art. cit.*, p. 314.

consequences—we shall easily see the difference between them. Gregory claims that the Origenist position is intimately connected with an idea of metempsychosis (the Greek equivalent of the Indian Samsara),[8] and argues that a fall into the material world would not imply purification, but rather successive falls leading to a complete destruction of the soul,[9] and that if this were not the case, it would, on the contrary, imply a superiority of sensual life over against spiritual life, since the latter would be the cause of the fall and the former of salvation.[10]

Maximus, however, argues in the opposite way. He states that the doctrine of the pre-existence of the soul would imply a merely negative and punitive function in the bodies, which God had been forced to create by the very existence of evil, without having intended to do so from the beginning. And the visible world, which reveals God, would then have its cause in evil.[11] But this is impossible, for all has been created according to God's foreknowledge,[12] and the λόγοι of all that exists pre-exist in God,[13] for else God would have had unwillingly to create things, the λόγοι of which he did not have from the beginning.[14]

Thus we see clearly, how Maximus, by stressing the co-existence of body and soul in the way that he does, while safeguarding this created unity, also safeguards very characteristically both God's sovereignty and a positive evaluation of the world in its differentiation.

But Maximus goes further and states that *body and soul cannot exist separately*,[15] for there is always a relation (σχέσις) between soul and body[16] and they are by necessity bound to each other.[17]

This is however immediately linked with our next point.

Body and soul as a composite nature and a complete species

Composite nature in relation to Christ had been affirmed by the monophysites, explicitly by Severus,[18] but denied by strict Chalcedonian and Neo-Chalcedonian theologians. The latter had, however, widely used the concept of "composite hypostasis" as a suitable expression for the

---

[8] *De hom. opif.* 28; PG 44, 232 AB. For Gregory's refutation of the metempsychosis idea in general, cf. *De anima et resurr.;* PG 46, 108 B ff.

[9] *De hom. opif.;* 232 D–233 A.

[10] *Ibid.;* 229 CD, 233 C.

[11] Amb 42; PG 91, 1328 A.

[12] *Ibid.;* 1328 D.

[13] *Ibid.;* 1329 B.

[14] *Ibid.;* 1329 D.

[15] Amb 7; PG 91, 1100 D.

[16] *Ibid.;* 1101 C.

[17] Ep 12; PG 91, 488 D.

[18] Cf. Lebon, La christologie du monophysisme sévérien, Chalk I, p. 488 and n. 92.

unity of divine and human in Christ.[19] Maximus does the same. But in relation to human nature he uses the expression "composite nature" (φύσις σύνθετος) deliberately.[20] This implies, however, in a very characteristic way, two aspects: mutual independence of the two elements, body and soul, *and* their indissoluble relationship to each other.

The independence of the elements is expressed in different ways. Thus, body and soul are said to have been brought into existence differently,[21] and man is said to be double in his nature,[22] so that the λόγος and τρόπος of body and soul are also different.[23] On the other hand, the unification of them—which takes place from the beginning—is not due to any intention or will on their own part. The ground is more basic: it is necessitated[24] by the will of God itself through the principle of one common, composite nature.[25] Maximus seems, thus, to stress the independence of the elements, not primarily in order to maintain the immortality of the soul in spite of its relationship to the body, but in order to underline the creative will of God as the only constitutive factor for both, as well as for their unity. It is thanks to the pre-existent principle of human nature alone that man consists, from the beginning, of body and rational soul,[26] and the content of this principle is simply that human nature should consist of these two elements, Maximus affirms. Therefore, both the independence and the union of body and soul—for which there exists no pre-existence of one in relation to the other but only co-existence—are based on the pre-existent λόγος of both in God.[27]

Here it is, however, of interest to compare Maximus with some of his Christian philosophical predecessors. For Aristotle, who raised the problem of what constitutes the unity of soul and body, the relationship between them had been one of form and matter,[28] and this understanding was still effective when Nemesius of Emesa tried to solve the problem by way of the concept of union of predominance. In both cases the unifying force was inherent in *one* of the elements, the soul, and exerted in

---

[19] Cf. MOELLER, Le chalcédonisme et le néo-chalcédonisme, Chalk I, pp. 680 and 692.
[20] See e.g. Ep 12; PG 91, 488 D.
[21] Amb 42; PG 91, 1324 CD.
[22] Amb 53; PG 91, 1373 C.
[23] Amb 42; PG 91, 1321 C.
[24] As VON BALTHASAR, KL², p. 240, n. 1, has pointed out, this necessity is also strongly emphasized by Sophronius, Maximus' venerated superior.
[25] Ep 12; PG 91, 488 D.
[26] Amb 42; PG 91, 1341 D.
[27] *Loc. cit.*
[28] The soul being the *entelecheia* of the body, see *De anima* 2, 1; 412 a, 19 ff.

relation to the other.[29] This way of thinking is, however, as we have seen, more or less excluded in Maximus.

More points of contacts may here be established in relation to the thinking of Leontius of Byzantium. In fact, a number of similarities can be noticed in relation to him, but also a number of very important differences. Leontius, like Maximus, stresses energetically the independence of the two elements in relation to each other. The soul is thus incorporeal and has a mobility of its own; it lives its own life, even when separated from the body—and this is the basic reason why it is also immortal and indestructible.[30] Maximus likewise says, that the soul never ceases to have or use its own intellectual forces. As soon as it has been brought into existence it will continue to exist, and its intelligible character is not for the sake of the body but for its own, and quite independent of its relationship to the body.[31]

Further, Leontius emphasizes that the unification of body and soul is not due to any quality inherent in the soul. It is not "natural" but due to divine power.[32] This reminds us of what Maximus says about the unification of body and soul as not caused by any inclination or will on their part but exclusively by the will of God.[33] But here, on the other hand, we also clearly see the difference. For where Leontius seems to be more interested to safeguard the independence of the soul, Maximus is interested in the independence of both body and soul; and where Leontius says that their unification is not of nature but of God's power, Maximus shows that it is of the λόγος of their *common* nature which is in fact the pre-existent creative will of God.

This difference between Leontius and Maximus goes in fact still deeper. This is most clearly shown, when we compare what the two writers have to say about the union of body and soul. Leontius speaks about a "common man" composed of soul and body in whom there is no confusion of qualities[34]—and this does not differ very much from the way Maximus expresses his ideas—but Leontius regards body and soul as two perfect substances or natures,[35] united in one hypostasis[36] (but also

---

[29] See WOLFSON, *The Philosophy of the Church Fathers*, pp. 405–407.

[30] *Lib. tres;* PG 86: 1; 1281 B.

[31] Ep 7; PG 91, 436 D–437 A.

[32] *Epilysis;* PG 86: 2; 1940 B.

[33] Ep 12; PG 91, 488 D. In Amb 7; PG 91, 1101 C Maximus says that their relationship is ἀκίνητος.

[34] *Lib. tres;* PG 86: 1; 1281 A. Already Nemesius talked about union without confusion in relation to soul and body; see *De nat. hom.* 3; PG 40, 596 AB.

[35] *Lib. tres;* 1281.

[36] *Ibid.;* 1281 C.

as two different hypostases).[37] The two elements are, thus, not imperfect in themselves but only in relation to this common hypostasis. Even if Leontius adds that the soul alone is no perfect man, though being itself a perfect substance,[38] it seems obvious that his main interest is to underline the distinction of body and soul, in order to safeguard the necessary independence and immortality of the latter. Maximus, on the contrary, stresses equally distinction and unity.[39]

Thus, body and soul, to Maximus, not only form a composite nature, with a λόγος φύσεως of its own as its natural ground of being[40]—in clear contrast to the Leontian form of the idea of a common hypostasis[41]—but also one species,[42] or a complete species.[43] This implies that body and soul cannot, separately, be complete species—cf. Leontius' statement that body and soul are both perfect substances—because they would then have to give up their identity when united.[44] But it implies also that there is no soul, which is without relation to its body,[45] a relationship which is preserved even after death, when the soul is separated from the body. This is illustrated, says Maximus, by the fact that one does not simply call a certain body "body" after death, but a human body or the body of this or that person.[46] Thus the human unity is to Maximus not of an accidental but of a natural character and quite undissoluble, in spite of the independence of its elements.[47] And we may also conclude that where Leontius stresses the distinction between body and soul in order to safeguard the immortality and dominance of the soul, Maximus is equally eager to prove the natural unity of body and soul in order to maintain the resurrection and permanent participation in created human life of the body.

---

[37] *Epilysis;* PG 86: 2, 1941 D–1944 A.

[38] *Lib. tres;* PG 86: 1; 1281 D.

[39] WOLFSON, *op. cit.,* p. 414, seems to be right, when he assumes that the common hypostasis of body and soul in Leontius is to be understood as the hypostasis of the soul, which remains even when it is united with the body and into which the body is thus "enhypostasized".

[40] Cf. on composite natures Ep 13; PG 91, 516 D.

[41] See further under 2 below.

[42] See Amb 42; PG 91, 1324 C.

[43] Amb 7; PG 91, 1101 A.

[44] Amb 42; 1324 A.

[45] Amb 7; 1101 C.

[46] *Ibid.;* 1101 B.

[47] This accords with some aspects of the anthropology of Leontius of Jerusalem who regards man as a new family (καινὸν γένος), but with the important difference that Leontius bases this idea on a natural orientation of body and soul towards each other; see further MOELLER, Chalk I, p. 706. Cf. the suggestions about an influence on Maximus, made by SHERWOOD, *The Earlier Ambigua,* p. 60 f.

The analogy between the unity of body and soul in man and the unity of divine and human nature in Christ

We have seen, that the most decisive difference between Leontius of Byzantium and Maximus concerning the human unity of body and soul lies in the fact that this unity is regarded by Leontius as hypostatic, and by Maximus as natural as well. Hypostatic union allows that both elements are perfect substances, while natural union implies that their completeness is in the end related to the whole as one species. Against this background it may seem surprising that Maximus nevertheless follows Leontius in establishing an analogy between the union of body and soul in man, and the union of the two natures in Christ,[48] though one of these is hypostatic and the other natural. How does this harmonize with the rest of Maximus' theology? Sherwood seems to regard it as a kind of inconsistency on the part of Maximus; but is this really a sufficient explanation?[49]

The intricacy of the problem becomes obvious, when we compare Leontius and Maximus further at this point. For in the two texts, to which Sherwood refers, Maximus seems to agree with Leontius, that the point of comparison in the analogy is the fact that in both cases there is a union of hypostatic character. Thus in Th Pol 13 Maximus compares the distribution of identity ($\tau\alpha\upsilon\tau\acute{o}\tau\eta\varsigma$) and otherness ($\dot{\epsilon}\tau\epsilon\rho\acute{o}\tau\eta\varsigma$) in three different kinds of union: Trinitarian, human and Christological, and states that in the Trinity identity refers to substance and otherness to persons ($\pi\rho\acute{o}\sigma\omega\pi\alpha$), while in the two other types of union otherness refers to substance and identity to person.[50] Similarly, in Ep 15 Maximus—in an argumentation to the conclusion that identity of nature implies otherness of persons and identity of person otherness of nature—makes clear that he regards the union of body and soul as a hypostatic union relating two different natures to each other.[51] How does this harmonize with his view that man is a composite nature and a complete species? Does it imply that, in using the analogy of man and Christ, Maximus falls back on a Leontian interpretation of both?

The question becomes still more pertinent, if we ask what Leontius himself may possibly imply in his use of the analogy. For it seems clear

---

[48] An early study of this similarity was made by GRUMEL, La comparaison de l'âme et du corps, EO 25 (1926), pp. 393–406. The difference between the two writers was also underlined by him, though less energetically than it should be.

[49] See SHERWOOD, in ACW, p. 52.

[50] PG 91, 145 B. In other places Maximus shows that $\pi\rho\acute{o}\sigma\omega\pi\sigma\nu$ and $\dot{\upsilon}\pi\acute{o}\sigma\tau\alpha\sigma\iota\varsigma$ are identical; see e.g. Th Pol 14; PG 91, 152 A; cf. ThPol 23; 261 A.

[51] PG 91, 552 D.

that to him the point of comparison in the analogy between union of man and union of Christ is not only the simple fact that both are hypostatic unions, but that in both cases hypostatic union means that one element, the non-dominant element, is enhypostasized into the other. While the union of body and soul lasts, the body has, thus, no hypostasis of its own, but the soul is its hypostasis.[52] But is it, then, we must ask ourselves, possible to avoid the conclusion, that the strict dichotomy of body and soul, which we find in Leontius, is sometimes also applicable to the anthropology of Maximus? And further, is it possible to avoid the impression that Maximus himself does not escape the Origenist idea that the soul is temporarily united with its body, for the purpose of purification and on account of the divine economy of salvation, but not on account of any persistent principle of its own created nature? We have seen that in the case of Leontius the main interest is precisely to maintain a strict distinction between body and soul, and a leaning towards Origenism on his part cannot be entirely ruled out.

Here we ought, however, to go back to Maximus himself and see, if there are other aspects of his use of the analogy. An indication of this is, in fact, to be found as early as in Ep 15, where we noticed the statement about body and soul as one hypostasis. For there we find, at the same time, that Maximus once more rules out the (Origenist) idea of the pre-existence of souls, and particularly that he qualifies the union of body and soul, not only as a hypostasis but as a union of composition ($\sigma\acute{u}\nu\theta\epsilon\sigma\iota\varsigma$).[53] In fact we get the impression that $\acute{u}\pi\acute{o}\sigma\tau\alpha\sigma\iota\varsigma$ is here simply a synonym for $\sigma\acute{u}\nu\theta\epsilon\sigma\iota\varsigma$. And this may lead to a solution of our problem. For if we go to the texts where Maximus expresses most clearly his idea of man as a composite nature ($\phi\acute{u}\sigma\iota\varsigma$ $\sigma\acute{u}\nu\theta\epsilon\tau\sigma\varsigma$), we also find two other characteristic features in the argumentation: 1) that the idea of a composite nature in the case of Christ is explicitly ruled out; 2) that the union of Christ is later described as a composite hypostasis ($\acute{u}\pi\acute{o}\sigma\tau\alpha\sigma\iota\varsigma$ $\sigma\acute{u}\nu\theta\epsilon\tau\sigma\varsigma$).[54] This putting together of the two alternatives is also a way of using the analogy, though with one particular condition: that the point of comparison is the fact that both are unions of composition ($\sigma\acute{u}\nu\theta\epsilon\sigma\iota\varsigma$). If hypostasis may be understood as a synonym to $\sigma\acute{u}\nu\theta\epsilon\sigma\iota\varsigma$, we may reconcile the different texts and conclude that Maximus' use of the analogy after all is different from that of Leontius. For $\sigma\acute{u}\nu\theta\epsilon\sigma\iota\varsigma$ is to

[52] See the discussion of this interpretation of Leontius in WOLFSON, *op. cit.*, pp. 412–415.
[53] PG 91, 552 D.
[54] See Ep 12; PG 91, 488 D–492 B; Ep 13; 516 D–520 D and 525 D–529 A.

Maximus obviously a more neutral term, applicable to different types of union, where his characteristic combination of independence of the elements and their indissoluble mutual relationship is at work.[55]

Here however, we may also get support from the tradition to which Maximus adheres. For it is a well-known fact that the use of the analogy of man to Christ was never restricted to Leontius of Byzantium. In the 6th century it was used widely in the most different circles and milieus. Thus for instance it has been emphasized that Severus, in his very subtle monophysitism, was able to use this analogy without introducing, by this very fact, any heterodox mixture or confusion.[56] This popularity was probably due to Cyril of Alexandria who, by his own use, seems to have authorized it as orthodox, though he might in fact have borrowed it from the Apollinarians.[57] Cyril's use of the analogy may sometimes be imprecise,[58] and sometimes he may see the point of comparison in the fact that in both cases there is a union of natures,[59] but more important for us is the fact that he qualifies the union as καθ' ἕνωσιν and "of composition", κατὰ σύνθεσιν.[60] It may be that Cyril understood union of composition as predominance in the Aristotelian sense, as Wolfson has argued,[61] but the most important thing in our context is that he does not use it in the sense of juxtaposition, and that he has introduced a more neutral term into the analogy. Another fact of similar importance is that this term, σύνθεσις, in relation to the Incarnation, was later accepted by the Council of Constantinople in 553 as an orthodox expression of the union in Christ (in contrast to those of confusion and mere relation), and at the same time there declared to be a synonym of hypostasis.[62] Maximus may thus very well have used the analogy man—Christ with the idea of composition as the dominant point of comparison on the authority of Cyril, and the word hypostasis as a possible synonym for it (under particular circumstances) on the authority of the Council of Constantinople.

In the light of Maximus' Christology this fact, however, implies a proper estimation of the body and of its permanent relationship to the soul. They are regarded as unconfused but indissolubly united, and, if we have been right in assuming that the *perichoresis* idea is at the heart of

---

[55] See VON BALTHASAR, KL², p. 230.
[56] See LEBON, Chalk I, pp. 450 and 539 f.
[57] To this last point, see LEBON, *art. cit.*, p. 447 and n. 91.
[58] See *Apol. contr. Theodoret.* 3; PG 76, 408 D.
[59] See *Ep 45 (ad Succens.); PG 77, 232 D and Ep. 46 (ad Succens.),* 4; 245 A.
[60] *Ep.* 45; 233 A and *Ep.* 46, 2; 241 B.
[61] WOLFSON, *op. cit.,* p. 409.
[62] Cf. *ibid.,* p. 417 f.

Maximus' Christology, then the analogy would imply to him even more, i.e. an interpenetration of body and soul as well. Is there any sign that it does? There is at least one text which makes us think so.

When Maximus in Amb 7 argues in favour of the initial co-existence of body and soul, he not only characterizes their union as a "complete species", but he also states, as a consequence of their constant co-existence, that the soul never ceases to transmigrate (μετεν-σωματοῦσθαι)[63] into the body, nor the body to transmigrate (μετεμ-ψυχοῦσθαι) into the soul.[64] Here Maximus not only makes an anti-Origenist use of the terms of transmigration in fact but understands by them, on the human level, what he means by *perichoresis* on the Christological level. The reciprocity is in both cases perfect, and the point of comparison is in the fact that both are unions of composition. But by doing so he further shows an evaluation of the body as an integral part of the whole, which—in a way similar to that which we have seen in Maximus' general cosmology—on the level of creation introduces standards of Christology, which, by analogy, give its final purpose to the created order.

2. Human trichotomy

We have seen, how Leontius regarded man in his earthly life as a hypostatic unity of two independent substances, body and soul, while Maximus defined human unity as a composite nature. We have tried also to show that, when on occasion he uses the idea of a hypostatic unity in relation to man, Maximus does so in the sense of "composition". It would, however, be misleading to stop there, pretending, as it were, that the idea of hypostasis would, in Maximus' case, be entirely out of place in relation to man. Our comparison between Leontius and Maximus must be more detailed and refined. We must define what Leontius means by a hypostatic unity of body and soul in man, and we must find out, where the idea of hypostasis becomes relevant to Maximus' anthropology. For only then shall we also be able to see, how man functions as a unity, in Maximus' view, in relation to his divine end.

---

[63] The term μετενσωμάτωσις is here, of course, not understood in the Origenist sense of transmigration of souls *(samsara)* which Gregory of Nyssa had already refuted.—In this context the problem of *Apokatastasis* is important. For a discussion of that problem in Maximus, see B.E. Daley, Apokatastasis and the 'honorable silence' . . . , in HEINZER-SCHÖNBORN, *Maximus Confessor,* pp. 309–339.

[64] PG 91, 1100 D.

Human hypostasis

As regards Leontius, it seems clear that to him the human hypostatic union is only of a temporal character. In accordance with his Origenist sympathies Leontius felt bound to stress the difference and independence of body and soul in relation to each other, to such an extent that he seems to have affirmed that they are not only two natures but two hypostases.[65] Their union into one hypostasis is only of an occasional and temporal character, not taking place "naturally" because of any natural inclination, but entirely on account of God's will.[66] The body is thus temporarily enhypostasized into the soul, in the same way as human nature is in Christ enhypostasized into the divine.[67]

For Maximus, as we have seen, the picture is quite different. He agrees with Leontius that body and soul, regarded separately, may be seen as different natures and that they do not form a unity because of their natural inclination towards each other but because of God's will. But against Leontius, on the other hand, he states that body and soul are one composite nature and a complete species, and that, thanks to God's will, they are brought into existence at the same time, and will remain inseparable from each other.

But do they, then, according to Maximus, also have one common *hypostasis,* and what in that case does the word hypostasis imply? One difference between man and the hypostatic union in Christ is evident from the beginning. In Christ two natures are united into one hypostasis, in spite of their difference. The concept of hypostasis transcends what is naturally differentiated. But if there is one common hypostasis in man, this must be so *because* body and soul form one composite nature. The transcending character of the human hypostasis, thus, cannot be manifested within the relationship between body and soul—for they form one nature—but only in relation to something which is not of human nature, i.e. superhuman. To the first part of our question—whether soul and body have one common hypostasis—the answer is, however, rather easy. The difference between Christ and man in this respect is not that one unity is hypostatic and the other is not, but that the hypostatic union in Christ is, as it were, *merely* hypostatic, i.e. non-natural, non-ontological, while the human unity of body and soul is *also* natural, ontological. Personal unity in Christ has its counterpart precisely in man as a person.

---

[65] See *Epilysis;* PG 88: 2; 1941 D–1944 A; cf. WOLFSON, *op. cit.,* p. 413 and VON BALTHASAR, KL², p. 238.

[66] *Epilysis;* 1940 B. This is, however, questioned by UTHEMANN, *art. cit.,* p. 229, n. 29.

[67] *Lib. tres;* PG 86: 1, 1277 D–1280 B.

For since no nature is without hypostasis, then certainly not human nature.[68]

Maximus in fact affirms this explicitly. He shows that not only human nature but also human hypostasis depend on the natural unity of body and soul.[69] Particularly when he stresses the difference between soul and body—for from one point of view they are, even to Maximus, two different natures—he affirms that they have one and the same hypostasis. They are "co-hypostasized"—which is not to say with Leontius that the body is enhypostasized into the soul.[70] Therefore, Maximus even once mentions the unity of body and soul to exemplify hypostatic union.[71] Finally, he states with emphasis that, if hypostasis means for the philosophers substance with its attributes, it means for the Fathers— who do not explicitly deny the philosophical definition, of course—an individual human being, separated as person from other human beings.[72] These statements together safeguard our conclusion that man as person is understood by Maximus in relation to his being a unity of body and soul.

The second part of our question—what the word hypostasis here implies—is, however, more difficult to answer. For man as a person cannot be isolated from the fact that human nature has, in Maximus' view, its hypostasis in the Logos, and thus is itself enhypostasized. Which is to say that a personal relationship to God cannot be excluded from human nature and is identical with fully realized human existence.[73] That is the reason why, to Maximus, man has full freedom, but his freedom is not fully realized until it finds its end in God. Divine and human nature are strictly kept apart and are yet—in that very separation —deeply interrelated.

Our question about the hypostatic character of the human unity grows, therefore, into a question about the spiritual human subject and its position. Here we may, however, take into consideration, that Maximus not only speaks of a human dichotomy of body and soul but also of a *trichotomy* in man. It is, of course, not a trichotomy in the strict sense of the word, nor a metaphysical distinction[74]—as ontological definition of man the expressions of dichotomy are sufficient to him—

---

[68] For definitions of hypostasis in Maximus, see ThPol 23; PG 91, 261 A; 264 AB and C; 265 D; Ep 15; PG 91, 545 A.
[69] Cf. von Balthasar, KL[2], p. 172.
[70] ThPol 14; PG 91, 152 A.
[71] ThPol 18; 213 A.
[72] ThPol 26; 276 B.
[73] Cf. von Balthasar, KL[2], p. 245.
[74] Cf. Loosen, *Logos und Pneuma*, p. 89, n. 19, and Sherwood, in ACW, p. 84.

but nevertheless Maximus often prefers triadic arrangements to describe the constitution of man. For the most part we meet a triad of ἐπιθυμία, θυμός, λόγος[75] with equivalents, entirely restricted to the psychological field, but sometimes also triads which, though primarily psychological, also introduce other aspects. The most important of these triads in this context[76] is that which consists of mind (νοῦς), soul (ψυχή) and body (σῶμα). For here, at least in some texts, mind is added to the other elements of man—those which are enough to define what man is—as a kind of personal aspect of individual human existence, representing the subject, as it were, of composite man. However this trichotomy also actualizes Maximus' relationship to some of his predecessors, especially Evagrius, and we are, therefore, more or less obliged to study its problems in some detail.

Mind, soul and body

Among the Fathers the idea of human trichotomy had been differently treated. The starting-point was partly philosophical, partly biblical. The three-fold distinction between the rational, irascible and concupiscible parts of the soul is a well-known element in Plato's anthropology,[77] but the type of trichotomy which interests us here is said to go back to Poseidonius. In Plotinus we find the same idea developed into a distinction between three men: sensible man, intelligible man and the one in between, who is in fact reasonable man.[78] The middle position of the soul, well illustrated in the last example, is characteristic of all these interpretations. On Christian ground this type of trichotomy competed with the Pauline triad of body, soul and spirit. Irenaeus e.g. used the latter,[79] while Clement of Alexandria has been regarded as the founder of a Christian trichotomist school in a more philosophical sense.[80] Origen seems mostly to have used the Pauline triad,[81] while Evagrius was probably the first writer to break entirely with the Pauline type, so that mind (νοῦς) became definitely substituted for the biblical term spirit

---

[75] See ch. IV: A, 2, p. 175 f. below.

[76] In ch. IV: A we shall deal with psychological trichotomy in the stricter sense.

[77] In ch. IV: A, 3 (see pp. 185–194) we shall study the Christian history of this distinction.

[78] See L. REYPENS, *art.* Ame, DSp I, col. 435.

[79] See CROUZEL, *Théologie de l'image de Dieu,* p. 65.

[80] See F. CAYRÉ, *Handleiding der Patrologie,* I, Paris—Doornik—Rome, 1948, p. 216. Clement at least divided the soul into an irrational and a dominating part; see VÖLKER, *Der wahre Gnostiker nach Clemens Alexandrinus* (TU 57), Leipzig 1952, p. 110.

[81] See VON BALTHASAR, ZkTh 63 (1939), p. 100. Cf., however, e.g. J. GAÏTH, *La conception de la liberté chez Grégoire de Nysse* (Études de Philosophie Médiévale 43), Paris 1953, p. 48, n. 1.

($\pi\nu\epsilon\hat{\nu}\mu\alpha$), though $\nu o\hat{\upsilon}\varsigma$ was understood more or less as the divine part of man.[82] From him Maximus now seems to have taken over the same trichotomy as a fixed terminology. But at the same time he seems to have been influenced to a great extent by Gregory of Nyssa, as far as its theological content is concerned. As we have seen, Gregory rejected the idea of the pre-existence of souls, and was also eager to stress the unity of man. He uses, though with a slight hesitation it seems, the trichotomy of spirit, soul and body, as he found it in Paul,[83] but also in Apollinaris,[84] and when he uses $\nu o\hat{\upsilon}\varsigma$ he makes clear, that the word has a spiritual and not an ontological sense. It is an aspect of the soul, and the soul is to him spiritual and incorporeal but always related to the body.[85] Maximus with his even stronger stress on the unity of man and his positive evaluation of the body, is bound to follow the Gregorian line, even when he uses the Evagrian terminology.

Maximus' use of the Evagrian type of human trichotomy and his understanding of $\nu o\hat{\upsilon}\varsigma$ in relation to it is, as a matter of fact, a good example of the subtle way in which he shows both his dependence and independence in relation to Evagrius. To a great extent he is able to use the same expressions and the same views, but at crucial points he turns them in another direction. One of these points seems to be with regard to the personal element of man as a total being.[86] At first, there are many similarities. Evagrius and Maximus not only use the same trichotomy of $\nu o\hat{\upsilon}\varsigma$, $\psi\upsilon\chi\acute{\eta}$, $\sigma\hat{\omega}\mu\alpha$ as a formal distinction in man.[87] In the way that $\nu o\hat{\upsilon}\varsigma$ is according to this distinction defined and described in its function and relationship to the best of man, the similarities are also striking. In both cases this fact gives to the trichotomy an integral function within their anthropology.

Thus, in both cases $\nu o\hat{\upsilon}\varsigma$ is often more or less identified with the higher part or capacity of the soul. Evagrius says, that it is called the head of the soul,[88] and contrasts it in different ways with the passible part of

---

[82] Cf. VON BALTHASAR, *loc. cit.*

[83] *De hom. opif.* 8; PG 44, 145 C.

[84] *Adv. Apoll.* 48; JAEGER 3: 1, p. 213.

[85] Cf. GAÏTH, *loc. cit.*

[86] It is characteristic that we find the majority of our examples of Maximus' use both of the trichotomy and of $\nu o\hat{\upsilon}\varsigma$ in relation to different aspects of man, in his ascetic writings, where his relationship to Evagrius is also most clearly to be seen. In works such as *Cent. gnost.*, *Liber asceticus* and *Cent. de char.*, etc. Maximus seems to have established a conscious connection with Evagrius in order to accept what he could accept and reject what he had to reject in this writer, so influential in monastic circles.

[87] See Evagrius, *Cent. gnost.* 1. 77, PO 28, p. 53; cf. FRANKENBERG, pp. 114–115; 2. 56, PO 28, p. 83; cf. FRANKENBERG, pp. 168–169; Maximus, *Char* 4. 46; CSC, p. 212; *Amb* 47; PG 91, 1360.

[88] *Cent. gnost.* 5:45; HAUSHERR, OCP 5 (1939), p. 231.

the soul.[89] We get, in fact, very often the trichotomy νοῦς, ἐπιθυμία, θυμός.[90]

Similarly Maximus contrasts νοῦς with anger and concupiscence,[91] or shows that a harmony must be established between νοῦς and the passible elements in man.[92] νοῦς is further, in both writers, primarily responsible for man's relationship to God. It is the contemplative part of man, and its highest function is to contemplate the divine realities and particularly the Holy Trinity. Thus Evagrius shows that it is νοῦς alone which contemplates spiritual things,[93] and affirms that spiritual knowledge is the wings of νοῦς.[94] νοῦς has its own five spiritual senses.[95] Evagrius further states that νοῦς possesses three kinds of light: knowledge of the Trinity, of its own incorporeal nature and the contemplation of beings,[96] and that νοῦς is able to see or receive the Trinity.[97] Likewise Maximus affirms in different ways that νοῦς, which is contemplative, is also the primary instrument of man's relationship to God. Prayer, particularly pure prayer, is, thus, connected with νοῦς,[98] and also hope and love for God.[99] νοῦς enjoys in fact a certain familiarity (παρρησία) with God.[100] Finally, purified νοῦς is attracted by knowledge of God,[101] is active in different kinds of spiritual contemplation[102] and occupied by the virtues of God,[103] whom it may sometimes even receive within itself.[104]

So far there are striking similarities between Evagrius and Maximus at this point. But comparing the two writers one discovers nevertheless that their differences are equally important. In Evagrius one notices the effects of the Origenist myth of a primitive henad of rational beings, the pre-existence of souls, the fall from the divine unity and a second creation. In Maximus these marks are eliminated. This means that in

[89] See e.g. *Cent. gnost.* 6. 55; HAUSHERR, OCP 5, p. 232.
[90] See *Cent. gnost.* 1. 84; PO 28, p. 57; cf. FRANKENBERG, pp. 120–121; 3. 35; PO 28, p. 111; cf. FRANKENBERG, pp. 212–213; 4. 73; PO 28, p. 169; cf. FRANKENBERG, pp. 304–305.
[91] See Char 1. 49; CSC, p. 66.
[92] Char 2. 48; CSC, p. 116.
[93] *Cent. gnost.* 1. 33–34; PO 28, p. 33; cf. FRANKENBERG, pp. 78–79.
[94] *Cent. gnost.* 3. 56; PO 28, p. 121; cf. FRANKENBERG, pp. 226–227.
[95] *Cent. gnost.* 2. 35; PO 28, p. 75; cf. FRANKENBERG, pp. 154–155.
[96] *Cent. gnost.* 1. 74; PO 28, p. 53; cf. FRANKENBERG, pp. 112–113.
[97] *Cent. gnost.* 3. 30; PO 28, p. 111; cf. FRANKENBERG, pp. 210–211, and 3. 71; p. 127; cf. FRANKENBERG, pp. 238–239.
[98] Asc 24; PG 90, 929 C; Char 3. 61; CSC, p. 122; 2. 100; p. 142.
[99] Char 1. 3; CSC, p. 50; 2.14; p. 96; cf. 1. 9–11; p. 52.
[100] Char 1. 50; CSC, p. 66 and 1. 68; p. 74.
[101] Char 1. 32; CSC, p. 60.
[102] Char 1. 87; CSC, p. 84; 1. 90; *loc. cit.*; 1. 97; p. 86; 2. 97; p. 142 and 3. 99; p. 190.
[103] Amb 10; PG 91, 1112 D.
[104] Char 3. 94; CSC, p. 188.

Evagrius one recognizes a certain dichotomy within the soul itself (leading even to a kind of ontological trichotomy in man) on the one hand, and a non-human affinity between νοῦς and the divine world on the other, while in Maximus a stronger stress is noticeable on the relationship between νοῦς and the rest of man, and on the whole of man as a created being, different from God and entirely relying upon His grace for the realization of its end.

Thus Evagrius often contrasts νοῦς with ψυχή in the sense of the passible part of the soul. The middle position of the latter is marked out. The mind (νοῦς) is, as it were, made heavy through its connection with sensibility. Thus, Evagrius says that detachment is the light of the soul, but knowledge the light of the mind,[105] and that the mind, if it advances on a road which belongs to the instruments of the soul, will be haunted by the demons.[106] Further, we learn that ψυχή is that νοῦς which has fallen away from its original Unity and has descended to the stage of the *vita practica*.[107] For this reason νοῦς should educate the soul and the soul should educate the body,[108] and when the νοῦς enters into the light of the Holy Trinity it should possess the soul as a fire possesses its body.[109] νοῦς cannot be united with its knowledge, until the passible part of its soul is united with its own virtues.[110] The mind has, thus, not only to become pure but "naked", i.e. freed from all worldly representations.[111] A naked mind is necessary to contemplate the Trinity, but also to contemplate intelligible beings.[112]

On the other hand it seems clear in Evagrius, that νοῦς has such an affinity to God and the divine world that it has a natural capacity for contemplation, even of the Holy Trinity, and may be undistinctively united with God. Thus we learn, that "second nature" is the sign of the body, "first nature" the sign of the soul, but νοῦς is Christ, united with the knowledge of Unity,[113] while the νοῦς which still contemplates secondary beings is not yet naked but wears the last garment,[114] and the νοῦς which requires a contemplation, acquired with the aid of bodily

---

[105] *Cent. gnost.* 1. 81; HAUSHERR, OCP 5, p. 230.

[106] *Cent. gnost.* 2. 48; PO 28, p. 81; cf. FRANKENBERG, pp. 162–163.

[107] *Cent. gnost.* 3. 28; PO 28, p. 109; cf. FRANKENBERG, pp. 206–207.

[108] *Cent. gnost.* 2. 56; PO 28, p. 83; cf. FRANKENBERG, pp. 168–169.

[109] *Cent. gnost.* 2. 29; PO 28, p. 73; cf. FRANKENBERG, pp. 148–149.

[110] *Cent. gnost.* 5. 66; PO 28, p. 205; cf. FRANKENBERG, pp. 348–349.

[111] VON BALTHASAR has noticed, that Philo already used the expression νοῦς γυμνός; see KL², p. 586.

[112] *Cent. gnost.* 3. 6; PO 28, p. 101; cf. FRANKENBERG, pp. 192–193; 3. 15; p. 103; cf. FRANKENBERG, pp. 198–199 and 3. 17; PO 28, p. 105.

[113] *Cent. gnost.* 1. 77; PO 28, p. 53; cf. FRANKENBERG, pp. 114–115.

[114] *Cent. gnost.* 3. 8; PO 28, p. 101; cf. FRANKENBERG, pp. 192–193.

nature, is imperfect.[115] Evagrius also tells us that the first movement of rational beings is that which has separated νοῦς from its (inward) unity.[116] Originally νοῦς was directly illumined by God with immaterial knowledge, but now the impressions of the senses give it material information.[117] Thus νοῦς is in itself immortal and incorruptible,[118] and of an inexpressible nature, being without either form or matter,[119] and therefore it is for itself to tell, what its nature is.[120]

In contrast to this—though he uses a number of Evagrius' expressions and thoughts—Maximus shows that he believes primarily in the created unity of man. When Evagrius contrasts mind and soul, Maximus rather stresses the tension between body and mind. They represent two competing tendencies, but no real split in man himself. He who turns his mind from attention towards God and binds it to sensible things, prefers body to soul and created things to God, Maximus says in a characteristic formulation.[121] A mind fixed upon charity for God may even scorn its own body,[122] but this is an expression of the fact that the soul is nobler than the body.[123] The important tension lies between mind/soul and body.[124] νοῦς may thus possess all the good fruits of the forces of the soul,[125] and not only the knowledge of God, but the virtues themselves, may be said to be the place where it should be.[126] The mind, not explicitly the soul, is said to be in the middle between angel and demon and has to choose,[127] and therefore the virtues of the soul naturally serve in its training.[128]

In relation to God νοῦς represents man as a whole and is not contrasted with the rest of man. It has to establish the true God-ward orientation of the entire man. Its end is in God alone, and therefore it should be pure and free from all feelings for creatures, filled with burning love for God. But being itself a creature it does not only have to experience an "ecstasy" out of all things—which is to Evagrius the all-important liberation of the mind—but also an "ecstasy" outside of

---

[115] *Cent. gnost.* 3. 10; *loc. cit.;* cf. FRANKENBERG, pp. 194–195.
[116] *Cent. gnost.* 3. 22; PO 28, p. 107; cf. FRANKENBERG, pp. 202–203.
[117] *Cent. gnost.* 3. 55; PO 28, p. 119; cf. FRANKENBERG, pp. 226–227.
[118] *Cent. gnost.* 3. 33; PO 28, p. 111; cf. FRANKENBERG, pp. 210–211.
[119] *Cent. gnost.* 3. 31; *loc. cit.*
[120] *Cent. gnost.* 3. 70; PO 28; p. 127; cf. FRANKENBERG, pp. 236–237.
[121] Char 1. 8; CSC, p. 52.
[122] Char 1. 6; *loc. cit.*
[123] Char 1. 7; *loc. cit.*
[124] Char 2. 92; CSC, p. 140.
[125] Char 1. 11; CSC, p. 52.
[126] Asc 18; PG 90, 925 C.
[127] Char 3. 92; CSC, p. 188.
[128] Char 2. 64; CSC, p. 124.

itself.[129] When Maximus speaks of a pure mind and a naked mind,[130] he makes it clear that this is achieved by the grace of God and does not imply a natural return of the νοῦς to an original unity, or a contemplation of God as He is in Himself. This knowledge is above created mind and is effected only in a mystical, supernatural communion.[131]

Νοῦς is, thus, to Maximus, both more or less identified with the soul, as representing the whole of man, and—in its relationship to God—called to be above human nature and above itself in a mystical sense. It is, thus, usually not regarded simply as a part of man but rather as his thinking subject,[132] or better: his spiritual subject. Maximus himself calls it "the inner man".[133] From this point of view νοῦς may be put over against *all* the elements of the soul, not only the passible ones.[134] This is most eloquently illustrated in Myst 5, where the complicated relationship between νοῦς as theoretical and λόγος as practical reason is described. Both are necessary parts of man's equipment and have parallel rôles to play in his sanctification. But λόγος is subordinated to νοῦς, and in the end will be fully integrated into the unity which the νοῦς represents.[135]

As man's spiritual subject νοῦς is active in different ways, and it is νοῦς which gives its consent to sin.[136] As such it has a leading rôle in man's spiritual development for better or for worse. It is said to advance in prudence by means of the development of the *vita practica,* as well as in knowledge by means of the development of the *vita contemplativa.* It requires the gifts of discernment and of participation in the essences of

---

[129] Char 1. 9–11; CSC, p. 52. On the difference between these two types of ecstasy, see below ch. VI: 10; cf. J. LEMAÎTRE, *art.* Contemplation ou "Science véritable", DSp 2, coll. 1830–55, 1862–72.

[130] See e.g. Gnost 1. 83; PG 90, 1117 BC; Asc 24; PG 90, 929 C; Char 2. 100; CSC, p. 142.

[131] See Char 1. 100; CSC, p. 88.

[132] The expression is taken from VON BALTHASAR, KL², p. 163.

[133] Char 4. 50; CSC, p. 214. In his commentary on this passage SHERWOOD, in ACW, p. 264, n. 218, refers to Evagrius, but the question is whether this is not an expression of a human unity, far more explicit than in Evagrius. The term "inner man" was probably taken from Origen, see *In Gen., hom.* 1, 13; GCS Orig. 6, p. 15.

[134] See e.g. Char 4. 80; CSC, p. 230.

[135] The goal of νοῦς is divine Truth, and the goal of λόγος divine Goodness. To νοῦς belong wisdom, contemplation, knowledge and unforgettable knowledge. To λόγος belong prudence, *vita practica,* virtues and faith (PG 91, 673 CD). These five elements form together five syzygies (676 A), but each of the qualities of νοῦς is able to be united with and thus to include its counterpart within the sphere of λόγος—and that is why νοῦς will in the end make the rest part of its own unity (680 B). The head of the soul will then be crowned with the Logos (681 B).

[136] Char 2. 31; CSC, p. 106; cf. 2. 1–6; pp. 90–92.

things. And finally it is fit for "theology", i.e. mystical contemplation of God, to the extent which is possible for a human (created) mind.[137]

Thus we see, that thanks to the trichotomy of mind, soul and body—which is to him no ontological trichotomy—Maximus is able to express his conviction that there is a personal aspect in man's life, which goes, as it were, beyond his nature, and represents his inner unity as well as his relationship to God. The idea of man as one hypostasis of body and soul is, at least sometimes, expressed in relation to the function of the mind or spiritual subject, as related to the whole of man but also characterized by a certain freedom over against the different elements of human nature, thanks to its grace-directed relationship to God; and for this relationship the same mind is in principle responsible. In contrast to Evagrius, Maximus is able to safeguard this aspect without denying the created character of the whole of man.

Here again a Christological aspect, that of "person", though different from a modern understanding of person, must have been effective in bringing about Maximus' anthropological understanding.[138]

3. The Image of God in Man

In an early article on the theological presuppositions of Maximus' thinking M.-Th. Disdier stated that the concept of image and likeness is at the very basis of all his theology and spirituality.[139] Later research has hardly rejected this statement. However, one has to bear in mind the fact that, at least as far as the concept of *imago Dei* is concerned, it is basic to such an extent, that its general content and consequences are simply taken for granted by Maximus himself. There are thus only few references to it in his writings, and most of them are of a general character. Maximus has, in fact, given no personal contribution to the theology of the image of God in man, as such. His main contribution in this field concerns the relationship between image and likeness and the important

---

[137] Char. 2. 26; CSC, p. 102.

[138] "The spirit (νοῦς) in human nature corresponds most nearly to the person", says LOSSKY, *The Mystical Theology*, p. 201, in relation to the orthodox Greek Fathers in general.—Maximus' freedom in relation to Evagrius is also revealed in the fact that he knows other human trichotomies. Thus in QuDub 22—according to the Migne text (PG 90, 801 D)—he uses the Pauline version: πνεῦμα, ψυχή, σῶμα, and from another point of view he may use the triad νοῦς, λόγος, πνεῦμα (Amb 7; PG 91, 1088 A; 10; 1196 A), which we find e.g. also in Gregory Nazianzen (see *Or.* 23, 11; PG 35, 1161 C–1164 A). For a detailed analysis of the relationship between pneumatology, ecclesiology, and eschatology, see A. RIOU, *op. cit.,* pp. 123–200. For the status of man as created in the image of God, consult further my own study *Man and the Cosmos*, pp. 59–65.

[139] DISDIER, Elie l'Ecdicos et les hetera kephalaia, EO 31 (1932), p. 36.

rôle which he ascribes to the concept of *likeness*. Before we enter this latter aspect of his anthropology, there is, however, a more basic question which has to be dealt with—in spite of Maximus' comparatively small interest in it—in connection with what we have said earlier in this chapter.

The place of the Image of God

Considering our conclusions concerning man as a complete species and the human mind as a kind of spiritual subject, it seems important to find out what Maximus' position is regarding the problem, where man's image character is most clearly manifested. This problem had been widely treated and very differently answered in the Christian tradition before Maximus, and in the great number of monographs devoted to the theology of the image of God in man for many years[140] due interest has been given to it. They, and other works, have clearly shown how different and differentiated are the attempts to "localize" the image character of man, and how far these attempts are representative of the general theological position of each writer. The answers differ from the whole of man, including the body, to a superior part or quality of man, his soul or mind or his rational capacity.[141] From what we have found about Maximus' anthropology we should expect to find him among those who refer the image character to the whole of man, soul and body alike. But is this conclusion as self-evident as it looks? The answer is linked with Maximus' relationship to his predecessors, and with the shape of the Christian tradition.

In very early Christian reflection upon the character of man as made in God's image, we find, in fact, frequent references to the body as marked by, or sharing in, this character.[142] But in such cases these

---

[140] Among those works, related to individual Church Fathers are: A. MAYER, *Das Gottesbild im Menschen nach Clemens von Alexandrien* (SA 15), Rome 1942; H. CROUZEL, *Theologie de l'image de Dieu d'après saint Athanase*, Paris 1952; H. MERKI, ΟΜΟΙΩΣΙΣ ΘΕΩΙ: *Von der platonischen Angleichung an Gott zur Gottähnlichkeit bei Gregor von Nyssa*, Freiburg 1952; R. LEYS, *L'image de Dieu chez Saint Grégoire de Nysse*, Brussels and Paris 1951, and W. J. BURGHARDT, *The Image of God in Man according to Cyril of Alexandria*, Baltimore, Maryland, 1957.

[141] Most ancient Christian writers would agree that man *is* not the image of God but has been created *in* the image of God, and with Paul that Christ alone is the Image of God (see Rom. 8: 29, 2. Cor. 4: 4), and man thus the image of the Image.

[142] Thus A. STRUKER, *Die Gottebenbildlichkeit des Menschen in der christlichen Literatur der ersten zwei Jahrhunderte*, Münster i. W. 1913, pp. 63–65 and 75, has pointed out, how in the Ps.-Clementines it is the body which carries the divine image, and how in the *Oracula Sibyllina* the whole man is seen as God's image. STRUKER, *op. cit.*, pp. 40–41, has further attempted to show that in Melito we find the idea that the human body has been shaped after a divine archetype used by God in his theophanies, and has finally, in relation

affirmations seem to have been connected with, or might at least lead to anthropomorphic conceptions of God. This is probably one of the reasons why this line of thinking was never fulfilled. For though Irenaeus for instance still claims that the whole of man, body and soul, is related to his image character,[143] and though both Cyprian and Lactantius give a similar impression,[144] not only the Alexandrian theologians—who took a lead in developing a theology of the image and likeness of God in man—but also writers of the most different schools seem later to have agreed that man's image character is principally linked with his soul and not with his body. Thus, both Eusebius of Caesarea and John Chrysostom profess that the image of God is *not* in the body,[145] while Cyril of Jerusalem[146] and the entire Western tradition in complete agreement localize the image in the soul.[147]

The most interesting expressions of this tendency are, however, found within the Alexandrian tradition; it is from here that we must conclude that Maximus got one of his main influences, even though modified by the Cappadocian understanding of the question. For here, as in the case of human trichotomy, Maximus reveals a strong terminological affinity to the Origenist Evagrius.

Within the Alexandrian tradition it seems to have been clear from the beginning, that the image character is related to the soul alone. This restriction was worked out already by Philo, who regarded the body simply as the sanctuary of the image.[148] Clement is equally restrictive,[149] and Origen clearly follows the Philonian line, professing the essential invisibility of the image, and thus its exclusive connection with the soul, regarding the body simply as the temple which contains the image.[150] The

---

to the *Letter to Diognetus,* suggested that its writer may have seen in the external appearance of man a mirror of divine perfection. A summary of these results is given in BURGHARDT, *The Image of God in Man,* pp. 15–17.

[143] Cf. STRUKER, *op. cit.,* pp. 97, 127; E. PETERSON, L'immagine di Dio in S. Ireneo, SC 19 (1941), pp. 3–11 and G. WINGREN, *Man and the Incarnation. A Study in the Biblical Theology of Irenaeus,* Edinburgh—London 1959, p. 95, who have all shown, that in Irenaeus the visibility of the divine image is closely connected with the bodily incarnation of the Logos.

[144] See BURGHARDT, *op. cit.,* p. 19.

[145] See Eusebius, *Contr. Marcell.,* I, 4; GCS Eus. 4, p. 25 and Chrysostom, *Hom. in Gen.* 8, 3–4; PG 53, 72 f. Cf. BURGHARDT, *op. cit.,* p. 17 f.

[146] Cyril, *Catech.* 4. 18; PG 33, 477. Cf. BURGHARDT, *op. cit.,* p. 17.

[147] Cf. BURGHARDT, *op. cit.,* p. 18 f., who refers to the following writers: Tertullian, Hilary of Poitiers, Zeno of Verona, Philastrius of Brescia, Ambrose of Milan and Augustine.

[148] Cf. e.g. CROUZEL, *Théologie de l'image de Dieu,* p. 55 f.

[149] Cf. e.g. CROUZEL, *op. cit.,* p. 67 (for a summary of Crouzel's study, see IDEM, L'image de Dieu dans la théologie d'Origène, SP 2 (TU 64), pp. 194–201) and BURGHARDT, *op. cit.,* p. 12 f.

[150] See CROUZEL, *op. cit.,* p. 45; ef. BURGHARDT,. *op. cit.,* p. 13.

same insistence on the soul alone may be followed in Athanasius and Cyril of Alexandria.[151] But we may go further. Already in Philo only the highest part of the soul, νοῦς, was regarded as of the image of God,[152] and in this restriction he was followed by the Christian Alexandrian writers. According to Clement νοῦς is thus the image of the Image,[153] and according to Origen man's image character is concentrated to the supreme part of his soul, i.e. where the pre-existent element of the soul is still to be found.[154] This last affirmation is, thus, closely linked with the idea of a prehistoric fall, and will be decisive for the position taken by the Origenists. Thus for Evagrius the image character is restricted to νοῦς, not because it is incorporeal, or less material, but because the mind alone is capable of receiving God (having once shared the divine Unity),[155] and the resemblance of the Image will consequently be given to it in the end—without any restrictions, it seems.[156]

In relation to this last aspect of the Alexandrian tradition, the Cappadocian theology of the image of God in man represents some modification. The anthropomorphic danger had obviously disappeared. The Cappadocians represented an apophatic understanding of God, to such a degree that they were free to express their conviction that the body, intimately related to the soul, is not entirely left out, when the image of God in man is under consideration. Through the mediation of the soul the body also shares to some extent in the image. This is at least the impression that one gets from Gregory Nazianzen[157] and Gregory of Nyssa.[158] In the last case this is particularly apparent in the way in which man's posture is seen as a kind of reflection of his spiritual position.[159] This modification of the Alexandrian view is, however, very restricted and does not interfere with the rôle played by the rational part of man.[160] Yet it may have been influential in the case of such a writer as Cyril of Alexandria, in whom Burghardt has found that the exclusion in principle

---

[151] Cf. BURGHARDT, *op. cit.,* pp. 13 and 19–21.

[152] Cf. e.g. CROUZEL, *op. cit.,* p. 56.

[153] *Strom.* 5, 14; GCS Clem. 2, p. 388. Cf. CROUZEL, *op. cit.,* p. 67 and BURGHARDT, *op. cit.,* p. 26 f.

[154] Cf. the summary given in CROUZEL, *op. cit.,* p. 179.

[155] See *Cent. gnost.* 6. 73; PO 28, pp. 247, 249.

[156] See *Cent. gnost.,* 6. 34; PO 28, p. 231.

[157] Cf. BURGHARDT, *op. cit.,* p. 14.

[158] Cf. J. T. MUCKLE, The Doctrine of St. Gregory of Nyssa on Man as the Image of God, MS 7 (1945), pp. 55–84; LOSSKY, *The Mystical Theology,* p. 116, and TH. CAMELOT, La théologie de l'image de Dieu, RSPT 40 (1956), p. 458.

[159] *De hom. opif.* 4; PG 44, 136; cf. BURGHARDT, *op. cit.,* p. 14.

[160] Basil e.g. makes it quite clear, that it is the mind which carries the image of the Creator; see *Ep.* 233, 1; PG 32, 864 C.

of the body—probably due to the influence of both the Alexandrian tradition and a new fight against contemporary anthropomorphism—is slightly modified by other tendencies.[161]

We have now seen how it was that Maximus inherited a rather fixed tradition with regard to the localization of the image character of man. Only slight modifications of a strict Alexandrian position invited him to include the body in this character.[162] It is thus not surprising to find that he also usually follows this tradition. More important than this localization of the image of God in man, however, is what we have said about Maximus' understanding of the position and function of the mind in relation to man as a whole. And there are other connections with Maximus' general anthropology which must not be forgotten—as we shall now see.

Different scholars have agreed that man's image character is in Maximus intimately linked with his *rational* nature and his mind. One has thus pointed out that the rational soul itself is the divine image,[163] or that man is image thanks to his reasonable nature alone,[164] and also that the image coincides with the very nature of $\nu o \hat{u}$ς.[165] This corresponds rather well with the dominant impression one gets from reading what Maximus himself has to say about the image of God in man.

According to Maximus every *rational* nature is made in the image of God. That is why man is destined not only to being but to ever-being.[166] *Mind* ($\nu o \hat{u}$ς) and *reason* ($\lambda \acute{o} \gamma o$ς) are both closely connected with the image of God in man.[167] The image and likeness of God are represented by the soul as marked by these two qualities ($\dot{\eta}$ λογικὴ τε καὶ νοερὰ ψυχή),[168] and every rational soul is said to be made in the image of God.[169] The image is, however, primarily related to the $\nu o \hat{u}$ς (while likeness is slightly more related to the $\lambda \acute{o} \gamma o$ς in man).[170] Thus, νοερὰ ψυχή and εἰκὼν θεοῦ are sometimes almost synonymous expressions.[171] In accordance

---

[161] BURGHARDT, *op. cit.*, p. 22 f.

[162] It may be added, that human reason seems to have represented the divine image also to such writers as Methodius, Cyril of Jerusalem, Theodoret of Cyrus and Isidore of Pelusium. Cf. BURGHARDT, *op. cit.*, p. 32.

[163] SHERWOOD, in ACW, p. 98.

[164] HEINTJES, BiNJ 6 (1942), p. 291.

[165] DISDIER, Les fondaments dogmatiques de la spiritualité de S. Maxime le Confesseur, EO 29 (1930), p. 302.

[166] Char 3. 25; CSC, p. 154.

[167] See Amb 7; PG 91, 1077 B.

[168] Myst 6; PG 91, 684 CD.

[169] Gnost 1. 11; PG 90, 1088 A; cf. Amb 7; PG 91, 1092 B (this text has a chiastic arrangement).

[170] See Amb 10; PG 91, 1193 D–1196 A and Myst 6; PG 91, 684 D.

[171] Amb 7; PG 91, 1096 A.

with this stress on the close connection between the rational functions of man and his character as image there is also the fact, that it is on account of the passions, which turn man away from the leadership of reason, that the image of God in fallen man has been replaced by a likeness to irrational animals,[172] while τὸ νοερόν can be said to be a reflection of the divine glory.[173] Likewise the new man, who is risen in Christ, is characterized by a γνῶσις acquired through the νοῦς, which is part of his restored image character.[174] Finally, while we see, e.g. in Ep 2, how it is charity alone which is capable of revealing man as created in the image of God, we must not forget that this is so, precisely because charity is able to subordinate human freedom to the λόγος of human nature.[175] This λόγος is, indeed, as we have seen, the creative will of God for man, but it functions at the same time as the *reasonable* principle, according to which human life should be orientated.

Freedom and the divine Image

There are, however, also other elements of Maximus' understanding, which may modify or complete the picture, and which show that when man's image character is connected with νοῦς, the latter is seen not only as a constitutive element of man's nature but first of all as his intellectual and spiritual subject. Thus this stress on the rational capacity of the soul as the primary reflection of man's image character is frequently balanced in Maximus by a similar stress on human freedom. Now, freedom had as such also been related to the mind by the Alexandrian tradition, but it is striking that Burghardt, in his study of the different motifs related to the image and likeness of God in man, has not found any explicit reference to the image in this context within the Alexandrian tradition until Didymus and Cyril of Alexandria. His main testimonies to the image character of human freedom are thus Irenaeus, Basil the Great, Gregory of Nyssa, Didymus and Cyril.[176] It looks, in fact, as if this lack of clear reference to freedom in the earlier Alexandrian writers coincides with their exclusive stress on νοῦς as carrier of the image. And thus, is it not rather the divine affinity of the mind in itself than its self-determination which for these writers is decisive of its image character?

The difference is certainly striking, when we come to such a writer as Gregory of Nyssa. For not only does he refer to human freedom more

---

[172] Thal 1; CCSG 7, p. 47.
[173] Amb 10; PG 91, 1204 A.
[174] Ep 32; PG 91, 625 D–628 A.
[175] Ep 2; PG 91, 396 C.
[176] BURGHARDT, *The Image of God in Man*, pp. 40–50.

frequently than others, but he also gives a decisive reason for the fact that freedom was given to man when he was created in the image of God: man was to find his self-fulfilment in the divine Good thanks to his own deliberate decision.[177] But this, again, is possible only if one does not conceive of the attainment of man's goal as a simple return to an original communion with God, such as we have reason to think that Origen, and still more the Origenists, did. And thus the emphasis on human freedom in relation to the image of God in man, as we find it in Gregory, is, in fact, in some way closely linked with his refutation of the idea of the pre-existence of souls and his affirmation of the unity between body and soul. For both reflect a view which sees in man's life on earth a positive call to realize the fact that he is created in the image and likeness of the Creator.[178] But if this close relationship between the idea of man as a unity and the emphasis on human freedom is true of Gregory of Nyssa, we should expect it to be no less true of Maximus, in whom we have already found a still stronger stress on the role of the body within this unity.

And certainly we do find in Maximus a clear stress on freedom in this context. To him also freedom is a sign of the image, which is to be used to acquire a divine good intended for man: spiritual sonship.[179] In his goodness God has created man as self-moved ($\alpha\dot{v}\tau o\kappa\acute{\iota}\nu\eta\tau o\varsigma$) according to His own image,[180] and human self-determination is at least in *Disp. c. Pyrrh.* regarded as a primary expression of man's image character, reflecting the self-determinative character of the divine nature, and at the same time—which is important—said to be necessarily implied in the rational character of human nature.[181] Likewise, it is also Maximus' conviction that the good of human nature, founded in its creation in the image of God, is fully realized only when made effective in an act of free will which also manifests the likeness of God in man.[182] But this means too, that the image character of the human will is not primarily due to its independence as such but to the good which is intended for it, and in relation to which alone it can be fully realized. Thus, as self-determination pertains in Maximus to the image, it is at the same time relative.[183]

---

[177] See *In Cant. cant., hom.* 2; JAEGER 6, p. 55 and *Or. catech.* 5; PG 45, 24 C.

[178] A similar interpretaton seems to be possible in relation to Cyril of Alexandria; cf. BURGHARDT, *op. cit.,* pp. 45–50.

[179] See Amb 42; PG 91, 1345 D.

[180] Gnost 1. 11; PG 90, 1088 A.

[181] PG 91, 304 C.

[182] Gnost 1. 13; PG 90, 1088 BC.

[183] Cf. SHERWOOD, in ACW, p. 56.

Dominion and the divine Image

Dominion over irrational creation is another modifying element in the theology of the divine image in man, which is connected with the aspects of the unity of the human composite and of self-determination. It is probably no mere coincidence that this motif is found in writers like Gregory of Nyssa and Cyril of Alexandria (though the Antiochenes with their realistic Bible interpretation seem to have been particularly fond of it).[184] Here man is seen as exerting his functions as rational being, and the human mind works as an intellectual subject. In Maximus at least this last aspect seems to be relevant. For we find in him the idea that it is natural to man as a spiritual being, both to subordinate himself to the Logos of God and to have dominion over the irrational part of himself.[185] Dominion, as a reflection of the image character of man, is, thus, realized already when the human mind, which is primarily responsible for the manifestation of this image, functions as the spiritual subject of the whole of man.

The body is in Maximus, therefore, in different ways implied—not in the localization of the image of God in man, but in relation to its realization—which is to Maximus a necessary consequence of its recognition. And, consequently, it can be said of Christ that he can save the body together with the soul, i.e. both save the image and immortalize the flesh. We recall that not only being but ever-being is intended for man as created in the divine image, and the body is thus called to share this vocation. The reasonable soul ($\psi v \chi \grave{\eta}$ $v o \epsilon \rho \acute{a}$) should in fact mediate divinity even to the body—and serve, we can add, as a true spiritual subject of the whole of man.[186] This involvement of the body is, however, most clearly seen, when we now come to the relationship between the image and likeness of God in the life of man—a point where Maximus' contribution is also more personal and original.

4. *From Image to Likeness*

One of the striking features of Maximus' anthropology is the energy and consciousness with which he stresses the difference between image and likeness. It seems clear that in this he is inspired by the earlier Alexandrian tradition, for which this distinction was of capital impor-

---

[184] See BURGHARDT, *op. cit.,* pp. 51–64, particularly p. 57.

[185] Char 2. 83; CSC, p. 134.

[186] See Amb 42; PG 91, 1336 A. Similar expressions are found in Thal 54; CCSG 7, p. 459.

tance, but it is still striking that he accepts this inspiration so unhesitatingly, since his acceptance of early Alexandrian anthropology is at other points not without reservation. Von Balthasar—even in the second edition of his *Kosmische Liturgie,* where he carefully avoids speaking of an Origenistic crisis in Maximus' life—evidently sees no problem here,[187] but the history of this theological—and exegetical—distinction shows that there must have been real problems connected with it. The important question for us is thus, not the mere fact that Maximus revives the distinction between image and likeness, but the grounds on which he feels free to do so and the interpretation he gives to it.

The background of Maximus' distinction

The history of this distinction cannot, of course, be traced in detail here, but a few indications should serve our purpose. Clement of Alexandria testifies to the distinction, and his own anthropology seems, at least to some extent, to be marked by it. An inspiration from Philo ought at this point probably to be excluded—since Philo himself did not attach any particular importance to the difference between the two terms in Gen. 1:26.[188] In fact Clement himself refers to other Christian teachers,[189] and though we do not know exactly who these other Christians were, we are more or less bound to think of the example of Irenaeus, who was, as far as we know, the first Christian writer to make the distinction.[190] For him—as we have pointed out already—the image is related to human nature as such—and to both body and soul—and cannot be lost, while likeness is something added to man, given to Adam but lost through his fall, and restored by Christ. And this likeness consists of the presence of the Spirit in the soul.[191] In Clement there is a certain affinity to this understanding. It has been emphasized that his distinction is similar to the later distinction between natural and super-natural. Likeness therefore for him means something more than what is naturally given.[192] Thus,

---

[187] Von Balthasar, KL², pp. 179 and 545f.
[188] See Philo, *De opif. mund.* 71; Cohn & Wendland, I, p. 24.
[189] Clement, *Strom. 2,* 22; GCS Clem. 2, p. 185.
[190] Cf. Bernard, *L'Image de Dieu,* p. 25 and Crouzel, *Théologie de l'Image de Dieu,* p. 65.
[191] The analyses of Irenaeus' thinking at this point are usually in reference to one single text—*Adv. haeres.* 5. 6, 1—and for that reason one must be careful not to draw too far-reaching conclusions. But on the other hand, this point is easily harmonized with the rest of Irenaeus' theology of human deification. Camelot, RSPT 40 (1956), p. 461, has also referred to *Adv. haeres.* 5. 16, 2 which may be interpreted in a similar way: likeness is a manifestation of the form of the image, effected through Christ.
[192] Cf. Crouzel, *op. cit.,* p. 67.

only a Christian believer can acquire this likeness, which is effected through the action of Christ.[193] It should be added, however, that the distinction is not absolute, for the image itself is dynamic and tends towards the likeness, so that the attainment of the likeness coincides with the perfection of the image.[194]

In Origen this line of thinking is fully developed. The distinction between image and likeness is noticeable in a number of texts. In one of the most representative of them we learn that man has received the dignity of image from the beginning but will gain likeness to God in the end, proportionate to his own efforts in the imitation of God.[195] Likeness is, thus, to Origen from one point of view an eschatological reality—it belongs to the coming glory[196]—but also a moral achievement, acquired by man's own efforts. It is a manifestation brought about through man's deliberate imitation of God. Image and likeness are thus, to some extent, related as potency to act, so that the image may be said to be realized in likeness after a long spiritual process.[197] Origen also makes clear that this imitation of God, as a moral act, consists of an imitation of His virtues,[198] though the "supernatural" character of the process is, on the other hand, underlined by the idea that it is the Sonship of God which is effected through the development of divine likeness, and that, thus, this process is at the same time to be regarded as Christ's formation in the soul of the believer.[199]

We may call this the classical form of the idea—striking similarities to it are found e.g. in Maximus and later in John of Damascus—but it is of particular importance to notice that it was far from being accepted by all orthodox writers. For already in the first part of the fourth century a change in attitude is evident. Even an Alexandrian writer like Athanasius seems quite uninterested in the distinction. In him at least there is no relation between likeness and the idea of a development towards perfection, such as we find in Origen.[200] Indeed, there are even indications that Athanasius consciously avoids speaking of likeness and prefers the term image, because the former for him has a negative tone: sin was introduced into God's world when man wanted to be like God.[201]

---

[193] See *Protr.* 12; GCS Clem. 1, p. 86; cf. *Paed.* I, 12; CGS I, p. 148.
[194] Cf. CAMELOT, *art. cit.*, p. 461.
[195] *De princ.* 3. 6, 1; GCS Orig. 5, p. 280.
[196] Cf. CROUZEL, *op. cit.*, p. 219.
[197] Cf. *ibid.*, p. 207.
[198] *Sel. in Gen.*; PG 12, 96 B; cf. CROUZEL, *op. cit.*, p. 158.
[199] *In Lev., hom.* 12,7; GCS Orig. 6, p. 466; cf. CROUZEL, *op. cit.*, p. 221.
[200] Cf. BERNARD, *L'Image de Dieu*, p. 27.
[201] Cf. *ibid.*, p. 28 f.

A similar lack of interest in the early Alexandrian distinctions has been noticed in Cappadocian writers, though in the case of Gregory of Nyssa the topic has been much debated. Gregory Nazianzen seems in any case to belong to those writers, who do not make any distinction between the two terms at all.[202] In relation to Gregory of Nyssa the problem is more difficult—and is partly linked with the question of the authenticity of certain texts attributed to him[203]—but there is at least general agreement among the scholars that Gregory does not make at all the same sharp distinction as Origen formerly had done. There is, in fact, for him no difference in principle between the terms,[204] there is *only a difference of perspective, so that likeness is more* often used in relation to the realization of man's image character.[205] The philosophical interpretation of Origen's distinction may perhaps be difficult to work out, but at least if it is understood as a distinction between an ontological image of God, given by the very nature of the mind as such, and a moral likeness acquired through man's deliberate efforts, it is, as von Balthasar has pointed out, rather characteristic of Gregory that he knows of no such distinction. For him the image itself is dynamic and the likeness is also of an ontological character.[206] It has, however, further been emphasized that, though the two terms often appear as synonyms, the term image represents on the whole a more static and the term likeness a more dynamic aspect of the same reality,[207] and Völker has seen in this double perspective of the image idea the important point of agreement between the older opinion and that of Gregory.[208] We may conclude that to the Cappadocian writers a clear-cut distinction between image and likeness of God in man is not self-evident, in the way it was for Origen.

This impression of a more reserved attitude is finally confirmed not only by a writer like Didymus the Blind, but by the whole Latin tradition.[209] Above all, however, the case of Cyril of Alexandria is

---

[202] Cf. DISDIER, EO 29 (1930), p. 301.

[203] Both the homily *Quid sit ad imaginem Dei et ad similitudinem* (PG 44, 1328–1345) and the much debated two homilies *In scripturae verba: Faciamus hominem ad imaginem et similitudinem nostram* (PG 44, 257–298; cf. among Basil's works *De hominis structura*, PG 30, 9–62) which have the distinction, are among the works attributed to Gregory; but they are mostly rejected as non-Gregorian. Cf. BURGHARDT, *op. cit.*, p. 5 f., n. 19, where the discussion is summarized.

[204] Cf. e.g. VÖLKER, *Gregor von Nyssa als Mystiker*, Wiesbaden 1955, p. 67.

[205] Cf. DANIÉLOU, *Platonisme et théologie mystique*, p. 48.

[206] VON BALTHASAR, *Présence et pensée*, Paris 1942, p. 89. Cf. GAÏTH, *La conception de la liberté*, p. 46.

[207] Cf. e.g. LEYS, *L'Image de Dieu*, p. 116.

[208] VÖLKER, *op. cit.*, p. 71 f.—MUCKLE, MS 7 (1945), p. 59 f., has not noticed any difficulties at all at this point. He simply regards the terms as synonyms.

[209] BURGHARDT, *op. cit.*, p. 5 f. has well summarized the situation, though he has also

important, since he simply refuses to accept any distinction at all. Cyril in fact shows a considerable irritation at the very idea of distinguishing between image and likeness of God in man, and regards them as synonyms, primarily because a difference of meaning is not demonstrable.[210]

Reasons for rejection and acceptance of the distinction

Against this clear evidence of the restricted influence of Origen's interpretation and the equally clear evidence of a new openness to it in Maximus—which we shall soon demonstrate—two questions appear as particularly important: why was this interpretation widely rejected, and for what reason did Maximus feel free to use it again? To the first question there is no easy answer. Here a few possible reasons may be indicated. A reaction against an exclusive stress on human effort might be suspected as one of these reasons. We have found traces of it in Athanasius. A reaction against excesses of Scriptural interpretation may be another reason. With Burghardt, we may assume that this was what caused the attitude of Cyril and Augustine.[211] But this is certainly not enough. In the case of Gregory of Nyssa his own understanding of the unity of man and his refutation of the pre-existence of souls must have been influential. For a too sharp distinction between image and likeness, as they were conceived by Origen, must have recalled the idea that something is lacking in created man as such and that the mind, which alone carries the divine image, is bound down by its relationship to the body and has to free itself through ascetic efforts in order to regain the divine likeness. But if this is the case with Gregory, an acceptance of Origen's distinction would not have been any easier in the 6th and 7th centuries, because inevitably it would have had to be linked with the Origenist myth as a whole. And this makes the answer to our second question still more difficult.

Von Balthasar has simply referred to the anonymous homily *Quid sit ad imaginem* . . . (PG 44, 1328–1345) as a sufficient testimony to the fact that the old distinction had been revived.[212] But without ignoring the importance of this text we must emphasize, on the other hand, that the

---

emphasized that in some writers, such as Chrysostom, we find other kinds of distinction between image and likeness than that of the early Alexandrians.

[210] See BURGHARDT, *op. cit.*, p. 7 f. A similar argumentation was put forward also by Augustine, see *Quæst. in Heptateuch.* 5, 4; CSEL 28: 2, p. 371 f.

[211] In this context it should also be noted that writers like Theodore of Mopsuestia and Theodoret of Cyrus do not discriminate between the terms at all, see BURGHARDT, *op. cit.*, p. 6.

[212] VON BALTHASAR, KL[2], pp. 179 and 545 f.

distinction which it makes between image and likeness does not seem to be identical either with that of Origen or that of Maximus. For it states that the naked soul is in the image of God, but that the synthesis of body and soul is in the likeness of the incarnate Logos,[213] and on the whole it seems less interested in distinguishing between the terms than in showing their parallelism.[214] More important probably are the homilies *In Scripturae verba . . .* (PG 44, 257–298) to which Burghardt has called attention as exceptions from the time of Gregory of Nyssa himself,[215] for there we learn that likeness is acquired through virtues,[216] though even in them the interest in developing this point of view does not seem to be particularly strong. This would be equally true of the longer recension of the same work, *De hominis structura,* falsely attributed to Basil.[217]

There is in fact only one writer, who really reminds us of Origen's interpretation, and who may possibly also have influenced Maximus, Diadochus of Photice.[218] In ch. 89 of his *Cap. gnost.* he develops what he means by image and likeness at some length. He sees likeness as above image. The divine grace in baptism restores the image of God in man, but when man sets his entire aspiration in movement towards the beauty of the divine likeness, then it also gives him the marks of this likeness. The perfection of the likeness is, however, effected only through illumination, an illumination brought about by spiritual charity, which alone makes the likeness to God perfect.[219] As we see, the "super-natural" character of likeness is here professed as in the early Alexandrian tradition, and also the idea that likeness is manifested through virtues. It is, however, more clearly seen as a work of divine grace, though it must be admitted, Origen's reference to the formation of Christ in the believer is lacking.

Maximus' personal understanding of the distinction

The position of Diadochus is striking, but it cannot give a fully sufficient solution to our problem. For the authority of Diadochus could in itself hardly outweigh that of the Cappadocians or of Cyril of Alexandria in the

---

[213] PG 44, 1329 B.

[214] It seems also more interested in the question of a certain trichotomy of the human soul as a reflexion of the Holy Trinity. We shall return to the Trinitarian aspect in an additional note to this section (see pp. 129–132 below).

[215] See BURGHARDT, *op. cit.,* p. 5 f., n. 19.

[216] PG 44, 276 CD.

[217] On the problem of authorship, see E. AMAND, Les états de texte des homélies pseudo-basiliennes sur la création de l'homme, RB (1949), pp. 3–54.

[218] BURGHARDT, *op. cit.,* p. 6, mentions him among the exceptions. To this problem, see E. DES PLACES, Maxime Le Confesseur et Diadoque de Photice, in HEINZER-SCHÖNBORN, *Maximus Confessor,* pp. 29–35.

[219] *Cap. gnost.* 89; DES PLACES, p. 149 f. Cf. the Introduction by the editor, p. 34 f.

judgment of Maximus. When he shows himself able to accept a similar distinction between image and likeness it must therefore be on the basis of considerations which are his own. And we must, consequently, go to Maximus' own texts to find out what these considerations may possibly be.

There are first of all clear similarities between Origen and Maximus at this point. Thus Maximus also says that the image of God was given to man in the beginning, but that the likeness of God is to be acquired through a spiritual process.[220] Maximus too professes that likeness is related to the divine sonship given to man,[221] and the formation of Christ in the believer may also in him be regarded as a development of the divine likeness.[222] Finally, the development of likeness is seen as a kind of imitation of God, a manifestation of divine virtues[223] and, on the whole, as a moral activity of man.[224]

Through this comparison however, it seems, we do not come to the core of Maximus' texts, or to the heart of his acceptance of the distinction. For the development of the idea in Maximus seems to be more consciously worked out and more intimately related to his entire theological position.

We need, thus, a key to understanding him at this point. It is difficult to find one, for Maximus never states systematically what he has to contribute in this field; it is not a matter of debate, nor the topic of an entire section in any of his works. But there are at least two short passages which primarily deserve our attention. First of these is a passage in Amb 10 (PG 91, 1112 D–1116 C), where Maximus deals with the three motions of the soul in men who are being deified. They are of mind, reason and sense, and each performs its own function in relation to the kind of knowledge it may acquire. These movements are interrelated and culminate in the function of the mind, which dwells in an unconceptual contemplation of God, supported "from beneath" by the functions of reason and sense. Ordered in such a way and related to God, man is now said to be deemed fit to "bear the image of the heavenly One, as much as men may".[225] After this section—which, as Sherwood has underlined, is not particularly original and could be found both in Evagrius and Ps.-Denis[226]—comes our key sentence (quoted already in ch. I above)

---

[220] See Amb 42; PG 91, 1345 D.
[221] See e.g. *loc. cit.* and Thal 6; CCSG 7, p. 71.
[222] See e.g. Char 4. 70; CSC, p. 224.
[223] Thal 53; CCSG 7, p. 435.
[224] See e.g. ThPol 1; PG 91, 12 A and Amb 7; PG 91, 1084 A.
[225] PG 91, 1113 B.
[226] SHERWOOD, *The Earlier Ambigua*, p. 143.

which runs like this (I use Sherwood's translation):[227] "For they say that God and man are exemplars (παραδείγματα) one of another; and that God makes himself man for man's sake out of love, so far as man, enabled by God through charity, deified himself; and that man is rapt up by God in mind to the unknowable, so far as man has manifested through virtues the God by nature invisible." We see here that the reciprocity between God and man—which already in ch. I we have noticed as a characteristic feature of Maximus' theology and found expressed particularly clearly in the relationship between Incarnation and deification and in the *tantum-quantum* formula—is presented as a kind of explanation of the fact that man in deification bears the image of God in perfection. The development of man's image character is an expression of this reciprocity in function—a divine-human function, in which man moves entirely towards God and is more and more established in him through the contemplative motion of his mind, but in which God also becomes incarnate in man through human virtues, which are reflections of divine attributes. Divine incarnation in the virtues and human fixity in God are two sides of the same process of deification, through which God is thus revealed in man.[228]

We may add, however, that this process of perfection may also be called the development of the likeness of God in man. Here our second key passage is illuminating. For in Char 3. 25 Maximus makes one of his most clear statements about image and likeness in relation to God's attributes. He says there that God in his goodness has communicated to rational beings four of his divine attributes, by which he supports, guards and preserves them. These attributes are being, ever-being, goodness and wisdom. Being and ever-being are given to their substance (for though created they are destined for eternal life) and pertain to the *image* of God in them, while goodness and wisdom are given for their will and judgment and pertain to their *likeness* of God. The first two are given by nature, the latter by grace.[229] We see in this passage not only that image is related more to man's being, while likeness is related to the use of his power of self-determination, but still more that this distinction between image and likeness is due also to a distinction in God's own properties. Being and ever-being are granted through the very constitution of rational beings; goodness and wisdom are qualities made available to

---

[227] Sherwood, *op. cit.*, p. 144. Cf. ch. I: A d (p. 32).
[228] The aspect of revelation in this context has also been underlined by Sherwood, *op. cit.*, p. 150 f.
[229] CSC, p. 154.—The difference between λόγος φύσεως and τρόπος ὑπάρξεως is well pointed out by Heinzer, *op. cit.*, p. 171.

their self-determinative power. They are related to their well-being.[230] Furthermore, goodness and wisdom are particularly related to God's activity towards created beings, for through and in Wisdom God has made all things, and out of Goodness he shows loving-kindness towards his creatures, glorifying the virtuous and being merciful to the bad.[231] Thus, likeness to God reflects divine attributes in man which express His particular relationship to differentiated creation.

We may conclude that Maximus must have felt particularly free to use the old distinction between the image and likeness of God in man, because through it he was able to express the reciprocity of God and man, and the different aspects of God's activity towards created rational beings. His interpretation was entirely free from connections with an Origenist understanding of man and creation. It is not because of any lack in the conditions of empirical man, that the image must be perfected through likeness, but only as a consequence of the fact that man is created with a self-determinative power, which should be used freely for his well-being. Nor is this development a mere reflection of the image character of the mind. It is a function through which aspects of God's own nature are manifested, aspects which are related to the freedom of man and to the incarnation of the divine in man's virtues, which has to take place in deification by grace. The whole of man is, thus, brought into the forefront of the discussion, through the concept of likeness, and not only by way of addition, as we might suspect to be the case in Origen, but also as part of a total relationship of man with God, initiated from the side of God.

This explains why in Maximus likeness is consistently related to the life of virtues and the *vita practica*. Thus we hear that likeness is linked with πρᾶξις ἐντολῶν[232] or with human goodness, as contrary to evil (i.e. the aspect of human, differentiated activity), while image is linked with truth and contemplation, as contrary to falsehood (i.e. the aspect of unifying divine fixity). Self-determination as such belongs to man's image character, as Maximus strongly underlines in his *Disputation with Pyrrhus*,[233] but its true development and use manifests the likeness to God. To what is naturally good (καλόν) according to the image, man is called to add through his free decision (προαίρεσις) a likeness through

---

[230] On Maximus' triad of being—well-being—ever-being, see further ch. VI: 5, pp. 368–373 below.

[231] Char 3. 22; CSC, p. 152 and 1. 25; p. 58.

[232] Thal 53; CCSG 7, p. 435.

[233] See PG 91, 304 C and 324 D.

virtues.[234] Thus a man who rightly uses the three movements of his soul, mind, reason and sense, has already added to the good (καλόν) of nature the voluntary good (τὸ γνωμικὸν ἀγαθόν) of likeness. Likeness perfects the image character of man in that it completes what is of nature, and is thus unchangeable, with what is of will, and thus differentiated according to everyone's personal choice and capacity. Maximus alludes to this duality again in the preamble to the *Ambigua*, where he speaks of a γνῶσις ἔμπρακτος and a πρᾶξις ἔνσοφος, which are the "beauty of Wisdom" and are marked by the principle of divine providence and judgment. Through them, he adds, is manifested, *how* God has made man after his image, in that he is incarnated in the virtues.[235] This incarnation is, however, also a formation of Christ in the believer, i.e. also an individual appropriation of the presence of the incarnate Logos in the world,[236] an appropriation which through the virtues includes the activities of the body and the senses.

Seen in the light of our two key passages Maximus' statements about the difference between image and likeness of God in man are, thus, yet another expression of his conviction that man is a totality of body and soul, entrusted with freedom, and that the aspect of unity, the image shared by all, should be balanced against the aspect of differentiation, likeness as acquired by those who are wise and good, within the perspective of God's economy for his creation.

Additional note: *Imago Trinitatis*

We have seen how the Maximian triad being, well-being, ever-being is related to the distinction of image and likeness in such a way that being and ever-being pertain to the image of God and well-being to the likeness of God in man. We have also seen, how the same distinction between image and likeness is connected with a distinction in the properties of God, so that God is said to communicate his Being and ever-being to man's nature as an image of Himself, and his Goodness and Wisdom to the likeness to Himself. If we combine these two viewpoints, we see clearly that both wisdom and goodness are seen as related to well-being (which is also the sphere of the development of the divine likeness in man).

Now, as Sherwood has shown, triads of this type indicate in Maximus the idea of some kind of Trinitarian reflections in creation and on the

---

[234] Amb 7; PG 91, 1084 A.
[235] PG 91, 1032 AB.
[236] Cf. Char 4. 70; CSC, p. 224.

human level. Thus from Amb 10[237] we should conclude that in combining ontological and moral terms in describing God's attributes as revealed through His relationship to the created world, Maximus establishes triads which reflect, in some measure, the mystery of the Holy Trinity. Such secondary triads in creation are motion, providence and position (θέσις),[238] or again difference, judgment and composition (κρᾶσις),[239] and they show both that God is, is wise and is living, that is to say they reveal His own being, well-being and ever-being.[240]

Sherwood has also shown, that this last triad of divine properties—being, wisdom, life—goes back to a four-fold distinction in Ps.-Denis: goodness, being, life and wisdom,[241] based on a triad of Proclus: being, life, mind,[242] where Denis has changed mind to wisdom and added his favourite divine attribute goodness. Maximus seems, in his turn, to have combined wisdom with goodness and put it in the second place and thus to have arrived at his own triad, where being corresponds to the Father, wisdom (and goodness) to the Son, and life to the Spirit.[243] These findings coincide, however, with what we have already found concerning the relationship between image and likeness as related to different attributes of God, and with our suggestion that likeness, which reflects the wisdom and goodness of God, is closely linked with the thought of God's incarnation or the formation of Christ in the believer, for it is exactly those two attributes, which pertain to likeness, which are also seen as reflexions of the Son as a divine Person.

But then we are bound to conclude that, when manifesting the divine image and likeness, man is in fact reflecting the Holy Trinity. Are there also other indications in Maximus of an *imago Trinitatis* in man, which may confirm this conclusion? Yes, and again Sherwood has pointed out the evidence. In Amb 7 Maximus emphasizes that the human mind, λόγος and spirit should be conformed to their archetype: the great Mind, Logos and Spirit, and in a passage of Amb 10, the same triad of the human soul is said to be an image of the Triune Archetype.[244] This triad as a reflexion of the Trinity in the human soul goes back to Gregory Nazianzen, who related its elements respectively to the unoriginate

---

[237] PG 91, 1136 BC. See further my own study *Man and the Cosmos*, pp. 46–49.
[238] Representing the aspect of unification, it seems.
[239] Representing the aspect of differentiation, it seems.
[240] See SHERWOOD, in ACW, p. 38 ff.
[241] *De div. nom.* 5, 2; PG 3, 816 C; the distinction is reflected also elsewhere, see e.g. *ibid.* 2, 3; 640 B and 2,5; 644 A.
[242] See SHERWOOD, in ACW, p. 40 f.
[243] Cf. *ibid.*, p. 41.
[244] PG 91, 1088 A, and PG 91, 1196 A; cf. SHERWOOD, in ACW, p. 41.

character of the Father, the birth of the Son and the procession of the Spirit.[245] Finally, Sherwood has found another example, which is, however, related more to the activities of sanctified man. It comes in a passage which we have already cited, Amb 10, and refers to an acquired simplicity and unity reflecting the divine simplicity, and an imitated goodness in virtues, reflecting the divine goodness, and a putting off of the individuality of naturally divisive forces through the power of divine grace, reflecting the unifying work of God.[246] In the last case the three functions seem to be easily recognizable as those of the Father, the Son and the Spirit respectively—and we can also add that the second element, characterized as the imitation of divine goodness, if we compare it with the other texts we have studied, alludes also indirectly to the free development of the likeness to God in man and to deification, seen as a divine incarnation in human virtues.

There are, thus, in Maximus clear indications of an *imago Trinitatis* conception related to the constitution and spiritual activity of man. But on the other hand, Maximus does not dwell very long on these aspects, probably because his apophatic theological position warned him against giving the impression that the mystery of the Holy Trinity is in any sense expressible in human terms. With Sherwood we are, therefore, bound to call them simply "adumbrations of the Trinity in creation".[247] As such they may, however, play an important role on the human level itself, as is shown in the example of Abraham, as we find it presented in Ep 2[248] and

---

[245] *Or.* 23, 11; PG 35, 1161 C–1164 A; cf. Sherwood, in ACW, p. 41 f.—In the anonymous homily *Quid sit ad imaginem* . . . this last aspect returns, but is developed in a different direction. The attributes of the persons of the Trinity are said to be reflected in the ἀγεννησία ψυχῆς, γέννησις λόγου and ἐκπόρευσις πνεύματος. The triad is thus here ψυχή, λόγος, πνεῦμα, but πνεῦμα is further identified with νοῦς, which makes the triad rather different from that of Gregory and Maximus (see PG 44, 1336 AB). The way the attributes are used is also interesting, since it sounds somewhat Origenist. For the ἀγεννησία ψυχῆς is easily referred to an idea of the pre-existence of souls, the γεννησία λόγου to a second creation including the lower parts of the soul, and the ἐκπόρευσις νοός to a return of the mind to an original 'supernatural' unity. It is also striking, that a second reflexion of the Trinity in the soul, namely in the three parts of the created soul: τὸ ἐπιθυμητικόν, τὸ λογικόν and τὸ θυμικόν, is referred to the *activities* of God (PG 44, 1336 B), which statement could be related to the Origenist idea of providence and judgment (see on Maximus' refutation of this understanding, ch. II: 3, pp. 67–70 above). The possible relationship between this little treatise of unknown origin and Maximus requires a particular study, which cannot be undertaken here.

[246] PG 91, 1196 B; cf. Sherwood, in ACW, p. 42.

[247] Sherwood, in ACW, p. 38.

[248] See PG 91, 400 C. Maximus' evaluation of Abraham in Ep 2 and Thal 28 is worked out in a most complicated dialogue with the earlier Christian interpretation of Gen. 18; see further my sketch of the history of this interpretation in the acts of the *Fourth International Conference of Patristic Studies,* Oxford 1963.

Thal 28. For as the visit of the three angels in Mamre is described there by Maximus, this story illustrates the relationship between the inner unity of man—established through the direction of the mind, freed from its dependence upon matter—and the revelation of the Holy Trinity to rational beings in the created world.[249] United in himself—and here one may think of the triads of the soul—Abraham was, thus, able to regard human multiplicity as oneness[250] and to receive the truth, that in the λόγος of the monad lies inherent the immaterial λόγος of the Triad.[251] The adumbrations of the Trinity in the human world may, therefore, serve at the same time as a kind of divine revelation *and* as a pattern for interhuman, as well as inner human, relationships. They are in fact another expression of the intimate connection and interdependence of true unity and multiplicity.

5. *Microcosm and mediator*

A dominant element in Maximus' general anthropology, which is related to his understanding of human nature as such, remains still to be treated, though it is evidently of the utmost importance for the whole perspective of this thesis; that is to say, Maximus' understanding of man as microcosm and—dependent on this—as cosmic mediator. There are a number of reasons for our delay in taking up this question.

First of all, man's rôle as mediator will be most appropriately dealt with in relation to Maximus' theology of deification, since it is part and parcel of the latter, and consequently belongs to a later section of this work. Secondly, the idea of man as microcosm presupposes an understanding of other elements of Maximus' anthropology, which we have had to treat first; not only his view of man as a natural unit, but also the different aspects of his theology of the image. Thirdly, the *explicit* references to the concept of microcosm are concentrated in a few particular texts. Finally, the practical implications of this idea are mostly seen in relation to Maximus' ascetic theology and will therefore only be fully treated in that context. It is for these reasons that not until this point have we arrived at a proper place to describe Maximus' use of the idea of man as microcosm, and for these reasons too, that we shall only indicate here—in a preliminary way—the task of mediation which is, in Maximus' opinion, set before man.

This task is his by virtue of the fact that he bears within himself the

[249] Thal 28; CCSG 7, p. 203.
[250] Ep 2; *loc. cit.*
[251] PG 90, 360 D.

elements of all creation, and still more is dignified by the presence within him of the divine image. It seems that there are at least three reasons why Maximus must have adopted rather readily the ancient idea of man as microcosm. First there is his profound understanding of unity and multiplicity. Then there is the fact that he, evidently, understood the created world in terms of Christological insights, which necessarily had powerful repercussions in his anthropology. Finally, the influence of the Cappadocians, as we shall see, at this point is particularly strong, and they had already explicitly made use of the idea on Christian grounds.

Man as microcosm in the tradition before Maximus

The view of man as microcosm, and the consequent interplay of this microcosm and the world as macrocosm, is an important and differentiated phenomenon in the world of religion.[252] Its presence in Greek antiquity was probably due to Oriental influences though in a number of ways it can be traced back to pre-Socratic times.[253] There seems, thus, to be a faint beginning of the idea in Anaximenes,[254] and a consequent development of it among the atomist philosophers. Democritus states explicitly that man is a microcosm,[255] and his development of the idea exerted a wide influence on later philosophy.[256] Its influence on Christian writers obviously depends on the fact that it was used by these later philosophers. Thus in Plato the whole dialogue of *Timaeus* is marked by it, since—reproducing older traditions—it describes a vision of the world as one great human being.[257] The term microcosm, however, does not appear in Plato. In Aristotle, on the other hand, we find the expressions $\mu\iota\kappa\rho\acute{o}s$ and $\mu\acute{e}\gamma as$ $\kappa\acute{o}\sigma\mu os$ and the idea of a reciprocity between them.[258] Here, however, the concept does not play a very important rôle, and the analogy is restricted to the constitution of the

---

[252] See G. LANCZKOWSKI, *art.* Makrokosmos und Mikrokosmos, in RGG³ 4, col. 624 f. and R. ALLERS, Microcosmus, from Anaximandros to Paracelsus, *Traditio* 2 (1944), pp. 319–407, where a very far-reaching differentiation (elementaristic, cosmocentric, anthropocentric, holistic, symbolistic and psychological microcosmism) is attempted.

[253] See W. KRANZ, Kosmos und Mensch in der Vorstellung des frühen Griechentums, NGWG, N.F., Fachgr. 1, vol. 2 (1936–38), pp. 121–161, and for the Oriental influence, the general summary of earlier research, p. 149 f.

[254] Cf. FR. UEBERWEG, *Grundriss der Geschichte der Philosophie*, I: K. PRAECHTER, *Die Philosophie des Altertums*, Berlin 1926, p. 51.

[255] See H. DIELS, *Die Fragmente der Vorsokratiker*, 2, 1954; no. B 34, p. 153, 1. 8; cf. 1. 13.

[256] Cf. KRANZ, *Kosmos*, 1 (Archiv f. Begriffsgeschichte 2: 1), 1953, p. 49 f.

[257] See particularly *Tim.;* 81 A and D; ef. also *Phileb.;* 29 B–30 A. A monograph has been devoted to the subject: A. OLERUD, *L'Idée de macrocosmos et de microcosmos dans le Timée de Platon*, Diss., Uppsala 1951. Cf. KRANTZ, *op. cit.*, p. 51 ff.

[258] See Aristotle, *Phys.* 8, 2; 252 b, 24.

human soul. Only within Stoic philosophy were there the decisive conditions, which caused the idea to flourish,—though this is, of course, not to say that we do not find it in e.g. Neo-Platonism[259]—for in Stoic philosophy it was intimately connected with a corresponding idea of God's immanence in the world. And so an all-embracing formula was reached on this basis: "What God is to the world, that is the soul to man."[260]

It should, however, be noticed, that it is a general tendency in the literature we have mentioned, as well as in the Oriental tradition, to understand the idea in such a way, that it is man who is formed after the pattern of the Cosmos and not the reverse,[261] though Plato, it is true, uses it primarily to describe the world in human terms.[262] This question now becomes of importance within the Christian tradition, for—as among Platonists—there will necessarily be a certain tension between the understanding of man as being, as it were, in the image of the material creation, and the idea that man was created in the image and likeness of God; the latter view implying, as it does, a super-human destiny, which could not be fulfilled within the function of a microcosm related primarily to the empirical world as macrocosm.

This difficulty is noticeable already in Philo, who probably paved the way for the Christian use of the idea. For in him on the one hand there is a clear parallelism between world and man, so that man may be regarded as a small world and the world as a single man in accordance with the understanding of the philosophers,[263] but, on the other hand, it is evident that it is not the Stoic concept which is relevant here but rather the Platonic.[264] For in Philo there is a strict distinction between the intelligible and the sensible world, and thus also between man created in the image of God and man formed from the earth.[265] The analogy between man and the world has in fact to include this dual perspective. And it is in their common *ideal* relationship to the Logos that man and world are equal, which fact implies a certain modification in the use of the concept

---

[259] Democritus' microcosm idea is reflected in Plotinus (see *Enn.* IV, 3, 1) and in Iamblichus, in both cases in connection with the idea of the Universe as being held together in a unity (ef. UEBERWEG—PRAECHTER, *op. cit.*, pp. 605 and 616).

[260] Cf. L. STEIN, *Die Psychologie der Stoa*, I, Berlin 1886, p. 208.—An important position within the same stream of tradition is held by Cicero, see *De nat. deor.* 2. 14, 37.

[261] Cf. H. HOMMEL, Mikrokosmos, RhM 92 (1943), p. 58, n. 7.

[262] Cf. KRANZ, *op. cit.*, pp. 16–20; 50–53.

[263] Philo, *Quis rer. div. haer.* 155; COHN & WENDLAND, 3, p. 36, 7 f.

[264] A slight parallel to Philo's dilemma may probably be found already in Poseidonius and the Middle Stoa, where there is room for a rather sharp distinction between body and soul. Cf. UEBERWEG—PRAECHTER, *op. cit.*, p. 480.

[265] Cf. DANIÉLOU, *Philon d'Alexandrie*, p. 172 f.

of man as microcosm. For in the end, the real analogy is that which exists between the Logos and the human mind ($\nu o \hat{v} \varsigma$) on the one hand, and the world and the human body on the other.[266]

Among Christian writers the idea of man as microcosm seems to have been used particularly by the Cappadocian Fathers.[267] We find it in fact in all three of them, though their point of emphasis is not always the same. Thus Basil of Caesarea, in one of his sermons, states that man is by self-attention able to see the wisdom of the Creator as in a microcosm. He obviously does not think of a mystical divine presence in the soul *or* of the universe in terms of the human body, but simply of the interplay between the different elements of man, as an analogy to the cosmic order, in both of which God's creative wisdom is reflected.[268] And in a different way Gregory Nazianzen on one occasion applies the very expression δ $\mu \iota \kappa \rho \delta \varsigma$ $\kappa \delta \sigma \mu o \varsigma$ to man, not, however, it would seem, referring first of all to the constitution of man as such, but to his receptive powers in their relation to the outside world, on account of which the human soul may be said to contain this world within itself.[269] Finally, Gregory of Nyssa uses the concept of man as microcosm in various places, sometimes explicitly, more often implicitly;[270] but here we recognize again, and more clearly, the *tension* which we have noticed in Philo. For when he assumes that man is a microcosm and is a mirror of the harmony of the universe, he does so, first of all, to stress that in both cases there is a certain imitation of the Creator, and that this is the reason why the mind finds in the microcosm what it discovers in the macrocosm, and why it may recognize the same harmony in itself as in the universe.[271] And then furthermore, he is eager to point out that man's likeness to the universe is not the reason of his greatness, which is due, on the contrary, to the fact that he is created in the image of the Creator.[272]

The multiplicity, which is an inescapable feature of creation as such, is thus to a Christian writer like Gregory an element in the analogy

---

[266] See Daniélou, *op. cit.*, p. 173 f.

[267] It should, however, be noted, that Jerome claims that Origen held the opinion that the four elements of the world corresponded exactly to the four traditional elements of man: flesh, breath, blood and heat (*Lib. contra Ioann. Hierosol.* 25; PL 23, 376 B). For other examples of the same close association between the elements of man and of the world, see further references given in Y. Lefèvre, *L'Elucidarium et les Lucidaires,* Paris 1954, p. 115 f., n. 1 (Prof. C.-M. Edsman has kindly drawn my attention to this study.)

[268] *Hom. in illud, Attende tibi ipsi,* 7; PG 31, 213 B–216 B.

[269] *Or.* 28 (*Theol.* 2), 22; Mason, p. 56.

[270] Cf. e.g. Völker, *Gregor von Nyssa,* p. 51 f.

[271] *In Psalm.* I, 3; PG 44, 441 CD.

[272] *De hom. opif.* 16; PG 44, 180 A. Cf. Allers, *art. cit.,* p. 370 f., where this position is understood (merely) as "symbolistic microcosmism".

between microcosm and macrocosm, which cannot be understood in its right proportion, until reference has been given to a more important doctrine: that of the image of God in man. For only in that is the unifying principle indicated, thus making the intended harmony of creation the crucial point of the analogy. Man is, in fact, called to mediate between the intelligible and the sensible world.[273] And thus the problem of the fall of man and the consequent disorder of creation is indirectly brought into the picture. The distinction between God and the world must necessarily be underlined in direct conjunction with the idea of man as microcosm. And this is all the more important in Gregory, where we have already found that the idea of the dignity of the soul, and particularly of the human mind, is more valuable than is the concept of the totality of man as created being, even though this totality is in principle defended.[274]

Man as both microcosm and mediator in Nemesius

In Maximus we shall see how this problem is felt just as keenly, but is tackled in such a way as to make possible a further development of the same tendencies. However, before we deal with him we should mention another writer, for whom the idea of man as microcosm is very relevant: Nemesius of Emesa. Nemesius is in fact important, not only because he accepts the classical understanding of man as microcosm—seeing the things of the external universe reflected in man as in a mirror[275]—but more particularly because of his attempt to reconcile the tension we have already mentioned. The dualism, which is such a characteristic feature of his philosophy—even implying, as we have pointed out, the idea of the pre-existence of souls—is the very pre-supposition of this reconciliation. For the idea of man as microcosm in Nemesius is not first of all related to an understanding of the universe as a harmonious whole, but to man's divine task to unite in himself the opposites of the world. Man is called to perform a function, to *act* as microcosm. For this reason he has been placed as the centre of the universe, a position which is first of all illustrated by the fact that he is created in the image and likeness of God.

The conclusions are thus drawn from man to the world rather than the other way round; the order which should regulate man's life—that the irrational element should be subordinated to the rational element—is equally valid for the world outside. It is in fact for man to exert this

---

[273] *Or. catech.* 6; PG 45, 25 B–28 B; ef. Gaïth, *La Conception de la liberté*, p. 50 ff.

[274] See p. 96 f. above our discussion of the difference between the argumentations of Gregory and Maximus in relation to their refutation of the pre-existence of souls.

[275] Nemesius, *De nat. hom.* 1; PG 40, 529 B.

rational rule over the world, and the fact that the things of the world are reflected in man as in a mirror implies a call to man to use them for his service.[276] Truths about the universe can be grasped from observations of man and *vice versa*, but the whole argument leads up to the conclusion that the lower creatures exist for man's sake.[277] And this task of man means that he has to join together things which are opposites: mortal creatures with immortal, rational beings with the irrational. This is the way in which he has to function as the "world in little", and thus it is that he "carries the image of the whole world".[278]

We are, therefore, bound to conclude that in Nemesius of Emesa the tension we have noticed between the idea of man as a microcosm, reflecting the outside world, and the idea of man as created in the image of God, is reconciled through the insistence on the *function* of man in the world. In other words: through a combination of the idea of the microcosm with that of man as *mediator*.[279] And it is this particular combination—though without the very strong dualism in relation to created beings, which is a Platonist, but perhaps also an Antiochene, element in Nemesius—which we find also in Maximus, though used in a personal way.

Maximus and man's middle position

Maximus, in fact, from the beginning sets out to reconcile, in a way which is in accordance with his Christological presuppositions, any tension that may exist between the idea of man as microcosm and the concept of the image and likeness of God, whether due to a dualism derived from a Platonist philosophical background or to the Christian dichotomy between Creator and creation. As in the case of Nemesius, so with him a dualistic outlook seems so far from being an obstacle for his acceptance of both conceptions, that it rather furthers their combination. The reason is again—as in Nemesius—that the emphasis lies on the *task* which man has to perform as microcosm—a task which is at the same time that of a *mediator*—a view which accords with Maximus' basic conviction that unity should, here on earth, be realized in diversity and diversity be fulfilled in unity.

---

[276] *Loc. cit.*

[277] *Ibid.;* 525 A. Cf. the commentary by Telfer, in *Cyril of Jerusalem and Nemesius of Emesa*, p. 254.

[278] *Ibid.;* 532 C–533 A. For the translation, see Telfer, *op. cit.,* p. 254.

[279] As far as Gregory of Nyssa is concerned, the solution of the problem is, as we have said, found in the same direction, though less explicitly. On this aspect see Gaïth, *La Conception de la Liberté*, esp. p. 50 ff.

What we have now said can be well illustrated by those texts in which Maximus explicitly develops or refers to the idea of microcosm. We find it already in Ep 6, where the concept is just slightly hinted at. This letter is entirely devoted to a refutation of those who claim that the soul is a body,[280] and only towards the end of it, does Maximus refer to man as ὁ μικρὸς κόσμος.[281] Nevertheless, an analysis of this section of his argumentation shows that a number of the elements which we have mentioned, are at play. Thus it is characteristic that what he wants to underline here, is that it is impossible to believe in the image of God in man, if the soul is corporeal, exactly because the analogy between the world and man, as microcosm, is then in fact not demonstrable. This is elaborated in a rather complicated manner, which may, however, through analysis be summarized in the following way.[282]

The analogy between man and the world, which is threatened by the idea of the corporeality of the soul, is one which is constituted by their common relationship to an immutable cause. For the whole world this cause is God, in relation to whom it naturally moves, but for man it is the substantial cause of movement (τὸ κινητικὸν αἴτιον), which is fixed in itself but in relation to which the organic existence of the body is moved. But this human cause of movement, represented in principle by the mind, at the same time bears the image of God, in relation to whom the whole of man moves, together with the whole of creation. Without the fixity in man, which is of the image of God in him, he would not truly reflect the world in its relationship to God as the first Cause. He would not truly serve as a microcosm—understood as mediator, we may add.[283]

In another shorter passage—in Amb 10—the emphasis lies on the opposite side, but the implications are the same. It is the mediating possibilities of man which are underlined, but the microcosm idea is presupposed. The tone is far more negative, since the context is a warning against the division which is caused by man, when he turns his attention towards the material world and not towards God. What is stressed, however, is the middle position of man, as represented by the human soul. Through the senses man is related to matter, and through

---

[280] His opponents can hardly have been the Origenists. SHERWOOD has discussed the problem but has not advanced beyond this negative conclusion; see *The Earlier Ambigua*, p. 193, n. 23.

[281] PG 91, 429 D.

[282] Since our interest here is focused on the way the analogy between man and the world is used, we leave the problem of moral and ontological mutability out of account, though this is an important object of Maximus' own attention. Cf. SHERWOOD, *The Earlier Ambigua*, p. 193 f.

[283] See Ep 6; PG 91, 429 B–432 A.

his mind to God. He has to choose, where he should turn his attention, and in that sense he must break with his dependence from matter. This break with matter in favour of the divine relationship, implies, however, in Maximus a right ordering of man as a totality, which is the presupposition for his work as mediator. Man's being a microcosm, his middle position, will always tempt him to break with God, as it once tempted Adam, but it does not deprive him of his ordering and unifying task within the universe, in relation to which he may even develop his likeness to the Holy Trinity.[284]

This last fact is made fully evident in a third passage, which may serve as a key illustration to Maximus' use of the ideas of man as microcosm and as mediator. This passage is the first section of *Amb 41* (PG 91, 1304 D–1313 B), which deals as a whole with the question, how five basic divisions (διαιρέσεις)—both unnatural and natural[285]—which are characteristic of the universe in which man dwells, may be overcome. It is made clear from the very beginning that this work of reconciliation and unification is a task, originally set before man, but now fulfilled—because of man's fall—by Christ on his behalf, in such a way that he has to live in accordance with this fulfilment and participate actively in it. It is thus the idea of man as mediator which is undoubtedly put into the foreground. But it is striking, how closely this idea is linked to a presentation of man as microcosm—though this last concept does not expressly appear in the text. For the moment we shall therefore leave this aspect of mediation and shall concentrate our attention upon the microcosmic aspect, and only towards the end of this section shall we return to the question how Maximus conceives of the task of mediation as such.[286]

Man is, first of all, presented here as being in all respects *in the middle* between the extremes of creation, to which he has a natural relationship. He was brought into being as an all-containing workshop, binding all together in himself.[287] As such he has also been given the power of unification, thanks to his proper relationship to his own different parts. Man was further brought into being as the last of God's creatures, because he was to be a natural *link* (σύνδεσμος) between all creation,

---

[284] See Amb 10; PG 91, 1193 C–1196 B.

[285] Cf. in ch. II: 1 (p. 56 f.) above, our discussion of Maximus' use of the term διαίρεσις in this text. Cf. also ch. VI: 6–10 below, where this text serves as the basis of systematization.

[286] The problem of mediation, i.e. of man's participation in the work of mediation, will attract all our attention in ch. VI, since this mediation in fact coincides with the process of deification.

[287] PG 91, 1305 A.

mediating ($\mu\epsilon\sigma\iota\tau\epsilon\acute{\upsilon}\omega\nu$) between the extremes through the elements of his own nature.[288] Man was thus called to bring into one unity in relation to God as Cause that which was naturally distinguished, starting with his own division, summarized in the distinction between man and woman. Overcoming this strictly human difference, man should let the one man be manifest in himself, i.e. the man who exists in fact even after the fall and who is not divided by the difference between man and woman, because he remains related to the common principle ($\lambda\acute{o}\gamma o\varsigma$) of human nature.[289] And from there he is in the position to go on and unite the world in itself and bring it into an harmonious relationship with God.[290]

This was the task set before man, but he did not fulfil it. He failed in his destiny and denied his relationship with God. He preferred to direct his natural movement towards the created world, which was itself moved, and thus he was rescued only thanks to Christ, the God incarnate, who fulfilled the unifying and mediating function of man, being himself man in true relationship to God. On this point Maximus dwells for a long time, developing the way in which Christ realized his task.[291] And he summarizes it once more, concluding with the statement, that Christ has thus demonstrated that the whole creation is one, as it were one new man, fulfilled through the coming together of its members and tending towards itself in a totality of existence, according to one simple and immutable principle: the coming into existence out of nothing, which from the very beginning unites the whole of God's creation in spite of its differences.[292] The fulfilment of the work of mediation thus never violates the basic principle of the gulf between Creator and creation.[293] Man as microcosm is a creature among creatures.

A fourth text is Myst 7, where the idea of the microcosm is again brought into the foreground. The concept of man as mediator is, however, implicitly present. From what we have examined already, we may conclude that the microcosm idea tends to be developed by Maximus in such a way, that it leads to the concept of the universe as a cosmic man, the $\mu\alpha\kappa\rho\acute{\alpha}\nu\theta\rho\omega\pi o\varsigma$ idea. In Myst 7 this is the very starting-point. Here, as in the rest of this work, Maximus refers to "an old man", who has given a mystical interpretation of the Holy Liturgy

---

[288] 1305 B.
[289] 1305 CD.
[290] 1305 D–1308 C. Cf. ch. VI: 6–10 below.
[291] 1308 C–1309 D.
[292] Cf. our study of the *creatio ex nihilo* idea in Maximus, ch. II: 1 above.
[293] See 1312 AB.

and whose ideas he only reproduces and elaborates.[294] Among those ideas is one which says, that both Scripture (ch. 6) and the universe may be called a man. Let us see, how the elements of this last concept are developed and how the analogy between man and the world is worked out.

The chapter starts with the *makranthropos*-idea, and only from there, though immediately, does it go on to the opposite aspect, the microcosm.[295] The analogy is then worked out in a way, which again reminds us of Nemesius, for a certain dualism is presupposed in both writers; as the world consists of visible and invisible things, so man consists of body and soul. And this dual constitution of both reflects each other, but this is not enough, for one must also say, that the intelligible things in the world represent the soul, as the soul represents the intelligible things in man, and the sensible things of the world are the type of the body, as the body is the type of the sensible things in man. And as the soul is present in the body, so also the intelligible world is present in the sensible world.[296] Thus, each forms a characteristic unity in diversity, so that, as there is one single man, made up of soul and body, kept together in their unity, so there is also one world consisting of these two different elements.[297]

The separate character of each element, however, should in neither case be so emphasized, that their unity is threatened, and this is safeguarded by a principle (λόγος), which does not allow it to happen. For there is a certain affinity between all, on account of which the Cause of created beings is mystically present in a manifold way, at the same time preserving and uniting all, so that it remains both unmixed and unseparated.[298] When this principle is followed the whole world may expect a final, eschatological change, a day when the world dies away like a man, and both man and the world experience a resurrection, where the dualism is finally overcome, in that the body is completely united with the soul and the sensible things with the intelligible things.[299]

---

[294] Who this is—if not a literary fiction—is hard to say. SHERWOOD, *The Earlier Ambigua*, p. 8 f., has called attention to the fact that such a person is referred to, not only in the *Liber asceticus,* but also in *Ambiguorum liber.* He mentions Sophronius as a possible suggestion, and we may add, that the existence of a non-authentic *Commentarius liturgicus,* attributed to him, is at least an indication that there was a tradition of regarding Sophronius as among the commentators of the Liturgy. VON BALTHASAR, KL², p. 365, thinks, however, that the problem is not to be solved.

[295] PG 91, 684 D–685 A.

[296] PG 91, 685 A.

[297] *Loc. cit.*

[298] 685 B. Notice here, how the Christological convictions are reflected in the interrelated cosmological and anthropological fields.

[299] 685 C.

The analogies thus also include that of a similar resurrection in the end. It is pointed out, however, that man should be careful, not to direct his attention to the flesh but to care for the soul as much as possible, for it is the higher and more valuable which ought to dominate in relation to Scripture, world and man.[300] A precondition for the work of unification is therefore that the proper order of things is preserved, and herein lies the function of man as mediator. Thus, even in this text there is an indirect reference to the task of man.

Man the mediator

We have seen, through the way it is used, how central to Maximus is the idea of man as microcosm, though it does not appear explicitly in very many texts. What is the main reason for this fact? From what we have now seen through an analysis of the texts, the answer seems rather near at hand. In a theology, where the Christological insights function as a paradigm for the understanding of the world as well as of man, the anthropology must appear as the decisive link. Only an understanding of man as the centre of the created universe does justice to the cosmic implications of Christ's position and work of reconciliation, at least within the context of Greek thinking. And in a theology, where a reciprocal relationship is professed between Incarnation and deification, there must needs be a close relationship between this deification of man and a transfiguration of the world, such as we have seen illustrated in our passages from Amb 41 and Myst 7.

In Maximus' system, however, the Incarnation represents the aspect of differentiation and limitation, while deification represents the aspect of union—aspects which we have found faithfully reflected through the whole cosmological field—and thus the idea of man as microcosm, reflecting the world in its manifoldness and diversity, has naturally in Maximus' writings to be combined with the idea of man as mediator, who unites in himself all that is differentiated without violating its integrity. But this work of mediation and unification is at the same time a fruit of man's relationship to God, of the fact that he is created in the divine Image. For both the establishment of the true order (within man through the direction of the mind which carries the image) and the work of mediation depend on the dominance of the higher principles, in relation to which the movable world is moved, and this leads in the end to God, who keeps all together in differentiated unity. The idea of man as

---

[300] 685 D.

mediator is, thus, a very appropriate expression of Maximus' whole theological intention, as it is to be felt throughout his work.

But what, then, are the opposed elements which need to be reconciled through man's work of mediation, and how are they reconciled? A few indications in response to this question should be given here at the end of our present section. We choose to do it in relation to the passage in Amb 41, which we have already mentioned, first because it is most clearly elaborated there, but also because this text shows how man's microcosmic position functions in this context.

Maximus distinguishes between five "divisions", which man is called to overcome. That between intelligible and sensible is just one of them, the second. The others are: 1) between created and uncreated nature; 3) within sensible creation, between heaven and earth; 4) within the sphere of the earth, between paradise and the world inhabited by men; and 5) within humanity, between man and woman.[301] In all these cases man has a specific function. He should start with his own particular division, the fifth, which to Maximus is contrary to the original divine intention for man. Since this division is upheld by an intercourse between the sexes characterized by lust, it should be overcome through the establishment of a passionless relationship, which manifests the common principle of human nature alone, and which in Christ is established by his birth of a virgin.[302] The fourth division is healed through man's holy conduct, which makes paradise and the inhabited earth into one land. The third division is overcome through an imitation of the angels, as far as this is possible for man, which fixes man entirely in the God-ward direction.[303] But as soon as man has, thus, acquired a knowledge equal to that of the angels, so that there is no more any difference between knowing and not knowing, man may also reconcile the division between the sensible and the intelligible world. In this state he lives by grace in an intimate communion with God, which leads in the end to the overcoming of the last division, to mystical union with God—though without, of course, any ontological identification.[304] Thus, a particular stress lies on the "gnostic" functions of man, as it were sharing with God, in the holding together of the whole universe through the contemplated principles of being. Deification and mediation on the cosmic level coincide, and the basis of both is the fact that man is a rational creature and as such carries in himself the image of God.

---

[301] PG 91, 1304 D–1305 A.
[302] See PG 91, 1305 C and 1309 A. See further ch. VI: 6, pp. 373–379 below.
[303] 1305 D. See further ch. VI: 7–8, pp. 381–398 below.
[304] 1308 AB. See further ch. VI: 9–10, pp. 398–427 below.

B.   The Fall of Man and Its Consequences

1. Adam and the original state of man

There is still a number of aspects of anthropology, which have not been treated so far: the original state of man, the fall, the consequences of the fall, etc. They will, however, be dealt with most appropriately in relation to Maximus' interpretation of the biblical narrative about the creation and fall of man. For it is within such an exegetical tradition—far more than within the field of philosophical considerations—that his opinions on these questions naturally belong.

The excellency of the primitive state

Thus, we should first ask, how Maximus conceives of man in his original state. We could of course also ask what properties the image of God in man contains, when it is still unaffected by sin and its consequences. The answer is provided by a combination of elements coming from different texts. Thus we learn that Adam enjoyed spiritual freedom,[305] which he was able to use in communion with God, since he also had an ability for spiritual pleasure;[306] moreover he was sinless,[307]—or perhaps better, without (ψιλός) sin, since he never acquired that actualized sinlessness, which Christ, the new Adam, manifested[308]—and incorruptible, since he had not yet sinned and fallen a prey to physical corruption.[309] For this last reason he was subject only to the law of "coming into being" (γένεσις), a law which harmonized with the principle of his nature, but not to that of physical birth (γέννησις) after sexual intercourse, which was introduced after the fall[310] as a means of relative preservation and the counterpart of death, the final sign of human corruptibility.[311] Finally, in a discussion of

---

[305] Amb 42; PG 91, 1316 D.
[306] Thal 61; CCSG 22, p. 85.
[307] Amb 42; PG 91, 1317 A.
[308] Amb 31; PG 91, 1276 C.
[309] Amb 42; 1317 AB.
[310] It should be noted, that Clement of Alexandria already regarded sexual propagation as a consequence of the fall; see *Strom.* 3. 17; GCS Clem. 2, p. 243.
[311] See Amb 31; PG 91, 1276 C; 42; 1316 B–1317 C and Thal 61; CCSG 22, pp. 85 and 93. Concerning Thal 61, where the term γένεσις is used about the way in which sinful men come into being, and the term γέννησις about Christ's sinless birth, it should be noted, that it is Maximus' opinion that after the fall sexual intercourse is the established way for human beings to come into existence (their mode of γένεσις) and may thus be called a γένεσις καθ᾽ ἡδονήν, while Christ took upon himself *freely* to be born in a human manner, though without sexual intercourse, thus pointing back to the original state of man. We shall later discuss the implications of this teaching.

Gregory Nazianzen's expression, that the first man was naked in his simplicity and his unartificial life and needed no clothing,[312] Maximus elaborates the idea that Adam was naked, not in the sense that he was without flesh or body, but to the extent that he was free from that which makes the human flesh heavier, mortal and resistant. He could live without the aid of any human technique and without any clothes, since he had detachment (ἀπάθεια) and thus had no need to have shame, and further was not subject to any extreme of cold or heat.[313] He was passionless by grace, free from needs caused by outward circumstances, and wise, since he enjoyed knowledge (γνῶσις) above the sphere of purely natural contemplation.[314]

Thus we may recognize that Maximus elaborates rather eloquently the excellency of the primitive state of man. This has been noticed by many scholars. A problem which remains, however, is how far this implies that the first man already enjoyed all the heavenly blessings, which are promised to saved sinners in the world to come. In other words we must ask how far Maximus conceives the process of salvation and deification simply in terms of a restoration to an original human state, or alternatively, how far he imagines a development of mankind which exceeds anything which characterized man in the beginning?

Heintjes takes a rather extreme position in discussing this point, claiming that it is Maximus' opinion that Adam had already acquired the full divine likeness, because he had given himself freely to God.[315] But this must be due to a misunderstanding of Maximus' own words, for according to them perfect likeness and deification are clearly put before man as a *purpose*, related to the fact that he has been created in the image of God. Only by an act of his free will could Adam realize this purpose.[316] And according to Maximus Adam failed in this destiny, since he made his wrong decision immediately (ἅμα τῷ γενέσθαι).[317] Disdier is more true to the texts, underlining that what God communicated to man in the beginning was a certain knowledge of God, linked with a desire and passion for Him, but he goes on and hazards the guess that Maximus may have regarded Adam as constituted in the state of mystical knowledge.[318] But is this not again an over-statement of the case, for spiritual life to

---

[312] Gregory Nazianzen, *Or.* 45, 8; PG 36, 632 C.

[313] Amb 45; PG 91, 1353 AB.

[314] *Ibid.;* 1353 CD.

[315] HEINTJES, BiNJ 6 (1943), p. 65 f., with ref. to Amb. 42; PG 91, 1345 D–1348 A.

[316] See Amb 42; PG 91, 1345 D.

[317] Thal 61; CCSG 22, p. 85. Cf. BLOWERS, *op. cit.*, p. 171 f., n. 154.

[318] DISDIER, EO 29 (1930), p. 305 and n. 2.

Maximus culminates in something which is above γνῶσις, a mystical union with God in love?[319]

Finally, Sherwood at one point feels bound to draw the conclusion that Maximus, at least sometimes, thinks rather simply in terms of an identity between beginning and end—in spite of his clear refutation of the Origenist myth of a primitive henad of rational beings, in which salvation consists in a return to the original unity in God. This point is all the more striking, since it is exactly this idea of identity between beginning and end which was anathematized as an Origenist error in the 15th anathema of Justinian, as Sherwood himself points out.[320] Sherwood adds, however, that Maximus' refutation of Origenism lies at a deeper level than this, and is not affected by his more or less accidental use of the cyclic argument. One could also add, that an identification of beginning and end of a kind such as we find e.g. in Amb 7, where the beginning and end of everything is identified with its intent and purpose,[321] does not necessarily imply the idea of simple restitution, since intent and purpose are terms which point forward beyond themselves. And if God is seen as the purpose of man, as well as his beginning and end, it must be borne in mind that to Maximus, God as beginning both establishes and over-bridges a distance and difference to himself. This difference is the very presupposition of movement towards Him as end and purpose; it applies to primitive man, and will never be annihilated except in a mystical sense.[322]

It is thus far from certain, that Maximus praises the state of Adam in order to give an accurate picture of the future blessings of deified man. One would rather suspect that he does so in order to under-line the unlimited possibilities which lie ahead, when man has been re-stored in Christ to his image character and is called to work out for himself, in grace, his divine purpose at the point where Adam failed to do so.

This question is, however, also linked with the problem of Maximus' relationship to some of his predecessors, for whom the concept of a double creation is particularly important in relation to the original state of the first man and the problem of restoration. We should, therefore, ask next: what is Maximus' view of this concept?

---

[319] See further ch. VI: 11 below on the process of deification.
[320] SHERWOOD, *The Earlier Ambigua*, p. 91, n. 40 and 86 with n. 34.
[321] PG 91, 1073 C. SHERWOOD, *op. cit.*, p. 91, n. 40 quotes this text.
[322] Cf. ch. II above and SHERWOOD, *op. cit.*, p. 95, n. 49, where the latter himself notices that sometimes in Maximus there is a difference between limit (πέρας) and end (τέλος).

The idea of a double creation in Maximus' predecessors

The idea of a double creation is already found in Philo, as an interpretation of the double biblical narrative of Genesis 1 and 2. Thus Philo distinguishes between the ideal man, created after the image of God (Gen. 1: 27), and the corporeal man, formed from clay (Gen. 2: 7). The first man is thus more or less identifiable with the idea of man, and is an object of thought only, incorporeal, incorruptible, neither male nor female, while the second man, who is the empirical man and is formed from matter (i.e. a πλάσμα) is the object of sensual perception, consists of body and soul, is mortal and either man or woman.[323] The first man belongs thus to the intelligible world and the second man to the sensible world.[324] No fall is here presupposed before the second creation, as there was later in Origen's interpretation, but there is a strong Platonist dualism in Philo's outlook. This dualism tends, however, to coincide with that of divine and human in a more biblical sense, since man after the image of God is to Philo also an aspect of the Logos (who contains the λόγοι).[325]

Philo's conception of a double creation was taken up by Origen but developed by him in a different direction. He gave it, on the one hand, a more Christian character by changing Philo's distinction between ideal and corporeal man into the Pauline distinction between inner and outer man, the former being identified with the soul, or particularly the mind. But on the other hand, it is a well-known fact that he combined this idea with his myth of a prehistoric fall in the intelligible world, so that this world was seen as brought into being through the first creation, while the second creation took place, when the fallen νόες had cooled down into souls, so that they needed bodies for their spiritual education.[326] There is thus, also for Origen, a man made (*factus*) after the image, who was created first, and a second man, who is formed from matter (*plasmatus*). The former was invisible, incorporeal, incorrupt, immortal; the latter corporeal, visible, etc.[327] The first man was further male and female, which means, in Origen's allegorical interpretation, that he possessed two elements constitutive of our inner man, namely the mind and the soul, while the second man consists of man and woman.[328] It is obvious,

---

[323] See Philo, *De opif. mund.* 134; COHN & WENDLAND, I, p. 46 and *Leg. alleg.* 1, 31; p. 68 f.; cf. WOLFSON, *Philo* I, p. 310.

[324] Cf. DANIÉLOU, *Sacramentum Futuri*, Paris 1950, p. 46 f., who also thinks that Paul in 1 Cor. may have reacted against this kind of understanding.

[325] This is particularly emphasized by DANIÉLOU, *Philon d'Alexandrie*, p. 173.

[326] Cf. CROUZEL, *Théologie de l'image de Dieu*, p. 149.

[327] Origen, *In Gen., hom.* 1, 13; GCS Orig. 6, p. 15.

[328] Cf. CROUZEL, *op. cit.*, p. 153.

that to Origen the doctrine of a double creation furthers an understanding of the complete work of human salvation in terms of a simple restitution and return to the original unity.

Evagrius, who is one of the most outstanding representatives of the Origenist tradition, of course follows Origen in his general interpretation. This conclusion may be drawn both directly and indirectly. Thus, also for him there is a prehistoric fall, which is defined as a movement of intelligible beings away from their original unity,[329] and afterwards a second creation, effected by God but due to the Evil One.[330] The first creation is that of the νόες,[331] the second one Christ's formation of the nature of our bodies.[332] A detailed description of the fall, causing this second creation, as disintegration of the original νοῦς, is explicitly given in the *Letter to Melania*.[333] The position of Evagrius is thus clear, and spiritual development is understood by him as a return to an original unity of intelligible beings, a conception which was one of the main points of accusation against the Origenists.

Among the Cappadocian fathers Gregory of Nyssa was most clearly influenced by the early Alexandrian writers. It is, thus, not surprising to find him also wrestling with the problem of a double creation. His understanding of it is, however, so modified in comparison with that of Origen, that it is a question of debate, whether he teaches a double creation, in the real sense of the word, or not. Gregory comes, as W. Völker has pointed out, far closer to Philo, whom he follows in referring Gen. 1 to an ideal state and Gen. 2 to the empirical man.[334] It is, however, doubtful whether one can speak about a real creation in the first case, since this ideal man—who is not yet Adam but the species of man—exists only in God's foreknowledge,[335] though as a type of a humanity, which will be realized in the body of Christ. There is, thus, to Gregory one ideal man, who is after the image of God, and who is in fact a type of a future blessed humanity. This man is not sexually differenti-

---

[329] See e.g. Evagrius, *Cent. gnost.* 1. 51; in PO 28, p. 41 f.; 6. 75; p. 249.

[330] *Cent. gnost.* 6. 36; PO 28, p. 231 ff.

[331] *Cent. gnost.* 3. 24; PO 28, p. 107.

[332] *Cent. gnost.* 3. 26; PO 28, p. 107; cf. GUILLAUMONT, *Les "Kephalaia gnostica"*, p. 109.

[333] See FRANKENBERG, *Euagrius Ponticus*, p. 617. The second part of the Syriac text of this treatise, which was unknown to Frankenberg, has been published in G. VITESTAM, *Seconde partie du traité, qui passe sous le nom de "La grande lettre d'Évagre le Pontique à Mélanie l'Ancienne".* Publiée et traduite d'après le manuscrit du British Museum Add. 17192. (Scripta minora Regiae Societatis Humaniorum Litterarum Lundensis 1963–1964:3.) Lund 1964.

[334] VÖLKER, *Gregor von Nyssa*, p. 64 with ref.

[335] *De hom. opif.* 16; PG 44, 185 B and 23; 204 D; cf. VÖLKER, *Op. cit.*, p. 64, n. 4.

ated ("male and female he created them" of Gen. 1: 27 is understood as an addition). The "second" creation, on the other hand, divides humanity into man and woman, though this does not change the pre-sexual character of the divine image in this "second" man, for the sexual distinction in the creation of Adam is made by God in view of the coming fall.[336]

In Gregory of Nyssa at least, we find no idea of a fall between the first and the second creation. The "first creation" is furthermore seen as a prefiguration of a future, blessed humanity. The decisive fall takes place *after* the second creation, though the latter is carried out with a view to the fall. In this way Gregory is able to combine a description of an original state related to the creation of the first empirical man—who is, however, himself only a representative of all the coming generations of men—with an anticipation of the blessed state to come, as it is realized through Christ. Thus in the beginning life was simple, according to Gregory, and matter—for there was, and will be matter—was light and transparent, and man possessed a spiritual body, was incorruptible, transcendent, immortal, and showed detachment, purity and absence of sexuality.[337] As this is at the same time a description of a state to come, one is tempted to draw the conclusion that Gregory, too, thinks of human spiritual development only in terms of a return. But if we bear in mind that the "first creation" is, to a greater or lesser degree, simply an anticipation, we shall see that man in Adam, empirical man, from one point of view, will never return to an original state which was his, since he has never experienced the ideal human life of the first creation. This seems to be the reason, why Adam is always regarded as similar to all other men.[338]

Whatever conclusion one may reach in relation to the question, whether Gregory of Nyssa really taught a double creation, one must agree that in him this concept has at least been modified to such an extent, that the idea of a spiritual development, which goes beyond anything which man has already experienced, is no longer excluded. This is, moreover, of importance to us, since it is at this very point, that Maximus, too, seems to have made a personal contribution.

---

[336] Cf. BURGHARDT, *The Image of God in Man*, p. 139, and VÖLKER, *op. cit.*, p. 64 with ref. It should be noticed that Gregory builds his idea exclusively on Gen. 1: 26 and 27, and not on Gen. 2: 7; cf. G. B. LADNER, The Philosophical Anthropology of Saint Gregory of Nyssa, DOP 12 (1958), p. 83.

[337] Cf. GAÏTH, *La conception de la liberté*, p. 52 ff.

[338] To Gregory he is simply the first man to have sinned. On this problem, cf. the discussion in GAÏTH, *op. cit.*, pp. 111–117, esp. p. 115 f., who has pointed out the originality of Gregory at this point.

The "garments of skin"

But before we compare Maximus with his predecessors, we should add a few remarks concerning another idea, which has been closely related to that of the double creation: the bodily interpretation of the "garments of skin" of Gen. 3: 21. From the texts of Origen, which are at our disposal, it is difficult to be sure that he identified these garments with bodies as such—though he stresses that they were taken from the animals, were fit for sinners and indicated the mortality and fragility of fallen man,[339] and argues that this interpretation is better than that of Plato: that the souls have lost their wings and fallen down[340]—but a great number of his later opponents testify unanimously, that he made this identification. We find polemics against it in Methodius, Epiphanius and other anti-Origenist documents.[341] It is, thus, quite clear that this interpretation was regarded as linked both with the doctrine of the pre-existence of souls and the prehistoric fall, and also with that of man's loss of the divine image after the fall.[342]

Evagrius—the main representative of later Origenism—however, does not provide any text, where the same identification is expressly stated, though he does know a blessed state of nakedness for the mind.[343] Macarius, on the other hand, follows Origen closely in interpreting the "garments" as the body as such.[344]

An allegorical interpretation of the "garments of skin" along the line of Origen—though in a modified form, prepared by Methodius[345]—is, however, to be found in Gregory of Nyssa, to whom this speculation became rather central. The garments are to him, of course, not the bodies as such—since he rejects the pre-existence of souls—but a certain quality of our bodily nature resulting from the fall, a bodily temperament, different from that of the ideal man of the first creation.[346] Gregory

---

[339] See Origen, *In Lev. hom.* 6, 2; GCS Orig. 6, p. 362, 14 ff. As J. QUASTEN, A Pythagorean Idea in Jerome, AJPh 63 (1942), pp. 207–215, has shown—in relation to Jerome—this interpretation contains a reference to the Pythagorean idea, that wool is a symbol of death, since it comes from an animal destined to die, a principle open to different degrees of spiritualisation; cf. BURGHARDT, Cyril of Alexandria on "Wool and Linen", *Traditio* 2 (1944), p. 486.

[340] *Contra Cels.* 4. 40; GCS Orig. 1, p. 313 f., 25 ff.

[341] See Methodius, *De resurr.* 1, 29; GCS, p. 258; and indirectly in a long quotation in Epiphanius' *Panarion,* particularly 64, 47; GCS Epiph. 2, p. 472 f.; and further Epiphanius, *ibid.* 64, 4, 9; p. 412, 12–15 and *Ancoratus* 62; GCS Epiph. 1, p. 74 f. For other documents see GUILLAUMONT, *Les "Kephalaia gnostica",* pp. 89 (Epiphanius) and 90 (Jerome).

[342] See GUILLAUMONT, *op. cit.,* p. 109, n. 131.

[343] See our discussion of the concept of mind, pp. 107–113 above.

[344] See Macarius Magnus, *Hom. in Gen.;* PG 10, 1400 C–1404 C.

[345] See *De resurr.* 1, 38–39; GCS, p. 281 ff.

[346] Cf. LADNER, *art. cit.,* p. 88 f.

agrees with Origen about the basic assumption, that "skin" symbolizes what man has in common with the animals, and the garments are thus that which was added to man as a result of his lustful sense experience of the world around him. They include all that is implied in animal nature—Gregory himself mentions sexual intercourse as the means of procreation and all the bodily characteristics of different ages in man's life.[347] The fall led through pleasure to shame and fear, and in the end to the covering of man with these garments, which Gregory calls dead and which are a sign of man's present mortality.[348] Sexuality is the most prominent sign of their existence to Gregory, who, for personal reasons, took an exceptionally negative attitude to marriage. But he presupposes a refined bodily character before the fall—garments of light[349]—renewed in Christ,[350] and a possible fulfilment of the destiny of mankind above sexual differentiation in accordance with this superior bodily nature.[351]

We find, however, a still more modified form of the same speculation in Gregory Nazianzen, which shows that the allegorical interpretation of the "garments of skin" along lines similar to those of Origen is not necessarily linked with Gregory of Nyssa's particular negativism in relation to sexual life. Gregory Nazianzen thus simply states that the specific resistence and slowness of human flesh, as we all know it, may be a consequence of the fall, symbolized by the "garments of skin", but that our present bodies are, in spite of this fact, not very different from that which man had before the fall.[352]

Maximus and the concept of a double creation

What now is Maximus' relationship to this tradition of *Genesis* exegesis? Sherwood is of the opinion that Maximus easily accepted "Gregory of Nyssa's doctrine of a double creation . . . which argues back from the state of man in heaven (Matt. 22: 30) to the state in paradise."[353] We have, however, already seen reason to doubt, whether Gregory holds a doctrine of a double creation in the real sense of the word, since the primitive state

---

[347] See *De anim. et resurr.;* PG 46, 148 C–149 A; cf. Daniélou, *Platonisme et théologie mystique*, p. 55 f.

[348] *De virg.* 12; Jaeger 8, 1, p. 302.

[349] Corresponding to the old idea of garments of linen; cf. Quasten, *art. cit.*, p. 212.

[350] The relationship between this idea and the baptismal rites has been elaborated by Daniélou, *op. cit.*, pp. 25–31.

[351] Cf. Daniélou, *op. cit.*, p. 56 f.

[352] See J. Plagnieux, *Saint Grégoire de Nazianze Théologien*, Paris 1951, p. 426 f. Cyril of Alexandria regarded garments of wool as a symbol of death, but does not seem to have made explicit references to the "garments of skin" of Gen. 3: 21; see Burghardt, *art. cit.*, p. 484.

[353] Sherwood, *The Earlier Ambigua*, p. 91, n. 40.

of man to which he "argues back" perhaps represents a divine intention more than an established reality.[354] And we have further seen, that Gregory Nazianzen—whose influence on Maximus is at least more explicit than that of Gregory of Nyssa—represents an element of the same tradition, but in a still more modified form. An easy acceptance of a double creation idea need, therefore, not at all be presupposed.

There is, in fact, one text, Thal 1, where Maximus comes at least very close to a doctrine of a double creation in the modified form we have found in Gregory of Nyssa, and where he also refers explicitly to Gregory as his teacher at this particular point. The question is whether the Stoic cardinal passions—desire ($\dot{\epsilon}\pi\iota\theta\upsilon\mu\dot{\iota}\alpha$), lust ($\dot{\eta}\delta o\nu\dot{\eta}$), fear ($\varphi\dot{o}\beta o\varsigma$) and grief ($\lambda\dot{\upsilon}\pi\eta$)—are evil in themselves or only through misuse. Maximus answers by referring to the idea that the passions were not created together with the rest of man, but introduced into the irrational part of his soul after the fall. In spite of this, they can, however, be good, if they are used in obedience to Christ, and this can be exemplified in relation to all the four passions mentioned.[355] We see that Maximus' interest is here very similar to that of Gregory. But in this text there is no reference at all to man's bodily character, nor is the word creation used in relation to the introduction of the passions into the life of man. One is, in fact, left free to guess for oneself, how these secondary conditions were brought about.

At this last point Thal 61, however, gives more information. For there we learn that sensible lust and pain were not created together with human nature. But there was in man a capacity for another lust ($\dot{\eta}\delta o\nu\dot{\eta}$), according to the $\nu o\hat{\upsilon}\varsigma$, a spiritual kind of pleasure. And we are informed that this very capacity was misused by man and directed towards the sensible world. It was, thus, itself turned into unnatural lust. God, then, in his providence inserted into man pain ($\dot{o}\delta\dot{\upsilon}\nu\eta$) as a necessary consequence and counterpart to sensible lust—in accordance with which the law of death was also rooted in man.[356] We see, therefore, that there is in Maximus' mind no idea of a real second creation, but rather of providentially introduced consequences of man's misuse of his capacity for true pleasure.

We learn further, here indirectly and in other texts, that after the fall, as another consequence, a law of procreation through conception and birth ($\gamma\dot{\epsilon}\nu\nu\eta\sigma\iota\varsigma$), is providentially introduced into man's life by God.[357]

---

[354] See above, p. 148.

[355] Thal 1; CCSG 7, p. 47 f. For a rendering of part of this text, see BLOWERS, *op. cit.*, p. 89, n. 172.

[356] CCSG 22, p. 85.

[357] See e.g. Amb 42; PG 91, 1317 A.

This is a secondary law of human nature—implying "conception through sowing and birth through destruction" (i.e. destruction of virginity)[358]—which is, however, later broken through Christ's coming into existence (his birth from a virgin), renewing the "first and truly divine" laws of human life.[359] Maximus also says explicitly that he takes it for granted that in the beginning there was another way of procreation available to man, had he not disobeyed God's commandment.[360]

It is, however, very difficult to say, whether these statements imply that Maximus regarded this secondary introduction of laws and consequences as a "second creation" even in the sense we have discussed in relation to Gregory of Nyssa. First of all, because of what he says in the text we have just cited; if another way of procreation other than that through lust was available to man, then the latter must have been potentially present, for neither of them was manifested until after Adam's decisive choice; secondly, because there seems to be a difference between Gregory's and Maximus' positions. What Maximus has learned from Gregory is, according to his own words, that something was introduced by God into man's nature after the fall, but, obviously, not that there was in the first place a divine conception of ideal man as mankind, and afterwards a creation of Adam as the first of all men. But if there is a real doctrine of double creation in Gregory, it must primarily be referred to this type of dualism. For the introduction of certain bodily elements into man's life after the fall—to which Maximus refers—is according to Gregory provisionally prepared for, when Adam is created. Adam is, as we have seen, not different from other men. In Maximus, on the contrary, the first man and Adam seem to be identical. We are thus almost forced to conclude, that where Gregory has a doctrine, which does resemble an idea of a double creation, Maximus probably does not follow him, and in those places where he follows him, he hardly professes the double creation at all. There is, then, no need for us to talk about an idea of double creation in Maximus.

Maximus and the "garments of skin"

Before we close this section with this negative conclusion we should, however, add a few words about Maximus and the interpretation of the "garments of skin". There is, it seems, only one text, Amb 45, where Maximus shows, indirectly, that he is aware of the Origenist and

---

[358] *Ibid.;* 1341 C.
[359] See Amb 31; 1276 B–C and 41; 1313 CD.
[360] Amb 41; 1309 A.

Gregorian interpretation. But it is rather characteristic, that his treatment of the problem there is made in relation, not to Gregory of Nyssa, but to a particular expression of Gregory Nazianzen, on whom he is commenting.[361] We have already presented its content: Adam was naked, not in the sense that he was without flesh or body—obviously a polemic against the Origenist interpretation—but in the sense that he was free from that which makes the flesh heavier, mortal and resistent. He was also free from worldly needs of different kinds. This last statement comes in fact very close to Gregory of Nyssa's understanding of the difference between the first man and sinful man, but it seems surprising, exactly for this reason, that Maximus does neither refer to Gregory's interpretation of the garments of skin nor to a double creation. On the contrary, he takes Adam's nakedness rather literally, in that he says that he needed no clothes, because he felt neither cold nor shame. Maximus seems, thus, to agree with Gregory that changes in man's bodily temperament took place after the fall—as well as agreeing with him about the non-sexual state of man in the beginning—but he does not refer this agreement to a common interpretation of the "garments of skin." At this point he bases himself on Gregory Nazianzen with his far more modified position.

It is difficult not to see in this attitude a certain cautiousness over against anything that could be suspected of Origenist heresies, even when he could rely upon the authority of Gregory of Nyssa. It is also difficult not to see in this cautiousness a rather high evaluation of man's bodily make-up, which would have been in harmony with his whole conviction about man as a composite nature.

2.   Adam's fall and its causes

Maximus' general opinions about the character of man's fall and its consequences do not distinguish him from other ancient Christian Fathers. It may, therefore, be sufficient here to give a short summary of what Maximus has to say at this point. There are, however, a few details in his presentation, which seem to be more personal or original, and in relation to them we shall try to mark out his relationship to earlier writers.

Man's fault and the Devil's seduction

Maximus shares, of course, a general Christian conviction, that God did not cause man to fall. The original sin is the fault of man, but it is also

---

[361] Gregory Nazianzen, *Or.* 45, 8; PG 36, 632 C.

due to the persuasive attacks of the Devil. Maximus refers explicitly both to man's misuse of his natural freedom and to the Devil's seduction, and sees no contradiction in this combination. In one and the same text (Thal 61) he speaks exclusively about man's fault in one place,[362] and about the seduction of the Devil as active cause of evil in another;[363] and in a short reference to the fall, he may either, as at the end of Amb 38, stress that the Devil wounded man through the thorn of pleasure and thus brought him to destruction,[364] or, in a similar passage, such as the summary given in Amb 8, not mention the Devil at all.[365] In either case an important element of human freedom is left: the Devil tries to persuade, or again man is tempted by his middle position in the world, but it is man who decides. Freedom belongs to human nature, is part of man's image character, but he uses it to his own destruction.

This view is, in its turn, connected with Maximus' understanding of evil. Evil is conceived in entirely negative terms. To Maximus, as to Ps.-Denis, evil has no substantial existence.[366] In the Prologue to *Quest. ad Thal.* Maximus defines evil either as ignorance of the Cause of things, or as failure to direct one's natural energies towards man's true End.[367] And it is nothing more than that, Maximus adds, before he goes on to a *formally* positive definition: an irrational movement of the natural faculties towards something else than this end.[368] Thus, the decisive point in evil is this failure, this non-fulfilment of natural human capacities, in which man turns away from God, and the whole story of the fall of Adam may be described accordingly.

Consequently, Maximus tells us that the Devil, who had fallen because of pride and was jealous of man, wanting him to share his fall,[369] covered his jealousy with benevolence and persuaded man to direct his desire towards other things than the Cause of all, and thus effected in him ignorance of this Cause.[370] The Devil thus seduced man through a stratagem, pretending to be benevolent and appealing to man's self-love (φιλαυτία).[371] But, on the other hand, the fall was also for this reason

---

[362] CCSG 22, p. 85.
[363] *Ibid.*, p. 95.
[364] PG 91, 1301 A.
[365] PG 91, 1104 AB.
[366] See the Scholies to Ps.-Denis; PG 4, 304 D; cf. von Balthasar, KL², p. 143.
[367] CCSG 7, p. 35 and p. 29, respectively.
[368] CCSG 7, p. 29 ff.
[369] Thal 61; CCSG 22, p. 95.
[370] Thal, *Prol.*, CCSG 7, p. 29 ff.
[371] Ep 2; PG 91, 396 D.

entirely man's fault, for he let himself be persuaded by the pleasure (ἡδονή) which the Devil suggested,[372] and thus he freely turned
his natural capacity for spiritual pleasure (ἡδονή) towards the
sensible world, preferring its pleasures to God. This perversion of true
enjoyment was made effective in relation to the sensible world.[373]
Man became not only ignorant but acquired a certain likeness to
the animals,[374] and he used his intellectual capacities for seeking
more pleasure, his self-love (φιλαυτία) always aiming at sensual lust
(ἡδονή).[375]

Sensual pleasure, however, always involves its negative counterpart,
pain (ὀδύνη),[376] a provision through which God has introduced a punitive
and purgative counter-force into fallen man's life.[377] This now causes
man—further inspired by the Devil—to find out methods, by which to
seek for pleasure and escape from pain, and these methods are the new
object of man's intellectual activity.[378] He tries to separate lust and pain,
but is always bound to cause pain by seeking lust, and to try to escape
from pain by seeking more pleasure,[379] and this is all in accordance with
the Devil's intention—who has now gained power over man through his
bodily temptations,[380]—for nothing pleases him more, says Maximus,
than to see man punished and plagued.[381] Man is no longer free, since he
has made his fatal decision and turned his attention to the pleasures of
the sensible world.

In the picture which we have now given, there are two elements which
are of particular interest, since they seem to be personal characteristics of
Maximus. One of them is the insistence on self-love (φιλαυτία) as the
root of evil in man. This aspect, however, will be treated at length in
connection with our study of Maximus' hierarchy of the vices. The other
element is Maximus' combination of pleasure with pain, in order to form
a pair—open to a play upon words—which summarizes, as it were in
one formula, the mechanisms of the fallen state of man. Here a few
remarks should be added.

---

[372] *Loc. cit.*
[373] Thal 61; CCSG 22, p. 85.
[374] Cf. Thal 1; CCSG 7, p. 47.
[375] Thal, *Prol.*, CCSG 7, p. 31.
[376] *Ibid.;* p. 31.
[377] Thal 61; CCSG 22, p. 85.
[378] Ep 2; PG 91, 396 D–397 A; cf. Thal, *Prol.;* CCSG 7, p. 31 ff.
[379] Thal 61; CCSG 22, p. 89.
[380] Thal 49; CCSG 7, p. 361.
[381] Thal 26; CCSG 7, p. 173 ff.

The dialectic of pleasure and pain

Maximus' opinion on pleasure and pain, seen in a general perspective, obviously has a background in Stoic thinking, for which ἡδονή, together with its counterpart grief (λύπη), belonged to the four basic passions of man and was entirely foreign to reason.[382] Maximus speaks, however, also of ἡδονή in a positive sense, since man is said to have a natural capacity for spiritual pleasure.[383] As we have underlined in our discussion of the problem of double creation, it is this capacity which is perverted, when man turns towards the sensible world. Maximus also uses the same word in a positive sense about the pleasure of the soul in relation to its virtues,[384] and thinks that even the sense of pleasure which is added to man after the fall may become valuable under obedience to Christ.[385]

Gregory of Nyssa, for whom the term ἡδονή plays a parallel rôle in describing the nature of the fall[386] and who regards it as one of the properties of the "garments of skin",[387] seems to be more hesitant than Maximus at this point. For Gregory says explicitly, that he usually restricts the term ἡδονή to bodily pleasure and avoids it in spiritual contexts.[388] This is, however, not to say that he excludes any positive use of passion in the service of Christian asceticism.[389] Here anyhow, is a characteristic difference between Gregory and Maximus, who appears as less 'Stoic' in this respect. Maximus seems to come closer to Nemesius, who attributes a positive function to ἡδονή taken in the true sense of the word.[390]

It is, however, the dialectic between pleasure and pain, which is of a special interest in this context, for it seems to be more energetically put forward by Maximus than by his predecessors. His play with the words ἡδονή—ὀδύνη is particularly original, but he shares with e.g. Gregory of

---

[382] See e.g. Diog. Laërt. in VON ARNIM, *Stoic. vet. fragm.* I, p. 51, no. 210; UEBERWEG—PRAECHTER, *op. cit.,* p. 429.

[383] Thal 61; CCSG 22, p. 85. The Cyrenaic school regarded ἡδονή as one of the basic desires of human nature, but the Stoics rejected this assumption (VON ARNIM, *op. cit.* 3, p. 54, no. 229 a). Cf. STÄHLIN, *art.* ἡδονή, φιλήδονος, in G. KITTEL, *Theologisches Wörterbuch zum Neuen Testament 2,* 1933–35, p. 916.

[384] Thal 58; CCSG 22, p. 37.

[385] Thal 1; CCSG 7, p. 47 ff. HAUSHERR, *Philautie,* p. 60 f., has underlined the importance of this positive aspect.

[386] *De virg.* 12; JAEGER 8, 1, p. 302.

[387] *De mortuis;* PG 46, 524 D.

[388] *In Psalm.* 1, 2; PG 44, 437 A; cf. DANIÉLOU, *Platonisme et théologie mystique,* p. 238.

[389] Cf. VÖLKER, *Gregor von Nyssa,* p. 118, n. 9.

[390] See Nemesius, *De nat. hom.* 18; PG 40, 680 C.

Nyssa the tendency to put ἡδονή at the very root of sin.[391] Yet, the background of the dialectic seems clear. In general Maximus may refer to a long philosophical and Christian tradition.

In Greek philosophy ἡδονή is usually regarded as a counterpart to, or in interplay with, an opposite negative feeling. The latter may either be toil (πόνος), as in Anaxagoras[392] or in the Cyrenaic school,[393] or grief (λύπη) as in Aristotle,[394] or among the Stoics, who divide the four basic passions into two couples, each consisting of one positive and one negative feeling: ἡδονή—λύπη and ἐπιθυμία—φόβος,[395] or in Porphyry, who regards ἡδονή and λύπη as two passions, growing out of sense perception (αἴσθησις).[396]

In Philo and among Christian writers this tradition may be further followed. Philo follows the Stoics in his considerations of the basic passions and upholds a dialectic between pleasure and grief.[397] Clement of Alexandria sees e.g. ἡδονή in close connection with sensual desire (ἐπιθυμία) and combines this connection with the affirmation, that ἐπιθυμία is a kind of grief (λύπη), which lacks something and thus longs for it.[398] Evagrius knows of a dialectic between ἡδονή and λύπη,[399] and the same dialectic is found later in the Evagrian tradition, in Nilus,[400] but is also an important element in Nemesius of Emesa's understanding of human passions. Finally, Nemesius' later excerptist, Meletius the Monk, defines λύπη as the state of a soul, deprived of pleasures (ἡδονίαι),[401] while earlier Gregory of Nyssa affirms that every ἡδονή is combined with toil (πόνος), thus returning to the older alternative expression.[402]

It seems clear that Maximus wants to elaborate the older Christian understanding, which was developed on a mostly Stoic basis, of pleasure

---

[391] This position of ἡδονή is developed in Alexandrian thinking to an extent, which is unknown in Stoic tradition; cf. VÖLKER, *op. cit.,* p. 88. Combining it intimately with self-love (which is to him the source of all vices), Maximus sees it as a force, which has—in its interplay with ὀδύνη—brought upon man all the slime of evils (Thal, *Prol.;* CCSG 7, p. 37 ff.).

[392] See DIELS, *Doxogr.,* p. 398, no. 16 ff.

[393] Cf. STÄHLIN, *art. cit.,* p. 914 f.

[394] *De anim.* 3, 7; 431 a, 9 ff.; *Eth. Nicom.* 2, 4; 1105 b, 23.

[395] UEBERWEG—PRAECHTER, *op. cit.,* I; p. 429.

[396] *De abst.* 1, 33.

[397] See e.g *Quod Deus sit immutabilis,* 98; COHN & WENDLAND 2, p. 77, and *Quod det. pot. insid. soleat,* 46; COHN & WENDLAND, I, p. 268 f.

[398] *Strom.* 3, 5; GCS Clem. 2, p. 215, 7.

[399] See *Pract.* 1. 10; PG 40, 1224 C; cf. the fragments of *Par. Gr.* 913 (no. 21) and 3098 (no. 5), Mus 44 (1931), pp. 376 and 381.

[400] *De monach. praest.* 11; PG 79, 1073 B. For Nemesius, see e.g. *De nat. hom.,* 16; PG 40, 673 A.

[401] *De nat. hom.;* PG 64, 1136 B.

[402] *In Christi resurr., or.* 1; PG 46, 604 A.

as at the root of evil and as always combined with its negative counter-part. But he does it by use of a dialectic, in which this counterpart is usually not called toil or grief but pain (ὀδύνη). That his intention is to put pain in the place of grief in the Stoic system seems to be manifested by the fact that he also combines a "positive" couple of passions, ἡδονή—ἐπιθυμία with a negative one, ὀδύνη—φόβος, where ὀδύνη has taken the place of λύπη.[403] In the same writing he shows, at the same time, that he is well acquainted with the four basic passions of the Stoic system.[404] But on the other hand, he establishes even a certain parallelism between the couple pleasure—pain and the division of the soul into concupiscible and irascible (ἐπιθυμία—θυμός)[405] which are natural ele-ments in man, thus pointing out—in a more Christian than Stoic way—that at least after the fall both pleasure and pain have become natural to man.

He is thus free to depict—in a personal way—all the grave conse-quences of the fall, pertaining to all men, as results of the function of this basic dialectic of pleasure and pain.

3. Consequences of the fall

All the disastrous consequences of man's fall may thus, according to Maximus, be seen as resulting from the dialectic between pleasure and pain in which man has been caught through his preference of sense pleasure to spiritual pleasure, the only pleasure which is truly satisfying for him as a rational being. Maximus develops this line of thinking with great consistency.

Laws of pleasure and destruction

The most basic consequence is the fact that the physical mode of man's life is changed and marked by pleasure and pain. Man was destined to live eternally, but through his choice of temporal, sensible pleasure he called upon himself—according to God's good counsel—a pain, which introduced into his life a law of death, which—seen from the aspect of

---

[403] Thal, *Prol.;* CCSG 7, p. 39. Occasionally the couple ἡδονή—ὀδύνη seems to be found also in Evagrius (see *Tract. ad Eul. monach.* 11; PG 79, 1108 B), but it is Maximus who has made it a fixed element in his system.

[404] Thal 1; CCSG 7, p. 47 ff. Maximus himself explicitly uses the couple ἡδονή—λύπη (as equivalent of ὀδύνη) and identifies πόνος and λύπη in Thal 58; CCSG 22, pp. 22–37.—On this dialectic in Thal, see SCHÖNBORN, Plaisir et douleur . . . , in HEINZER-SCHÖNBORN, *Maximus Confessor,* pp. 273–284.

[405] DALMAIS, Un traité de théologie contemplative, RAM 29 (1953), p. 135, has noticed this parallelism.

the divine purpose—is there to put an end to his destructive escape from his natural goal.[406] Death is thus the culmination of pain. On the other hand, man is still created to live, and mankind gains its life, after the fall, by means of that very lust, sexual intercourse, which is an excellent example of sense pleasure, and which also leads to a birth through pain. The law of death, putting an end to individual life, has its counterpart in a law of pleasure, regulating new physical life.[407] These laws constitute the collective imprisonment of fallen man, from which he cannot escape,[408] except through Christ, who took upon himself freely to be born as man without lust[409] and die as a sinner without necessity.[410] Adam's coming into existence ($\gamma \acute{\epsilon} \nu \epsilon \sigma \iota \varsigma$) has been transformed by his fall into a law of conception and birth ($\gamma \acute{\epsilon} \nu \nu \eta \sigma \iota \varsigma$)—another play upon words—but through Christ's birth ($\gamma \acute{\epsilon} \nu \nu \eta \sigma \iota \varsigma$) without pleasure this law of lust was broken and the law of death was, through his voluntary death without sin, transformed from a judgment of death because of sin, into judgment upon sin.[411] Christ alone could break what Maximus calls the tyrannical rule of beginning and end, characteristic of human nature after the fall.[412]

There are, however, also other and more individualized consequences of the fall, equally related to the dialectic of pleasure and pain. Hausherr has justly entitled a central section of his work on self-love in Maximus "La philautie en quête de plaisir . . . et manquant le bonheur."[413] For having turned his attention to the sensible world of corruptible things man will always experience that they cannot satisfy his desire, and by trying to make them steadfast and lasting, he will simply increase their corruptibility.[414] And yet, he cannot escape from seeking his satisfaction there. His nature has been turned towards passion, corruptibility and death. This is his judgment, his curse.[415]

Maximus elaborates the sense of Adam's curse through an allegorical interpretation of Gen. 3: 17–19. The cursed ground is Adam's flesh, which through the works of Adam, i.e. the passions and vices of his earth-bound mind, always remains cursed with infertility in relation to virtues, i.e. the works of God. And he will eat of this soil in great pain

---

[406] Thal 61; CCSG 22, p. 85.
[407] Loc. cit.
[408] Ibid.; CCSG 22, p. 87.
[409] Ibid.; CCSG 22, p. 91.
[410] Ibid.; CCSG 22, p. 91 ff.
[411] Ibid.; p. 93. Cf. Amb 42; PG 91, 1317 A.
[412] Thal 61; ibid., p. 93.
[413] HAUSHERR, Philautie, p. 60 f.
[414] Thal, Prol.; CCSG 7, p. 39.
[415] Thal 42; CCSG 7, p. 287.

(ὀδύνη) and grief (λύπη), enjoying just that small amount of pleasure (ἡδονή), which it has to give.[416] This flesh brings forth to him troubles and anxieties as thorns and thistles; he has to eat his bread in the sweat of his face, i.e. in the toil and labour of the inquisitive act of sense perception, and to find his temporal sustenance through self-invented means and techniques.[417]

Three fundamental evils

Maximus can also say, that fallen man suffers from three fundamental evils, from which spring the whole company of vices and passions: *ignorance, self-love* and *tyranny*, which depend on one another and sustain one another.[418] Ignorance (ἄγνοια) is lack of knowledge of God as the good Cause of all things, and implies entire absence of divine perception and of the healthy movement which is connected with the virtues. It means that there is no understanding of what is truly good and no reasonable motion according to the divine purpose.[419] This ignorance causes man to go on searching for satisfaction in the corruptible world of the senses. And this strengthens man's self-love (φιλαυτία), which is the root of all the vices, which though they can be enumerated in different ways always first of all include passions of bodily lust and expressions of human pride.[420] Through the senses man continually receives sensations, impulses and suggestions, to which he is moved in diverse directions, as his will is inspired. And there arises in the individual, as well as in humanity as a whole, a number of competing opinions and imaginations, which divide the one human nature and cut it asunder.[421] It is divided into thousands of pieces.[422] This is the expression of the third principal evil: tyranny (τυραννίς), which implies both a tyranny of the passions in the individual soul (this is the classical use of the word in relation to human vices) but also—through a division of mankind—tyranny against other human beings, sharing the same nature. When love for God—which was in the beginning open to man—was transformed by him into constant self-love, it also immediately excluded love for the neighbour.[423]

---

416 Thal 5; CCSG 7, p. 65.
417 *Ibid.;* CCSG 7, p. 65.
418 Ep 2; PG 91, 397 A.
419 Thal 64; CCSG 22, p. 193.
420 Thal: *Prol.;* CCSG 7, p. 33. See further ch. V: A, 1, pp. 243–246 below.
421 Ep 2; PG 91, 396 D.
422 Thal, *Prol.;* CCSG 7, p. 33.
423 See the whole of Ep 2 and especially PG 91, 397 A.

Maximus thus develops the consequences of fallen man's dependence upon the dialectic of pleasure and pain in a personal way, though he is in general agreement with the ascetic Christian tradition before him. We shall follow aspects of this dependence in the next chapters; here it may be sufficient just to state the fact. There is, however, one more point of particular interest in Maximus' view of the original state and fall of man, which ought to be treated before this chapter is closed—his interpretation of the trees of Paradise—because it helps to distinguish his personal position.

4. The trees of Paradise

Maximus says in one place that in relation to the interpretation of the two principal trees of Paradise, the doctors of the Church, though capable of dwelling at length on this element of Scripture, have found it wise to honour most of this mystery in silence.[424] This statement contains a remarkable historical truth. There are, in fact, comparatively few interpretations of the trees of Paradise to be found in the writings of the Fathers of the Church. This is rather surprising, since speculation upon this theme ought to have been central. A certain hesitation before the mysteries of the economy of salvation seems to have exerted a restricting influence.

Earlier Christian interpretations

Before we go to Maximus himself, we ought, however, to mention a few instances, where an interpretation is given. First of all there is an early typological interpretation of the tree of life as prefiguring Christ, e.g. in Ambrose,[425] or the Cross of Christ, e.g. in Irenaeus,[426] but there is also an antithetic parallelism between the tree of disobedience, which was the beginning of sin, and the tree of the Cross, which put an end to sin, in Cyril of Jerusalem.[427]

Within the field of allegorical interpretation a foundation had been laid already by Philo, for whom Paradise symbolizes virtue in general. The trees of Paradise are, thus, interpreted by him as different virtues, and the tree of life as the principal virtue, goodness.[428] Of specific

---

[424] Thal 43; CCSG 7, p. 293.

[425] Cf. DANIÉLOU, *Sacramentum futuri*, p. 16.

[426] Cf. *ibid.*, p. 34.

[427] Cf. *ibid.*, p. 31.

[428] See e.g. *Leg. alleg.* 1, 59; COHN & WENDLAND, I, p. 75 f. and *De migr. Abr.* 37; COHN & WENDLAND, 2, p. 275. Cf. DANIÉLOU, *op. cit.*, p. 47, with other references.

interest, however, is Philo's interpretation of the tree of knowledge; he says of this, that one cannot quite gather from the text, whether it is inside or outside Paradise, but concludes, that in its essence it is inside but in relation to its power it is outside. It is in fact closely linked with the authoritative part of the soul, τὸ ἡγεμονικόν (in the Stoic sense), and this does not function within Paradise in man at present.[429]

Philo's influence is, however, hardly noticeable in Clement of Alexandria. (It comes back most clearly as late as in Gregory of Nyssa.) In interpreting the tree of knowledge Clement refers to the fact that Scripture itself denotes sexual intercourse as a kind of "knowing". This is, he concludes, the secondary knowledge, which the tree of knowledge represents. The tree of life represents another kind of knowledge, i.e. of the truth itself.[430] But Clement also gives a Christological interpretation of the tree of life. Thus he interprets Paradise as the created world, in which the Logos has grown up (as the tree of life) and has borne fruit in becoming man, and on his cross the life of men is fixed.[431]

Origen, who points out that the trees of Paradise should not be interpreted literally,[432] follows quite another line.[433] He goes back to the earlier understanding, which we found in Irenaeus, of the tree of life as referring to the Cross, but combines it with reference to the double character of the tree of the Cross, on which not only the Good (Christ) but also the Evil (the powers of this world) have been fixed, according to Paul (see Col. 2: 14–15). This interpretation thus logically leads to an identification of the tree of life and the tree of knowledge of good and evil, which in its turn serves as an argument among others in favour of Origen's idea of general restoration, or *apokatastasis*.[434]

This last interpretation seems to have been of importance for Gregory of Nyssa, who elaborated and refined it. In Gregory we also recognize Philo's interpretation of Paradise as a place of virtues,[435] but his interpretation of the two trees as virtually one is his most important contribution in this context. The argumentation is rather complex and is elaborated in relation to the Song of Songs 5: 5, the myrrh being

---

[429] *Leg. alleg.* 1, 59; COHN & WENDLAND, I, p. 75 f.
[430] *Strom.* 3, 17; GCS Clem. 2, p. 244.
[431] *Strom.* 5, 11; GCS Clem. 2, p. 374 f.
[432] *Sel. in Gen.;* PG 12, 100 A.
[433] Correctly or not, Jerome accuses Origen of having interpreted the trees in Paradise, allegorically, as angels (*Lib. contra Ioann. Hierosol.* 7; PL 23, 360 C).
[434] Origen, *In lib. Iesu nave, hom.* 8, 6; GCS Orig. 7, esp. p. 342; cf. VON BALTHASAR, KL[2], p. 356 f. and SHERWOOD, *The Earlier Ambigua*, p. 210 f.
[435] *In Cant. cant., hom.* 9; PG 44, 965 B; Cf. DANIÉLOU, *Sacramentum futuri*, p. 50 f.—On Paradise as a place of virtues, see further ch. VI: 7, p. 383 f. below.

understood as a symbol of death, and it leads Gregory to show how the soul may rise from death through death.[436] In Paradise, he says, God's commandment was the law of life, announcing that man should not die,[437] and the tree of life stood in the middle of Paradise. But also the death-promoting tree is said to have been in the middle, though there could be no room for both trees in the very middle.[438] Gregory argues further, that one and the same circle cannot have two centres.[439] Thus, the middle of God's plantation is life, and death has no root and no place of its own to grow.[440] This is to say, that death has no substance of its own, it is just absence of life. When the tree of knowledge is said to be of good and evil, it does not interfere with this interpretation, for what is called good is that which appears as good from the point of view of lust ($\dot{\eta}\delta o\nu\dot{\eta}$), and what is called evil is that which gives the opposite feeling. The name which the death-giving fruits of this tree are correctly given is sin.[441] Life is gained through participation in life, and death through the removal of life. But since one who is dead to virtue, lives in evil, also one who is dead in evil, comes to life for virtue. This is the way in which the Maiden opens to her friend, the Logos, her hands dropping with myrrh.

Maximus' interpretation

We have dwelt in detail upon this interpretation of Gregory, because there are indications which show, that it must have been present to the mind of Maximus in relation to his own interpretation. We may leave the question of Gregory's acceptance of Origen's conclusions regarding *apokatastasis,* which has been the dominant interest in von Balthasar's and Sherwood's discussion of Origen's and Gregory's influence upon Maximus at this point,[442] until a later moment,[443] but we cannot avoid a comparison between Gregory and Maximus in relation to their understanding of the trees of Paradise as such.

For what is interesting to us in this respect, seems to be the primary point of contact between their interpretations. We saw that Gregory felt bound to conclude that what is referred to as good concerning the tree of knowledge is just what seems good to sensual lust ($\dot{\eta}\delta o\nu\dot{\eta}$). Now, this is

---

[436] *In Cant. cant., hom.* 12; PG 44, 1020 B.
[437] 1020 C.
[438] *Ibid.;* 1020 D.
[439] 1021 A.
[440] 1021 B.
[441] 1021 CD.
[442] For this discussion in relation to Maximus, see VON BALTHASAR, KL², pp. 355–359 and SHERWOOD, *The Earlier Ambigua,* pp. 210–214.
[443] See our short indications in ch. VI (p. 371 ff., esp. p. 372, n. 256).

exactly the starting-point of Maximus' understanding. It harmonizes well
with his own dialectic of pleasure and pain. And thus he affirms that what
is characteristic of the tree of knowledge, is that it gives a mixed
experience, referring to the experience of both pleasure and pain through
sense perception.[444] He thus agrees with Gregory in his basic assumption
about the tree of knowledge, and he accepts as a possible conclusion, that
this tree may be interpreted simply as the sensible and visible world,
which gives to fallen man this mixed experience.

But unlike Gregory, he does not stop at this point, but goes on to give
this fact a positive interpretation. In a sense, he obviously wants to accept
good as good and evil as evil. This discernment of the senses is, therefore,
to him not only an illusion, as one might expect Gregory to conclude, but
also refers to a reality, which should be rightly understood. Maximus
does not want to accept such an identification between the tree of
knowledge and the visible world, as is combined with a denial of the
reality implied in the tree of knowledge, and in the end a depreciation of
the created world.

And thus he goes on to say, that *what* he has accepted is true also from
another point of view: since creation possesses λόγοι of visible things,
which nourish the mind, and a natural power, which delights the senses,
it may be called the tree of knowledge of good and evil, for contemplated
spiritually it contains knowledge of good, but grasped according to the
flesh, it gives knowledge of evil.[445] The tree of knowledge opens in itself
an alternative. Identified with the visible creation—which to Maximus is
one way of interpreting it—it offers the good fruits of spiritual contemplation of the λόγοι, and the evil fruits of mere sense perception. The
view-point of Gregory has slowly been transformed.

In the rest of the same text Maximus draws further logical conclusions
within the field of the economy of salvation. The two trees represent two
different ways of human development, which are both intended for man.
God, forbidding man to eat of the tree of knowledge, postponed its use,
i.e. contemplation of the created and visible world, and put before man
the other alternative: knowledge of God as man's Cause through intellectual and practical reflection upon himself (i.e. probably as bearing the
image of God), a way which would lead to detachment and unchangeableness, strengthened through immortality by grace, and finally to
deification. Only then would man as god and united with God be
prepared to contemplate the visible world.[446] But man failed, disobeyed

444 Thal, *Prol.;* SSCG 7, p. 35.
445 *Ibid.,* p. 37.
446 Thal, *Prol.;* CCSG 7, p. 37.

the commandment and fell into the grip of the senses. The tree of life, which should safeguard man's immortality by grace, was rejected in favour of the tree of knowledge, which then becomes a tree giving both good and evil. In the end Maximus indicates that there are other, and deeper interpretations, but he passes them over in silence, without giving a hint at their content.

In his answer to Question 43 of Thalassius, Maximus is, however, forced to return to the problem, and we get more details of his view. Thalassius has asked directly about the difference between the trees, referring to Prov. 3: 18, where Wisdom is said to be the tree of life, a text which thus implies that the latter is also a tree of discernment, and now Maximus cannot wholly avoid the problem. In his answer he shows again that Gregory's interpretation is in his mind, for here he seems to go back to what Gregory said about life and death: death is absence of life. There is, thus, a big difference between the trees, since one is the tree of life, and the other must be of non-life, the death-giving tree,[447] and if one is wisdom, the other is not. The tree of life is, therefore, also mind, and the tree of knowledge (the senses) of the body, for mind and reason are characteristic of wisdom, while the contrary contains only absence of reason, and sensibility. This argumentation, however, does not lead Maximus immediately to Gregory's conclusion, that the tree of knowledge is a kind of nullity, or that there is no separate tree of knowledge.

Maximus prefers to continue, in a characteristic way, by demonstrating a similarity in relation to a differentiation, and a difference in relation to this similarity: Thalassius has put a correct question, for what is common to the two trees is that both are trees of discernment, of differentiation, but what makes them different in their discernment is the object of it. Thus the mind, which is related to the tree of life, discerns between intelligible and sensible, temporal and eternal; but the senses discern—and here Maximus comes back to his earlier interpretation—between pleasure and pain. Therefore, if man discerns only between pleasure and pain in a bodily sense, he breaks the divine commandment and eats of the tree of knowledge of good and evil, but if he discerns only between eternal and temporal, he keeps the commandment and eats of the tree of life.[448]

Having made these distinctions Maximus, however, also adds a modifying statement. The exact sense of this statement is not easy to find out. What Maximus says is, that harm may be done to those who read the

---

[447] Thal 43; CCSG 7, p. 293.
[448] CCSG 7, p. 295. On this whole text, see further Blowers, *op.cit.*, p. 189 f.

words of the Spirit unwisely, but that his correspondent knows that what is simply called evil is not entirely evil, and what is simply called good is not entirely good, but good only in a particular respect. Sherwood guesses that this warning is an indirect reference to Origen's easy identification of Christ and the Good, and the Devil and the Evil in relation to the tree of knowledge.[449] This is a possible solution, which might imply a refutation also of Origen's idea of *apokatastasis,* but it is not the only one.

What Maximus warns against is a too literal understanding of the words good and evil in relation to the tree of disobedience. This would, in fact, imply that, when good is identified with pleasure and evil with pain, pleasure is regarded as entirely good and pain as entirely evil, and further that the tree of life had nothing whatsoever to do with them. But now through Christ there is introduced into the world a healthy pain[450]—of mortification—and a demonstration of the results of vicious pleasure—of egoistic desire—so that both, turned into their opposite, are linked with the economy of salvation, and thus indirectly with the tree of life. Fallen man gains eternal life through abstaining from a vicious pleasure and accepting a healthy pain, and though this is not the way God had indicated from the beginning, it is not entirely outside of God's plan and intention.

Thus Maximus may very well hint at an identification between the trees, as von Balthasar has suggested (this would be the doctrine which he honours in silence),[451] but this would not necessarily lead either to a positive evaluation of the fall or to the idea of *apokatastasis* in Origen's sense. For Maximus has already indicated that there are two ways, equally important and valuable in themselves: the way of self-knowledge and participation through divine grace, and the way of contemplation of God's creation, postponed by God till after man's deification. Man has chosen the latter way and gone astray in the world of sense experience, but the means by which he is brought back to a true relationship to God are not contrary to God's intentions, but simply applied to the conditions of man's freedom.

This last interpretation may be correct or not; it remains a fact that, in relation to the problem of the trees of Paradise as in so many other respects, Maximus has succeeded in preserving a necessary distinction between two extremes without absolutising it, and thereby also safe-

---

[449] SHERWOOD, *The Earlier Ambigua,* p. 213.

[450] On Maximus' positive evaluation of pain in relation to mortification, see also ch. VI: 7, p. 388 ff. below.

[451] VON BALTHASAR, KL², p. 179.

guarded a positive evaluation of the created world, of man in his totality and of human freedom. This vision of unity without violation of the individual elements, of totality in differentiation, is, as we have seen in this chapter, in accordance with Maximus' anthropology in general, in the same way as we saw it to be in accordance with his cosmology in Chapter II. And this conclusion is, in its turn, a necessary presupposition for what we shall study in our next chapter on Maximus' psychology.

CHAPTER FOUR

Some Elements of Maximus' Psychology

A. The Trichotomy of the Soul

We have noted that man's microcosmic position in the centre of the created world is regarded by Maximus as a positive starting-point for the fulfilment of his task of mediation. In Christ fallen man is in principle restored to this task, which now as in the beginning, lies ahead of him. Before he can undertake it however, he is first of all called to respond freely to the act of Christ and thus to re-establish within himself the order of the microcosm, which is the presupposition of his work of mediation. In chapters V and VI we shall pay full attention to the two themes of man's call to personal re-establishment and general mediation, but before we come to them there are some elements of Maximus' psychology, which need to be treated.

The first of these is the fact that man is, in Maximus' opinion, not only composed of body and soul but also of different and distinct 'parts' and powers or faculties of the soul, which in fallen man are contradictory to one another, and in the Christian are thus to be restored to their unity and order. Another element is related to the fact that these different faculties can be said to have a good as well as a bad use and function, and these functions have to be analysed in relation to the task set before man. Finally, there is the whole aspect of man's assent to the process of restoration and mediation, in other words Maximus' psychology of the will.

The basic dichotomy between the intelligible and the sensible world which is common to most Greek thinking and is shared by the Fathers of the Church, is an evident presupposition for what Maximus has to say on the subject of man's middle position in creation—and in relation to the question of human unity in its different aspects. It is man's double relationship to God and the intelligible world on the one hand, and his bodily relationship to the world of senses on the other, which constitutes his microcosmic character. This fact, however, is in principle seen in a positive perspective. We have already noticed, in relation to the human trichotomy of mind, soul and body, that there is a primary concern on the part of Maximus to avoid too sharp a distinction between the different parts of man and to underline the human unity as integrating both the mind and the body into a common whole, of which the mind is regarded as the spiritual subject.[1]

This view-point must be borne in mind when we now come to deal with Maximus' understanding of the soul and its 'parts'; first of all, because there is an analogy between man as a whole and the human soul. The middle position which is given to man within the order of the created world has its counterpart in the place of the human soul within the order of man, regarded in the perspective of human trichotomy. The soul is called to mediate the spiritual call of man to the body, and this inherent ability of the soul is seen as being decisive for its constitution. And secondly, the different 'parts' of the soul are in their turn to be understood in relation to what is common to the soul as a whole, and in relation to the call and position of the soul within the human unity.

Consequently, *the trichotomy of the soul,* with which we shall deal in this section, is in Maximus, with his strong stress on the unity of the human composite, always to be related to this unity. And furthermore, the same human unity is to be interpreted in the light of Maximus' understanding of man as microcosm and mediator, called to unite and reconcile through himself all that, naturally as well as unnaturally, is divided, and thus to bring about, through his own relationship to the divine world, a higher unity which by interrelating in a proper way the intelligible and the sensible world, will transcend the basic dichotomy of God's creation without violating or annihilating its natural differences.

1.   The human soul and the basic dichotomy

Man's position in the universe makes the basic dichotomy of creation particularly noticeable in relation to him. This conviction seems more or less to be a commonplace in the Christian anthropology of the patristic period. Let us therefore study first of all how this basic understanding is reflected in Maximus' writings.

Its importance is illustrated in different ways. Thus, in Thal 32 Maximus shows that the same dichotomy is applicable to Scripture, to creation and to man, and that man himself as both a rational and sensible being is precisely in the position to discriminate between the opposites.

---

[1] See pp. 109 and 112 above.

In relation to Scripture it is a dichotomy of spirit and letter, in relation to creation, of inner principle (λόγος) and outward appearance, and in relation to man himself of mind and sense.[2] And in Thal 58 he states that these two elements in man, mind and sense, have an opposite energy in relation to each other, because of the extreme difference which exists between their natural relationships. Thus mind (νοῦς) is related to intelligible and incorporeal substances, which it apprehends by its own substance, while sense (αἴσθησις) is related to sensible and bodily natures, which it even grasps itself by nature.[3] Finally for Maximus, this dichotomy is explicitly relevant to the human soul, which is characterized by its middle position. Thus in Amb 10 he underlines that the saints, knowing that the soul puts on an earthly form, when it is unnaturally moved towards matter by means of the flesh, as a consequence, by means of what is natural to the soul itself, when moved towards God, have wished to make the flesh acquainted with God, seeking to adorn it with divine reflections.[4]

The soul has thus, according to Maximus, a call to fulfill precisely this mediating function. It is intended to relate the flesh, with which it is connected—through its natural relationship with the body—to the divine purpose for man, but it may on the other hand itself be made dependent on and become formed by the flesh. Man possesses in his soul an intelligible and reasonable faculty (νοερὰ τε καὶ λογικὴ δύναμις), and thus before the fall he was able to grasp and experience the Divine. In his fall however, man misused this capacity and turned this faculty towards the world of the senses, so that now it can be restored in him only thanks to Christ by divine grace and through the Holy Spirit.[5] Man's relationship to the sensible world, which he was called to use in a positive way in his function as mediator, in fallen man has developed into a slavery to sensibility from which he must be liberated. In his commentary on the Lord's Prayer, Maximus points out that man now must re-orientate the activity of his soul and turn his whole desire towards God, so as to know only one pleasure (ἡδονή), the pleasure which is contrary to that of the senses and consists entirely of the living communion (συμβίωσις) of the soul with the *logos*.[6] Or as Maximus says in an allegorical interpretation of the story of the marriage feast at Cana, the human mind must be

---

[2] CCSG 7, 225. A substantial study of this position is worked out by BLOWERS, *op.cit.*, e.g. p. 101.
[3] CCSG 22, p. 33.
[4] PG 91, 1112 C.
[5] Thal 59; CCSG 22, p. 45.
[6] OrDom; CCSG 23, p. 56.

united with virtue as with its bride, and it is this communion (συμβίωσις) which the Logos, born by faith, honours with his presence.[7]

The basic dichotomy, characteristic of creation and most deeply influential in relation to the human soul, is however not regarded by Maximus as evil in itself but rather as a *starting-point* for man's mediating function and thus for a movement. It is to this starting-point that by faith he is restored in Christ. Thus, when Maximus—using a trichotomist perspective within the framework of the dichotomy—speaks in Amb 10 of three *movements* of the soul, which are natural to man, he does so without any negative or Origenistic understanding of motion.[8] He simply refers to the fact that man—and we can add, precisely in his central position related to the basic dichotomy—may be said to consist of *three* parts, mind, reason (in the middle), and sense, and that each of these parts possesses a motion natural to itself. Thus the motion of the mind is simple and direct, that of reason is analytic and distinguishes according to causality, while the motion of sense is synthetic and yet receives from visible things, in the form of symbols, some insight into their *logoi* which itself it refers to reason.[9] And by doing so Maximus also makes it clear that in the end the true natural motion in all this is from the lower to the higher, so that what is grasped by one functions in the other to serve the final consummation of all the movements in God—and thus the final transcendence even of the basic dichotomy.[10]

To Maximus the basic dichotomy is thus a presupposition for these natural movements of the parts of the soul, which are themselves willed by God, and for this reason one aspect of it corresponds to each part. And this analogy between the different parts, in regard to their dichotomy, is so far from dividing the human soul into separate entities, that it serves the unifying movement of the whole. For—in virtue of the dichotomy—the *sensible* part of the soul is in fact not only sensible but also intellectual. It receives from the visible things a "symbolic" insight into their *logoi,* which it refers to the rational part of the soul. And this *rational* part is not only immanent but also transient, which is to say that its analytic knowledge is referred by it to the element of the mind. And the *mind* itself knows of a dichotomy, since it is not only intellectual but also passible.[11] It can receive imaginations from the lower parts of the

---

[7] Thal 40; CCSG 7, p. 273.
[8] Cf. ch. II: 6, pp. 81–83 above.
[9] PG 91, 1112 D–1113 A.
[10] Cf. SHERWOOD, *The Earlier Ambigua,* pp. 35 and 143.
[11] Amb 10; PG 91, 1116 A.

soul. And thus, the motion of the soul is conditioned by a dichotomy of each of its parts, which not only safeguards their individual characteristics but also serves the on-going motion from lower to higher. It is not difficult to see here, in the field of psychology, a further expression of Maximus' basic faithfulness to his understanding of *the Chalcedonian principle* of union without violation, and of difference as a prerequisite for unification.

That this view-point is not just occasional is further at least indirectly shown by Thal 25, an exegesis of 1 Cor. 11:3 and 10. Maximus there gives an allegorical interpretation of the words "man", "woman", "head", and "Christ", applied to the different stages of Christian spiritual development. *Man* is thus interpreted as the *mind,* engaged in either *vita practica,*[12] *vita contemplativa*[13] or *vita mystica,*[14] and *woman* is likewise interpreted as the *habitus* (ἕξις) or the accompanying conditions of these three spiritual stages.[15] The most interesting element in this interpretation from our point of view, however, is that this "woman" element implies at the same time what we might call the sensible aspect of each of these stages. Thus, the "woman" related to the practical mind is the *habit* of the *vita practica* itself, covered by practical thoughts and actions, and the "woman" related to the theoretical mind, is the *sense* itself which is always combined with natural contemplation, while the "woman" related to the mystical mind represents the *notion* linked with mystical knowledge, though, at this stage, cleansed from all sensible imagination. Thus, "woman" in all these cases symbolizes the relationship which exists at all levels with the 'lower' parts of the soul and their kinds of knowledge, and this fact is presented as the reason why the text says that the woman should have a "power" on her head.[16] The differentiated make-up of man thus serves the whole.

2. *Different forms of 'trichotomist' psychology in Maximus*

We have seen how a basic dichotomy in creation is recognized by Maximus, and how he develops the accompanying idea that this fact particularly affects man in the world and the human soul in man, so that both have a call to use this position in a work of mediation. We have also

---

[12] CCSG 7, p. 159.
[13] *Ibid.,* p. 161.
[14] *Loc. cit.*
[15] *Ibid.,* p. 161 ff. For a rendering and some discussion of this text, see BLOWERS, *op.cit.,* p. 200 ff.
[16] *Ibid.;* CCSG 7, p. 165.

seen that this dichotomy is supposed to be related to the different 'parts' of the soul, but that whether seen in relation to each of these 'parts', or to the whole of the human soul, this fact can be evaluated positively as a starting-point and presupposition for the motion which is natural to each of the parts, as well as for that which is natural to the soul and man as a whole. This natural motion, when not perverted as it is in the fall of man, is able to transcend the dichotomy without violation and thereby to unite the different parts of the soul in one single, God-ward direction. Differentiation and unification go together.

This fact, however, also provides the right background for an interpretation of Maximus' treatment of the trichotomist aspects of human psychology. These aspects are, in fact, dominant in Maximus' anthropology, especially in his ascetic theology and in his speculations about man's spiritual development. He favours triadic arrangements closely linked with the different trichotomies of the soul. This tendency however is always combined with a strong stress on the unity of the soul and the unification of its movements for one single purpose, the communion between human and divine which is the core of God's providential economy.

It is, therefore, not surprising that Maximus feels free to use different types of three-fold distinctions in relation to the human soul. None of them is absolute. We have already met the classical distinction of *mind, reason, sense,* to each of which belongs a corresponding motion.[17] But he also uses a distinction, based mainly on Aristotelian ground, between a *rational,* a *non-rational* and a *non-sensible soul,* corresponding to souls of rational beings, animals and plants respectively. Man shares all these souls, of which the third one is vegetative or nutritive, the second is appetitive and sensible, and the first is reasonable and intellectual but also imperishable and immortal.[18] Maximus also uses the Pauline distinction between *carnal, psychic* and *spiritual* man and interprets it with reference to different moral modes of man.[19] The dominant trichotomy which we find in Maximus is, however, that between the *rational, irascible* and *concupiscible* elements of the soul—a distinction which is found almost everywhere in ancient Greek philosophical, theological and

----

[17] Amb 10; PG 91, 1112 D. On the importance of this triad, cf. VON BALTHASAR, KL², p. 287 f.

[18] Char 3. 30–31; CSC, p. 158. This trichotomy had been developed on Christian ground by Gregory of Nyssa, who also related it closely with the Pauline trichotomy of spirit, soul and body; see LADNER, The Philosophical Anthropology, DOP 12 (1958), p. 70 f.; cf. p. 74.

[19] See Ep 9; PG 91, 448 A–C.

ascetic literature, and not least in Evagrius from whom Maximus probably took it in the first place. Its importance goes, however, beyond that of the Evagrian influence, and the variety and freedom with which it is used is wider than that which we find in Evagrius.[20]

This variety is well illustrated by Maximus' variations of terminology within the last trichotomy itself. Here his freedom, in comparison with Evagrius, is immediately striking. Thus for the most part Evagrius identifies the reasonable part of man with the mind (νοῦς) and establishes a trichotomy of mind (νοῦς), anger (θυμός) and concupiscence (ἐπιθυμία)—this is always so in *Cent. gnost.*[21] While Maximus certainly knows of this form,[22] in most cases he does not identify the mind as spiritual subject with any particular element of the soul and thus he most often uses a trichotomy of rational, irascible and concupiscible.[23] It is further within this second and dominant form of the trichotomy, that Maximus elaborates his personal variations.

He, thus, sometimes speaks of θυμός, ἐπιθυμία, λόγος, to which the mind (νοῦς), as a fourth or rather integrating element, is added,[24] and sometimes of λόγος, τὸ θυμικόν, ἐπιθυμία, to which the mind is likewise added.[25] In some texts Maximus uses neuter, substantive expressions, which indicate that the three elements may be regarded as different '*parts*' of the human soul—though this distinction is, of course, in Maximus never of a metaphysical or ontological character.[26] In such cases he refers to τὸ ἐπιθυμητικόν, τὸ θυμικόν and τὸ λογικόν,[27] or, more often, to τὸ θυμικόν, τὸ ἐπιθυμητικόν and τὸ λογιστικόν.[28] In a number of other texts he prefers to speak of three powers or *faculties* (δυνάμεις) of

---

[20] SHERWOOD, in ACW, p. 84, almost exclusively stresses the Evagrian influence at this point. Evagrius' system of ascetic theology was obviously of the utmost importance for Maximus' ascetic writings, and in these writings we find the majority of references to this trichotomy. This fact does not however exclude a wider range of influences at this particular point than Sherwood seems to believe. As we shall see in section 3, there are, in fact, considerable differences between Evagrius' and Maximus' understanding of the trichotomy.

[21] See p. 199 f.

[22] See Thal 16; CCSG 7, p. 105 and Ep 24; PG 91, 609 D–612 A.

[23] This most important difference between Maximus and Evagrius is hardly noticed by SHERWOOD, who mentions, however, the alternatives (see in ACW, p. 84 f.).

[24] See Thal 16; CCSG 7, p. 109.

[25] *Ibid.;* CCSG 7, p. 107. Cf. BLOWERS, *op.cit.,* p. 236, n. 78.

[26] Cf. SHERWOOD, in ACW, p. 84.

[27] See e.g. Thal 27; CCSG 7, p. 197.

[28] This version is frequent in *Cent. de char.,* probably on account of the influence from Evagrius' *Praktikos* which is recognizable here, since in it Evagrius once uses the same distinction (see *Pract.* 1. 58; PG 40, 1233 D–1236 A). For Maximus' use, see Char 1. 67; CSC, p. 74; 2. 12; p. 94; 3. 20; p. 150; 4. 15; p. 200; 4. 44; p. 212 and 4. 80; p. 230.

the human soul,[29] described either as ἐπιθυμητική, θυμοειδής and λογιστική,[30] or as λογική, ἐπιθυμητική and θυμική.[31]

We shall later study how Maximus understands this particular trichotomy and its different elements. However, the variations of human trichotomy which we have now demonstrated in Maximus—different systems of trichotomy, differences of terminology within the dominant system and flexibility in relation to the question whether these elements are 'parts' or faculties within the human soul—are a clear indication that Maximus is not bound by any particular form of trichotomy and does not regard his distinctions between the different elements as metaphysical or ontological. The decisive distinction to him is that between the intelligible and the sensible world, and the human soul by its middle position shares this basic dichotomy in all its elements.

The most important point in Maximus' view is, therefore, that God has, in spite of the basic dichotomy, created man and his soul as a unity, empowered with a certain call to be a microcosm and to act as a mediator in the world. For according to this understanding neither the dichotomy as such, nor the divine call of man does violence to the human unity. And consequently, not even the passible parts of the human soul can in principle be seen in a negative perspective. All elements have a positive function set before them, which is restored in Christ, and all elements are equally perverted in fallen man, even if it is from the sensible element that man in the very beginning received such disastrous influences.

Before we go on to demonstrate how in Maximus' thought unity and differentiation are in this way balanced with regard to the trichotomy of the human soul, we ought, however, to give a general survey of the background of thinking against which Maximus' position has to be understood; in general as regards his dominant trichotomy, and more particularly as regards its distinction between the concupiscible and the irascible element.

3.   The general background of Maximus' dominant psychological trichotomy

In the Christian tradition which influenced Maximus, the trichotomy of *reasonable, irascible* and *concupiscible* obviously goes back first of all to Plato, but Aristotle's reflections on the same subject should also be kept in mind. Of utmost importance further is the Stoic understanding of the

---

[29] See e.g. Thal 39; CCSG 7, p. 259 and *Expos. in Ps. LIX;* CCSG 23, p. 7.
[30] See Char 3. 3; CSC, p. 144.
[31] See Thal 49; CCSG 7, p. 355.

powers and passions of the human soul. And finally, the later modifications between these different standpoints should not be neglected, when we now first try to outline the general philosophical background of the 'trichotomist' psychology of Maximus' predecessors. For all these elements have certainly been influential in relation to the Christian tradition which Maximus reflects and elaborates.

Plato's position

Plato's use of the trichotomy finds its most well-known expression in the Fourth book of *The Republic,* where he establishes an analogy between the three faculties of the human soul on the one hand, and the three classes of society as well as their cardinal virtues on the other.[32] Here the psychological interpretation of the three parts of the human soul, τὸ λογιστικόν, τὸ θυμοειδές and τὸ ἐπιθυμητικόν, is very clearly presented. A double faculty—one intellectual and one volitional—is here referred to each part: the rational element contains both rational apprehension and rational aspiration, the irascible element both conviction and arduous striving, and the concupiscible element both conjecture and appetite.[33] The trichotomy can, however, be followed through most of Plato's dialogues.[34] But this fact does not imply that the picture is completely free from ambiguity, since there are also other elements of systematization in Plato in relation to the faculties of the soul.[35]

If we try to interpret what Plato says about our triad and its elements, what is striking first of all, is that its totality is to a great extent positively evaluated. The irascible and concupiscible elements are not bad in themselves. The cardinal virtues of the state find their proper place in them.[36] The most well-known illustration of this understanding is, of course, given in the *Phaedrus,* where τὸ ἐπιθυμητικόν and τὸ θυμοειδές

---

[32] See e.g. *Res publ.* 4; 435 e–436 b.

[33] Cf. J. WILD, *Plato's Theory of Man,* Cambridge, Mass., 1946, p. 152 ff.

[34] Already in 1909 A. LEISSNER in his dissertation, *Die platonische Lehre von den Seelenteilen nach Entwicklung, Wesen und Stellung innerhalb der platonischen Philosophie,* Nördlingen, gave a most detailed account of all the traces of this trichotomy in Plato's works.

[35] A certain complication is provided by the fact that it happens that Plato, in relation to different moods of the soul, seems to use another triad: grief (λύπη), fear (φόβος), and desire (ἐπιθυμία); see *Res publ.* 4; 430 b. Yet it becomes immediately clear that these three elements (with the addition of ἡδονή) are part of a tetradic arrangement (see *ibid.;* 430 ab), which is also later known as the Stoic tetrad of cardinal passions. (Cf. Plato, *Laches;* 191 d; *Symp.;* 207 e; *Theaet.;* 156 b and also *Res publ.* 4; 429 c.)

[36] Wisdom is thus to be found in the rational part, courage in the irascible and moderation in the concupiscible part, while righteousness should characterize their unity; see Plato, *Res publ.* 4; 428 b–429 a; 429 a–430 c; 430 c–432 b and 435 b. These elements may thus be used either for a good or for a bad purpose.

are described as the two horses of a human chariot, the driver of which has, however, to be the rational part of man.[37] The general view of this dialogue seems to be that the two passible elements are not separated from the immortal part of the soul,[38] though on the other hand, Plato presupposes, of course, everywhere that there are in the soul two different elements, one immortal and one mortal, one rational and one non-rational, and that it is in the latter element that we can distinguish between an irascible and a concupiscible part. The basic dichotomy thus underlines and conditions the trichotomy.[39] This fact however does not exclude the conclusion that within the triad, the irascible part is given a middle position and a mixed character.[40] For in the first part of the triad we meet a non-divisible substance and in the last part a divisible substance, but in the middle part, the irascible, a mixed substance.[41]

This middle position of the irascible part is of a certain interest to us, since it serves to make the basic dichotomy less absolute as far as the human soul is concerned, and also seems to have exerted a certain influence upon the understanding of the irascible element among Christian writers. The faculty of the irascible element is to Plato of a self-expansive character, equally fit for both true courage and passionate anger, as we notice in *The Republic*. The irascible element is also more naturally inclined to be subordinated to reason.[42]

A few other aspects of Plato's view should be mentioned in this context. First of all, it seems clear, that Plato regards the three elements more or less literally as *parts* of the soul, though he also speaks of their corresponding faculties. The latter are distinguished from the parts, for when he uses the neuter expressions, τὸ ἐπιθυμητικόν, etc., he refers to these elements as parts of the soul, while the functions of these parts,

---

[37] Plato, *Phaedrus;* 246 a ff., 253 cd, etc.

[38] See *Phaedrus;* 246. This is of importance, since it makes it impossible to see in Plato's works a development towards a more rigorous evaluation at this point. It was still possible to uphold such a hypothesis, as long as the *Phaedrus* was regarded as an early work. Now, since the question of its date of composition is reversed, this is no longer possible. Cf. here also E. Zeller, *Die Philosophie der Griechen,* II: 1, Leipzig 1889, p. 843, n. 3, and p. 820, where it is argued that according to Plato in the *Phaedrus* the lower parts of the soul also belonged to it in its pre-existence.

[39] See e.g. *Res publ.* 4; 439 e; cf. R. Arnou, *art.* Platonisme des Pères, DTC 12: 2, col. 2267.

[40] In the *Phaedrus* the irascible part is thus called "the good horse" and the concupiscible part "the non-good horse", see 253 d.

[41] Cf. A.-J. Festugière, *Contemplation et vie contemplative selon Platon,* Paris 1936, p. 121, where this problem is discussed in relation to *Timaeus;* 35, where it seems clear that the sensible part of the soul in its strictest sense is regarded as foreign to the real soul.

[42] See *Res publ.* 4; 440 b; cf. Zeller, *op. cit.,* p. 884 and Festugière, *op.cit.,* p. 149 f.

ἐπιθυμία, etc., are designed as faculties (δυνάμεις).[43] Secondly, it is obvious that what interests Plato in relation to the three elements of the soul is not their formal definition, but the object of their activity,[44] though an analysis of this activity also shows the difference of their faculties. And both aspects of this question are closely connected with the problem of the localization of the elements.

They are bound to different organs of the body, and are thus, as it were, at a different distance from the higher world. This position expresses both the orientation and the psychic character of each element, which is obvious e.g. in relation to the middle position of the irascible part. In localizing the different elements Plato reflects, of course, older speculation. Thus reason is related to the head, anger to the chest and concupiscence to a particular area between the diaphragm and the navel.[45] The mediating organ between the rational and the appetitive part is the liver (as θυμός is the mediating psychic activity), and—in accordance with an old tradition—Plato is of the opinion that the reason projects images on to the smooth surface of the liver, even though he rejects the investigation of the livers of sacrificed animals.[46] Finally, it is also clear that to Plato plants possess ἐπιθυμία and animals both ἐπιθυμία and θυμός.[47]

Aristotle's understanding

Aristotle's position in relation to this trichotomy is not radically different from Plato's. Like Plato he distinguishes between an immortal and a mortal part of the soul. The relationship between body and soul is, however, more complicated and also more 'positive' in Aristotle than in Plato, since they are regarded as form and matter,[48] and the soul is understood as the *entelecheia* of the body,[49] which is of importance also for the trichotomy.

Four aspects of Aristotle's understanding are of a particular interest in our context. θυμός and ἐπιθυμία are, first of all, integrated into Aristotle's general view of will and desire. In this field we thus arrive at

---

[43] Cf. LEISSNER, *op.cit.*, p. 62. This position is illustrated by Plato's terminology. The elements are thus often called "parts", μέρη (see *Res publ.* 4; 442 b and 444 b), "forms", εἴδη (see *ibid.*; 435 c, 439 e, 504 a; *Phaedr.*; 253 c; *Tim.*; 69 c and 77 b) and "species", γένη (see *Res. publ.* 4; 441 c, 443 d, 444 b and *Tim.*; 69 e).

[44] Cf. ZELLER, *op. cit.*, p. 884 and also LEISSNER, *op. cit.*, p. 63.

[45] See *Tim.*; 69 e, 70 d, 77 b and 90 a.

[46] See *ibid.*; 71 a–72 d.

[47] See *ibid.*; 77 ab and *Res publ.* 4; 441 b respectively.

[48] See *De anima* 2, 1; 412 a.

[49] *Ibid.*; 412 b.

another triad of βούλησις, θυμός and ἐπιθυμία, in which the first element represents a reasonable desire, the second an arduous striving of a more general (and impulsive) kind and the third concupiscence in the proper sense.[50] Of these three forms of appetency only the wish (βούλησις) however is free,[51] while concupiscence gives the most striking example of a desire which is not free.[52]

Secondly, we also find in Aristotle that the trichotomist distinction is strictly subordinated to the dichotomy. The irascible and concupiscible elements are even brought nearer to each other in Aristotle, than we found them to be in Plato, though θυμός preserves a middle position.[53] θυμός is sometimes presented as even more foreign to reason than concupiscence.[54]

Thirdly, this rather negative view of the irascible element as foreign to reason, together with the stress on the bodily character of all passions, has effected a certain change in the understanding of θυμός, so that this term is more often than in Plato interpreted simply as "wrath".[55] But, fourthly, this nevertheless does not imply that θυμός loses its middle position. It remains in principle a servant of reason and is in fact far more capable of following reason than concupiscence is.[56]

Aristotle's stronger stress on the unity of the human composite, which to some extent relativizes the basic dichotomy in man, is thus balanced by a rather negative evaluation of both elements of the non-rational part of the human soul, though particularly of the concupiscible element.

The Stoic view

In Stoic philosophy the negative view of the passible part of the soul becomes quite dominant, and at the same time it was the Stoic outlook which was perhaps the most influential force in ancient Christian ascetic thinking regarding our trichotomy. It is a well-known fact that the Stoics regarded all kinds of passions as disastrous and saw complete detachment (ἀπάθεια) as an ideal human attitude. It is true that these passions were systematized differently; the Stoic analysis of them is dominated by the *tetrad,* which we also meet occasionally in Plato: pleasure (ἡδονή),

---

[50] See *De anima,* 2, 3; 414 b; cf. P. WILPERT, *art.* Begierde, RACh 2 (1954), col. 64.

[51] See *Magna Mor.,* 1, 13; 1188 a.

[52] Cf. e.g. WOLFSON, *The Philosophy of the Church Fathers,* p. 464.

[53] *All* 'passions' of the soul imply the participation of the body; cf. F. NUYENS, *L'Évaluation de la psychologie d'Aristote,* The Hague/Paris 1948, p. 224 f.

[54] See *Eth. Nicom.* 3, 11; 1116 b.

[55] See *Eth. Nicom.,* 3, 3; 1111 a and 4, 11; 1126 a, and *Eth. Eudem.,* 3, 1; 1229 a.

[56] *Eth. Nicom.* 7, 5; 1147 b and 7, 7; 1149 a. The incontinence of ἐπιθυμία is greater, see *ibid.,* 7, 7; 1149 b.

grief (λύπη), desire (ἐπιθυμία) and fear (φόβος).[57] But the use of the triad among Stoic writers is also well testified to in the literature of the period.[58]

Characteristic of the Stoic use of the triad is, of course, first of all the fact that it depends directly on the Stoic understanding of the passions. To some extent this limits the scope of the trichotomy and has facilitated a simple identification between θυμός and wrath, rage, fury. Anger and concupiscence are also brought into a very close relationship to each other. An expression of this relationship is the fact that both are localized in the same place, the chest.[59] According to Stoic understanding all passions may be subsumed under the category of sensibility. For this reason there is no clear difference of character between passions referred to the irascible part of the soul and those referred to the concupiscible part in the stricter sense.[60]

The picture of the Stoic understanding of the trichtomy is, however, still more complicated than we have indicated so far. In the first place the basic dualism which we have studied in Plato and Aristotle is absent in Stoic philosophy. The soul is regarded as corporeal in a refined sense. This view of course influences the Stoic understanding of the trichotomy. The three elements are thus not distinct parts of the soul but *powers* and *motions* within it.[61] Consequently, we notice on the one hand what we might call a more 'positive' tendency; man is seen as a unity, and the animals do not share with man his irascible and concupiscible faculties.[62] The passion of concupiscence for example is simply an irrational motion within the rational soul.[63] But on the other hand, the Stoic stress on the close relationship between the movements of the soul and the human

---

[57] For the use of this tetrad already in Zeno, see the testimony of Diogenes Laërtius in VON ARNIM, *Stoic. vet. fragm.* 1, p. 51, no. 211. Cf. also VON ARNIM, 3, p. 92, no. 378 and p. 95, no. 394 (Chrysippus) as well as *ibid.* 3, p. 95, no. 391 (Andronicus). For the platonizing philosopher Poseidonius the combination of this tetrad and our triad (both found in Plato) obviously caused some difficulties; see M. POHLENZ, *Poseidonios' Affektenlehre und Psychologie*, NGWG (1921), p. 181 f.

[58] See e.g. the testimony of Galen in VON ARNIM, *op. cit.*, 1, p. 129, no. 570. Cf. also what is referred from Alex. Aphrod., in VON ARNIM, *op. cit.*, 2, p. 225, no. 823, where we find an interesting equivalent of verbs (showing that a negative evaluation of the passible functions dominates the picture): διανοεῖσθαι, ὀργίζεσθαι, ἐπιθυμεῖν, though the common power of the soul is said to be developed beyond the "parts".

[59] See the testimony of Galen, VON ARNIM, *op. cit.*, 2, p. 250, no. 903.

[60] This position may be exemplified by Chrysippus, see VON ARNIM, *op. cit.*, 3, p. 96, no. 396.

[61] This holds true also when the Stoics point out that the soul is eight-fold; see STEIN, *Die Psychologie der Stoa*, 1, p. 122 with n. 222.

[62] See the testimony of Galen, VON ARNIM, *op. cit.* 2, p. 255, no. 906.

[63] Cf. WILPERT, *art. cit.*, col. 63.

body indirectly strengthens the negative aspect. The passible elements lose the neutral sense which they had in Plato and also in Aristotle.[64] θυμός and ἐπιθυμία are certainly both localized in the chest together with the ἡγεμονικόν,[65] but θυμός is at the same time often subordinated to ἐπιθυμία[66] and thus understood exclusively as wrath.[67]

Later modifications

Even though the Stoics from the outset regard anger and concupiscence as passionate powers of the human soul, it is not until the later Stoa that the problem of a polarity between them is again brought into the foreground. Thus Poseidonius goes back to an older trichotomy of body, soul and spirit and combines it with the Platonic understanding of the three parts of the soul. The result is that the concupiscible part is now regarded as the concupiscence of the flesh, while the mind is identified with the older concept of spirit, but thereby the irascible part regains its middle and ambivalent position,[68] in spite of the fact that θυμός in Poseidonius is practically subordinated to ἐπιθυμία.[69] Against this background it is certainly not surprising that, influenced by Plato through Panaetius, he is also willing to allow for ἐπιθυμία in plants and both ἐπιθυμία and θυμός in animals.[70] It should also be added that Poseidonius holds the opinion that the soul is united to the body only during its earthly existence and develops its irascible and concupiscible faculties only under these conditions. This non-Stoic opinion he shares not only with Plato but also with Plotinus.[71]

Here we have touched upon another important stream of thinking,

---

[64] Cf. WILPERT, loc. cit.

[65] According to Nemesius, the Stoics saw θυμός as concentrated in the bile—a sign of its identification with wrath—and regarded it as caused by an act or sense of injustice, see VON ARNIM, op. cit., 3, p. 101, no. 416.

[66] According to Andronicus both ὀργή and θυμός belong to the forms (εἴδη) of ἐπιθυμία, so VON ARNIM, op. cit., 3, p. 96, no. 397. Cf. in Diogenes Laërtius, see ibid., no. 396.

[67] A clear tendency to identify θυμός and ὀργή and to link them closely with hatred (μῖσος) can be recognized in the Stoic tradition, see e.g. in VON ARNIM, op. cit., 3, p. 96 f., no. 396 and 397. Thus θυμεῖσθαι may be substituted by ὀργίζεσθαι, see VON ARNIM, op. cit., 2, p. 225, no. 823.

[68] Cf. WILPERT, art. cit., col. 68.

[69] Cf. STEIN, op. cit., p. 190.

[70] The concupiscible element in Poseidonius' view is characteristic of all forms of vegetative and animated life, to which the irascible is added in the case of animals. The latter is described as a desire for dominance and victory. In man these two elements are recognizable before the rational faculty. In an adult man they will, however, acquire a new function, since they have to subordinate themselves to reason, though they will preserve their own character. For this summary, see POHLENZ, Die Stoa, I, Göttingen 1948, p. 225.

[71] Cf. POHLENZ, op. cit., I, p. 394.

which ought to be considered in this context, that of Middle and Neo-Platonism. Its contribution however lies mostly within the field of *terminological refinement*. In Albinus e.g. we find, that the Stoic concept of ἡγεμονικόν and the Platonic concept of λογιστικόν are both localized in the head and are partly identified.[72] The distinction between the reasonable and the passible part of the soul is further developed on Platonic ground, and in the passible part Albinus distinguishes between an irascible element (for which he uses the Aristotelian term τὸ θυμικόν instead of Plato's word τὸ θυμοειδές) and a concupiscible element.[73] In the realm of pre-existence these two passible elements are further said to have had their counterparts, which are transformed when the soul is united with the body.[74] Finally, Albinus—like the Stoic writer Chrysippus—underlines the inner struggle between the two passible elements themselves. The aspect of disorder is thus brought into the foreground.

Plotinus emphasizes more strongly the indivisibility of the soul, but cannot deny that it has yet to put up with a certain divisibility on account of its affinity to the body and the sensible world.[75] Plotinus' trichotomy, however, does not coincide with that of Plato, though it is probably influenced by it.[76] He thus distinguishes between sensible man, intelligible man and the man in between, who is the reasonable man;[77] but in relation to the four cardinal virtues we notice that our triad too is relevant to him in its Platonic, more neutral sense.[78] It should finally be noted that Porphyry later, in conjunction with Poseidonius, again understood the Platonic "parts" of the soul as "powers" and faculties rather than real parts.[79]

Within Neo-Platonism one may consequently recognize ambivalence in relation to some problems. On the one side there is the influence of Plato, resulting in a neutral, and even positive, understanding of the irascible element in the human soul, but on the other we find a tendency to stress the unity of the human composite, resulting not only in an understanding of the different elements as faculties rather than parts, but

---

[72] Cf. UEBERWEG-PRAECHTER, *op. cit.*, p. 529.

[73] Cf. *ibid.*, p. 543.

[74] τὸ ὁρμητικόν becomes τὸ θυμικόν, and τὸ οἰκειωτικόν becomes τὸ ἐπιθυμητικόν; see UEBERWEG-PRAECHTER, *loc. cit.*

[75] Cf. ARNOU, *art. cit.*, col. 2279.

[76] Cf. UEBERWEG-PRAECHTER, *op. cit.*, p. 605 f.

[77] Cf. REYPENS, *art.* Ame, DSp I, col. 435; cf. also ch. III: 2 above.

[78] φρόνησις is thus said to be the virtue of τὸ λογιστικόν, ἀνδρεία still the virtue of τὸ θυμούμενον and σωφροσύνη that of τὸ ἐπιθυμητικόν, while δικαιοσύνη as in Plato is the virtue of the whole; see Plot., *Enn.* I. 2, 1.

[79] Cf. UEBERWEG-PRAECHTER, *op. cit.*, p. 610.

also in a stress on the relationship to a body as a necessary prerequisite for their use.[80] This position also summarizes rather well the situation in which the influential Christian writers had to work out their theological understanding of the trichotomy.

We have dwelt rather long on the philosophical discussion of the nature of the human soul. We have done so, first of all in order to show the complexity of this tradition, as well as the terminological development which it reveals. But we have, be it noted, only pointed out elements which are of a particular importance for the Christian tradition in this respect, and for the problems which we meet in Maximus. The idea of the middle position of man and the view of an establishment of a truly ordered human microcosm, which we find in Maximus, can only be understood against the background of the discussion about the unity and differentiation of the human soul which we have here outlined. That this is so, will be further illustrated when we turn our attention now to those writers, who may possibly have influenced Maximus more directly.

Before we study the Christian understanding of the trichotomy—where we shall concentrate on the Alexandrian and Cappadocian writers and on Evagrius, Ps.-Denis and Nemesius—we must add, however, a few words on Philo's use of the trichotomy. The reason for this is obvious: Philo exerted a wide influence on a number of these writers—and his influence is equally felt in Maximus himself.

Philo and Clement—the earlier Alexandrian position

In Philo we find an *eclectic attitude* to the philosophical considerations. For example, his conception of the soul is deeply marked by the Platonic dichotomy. Thus he distinguishes between a rational and an irrational soul. He also rejects the Stoic idea of the corporeality of the soul, but only so far as the rational soul is concerned.[81] With the Stoics he agrees in talking of an ogdoad of psychic faculties.[82] The triad of the reasonable, irascible and concupiscible parts of the soul he took over from Plato, but with Aristotle he also distinguishes between nutritive, sensible and reasonable soul.[83] Finally, there is even a Jewish element in his under-

---

[80] This last tendency may perhaps be illustrated by the case of Proclus, who supposed not only a material body and a body of light but also a third body in between, thus establishing a particular kind of triad; see e.g. UEBERWEG-PRAECHTER, *op. cit.*, p. 629 f.

[81] See WOLFSON, *Philo*, I, pp. 385–391 and ZELLER, *Die Philosophie der Griechen* III: 2, Leipzig 1903, p. 447.

[82] The dichotomy interferes, however, in so far as there is a heptad of faculties of the irrational soul, while the rational soul consists of the undivided mind; cf. WOLFSON, *op. cit.*, pp. 389 and 392.

[83] Cf. e.g. ZELLER, *op. cit.*, p. 447.

standing of the soul. Thus for instance he is based on Jewish tradition when he opposes the Aristotelian idea that the lower powers of the soul do not share in free will.[84]

The classical terminology in relation to the trichotomy is well preserved in Philo. Thus he reproduces the Platonic distinctions of three "parts" and three "forms" in the human soul.[85] He further uses Plato's image of the chariot and the two horses (emphasizing at the same time that the symbol of concupiscence is female and the symbol of anger male), and like Plato he underlines, of course, that reason ought to be the chariot-driver.[86] On the other hand he shows a certain affinity to the Stoics in underlining the negative rôle of the passions of the passible elements, and in bringing the two types of passions very close to each other.

The most interesting aspect in Philo's understanding of the trichotomy in our context is, however, that which is related to the irascible element. Basing himself on Plato, Philo obviously regards it as a neutral counterpart to the concupiscible element, as is illustrated by the image of the chariot.[87] But at the same time it is also obvious, that θυμός by this time had to a great extent become identified with ὀργή, wrath, and this combination of influences from Plato and the Stoics which we recognize in Philo, leads to the striking result that ὀργή itself partly loses its negative meaning and becomes more ambivalent. On the other hand, however, this development in Philo is also due to the Jewish tradition, where *a justified wrath* has always had a proper place and is ascribed to God himself. This integration of a *biblical element* into the philosophical discussion of the human trichotomy was certainly of importance for the Christian interpretation.[88]

Among the Christian Alexandrian writers Clement of Alexandria seems to be of immediate interest in the same context. For his eclectic

---

[84] See WOLFSON, *Philo*, 2, pp. 231–235 and particularly 234.

[85] The three μέρη are τὸ λογικόν, τὸ θυμικόν (the Aristotelian term used also by Albinus) and τὸ ἐπιθυμητικόν, see *Leg. alleg.* I, 71; COHN & WENDLAND, I, p. 79 f. The three εἴδη are λόγος, θυμός and ἐπιθυμία, see *De spec. leg.* 4 (*De Concupiscentia*), 92; COHN & WENDLAND, 5, p. 229.

[86] See *De migr. Abr.*, 67; COHN & WENDLAND, 2, p. 281 and *De agricult.* 73; *ibid*, p. 109 f. Either νοῦς or λόγος are said to have this leading function. Anger and concupiscence are further described as brother and sister, see *De migr. Abr.*, 66; p. 280 f.; and reason is also called arbitrator and guide (cf. Plato, *Phaedrus;* 247 c), see *Leg. alleg.* 3, 118; COHN & WENDLAND, I. p. 139. On the Logos as ἡνίοχος in Philo and early Christian speculation, cf. further P. BESKOW, *Rex Gloriae. The Kingship of Christ in the Early Church*, Uppsala 1962, pp. 200–206.

[87] Cf. *De agricult.*, 73; COHN & WENDLAND, 2, p. 109 f.

[88] On this problem in Philo, see WOLFSON, *Philo*, 2, p. 109 f.

position is very close to that of Philo. He maintains the basic dichotomy and distinguishes between a reasonable and a non-reasonable part of the human soul,[89] but also—in accordance with the Platonic tradition—within the latter between anger and concupiscence.[90] He constitutes a triad, usually called θυμός, ἐπιθυμία, λογισμός, which is in its turn, somewhat inappropriately but on biblical grounds, closely linked with the Pauline triad of flesh, soul and spirit.[91] Clement further, in a Stoic way, subordinates anger to concupiscence terminologically,[92] and consequently names the former "impulse of desire" (ὁρμὴ ἐπιθυμίας).[93] In a way which reminds us of Philo, θυμός is also seen as a male and ἐπιθυμία as a female impulse.[94]

In Clement we should, in fact, allow for a rather strong influence from a Stoic understanding of human passions, which his use of the concept of detachment (ἀπάθεια) most clearly reveals.[95] The Stoic tetrad of passions is, however, not particularly underlined by Clement, though he uses it with interesting modifications.[96] His triad of ἐπιθυμία, θυμός, λογισμός is more frequently used.[97] More definitely Stoic, however, is the close relationship which Clement establishes between θυμός and "wrath", which indicates a plainly negative evaluation of the former,[98] but, like Philo, he allows for a righteous wrath in God.[99] The ambivalent character

---

[89] J. WYTZES, The twofold way II; Platonic influences in the work of Clement of Alexandria, VC 14 (1960), pp. 129–153, emphasizes that Clement preserves the Platonic distinction between the sensible and intelligible world, though—like all Christian followers of Philo, he says—on religious rather than philosophical grounds (p. 133).

[90] See *Strom.* 3. 10; GCS Clem. 2, p. 227, 22; *ibid.* 4. 6; p. 264, 9 ff. and 5. 8; p. 362, 7 ff.—On this eclecticism of Clement's anthropology, cf. VÖLKER, *Der wahre Gnostiker nach Clemens Alexandrinus* (TU 57), Berlin 1952, p. 110 f.

[91] See *Strom.* 3. 10; GCS Clem. 2, p. 227, 9 f. The same triad is found in e.g. *ibid.* 13; p. 238 f. and 4. 6; p. 266, 11 f.—Here we ought also to recall Poseidonius' use of Plato's triad in combination with that of body, soul and spirit.

[92] See *Strom.* 4. 23; GCS Clem. 2, p. 315, 24.

[93] *Ibid.* 5. 5; p. 343, 17. Cf. VÖLKER, *op. cit.,* p. 131 with n. 2.

[94] See *ibid.* 3. 13; p. 238, 29 f.

[95] On the place and function of this concept within Clement's theology and in Christian thinking before him, see TH. RÜTHER, *Die sittliche Forderung der Apatheia.* (FThSt 63.) Freiburg i. Br. 1949.

[96] We may thus find πόθος as a substitute for ἐπιθυμία (see *Strom.* 6. 14; GCS Clem. 2, p. 488, 8) or even ὁργή or θυμός as a substitute for ἐπιθυμία (see *ibid.* 6. 9; p. 469, 3).

[97] See *Strom.* 3. 10; GCS Clem. 2, p. 227, 9; 13; p. 238, 31 ff.; 4. 6; p. 266, 11 f. and 5. 8; p. 362, 8 f. (combined with Plato's image of the two horses and the chariot).

[98] Thus Clement sees θυμός and ὁργή more or less as equivalents, see *Strom.* 6. 9; GCS Clem. 2, p. 469, 3. He further underlines its physical connection with the bile, see e.g. *Paed.* I. 11; GCS Clem. I, p. 147, 11 f. Like the Stoics he also attributes a great importance to wrath, see *ibid.* 3. 12; p. 286, 25 f. and p. 290, 18; and *Strom.* 6. 16; GCS Clem. 2, p. 500, 25.—For the lively Stoic discussion on problems of wrath, cf. e.g. J. STELZENBERGER, *Die Beziehungen der frühchristlichen Sittenlehre zur Ethik der Stoa,* Munich 1933, p. 250 ff.

[99] Divine wrath differs, however, from human wrath, in that it is φιλάνθρωπος, see

of the concept of wrath, which we noticed in Philo, is in Clement, however, more exclusively related to the idea of a righteous wrath of God, entirely different from the human passion of wrath.[100]

Origen's view—a more elaborated standpoint

When we turn to Origen, we find that he uses the different terminologies with greater care than either Philo or Clement did. He finds e.g. obvious difficulties in combining the Platonic and Pauline trichotomies,[101] and thus he arrives at a *tetradic arrangement,* where the biblical term "spirit" is added to the philosophical triad. This tetrad is particularly reflected in his allegorical interpretation of Ez. 1: 10, where the face of man is referred to the rational element (*rationabile*), the face of the lion to the irascible element (*iracundia*) and the face of the bull to the concupiscible element (*concupiscentia*), while the face of the eagle is referred to the spirit of man (*spiritus*), which guides the soul.[102] With this modification Origen is then free to use the triad, but here as in Clement the negative aspect seems to be dominant, as far as the passible elements are concerned.[103] The reason for this is, that the basic dichotomy between the intelligible and the sensible world, which is observable in the tetrad itself, in Origen's view, imparts a primarily tragic character to the existence of empirical man, which is overcome only through his return to an original spiritual unity. The mind (νοῦς) is thus the light of the soul, while the irascible and concupiscible parts—the place of imaginations and passions—are darkness without this light.[104]

A number of tendencies, which we noticed in Clement, are further found also in Origen. Thus there are similar modifications in his use of the Stoic tetrad of passions. Anger (θυμός) or wrath (ὀργή) tend to occupy the place of grief (λύπη),[105] or even of desire (ἐπιθυμία).[106] The negative evaluation of the irascible element, which we found both in the Stoic tradition and in Clement, may, of course, be noticed also in Origen.

Paed. I. 8; GCS Clem. I, p. 127, 31 ff. and particularly 8; p. 133, 23 f. In relation to this problem, cf. also Lactantius' polemic in *De ira Dei,* 17, 1 ff.; CSEL 27, p. 110 ff.

[100] Human wrath is usually not righteous but causes injustice, see *Quis dives salvetur?* 8, 3; GCS Clem. 3, p. 165, 4.

[101] He notices that it is difficult to verify the Platonic triad by Scripture, see *De Princ.* 3. 4, 1; GCS Orig. 5, p. 264, 12 ff.

[102] *In Ezech., hom.* 1. 16; GCS Orig. 8, p. 339 f.

[103] Origen speaks of a παθητικὸν μέρος, divided into τὸ θυμικόν and τὸ ἐπιθυμητικόν, see *In Luc.,* fragm. no. 187; GCS Orig. 9, p. 307.

[104] *Ibid.;* cf. CROUZEL, *Théologie de l'image de Dieu,* pp. 130 f. with n. 9 and 159.

[105] *Comm. in Matth.* 15. 18; CGS Orig. 10, p. 402, 29 ff.

[106] *In Cant. cant., lib.* 2; GCS Orig. 8, p. 143, 22 ff.

θυμός is thus regarded e.g. as a "paralysis of souls",[107] or as an intoxication.[108] θυμός and wrath are almost identified.[109] This tendency becomes particularly apparent, when Origen demonstrates his eagerness to avoid misunderstandings concerning divine anger, which is said not to interfere with the fact that God is above all passions.[110] The negative understanding of the irascible element of the human soul is thus hardly weakened by the reference to the anger of God.

Evagrius and later Origenism

The restrictive attitude of Origen in relation to a Christian use of the trichotomy, with which we are here concerned, is not found in later Origenism. The Platonic trichotomy grows into a fixed element of its tradition. This is quite clear in Evagrius, who also carried his speculation on this theme much further than his predecessors. Since Evagrius greatly influenced Maximus at this point, we must devote more detailed attention to him.

The most decisive sign of this development from Origen to Evagrius is the fact that Evagrius not only substitutes mind (νοῦς) for spirit, but also reduces Origen's tetrad to a triad, where νοῦς is more or less identified with the rational part of the soul. The dominant Evagrian trichotomy of the soul thus consists of *mind, anger* and *concupiscence,*[111] though it also happens that he speaks of the concupiscible, irascible and reasonable parts of the soul without identifying the last one with the mind.[112]

---

[107] *Cat. fragm.* to Matth. 4: 23–24; no. 77; GCS Orig. 12, p. 46.

[108] *In Lev., hom.* 7, 1; GCS Orig. 6, p. 372, 20 f. and *In Ierem., hom.* 2, 8; GCS Orig. 8, p. 297, 16 f.

[109] *Iracundia* is intimately connected with *furor* (see *In Lib. Iesu nave, hom.* 12, 3; GCS Orig. 7, p. 370, 11) and θυμός with ὀργή (see *Comm. in Io.* 20, 36; GCS Orig. 4, p. 376, 25).

[110] *In Ierem., hom.* 18, 6; GCS Orig. 3, p. 160, 12 ff. The anger and wrath of God should be understood in a figurative sense and not as expressions of an anthropomorphic idea of God, see *Comm. in Matth.* 17, 18; GCS Orig. 10, p. 636, 14 ff. God's anger is an expression of his mercy, it belongs to his goodness, and his wrath serves the cause of human education (παιδεία), see *ibid.* 15. 11; p. 379, 14 ff. and *De or.*, 29, 15; GCS Orig. 2, p. 390, 12 ff. (On the same problem in Origen, cf. also e.g. *In Ezech., hom.* 10, 2; GCS Orig. 8, p. 419, 30 ff.; *In Num., hom.* 8, 1; GCS Orig. 7, p. 49, 14 ff.; *In lib. Iud., hom.* 2, 4; GCS Orig. 7, p. 477, 23 ff. and *Comm. in Io.* 6, 58; GCS Orig. 4, p. 167, 14 ff.)

[111] See e.g. *Cent. gnost.* 1. 53; OCP 5 (1939), p. 230; 1. 68; PO 28, p. 49; 1. 84; p. 57; cf. Frankenberg, pp. 120–121; 3. 35; in Muyldermans, *A travers la tradition manuscrite d'Évagre le Pontique* (Bibl. du Mus. 3), Louvain 1932, p. 85; 3. 59; OCP 5, p. 230; 4. 73; PO 28, p. 169; cf. Frankenberg, pp. 304–305; and 6. 83; p. 253; cf. Frankenberg, pp. 416–417.

[112] See e.g. *Pract.* 1. 58; PG 40, 1233 D–1236 A.—The relationship of the mind to sensibility is to Evagrius only accidental—as is the three-fold unity of mind, soul and body (cf. Refoulé, Immortalité de l'âme et la résurrection de la chair, RHR 163 (1963), p. 19 f.)—and this fact necessarily characterizes his use of the trichotomy.

Evagrius' triad is furthermore, in a characteristic way, related to his general speculations on physical and spiritual realities. Thus, νοῦς is associated with fire and is said to dominate among the angels, while ἐπιθυμία is associated with earth and dominates among men, and θυμός is related to air and dominates among demons.[113] This does not imply however, that Evagrius regards anger in a more negative way than concupiscence[114]—rather the opposite. Distinguishing among the demons between those who attack the different parts of the soul, at least he calls demons related to the mind "birds" and those related to anger "wild animals", while those related to concupiscence he names "domestic animals",[115] which is probably to say powers attacking man from within his own lower self.

Through his frequent identification of νοῦς with the reasonable part of the human soul, Evagrius obviously allows the basic dichotomy to interfere decisively with the unity of the soul. For this reason we should expect him to exclude the very possibility of any positive function of the passible parts. However this is not the case. Evagrius gives a positive rôle to all the three parts in relation to man's purification. He is able to do this, because his Origenist speculation allows for the idea that the mind itself is affected by its primitive fall and consequent attachment to the bodily world of the senses.

For this reason there is, within Evagrius' ascetic thinking, a certain room for both a good and a bad use of all the three parts of the soul. Thus, we learn that the mind may be united with either knowledge or ignorance, and that, consequently, the concupiscible part is susceptible either to chastity or luxury, and the irascible part united either with love or hatred.[116] All the three parts have likewise, according to Evagrius, to be healed of their disease: the mind through knowledge, the concupiscible part through chastity and the irascible part through love.[117] In this case a positive task lies open to each of these parts of the soul, which latter is then altogether reasonable: the concupiscible part is free to desire virtue, the irascible part to fight for this virtue and the rational part can devote itself to natural contemplation.[118] Evagrius even goes on to say that there is a situation where man need have no fear of any demons, because his

---

[113] See *Cent. gnost.* 1. 68; PO 28, p. 49.

[114] It requires, however, more medicine, see *Pract.* 1. 26; PG 40, 1228 D.

[115] *Cent. gnost.* 1. 53; OCP 5 (1939), p. 230. Demons are, in fact, the reasonable nature, which, because of too much θυμός, is no more in the service of God, see *Cent. gnost.* 3. 34; PO 28, p. 111.

[116] *Cent. gnost.* 1. 84; PO 28, p. 57; cf. FRANKENBERG, pp. 120–121.

[117] *Cent. gnost.* 3. 35; MUYLDERMANS, *op. cit.*, p. 85.

[118] See *Pract.* 1, 58; PG 40, 1233 D–1236 A. Cf. also *ibid.* 1. 61; PG 40, 1236 AB.

mind is all the time with the Lord, his irascible part is humble and his desire (ἐπιθυμία) is directed toward God.[119]

We ought, however, to remember that as regards the passible parts in most cases this positive aspect is restricted to man's purification and mortification, though, of course, it is Evagrius' conviction that it is the misuse of the *three* faculties which introduces vices into man's life.[120] It is, however, the temptations arising from the passible parts which prevent the human mind from the knowledge of God,[121] and each of them in its own way makes it blind.[122]

It should perhaps also be noted that Evagrius, following both Platonist and Stoic traditions, localizes θυμός in the chest, while he relates ἐπιθυμία to the blood.[123] Also Platonic is the idea that animals possess both these faculties, which for Evagrius accords well with his Origenist conviction that man's passible nature is of a secondary character, due to the second creation.[124] Evagrius' negative understanding of "anger" is particularly revealed in his conviction that it is a blindness, a passionate disturbance of the balance of the soul.[125] Connected with this too is his insistence on the close connection between θυμός and wrath.[126]

Later Evagrian asceticism presupposed Evagrius' own position, but hardly contributed much to the development of the tradition. *Tractatus ad eumdem Eulogium*—which is hardly to be attributed to Evagrius himself—however defines wrath in a characteristic way as the "law of θυμός",[127] and in the compilation from Cassian called *De octo vitiosis cogitationibus* the negative evaluation of these two terms—which are practically identified—is strongly emphasized.[128]

The Cappadocian Fathers and the trichotomy

When we now turn our attention to the Cappadocian Fathers, it becomes evident from the beginning that they naturally take the trichotomy for

---

[119] *Cent. gnost.* 4. 73; PO 28, p. 169.

[120] See *Cent. gnost.* 3. 59; OCP 5 (1939), p. 230.

[121] *Cent. gnost.* 6. 83; PO 28, p. 253.

[122] *Cent. gnost.* 5. 27; OCP 5 (1939), p. 231; cf. Ps.-Orig., *Sel. in Psalm.* 149, 6; PG 12, 1681 B.

[123] *Cent. gnost.* 6. 85; PO 28, p. 253.

[124] *Loc. cit.*

[125] See e.g. *Cent. gnost.* 5. 27; OCP 5 (1939), p. 231.

[126] See *De octo vit. cogitat.* 6; PG 40, 1273 A.

[127] See PG 79, 1144 A.

[128] Wrath is defined as μήτηρ μανίας. Here we also find the Evagrian idea that θυμός requires a stronger medicine than ἐπιθυμία. See PG 79, 1453 A–C.—It should be noted here in addition that an ascetic writer such as Diadochus of Photice, on the other hand, does not seem to be familiar with the trichotomy.

granted. Thereby a certain polarity between the irascible and the concupiscible elements is also presupposed by them. The trichotomy itself, however, presupposes the basic dichotomy which we have mentioned as a general characteristic of the Greek Christian writers. Thus Basil e.g. reckons with a duality in man between a principle of vitality (ζωτική) and a principle of intellect (θεωρητική), which corresponds with the Platonic duality between the intelligible and the passible elements. Basil's adherence to this tradition is further demonstrated by his possible use of the Platonic image of chariot and driver.[129] His analysis of the triad of anger (θυμός), grief and fear, which are all regarded as an intoxication of the soul,[130] is on the other hand, probably partly Stoic in origin. θυμός is further very closely linked with wrath,[131] though when defining their relationship he calls θυμός a disposition (διάθεσις) and wrath an impulse (ὁρμή).[132]

The most important example of the Cappadocian understanding of our trichotomy is, however, provided by Gregory of Nyssa in his *De anima et resurrectione.* There we are allowed to follow a conversation between Gregory and his sister, "the teacher" Macrina, where the latter discusses the question whether the concupiscible and irascible elements in man are of the same nature as the soul and really belong to it. She underlines, that one should make the Holy Scriptures the rule and therefore neglect the Platonic image of the chariot, the pair of horses and the driver.[133] But since the Bible sees the soul as the image of God, she concludes that all that is foreign to God has no natural relationship to the soul.[134] Thus it is already clear that the two terms are seen in a *negative perspective.* According to Macrina this negative understanding is further favoured by the fact that even the animals possess irascible and concupiscible faculties.[135] In reply to a question of Gregory, Macrina

---

[129] *Const. asc.* 2, 1; PG 31, 1340 C–1341 C. (This text however, has been regarded as spurious, see QUASTEN, *Patrology* 3, Utrecht/Antwerp—Westminster, Maryland 1960, p. 213.)

[130] See Basil, *De Jejun., hom.* 1; PG 31, 181 B.

[131] θυμός is called a μανία, see *Hom. adv. irat.* 1; PG 31, 356 B.

[132] See *Reg. brev., interr.* 55; PG 31, 1120 B. On the development of the concept of ὁρμή within Stoic thinking, see e.g. R.-A. GAUTHIER, S. Maxime le Confesseur et la psychologie de l'acte humain, RTAM 21 (1954), p. 65 f. An analogous definition of Basil is that of θυμός as νεῦρον τῆς ψυχῆς, preventing the τόνος of the soul from being directed towards the good, see *Hom. adv. irat.* 5; PG 31, 365 B.

[133] *De anima et resurr.;* PG 46, 49 BC.

[134] PG 46, 52 AB.

[135] PG 46, 53 A. Here the Platonic understanding is obviously no obstacle. In other contexts Gregory rather follows Aristotle in his distinctions between the nutritive, sensible and rational soul, which triad he identifies with both the Pauline and the Platonic trichotomy, see LADNER, DOP 12 (1958), p. 70 f. and 74.

then argues that since Moses, who has himself given the definition of the image of God, according to Scripture was superior to anger and concupiscence, it is impossible that those two latter elements should belong to the nature of the soul.[136] They are *merely accidental*, their passions arrive from outside and man may thus be liberated from them.[137]

We see here that to Gregory, whose real ideas Macrina obviously expresses, the negative understanding of the concrete passible elements has led to a denial of their consubstantiality with the human soul. The Platonic ambiguity at this point has given way to a more or less Stoic evaluation of the passible faculties.[138] We shall see later how such an entirely negative conclusion is excluded in Maximus' thinking.

Nemesius and Ps.-Denis—a more positive approach

This last suggestion, which we shall later exemplify, leads us naturally to ask whether there are no other writers, in whom a more positive evaluation, which might have also influenced Maximus, is to be found. The answer is that there are at least two writers, who should be brought into the foreground when we thus ask for a more positive approach: Nemesius of Emesa and Ps.-Denis.

In Nemesius we find, first of all, a *basic dichotomy* between a rational and an irrational element. The rational element contains thought, memory and higher imagination, while the irrational element is itself differentiated into two categories, that which is susceptible to reason and that which is entirely uncontrolled by reason. Through this arrangement Nemesius is obviously in the position to affirm both the possible obedience of the passible part to reason, and its close relationship to the body. Both the irascible and the concupiscible element of the human soul thus belong to that part which is *susceptible to reason,* while the physical appetites do not.[139] In this way Nemesius gives room for a more positive evaluation of the passible faculties than we usually find in Christian writers.

Nemesius, who localizes concupiscence in the liver and anger in the heart, goes far enough on this line to state that in men who live in

---

[136] PG 46, 53 C.

[137] PG 46, 53 D–56 A.

[138] Being a counterpart to Plato's *Phaedo* this dialogue otherwise in general provides a good opportunity for a comparison between Platonism and Gregory's position; see the special study on this topic: M. PELLEGRINO, Il Platonismo di San Grigorio Nisseno nel Dialogo intorno all' anima e alla risurrezione, RFN 30 (1938), pp. 437–474.

[139] See e.g. B. DOMANSKI, *Die Psychologie des Nemesius,* Münster 1900, p. 74, where a summarizing picture is given of how Nemesius differentiates the soul.

harmony with nature, it is in the very nature of these two passions to obey reason. In this case the Stoic ἀπάθεια is apparently far from the only possible attitude, for Nemesius goes on to say that they submit or rouse themselves as reason commands. In fact, life could not continue without them.[140] Another expression of this positive evaluation is Nemesius' insistence that as transgressions anger and concupiscence are not involuntary.[141] The fact that they lead to pleasure (ἡδονή) or grief prove that they are not.[142]

This positive view, however, does not imply that the Stoic perspective is entirely left out. One can, in fact, say that the mainly Stoic element of the four cardinal passions is integrated with the Platonic trichotomy into a mainly Aristotelian scheme.[143] As a vice θυμός is further identified with wrath, vindictiveness and rancour.[144]

Nemesius of Emesa thus obviously belongs among those Christian writers who were in a position to modify the Alexandrian and Nyssene Christian influence on Maximus in relation to his interpretation of the trichotomy.[145] Ps.-Denis is another. The triad of reason, anger and concupiscence is a normal element in his system.[146] As such, anger and concupiscence are further regarded as characteristic of irrational creatures. But when we find them in reasonable beings, they must be interpreted in another way.[147] The irascible and the concupiscible elements in man include valuable possibilities.

Thus, we are not only allowed to speak of a righteous anger in relation to God himself,[148] but we must, according to Ps.-Denis, allow for a *spiritual interpretation* of these faculties, a spiritual counterpart to them even on the heavenly level. Thus, the anger of animals may be a symbol of

---

[140] *De nat. hom.* 16; PG 40, 672 B–673 A.

[141] *Ibid.* 30; 724 AB.

[142] *Ibid.* 32; 729 B.

[143] The Stoic tetrad reveals its influence in the disposition of Nemesius' treatment of these problems. Thus ch. 17 deals with desire, ch. 18 with pleasure, ch. 19 with grief and ch. 20 with fear, to which is added ch. 21 on anger.

[144] *De nat. hom.* 21; PG 40, 692 A.

[145] We shall soon discuss the amount of Nemesius' influence at this particular point. In fact, Maximus quotes Nemesius literally from time to time; cf. GAUTHIER, *art. cit.,* p. 71 f. and n. 67–68.

[146] See *Ep.* 8, 3 f.; PG 3, 1093 A and C. In *De div. nom.* 4, 23 he mentions, however, an evil triad of anger, desire and occasional imagination, characteristic of demons (PG 3, 725 B).

[147] *De coel. hier.* 2, 4; PG 3, 141 D–144 A. However, Ps.-Denis is eager to emphasize that there are no parts of the soul as there are parts of the body, but he follows Plato by referring—though only symbolically—θυμός to the chest and ἐπιθυμία to the belly; see *De div. nom.* 9, 5; PG 3, 913 A.

[148] *Ep.* 8, 1; PG 3, 1085 A and 1089 C.

spiritual courage, and their desire a symbol of love (ἔρως) for God.[149] And on the human level, Ps.-Denis goes so far as to affirm that a person who is deprived of what is good because of his unreasonable concupiscence, has nevertheless a share in the good, in virtue of the reflection of a true good which is inherent in his evil alliances themselves. Again he asserts that a person who is filled with anger shares in the same way in the good, in virtue of the aspiration which anger itself exemplifies, though this aspiration ought to have been directed towards God.[150]

We may thus conclude that a Platonic ambiguity in relation to the concepts of the irascible and the concupiscible elements in man returns in Ps.-Denis. This, of course, does not exclude the fact that concupiscence is usually seen as something evil and θυμός is usually identified with wrath. This tendency is demonstrated not only by the fact that Ps.-Denis agrees to denote the wrath of God by the word θυμός,[151] but also by his use of a combination of words such as strife and anger (ἔρις καὶ θυμός).[152] There is also a Platonic element in his conviction that even the animals are provided with anger and concupiscence,[153] and that the irascible element is related to the chest or the heart, and the concupiscible element to the belly, while the reasonable element is related to the head.[154]

The background of Maximus' use of the trichotomy of rational, irascible and concupiscible is, as we have now seen, both rich and complicated. Where the Stoic tradition dominates, the last two faculties are entirely regarded from the point of view that they give rise to irrational passions which must be overcome in complete detachment (ἀπάθεια). The idea that man is a unity does not prevent this conclusion. Where the Platonic tradition dominates, on the other hand, a certain ambivalence characterizes the passible faculties, in spite of the fact that they belong to the bodily and irrational side of the basic dichotomy between intelligible and sensible, rational and irrational. In most Christian writers a Stoic, negative evaluation of anger and concupiscence is combined with a Platonic insistence on both the trichotomy and the dichotomy. This combination strengthens the negative evaluation, as we have found in a number of Alexandrian writers. This tendency is apparent in Evagrius,

---

[149] *De coel. hier.* 15, 8; PG 3, 337 B.
[150] See *De div. nom.* 4, 20; PG 3, 720 BC.
[151] Cf. p. 186, n. 99.
[152] *De div. nom.* 11, 5; PG 3, 953 A.
[153] *Ibid.* 4, 25; PG 3, 728 B.
[154] In *De div. nom.* 9, 5; PG 3, 913 A, these references are at least regarded as filled with symbolical meaning.

who usually identifies νοῦς with the reasonable element, though, on the other hand, with his practical and ascetic experience of man's position, he never oversimplifies the issue. In such a writer as Nemesius of Emesa, however, we have found a more genuine insistence both on the basic dichotomy and on a positive evaluation of the passible faculties as such.

The way was thus prepared for Maximus to work towards an integration of Evagrius' practical experience and systematic treatment of the life of the human passions, related to the trichotomy, into a synthesis, which gives to man a central and mediating position, and thus allows for the positive opportunities inherent in *all* the elements of the human soul.

We shall soon see, how the balancing aspects of differentiation and unity are at play in Maximus' use of the inherited idea of a trichotomy of the human soul.

4. The trichotomy and Maximus' allegorical Scripture interpretations

The importance which Maximus attaches to the triad of the rational, irascible and concupiscible elements or faculties of the human soul is demonstrated in different ways. The differentiation which this triad implies and the discernment which it requires is obviously dear to him. It may be all the more so, since it does not—according to Maximus' general understanding of created differentiations—interfere with the unity of man, which he affirms in principle. An excellent example of how this differentiation in the human soul appeals, in Maximus' view, to the power of spiritual discernment, is the extent to which it is used in his allegorical Scripture interpretations—which allow, at the same time, for a characteristic insistence on man as a spiritual unity willed by God. Let us give some examples.

The negative aspect of disintegration through the trichotomy

The idea of a three-fold spiritual discernment related to the negative aspect of the faculties of the soul—i.e. to their misuse in fallen man—is perhaps best illustrated by Maximus' allegorical interpretation of Acts 10: 12 ff. The sword with which Peter was supposed to kill the animals on the great sheet is thus interpreted as the sword of the Spirit, the word of God, and the variety of animals as the variety of human passions.[155] Peter

---

[155] Thal 27; CCSG 7, p. 195 ff.—Cf. Origen who says in a fragment of the *Catenae* that the differentiation of animals in the text serves to distinguish between different kinds of "sins" (*In Matth.*, fr. 137 II; GCS Orig. 12, p. 69).

now both distinguishes between them and sacrifices them. The creeping animals thereby symbolize those who have their concupiscible element attached to worldly things, the wild beasts those who stir up their irascible element to one another's destruction, and finally the birds those who puff up their rational element entirely for pride.[156]

Here we see that the differentiation dealt with, is first of all regarded as one of passions. Maximus' use of the symbolism of animals underlines this tendency. The reference to birds and to the different kinds of animals we have found to be Evagrian.[157] However, we should notice that the reasonable element is also included in this perspective.[158] And more important, Maximus immediately goes on to say that, through Peter's sacrifice, they are all transformed, so that souls filled with desire now long for heavenly things, those filled with anger are mild and benevolent towards other human beings, and those filled with pride are meek and God-loving.[159] Thus, the three faculties are not evil in themselves. Everything depends on their *use*. Put in the right order and perspective, they may serve the real purpose of the whole of man.

But then we also see clearly, why Maximus distinguishes so conscientiously between the different parts; they are expressions of the different relationships into which man has been introduced: the concupiscible element represents man's relationship to the lower world and thus is called to express his basic direction of being, attachment to a higher cause; the irascible element represents primarily the inter-human relationship; and the rational element the relationship to God as Intellect and Spirit.

Other allegorical interpretations where the negative aspect is predominant, are for instance related to 1 Sam. 17:34–37, where the lion and the bear slain by David (figure of Christ) are interpreted as anger and concupiscence, and the sheep as the reasonable element of the soul, always in danger of being swallowed up by the sensible passions,[160] or

---

[156] Thal 27; CCSG 7, p. 197.

[157] See Evagrius, *Cent. gnost.* 1. 53; OCP 5 (1939), p. 230; cf. p. 189 above. This tradition goes back at least to Plato who in *The Republic* calls the passible elements τὰ θηριώδη (589 d) and the concupiscible element τὸ ὀφεῶδες (590 b).

[158] Even Evagrius includes it, but the important difference is that this element in Evagrius' view is represented by the fallen mind (νοῦς); see p. 189 above. Of particular importance also, of course, is the general Origenist background to all that Evagrius has to say about the constitution of man.

[159] Thal 27; CCSG 7, p. 197.—About Peter as a model of the ascetic, see BLOWERS, *op.cit.*, p. 66.

[160] Thal 53; CCSG 7, p. 431 and QuDub. 1 37; CCSG 10, p. 153. Already Plato called the irascible element τὸ λεοντῶδες (*Res. publ.* 9; 590 b). Cf. also Origen, *In Ezech., hom.* 1, 16; GCS Orig. 8, p. 340, where *iracundia* is symbolized by the face of the lion.

again to Ps. (90) 91:13, where the lion and the dragon are interpreted as anger and concupiscence.[161]

The negative perspective is also predominant when "male and female", overcome in Christ, in Gal. 3: 28 are interpreted in Maximus' commentary to the Lord's Prayer as anger and concupiscence.[162] This has further to be combined with Maximus' insistence, in the same text, on the idea that the only one who fulfils the will of God on earth as it is in heaven is he who, mystically, pays service to God with his reasonable power alone, separated from anger and concupiscence. For in heaven there is "no concupiscence, dissolving the mind through pleasure", and "no furious anger which barks indecently" at those of the same race, but only reason (λόγος) which leads reasonable beings naturally to the first Logos.[163] Similar too is the idea that the "flesh and blood" of 1 Cor. 15: 50, which cannot inherit the kingdom of God, is to be understood as concupiscence and anger.[164]

The positive or neutral aspect of unity in trichotomy

A *positive* perspective is dominant in other Maximian interpretations of a similar kind. In these cases the relationship between the triad and the mind as man's spiritual subject is usually also pointed out. Thus Hezekiah of 2 Chron. 32:2 is interpreted as the mind, ruling in Jerusalem, i.e. the soul,[165] and the seniors and chiefs with whom he is said to have taken counsel (v. 4) are consequently the three faculties of the soul. They are called seniors, because they are the first powers of the soul, and chiefs because they provide a starting-point for other movements. And a right use of these faculties includes faith (the rational element), charity (the concupiscible element) and peace (the irascible element) respectively.[166]

---

[161] Ep 34; PG 91, 628 D–629A.

[162] OrDom; CCSG 23, p. 47. The idea of anger as male and concupiscence as female is found e.g. in Philo (see *De agricult.* 73; COHN & WENDLAND, 2, p. 110) and in Clement of Alexandria (see *Strom.* 3. 13; GCS Clem. 2, p. 238, 29).—On this interpretation in Maximus, see further ch. VI: 6 (pp. 376–380) below.

[163] OrDom; CCSG 23, p. 57 f. In this text the negative aspect—and the Evagrian influence—seem to be particularly dominant, though it also indirectly does give a place to the idea of a transformation, in asceticism, of all three faculties (896 C).

[164] QuDub 72; CCSG 10, p. 55. Cf. also Thal 62; CCSG 22, p. 129, where the wood and the stones, that are broken down by the Lord in the house of the soul, are said to be concupiscence and anger.

[165] Thal 49; CCSG 7, p. 351. In the *onomastica sacra* Hezekiah is regularly interpreted as power, strength or rule, see F. WUTZ, *Onomastica sacra* 1 (TU 41: 1), Leipzig 1914, p. 358. Cf. also BLOWERS, *op.cit.*, p. 116.

[166] CCSG 7, p. 355.

Likewise, the "city" of Mark 14: 13 is interpreted as the soul,[167] and the master of the house of Luke 22: 11 as the mind.[168] The unity of the soul, as well as its image character, is further underlined by Maximus, when he interprets the robe of Jesus, woven from the top throughout, of John 19: 23, as referring to the soul, having its kinship with the heavenly world.[169] From there it is no great step to the interpretation of the three days in which the multitudes were with Jesus in the desert (Matth. 15: 32) as symbolizing the three faculties of the soul, through which man *seeks, longs* and *fights* respectively.[170]

Finally, a *double* perspective is present for example in Maximus' interpretation of the different sacrificial animals of the old Israel as the different elements and spiritual qualities of the soul. Thus the ram, in Maximus' view, refers to the rational part, the bull to the irascible part, the goat to the concupiscible part, while the turtledove symbolizes moderation and the pigeon sanctification. These elements are thus presented in a neutral sense, but Maximus adds also that the pupil of the eye should be referred to the Sun of righteousness, which is in its turn to be identified with the mind ($\nu o \hat{v} \varsigma$). Therefore, it is once more the relationship to the mind which is the decisive factor.[171]

The same is true of Maximus' interpretation of Neh. 7: 67, where the foreign servants of both sexes are interpreted as anger and concupiscence, for which the mind should care, so that concupiscence is turned into a desire for divine things, and anger into an incessant energy of desire. Thus these foreign servants may be made by grace into true Hebrews.[172] The rôle of the mind is decisive. But the insistence on the fact that the servants are foreigners and are made into Hebrews only by grace, shows how important the basic dichotomy is to Maximus, and reveals too that the split caused by sin, which is always related to this dichotomy, is not overcome by man's efforts but by the grace of God.

It is thus clear, that Scripture itself, at least when it is interpreted tropologically,[173] refers, in Maximus' opinion, to the trichotomy of man, and this triad is thus not merely accidental. It is based on the purpose which God has set before man, and in the end that is why it allows for an allegorical interpretation. But this leads, in its turn, to the fact that it is as

---

[167] Thal 3; CCSG 7, p. 57.
[168] CCSG 7, p. 59.
[169] Thal 4; CCSG 7, p. 63.
[170] Thal 39; CCSG 7, p. 259. In the text there is no explicit reference to our trichotomy, but the scholies provide one without hesitation, see PG 90, 393 B.
[171] See QuDub 17; CCSG 10, p. 13 f.
[172] Thal 55; CCSG 7, p. 499 ff.
[173] See Thal 62; CCSG 22, p. 129 ($\tau \rho o \pi \iota \kappa \hat{\omega} \varsigma$).

important to point out the aspect of unity in this context as the aspect of differentiation.

5. *The trichotomy and human differentiation*

We have seen that Maximus frequently and consistently uses the trichotomy with which we are dealing in this section. The differentiation of the human soul which it implies, however, may be seen either in a negative or in a positive perspective. In the first instance it leads to an analysis of the human passions, in which Maximus often follows Evagrius and the Alexandrian tradition, and in the second instance it leads to an affirmation of the rôle which the different faculties of the soul have to play in man's ascetic endeavour, his sanctification and restoration to a positive relationship to his divine Cause and End. Here also Maximus to some extent follows Evagrius, but he even introduces view-points earlier represented by such writers as Nemesius and Ps.-Denis, and puts them into his general view of man's middle position and task of mediation.

This double perspective of the trichotomy can, of course, be illustrated in relation to each of its elements. A short study of Maximus' treatment of these different elements will show this.

The concupiscible element in human differentiation

The concupiscible element is *the element of desire* which is mainly responsible for the *fall* of man.[174] In fallen man this is further a constant fact, so that when the concupiscible element is frequently disturbed, its result is a fixed habit of pleasure ($\dot{\eta}\delta o\nu\dot{\eta}$).[175] For this reason the old man may be said to be corrupt according to his deceitful lusts (Eph. 4: 22).[176] Symbolized by armlets, concupiscence denotes acts made for the sake of lust, though ignorance is often said to be the real root of passions.[177] As we shall see in Chapter V, which is devoted particularly to catalogues of vices and virtues, these different acts may be clearly distinguished from each other and labelled as distinct vices.

The general psychological process by which this evil becomes active, is also analysed by Maximus in a way which is in good general accord with the Greek Christian tradition, influenced by Stoic teaching, to which he also adheres.

Thus in Amb 10 he puts the question how (bad) pleasure is born, and

---

[174] See e.g. Thal 62, CCSG 22, p. 129.
[175] Char 2. 70; CSC, p. 126.
[176] Ep 32; PG 91, 625 D.
[177] Thal 16; CCSG 7, p. 107 ff. (the passage refers indirectly to Ex. 32: 2–3).

answers that all pleasure derived from what is forbidden comes from a passion for something sensible mediated by sensation. Pleasure is, in fact, a kind of sensation formed in the sense by the sensible object, or a sense activity related to an irrational desire.[178] For a desire (ἐπιθυμία) combined with a particular sense, is changed into pleasure, when it brings a certain experience to the sense, and a sense moved by desire effects pleasure, when it attains to the sensed object.[179] On account of the fact that the human soul in its middle position is related both to God and to the sensible world, this process has to be transformed, through asceticism and the development of virtues, into a God-ward movement, establishing a true order and unity in man.

The *good* use of the concupiscible faculty is, in fact, strongly underlined by Maximus. For in the same way in which he allows for a true pleasure (ἡδονή) related to the divine realities, so also he allows for *a true desire,* implying a good use of the concupiscible element. Basically this possibility is inherent in God's purpose for man, the microcosm.

Maximus thus points out that all the faculties of the soul can be "logicized", and when that happens, the concupiscible desire is transformed into *joy,* a legitimate use of man's capacity for pleasure in accordance with the will of God.[180] In another text Maximus shows that when the concupiscible faculty is properly used, it is the vehicle of divine love, through which man in ardent desire (πόθος) for God is kept in indissoluble relation to that which he desires.[181]

Thus Maximus' statements about the positive use of the concupiscible element obviously imply that the passionate attachment to the world of the senses which is characteristic of its use in fallen man, may be restored to an attachment to God, where the element of passionate affection is preserved, but the object is different.[182]

---

[178] This understanding of sensation corresponds at the same time—*mutatis mutandis* —to what, in Aristotle's analysis, happens in relation to any kind of wish; see *Met.* 6, 7; 1032 b; cf. GAUTHIER, *art. cit.,* p. 59.

[179] PG 91, 1112 C; cf. HAUSHERR, *Philautie,* p. 61.

[180] Amb 6; PG 91, 1068 A. Reference is given here to two biblical examples of true joy: the joy of John the Baptist in his mother's womb (Luke 1: 41) and David's joy at the entry of the ark (2 Sam. 6).—It should be noticed here that the Epicurean distinction between joy of the mind and pleasure of the body had earlier been mentioned but hardly accepted by Nemesius, see *De nat. hom.* 18; PG 40, 681 A–684 A. The decisive difference according to Maximus is, of course, not *where* the pleasure is experienced, but what *object* it is which causes the pleasure, and that it is in accordance with the will of God and not with the egoistic will of man.

[181] Thal 49; CCSG 7, p. 355; cf. Ep 2; PG 91, 397 B, where in the same context the same aspect of πόθος is underlined.

[182] Evagrius also allows for some positive function of the concupiscible element.

The irascible element in differentiation

The irascible element is perhaps not as frequently put into a *negative* perspective as the concupiscible element.[183] There is, however, no difference in principle, such as would make the irascible element more ambiguous than the concupiscible element, as in the case of Plato. As with the concupiscible faculty, all depends on its use. However, the irascible faculty is usually directed towards *other human beings*.[184] The power of aggression is, of course, an inner quality, but it is most frequently exercised on the horizontal level. When put into the service of self-love—which is exercized primarily in the activities of the concupiscible element—it leads to a *tyranny,* which is not only the tyranny of the passion itself within one's own soul but, in Maximus' opinion, first of all a tyranny over others.[185]

Maximus' insistence on this inter-human character of anger seems to be particularly strong, though this aspect is also to be found in some of his predecessors, such as Evagrius,[186] Nilus,[187] Cassian,[188] and particularly Basil.[189]

Maximus' affirmation that anger tyrannically leads to imagination and establishes a manner of thought which is outside the law of nature, probably lies on the same line, since "nature" may here refer particularly to human nature as common to all men.[190]

Sometimes the stress lies, however, more on the inner condition of the soul. Such is the case, when Maximus emphasizes that a temper, which is constantly stirred, has as its result a cowardly and unmanly mind, though he goes on to say that such a disease of the irascible element is healed through a number of virtues, which are entirely active in the field of neighbourly relations.[191] Of a similar character—and

[183] This difference of evaluation has been noticed by DALMAIS, Un traité de théologie contemplative, RAM 29 (1953), p. 136, who says that Maximus is particularly concerned with "les désordres de l'affectivité", but that ". . . ceux de l'agressivité semblent l'avoir beaucoup moins frappé". Maximus thus—practically—preserves to some extent the middle position of anger which we found in the Platonic tradition as well as in Aristotle (see pp. 177 and 179 above), though his principle of an equal evaluation is clear.

[184] Its misuse results in hate, says Maximus in Char 3. 3; CSC, p. 144. See further ch. V: A below.

[185] See e.g. Ep 2; PG 91, 397 A and Ep 27; 620 C. Cf. ch. III: B, 3 (p. 161) above.

[186] See e.g. *De octo vit. cogitat.* 6; PG 40, 1273 A and *De mal. cogitat.,* in MUYLDERMANS, À travers la tradition manuscrite, p. 47 (no. 22).

[187] See *De octo spir. mal.* 9; PG 79, 1153 CD.

[188] *De octo vit. cogitat.;* PG 79, 1453 A–C.

[189] See e.g. *Hom. adv. irat.* I; PG 31, 356 A; 3; 360 D and 4; 364 A.

[190] OrDom CCSG 23, p. 47.

[191] Char 2. 70; CSC, p. 126.

equally ambivalent—is the allegorical interpretation of the neckpiece as referring to anger, since the neck is the τύπος of "majesty and tyranny".[192]

The inter-human perspective is, of course, also preserved by Maximus when he deals with the *positive* use of the irascible faculty. However this is not exclusively the case. The neighbourly relationship obviously dominates the picture, when he affirms—in a way which reminds one of Evagrius[193]—that the positive counterpart to a misuse of this element is provided by charity.[194] Of a different character however is his emphasis on the preservation of the full vigour of the irascible element within the life of virtues, for here the stress is on the inner quality which this element represents.[195]

But more important, the good use of this element, like that of the concupiscible part, also implies a particular quality in the *relationship to God*. This is made clear in Thal 49, where it is said that thanks to the faculty of the irascible element, the human soul may cling to the divine peace and thereby strengthen the movement of desire (ἐπιθυμία) towards the divine love (ἔρως), which thus should animate the concupiscible element.[196] And it is most explicitly affirmed in Ep 2, where the transformed power of anger is supposed to result in a fighting spirit for the attainment of the divine end, which is God himself.[197] It should be noted that Evagrius hardly goes so far.[198]

The rational element in differentiation

When we now turn our attention to the rational element, it must be mentioned first of all that the positive and negative aspects are both equally relevant to this highest element, just as they were to the lower parts of the human soul. At this point particularly Maximus shows his independence in relation to Evagrius. Not that Evagrius would deny that

---

[192] Thal 16; CCSG 7, p. 107.

[193] See *Pract.* 1. 26; PG 40, 1228 D; *Cent. gnost.* 1. 84; PO 28, p. 57 and 3. 35; p. 111.

[194] Amb 6; PG 91, 1068 A.

[195] See Thal 55; CCSG 7, p. 503. A corresponding idea in Evagrius is that the irascible element has to be "hardened", *Cent. gnost.* 6. 41; PO 28, p. 235. Evagrius stresses also the duty of the irascible part to "fight" for the virtue, see p. 189, n. 118 above and n. 198 below.

[196] CCSG 7, p. 355.

[197] PG 91, 397 B.

[198] When Evagrius mentions the good use of the irascible element, he only underlines that it may fight for those virtues, which the concupiscible element desires (*Pract.* 1. 58; PG 40, 1233 D–1236 A), that it may be transformed into courage and endurance (*Pract.* 1. 61; 1236 AB) and that it should be filled with humility (*Cent. gnost.* 4. 73; PO 28, p. 169).

the reasonable element in fallen man is deeply marked by sin, but that through his identification of this element with the mind ($\nu o\widehat{\upsilon}\varsigma$),[199] this truth is to a great extent obscured by his equally important insistence on the "divine" character of the mind.

Maximus, on the contrary, distinguishes the mind from the reasonable element and regards it as man's spiritual subject, of course affected by sin, but with a more direct relationship to all three parts of the soul.[200] Thus, the mind is to him never considered as the only true "part" of man, fallen into the trap of sensible creation and trying to return to its true home,[201] but it is the self of man entrusted with a divine call to restore, through its own unity, the created world which has been rent asunder by sin. The need for a transformation of the reasonable element is thus equally great as for the other faculties.

It should, of course, not be denied that there is a difference between the *negative* perspective as it is applied to the rational element and as it is applied to the other elements. For the rational element is not passible in a direct sense, and thus it depends, as far as its vices are concerned, upon the impulses which it receives from the other elements. It is from the testimony of the senses that it arrives at the false opinions and imaginations which darken its true faculty. Its primary vice is therefore expressed in a negative term, ignorance ($\mathring{\alpha}\gamma\nu o\iota\alpha$), i.e. ignorance of its divine Cause and End, which prepares it to fall a prey to all these imaginations from outside. But since all this depends on the decisions of the will of man, the passible parts are in principle not more responsible for his fall than the rational part.[202] By an act of will man turns his attention from God to the world of the senses. He empties himself of the natural relationship to God, which exists already thanks to the pre-existent relation between the Logos and the *logos* of his human nature. Thus Maximus can say, not only that self-love, which is primarily the vice of the concupiscible element, is the mother of passions and vices,[203] but also that ignorance is the cause and mother of the vices.[204] Ignorance and folly can be said to be the result of the misuse of the rational faculty.[205]

---

[199] This identification is particularly apparent in *Cent. gnost.;* in *Pract.* it happens that he speaks of the reasonable element in the same way as Maximus.

[200] Cf. ch. III: A, 2; p. 112 f. above.

[201] This is the Origenist view which lies behind Evagrius' statements at this point.

[202] See particularly the short psychological analysis of Ep 2; PG 91, 396 D–397 A.

[203] Char 2. 8; CSC, p. 92 and 2. 59; p. 122. See further on self-love, ch. V: A, 1 (pp. 232–248 below).

[204] Thal, *Prol.* CCSG 7, p. 31 and 16; CCSG 7, p. 107 ff.

[205] Char 3. 3; CSC, p. 144.

Another result is pride, because forgetful of God man elevates himself in an unfitting way.[206]

A *good* use of the rational faculty, consequently, establishes a direct relationship to God. Thus, according to Maximus, it gives birth to faith, which implies knowledge and information about God,[207] and is filled with knowledge and prudence.[208] Converted and transformed it is engaged in an enlightened search (ζήτησις) for God alone,[209] devoting itself to the different degrees of true rational examination (ἐρεύνησις and ἐξερεύνησις)[210] and aided to a greater or lesser degree by virtues implied in a good use of the other faculties.

The "earrings" of Ex. 32: 3 are interpreted as referring to the rational faculty, since the ear is a symbol of the *logos*,[211] and among the sacrificial animals of Israel the ram as the most important of them symbolizes the rational faculty, but also man as a whole as a "rational sheep".[212] The rational element has finally to be nurtured by spiritual contemplation and prayer.[213]

We have seen how the aspect of differentiation, as it is applied to the trichotomy of the soul, pertains both to the negative and the positive perspective of each of the elements of the triad. In the first place differentiation leads to passions and vices characteristic of each element respectively, and thereby to a dissolution of the soul, torn asunder by these passions. In the second place, however, differentiation is the starting-point for a process of the reintegration of man, in which each element may contribute what is proper to it, establishing and strengthening a true relationship of the whole of man to God, other human beings and the created world. This positive implication will become still more clear, when we come to consider the opposite aspect.

---

[206] Thal 27; CCSG 7, p. 197.

[207] Thal 49; CCSG 7, p. 355.

[208] Char 3. 3; CSC, p. 144.

[209] See e.g. Thal 39; CCSG 7, p. 259; OrDom; CCSG 23, p. 58 and Ep 2; PG 91, 397 B.

[210] See Maximus' analysis of these and their corresponding terms, related to the function of the mind, in Thal 59; CCSG 22, p. 65.

[211] Thal 16; CCSG 7, p. 107.

[212] QuDub 17, CCSG 10, p. 13 f.

[213] Char 4. 15; CSC, p. 200 and 4. 44; p. 212. It should be noted that Evagrius, speaking in *Pract.* on the good use of the reasonable faculty, says that it should devote itself to natural contemplation and contain φρόνησις, σύνεσις and σοφία (see *Pract.* 1. 58 and 61; PG 40, 1236 A).

6. The trichotomy and the mind in human unity and unification

In our last section we found it necessary to refer to Evagrius and to compare Maximus with him, for it seemed obvious that, as far as the analysis of the function of the trichotomy is concerned, Maximus must have taken over a considerable amount of material from Evagrius and the Evagrian tradition. In this section we should rather turn our attention to Nemesius and Ps.-Denis, since they have both made important contributions to the Christian understanding of the created unity of the human soul and the function of integration, which is to be performed by man through the faculties of his soul. Here Maximus' immediate dependence is not as easily demonstrated as in the case of Evagrius. As regards Ps.-Denis, however, we must allow for a general influence observable everywhere in Maximus' writings.[214] As regards Nemesius, there is a section of Amb 10, which consists of quotations from Nemesius precisely in relation to the different powers and faculties of the soul, and which at least proves that Maximus was well acquainted with Nemesius' analysis.[215] Yet, the real influence of these writers at this particular point is difficult to demonstrate, and we shall have to be content with general references.

But more important, as we have already emphasized,[216] is Maximus' understanding of the mind (νοῦς) as the spiritual subject of man, related to the whole of the human composite. This is, of course, of equal importance in relation to the trichotomy of the soul. Our primary task in this section is therefore to show, how this function of the mind in relation to the different elements of the triad—negatively as well as positively— underlines the aspect of unity *in* trichotomy and of unification *through* trichotomy.

Negatively Maximus' insistence on the mind as man's spiritual

---

[214] As regards Ps.-Denis' positive understanding of the elements of the trichotomy, see p. 193 f. above.

[215] The quotations are extensive and relate to a central analysis of the constitution of the soul. Their correspondence is almost perfect. The section is constructed as follows: Amb 10; PG 91, 1196 C = a combination of quotations from Nemesius, *De nat. hom.* 22; PG 40, 692 D–693 A, 16; 672 B and 672 B–673 A; PG 91, 1196 D = 17; PG 40, 676 B and C; PG 91, 1197 A = 17; PG 40, 676 C and 19; 688 A; PG 91, 1197 B = 20; PG 40, 688 B–689 A and 21; 692 A; PG 91, 1197 C = *De nat. hom.* 21; PG 40, 692 B. The isolated character of this complicated quotation in Maximus' own context leads, however, to the suspicion that Maximus has quoted from a florilegium rather than that he has combined the extracts himself. This suspicion is further strengthened by the fact that the Nemesian dialectic of pleasure—grief (ἡδονή—λύπη) is preserved and not replaced by the Maximian dialectic of pleasure—pain (ἡδονή—ὀδύνη).

[216] See ch. III: A, 2; p. 111 ff.

subject leads to the conclusion that the misuse of any of the elements of the human soul involves the mind itself, as well as the other elements of the soul, and leads in the end to a disintegration which is against the purpose placed before man. Thus, Maximus can say that it is the mind which in a sense sets the fire of the passions to all the elements,[217] and that the vigour of the mind itself is dissolved by concupiscence through pleasure.[218] The paralysed man of Luke 5: 19 is further anagogically interpreted as the mind, which, sick in sins, cannot see the Logos through the door, i.e. natural contemplation.[219] And in Char 1. 84 Maximus analyses the psychological process, by which this increasing darkness and disorder of the mind is brought about. It happens when the memory of something which has an appeal to the passible faculty of man calls forth a thought (λογισμός, in the Evagrian ascetic tradition usually the term for a thought, which includes a temptation) in the mind and this rouses the corresponding passion, which leads in the end to the necessary consent of the mind, after which the actual sin is an immediate result.[220]

This *active function of the mind* also in relation to man's misuse of the three elements of the soul is due to the fact that the mind itself is characterized by man's middle and mediating position. For it is Maximus' conviction that the human mind is not only intellectual but also passible, and that likewise the human faculty of sensation is not only sensible but also intellectual.[221] Now, this reminds us clearly of Nemesius of Emesa, who affirms that both the irascible and the concupiscible elements are susceptible to reason, a conviction which Maximus explicitly quotes in Amb 10.[222]

Against the background which we have now indicated, it becomes obvious that the relationship of the different parts of the soul to the mind is of equal importance also for the *positive* aspect, the unification and reintegration of man through Christ. Each mind, living by divine power, has these three "seniors and chiefs" at its positive disposal, Maximus underlines.[223] It is at once the head of man, which has to be washed (Matth. 6:17), i.e. illuminated by divine knowledge,[224] in order to

---

[217] Thal 16; CCSG 7, p. 107.

[218] OrDom; CCSG 23, p. 58.

[219] QuDub 162; CCSG 10, p. 113.

[220] CSC, p. 82. Cf. Nemesius' conviction that the transgressions of anger and concupiscence are not involuntary, see e.g. *De nat. hom.* 30; PG 40, 724 A.

[221] See Amb 10; PG 91, 1116 A and the whole of Thal 25; CCSG 7, p. 159–171 (cf. A, 1; p. 172 f. above). Sensation is "synthetic", says Maximus, Amb 10; 1113 A.

[222] See PG 91, 1196 C, where Maximus quotes Nemesius, *De nat. hom.* 16; PG 40, 672 B–673 A.

[223] Thal 49; CCSG 7, p. 355.

[224] QuDub 70; CCSG 10, p. 54.

function as a true spiritual subject. And it is also engaged in a search for God (ζήτησις and ἐκζήτησις), which is not only encouraged by this knowledge (integrated into man through his rational faculty), but also strengthened by the desire and vigour which fill his passible parts.[225]

Anger and concupiscence have certainly to be "logicized",[226] and even, as Dalmais has pointed out, in the end to be in some way transcended (i.e. subsumed) by the supreme simplicity of the λόγος.[227] But this in itself is not all that has to be said. For Maximus also states that when it is emphasized that as man's reason should be directed to the search for God, so the concupiscible faculty should move in ardent desire for Him and the irascible faculty should fight to hold Him fast, all this could be better expressed in the following way: the mind should tend towards God, strengthened as it were by its irascible element and aflame with love through the extreme desire of the concupiscible.[228] In other words, the mind as man's spiritual subject should use *all* its faculties— and in this context the passible ones play an important rôle. The reintegration of man and the fulfilment of his purpose through Christ is a matter not only of the intellect but also of will, emotion and temper—in order that he may arrive at a true relationship to God as man's Cause and End, a relationship carried by the will and manifested not only in "reasonable" communion, though this is primary, but also in virtues, which engage the whole of man.

When we apply this aspect of unification to the trichotomy of man as we find it in Maximus' writings, it thus reveals that the rôle of the mind as spiritual subject and as integrating factor is of the utmost importance. For through the mind consent is given either to a negative process which affects the whole of man and leads to disintegration, or to a positive process which also affects the whole of man and leads to a saving relationship with God, through which man is able to fulfil his task of integration and mediation. And in both perspectives, each element of the soul plays its part and effects the final result. Here as in other sections of Maximus' theology, created differentiation, represented by the trichotomy of the soul, is so far from in itself threatening the unity of man, that it may serve the development of this unity by its differentiated power. *The unity and the trichotomy of the human soul condition each other.*

But the mind as man's subject and the will of man are always of decisive importance. For this reason we must now turn our attention to Maximus' psychology of the will.

---

[225] Thal 59; CCSG 22, p. 65.
[226] Amb 6; PG 91, 1068 A.
[227] See DALMAIS, RAM 29 (1953), p. 139; cf. OrDom; CCSG 23, p. 57 f.
[228] *Ibid.;* CCSG 23, p. 58.

B.   The Psychology of the Will

We have seen how Maximus ascribes to the mind as man's spiritual subject an important integrating function. In fact, it is the task of the mind to direct the whole of man towards his God-given end, and thereby both to integrate the different parts of man with one another by relating them to this end—i.e. to establish a true microcosm—and to help this microcosm to fulfill a reconciling function in relation to the whole of God's creation—i.e. to act as a mediator between Divinity and created beings. The mind needs for this purpose the positive support of the three 'parts' of the human soul, not only the rational but also the passible 'parts' (or better: faculties). However, it goes without saying that the volitional capacity of man plays a most important rôle in this process. The integration of the different elements of the human composite (not least the psychic composite) through the establishment of a true relationship to man's divine end is not only an intellectual adventure but in equal degree a matter of intention, desire, good will, longing and love. For this reason the question of Maximus' psychology of the will is of primary importance for our study.

But on the other hand, since this theme is in itself very vast and leads to detailed discussions of its Christological consequences—for it was not until Maximus had become deeply involved in the heated discussions on the two wills of Christ that he developed his very differentiated psychology of the will—and since nevertheless Maximus' doctrine at this point permits of a shorter and more summary description, we shall in this general study of Maximus' anthropology try to deal with this topic rather briefly.

1.   Will, mind and human nature

For obvious reasons our first question concerns the relationship between mind and will in Maximus' understanding. Sherwood, who has convincingly emphasized the importance of the positive concept of motion in Maximus' thinking, affirms first of all that a "prominence of the volitive faculty" seems to be characteristic of the 7th century in general,[229] but then also that Maximus' system in the end lacks a perfect harmony between the elements of will and mind.[230] This is certainly true in the first case and may be true in the second, but are we not forced to add that it is

---

[229] SHERWOOD, *The Earlier Ambigua*, p. 130, n. 8.

[230] SHERWOOD, *op. cit.*, p. 154, n. 57—For a recent analysis of the understanding of the status and activity of the will in Maximus, see PIRET, *op.cit.*, pp. 305–329 (particularly based on *Disp. c. Pyrrho*).

this stress on the volitional faculty of man which deprives the concept of mind (νοῦς) of its purely intellectual character? Here we have already tried to show that this fact is closely connected with the idea of the mind as man's spiritual subject, i.e. as subject also in relation to man's passible and affective capacities. But if this is true, what Sherwood describes as Maximus' "weakness" is put into another perspective.

In fact, there is in Maximus' thinking a very close relationship between mind and will, or better: between the intellectual and the volitional faculties of man as they are both related to the mind as spiritual subject. The positive evaluation of the *three* faculties of the human soul as such, which we have demonstrated in section A of this chapter, leads inevitably to an understanding of both mind and will as superior to these three parts. The 'volitional' life of man, therefore, cannot be identified with the functions of the passible elements alone, nor can the 'intellectual' life of man be identified with the rational faculty alone.

Reason and will in human nature

This close relationship between intellect and will may now be observed at two levels: on the level of human nature and on the level of man's use of his human nature. On the level of human nature we notice clearly how Maximus combines the aspect of reason with the aspect of will. And this is further made in relation to a term, θέλησις, the use of which Maximus himself develops considerably and in a rather personal way.[231] In the *Letter to Marinus* Maximus defines θέλησις as a faculty of desire inherent in human nature itself,[232] regarded as "a rational appetency" (ὄρεξις λογική)[233] like the Aristotelian term wish (βούλησις),[234] and at the same time as a basic natural desire—and as such to be distinguished from βούλησις[235]—which belongs to man in virtue of his (intelligible) nature (θέλησις τῆς νοερᾶς ψυχῆς).[236]

---

231 Cf. GAUTHIER, RTAM 21 (1954), p. 77 ff.

232 ThPol 1; PG 91, 12 C.

233 PG 91, 13 A.

234 On this concept in Aristotle, see e.g. GAUTHIER, *art. cit.,* p. 58 f.

235 For this distinction, unknown to Aristotle, Maximus refers in *Disp. c. Pyrrh.* to a lost work, *De Providentia,* of Clement of Alexandria (which he, however, calls *Stromateis*), see PG 91, 317 C; cf. GCS Clem. 3, p. 220, 11 ff. and WOLFSON, *The Philosophy of the Church Fathers,* p. 465 and n. 16. In ThPol 26 (PG 91, 276 C) he refers a similar definition explicitly to Clement's *De Providentia.* (E. F. OSBORN, *The Philosophy of Clement of Alexandria,* TSt 3, Cambridge 1957, p. 190 f. discusses Maximus' references to *De Providentia* but thinks it is a work of a later writer. He does not seem to know the problem of the authorship of the scholies to Ps.-Denis, however, and his conclusions about Maximus' very limited knowledge of Clement are hasty.)

236 ThPol 1; PG 91, 21 D.

Maximus affirms in fact that reasonable nature possesses reasonable desire as its natural faculty which is also called "will of the intelligible soul", and adds that, therefore, "we reason willingly, and reasoning we wish according to our willing faculty".[237] Thus, according to Maximus, no human being wills without reasoning or uses his rational faculty without being moved in his faculty of desire. In virtue of his rational nature man is both *reasoning and desiring,* willing and seeking, etc.[238]

Human nature is, thus, to Maximus not only reasonable ($\lambda o \gamma \iota \kappa \acute{\eta}$) but at the same time volitional ($\theta \epsilon \lambda \eta \tau \iota \kappa \acute{\eta}$).[239] Man is volitional ($\theta \epsilon \lambda \eta \tau \iota \kappa \acute{o} \varsigma$) in his very substance, in virtue of his being a reasonable creature.[240] This combination of the aspects of reason and will is, however, further supported by Maximus with a definition of Diadochus of Photice, according to which self-determination is a faculty of will ($\theta \acute{\epsilon} \lambda \eta \sigma \iota \varsigma$) which belongs to the rational soul.[241] Through this affirmation the freedom and dignity of man as created in the image of God are shown to be bound up with his being a creature with both reason and will.[242] Thus for Maximus the fulfilment of man's purpose is immediately linked with his being not only reasonable and intelligible—it is his $\nu o \hat{u} \varsigma$ which carries the image of God—, but also willing, for self-determination is the core of this image of God.

Finally, the centrality of this theme is also shown by the fact that in his florilegium ThPol 26 Maximus brings together a number of quotations which manifest the same combination of the ideas of reason and will as related to the freedom of man. Among these there should be mentioned particularly one from Clement of Alexandria where—as in the quotation mentioned above—$\nu o \hat{u} \varsigma$ itself as moved freely is identified with $\theta \acute{\epsilon} \lambda \eta \sigma \iota \varsigma$ and also with self-determination,[243] but also quotations from Athanasius[244] and from Gregory of Nyssa,[245] which express virtually the same view. It is characteristic of Maximus, as a

---

[237] Pyrrh; PG 91, 293 B.

[238] ThPol 1; PG 91, 24 A.

[239] *Ibid.;* 12 D.

[240] Pyrrh; PG 91, 301 C. This expression, $\theta \epsilon \lambda \eta \tau \iota \kappa \acute{o} \varsigma$, seems to have been introduced for Christological purposes by Maximus in his dispute with Pyrrhus; cf. E. CASPAR, *Geschichte des Papsttums,* 2, Tübingen 1933, p. 547.

[241] Αὐτεξουσιότης ἐστὶ ψυχῆς λογικῆς θέλησις . . ., Diadochus, *Cap. gnost.* 5; DES PLACES, p. 86, 18.

[242] See particularly Pyrrh; PG 91, 301 C and 324 D. The quotation from Diadochus is also found in ThPol 26; PG 91, 277 C.—It is through this kind of an argumentation that Maximus proves that acceptance of the two natures in Christ leads inevitably to the further affirmation of two natural wills in him.

whole that he draws as much support as possible from the Fathers for this combination of the intellectual and volitional aspects, which seems particularly important to him. Such support was obviously to be found within the Christian tradition, though the exact value of it is still difficult to estimate because of the fragmentary character of Maximus' own quotations (an indirect sign of Maximus' personal involvement in the question?).

The mind and man's use of his self-determinative nature

θέλησις is thus to Maximus a rational desire which belongs to man as such, a capacity for self-determination inherent in his human nature. Sometimes Maximus also calls it *"natural will"* (θέλημα φυσικόν).[246] This term, however, immediately actualizes the second level on which the close relationship between mind and will may be observed in Maximus, i.e. man's use of his self-determinative nature. For "natural will" is in Maximus' later writings explicitly compared and contrasted with a corresponding expression, *"gnomic will"* (θέλημα γνωμικόν), which denotes exactly this individual human use of the θέλησις.

"Natural will" is the *rational* faculty of self-determination inherent in man, "gnomic will" is the free and *ambiguous* (ἐφ' ἑκάτερα) desire and motion active in concrete man,[247] and called forth by man's sense of pleasure (spiritual or bodily).[248] "Natural will" is based on God-given human nature and thus closely related to the λόγος of human nature; "gnomic will" is based on γνώμη, i.e. the *habitus* of desire which man has acquired through his use of his capacity for self-determination.[249]

This ambiguous character of the "gnomic will" does not, however, exclude a relationship on its part to the mind. For, as we have seen, the mind is deeply involved and active in man's life, whether sinful or righteous, whether full of irrational passions or God-directed and rational. Thus Maximus clearly points out that it is the mind which gives its consent to the impulses of the senses. It consents to impassioned

---

243 PG 91, 276 C; cf. note 235, p. 209 above.
244 PG 91, 277 A; cf. Athanasius, *Fragm. var.;* PG 26, 1292 D.
245 PG 91, 277 B. I have not found it elsewhere.
246 See ThPol 1; PG 91, 12 C; cf. ThPol 26; 280 A.
247 ThPol 14; PG 91, 153 AB.
248 ThPol 26; PG 91, 280 A.
249 See further the next section on the term γνώμη.

thoughts and imaginings,[250] to the suggestions of the demons,[251] to sin,[252] etc. There is however no reason to suppose that this concept of consent (συγκατάθεσις) has entirely lost its positive Stoic sense as a characteristic of human freedom,[253] though Maximus does use other ways to express the positive function of human freedom of choice, or to denote a more neutral relationship of mind and will.

What is important in this respect is first of all the fact that the mind is seen as active in relation to the goals to which it is directed. Thus Maximus emphasizes that the expanding mind directs its desire (ἐπιθυμία) and love either towards divine and intelligible things or towards the things of the flesh and the passions.[254] It stands between virtue and vice, angel and demon, but has power to follow or resist which one it wills.[255]

Even if Maximus obviously often sees the will as an independent element and the mind primarily as the intellect—this is not least the case in *Cent. de char.* and *Cent. gnost.*—the mind has nevertheless a coordinating function in relation to all the elements and faculties of the human soul. Therefore, on the one hand the mind should always try to be free from its dependence upon outward impressions and strive to become a "naked mind", but, on the other hand, it should also integrate the whole of man with itself and use all the elements of the human composite for a good purpose. For this reason Maximus emphasizes in *Cent. de char.* not only that the mind, which tends either towards God or to the flesh,[256] should advance in love for God[257] and should be God-loving,[258] or that it should operate according to its nature,[259] but also that it should *love* both the Saviour and *its neighbour*,[260] and pass through the observances of active and contemplative life to "theology".[261] Man should join knowledge to action and thereby deprive anger and concupiscence of their (negative) strength and give wings to the mind,[262] and the mind may

---

[250] Char 1. 84; CSC, p. 82; 2. 56; p. 120.
[251] *Ibid.* 2. 19; p. 98.
[252] *Ibid.* 3. 34; p. 160.
[253] Cf. GAUTHIER, *art. cit.*, pp. 64 and 71, n. 68.
[254] Char 3. 71; CSC, p. 176 ff.
[255] *Ibid.* 3. 92; p. 188.
[256] *Ibid.* 3. 12; p. 148.
[257] *Ibid.* 2. 14; p. 96.
[258] *Ibid.* 3. 40; p. 162.
[259] *Ibid.* 4. 45; p. 212.
[260] *Ibid.* 4. 56; p. 218.
[261] *Ibid.* 2. 26; p. 102.
[262] *Ibid.* 2. 28; p. 104.

even make the passible element one with itself and so turn it into a divinely burning love and endless charity.[263]

The "gnomic will" is closely related to the activities of the mind. The ambiguity which characterizes it is due to the same factor which gives its ambivalent position to the mind, allowing it to turn its attention either to God or to the world of the senses and passions. The only difference is that the relationship between the mind and "natural will" is one which is coherent with the rational character of both as signs of the divine image in man, while the relationship between the mind and "gnomic will" may lead either to an irrational disintegration of man (fallen and individualized), or to a restoration of man as directed in accordance with the rational principle of the human nature (its λόγος φύσεως). This leads us, however, to a closer analysis of the term γνώμη itself.

2. Γνώμη—an ambiguous term

As we have indicated already, γνώμη—a favourite term of Maximus'—does not denote an act of the will but a disposition or *habitus* of will, such as man as individual and as fallen creature may establish for himself. From it spring different acts of will, but by itself it is an ambiguous reflexion of man's basic capacity for self-determination. Sherwood has studied Maximus' use of this term in detail and has revealed a certain development in Maximus' thinking at this point.[264] There is therefore no need to do his valuable work again; rather we shall content ourselves with pointing out a few things which are of particular interest within the context of our study.

Its use before Maximus

First of all it should be noted that the word γνώμη, which had originally a very varied use and the rather general sense of "opinion",[265] "mind", etc., had received in some of the Fathers of the Church a slightly more defined theological content. However it is not until Maximus that this term gains so dominant a position and so fixed a use. This development is partly reflected even in Maximus' own writings, so that the sense of the term is much more clear in his later works.[266] Let us simply indicate some of the possible roots of Maximus' understanding of the term.[267]

---

[263] *Ibid.* 2. 48; p. 116.

[264] See SHERWOOD, in ACW, pp. 58–63.

[265] This use of the term is also found in Maximus, see e.g. Char 1. 70–71; CSC, p. 76; cf. SHERWOOD, in ACW, p. 59.

[266] This is, however, true of all his volitional terminology and is, of course, a result of

Maximus says himself, that he has found 28 different understandings of the term in biblical texts and in the Fathers,[268] but all of this material can hardly have been of equal importance to him. The characteristic ambiguity of γνώμη is, however, reflected in a number of Christian writers. Thus already Denis of Alexandria seems to have discussed the difficulty in attributing a "gnomic will" to Christ—though some of the Fathers are said to have done it—since Christ stands above all deliberation,[269] and according to Didymus the Blind sin is due to human beings because of their γνώμη as well as their works.[270] The term often expresses man's free consent,[271] but this at the same time implies a choice between good and evil.[272] In a writer like Theodoret of Cyrus this fact does not lead to a denial of a γνώμη in Christ,[273] but at least to an affirmation of the difference between Christ's γνώμη and that of human beings in general.[274] In Basil of Seleucia γνώμη means good or bad intention.[275] Finally, it should also be noted that Nestorius' proposal that there is a "gnomic" union in Christ and thus a gnomic will, though no union of natures, had been refuted in Ps.-Leontius with the argumentation that what γνώμη possesses, "nature" also possesses, and that if there is a "gnomic union" in Christ, there must all the more be a "union of natures" in him.[276]

Its note of ambiguity in Maximus' understanding

Thus the term γνώμη had already acquired a sense of a human, and relative, intention and a certain ambiguity regarding its direction, when Maximus began to use it widely in his writings. It is also quite clear that the development and change which this term underwent in Maximus himself is not so radical as to mean that there is no consistency in his use and understanding of it.

---

his contributions to the discussions about one or two wills in Christ.

[267] Regarding the use and frequency of the term γνώμη in early Christian writers, I am most grateful to Miss Hilda GRAEF, Oxford, who kindly made her studies of the subject for the *Oxford Patristic Greek Lexikon* available to me by allowing me to consult all her preparatory material. See now F.L. CROSS, *A Patristic Greek Lexikon*, p. 317 f.

[268] Pyrrh; PG 91, 312 C.

[269] See *Interpret. in Luc.;* PG 10, 1593 C.

[270] *De Trin.* 3, 10; PG 39, 857 C.

[271] So in Chrysostom, *In Matth.*, hom. 76 (77), 4; PG 58, 699 and *In Ep. 1 ad Cor.*, hom. 3, 1; PG 61, 23 (here also in the sense of "opinion").

[272] See Cyril of Alexandria, *De ador. et cult. in spir. et verit.* 6; PG 68, 456 D.

[273] It may denote Christ's free consent to his sufferings, see *In. Zach.* 13; PG 81, 1949 A.

[274] See *Interpret. Ep. ad Rom.* 8; PG 82, 128 D.

[275] See *Or.* 4; PG 85, 68 D, 69 A, C and 72 A.

[276] *Adv. Nestor.* I, 41; PG 86, 1501 A–C.

The most obvious change is in relation to Christ, so that while Maximus in his earlier thinking is able to attribute γνώμη (though without passion) to Christ,[277] during the Christological debates about the two wills he denies it of Christ, because uncertainty and ambiguity belong to γνώμη as such but are in principle excluded in Christ.[278] In his *Dispute with Pyrrhus* Maximus even regards it as a blasphemy to attribute γνώμη to Christ, since Christ is never "pure man" (ψιλὸς ἄνθρωπος) but always hypostatically one with God.[279] The difference between these two positions is, however, not so great as it may look, for already in *Expos. or. Dom.*, where Maximus affirms a γνώμη in Christ, he distinguishes it by describing it as being without passion and revolt in relation to human nature (i.e. the principle and purpose of human nature) from the very beginning.[280] It thus denotes a character of will which is always susceptible to the rational principle underlying created human nature, in spite of the fact that it is usually characteristic of γνώμη in man that it is unfixed and uncertain.[281] And this implies—to use a later Maximian terminology —that Christ's γνώμη in these earlier statements coincides more or less with what Maximus calls "natural will". Whenever Maximus attributes a γνώμη to Christ he thus underlines the uniqueness of its character in him.

It is, in fact, the ambiguous character of γνώμη in ordinary human beings which Maximus constantly stresses. For this reason the clue to a virtuous life in Christ is to Maximus, not least in his early writings, the establishment of a peaceful and harmonious relationship between γνώμη and that nature which is shared by all human beings,[282] since the tyranny of passions is exerted "gnomically"[283] and a sinful γνώμη always cuts the one human nature into pieces.[284] Thus there is always to be found in Maximus a clear distinction between γνώμη (and "gnomic will") on the

---

[277] See OrDom; CCSG 23, p. 34, this opinion is repeated as late as in ThPol 7; PG 91, 80 A (for the dating of this text, see SHERWOOD, *An Annotated Date-list*, p. 51). On this problem, cf. LÉTHEL, *op. cit.*, p. 127 ff.

[278] This position is first indirectly presented in ThPol 16; PG 91, 193 A. This opuscule is translated by LÉTHEL, *op. cit.*, p. 124, who regards it as the mature key text on Christ's freedom of will.

[279] PG 91; 308 D–309 A.

[280] CCSG 23, p. 34.

[281] This idea is present also in ThPol 7; PG 91, 80 A.

[282] See e.g. OrDom; CCSG 23, p. 55 and p. 65 f., Thal 64; CCSG 22, p. 233 and Ep 2; PG 91, 396 C and 400 D–401 A; cf. Thal 6; CCSG 7, p. 69 and Ep 14; PG 91, 533 B.

[283] OrDom; CCSG 23, p. 69.

[284] See *ibid.*; CCSG 23, p. 65 (cf. e.g. CCSG 23, p. 37) and Ep 2; PG 91, 396 D. It should be added here that I am, therefore, opposed to any identification of γνώμη with *liberum arbitrium* in an inclusive sense, moderately discussed by LARCHET, see *op. cit.*, (forthcoming), p. 69 ff.

one hand and nature (and "natural will") on the other. However this does not imply that γνώμη must be defined in opposition to nature (see below).

Γνώμη and the aspect of differentiation

This last point is of a particular interest in our study. For since nature (and "natural will") represents the aspect of unity—and thus conformity with the principle of nature and the corresponding aspect of unification —while γνώμη represents the aspect of individuality and differentiation, a diametrical opposition between nature and γνώμη would, at this very point, introduce, for the first time, an entirely negative evaluation of the aspect of differentiation into Maximus' thinking. It seems, however, quite obvious that such an opposition is *not* what Maximus intended. His willingness in the beginning to attribute a γνώμη (though entirely without passion) to Christ shows this, while his later denial of a γνώμη in Christ was probably also due to the fact that he regarded the incarnate Christ not only as one human being among many but as Man, representative of all humanity. For according to Maximus, it is always the same Christ, who is present in a differentiated manner in the individual virtues of the believer, as it is through one and the same Logos that all are created in the beginning.

The ambiguity of γνώμη is, of course, a consequence of the fall. It is formed by the acts of deliberation about good and evil, which are characteristic of fallen man, because of ignorance of the true good and because the evil alternative is always present. But this ambiguity neither excludes a positive relationship to human nature and to the power of self-determination which is the dignity of this nature, nor does it lead to an entirely negative evaluation of the acts of γνώμη. These are all expressions of man's free will, and rightly used they lead to goodness and a virtuous life.[285]

Sherwood has correctly underlined that though γνώμη cannot affect the nature and substance of things, it is related to that motion which is consequent upon nature.[286] For this reason γνώμη is defined as a "mode of use" (i.e. of the human faculty of willing) and not a principle of nature".[287] It is a mode of life,[288] i.e. a personal and *individual* disposition

---

[285] Cf. GAUTHIER, *art. cit.,* p. 80 ff., who has seen this positive relationship to human free will, but nevertheless opposes γνώμη too strongly to nature and seems to take the negative acts of decision, emanating from γνώμη, almost exclusively into consideration. The discussion by LARCHET, *op. cit.,* p. 69 ff., is far more balanced.

[286] SHERWOOD, in ACW, p. 58.

[287] Pyrrh; PG 91, 308 D: τρόπος οὖσα χρήσεως, οὐ λόγος φύσεως.

[288] *Ibid.;* PG 91, 308 B.

(διάθεσις)[289] or *habitus* (ἕξις),[290] acquired through free human acts of decision, though always changeable. It thus belongs to the field of personal existence (ὕπαρξις), though as such it stands in a constant relationship to the sphere of nature (φύσις).[291]

However, there is a certain fixity also of the "modes" in relation to nature, in that the modes are meant to be in accordance with nature.[292] There is, in other words, a divine plan which awaits fulfillment. And this pertains also to γνώμη as "mode of use", a fact which is particularly well brought out in *Expos. or. Dom.*, where Maximus states explicitly that a γνώμη which is in revolt, causes as it were an inward revolt in nature.[293] It belongs to nature itself that its purpose should be fulfilled. A lack of realization does not affect this purpose as such, but human self-determination is certainly divided against itself.

Man is, consequently, always called to present not only a γνώμη which abstains from revolt, but also a good γνώμη.[294] Thus in *Cent. de char.* Maximus emphasizes that a virtuous man is loved by God as one who has made himself closely acquainted with God through his γνώμη, and who loves his fellow-beings in a similar way,[295] and furthermore that the imitator of God alone is good, not by nature as is God, but through the conformity of his γνώμη.[296] Likewise, in *Amb. lib.* the middle state of well-being (εὐ-εἶναι) is said to be acquired, not only through the grace of God but also through the acts of γνώμη.[297] Virtue and the human relationship to the good as a whole are closely attached to the realm of γνώμη.[298]

The function of γνώμη and the aspect of individuality and differentiation which is linked with it, is thus far from being seen in a purely negative perspective. On the contrary, it is a necessary and in itself positive counterpart to the will of nature and the aspect of unity which the latter represents. Here as elsewhere Maximus is eager to stress both

---

[289] Ep 6; PG 91, 428 D.

[290] ThPol 1; PG 91, 17 C.

[291] Cf. SHERWOOD, in ACW, p. 57 f.

[292] See above ch. II, p. 91 and n. 267. There is an individual "mode of use" among human beings, and a common human "mode of existence" of mankind, but the individual "mode" is meant to be in accordance with the common "mode", and the common human "mode" is called to share with Christ in his "divine mode" of human existence. Cf. also SHERWOOD, in ACW, p. 35 f.

[293] CCSG 23, p. 55.

[294] Man is called to "gnomic reform", says SHERWOOD, in ACW, p. 81.

[295] Char 1. 25; CSC, p. 58.

[296] *Ibid.* 4. 90; p. 234.

[297] Amb 10; PG 91, 1116 B; cf. Amb 7; 1073 C.

[298] See e.g. Ep 1; PG 91, 364 A and 365 B, and Thal 64; CCSG 22, p. 233 ff.

sides. Man's power of self-determination must be exerted on the personal and "existential" level. But if it is, at the same time it should serve the purpose of higher unification. This is most eloquently illustrated by a passage in Amb 7, where Maximus shows that true fixity in the good is finally achieved only through a surpassing of γνώμη, a voluntary transcendence of conditioned human self-determination, which is, however, at the same time "its perfect fulfilment according to the capacity of its nature".[299]

3. *Stages of volitional activity*

We have seen, how closely the affective and rational faculties of the human soul are combined in Maximus' understanding of man's volitional activity, and we have also seen, how he balances the aspect of unity and unification (natural will in its relationship to the principle of human nature) and the aspect of individuality and differentiation (gnomic will and its fulfilment in acts of self-determination) against each other.[300] When we now turn our attention to the different stages of the volitional activity (the differentiated terminology of the human will), as Maximus conceived of them in the course of the dyothelite debates, we shall be able to notice how these elements all enter into the picture and form a whole.[301]

Let us therefore study the different moments of this human process of willing, to be found in its clearest expression in Maximus' *Letter to Marinus,* but also elsewhere.[302]

The basic presupposition for all later stages of volition is, as we have indicated, the fundamental *capacity for willing* (θέλησις), which is to Maximus a pre-eminent expression of the image character of human nature.[303] Man is a creature who wills and he always expresses his nature in acts of the will. This capacity is at the same time a rational and vital

---

[299] Maximus calls this transcendence an ἔκχωρησις γνωμική, see PG 91, 1076 B; cf. SHERWOOD, in ACW, p. 59, and also *The Earlier Ambigua,* p. 129. See further also ch. VI: 10, p. 424 below.

[300] See section 1, pp. 211 and 213 above.

[301] GAUTHIER, *art. cit.,* pp. 71–82, has discussed and systematized the scheme of this terminology. We shall rely to a great extent on his presentation and criticize it at particular points.

[302] The order of the different stages may be constructed through a study of the following texts: ThPol 1; PG 91, 12 C–16 C; 13 A; 16 B; 17 D–20 A; 21 D–24 A and Pyrrh; PG 91, 293 BC. LARCHET, *op. cit.,* p. 71 f. discusses this scheme of stages in a very interesting, but not uncontestable, way.

[303] See above under 1, p. 209 f. On Maximus' use of the term θέλησις, see J. D. MADDEN, The Authenticity . . . , in HEINZER-SCHÖNBORN, *Maximus Confessor,* pp. 61–79.

will, which obviously wills according to nature and the λόγος of nature. Therefore, it is also called "natural will" (θέλημα φυσικόν).[304]

Man is thus by his very nature bound to desire as well as to rationalize. There is, however, also a disposition other than that of nature, which guides man's willing activity, and this is, as we have seen, the personal disposition or *habit* of γνώμη, which is developed through man's actual willing. γνώμη represents the personal and actualized aspect of man's capacity for self-determination. It is thus not identical with choice but leads to choice.[305] All acts of the will presuppose, according to Maximus, these two conditions, one directly of nature, the other of the *habitus* of the individual.

The wish

The starting-point of *actual willing*, however, is βούλησις, *wish*, Maximus' definition of which is particularly interesting, since it shows that he conceives of the human soul as a unit, more in the sense of the Stoic understanding than of the Aristotelian one. Aristotle regarded βούλησις as "a rational desire", different from "concupiscence" which is a desire mingled with sensible imagination (φαντασία),[306] but Maximus defines it exactly as an *"imaginative appetency"* (ὄρεξις φανταστική).[307] For the Stoics, on the contrary, who denied the basic dichotomy of man, all action implied an element of imagination, though human action was distinguished by rational consent (συγκατάθεσις).[308] One should also add that with Nemesius—who builds primarily on Aristotle but had also undergone an important Stoic influence, since he was dependent on both Galen and Poseidonius—Maximus obviously does not see imagination as in itself contrary to reason.[309] This is important, since it is one of the expressions of the middle position of man in Maximus' thought. The wish is further related to its object, which is the *goal* (τέλος) of the act of willing, while choice (προαίρεσις) is only related to the means by which this goal may be reached.[310] For this reason "wish" is a concept which

---

[304] See ThPol 1; PG 91, 12 D–13 A; cf. ThPol 26; 280 A.
[305] ThPol 1; PG 91, 17 C.
[306] Cf. WOLFSON, *The Philosophy of the Church Fathers*, p. 463 f.
[307] ThPol 1; PG 91, 13 B.
[308] Cf. GAUTHIER, *art. cit.,* p. 64 ff.
[309] For Nemesius, cf. however DOMANSKI, *op. cit.,* p. 74 f., n. 1, where Nemesius' ambiguity at this point is discussed, but the conclusion is drawn that the imaginative element rather belongs to the irrational soul.
[310] ThPol 1; PG 91, 13 C.

comes close to γνώμη. It manifests the intention itself of an acting human being.[311]

The enquiry

The next stage in a human psychology of willing in Maximus is expressed by the term *search* (ζήτησις). Gauthier notices the distinction which Nemesius, following Aristotle, had made between a more general category of enquiry (ζήτησις), which includes questions as to whether the sun is greater than the earth, and deliberation (βούλευσις), which is directly related to man's use of his free will and leads to a practical decision.[312] He draws the conclusion that Maximus, when introducing ζήτησις as a stage in a *chronological* order, which later leads up to deliberation (βούλευσις), simply misunderstands Nemesius' logical distinction.[313]

This explanation, however, seems to be over-simplified and hardly convincing in relation to a thinker of the type of Maximus. Nemesius' position is, in fact, very clear. The question is, therefore, whether Maximus really combines "search" and "deliberation" as closely as Nemesius evidently does, or whether Maximus rather uses Nemesius' terminology but interprets it differently. Maximus' use of the term ζήτησις in other contexts, as a matter of fact, suggests the second alternative. In Thal 59 Maximus defines ζήτησις, though in a higher sense, explicitly as a simple, affective movement of the mind towards something known.[314] The term can thus hardly be identified with deliberation of any kind, for it denotes no weighing of alternatives, as in the case of Nemesius.

On the other hand, it is of reason rather than of desire, for Maximus relates ζήτησις to the rational part of the soul,[315] though—like all other volitional acts of man—it is carried by desire. ζήτησις is at best described as *a consistent effort* of the rational faculty in general, when it is conscious of its goal.[316] But then it has also, quite naturally, its place in the chronological order of volitional acts between the basic wish (βούλησις) and deliberation (βούλευσις), which enquires about the means to reach this goal. It involves the rational faculty which sets out for the goal, but it is also carried by desire.

---

[311] See e.g. Char 3. 27; CSC, p. 156.
[312] Nemesius, *De nat. hom.* 34; PG 40, 736 B–737 A.
[313] GAUTHIER, *art. cit.*, p. 72.
[314] CCSG 22, p. 65.
[315] See Thal 39; CCSG 7, p. 259.
[316] See Ep 2; PG 91, 397 AB.

Consideration and deliberation

In one place Maximus seems to indicate that the stage of "search" leads straight on to that of deliberation,[317] but elsewhere he introduces between these two a middle stage of *consideration* (σκέψις).[318] Here another of Nemesius' logical distinctions—between "consideration" about such things as mathematical propositions and "deliberation" as pertaining to practical decisions of will[319]—has been transformed into a *chronological* succession, and Gauthier explains it in the same way as in the case of ζήτησις.[320]

The term σκέψις however, is not widely used by Maximus, and for this reason it is difficult to present corresponding evidence to show that Maximus had not simply misunderstood something which he had taken over from Nemesius. It is further true to say that the whole scale of stages has a rather formal appearance in Maximus, and he does not try to explain its elements in detail. Nevertheless it seems doubtful whether such an easy solution as Gauthier's is acceptable. Maximus says explicitly that the object of "consideration" is that which was "searched for" and the object of "deliberation" that which has been "considered", and that nobody deliberates without having considered.[321] Since we have found that ζήτησις denotes a general direction of the rational power towards a goal, and since deliberation concerns the means to reach this goal,[322] it is not difficult to suppose that Maximus brought in the term σκέψις between them to describe *the general survey* in which the mind is engaged in view of these means.

The next stage is thus that of *deliberation* (βούλευσις or βουλή). Its background in Aristotle and in Nemesius seems clear.[323] Deliberation concerns the *means* by which the wished for good may be reached. Maximus calls it a "searching appetency" (ὄρεξις ζητητική), i.e. a desire guided by the searching for a desired goal which goes on in the mind.[324] It concerns things which may be effected by human beings. In a further analysis of what is and what is not an object of deliberation Maximus follows closely Nemesius in Chapter 34 of his *De natura hominis*.[325]

---

[317] ThPol. 1; PG 91, 16 B.
[318] See *ibid.;* PG 91, 24 A and Pyrrh; PG 91, 293 C.
[319] *De nat. hom.* 34; PG 40, 736 C–737 A.
[320] GAUTHIER, *art. cit.,* p. 72.
[321] ThPol 1; PG 91, 24 A.
[322] *Ibid.;* PG 91, 17 A.
[323] GAUTHIER, *art. cit.,* pp. 59 and 72, has convincingly demonstrated this line of dependence.
[324] See ThPol 1; PG 91, 16 B.
[325] See *ibid.;* PG 91, 16 D–17 B and Nemesius, *De nat. hom.* 34; PG 40, 737 A–741 A.

The judgment

As is the case in *Aristotle,* deliberation concerning possible means leads to judgment (κρίσις) about them, which is thus the next stage in the process. Judgment is in fact a fixed and necessary element, which is always mentioned, when Maximus discusses the different acts of willing.[326] It is further a decisive proof of a man's capacity for true and virtuous action. The term is probably also used to denote a *discernment* of thoughts,[327] which is bound also to testify to the γνώμη which man has acquired. Mistakes in judgment are due to a wrong attitude in general. It is at the same time a strictly rational function, and κρίσις comes as such close to a similar term, διάκρισις (discernment), which implies a good use of the same faculty.[328]

Finally, Gauthier has correctly emphasized the close correspondence between the terms judgment and *consent* (συγκατάθεσις),[329] for judgment depends to a great extent on a man's disposition for different kinds of impressions and representations. We have, however, seen earlier that Maximus uses the term consent mostly in a negative context, as consent to sensual instigations and passions.[330]

The choice

Judgment now leads—according to Maximus as according to Aristotle— to choice or decision (προαίρεσις), a term which also summarizes the efforts of personal willing.[331] Gauthier points out that in Aristotle it is not a separate act but simply the conjunction of wish and judgment.[332] Is this also the case in Maximus?

An answer to this question is directly linked with the problem of ὁρμή, "appetite" or "impulse", which is the next stage in Maximus'

GAUTHIER has not noted Maximus' dependence on Nemesius at this particular point.

[326] See ThPol 1; PG 91, 13 A; 16 B; 20 A; 24 A and Pyrrh; PG 91, 293 C.

[327] See Char 2. 17; CSC, p. 98; cf. n. 1.—CERESA-GASTALDO (*ibid.,* p. 99, n. 7) does not accept the reading of the manuscripts here, but conjectures that κρίσις should be read χρῆσις. He refers to the possible effects of itacism and to the fact that the expression χρῆσις τῶν νοημάτων is well-known in Maximus. His argument is, however, not entirely convincing, since the combination χρῆσις—παράχρησις seems too simple for Maximus and κρίσις obviously is the *lectio difficilior* in this passage.

[328] διάκρισις distinguishes between virtue and vice (see 2. 26; CSC, p. 102; cf. 2. 67; p. 124 ff.) and is intimately related to detachment (ἀπάθεια), of which it is regarded as a fruit (*ibid.* 2. 25; CSC, p. 102) or *to* which it is said to give rise (*ibid.* 4. 91; p. 234).

[329] GAUTHIER, *art. cit.,* p. 82.

[330] See p. 212 above.

[331] Cf. GAUTHIER, *art. cit.,* p. 60 f.

[332] GAUTHIER, *loc. cit.*

system and which he himself has introduced as a separate element. We shall deal with this particular problem below. For the moment it may be sufficient to point out that if Nemesius, like the commentators of Aristotle, by his insistence on "choice" as a composition of judgment and a desire which is added to it, more or less identifies the Aristotelian term choice with the Stoic term appetite (ὁρμή), as Gauthier is inclined to believe,[333] then Maximus must be suspected of doing the same, since he quotes Nemesius literally at this point.[334] Furthermore, in order to illustrate the composition of judgment and appetency he even refers— exactly as the commentators of Aristotle and Nemesius had done—to the human composite of body and soul.[335] And yet, one must ask whether this dependence on Nemesius should not be distinguished from the problem of ὁρμή.

Nemesius' stress on "appetency" (ὄρεξις) in addition to "judgment" in the make-up of "choice" is seen by Gauthier as an expression of a tendency to combine Aristotelian προαίρεσις and Stoic ὁρμή, whereby the freedom of desire is in fact distinguished from the rational deliberations which result in judgment. But Maximus' interest can hardly be the same. He agrees with Aristotle that there is an element of appetency involved already in the process of wish and deliberation, and he does not distinguish sharply between judgment and a desire added to it in order to form the "choice". But this does not mean that the element of desire is neglected by Maximus in relation to "choice". On the contrary, its great importance is self-evident to him.

This becomes clear when we compare his definition of choice with his definitions of factors like wish and deliberation. Wish is thus to him, as we have seen, "imaginative appetency" (ὄρεξις φανταστική),[336] and deliberation a "searching appetency" (ὄρεξις ζητητική),[337] to which Maximus now adds the definition of choice as *"deliberating appetency"* (ὄρεξις βουλευτική).[338] There is a clear similarity between these definitions. The element of appetency is marked in them all. They are all composite of this element and something else. In the cases both of deliberation and choice this second element is of a rational character. What is unique about προαίρεσις in Maximus' presentation is only the

---

[333] *Ibid.,* p. 69 ff.
[334] See Nemesius, *De nat. hom.* 33; PG 40, 733 B–736 A and Maximus, ThPol 1; PG 91, 16 BC; cf. GAUTHIER, *art. cit.,* p. 71, n. 67.
[335] ThPol 1; *loc. cit.*
[336] *Ibid.;* 13 B.
[337] *Ibid.;* 16 B.
[338] *Ibid.;* 16 BC.

fact that he gives here a further explanation of this composite character, an explanation which he has obviously taken over from Nemesius.[339]

The conclusion is, therefore, that *all* the major acts of human willing are seen by Maximus as a kind of *desire*, and that this idea is particularly explained in relation to "choice", since "choice" is the decisive and final act of the process of willing. Maximus may therefore be said to follow Aristotle more closely than Nemesius, in so far as he does not feel the need to add a particular element of desire in relation to "choice", but this must be seen to be so, only because he stresses this element of desire throughout the whole process of willing. And since "choice" is the decisive and final act of the process of willing. Maximus may therefore be said to follow Aristotle more closely than Nemesius, in so far as he does not feel the need to add a particular element of desire in relation to "choice", but this must be seen to be so, only because he stresses this element of desire throughout the whole process of willing. And since "choice" summarizes this process up to the point where action itself is born, we may add that the term "choice" consequently comes rather close to γνώμη. In a both concrete and summarizing way it expresses a man's intention,[340] moving him, in the field of action, either towards the good or towards its opposite.[341]

The decisive impulse

But if this solution is correct, Maximus' addition of the term *appetite*, or better: *impulse*, effort (ὁρμή)[342] as the next step on the scale—which Gauthier sees as another misunderstanding of Nemesius on Maximus' part[343]—must have an independent explanation. Gauthier thinks that Maximus regards this term as an equivalent of decision, as almost identical with choice. But is this true?

Here, as in the case of ζήτησις, we must find the solution through a study of Maximus' general use of the term.[344] It seems probable that ὁρμή is in Maximus' writings a fairly *neutral* word. For though Maximus obviously knows it to be a Stoic term, he uses it differently on different occasions. Thus in Char 2. 56 he uses the Stoic triad of imagination,

---

[339] προαίρεσις as composite of three elements: ὅρεξις, βουλή and κρίσις, comes also from Nemesius.

[340] See Char 1. 25; CSC, p. 58 and 1. 69; p. 74.

[341] See *ibid.* 2. 32–33; p. 108; cf. 3. 93; p. 180.

[342] ThPol 1; PG 91, 20 A, 24 A and Pyrrh; PG 91, 293 C.

[343] GAUTHIER, *art. cit.,* p. 72 f.

[344] GAUTHIER, *art. cit.,* p. 71 f., n. 68 has done such a study but only found his own suggestions confirmed.

appetite and consent,[345] but exactly in the order mentioned here, and not in the order imagination, consent, appetite, which Gauthier argues to be more truly Stoic.[346] In Maximus' order imagination and appetite come very close to each other, and ὁρμή is thus, in this particular text, not understood as an expression of man's free will. It is an *impulse* to which the mind has to consent before there can be any decision.[347]

On the other hand, however, Maximus affirms in other texts that man can show forth "a self-determinative impulse" (αὐθαίρετος ὁρμή), though this impulse is not to be identified with the particular element of choice but rather with "gnomic will", in general.[348] Finally, ὁρμή is used in relation to "natural will", both when it reaches outside itself in Christ[349] and when it is activated in ordinary human beings.[350]

What then is ὁρμή in Maximus' writings, and what does it mean, when he introduces it as a new stage in the volitional process immediately after "choice"? ὁρμή seems first of all to be combined with another neutral term in Maximus, *movement* (κίνησις), which often serves to express the totality of the volitional process from wish to practical action.[351] And in this context it seems not least to be related to action.[352] It is an out-going activity which sets out for its goal, the performed action itself. And when it is introduced as a particular stage, it seems to carry the same characteristics.

Maximus says explicitly in this context that he regards προαίρεσις as the end of the volitional process as such, a process which is itself a both affective and rational movement towards a goal. To reach this goal choice has, however, to be combined with "impulse" (ὁρμή) and "use" (χρῆσις).[353] The basic element of desire, which may be involved in the term, is thus according to Maximus necessary for the realization of the decision in *practical action,* but it has, at the same time, its counterpart at all the earlier stages of wish, deliberation and choice. What leads to action is a προαιρετικὴ ὁρμή.[354]

---

[345] CSC, p. 120.
[346] GAUTHIER, *art. cit.,* p. 65, n. 53.
[347] GAUTHIER himself has also noticed that in Maximus ὁρμή is often substituted by πάθος, see *art. cit.,* p. 90, n. 136.
[348] See ThPol 16; PG 91, 192 BC and 14; 153 AB.
[349] ThPol 3; PG 91, 48 C.
[350] ThPol 26; PG 91, 280 A.
[351] ThPol 14; PG 91, 153 B.
[352] See Thal 54; CCSG 7, p. 461.
[353] See ThPol 1; PG 91, 21 D.
[354] Amb 10; PG 91, 1136 A. With Nemesius (*De nat. hom.* 12; PG 40, 660 B) Maximus is free to regard these ὁρμαί even as belonging to the field of the intellect (see Amb 10; PG 91, 1109 A).

The action

And so we are at the final stage of volitional activity, the *use* (χρῆσις). This term is unknown in both Aristotelian and Stoic analyses of the volitional process. Gauthier has however referred to the rôle which the idea of a use of imaginations and notions had in Epictetus, but particularly to Maximus' own wide and varied idea of a "use", either of thoughts or of things, or of our bodily or psychic faculties.[355] He comes finally to the conclusion that in this context Maximus thinks specifically of a *use of the things,* which implies that he refers by the term "use" simply to action itself.[356] This conclusion is evidently thoroughly convincing. What we have said here—in opposition to Gauthier—about ὁρμή as an impulse to action itself strengthens it.

Maximus thus ends his analysis of the human acts of willing with a reference to action itself, an action which for its preparation has involved the psychic faculties of man, his desire as well as his rational capacity, and now involves also his body. Maximus' regular insistence on the co-operation of the different elements of the human composite is again confirmed.

4. *Fall and restoration of the human will*

Man's fall according to Maximus is caused both by the Devil's seduction and by man's free consent to this seduction.[357] Man turned his natural capacity for true, divine pleasure into an enjoyment of sensual pleasure, an interest in temporal, transient goals, because he fell a prey to his own self-love, turned towards egoistic self-satisfaction, and preferred ignorance of his divine Cause and End to true knowledge. This is the general picture which Maximus presents at different occasions when he deals with the rise of sin and the fall of man.[358]

It is clear from this picture, that the human will is at the very root of sinful life. Man is guilty of his own fall, which is due to his misuse of his capacity for self-determination. We have seen that according to Maximus self-determination as such is of the nature of man, a created good which is a sign of the divine image in him and is thus in itself indestructible.[359] The principle of nature is not affected by the fall, and the "natural will",

---

[355] GAUTHIER, *art. cit.,* pp. 74–76 with references.
[356] *Ibid.,* p. 76 f.
[357] Cf. ch. III: B, 2; p. 154 ff. above.
[358] See ch. III: B above.
[359] See p. 209 f. above.

consequently, never disappears, for it is positively related to this principle.

What happens through the fall is that a *perversion* of man's capacity for self-determination takes place—not an annihilation of it—a perversion which predisposes man for its constant misuse, and even new misjudgment. That is to say, it forms in man a sinful disposition of will (γνώμη). This, in its turn, affects nature as far as it is misused, and it is only through Christ's Incarnation that the human composite is again freed from its slavery, and man's volitional capacities can be freely used in a converted γνώμη. A few words therefore should be added here at the end of the chapter, about Maximus' conception of the human will, particularly γνώμη, in relation to the fall and restoration of man.

The individual will in man's fall and restoration

Already in one of his early writings, Ep 2, Maximus makes his own position at this point perfectly clear.[360] He shows there and elsewhere, that the whole drama of human destiny is centered around the problem of man's *use* of his capacity for self-determination. The disastrous fruits of sin are conveyed to him, when he *freely* accepts this misuse, and the gifts of grace are received by him when he turns *freely* to God. To the seduction of the Devil, to which man's will consents in the fall, corresponds the persuasion of divine Love, which alone can lead man's will back to harmony with the principle of nature.[361]

Sin is thus to Maximus not of human nature but of γνώμη, for γνώμη is always an expression of man's use of his self-determinative faculty.[362] And it is, consequently, according to γνώμη that the fall has separated God and man from each other.[363] But since γνώμη is always of an individual character, this separation immediately also concerns inter-human relations. An attention, and therefore also a will which is directed towards the world of the senses is itself split up by the variety of impressions which is caused by the manifoldness of this world. Thus, the fallen γνώμη as it were *cuts the common human nature into pieces,* since it divides men from each other because of their different opinions and imaginations, which again instigate contrary actions.[364] And this split is, at the same time, a revolt through γνώμη within nature itself, since there

---

[360] Later modifications concern the terminology but not the content.
[361] PG 91, 396 CD.
[362] See e.g. ThPol 16; PG 91, 192 A.
[363] Ep 2; PG 91, 396 D. Cf. LARCHET, *op. cit.,* p. 105 f.
[364] *Ibid.*

is *no consistency* in its appearance.[365] Likewise, the tyranny of the passions is exerted "gnomically".[366]

In relation to the restoration of man in sanctification and deification a corresponding stress on the role of γνώμη can be observed. Unity corresponds to division. The individuality of the human freedom of γνώμη is fulfilled in a *free relationship to a common goal*. In the early writings Maximus' stress on the unity of will in this respect was put forward in a passionate way, so that one might get the impression that Maximus was arguing in favour of the idea that the human will should in the end be entirely swallowed up by the divine will. An analysis of what he says, e.g. in Ep 2, shows, however, that this was never his intention.

Unification of will

In Ep 2—in a passage[367] which Sherwood presents as an example of Maximus' terminological difficulties at the outset[368]—the main emphasis lies, in fact, on the unification of the will on the basis of one common human nature. All men share the same nature, and a mind which moves according to the principle of this nature, so Maximus would say, can be in no separation either from God—towards whom human nature is directed, in order to find its hypostatic rest there—or from other men, with whom this call and direction is shared. The point is that there is *a common human principle of nature*, to which men may freely give their assent. This is clearly demonstrated by the fact that when Maximus says here that men "can have one γνώμη and one will with God and each other" (a formulation which is in itself bound to cause misunderstandings), he introduces this sentence by the comparison "as they have one nature".[369]

It is thus very doubtful whether Maximus ever intends to say that there is only one will at work. The comparison with "nature" shows rather that he thinks of a *co-ordination of wills under the principle of nature,* which indicates the divine purpose of man. For if we should argue that Maximus here speaks in a "monothelite" way, we should also have to conclude that he does so on the basis of monophysite presuppositions! It is thus rather of a harmony of wills—and of a life in harmony with the God-directed principle of human nature—that he speaks, not of the

---

[365] OrDom; CCSG 23, p. 55.
[366] *Ibid.;* p. 69.
[367] PG 91, 396 C.
[368] See SHERWOOD, in AWC, p. 7 f.
[369] Ep. 2; *loc. cit.* For a constructive discussion of Maximus' position in regard to the conflict about monothelitism, see FARRELL, *op. cit,* pp. 155–190.

✗ extinction or annihilation of the human will. Sinful γνώμη divides and is itself divided; restored γνώμη is so intimately related to the principle of nature, that it is hardly distinguishable from what Maximus calls "natural will". And "natural will" is itself an expression of man's image character; it implies a relationship to the divine will.

The passage in Ep 2 has, however, a parallel from about the same time in Amb 7,[370] which Maximus had himself to interpret later in defence against misunderstandings.[371] Here he speaks openly of "one energy of God and those worthy of God, or better: of God alone", but even here the monenergetic tone is in the end accidental. For what Maximus wants to stress is that deification is not the fruit of man's activity but of God's. Man can only—voluntarily—receive it. He speaks of the rôle of the will in this process as a "voluntary outpassing" and affirms clearly that he is not doing away with free will. There is a divine *perichoresis* into those who are holy, but it has its counterpart in a *human consent to this process*. Man as it were suffers it to happen.

Maximus' way of stressing the divine power and energy in this context was again open to misunderstandings, which his monothelite opponents were obviously eager to use in their favour. And thus, he had to defend himself in a passage where he underlines that he has been speaking of "the future state of the saints", and that he has concentrated his attention on the deifying action of God. He goes on to show that it would be false to say that the power of deification is itself inherent in man's nature or its operation, and thus it is obvious that this power is of God alone.[372] And he concludes by saying: "I therefore did not do away with the natural operation of those who will suffer this (deification) . . . but I did show the supersubstantial power as alone effective of deification . . ."[373]

Maximus' position in relation to the unification of wills is thus clear: the human "gnomic" activity has to be directed towards what is common to all men, the λόγος φύσεως. In following this direction man's will is subordinated to the divine will, and in deification its whole activity is concentrated on a free acceptance—a "suffering"—of this deification to take place. The purpose of human self-determination is to lead to this transforming relationship with God, and therefore this "voluntary outpassing" is not the annihilation of the human will but the only true fulfilment of it.

---

[370] PG 91, 1076 C.

[371] See ThPol 1; 33 A–36 A.

[372] *Ibid.;* 1, 33 C.

[373] PG 91, 33 CD; cf. SHERWOOD, *The Earlier Ambigua,* pp. 128 ff. and 135 f., where the translation used here is found.

The aspect of individuality thus in the end finds its own purpose in a unification which harmonizes the intentions of God and man and of human beings among themselves to an extent which is only made possible by the full working out of Maximus' Chalcedonian vision.[374]

[374] In ch. VI: 10 and 11 this perspective will be worked out more in detail.

CHAPTER FIVE

Establishing the Microcosm

A. Disintegration through the Passions

We have seen, that Maximus follows the widespread philosophical and Christian tradition which sees man, composed of body and soul, as forming a microcosm which in its constitution reflects the created world, and who thus receives the further call to act as a mediator between all that is separated and divided. We have also seen how in Maximus' view, the fall prevented man from carrying out this task. Man has turned his attention from the principle of his own nature, from his own integrating centre, and has chosen to pursue the pleasure of the senses instead of his true spiritual pleasure. Thus he has also fallen a prey to the host of passions, which stir up the passible parts of his soul, instigate wrong thoughts and disturb his mind.

Man still reflects the world around him, but now in a disordered way. A disintegration within man, the microcosm, takes place, which can be arrested only through the use of his new freedom in Christ, and through an active assimilation to Christ through positive virtues. It is this double process first of disintegration, and then of restoration involving the true re-establishment of the microcosm, as presented in the writings of Maximus, which we shall study in this chapter. And we shall see how the aspect of differentiation, which in Maximus' anthropology is represented by his idea of man as a microcosm reflecting the variety of the created world, may be applied both *negatively*, i.e. in relation to the disintegrating effect of the variety of passions and vices, and *positively*, i.e. in relation to the reintegrating effect of an ascetic life (in imitation of Christ), where the virtues abound in their variety and diversity. We shall also see, how the first of these applications may be summed up in the principle of self-love, and the second in the corresponding principle of love or charity.

1. Self-love—mother of vices and passions

In Maximus' writings self-love (φιλαυτία) occupies a position in relation to the vices which to a great extent corresponds to that of charity (ἀγάπη) in relation to the virtues. It gives a summary description of a general attitude which finds expression in all vices. But at the same time in at least some cases, it is also regarded as itself being *one* of the vices, the basis or summit of them all. The position of charity differs from that of self-love in that charity is never regarded simply as the first of the virtues but rather as their culmination. Nevertheless as fundamental expressions of the two opposite attitudes of man, self-love and charity correspond to each other. In fact, the correspondence between the two terms indicates that while charity is in accordance with the purpose of man's life, self-love as its evil counterpart, in Maximus' view represents a failure to recognize this truth, and thus a misuse of man's natural capacity to find out what is best for himself. Charity implies a true relationship to God and to the purpose and principle of man, which is of service to his function as mediator and co-ordinates the human microcosm; self-love is the perversion of this, which causes the tyranny of the passions and human disorder.

On different occasions Maximus presents different and distinct definitions of self-love, particularly in its relationship to other vices. For the most part we find them in *Cent. de char.* (and in *Quæst. ad Thal.*), where Maximus' concern with problems of *vita practica* is often predominant. Thus, we learn that self-love is the "mother of the passions",[1] or "mother of the vices",[2] or "the beginning of all the passions",[3] and also that a person who is filled with self-love has in fact all the passions.[4] These definitions leave us in no doubt as to the position of self-love in Maximus' system of thinking, even though it is true that in all the Fathers the question as to the "mother" of the vices is answered differently in different contexts, and that in general there is a tendency to give priority to the vice with which one is dealing at the moment.[5] This formal definition is, however, in Maximus often confirmed by an elaborated hierarchy of vices, of which self-love forms the basis. We find the clearest expression of this in the Prologue of *Quæst. ad Thal.*, but the general scheme is also to be found elsewhere.

---

[1] Char 2. 8; CSC, p. 92.
[2] *Ibid.* 2. 59; p. 122.
[3] *Ibid.* 3. 57; p. 170. To the fight against the passions, cf. W. VÖLKER, *Maximus Confessor*, pp. 174–190.
[4] *Ibid.* 3. 8; p. 146.
[5] "En somme, une maternité très disputée", see HAUSHERR, *Philautie*, p. 64.

Thus, we can see, how self-love gives rise to two or three more basic vices, from which the rest are developed further. The first off-spring of self-love is either avarice and vainglory,[6] or a triad of *gluttony, avarice and vainglory,* all expressions of concupiscence (ἐπιθυμία),[7] or gluttony, pride and vainglory.[8] The first of these triads gives rise in Char 3. 56 to a catalogue which includes 9 more vices,[9] while in the Prologue of *Quæst. ad Thal.* Maximus arrives at a systematization, which includes 27 vices, caused by the search for pleasure (ἡδονή), 24 vices, caused by escape from pain (ὀδύνη), and 6 vices, due to a combination of these two desires.[10] We shall return to the problems involved in these and other hierarchies of vices in Maximus' writings and their relationship to the classical system of eight or seven cardinal vices,[11] but for the moment it is sufficient to conclude that it seems to be Maximus' opinion, that there is no vice which cannot in the end be traced back to the basic passion and vice of self-love.

The position of self-love in the theology of Maximus' predecessors

The dominant position given to self-love is striking. The frequency with which the concept appears in Maximus is, in fact, original. It is with good reason that Hausherr has called his study of Maximus' ascetic theology *Philautie,* for the term belongs to Maximus more than to any of the Fathers before him. Thus the question arises, whether Maximus' originality at this point is total, or whether he received his inspiration from others, and if so from where. The answer to this question is also in large measure given by Hausherr, on whose results therefore we shall have to rely, though some supplementing references and systematic aspects need to be added.[12]

At the outset reference should be made to Evagrius and the Evagrian tradition.[13] For in a text, ascribed to Nilus but possibly of Evagrius

---

[6] Char 3. 7; CSC, p. 146.

[7] *Ibid.* 2. 59; p. 122 and 3. 56; p. 170.

[8] Thal, *Prol.;* CCSG 7, p. 33.

[9] CSC, p. 170.

[10] CCSG 7, p. 33.

[11] See section 2, pp. 248–259 below.

[12] See HAUSHERR, *op. cit.,* pp. 11–42.

[13] In this thesis the term "Evagrian tradition" is restricted to those ascetic writers who were directly influenced by Evagrius' systematizations of the practical experiences of the Desert Fathers: Palladius, Nilus, Cassian and the authors of such writings as *Tractatus ad eumdem Eulogium* (PG 79, 1140 B–1144 D) and the compilation *De octo vitiosis cogitationibus* (PG 79, 1436–1464). The Syrian Evagrian tradition is thus left out, since it is of no interest in relation to Maximus, and so is for similar reasons the wider Evagrian influence on Greek-speaking ground. On Evagrius and his influence in general, see

himself, which is found in different versions in two Parisian manuscripts, the idea of self-love as *the basis of all the vices* is explicit. We learn that self-love is the first of the tempting thoughts ($\lambda o \gamma \iota \sigma \mu o i$) and that the eight vices of the Evagrian hierarchy depend upon it.[14] This passage may very well have served as a starting-point for Maximus, who used Evagrius considerably in his ascetic theology. The problem is, however, that it seems to be isolated in Evagrius' own writings. The idea is not further developed in them. Furthermore the rest of the Evagrian tradition is also restrictive at this point. The hierarchy of eight vices, which is a dominant element both in Nilus and in Cassian, is not there combined with statements about self-love as its basis.[15] The supposition that Evagrius nevertheless has served as Maximus' primary source of inspiration is, however, to some extent supported by an exclamatory statement in Evagrius, in which self-love is presented as a universal evil of hate.[16]

However, Evagrius is certainly not entirely isolated, since before him there already existed a certain stress on the importance of self-love particularly in the Alexandrian tradition. This is clear in Clement of Alexandria who expresses directly the idea that self-love ($\phi\iota\lambda\alpha\nu\tau\iota\alpha$) is always the cause of all sins,[17] an expression which in its turn, however, goes back almost literally to Plato, though with the difference that Plato uses the expression $\grave{\epsilon}\alpha\upsilon\tauo\hat{\upsilon}\ \phi\iota\lambda\iota\alpha$ instead of $\phi\iota\lambda\alpha\nu\tau\iota\alpha$.[18] The insistence on the disastrous effect of human love for self is thus probably originally of Platonic inspiration. It is also on account of this Platonic influence, that the concept of self-love plays an important rôle in Philo. Here too Clement might have found some support.

It is at least clear that Philo gives to self-love a central position among

---

particularly A. and C. GUILLAUMONT, art. Évagre le Pontique, DSp. 4 (1961), coll. 1731–1744 and HAUSHERR, *Les leçons d'un contemplatif,* Paris 1960.

[14] See these texts from *Par. Gr.* 913 (no. 53) and *Par. Gr.* 3098 (no. 10), in MUYLDERMANS, Note additionelle à: Evagriana, Mus 44 (1931), pp. 379 and 382. HAUSHERR, *Philautie,* p. 39 has noticed this text but has not given it the importance which it deserves.—A background to Evagrius' statement is perhaps provided by Sextus in *Enchiridion* 138: $\grave{\epsilon}\kappa\ \phi\iota\lambda\alpha\upsilon\tau\iota\alpha\varsigma\ \grave{\alpha}\delta\iota\kappa\iota\alpha\ \phi\upsilon\epsilon\tau\alpha\iota$. For this sentence and the possible relationship between Sextus and Evagrius, see H. CHADWICK, *The Sentences of Sextus* (TSt, N. S. 5), Cambridge 1959, pp. 28 and 161 f.

[15] The only reference might be given to Cassian's teaching about the three sources of human thoughts: God, the demon and man himself. But it is from the demon that the primary attachment to vices is derived. See *Coll.* 1. 19; PICHÉRY, pp. 99–101.

[16] *Sent. alph.* 25; PG 40, 1269 B: $\Omega\ \check{\alpha}\pi o\ \tau\hat{\eta}\varsigma\ \phi\iota\lambda\alpha\upsilon\tau\iota\alpha\varsigma\ \tau\hat{\eta}\varsigma\ \pi\acute{\alpha}\nu\tau\alpha\ \mu\iota\sigmao\acute{\upsilon}\sigma\eta\varsigma$. The metrical form of this sentence which is placed at the very end of *Sent. alph.*, since it begins with the letter Ω, may be an indication that Evagrius has in fact taken it from somewhere else.—John of Damascus quotes it in *Sacra parallela,* Φ, 13; PG 96, 420 D.

[17] *Strom.* 6. 7; GCS Clem. 2, p. 460, 13 f.

[18] Plato, *Leges* 5; 731 d–732 a.

the vices,[19] though he does not explicitly affirm that it is the root of all human evil. He presents self-love as a passion which is deadly or difficult to heal,[20] and he calls it a great vice, the opposite of which is true piety.[21] The importance of self-love to Philo is further illustrated by the fact that the construction of the tower of Babel for instance is regarded as an expression of self-love.[22] Though Philo does not make it explicit, we are therefore inclined to agree with Hausherr's conclusion that he does in fact regard self-love (φιλαυτία) as the origin of the vices.[23] Philo may even have influenced Maximus directly at this point. We have at least an indirect indication which points in this direction in the fact that in the *Loci communes* attributed to Maximus a statement of Philo's is quoted where self-love is called a great vice.[24]

Maximus thus had the support of certain of his predecessors when he attributed such an important rôle to self-love. A few more references will show that this support was not confined to the Alexandrian tradition and its inheritor Evagrius. In at least two of the Cappadocian writers also the idea of self-love seems to have played a rather important rôle, even though they do not—as is true also of Clement and Evagrius—very often mention it explicitly. Thus Basil the Great, in his shorter monastic rule, deals with self-love (φιλαυτία) in a way which shows that he regards it as a decisive expression of man's sinfulness, though its rôle seems to be restricted to the sphere of inter-human relations. Furthermore the answer to the question about self-love which is given in this passage is presented with reference to a biblical statement, which is central to monastic thinking, and the vice of self-love is said to lead to destruction.[25] Secondly, a statement of Gregory Nazianzen reveals a similar stress on self-love as a cardinal vice. From him we learn that man in his "insight" and self-love tries to escape being defeated and made inferior,

[19] See e.g. *De sacrif. Ab. et Caini* 58; Cohn & Wendland 1, p. 225, 11, and *De poster. Caini* 52; 2, p. 11, 22.
[20] See *De spec. leg.* 1 (*De victim.*) 196; Cohn & Wendland 5, p. 47, 20, and *De Ioseph.* 118; 4, p. 86, 2 f.
[21] *De spec. leg.* 1 (*De sacrificant.*) 133; Cohn & Wendland 5, p. 80, 20, and *De congr. erud. grat.* 130; 3, p. 99, 1 f.; cf. *De praem. et poen.* 12; 5, p. 338, 23 and *Quis rer. div. haer.* 106; 3, p. 24, 16 f.
[22] *De confus. ling.* 128; Cohn & Wendland 2, p. 253, 15 f.; cf. *De agr.* 173; 2, p. 130, 11.
[23] Hausherr, *Philautie* p. 21 f.
[24] *Loci comm.* 69; PG 91, 1012 D. As Hausherr, *op. cit.,* p. 41 f., has pointed out, this subject occurs also in John of Damascus (*Sacr. parall.* Φ, 13; PG 96, 420 D)—in a longer extract which clearly shows that self-love is regarded as the root of all passions, at least those which concern inter-human relationships—but is there attributed to Abba Isaias. Hausherr thinks, however, that it is a quotation from Philo.
[25] *Reg. brev., interr.* 54; PG 31, 1120 A. Love for one's neighbour and self-love are the two opposites.

and for this reason creates obstacles for the leading of a virtuous life. Here self-love is taken almost as a synonym for man's basic pride.[26]

However between Evagrius and Maximus very few expressions of an estimate of self-love which resembles that of earlier writers are to be found. Nevertheless there may be some. Hausherr notices that in Ephrem of Syria self-love is presented as the source of all the vices and as the negative counterpart of charity, though he suspects that the passage which he quotes is of a later date and even influenced by Maximus.[27] Further he emphasizes that Ps.-Denis uses the term self-love only once,[28] but holds that this fact may nevertheless have been of some importance for Maximus, since he commented upon this very text,[29] and thus gained support for his acceptance of the position of Evagrius at this point. We may agree with Hausherr that Maximus knew the text and might have felt supported by it, even though it is difficult to agree that he did in fact comment upon it.[30] We might, however, add another witness, that of the Abba Dorotheus, who seems to have regarded self-love as a summary description of man's sinfulness.[31] Finally, Thalassius, the friend of Maximus, should be mentioned, though probably he was far more influenced by Maximus than himself an influence upon Maximus. In Thalassius we find anyhow a clear theology of self-love, which summarizes well the position taken by Maximus, but also gives an expression of the kind of support which Maximus must have received from his friend. Here self-love is explicitly called the mother of the vices,[32] and said to lead the way to all the passions.[33]

Maximus thus had a fairly wide support in his predecessors, and probably particularly in Evagrius, for his estimate of the importance of self-love.[34] The further development of the idea and its systematic

---

[26] *Or.* 2, *apol.* 19; PG 35, 428 C. Cf. HAUSHERR, *op. cit.,* p. 38 f., who seems indeed to reckon with a more elaborate speculation about φιλαυτία on Gregory's part than the text itself warrants.

[27] See HAUSHERR, *op. cit.,* p. 40 f.

[28] *De coel. hier.* 9,3; PG 3, 260 C.

[29] HAUSHERR, *op. cit.,* p. 41.

[30] HAUSHERR is thinking of the passage of comment in the scholies to Ps.-Denis (PG 4, 84 D), where φιλαυτία is regarded as a synonym to αὐθάδεια and is said to denote τὸ αὐτάρεσκον, but it is very doubtful whether this commentary is really by Maximus. It reveals at least no trace of Maximus' own concept of self-love, and VON BALTHASAR, KL², p. 665, seems to regard the context as pointing in the direction of John of Skythopolis as being the scholiast here.

[31] *Doctr.* 1, 7; PG 88, 1625 B.

[32] *Cent.* 2. 1; PG 91, 1437 B.

[33] *Cent.* 3. 86; PG 91, 1456 CD; cf. 3. 87; 1456 D.

[34] HAUSHERR, *op. cit.,* p. 42 refers correctly to the ideas of Diadochus of Photice, e.g. as expressed in *Cap. gnost.* 12; DES PLACES, p. 90.

elaboration however is his own. The influence which he himself exerted in this respect, not only in relation to Thalassius but also to a whole important later tradition, not least reflected in John of Damascus, shows indirectly the importance of his personal contribution to this concept.[35]

A Western parallel—Augustine's evaluation of self-love

We cannot, however, end our survey of the predecessors of Maximus at this point without discussing one more writer, though he is a representative of the Western Christian tradition, of which we have usually no reason to believe that it influenced Maximus. This writer is Augustine. Can Maximus possibly have known Augustine, and even have been influenced by him? Maximus' frequent contacts with Rome and the West, and his long stay at Carthage make it improper to exclude such a possibility. Such a relationship is, however, very difficult to demonstrate. General similarities are in themselves no proof, since Maximus' dependence on the Greek Christian tradition can be demonstrated with a far greater amount of certainty. Furthermore he does not quote from Latin Christian writers, nor are there any such quotations in the *Loci communes.* But on the other hand, we must not rule out the possibility of a certain knowledge of Augustine's work and thinking on Maximus' part, and thus of some degree of Augustinian influence.[36]

For at least in relation to the position and rôle of self-love there are

[35] In John of Damascus reference should be made particularly to *De octo spir. nequ.,* where John's presentation of the eight cardinal vices includes an emphasis on the fact that the mother of all vices is after all φιλαυτία (PG 95, 88 D–89 A).—One should further notice, not only the text by Philo which we observed above as later known and evaluated under the name of Isaias (see p. 235 and n. 24), but also a passage to which Hausherr, *op. cit.,* p. 39 f., has called attention and which is found in the *Philocalia* under the name of Theodore of Edessa. There again we find the idea—with an anonymous reference to Evagrius—that φιλαυτία is the source of the eight vices, which are even divided—as often in Maximus—into a group of three (gluttony, avarice and vainglory) and the rest (see Theodore, *Cent.* 65; *Philocalia* 1, Venice 1782, p. 274). It is also said to give rise to a number of other vices (*Cent.* 92 and 93; *ibid.,* p. 279). Now Theodore has been shown to be a name chosen to authorize Evagrian ideas (see P. GOUILLARD, Supercheries et méprises littéraires: L'oeuvre de Saint Théodore d'Edesse, REB 5, 1947, pp. 137–157, particularly pp. 144–149) and thus the circle is in fact closed. For the possibility can hardly be excluded that the evaluation of this element in Evagrius' thinking which Maximus worked out so far, has here in the *Philocalia* led to passages which combine Evagrius' own statements with a 'Maximian' interpretation. (It may even be that ch. 92 and 93 of Theodore's century are in fact compiled on the basis of Maximus' own statements on φιλαυτία; cf. VILLER, Aux sources de la spiritualité de Saint Maxime, RAM 11, 1930, p. 266, n. 210, and GOUILLARD, *art. cit.,* p. 148.) That GOUILLARD does not believe in Maximus' originality either, is no argument against this conclusion and is even hardly convincing (see *art. cit.,* p. 144).

[36] VON BALTHASAR, KL², p. 13 emphasizes that Maximus' possible relationship to Augustine ought still to be studied. To this problem, see G. BERTHOLD, Did Maximus the Confessor Know Augustine?, *Studia patristica* 17, p. 16 f.

striking similarities between Maximus and Augustine. Von Balthasar has pointed out that what Augustine calls *concupiscentia* corresponds to Maximus' term φιλαυτία,[37] and that both writers conceive of this basic vice as a movement away from God to matter.[38] We can add that Augustine—like Maximus[39]—beside this evil self-love is also acquainted with a general *amor sui*, which is good and in accordance with nature. This idea in Augustine is developed in connection with the Stoic understanding of *amor sui* as an instinct for self-preservation.[40] This self-love must, however, have a right direction, in order not to become perverted into its opposite, an evil self-love which expresses *the very nature of sinfulness*.[41] This makes it possible to use very strong expressions to describe the detestable character of self-love, formulations which are in good harmony with the Eastern tradition which we have examined.

Augustine thus underlines, with reference to John 21: 12–19, that one should love the Lord and not oneself, for in so doing one truly loves oneself. He who does not love God, on the other hand does not really love himself either.[42] And in *The City of God* we find even stronger, well-known formulations to express a superficial self-love, which is to be rejected. The heart should not be directed towards itself—as is the case in pride—but towards the Lord.[43] Thus the city of God is characterized by love for God, but the city of this world by self-love. Both are built on a kind of love, but the city of the world on a self-love which ends in a contempt of God, and the city of God on a love for God which reaches as far as to a contempt of oneself.[44] But on the other hand, when the love for God predominates, there is also room for a true self-love.[45] The only kind of self-love which is acceptable, is that which depends on the love for God. By loving God man shows true self-love (*dilectio sui*).[46] Though Maximus' starting-point is different—and though he does not regard

---

[37] KL[2], p. 181.

[38] KL[2], p. 412.

[39] On good self-love in Maximus, see p. 248 below.

[40] Cf. R. HOLTE, *Béatitude et sagesse. Saint Augustin et le problème de la fin de l'homme dans la philosophie ancienne* (Études Augustiniennes), Paris 1962, p. 238 f., with reference to G. HULTGREN, *Le commandement d'amour chez Augustin*, Paris 1939, pp. 237 ff. and 251 ff.

[41] For the relationship self-love—love for God, cf. HOLTE, *op. cit.*, pp. 251–273, particularly p. 263 f.

[42] *In Io., tract.* 123, 5; PL 35, 1967 f. This kind of argumentation on the basis of the double commandment of love might also express Maximus' thoughts, but it is not usually found in him.

[43] *De civ. Dei* 14, 13; CSEL 40: 2, p. 31.

[44] *Ibid.* 14, 28; p. 56, 30 ff.

[45] See *De doctr.* 1, 26; PL 34, 29.

[46] See *Ep.* 155, 15; CSEL 44, p. 445 f.

pride as the source of the vices—he would have been in the position to express himself in a similar way. For Maximus also accepts this kind of true self-love.[47]

Self-love as sensuality and pride in Maximus' predecessors

This last indication of Augustine's position in comparison with that of Maximus leads us naturally to our next question: What is self-love in itself for Maximus and his predecessors? So far, we have restricted our interest mostly to those definitions of the term which are of a formal character, and which express its relationship to other vices. Now we must turn to those descriptions of self-love which concern its psychological content. But here it should be said from the beginning that the clearest indications of this content in many of the authors whom we have mentioned as influential in relation to Maximus—even in the case where a writer explains to some extent what he means by self-love as such—are to be found either in the order of the separate elements in their hierarchy of sins or vices, or in the writers' understanding of the nature of human sinfulness. Those who regard self-love as fundamental in relation to such a hierarchy[48] or to vices in general, can thus be expected to reveal their understanding of it already by the way in which they denote the first and most basic of these vices.

In general, we have to reckon with two traditions here: one, an Eastern tradition which regards the "bodily" vice of gluttony as the first of the vices, and one, a Western tradition which regards the more "spiritual" vice of pride as the basis of all the rest.[49] And this leads to the result that sinful self-love tends in the Eastern tradition to be more or less identified with a desire for bodily lust and in the Western tradition with an attitude of pride over against God and other human beings. How far this is true also of individual authors, and in what sense Maximus is to be identified with either of these tendencies, we have now to try to find out.

When Plato in his late work *The Laws* attacks self-love (φιλία ἑαυτοῦ), in a passage which we have mentioned earlier and on which Clement of Alexandria seems to depend, he seems to do so in order to avoid the idea that one can refer everything to one's own "nature", and thus escape from having a higher aim.[50] The statement also includes a

---

[47] He calls it a φιλαυτία νοερά; Thal, *Prol.;* CCSG 7, p. 39; cf. *Quinquies cent.* 1. 50; PG 90, 1197 B. See further p. 248 below.

[48] This is particularly relevant in Evagrius, to whose hierarchy of eight vices we shall return in the next section, p. 248 ff.

[49] See next section.

[50] *Leges* 5, 731 e.

criticism of a lack of concern for one's neighbour, but in itself self-love implies here nothing more specific than an absence of an interest in higher values in general. When Clement uses the idea in his own context, however, he shows clearly that he regards it differently. Self-love is to him almost the equivalent of sinful vainglory.[51] He has thereby, it seems, transferred a predominantly philosophical discussion into the field of Christian ethics. But he has also shown how close he is to the idea that the nature of sin is itself a kind of *pride*.

This tendency, however, should be compared with the understanding of self-love which we find in Philo, Clement's Alexandrian predecessor, who uses the term much more frequently than Clement does, and thus gives a more complete picture of how it is conceived within this tradition. In Philo there is a clear combination of the aspect of *pride* and the aspect of *sensual lust*. Thus Philo makes self-love almost into an equivalent of desire ($\dot{\epsilon}\pi\iota\theta\upsilon\mu\dot{\iota}\alpha$),[52] or he indicates at least that there is one kind of self-love which consists of sensuality.[53] At the same time, he establishes a very close relationship between self-love and the desire for worldly glory.[54] In this connection he speaks of a "glory of self-love" ($\delta\dot{o}\xi\alpha$ $\phi\iota\lambda\alpha\upsilon\tau\dot{\iota}\alpha\varsigma$)[55] and combines it with such vices as "boasting" and "false glory".[56] He even directly describes the sin of the tower of Babel as self-love.[57] This shows that at least in the early Alexandrian tradition self-love was regarded *both* as a desire for sensual lust and as an attitude of pride.

If we now follow the Alexandrian tradition in its influence on Evagrius, we at once arrive at the conclusion that the hierarchy of the eight vices, the basis of which is said to be self-love, shows clearly that the aspect of *sensuality* and attachment to the body is the dominant one, since gluttony and fornication are its first two vices, while vainglory and pride are the final ones. This dominance is probably bound up with the monastic outlook, which Evagrius so exclusively represents. It does not however exclude the fact that the vices of pride are also of a particular importance in Evagrius.[58] In Ps.-Nilus', i.e. Evagrius', treatise *De*

---

[51] Clement (*Strom.* 6. 7; GCS Clem. 2, p. 460, 14 f.) says that one should not demonstrate one's $\phi\iota\lambda\alpha\upsilon\tau\dot{\iota}\alpha$ by preferring $\tau\dot{\eta}\nu$ $\dot{\epsilon}\iota\varsigma$ $\dot{\alpha}\nu\theta\rho\dot{\omega}\pi\upsilon\varsigma$ $\delta\dot{o}\xi\alpha\nu$ to the love for God.

[52] See e.g. *De spec. leg.* 4 (*De concupisc.*), 131; COHN & WENDLAND 5, p. 238, 24 ff.

[53] *De spec. leg.* 1 (*De sacrificant.*), 133; COHN & WENDLAND 5, p. 80, 20 ff.

[54] See e.g. *De spec. leg.* 1 (*De victim.*), 196; COHN & WENDLAND 4, p. 47, 18 ff.

[55] *De decal.* 72; COHN & WENDLAND 4, p. 285, 10.

[56] *De poster. Caini* 52; COHN & WENDLAND 2, p. 11, 22 f.

[57] *De confus. ling.* 128; COHN & WENDLAND 2, p. 253, 15 f.; cf. p. 235 above.

[58] Evagrius uses e.g. the striking expression $\dot{\eta}$ $\pi\rho\dot{\omega}\tau\eta$ $\dot{\upsilon}\pi\epsilon\rho\eta\phi\alpha\nu\dot{\iota}\alpha$, see *Par. Graec.* 913 (no. 44); MUYLDERMANS, *Mus* 44 (1931), p. 378.

malignis cogitationibus it is thus made obvious that the whole hierarchy is built upon a *triad* of more capital vices: gluttony, avarice and vainglory,[59] and in the same text we also learn that *pride* is the first offspring of the Devil.[60]

We shall soon return to this question in our discussion of the origin and structure of the hierarchy,[61] but here already it must be underlined that the important position of vainglory and pride in Evagrius is of a particular interest. This fact is further emphasized when Evagrius says of these two vices that they appear (in the monk), when the others are overcome.[62] There is, in fact, in Evagrius, what we might call an antithetical relationship between these two types of vices.[63] Later Cassian too gives an outstanding position to pride, though he uses the Evagrian hierarchy.[64]

In Basil, however, the dominant thought is different. For him self-love is first and foremost opposed to love of one's neighbour.[65] For this reason one cannot in his writings draw any conclusion as to the dominance either of the perspective of sensuality or of that of pride. It should, however, be noted that in the Fathers pride is usually said to separate man from his fellow men. In Gregory Nazianzen this last view-point is apparently brought into the foreground in relation to self-love. For according to him the effect of self-love is often recognizable in the fact that human beings cannot tolerate their fellow human beings to be spiritually superior to themselves.[66] In the Abba Dorotheus also we find that the passage on self-love, which we have mentioned, is part of a treatment of humility and its opposite, pride.[67]

We can thus conclude that the aspects of sensuality and pride are *both* connected with the concept of self-love as it is presented in the writings of

[59] Ch. 24; PG 79, 1228 B.

[60] Ch. 1; 1201 A.

[61] See pp. 248–259 below.

[62] See *Par. Graec.* 913 (no. 57); MUYLDERMANS, *art. cit.,* p. 380.

[63] See e.g. *Pract.* 2. 58; PG 40, 1248 C and *Tract. ad Eul. monach* 22; PG 79, 1121 B f.

[64] He calls *superbia* "omnium peccatorum et criminum . . . principium", see *De institut. coenob.* 12, *De spir. superb.* 6; PL 49, 432 A. O. CHADWICK, *John Cassian. A study in Primitive Monasticism,* Cambridge 1950, regards pride and vainglory in Cassian's opinion to be immanent in all vices and for this reason placed at the end of the hierarchy, while gluttony as "the root instigator" acquires its place in the beginning (p. 94 f.).

[65] *Reg. brev.* 54; PG 31, 1120 A. It should however also be noted here that Basil even leaves room for the idea of a true love for self which coincides with the love for God; cf. e.g. TH. ŠPIDLÍK, *La Sophiologie de S. Basile* (Orientalia Christiana Analecta 162), Rome 1961, p. 150. We have noticed the same idea in relation to Augustine and Maximus, p. 237 f. above; cf. also p. 248 below.

[66] See *Or. 2, apol.* 19 f.; PG 35, 428 C–429 B.

[67] *Doctr.* 1, 7; PG 88, 1625 B.

those Greek predecessors of Maximus who devoted some noticeable consideration to it. This is also true of Evagrius, though he emphasizes most strongly the primary connection with sensual lust by making it the basis of his hierarchy of vices.

A similar combination finally is characteristic of Augustine also. For on the one hand he builds on the Stoic idea of *amor sui,* the aim of which was originally bodily health.[68] Consequently good self-love can exist only in so far as it is an 'ordered' love, while the revolt against true order which an evil self-love represents, necessarily includes a predominance of *sensuality,* a false attachment to the body.[69] And on the other hand, *pride* is always involved when self-love is manifested, for it implies a self-sufficient escape from true inclination towards God. It is in this latter sense that the two kinds of love are contrasted with each other in *The City of God.*[70] Furthermore pride is usually seen by Augustine as the basic sin.[71] *Superbia* is, therefore, often presented as an equivalent of evil self-love. Thus the passions of the body and the apostasy of pride are *both* closely connected with the Augustinian concept of self-love.[72] The sin of sensuality and the sin of pride coincide in Augustine, even though the former is logically subordinated to the latter. Augustine is a Western counterpart to Evagrius; both writers stress the role of sensuality *and* pride, but where Evagrius subordinates pride to sensuality, Augustine does the opposite.

A similar understanding in the tradition influenced by Maximus

Before we advance to Maximus' own understanding of self-love, we shall note here in addition, that the same combination of the aspects of sensuality and pride is also present in those later writers who were themselves probably influenced by Maximus—though with some predominance of the aspect of sensuality. Thus, Thalassius defines self-love

---

[68] See HOLTE, *op. cit.,* p. 239.

[69] An excellent example of this aspect in Augustine is provided by *De mus.* 6. 5, 12; *Bibl. Aug.* 7, p. 444: a love which turns towards the passions of the body, directs the soul away from contemplation of eternal things.

[70] *De civ. Dei* 14, 28; CSEL 40: 2, p. 56 f. and particularly 14, 13; p. 31, where self-love and pride are explicitly connected.

[71] See e.g. *De Gen., adv. Manich.* 2. 9, 12; PL 34, 203, where it is explicitly stated of *superbia:* "initium omnis peccati"; on this subject in Augustine see W. M. GREEN, Initium Omnis Peccati Superbia, Augustine on Pride as the first sin, *Univ. of California Publ. in Class. Philol.* 13: 13 (1949); pp. 407–432.

[72] See e.g. *De doctr.* 1, 23; PL 34, 27, where Augustine, with reference to Ps. 10: 6, argues that the soul should not love the body but God, and at the same time underlines the fact that he who wants to exert an egoistic rule over somebody else falls a prey to pride.

[73] HOLTE, *op. cit.,* p. 249 f.

explicitly as affection for the body.[74] But at the same time, in Thalassius, as in Evagrius, gluttony (which is immediately connected with self-love) and pride as the first and the last vices of the hierarchy are both in a particular way expressions of the nature of self-love.[75] In its most refined form self-love turns out to be pride. And when Thalassius—like both Evagrius and Maximus—uses a basic triad of *gluttony, avarice* and *vainglory,* the first and the last of these vices are particularly emphasized.[76]

In John of Damascus we find the same tendency: a close affinity to the Evagrian tradition—with a preservation of the order of its hierarchy of vices—and at the same time a certain stress on both sensual pleasure and vainglory or pride as the most representative expressions of self-love.[77] And finally, in Ps.-Theodore this combination is even more obvious. There self-love is, as in Maximus and Thalassius, defined as affection for the body,[78] while at the same time a basic triad of gluttony, avarice and vainglory appears,[79] and more important, self-love is in a summarizing way described as both love for (sensual) pleasure *and* love for (human) glory.[80]

Also in view of what we are now going to study more closely in Maximus himself, it is difficult to deny here a direct Maximian influence.

Self-love as love for the body in Maximus' understanding

What then is Maximus' own understanding of self-love? We have seen that in his formal definition it is described as the mother of all vices,[81] but what is it in itself? In the case of Evagrius this question was best answered by a reference to the fact that gluttony is the first of the vices, and thus directly derived from self-love.[82] In Maximus a similar attachment to the body is characteristic of self-love. He defines it explicitly as a bodily and sensual weakness. It is to him *man's passionate attachment to the body,*[83] an irrational affection *for* the body, or *of* the body.[84] This may, in fact, be an elaboration of Evagrius' understanding of the question, since

---

[74] *Cent.* 1. 4; PG 91, 1437 B.
[75] See *Cent.* 3. 86 and 88; PG 91, 1456 CD.
[76] *Cent.* 3. 89; PG 91, 1456 D.—We shall return to this subject in the next section of this chapter.
[77] *De octo spir. nequ.;* PG 95, 88 D–89 A.
[78] *Cent.* 93; *Philocalia* 1, p. 279; cf. HAUSHERR, *Philautie,* p. 40.
[79] *Cent.* 65; *ibid.,* p. 274.
[80] *Cent.* 92; *ibid.,* p. 279; cf. HAUSHERR, *op. cit.,* p. 40.
[81] See p. 232 above.
[82] Cf. p. 234 above.
[83] Char 3. 8; CSC; p. 146.
[84] *Ibid.* 3. 57; p. 170 and 3. 59; p. 172.

Maximus thus preserves the close relationship between self-love as the root of the vices and gluttony as the first of them.[85] This impression is further confirmed by the scholies to *Quæst. ad Thal.*, which explicitly identify the thoughts of self-love and gluttony.[86] We are thus bound to conclude that self-love, in Maximus' opinion, manifests itself *primarily in an inner affection for bodily sensations and the sensible world*, and thus is also primarily linked with *the concupiscible faculty of the soul*.[87] Concupiscence in an evil sense and self-love in its primary manifestation are, in fact, regarded as synonymous expressions of human sinfulness. Self-love in a more restricted sense summarizes a sinful use of the concupiscible faculty.[88]

In Chapter III we noted that Maximus regards the fall of man as a misuse of his natural capacity for spiritual pleasure and a preference for sensual pleasure. We have also noticed that this failure resulted, by God's providence, in a double experience of pleasure and pain, so that fallen man is always bound to seek for a pleasure, which can never satisfy him, and to try to avoid the consequent pain.[89] Now this perspective is, of course, also related to the character of self-love. Consequently, Maximus concludes that self-love, being both the root of the vices and manifested through all the vices, is linked with this double process in fallen man. It may thus be combined either with pleasure—as it was when man fell[90]—or with pain, or even with a mixture of both.[91] And different vices are caused by these different kinds of combination. Self-love is primarily related to pleasure, which is both the offspring and the end of self-love,[92] but in this world it can never avoid being also related to pain.[93]

This fact, however, obviously implies that for Maximus the nature of self-love is not sufficiently described by a reference to sensual lust. The whole set of vices is involved in the activity of self-love. The unreasonable affection for the body, which primarily constitutes self-love, leads to all the other vices, and the end of them all is pride, so Maximus affirms;

---

[85] See e.g. Thal, *Prol.;* CCSG 7, p. 33; Char 2. 59; CSC, p. 122; 3. 7; p. 146 and 3. 56; p. 170.—Maximus' principles of further differentiation among the vices will be treated in section 2 below.

[86] Thal 49, schol. 20; CCSG 7, p. 377. HAUSHERR, *op. cit.,* p. 44 has emphasized the importance of this commentary.

[87] Cf. SHERWOOD, in ACW, pp. 62 f. and 85.

[88] In the same way "tyranny" summarizes the sinful use of the irascible faculty, see Ep 2; PG 91, 397 AB.

[89] See pp. 158 f. and 162 above.

[90] See e.g. *ibid.;* 396 D.

[91] See Thal, *Prol.* CCSG 7, p. 33.

[92] *Ibid.;* CCSG 7, p. 31 ff.

[93] *Ibid.;* CCSG 7, p. 33.

adding that he who roots out self-love, roots out at the same time all the passions that come from it.[94]

We can thus see, how the aspect of *pride* enters into the picture in a way which reminds us of what we have found in the predecessors of Maximus. As the conclusion of the hierarchy of vices, pride manifests the inevitable consequences of self-love itself. Maximus' use of *a basic triad of vices*, identical with that of Evagrius, points in the same direction. For in this triad, which is a noticeable element in *Cent. de char.* and which consists of *gluttony, avarice* and *vainglory*, the aspect of pride plays an important rôle.[95] This fact is further emphasized, when Maximus states in Char 3. 7 both that licentiousness, caused by gluttony in its two aspects of excessive and delicate eating, and hate for one's neighbour, caused by avarice and vainglory, are themselves caused by self-love.[96] For by relating vainglory and hate for one's neighbour to each other, Maximus at the same time establishes a close relationship between self-love, as contrary to love for one's neighbour, and vainglory. The aspect of pride is still more emphasized in the Prologue of *Quæst. ad Thal.*, where Maximus makes gluttony together with vainglory and pride the first three vices, and all three result from self-love combined with pleasure.[97]

In this last example, there is however another tendency which ought to be observed in this context. *Vainglory and pride as vices are to Maximus not very different from gluttony.* All three are expressions of man's basic search for sensual pleasure. Maximus even states explicitly that not only gluttony and possibly avarice but also vainglory have their origin in a *demand of the body*.[98]

The vices of pride are, in fact, closely related to the other vices, though they must be kept distinct from them. They take a different shape in the monk and in a man of the world, but they are in both cases at least negatively bound to the other vices. For in the monk, vainglory is the pleasure he takes in demonstrating his own virtue, and pride is this attitude as manifested over against his fellow monks. In both cases he thus abstains from lower pleasures only in order to enjoy those of pride. And for a man of the world the vices of pride imply boasting about himself on account of earthly riches or social prestige.[99]

We can thus conclude that Maximus, in developing the concept of

---

[94] Char 3. 57; CSC, p. 170.
[95] See *ibid.* 2. 59; p. 122; 3. 7; p. 146 and 3. 56; p. 170.
[96] CSC, p. 146.
[97] CCSG 7, p. 33.
[98] Char 2. 59; CSC, p. 122.
[99] See the important statements in Char. 3. 84; CSC, p. 184.

self-love, emphasizes strongly both a primary attachment to the body and also the great impact of the vice of pride on sinful human life. There is in fact in Maximus a close relationship between these two aspects. In one sense certainly they are contrary to each other, in so far as the 'higher' vices of pride usually exclude a simultaneous manifestation of the 'lower' ones. This latter idea—which is present already in Evagrius[100] and Cassian[101]—is expressed in different ways in *Cent. de char.*[102] But a combination of the two aspects is also frequent.

Maximus and the Eastern alternative

We noticed above that a similar combination is characteristic of the whole tradition to which Maximus adheres. But within this common tradition we found a clear difference of emphasis: in Evagrius and the Eastern monastic line of thinking the sin of pride is subordinated to the sin of sensuality, but in Augustine and the Western tradition it is the sin of sensuality which is subordinated.[103] We must therefore go further and ask: Which of these alternatives within the common tradition does Maximus follow? From what we have seen, the answer must be that Maximus stands closer to the Evagrian and Eastern alternative. The concept of an attachment to the body as decisive for a vicious life is never abandoned by him, not even in relation to the 'higher' vices of pride, for these are negatively bound to the 'lower' vices and are thus indirectly dependent on sensual affection, though this, of course, does not imply a negative evaluation of the body and the sensible world in themselves.[104]

This predominance of the aspect of sensible attachment, which is first of all noticeable in Maximus' different descriptions of the fall of man, may finally be illustrated by a passage in Thal 55, where Maximus allegorizes the story of David and Absalom in 2 Sam. 18. David is interpreted here as the practical mind, i.e. the mind which is active in a virtuous life, while Absalom, with whom he ought to fight but from whom he has fled into the land of Gilead, is interpreted as a kind of pride or self-conceit (οἴησις), because his name means that he was regarded as "the peace of his father", and when we think that we have peace from the passions we bring about self-conceit. Thus Absalom means no freedom from passions, and Maximus gives a genealogical reason for this. Absalom was the son of David, but his mother was the daughter of the

---

[100] *Pract.* 2. 58; PG 40, 1248 C.
[101] *Coll.* 5. 10; PICHÉRY, p. 197 f.
[102] *Char* 2. 40; CSC, p. 112 and 3. 59–60; p. 172.
[103] See p. 242 above.
[104] *Char* 1. 65; CSC, p. 74; cf. Amb 10; PG 91, 1112 AB.

king of Geshur. And Geshur means, says Maximus, "the guiding of the wall", and since the wall is the body, the guiding of the wall is "the law of the body", i.e. sense or sensation, out of which Absalom, or self-conceit, is born.[105] Maximus could hardly be more definite about the close relationship between bodily and nonbodily vices. Thus the basic attachment to the body remains for Maximus a characteristic of all vices, though the importance of the vices of pride is always emphasized. If Augustine may be said to subordinate sensual sin to the sin of pride, Maximus, following Evagrius and the Eastern tradition, rather does the opposite: he assigns an important place to the sin of pride within the sphere of sinful life, the primary characteristic of which is, however, attachment to the body and disordered concupiscence.

Negative and positive self-love

The passions and vices exert a disastrous effect on man. The intended order and use of man's faculties is destroyed. The intended unity of the human composite, the created microcosm, is transformed first into disunity and then chaos, both within the individual and within the human race. This view is common to Maximus and the whole Christian tradition to which he adheres. But more strongly than his predecessors he emphasizes that all this disorder of sinful life is caused by man's self-love, i.e. his disobedience to the divine commandment of love for God and one's neighbour. Without self-love the differentiation of the human faculties, and man's microcosmic character, would have been able to serve the purpose of human life and to favour a more complete integration of the whole. But with self-love these different faculties are used in a way which disintegrates man and mankind.[106]

Unity and differentiation are thus, here as elsewhere in Maximus' speculation, contrary to each other only in the perspective of sin. It is not the body itself, nor the senses nor the passible faculties themselves which are evil, but only their wrong use. This is Maximus' conviction, which he states—in spite of his Evagrian understanding of the psychology of the vices—in clear contrast to all Origenist tendencies. Self-love is defined as love for the body, not because the body is linked with evil, but because

---

[105] CCSG 7, p. 507. The etymological interpretation of Absalom as "the peace of the father" is not unknown in the ancient Christian *onomastica sacra,* see WUTZ, *Onomastica Sacra* 2, pp. 827 and 963. With regard to Geshur there is at least a slight parallel to Maximus' interpretation in Origen, *In Genes., fragm.;* PG 12, 121 AB, where Σούρ is interpreted to mean "wall"; cf. R. P. C. HANSON, Interpretation of Hebrew names in Origen, VC 10 (1956), p. 111. BLOWERS, *op. cit.,* p. 219 sees Thal 55 as a "consummate example of the spiritual paedagogical nature of Maximus' exegesis of Scripture".

[106] See further sections 2 and 3 below.

attachment to the body prevents man's entire attachment to his divine
end.

But if this is Maximus' conviction, one would also expect him to
allow for *a positive kind of self-love*, which would be involved in a love for
the true purpose and end of man. In fact he does speak of such a good
self-love. He calls it spiritual (νοερά) self-love, i.e. a self-love which is of
the mind when the mind is attached to its divine end, and which is thus
entirely free from affection for the body and for this world. It is elevated
above the sinful search after pleasure and attempts to escape from pain.
It never ceases to adore God, seeking in him the consistency of the
soul.[107] Such a love is a self-love in so far as it searches for that which is
good for man, but in the sense of isolation and separation it is not
self-love, since what is good for man, is transcendent in relation to him.[108]

Thus it orientates and orders the whole of man towards an end, which
is outside of man. Filled with such a good self-love the ordered
microcosm is also in the position to act as a universal mediator.

2. The Evagrian hierarchy of eight vices and Maximus' differentiations of vices

We have suggested that Maximus probably found one of the main sources
of his own understanding of self-love in some Evagrian texts.[109] These
texts clearly set out a view of self-love which regards it as the root of all
the vices, and link this view directly with the Evagrian hierarchy of eight
cardinal vices, presenting self-love as the very basis of this hierarchy.
This fact, however, leads us immediately to another question: Is this
combination of the idea of self-love as the root of the vices and the idea
of the eight cardinal vices to be found in Maximus also? The answer to
this question is not quite simple. We have seen that Maximus regards
self-love as the basis of all the vices, but the system of eight vices does not
seem to be a fixed element in his ascetic teaching, as it is in Evagrius and
in the Evagrian tradition. On the other hand, Maximus shows clearly that
he knows of Evagrius' hierarchy, though he develops it further, and he
sees self-love as the basis of his own hierarchy of vices.

This last conclusion is best illustrated by a reference to Char 3. 56,
where Maximus 1) affirms in an Evagrian way that self-love is the cause
of impassioned thoughts (λογισμοί), 2) presents the basic Evagrian triad
of the vices gluttony, avarice and vainglory, and 3) finally presents a list

---

[107] Thal, *Prol.;* CCSG 7, p. 39 ff.; cf. HAUSHERR; *Philautie,* p. 49 f.
[108] At this point Maximus is very close to Augustine; cf. p. 238 above.
[109] See p. 234 above.

of nine more vices, which includes all the rest of the Evagrian hierarchy.[110] The relationship between self-love and the scale of vices is thus understood by Maximus in an Evagrian way. Char 3. 56, and still more Maximus' treatment of the problem in *Cent. de char.* as a whole, however, raise a number of other problems.

First of all, in Char 3. 56 Maximus says that the basic triad of vices are "of concupiscence", but in other instances he differentiates more explicitly between the vices according to the whole trichotomy of the human soul,[111] and also in other ways. This leads to the question how Maximus' understanding of the hierarchy of vices is linked with his understanding of man's use of his three psychic faculties, and further, how this fact is related to different aspects of self-love. Secondly, the addition in Char 3. 56 of four other vices to the original Evagrian hierarchy of eight raises the question, whether this fact expresses a deliberate Maximian alternative to the Evagrian hierarchy or to any fixed number of vices at all, or whether it is rather a natural elaboration of the Evagrian hierarchy, perhaps particularly understandable in the light of the changes which had taken place within the original hierarchy during the centuries since Evagrius, both in the East and in the West. And finally, the answers to these questions will inevitably lead us to the problem of how Maximus' position possibly serves to illustrate the disintegrating function of vices and passions within the human unity, i.e. the negative aspect of the idea of man as microcosm.

In order to arrive at an answer to these questions we must, however, first of all present a short account of both the problem of *the possible context of the Evagrian hierarchy*, seen from one particular aspect, and of *the historical development of the idea of cardinal vices*. In the first case we shall see that there may have existed a relationship between the idea of the trichotomy of the human soul on the one hand and the Evagrian hierarchy of vices on the other from the very beginning, and in the second case that Maximus' contribution to the Christian systematization of vices is well illuminated by the historical development of the hierarchy.[112]

The context and roots of the idea of the eight cardinal vices according to earlier research

This question has been widely discussed among the scholars, and so far

---

[110] CSC, p. 170.

[111] See further section 3 below.

[112] A number of problems concerning the psychological understanding of the hierarchy must here be left out. They do not immediately touch the main theme of this thesis.

no consensus has been reached. Evagrius presents the hierarchy as a fixed system, and one gets the impression that he builds on an older and accepted tradition. But this is often the case with Evagrius. No such tradition in literary form has been found however, in this particular case, and none of the suggestions concerning the possible roots of the Evagrian hierarchy have been altogether convincing. It thus remains a fact that Evagrius' own literary contribution must have been decisive,[113] though Cassian, who in general follows Evagrius very closely, refers his section on the eight vices to the teaching of Abba Serapion, and for the actual number eight quotes directly his own two authorities, Abba Germanus and Abba Serapion.[114] The names of the eight vices—in Evagrius' hierarchy they are: gluttony ($\gamma\alpha\sigma\tau\rho\iota\mu\alpha\rho\gamma\iota\alpha$), fornication ($\pi o\rho\nu\epsilon\iota\alpha$), avarice ($\varphi\iota\lambda\alpha\rho\gamma\upsilon\rho\iota\alpha$), grief ($\lambda\upsilon\pi\eta$), wrath ($\dot{o}\rho\gamma\dot{\eta}$), weariness ($\dot{\alpha}\kappa\eta\delta\iota\alpha$), vainglory ($\kappa\epsilon\nu o\delta o\xi\iota\alpha$) and pride ($\dot{\upsilon}\pi\epsilon\rho\eta\varphi\alpha\nu\iota\alpha$)[115]—are well known from earlier speculation, but their combination is not found in any of Evagrius' predecessors. Thus the problem remains: what are his sources and what is his principle of systematization?

The answers to these questions have varied considerably among the scholars. It has been argued that the system is derived from the doctrine of the seven planets, or that it was composed of the (Stoic) four cardinal passions, combined with an interpretation of the four cardinal vices, or that it was composed by Evagrius himself on the basis of a number of varying catalogues of vices in Origen. Again it has been held that it was the result of a systematization of the negative counterparts to the four cardinal virtues, arranged according to the principle of the trichotomy of the human soul.[116] All these suggestions have finally been rejected by A. Vögtle, who has presented considerable reasons for thinking that the hierarchy of eight vices was constructed in monastic circles for practical purposes and built virtually upon a common teaching about the power of passions, and on concrete experiences and traditional Biblical exegesis (interpretation of particularly Deut. 7: 1), and who maintains as a consequence that the rôle of Evagrius himself is not as decisive as some

---

[113] Cf. e.g. HAUSHERR, L'origine de la théorie orientale des huit péchés capitaux, OCh 86 (1933), p. 171.

[114] Cassian, *Coll.* 5, 17–18; PICHÉRY, p. 210.

[115] This system is presented by Evagrius particularly in *Antirrhetikos* (Syriac text and Greek retranslation in FRANKENBERG, *Euagrios Ponticus*, pp. 472–545) but also in *De octo vit. cogitat.*, a part of *Praktikos* (PG 40, 1272–1276); cf. also Ps.-Nilus (Evagrius), *De mal. cogitat.* 1 (PG 79, 1200 D–1201 A).

[116] For this summary, cf. VÖGTLE, Woher stammt das Schema der Hauptsünden?, ThQ 122 (1941), p. 218, and *art.* Achtlasterlehre, RACh 1 (1950), col. 75 f.

scholars[117] have thought.[118] On this argument the roots of the hierarchy are not of one particular philosophical type, nor the principle of construction a definite systematic speculation. What interests us here specifically however are the reasons which may still be brought forward to support *the idea that the trichotomy of the soul may have served as one of the principles of systematization* from the very beginning, since at least Maximus, who builds on Evagrius, obviously attempts to make a differentiation of the passions and vices according to the trichotomy of the soul.

The idea of the trichotomy of the soul as background to the hierarchy

The idea that the hierarchy of eight vices was constructed on the basis of the Platonic trichotomy of the soul and on the corresponding system of cardinal virtues was particularly advocated among older scholars by S. Schiwietz.[119] His arguments are not entirely convincing,[120] and Vögtle is probably right in rejecting them, at least as a proof for a single source of the hierarchy.[121] On the other hand, we cannot deny the importance which Evagrius himself attributes to the differentiation of the faculties of the soul in relation to passions and vices in general. It is true that Evagrius never indicates that the idea of the trichotomy is the source of the hierarchy, but it is not very convincing to argue that there is no connection at all, since the trichotomy (especially the division of the passible part) and the hierarchy are both of a great importance to Evagrius, who is regarded by all scholars as the first literary exponent of the doctrine of eight vices. What particular reasons are there, then, for allowing for such a connection?

First of all, Evagrius says explicitly, that the impassioned thoughts grow from the two passible parts of the soul;[122] furthermore he constructs a hierarchy of *virtues* on the basis of the trichotomy.[123] Secondly, there are a number of cases where Evagrius speaks of the passions and vices in general, in combination with a reference to the trichotomy, or to the double faculty of the passible part of the soul. Thus, he underlines the

---

[117] See particularly HAUSHERR, *art. cit.,* p. 173.
[118] VÖGTLE, ThQ 122 (1941), p. 237; cf. IDEM, RACh I, col. 77 ff.
[119] See S. SCHIWIETZ, *Das morgenländische Mönchtum* 1, Mayence 1904, pp. 269–273 and 2, Mayence 1913, pp. 80–84.
[120] His comparison between *Pract.* 1, 61 and the Ps.-Aristotelian treatise *De virt. et vit.* is striking, but his conclusions about the origin of the hierarchy are too quickly drawn; see SCHIWIETZ, *op. cit.* 2, p. 82 ff.
[121] VÖGTLE, ThQ 122 (1941), p. 221 ff.
[122] See e.g. *Pract.* 1. 63; PG 40, 1236 CD.
[123] *Ibid.* 1. 61; 1236 A–C.

close relationship between desire (ἐπιθυμία) and the rise of passion, for both have their root in sensation,[124] and he also stresses that when the concupiscible part of the soul has been quenched in detachment, the irascible faculty of the monk is usually stirred.[125] Evagrius further points out on several occasions that the thoughts of concupiscence and anger are opposed to one another,[126] and therefore that a good use of these two faculties may keep the soul in a proper balance.[127] Thus Evagrius' understanding of the trichotomy of the human soul always comes into his discussion of the passions, in spite of the fact that he never bases his hierarchy of vices explicitly on the idea of the trichotomy.

There are, further, quite a number of indications of the possible relationship between the two concepts. A good illustration of this fact may be found in a passage, which is probably by Evagrius and at least belongs to the Evagrian tradition, where it is said that during the night, when neither anger nor concupiscence is stirred, the demons attacking the monk form dreams of vainglory in his mind.[128] Here the idea seems to be that vainglory is mainly related to the rational faculty, and it can hardly be denied that the writer regards the vices which appear before vainglory as bound either to anger or to concupiscence.

This conclusion is finally affirmed in the later Evagrian tradition, particularly in a text, which Schiwietz found to be decisive: a passage in Cassian, *Coll.* 24, 15, which explicitly divides different vices according to the trichotomy of the soul.[129] It is true that this kind of systematization is not found elsewhere in Cassian. Thus in *Coll.* 5 e.g., where he deals with the eight vices, he makes another differentiation.[130] But what Cassian tells us here in *Coll.* 24, referring to a certain monk named Abraham, shows that this kind of speculation was at least found within the monastic tradition which accepted the hierarchy. It is further true that Cassian here mentions a number of vices other than those which belong to the original Evagrian hierarchy, but at the same time all the vices of

---

[124] *Ibid.* 1. 15; 1221 D–1224 A.

[125] *De mal. cogitat.* 16; PG 79, 1217 D–1220 A.

[126] See e.g. on the power of anger and the thoughts of fornication *Antirrhet.* 2. 22; FRANKENBERG, p. 488 f.

[127] *De mal. cogitat.* 17; PG 79, 1220 B: the good shepherd (i.e. the virtuous man) escapes from the wolves by virtue of his irascible faculty, but loves the sheep (i.e. the true thoughts of man) by virtue of his concupiscible faculty.

[128] See the addition to *De mal. cogitat.*, published in MUYLDERMANS, *À travers la tradition*, p. 51, no. 28.

[129] Cassian, *Coll.* 24, 15; CSEL 13, p. 690 f.; SCHIWIETZ, *op. cit.* 1, p. 270 f. and 2, p. 80 f.

[130] See *Coll.* 5, 3; PICHÉRY, p. 190, where the vices are divided into those which need the co-operation of the body and those which do not, and into those which are due to an outward and those which are due to an inward impulse.

the hierarchy *are* included, and those which are added are easily related to the eight. We find, thus, that at least there was speculation within the Evagrian monastic tradition about a trichotomist differentiation of the vices, and that the way in which the vices of the hierarchy are distributed here is also in accordance with the presentation of the individual vices in the rest of the Evagrian tradition. And in *Coll.* 24, 15 we learn explicitly that of the eight vices *cenodoxia* and *superbia* belong to the rational part, *furor, tristitia* and *acedia* to the irascible part, and *gastrimargia, fornicatio* and *avaritia* to the concupiscible part.[131] The details of this scheme may be questioned from the point of view of Evagrius himself, but not the general understanding.

This clear systematization leads, however, in the third place to an evaluation even of those indications of the trichotomist context, which we may find in the descriptions of individual vices in Evagrius himself and in the rest of the Evagrian tradition. The very structure of the hierarchy, in fact, invites us to make such an evaluation, for it starts with the bodily vices of gluttony and fornication, which it goes without saying are related to the concupiscible element; it continues later with a vice like wrath (ὀργή), which is often, as we have seen, simply identified with anger (θυμός), and it ends with pride which is possibly closely related to the rational element. Many details of the Evagrian treatment of the individual vices, as a matter of fact, clearly affirm this general feeling. And the same is true of the later tradition, though in neither case is the differentiation absolutely fixed.

Examples of 'trichotomist' differentiation between the vices in Evagrius

A few examples may be illuminating. When Evagrius says that alms (or mercy) heal anger, prayer purifies the mind and fasting quenches concupiscence, not only do we recognize the characteristic Evagrian form of the trichotomy, but it is also obvious at least that *gluttony* is a vice of the concupiscible element, while vices like wrath, hate etc. are referred to the irascible element.[132] Later in the same text it seems clear that both gluttony and *fornication* are naturally referred to concupiscence.[133] A trichotomist differentiation in relation to individual vices (though vices not explicitly included in the hierarchy) is also found in *Cent. gnost.* Thus we learn that ignorance is related to the mind, luxury to concupiscence and hate to anger.[134]

---

[131] *Coll.* 24, 15; *loc. cit.*
[132] *Pract.* 1. 63; PG 40, 1237 B.
[133] *Ibid.* 2. 54; 1245 D.
[134] *Cent. gnost.* 1. 84; PO 28, p. 57; cf. 3. 35; p. 111, where it is said that chastity (related

In Evagrian texts we further find that concupiscence receives thoughts of fornication,[135] while the thoughts which arise from anger are insinuation, hate and resentfulness.[136] *Wrath* (and hate) are further clearly related to the irascible element.[137] More ambiguous is the position of *grief*. On the one hand it is defined as "lack of pleasure", and thus at least indirectly related to concupiscence,[138] but on the other hand it seems clear from a number of instances that in Evagrius' opinion it is equally, if not more, related to anger.[139] The reason behind this ambiguity seems to be indicated by Evagrius himself: grief comes either from lack of desires (ἐπιθυμίαι) or succeeds wrath (ὀργή).[140] The case of *acedia* is similar. It has a middle position and is, in fact, a false balance between the passions of concupiscence and anger and as such a negative counterpart to detachment (ἀπάθεια).[141]

Vainglory, finally, also has an ambiguous position. It is part of the Evagrian triad of gluttony, avarice, vainglory, the three elements of which, however, can hardly be distributed according to the trichotomy. We should expect vainglory to be related to the rational element, but Evagrius seems to prefer to relate it to the body and to concupiscence. It stands close to gluttony and fornication. This is surprising at first sight, but perhaps less surprising when we realize that Evagrius also has a tendency to identify the rational element with the mind, as we have pointed out several times. This idea ought to lead to the conclusion that the rational part is only indirectly affected by the passions, and that ignorance is *the* vice of the mind. Thus though Evagrius often allows for the trichotomy in relation to the vices, he works mostly with a dichotomy of the passible elements.[142]

Examples of 'trichotomist' differentiation in the later Evagrian tradition

In the later Evagrian tradition similar observations can be made. Nilus

---

to concupiscence) gives rise to love (related to anger), and love to knowledge (related to the mind). Cf. also Maximus, Ep 2; PG 91, 397 A with the corresponding triad of ignorance, self-love and tyranny.

[135] See MUYLDERMANS, *À travers la tradition*, p. 51 (no. 27); cf. *Antirrhet.* 2. 7; FRANKENBERG, p. 484 f.

[136] MUYLDERMANS, *op. cit.*, p. 53 (no. 32).

[137] See *Pract.* 1. 11; PG 40, 1224 C and *De octo vit. cogitat.* 6; PG 40, 1273 A.

[138] See *Pract.* 1. 10; PG 40, 1224 C.

[139] See *Pract.* 1. 13; PG 40, 1224 D; 2. 54; 1245 D–1248 A and *Ad Eulogium mon.* 5; PG 79, 1100 D and 10; 1105 D.

[140] *De octo vit. cogitat.* 5; PG 40, 1272 C.

[141] This is made clear in *Sel. in Psalm.*; see the commentary by VON BALTHASAR, ZKTh 63 (1939), p. 188, γ.

[142] See e.g. *De mal. cogitat.* 1; PG 79, 1201 A and 5; 1205 D.

speaks of gluttony, fornication and avarice as desires (ἐπιθυμίαι),[143] while the passion of wrath, and explicitly that of grief also, concerns the irascible element.[144] *Acedia* occupies just as ambiguous a position as it does in Evagrius, though it might perhaps be argued that Nilus regards it as belonging to the irascible element.[145] It is of interest, however, that *acedia* is related to the soul, while vainglory is primarily related to the mind, though also to the soul.[146] And finally, in the *Tractatus ad eumdem Eulogium*, the authorship of which is uncertain, the different vices are interrelated in such a way that it seems more or less obvious that gluttony and fornication belong to the concupiscible element,[147] while grief, wrath and *acedia* belong to the irascible element.[148] Also of particular interest is the fact that vainglory is defined as "opposite to truth" and thus referred to the rational element.[149] It should perhaps also be added, that the very fluctuation of order between wrath and grief, which one can observe throughout the Evagrian tradition, may probably be best explained by a reference to the idea of the trichotomy of the soul, since grief is either regarded as caused by a lack of pleasure, and thus comes close to concupiscence, or as a counterpart to wrath, and thus is a kind of envy, linked with the irascible element.[150]

As a matter of fact, we come to the conclusion that the idea of the trichotomy of the human soul, which belongs to the context of general speculations about the passions of man, must have been of importance for the understanding of the hierarchy of eight vices within the Evagrian tradition. We may agree with Vögtle and others that this idea is not *the* root of the concept of the hierarchy, since Evagrius and the Evagrian tradition, except in one case in Cassian, never explicitly build it upon the trichotomy. But we are convinced that the monastic speculation on the hierarchy of vices was from the beginning closely integrated with the

---

[143] See *De octo spir. mal.* 1; PG 79, 1145 B; 6; 1152 B and 8; 1153 A.
[144] *Ibid.* 9; 1153 C and 11; 1156 BC.
[145] *Ibid.* 13; 1157 CD.
[146] See *ibid.* 16; 1161 B and 15; 1160 D.
[147] *Tract. ad eumdem Eul.* 2; PG 79, 1141 AB.
[148] *Ibid.* 3–4; 1141 D–1144 C.
[149] *Ibid.* 4; 1144 C.
[150] In Evagrius' *De octo vit. cogitat.* grief occupies the fourth and wrath the fifth place in the hierarchy (PG 40, 1272 A), but in *De mal. cogitat.* 1 (PG 79, 1200 D–1201 A), the order is reversed. In Nilus' *De octo spir. mal.*—except in the manuscript E of the recension B (cf. MUYLDERMANS, Une nouvelle recension du *De octo spiritibus malitiae* de S. Nil, Mus 52, 1939, p. 247)—grief occupies the fifth place and is said to spring from wrath (PG 79, 1156 B), but in *Tract. ad eumdem Eul.* we notice that grief and wrath are almost parallel, though grief precedes wrath (PG 79, 1141 D–1144 A). In Cassian's *Coll.* 5, 2 *ira* precedes *tristitia* (PICHÉRY, p. 190), and this is also the case in the compilation, called *De octo vit. cogitat.* (PG 79, 1436).

'trichotomist' understanding of the soul. There are too many indirect indications of this relationship to allow us to deny it altogether. And when we find direct and indirect references to both in Maximus, we must bear this background in mind. If there is a difference at this point between Maximus and Evagrius—as we shall try to find out in our next section—it does not, therefore, lie in the fact of this integration as such, but rather in the way in which it is understood.

The later history of the Evagrian hierarchy and Maximus' list of vices

But did Maximus really refer to the hierarchy of eight vices? We have called attention to Char 3. 56 as evidence, but there Maximus not only mentions the eight vices of the hierarchy but also four other vices, namely rapacity ($\pi\lambda\epsilon o\nu\epsilon\xi\acute{\iota}\alpha$), resentfulness ($\mu\nu\eta\sigma\iota\kappa\alpha\kappa\acute{\iota}\alpha$), envy ($\varphi\theta\acute{o}\nu o\varsigma$) and slander ($\kappa\alpha\tau\alpha\lambda\alpha\lambda\iota\acute{\alpha}$).[151] This text can therefore only be understood as a reference to the hierarchy of eight vices, if the additional vices are accepted as elaborations or synonyms of the original vices. It is here, however, that we may be helped by a short study of the history of the Evagrian hierarchy of vices.

Already within the Evagrian tradition itself we may recognize a tendency to go beyond the fixed number of eight, and from the beginning it is made clear that the vices of the hierarchy are only a kind of starting-point for the description of an innumerable host of vices. It is, however, a well-known fact that the system of seven deadly sins in the West, which was established by Gregory the Great on the basis of the hierarchy of eight vices, not only represented a reconstruction of the order of the vices, but also a more restrictive systematization of them. When pride (*superbia*), according to a Western tradition represented by writers like Tertullian and Augustine, was made the basis of the hierarchy in the West, this reform could receive some support from the fact that the vices of vainglory and pride occupied a particular position within the Evagrian tradition itself. They were said to attack the monk, after he had overcome the first six vices, and so could be understood to be more fundamental than the others as expressions of human sinfulness. Evagrius would hardly have said so explicitly, but in the Latin writer Cassian this idea is close at hand. He calls *superbia* "omnium peccatorum et criminum . . . principium".[152] And now the restrictive attitude of the Western tradition manifests itself in the fact, that since

---

[151] See CSC, p. 170.
[152] PL 49, 432 A. Cf. also our discussion on the sins of pride in the first section of this chapter.

both vainglory and pride express the same human sinfulness, which is regarded as basic, they are brought together into one vice, and the number is reduced to seven.[153]

In a characteristic way this reform was, in fact, supported by John of the Ladder who, though representing Eastern monastic piety, argued in a rather formal way in favour of seven vices instead of eight.[154] The general tendency of the Eastern tradition however was the opposite: for particular purposes one could add other vices to the hierarchy. It is only very late that the Western system became dominant in the East. However, we find it clearly expressed in Peter Moghila's *Confessio Orthodoxa* for instance, where the number of vices is reckoned as seven, pride being the first of them.[155]

If we follow the Evagrian tradition, what we notice first of all is in fact that there are certain fluctuations within the fixed system of the hierarchy from the very beginning. In Evagrius' *De malignis cogitationibus* e.g. *acedia* is missing, and the number of vices is, in fact, just seven,[156] but in the *Tractatus ad eumdem Eulogium* the number is nine, or ten, for there envy ($\varphi\theta\acute{o}\nu os$) is added, and slander ($\kappa\alpha\tau\alpha\lambda\alpha\lambda\iota\acute{\alpha}$) is treated almost as a tenth vice: envy is called both "the garment of pride" and "the root of slander".[157] Envy and slander are however, as we have seen, two of the additional vices on Maximus' list also.

But further, in the same treatise both pride and envy are said to come from vainglory. The close relationship between envy and the sins of pride, which is thus noticeable in the Evagrian tradition, probably forms on the other hand the basis of the introduction of *invidia* as one of the seven vices of the Western hierarchy. And these two facts together show that Maximus' addition of the vice of envy to his list is rather a sign which indicates that he does refer to the hierarchy than a proof that he does not. In the end envy found its place in the East as well: in the *Confessio Orthodoxa* it is the fourth of the vices.[158] The position of slander is weaker but we have seen that it is closely attached to the hierarchy within the Evagrian tradition.

---

[153] On this historical development, see e.g. O. Zöckler, *Das Lehrstück von den sieben Hauptsünden,* Munich 1893, III, 41 f., and Vögtle, RACh I, col. 74.

[154] *Scala Paradisi, gr.* 22; PG 88, 948.

[155] *Confessio Orthodoxa,* 3, *quaest.* 23 and 24–37; cf. Zöckler, *op. cit.* III, 107. On Peter Moghila, his work, its Latin version and his relationship with the West, see e.g. A. Malvy—M. Viller (ed.), *La Confession Orthodoxe de Pierre Moghila* (Orientalia Christiana 39), Rome—Paris 1927.

[156] PG 79, 1200 D–1201 A.

[157] PG 79, 1141 A and 1144 D.

[158] See *Conf. Orth., ibid., quaest.* 23 and 30; cf. Zöckler, *loc. cit.*

But what about rapacity and resentfulness? Here too the historical development is of interest. In Maximus' list rapacity (πλεονεξία) is said to grow out of avarice, for which reason these two vices come very close to each other. In the Western hierarchy *avaritia* is preserved, but in the *Confessio Orthodoxa*, where the hierarchy is modelled on the Western system, we notice the striking fact that avarice (φιλαργυρία) has disappeared and been replaced by rapacity (πλεονεξία).[159] The reason must be that the latter vice was frequently combined with avarice, and again we must conclude that Maximus represents a middle phase in this development, and that the addition of the vice of rapacity is another sign that he is referring to the Evagrian hierarchy.

The same conclusion can be drawn regarding resentfulness (μνησικακία). In the Western scheme *ira* occupies the place of ὀργή, but when this scheme is finally translated to the East, as we see in the *Confessio Orthodoxa*, wrath (ὀργή) is replaced by resentfulness (μνησικακία).[160]

The only possible conclusion from what we have now said is that Maximus shows, particularly in Char 3. 56, that he is well acquainted with the Evagrian hierarchy of the eight vices, and also that his treatment of this idea reflects a particular phase in its historical development. This is, of course, not to say that this historical development can be followed in its different stages, nor that the original form of the Evagrian hierarchy had already lost its importance by the time of Maximus. John of Damascus is a perfect example of a later writer, in whom the influences of both Maximus and the original Evagrian system are apparent.[161] What we might say, however, is that the monastic character of the hierarchy, which probably indicates its roots in practical ascetic experiences and which is dominant in writers like Evagrius, Nilus and Cassian—though one does not deny that these temptations attack worldly men as well as monks—disappears in the Western system, and consequently also in the East, in so far as the Western understanding gained influence there. But in the case of Maximus, the monastic character, which included a tendency to allow for additional vices in the system, still predominated,

---

[159] See *Conf. Orth., ibid.*, 23 and 26; cf. ZÖCKLER, *loc. cit.* In the Latin version this vice is translated *auaritia*, see MALVY—VILLER, *op. cit.*, p. 104 f.

[160] See *Conf. Orth., ibid.*, 23 and 34; cf. ZÖCKLER, *loc. cit.* In the Latin version this vice is called *ira*, see MALVY—VILLER, *op. cit.*, p. 104 and 107.

[161] See *De octo spir. nequ.* 1; PG 95, 80 A, where even the older order of grief—wrath is preserved.

and this to a great extent explains the way in which the hierarchy is treated in his writing.

We have thus shown a) that there is a relationship between the hierarchy of the vices and the idea of the trichotomy of the human soul, and b) that Maximus' treatment of human passions and vices includes an attachment to the Evagrian hierarchy of eight vices. This leads us, however, to a closer study of Maximus' treatment of vices and passions in a 'trichotomist' perspective. Such a study will demonstrate, how he conceives of the disintegrating function of passions in terms of a misuse of the psychic faculties.

3. The trichotomy of the soul and the work of passions in general

We have seen that an emphasis on the relationship between the trichotomy of the human soul and the differentiations of passions and vices is in harmony with the Evagrian hierarchy of eight cardinal vices or passionate thoughts, and we have also seen that teaching on passions and vices which includes extended or varying hierarchies, such as we find in Maximus, may very well be closely attached to the Evagrian system. This fact gives us the right to see Maximus' treatment of vices and passions in the perspective of his stress on the trichotomy of the soul, and at the same time as involving an elaboration of the Evagrian psychology of the eight vices.[162] This in its turn is of importance for our specific subject, since it may help us to understand how Maximus' strong emphasis on the unity of the soul of man, as well as of the human composite as a whole, can be combined with an equally strong stress on the disastrous effect of disintegrating passions and vices.

'Trichotomist' and other principles of differentiation among the vices

Against the background of our short study in Evagrius and the Evagrian tradition at this point, it seems first of all obvious that Maximus, when differentiating between the vices and passions which he mentions, refers rather frequently to the three faculties of the soul. This reference is, in

---

[162] It should be clearly underlined here that the trichotomist differentiation between vices (and virtues) in general is, of course, not in itself original in Maximus or his Christian predecessors. It is already an obvious fact in Ps.-Aristotle, *De virt. et vit.* 1–3, where explicit reference is made to the Platonic trichotomy (1249 a) and the application is worked out, first in relation to virtues and then to vices (1250 a). What interests us here is Maximus' use of it in relation to the Evagrian hierarchy.

fact, more apparent in Maximus than in the tradition to which he is attached.

Thus in *Cent. de char.* Maximus stresses on several occasions that the passions and vices should be differentiated according to the psychic trichotomy, or to the dichotomy of the passible part of the soul. In some cases—in an Evagrian way—the mind represents the rational part of the trichotomy, in other cases the mind is more clearly presented as being above all the elements, and in yet others the whole stress lies on the two elements of the passible part, since the problems of the mind and the rational faculty are for the moment left out of the picture. In isolated passages these variations may look puzzling, but seen as a whole *Cent. de char.*, like the rest of Maximus' writings, shows that Maximus conceives of the three parts of the human soul, in relation to passions and vices, as mutually related elements of a whole, of which the mind is called to serve as a spiritual subject.[163]

Before we exemplify this general understanding and try to illustrate the extent to which Maximus relates his teaching on the passions and vices to the idea of the trichotomy, however, we ought at least to indicate that there are also other principles of differentiation which Maximus uses, just as we found that there are other principles represented in the Evagrian tradition.

Thus, first of all we find isolated references to the classical *four cardinal virtues*—those of Plato's *The Republic*—with their corresponding vices, which serve as a basis for a classification of vices different from that of the Evagrian hierarchy.[164] Secondly, there is the general ascetic differentiation between passions and vices *of the body and of the soul*,[165] an idea which, in a more inclusive form, is expressed in a three-fold differentiation of good and bad conditions of life, i.e. between those in the soul, those in the body and those concerned with the body.[166] A third differentiation, also three-fold, is related to *the senses, the condition of the body and the memory* as different sources of impassioned thoughts.[167] The Stoic understanding of passions, with its stress on *the dialectic between pleasure and grief, present conditions and future expectations*, forms the background of a fourth principle of differentiation,[168] and this

---

[163] Cf. ch. III: A, 2; pp. 108–113 above.

[164] See e.g. Char 2. 79; CSC, p. 132; cf. QuDub 1, 68; CCSG 10, p. 158 and Myst 5; PG 91, 680 A.

[165] See Char 1. 64; CSC, p. 72; cf. the corresponding differentiation among virtues in 2. 57; p. 120.

[166] *Ibid.* 2. 76; p. 130.

[167] *Ibid.* 2. 74; p. 128.

[168] *Ibid.* 2. 65; p. 124; cf. 2. 44; p. 114.

principle, in its turn, is closely connected with a more genuinely Maximian differentiation between those vices which are born out of man's search for pleasure and those vices which are related to the subsequent pain, and finally those vices which are the result of a mixture of both.[169] A fifth principle of differentiation, which distinguishes between passions which manifest an *irrational love or hate* for something is probably equally genuinely Maximian.[170] And finally, there should also be mentioned the idea of a *seven-fold fall of human nature*, exemplified through the history of mankind, as it is reflected in the Bible, and which manifests, though implicitly, a system of human vices which is certainly in some way related to Maximus' understanding of human passions in general.[171]

There is, thus, in Maximus quite a variety of systematizations of passions and vices. But the direct and indirect references to *the trichotomy of the soul* in this context are, nevertheless, frequent and seem to be rather deeply integrated into the whole of his thinking. They are, however, of different kinds and represent different degrees of connection with the idea of the trichotomy. There are a) direct references to the whole trichotomy; b) direct references to the dichotomy of the passible part of the soul, with or without a mention of the mind (νοῦς), or possibly of the rational faculty, as a third element; c) indirect or implicit references to the trichotomy or to parts of it; and finally, d) descriptions of isolated vices which indicate that they are conceived as a kind of misuse of the faculties of the trichotomy.[172] Let us deal with these types of references here in the same order.

Direct references to the whole trichotomy

The direct references to the trichotomy are not frequent but clear. A good example is given in Char 1. 64–67, a section entirely devoted to the problem of passions, which shows that the reference to the trichotomy is not at all accidental. Here Maximus first of all underlines that some passions are of the body and some of the soul.[173] He then advances to the passions of the soul, dividing them into those of the irascibile and those of the concupiscible part, thus referring only to the dichotomy of the

---

[169] Thal, *Prol.;* CCSG 7, p. 33.

[170] Char 2. 16; CSC, p. 96; cf. 1. 51; p. 66 ff.

[171] See QuDub 59; CCSG 10, p. 46 f.

[172] This fourth type of reference will be treated separately under 4 (pp. 267–278) below.

[173] 1. 64; CSC, p. 72.

passible element,[174] but he ends by relating the rest of the passions to various parts of the *whole* trichotomy.[175] This procedure clearly shows that Maximus intends to underline both that it is from the relationships which involve the body and the exterior world of the senses that passions arise, and that the grip of passions takes hold of the whole of man. No human element is excluded; to all of them certain passions belong. And as far as the soul is concerned, it is also clear that the idea of the trichotomy serves to underline this involvement of the whole of the human composite.

Equally clear is Char 3. 3, where Maximus explicitly emphasizes that the vices arise from a misuse of the three powers of the soul, and though the types of vices which are here referred to the different elements are not to be found as such in the Evagrian hierarchy, it is not difficult to equate them with corresponding vices in the hierarchy. Thus Maximus says that the vices of the rational faculty are ignorance and folly, a couple which is not very far from that of pride and vainglory, and he goes on to say that hate and intemperance are vices of the irascible and the concupiscible parts respectively.[176] Here we must say that hate comes very close to wrath and intemperance to both gluttony and fornication. We may thus notice that Maximus again underlines that all the three faculties are involved, and also that the vices are explicitly called a *misuse* of these faculties.

Finally, we are inclined to suspect an indirect reference to the hierarchy of vices also. This last suspicion is, in fact, partly confirmed in the next chapter of the same century, for there Maximus presents a tetrad of gluttony, fornication, avarice and vainglory, which to a great extent resembles similar arrangements within the Evagrian tradition, which are there closely linked with the hierarchy of eight vices.[177] A similar passage is also provided by Char 3. 20, where Maximus once more distributes the different passions among the three parts of the soul, but also underlines the close relationship to the body on the one hand, and on the other the serious effects which the passions have on the mind.[178]

These three examples of a clear reference to the trichotomy in connection with passions and vices, should be enough to make certain that the 'trichotomist' principle of differentiation is central to Maximus,

---

[174] 1. 65–66; p. 74.

[175] 1. 67; *loc. cit.*

[176] CSC, p. 144.

[177] See *ibid.* 3. 4; *loc. cit.* It should, however, also be noticed that Maximus' reference to the trichotomy is supported by a citation of one of Maximus' accepted authorities, Ps.-Denis; see *ibid.* 3. 5; p. 146.

[178] CSC, p. 150 ff.

and serves to underline the fact that the *whole* of man is involved in the process of a life of passions, as much as in a Christian life in virtues.[179]

Direct references to the dichotomy of the passible part of the soul

Here the number of striking examples can immediately be extended. Now these references are often combined with a mention of the mind as a kind of third element, which seems to leave out the rational faculty as a separate element and to imply an identification of the mind and the rational faculty. This Evagrian tendency however, is not as strong as it might look at the beginning. One must remember that the mind as spiritual subject acts primarily *through* the rational faculty, and from the point of view of the basic dichotomy of man, i.e. that between the sensible and the intelligible element, the effects of the passions of concupiscence and anger on the rational part of man very easily coincide with the same effects on the mind. And this fact makes it quite natural for Maximus to mention these later effects without mentioning at the same time the rational element as such.

Thus for example it comes about that he describes how the mind, stirred by the impassioned activities of concupiscence, dreams of objects that give pleasure, but stirred by the activity of anger, looks on things which cause fear.[180] The mind is thus presented as enslaved by the passions of the passible elements, and as human subject it engages the whole of man in a search for pleasure and an escape from that which causes fear. A licentious and unmanly attitude characterizes such a man.[181]

In other instances Maximus points out, with an indirect reference to the same dichotomy, that hate and intemperance—notice the similarity between this couple and that of fear and pleasure—stir the mind of a man who suffers from passions, and that he has to be purified through love and self-mastery, their positive counterparts.[182] Consequently, the virtues and activities, which conquer the passions, are presented as powers to heal and transform the two passible parts of the soul.[183] Freedom from passions and divine charity are the effective powers

---

[179] Other references of the same kind could be enumerated; see e.g. *ibid.* 2. 12; p. 94 and Ep 2; PG 91, 397 AB; cf. also references to the trichotomy in relation to corresponding virtues or to a good use of the faculties, see e.g. Char 4. 15; p. 200; 4. 44; p. 212 and QuDub 126; CCSG 10, p. 93.

[180] Char 2. 69; CSC, p. 126.

[181] Both Platonic and Stoic ideas have obviously coloured these reflections. See also Char 2. 70; *loc. cit.*

[182] *Ibid.* 4. 72–73; p. 226.

[183] See e.g. *ibid.* 2. 47–48; p. 116.

behind this restoration of the faculties of the soul,[184] which is worked out through such means as spiritual reading for the mind, self-mastery for concupiscence, and prayers and alms for anger,[185] or, according to another version, through prayer for the mind, self-mastery for concupiscence and love for anger.[186]

The references to the dichotomy of the passible part of the soul in relation to the different kinds of lower passions and vices are, speaking generally, very frequent in Maximus' writings, and it is obviously his conviction, that any differentiation of them has to take this dichotomy into account.[187] If we also bear in mind his clear references to the trichotomy in this context, we can hardly escape the impression that references to the dichotomy are part of this greater system, which allows for a strong stress on the involvement of the whole of man, by mediation of the soul, in the disastrous process of a life in passions—a life where differentiation means harmful separation, and the mutual dependence of the different elements means common destruction.[188]

Indirect or implicit references to the trichotomy

This third kind of references is, of course, difficult to demonstrate with full certainty. Against the background of what we have now presented, at least a considerable number of these references are, however, illuminated.

But there is a particular problem here, which needs to be dealt with first of all, since it is of a special importance, i.e. the problem of the understanding of *the basic triad of vices*, which we have discovered already in Evagrius and which consists of *gluttony, avarice* and *vainglory.*[189] It is hardly possible to understand these three vices as an implicit reference to the trichotomy, for though gluttony is related to concupiscence and vainglory is at least sometimes possible to relate to the rational element, avarice is difficult to refer to the irascible part. And if this is the case, the apparently ambiguous position of vainglory[190] adds considerably to the general hesitation. But on the other hand, it would be

---

[184] See *ibid.* 1. 34; p. 60.

[185] See e.g. Ep 24; PG 91, 609 D–612 A; cf. the same formulation in Ep 43; 640 CD.

[186] Asc 19; PG 90, 925 D.

[187] For further examples, see e.g. Asc 15; PG 90, 924 A and Gnost 1. 16; PG 90, 1089 A.

[188] See further section 4 below.

[189] Cf. p. 241 above.

[190] An excellent illustration of this ambiguity is provided within the Evagrian tradition by the compilation *De octo vit. cogitat.*, where vainglory is explicitly said to be connected with all the three parts of the soul; see PG 79, 1461 C.

surprising if there were no connection at all between this triad and the elements of the trichotomy.

Already Evagrius presented this triad as a kind of basis for the rest of the hierarchy, i.e. of fornication, anger, grief and pride—which must be suspected to be arranged according to the trichotomy of the soul.[191] But at the same time it becomes clear that the triad itself is not arranged according to the same principle. It is presented as more basic than the rest of the vices, and as such, if we take Evagrius' general position into consideration, obviously also more basically related to the body. Evagrius seems to think of a straight development from gluttony to vainglory. The reason behind this arrangement, which probably goes back to older speculations about man's basic needs, is not apparent, but a most interesting biblical foundation is presented: the three vices of gluttony, avarice and vainglory are those which the Devil suggested to Christ in the desert. This last interpretation is also found elsewhere in the Evagrian tradition. Thus Cassian reproduces it, even noticing the difference between Matthew and Luke in regard to the order of the tempta-tions.[192] This tradition partly underlines, it seems, the basic and bodily understanding of these three vices.

But how are we to interpret the same triad, when it appears in Maximus? A short study of the passages in which the triad is found shows immediately that the Evagrian tradition at this point was known to Maximus. He presents the same elements of interpretation, and he does

---

[191] See *De mal. cogitat.* 1; PG 79, 1200 D–1201 A and 24; 1228 B.

[192] *Coll.* 5, 6; Pichéry, p. 194 f.—It is worth noticing that this rather precise interpretation of the story of Christ's temptations in the desert seems to have no explicit foundation in Origen, whose interpretation is of a wider and more general character. (On Origen's exegesis of the story, see particularly M. Steiner, *La tentation de Jésus dans l'interprétation patristique de saint Justin à Origène*, Paris 1962, pp. 107–192.) However, an interesting parallel is to be found in the *Canons of Hippolytus* 30 (see H. Achelis, *Die ältesten Quellen des orientalischen Kirchenrechts, 1. Die Canones Hippolyti*, TU 6, 4, Leipzig 1891, p. 281 f.), where the three temptations are said to aim at *cupiditas, superbia* and *amor auri;* cf. K.-P. Köppen, *Die Auslegung der Versuchungsgeschichte unter besonderer Berücksichtigung der Alten Kirche* (BGBE 4), Tübingen 1961, p. 37. Ambrose, *Expos. ev. Luc.* 4. 33; CSEL 32, 4, p. 155, 13–21, offers another parallel: *gula, facilitas* and *ambitio;* cf. Köppen, *op. cit.,* p. 83 f. Finally, Gregory the Great, *Hom. in Evv.* 16. 2, 3; PL 76, 1135 D–1136 A, reflects the influence of the Evagrian tradition itself: *gula, vana gloria, avaritia;* cf. Köppen, *op. cit.* p. 84. It is surprising that Köppen, who has noticed these interpretations and clearly seen that they are part of a wider parallelism between the temptations of Adam and Christ (see Idem, *op. cit.,* pp. 79–85), does not mention the contributions of Evagrius, the Evagrian tradition and later Maximus the Confessor at this point.—From the point of view of the New Testament itself the Evagrian ascetic interpretation is, of course, rather remote. There the Messianic perspective clearly dominates the presentation. On this perspective, see H. Riesenfeld, *Le caractère Messianique de la tentation au désert,* in E. Massaux etc., *La venue du Messie* (Recherches Bibliques 6), Louvain 1962, pp. 51–63.

not advance much further. Nevertheless, Maximus' statements about the triad allow for some larger amount of clarity. First of all, there is a strong stress on the view that all the three vices are connected with the body. Maximus says explicitly that they all have their origin in some demand of the body, though he does not indicate in what way.[193] Secondly, Maximus makes clear that as such, they rise more or less immediately from self-love.[194] And in the third place, he also points out that the vices of anger are not included in, but caused by, the vices of the triad.[195]

This last conclusion, which is of a particular importance in the context of our study, is most perfectly illustrated by Maximus in the *Liber asceticus,* where he follows the Evagrian interpretation of *Christ's temptations* in the desert as those of gluttony, avarice and vainglory,[196] but also demonstrates that the vices of the irascible faculty are not suggested to Christ in the desert but are confronted and overcome by him later during the course of his passion.[197] And this fact now gives us the right to conclude that the triad of basic vices, which Maximus presents in accordance with the Evagrian tradition, includes no explicit reference to the trichotomy of the soul, but that in their fundamental relationship to the body, and as vices which cause the vices of anger to rise in the second place, the elements of the triad are nevertheless connected with the trichotomy. They express primarily the *passions of concupiscence,* which lead to passions of anger.

The position of vainglory in this context may be difficult to understand, but it seems to be the conviction of both Evagrius and Maximus that vainglory should, at least sometimes, be understood as an expression of concupiscence, i.e. as a refined concupiscence which, however, in giving rise to the vice of pride, affects the rational element of the soul more directly.[198]

However, there are also more apparent indirect references to the trichotomy, or to the dichotomy of the passible part. This is not least the case when Maximus deals with virtues and other means for the restoration of the human composite. In this context charity can easily be referred to the irascible element, self-mastery to the concupiscible element, and reading and contemplation to the mind through the

---

[193] Char 2. 59; CSC, p. 122.
[194] *Ibid.* 3. 56; p. 170.
[195] *Ibid.* 1. 75; p. 78 and 3. 7; p. 146.
[196] Asc 10; PG 90, 920 C.
[197] See *ibid.* 11–12; PG 90, 920 C–921 B.
[198] A similar, though implicit, reference to the triad is also given in Char 4. 41; CSC, p. 210.

rational element.[199] Statements of this kind are further illuminated by passages where the perspective is an opposite one: Maximus speaks of the elements of the trichotomy and refers to the virtues in general. Thus in Thal 55 Maximus underlines the fact that anger and concupiscence must be subordinated to reason and be used by the mind in the service of the virtues.[200] Likewise, passions in general are both negatively and positively referred to the three parts of the soul.[201]

Finally, in Ep 5 Maximus alludes clearly, in one and the same text, both to the dichotomy, with its means of restoration, and to the Platonic virtues, including not only a reference to Plato's image of the two horses and the chariot, but also an enumeration of a great number of vices and virtues, of which the first ones at least could be divided according to the trichotomy. Thus prudence and ignorance should belong to the rational part, courage and fear to the irascible part, and moderation and intemperance to the concupiscible part. Though the rest of the virtues and vices mentioned may be more difficult to distribute in the same way—a number of them seem, however, to belong to the irascible faculty—this text is another example of the importance which Maximus obviously attaches to the trichotomy.[202] But then at the same time it also shows that this importance is intimately connected with Maximus' idea that the whole of man is involved in the activities of both vices and virtues, and that passions and vices are examples of a disastrous misuse of human faculties, which are meant to be used in a positive context. The indirect references to the connection between the host of vices and the trichotomy of the soul show that Maximus is here dealing not only with a formal principle of differentiation but also with an important element of his understanding of man.

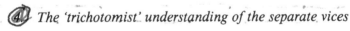 *The 'trichotomist' understanding of the separate vices*

Maximus' 'trichotomist' understanding of the vices is, of course, illustrated also by the descriptions of the separate vices, since these are understood as forms of misuse of any of the three faculties. This understanding can be demonstrated in different ways, but we shall here

---

[199] See e.g. *ibid.* 4.86; p. 232; cf. 4. 80; p. 230, where a similar differentiation is explicitly referred to the trichotomy.

[200] CCSG 7, p. 499.

[201] QuDub 126; CCSG 10, p. 93.

[202] See Ep 5; PG 91, 421 A–C. Justice and injustice refer, of course, in a Platonic way to the whole of man. To the same category also μακροθυμία and ὀλιγοψυχία should probably be referred; cf. the corresponding position of μεγαλοψυχία and μικροψυχία in Ps.-Aristotle, *De virt. et vit.* 1–3; 1249 b–1250 a.

concentrate our attention on those vices which belong to the Evagrian hierarchy. In fact, this limitation is desirable on other grounds as well as those of our present study.[203] For it seems clear that in general Maximus devotes more time and attention to these vices—and those closely linked with this hierarchy—than to others, and this is another indication of the close relationship which exists between the concept of the hierarchy and Maximus' understanding of the passions and vices of the soul. Let us then study Maximus' descriptions of each of the vices.

Gluttony (γαστριμαργία)

is the first, most basic and most bodily of the vices of the Evagrian hierarchy. Seen in a 'trichotomist' perspective it belongs to *the concupiscible faculty* of the human soul. In Maximus' interpretations of this vice these tendencies are confirmed. Thus Michal, the daughter of Saul (incorrectly called Merob[204] by Maximus),[205] is allegorically interpreted as gluttony, because she had brought up five sons, i.e. a five-fold misuse of the senses, for Adriel, i.e. the intellectual part of the soul.[206] The position of gluttony is, in fact, so fundamental that it is able to remove all the fruits of a virtuous life.[207]

In the only separate piece of writing which Maximus devoted to the passion of gluttony, he recalls that Aristotle, in his book about animals, mentions an animal which is born from decay, between land and water, and consumes earth until it appears in the daylight. In three days it dies, but after these three days a cloud pours rain upon it, and it comes to life, and will never be an "ever-eater" again. This is, says Maximus, an indirect reference to gluttons. For any passion—of which gluttony is obviously the basic example—is born from decay and does not stop eating until it is revealed. And then it dies *in the three faculties of the soul,* but it comes to life again thanks to the grace of the Spirit, but not to a life of passion, but to a virtuous life instead.[208]

Gluttony is thus to Maximus the most basic, and therefore most

---

[203] Cf. HAUSHERR, *Philautic,* p. 70.

[204] Jerome interprets Merab as "de multitudine", see *De nom. Hebr., De Regn. lib.* III; PL 23, 821–822.

[205] See 2 Sam. 21: 8.

[206] See Thal 65, CCSG 22, p. 257 ff. Cf. also p. 297, where Maximus presents an allegorical interpretation of I Sam. 15: 33. Samuel says to Agag: "As your sword has made women childless, so shall your mother be childless among women." Here the sword is interpreted as gluttony, the women as basic virtues and the children as the offspring of the virtuous soul.

[207] *Op. cit.;* CCSG 22, p. 297 ff.

[208] QuDub 126; CCSG 10, p. 92 f.

representative of all vices. It is born from the relationship of the human soul to the world of the body and the senses, but it affects the whole of man, and may consequently be converted into virtuous activity.

Fornication (πορνεία)

is the second vice of the Evagrian hierarchy. As such it comes very close to gluttony and is said to be born from gluttony. The Evagrian tradition seems to be unanimous at this point.[209] As a matter of fact, this understanding has also a wider background of physiological specula-tion,[210] which cannot, however, be treated within the limits of this study.[211] From this it follows naturally that fornication belongs to *the concupiscible element* of the soul.[212]

In Maximus this same tradition is clearly reflected. Once he even quotes authorities who say that demons touch the hidden parts of the body in sleep and rouse the passion of fornication.[213] And the descent from gluttony is also emphasized. He thus calls gluttony mother and nurse of fornication,[214] and in the *Liber asceticus* Maximus states that surfeit of food and drink heat the stomach and inflame the appetite to shameful desires, a process which leads logically to fornication. But in

---

[209] This is clear already in the catalogue of Evagrius itself, where fornication naturally follows gluttony. In *Tract. ad eumdem Eul.* it is explicitly stated that gluttony is the mother of fornication (2; PG 79, 1141 AB), and in Nilus' *De octo spir. mal.* gluttony is called "mother of licentiousness", i.e. in the first place fornication (4; PG 79, 1148 D). Finally, in Cassian gluttony and fornication do not merely belong to those vices which are bound to the body (*Coll.* 5. 3; PICHÉRY, p. 190), but their relationship is defined as that of fruit, fornication, and seed, gluttony (*Coll.* 5. 6; PICHÉRY, p. 194).

[210] Its general background in antiquity seems to be provided by the idea that dry and clean air is positive to thinking activities, while wet air is an obstacle to it. Humidity prevents reason from functioning, and therefore thinking is not favoured by sleep, intoxication and plenty of food, as Diogenes of Apollonia already held (see DIELS, *Fragmente der Vorsokratiker* 2, p. 56, 13 ff.); cf. C.-M. EDSMAN, Arbor inversa, *Religion och Bibel* 3 (1944), p. 22.

[211] To demonstrate the impact of these speculations in Eastern Christian asceticism, it may perhaps be sufficient to mention the realistic descriptions of gluttony and fornication presented by John of the Ladder. This important ascetic writer underlines in his *Scala Paradisi* that the demon of gluttony is often seated upon the stomach and constantly irritates man, and that the sin of impurity commonly follows after gluttony. He seems to presuppose a fixed line of development from gluttony to a sleep which instigates the sin of fornication (*gr.* 14; PG 88, 868 C).

[212] See e.g. in Evagrius' own texts: *Antirrhet.* 2. 22; FRANKENBERG, p. 514 f.; *Cent. gnost.* 1. 84; PO 28, p. 57; *Pract.* 2. 54; PG 40, 1245 D and *De mal. cogitat.* 27, in MUYLDERMANS, *A travers la tradition,* p. 51. Cf. also Nilus, *De octo spir. mal.* 6; PG 79, 1152 B and Cassian, *Coll.* 24. 15; CSEL 13, p. 691.

[213] Char 2. 85; CSC, p. 136.

[214] *Ibid.* 1. 84; p. 82; HAUSHERR, *Philautie,* p. 72, has noticed that he even interprets 1 Tim. 6: 10 in this direction.

the same context he also makes clear that self-mastery (ἐγκράτεια) is the means by which man may avoid this vicious development, since self-mastery quenches *concupiscence.*[215] In *Cent. de char.* he likewise underlines that carelessness in eating and contact with women are the weaknesses through which the demon of fornication gets hold of the monk, since they help him to inflame the body.[216]

Avarice (φιλαργυρία)

The position of avarice within the Evagrian tradition is more ambiguous. In Cassian's *Coll.* 24, 15 this vice is without hesitation referred to the concupiscible element,[217] but the earlier tradition is less fixed. Evagrius' own stress on alms as a means to heal anger seems at least to have some secondary reference to avarice also.[218] The general tendency however, coincides with the understanding presented by Cassian. This fact is particularly confirmed, if we have been right in supposing that the Evagrian triad of gluttony, avarice and vainglory is as a whole closely related to the body, and thus primarily also to the concupiscible element. Even Nilus seems to relate avarice to concupiscence.[219]

Maximus also seems to stress the connection between avarice and the body, as we have underlined in relation to his use of the Evagrian triad of basic vices. At the same time this implies however that avarice—which Maximus describes as the passion of a man who receives with joy but gives away with grief[220]—is very closely connected with vainglory. He says that these two vices condition each other in the man of the world, while the monk, who is without possessions, often grows all the vainer.[221] And since vainglory is also related to pride, avarice to some extent occupies a *mediating position.* Avarice is at least presented as often a secret vice, which, in the monk, is only revealed when a particular occasion appears. It is often combined with pride, but when it is revealed, it also shows its connection with bodily affections.[222]

We may, therefore, be allowed to conclude that avarice belongs, in Maximus as well, primarily to the sphere of *concupiscence,* but is of such

---

[215] Asc 23; PG 90, 929 AB.
[216] Char 2. 19; CSC, p. 98.
[217] CSEL 13, p. 691.
[218] *Pract.* 1. 63; PG 40, 1237 B.
[219] See *De octo spir. mal.* 8; PG 79, 1153 A. It should be noted in this context that Nilus here explicitly follows Paul (1 Tim. 6: 10) in calling avarice the root of all evil.
[220] Char 3. 76; CSC, p. 180.
[221] *Ibid.* 3. 83; p. 184.
[222] See e.g. Gnost 1. 64; PG 90, 1105 D.

a character that it underlines the involvement of the whole of man in the process of the passions.

Grief (λύπη) and wrath (ὀργή)

These two vices are closely related to each other in the Evagrian hierarchy. Their order in relation to each other fluctuates. Since wrath is, of course, the most characteristic vice of the irascible faculty, this close connection would logically lead to the affirmation that both belong to this faculty, when seen in a 'trichotomist' perspective. In Cassian's *Coll.* 24, 15 this is the case,[223] but in the earlier Evagrian tradition the picture is more complicated.

In the case of wrath there is, of course, no difficulty. ὀργή and θυμός are almost synonymous expressions both in Evagrius and in the later tradition.[224] But in the case of grief the situation is slightly different.[225] For when Evagrius places grief before wrath in his hierarchy, he obviously does so in order to underline how man moves from the more bodily vices to those of an inner aggression, i.e.—in a 'trichotomist' interpretation—how he moves from vices of concupiscence to vices of anger. And in this perspective grief seems to occupy a middle position. Evagrius defines it as a lack of pleasure.[226]

This "lack" may, however, be caused either by some outward circumstances or by e.g. a monk's fight against his own vices of concupiscence. Thus Evagrius points out that when the concupiscible element is moderated by detachment, then the irascible element of the monk is tempted.[227] But on the other hand, in Evagrius' opinion, grief in its middle position is also very closely connected with wrath. In fact, he says that grief is *either* caused by a lack of desire—an interpretation which has, of course, a Stoic background—*or* is a fruit of wrath.[228] For this reason it should in the end rather be related to *the irascible element* than to the concupiscible element. It is a passion of the former, which establishes the relationship with the latter.[229]

---

[223] See CSEL 13, p. 691.

[224] See Evagrius, *De mal. cogitat.* 1; PG 79, 1201 A and 14; 1216 BC, where wrath is replaced by θυμός; *De octo vit. cogitat.* 6; PG 40, 1273 A; *Antirrhet.* 5. 11–12 and 17–18; FRANKENBERG, p. 514 f. and 5. 30; FRANKENBERG, p. 516 f.; and *Pract.* 1. 11; PG 40, 1224 C and 2. 54; 1245 D–1248 A; further Nilus, *De octo spir. mal.* 9; PG 79, 1153 C and finally *Tract. ad eumdem Eul.* 3; PG 79, 1144 A, where wrath is called "the law of θυμός".

[225] On the place and interpretation of λύπη in general in ancient Christian writers, see further *art.* λύπη, G. W. H. LAMPE (ed.), *A Patristic Greek Lexicon* 3, Oxford 1964, p. 814.

[226] *Pract.* 1. 10; PG 40, 1224 C.

[227] *De mal. cogitat.* 16; PG 79, 1217 D–1220 A.

[228] *De octo vit. cogitat.* 5; PG 40, 1272 C.

[229] See e.g. *Pract.* 1. 10; PG 40, 1224 D and 2. 54; 1245 D–1248 A.

For this reason charity is a remedy for both grief and wrath,[230] or for grief in the same way as long-suffering is a remedy for wrath.[231] In Nilus grief is directly related to wrath and ought therefore to be connected with the irascible element,[232] and in the *Tractatus ad eumdem Eulogium* the situation seems to be the same, since the vices of grief, wrath and *acedia* are brought closely together.[233]

In Maximus the same psychological mechanism in relation to wrath and grief is presupposed. Grief is, however, in Maximus a vice which is far more discussed than wrath. In general and as a whole it is very frequently treated. Grief separates man both from God and from his neighbour.[234] In the latter case it is very closely related to both resentfulness and envy, and creates serious problems within the monastic community.[235] When we consider the cause of grief, however, we must bear in mind that the dialectic between pleasure ($\dot\eta\delta o\nu\dot\eta$) and pain ($\dot o\delta\dot v\nu\eta$) plays a most important rôle in Maximus' understanding of sinful human life, for this dialectic undoubtedly colours Maximus' view of grief ($\lambda\dot v\pi\eta$), which, as we have seen, in the tradition before Maximus, influenced by Stoic thinking, is the regular counterpart to pleasure ($\dot\eta\delta o\nu\dot\eta$). And this fact predisposes Maximus to accept the Evagrian understanding of grief as lack of pleasure.[236]

Thus he defines it explicitly as a disposition of the soul, characterized by lack of pleasure, adding that lack of pleasure necessarily implies an acquisition of toil.[237] Consequently, here too grief occupies a middle position, which does not however exclude the possibility that it belongs logically to the irascible element.

But even more important, the connection between Maximus' understanding of grief and his stress on the dialectic of pleasure and pain, leads him to an affirmation of a positive use of $\lambda\dot v\pi\eta$. Thal 58 deals particularly with a grief, which is combined with true pleasure. Toil belongs to the conditions of this life. For a virtuous man there is thus a useful grief in the same sense as there is a healthy pleasure.[238] In the end however, grief

---

[230] *Tract. ad Eul. monach.* 10; PG 79, 1105 D.
[231] *Ibid.* 5; 1100 D.
[232] See *De octo spir. mal.* 11; PG 79, 1156 BC.
[233] See 3; PG 79, 1141 D–1144 A and 4; 1144 BC.
[234] See Char 1.41; CSC, p. 62 and 1. 53; p. 68.
[235] See *ibid.* 3. 89 and 91; p. 186 ff.
[236] Cf. HAUSHERR, *Philautie*, p. 80.
[237] Thal 58; CCSG 22, p. 27.
[238] See particularly CCSG 22, p. 37.

and joy will be entirely separated,[239] in the same way as grief may be transformed into joy already in this world when peace is established.[240]

Listlessness (ἀκηδία)

In the Evagrian tradition *acedia* comes close to grief, and seen in a 'trichotomist' perspective this very monastic vice should naturally be related to the irascible faculty. *Acedia* is a kind of false balance in the soul, a negative counterpart to detachment (ἀπάθεια). It is a spleen, which paralyses man instead of setting him free.[241]

As such in Nilus it primarily concerns the faculties of the soul, and not the mind,[242] and is defined as a slackness (ἀτονία) of the soul.[243] The problem of psychic slackness and tension however belongs clearly to the sphere of *the irascible element*,[244] and consequently the vice of *acedia* should be referred to this element. In fact, Evagrius himself relates it very closely to anger and grief.[245] The same thing is found in the *Tractatus ad eumdem Eulogium*, where *acedia* is coupled with grief.[246] Finally in Cassian's *Coll.* 24, 15 *acedia* belongs, together with *furor* and *tristitia*, to the irascible element.[247]

Maximus too connects *acedia* very closely with grief,[248] but he stresses even more its middle position.[249] He thus emphasizes that a monk who tolerates thoughts of concupiscence and anger will easily fall from pure prayer and suffer from *acedia*.[250] And since pure prayer is an occupation of the mind it certainly has its effects on it, in Maximus' opinion. In this context, however, it is particularly interesting that Maximus goes even further and stresses explicitly that *acedia* grasps *all the faculties of the*

---

[239] QuDub 123; CCSG 10, p. 91.

[240] For such a use of the couple grief—joy, see Ep 24; PG 91, 608 C.

[241] On the position and interpretation of *acedia* in general in ancient Christian writers, see further G. BARDY, *art.* Acédia, DSp 1 (1937), coll. 166–169, and *art.* ἀκηδία, LAMPE, *A Patristic Greek Lexicon* 1, Oxford 1961, p. 61 f,.

[242] See *De octo spir. mal.* 16; PG 79, 1161 B.

[243] *Ibid.* 13; 1157 CD.

[244] Cf. what Maximus says in this context about the good tension in the irascible element of a virtuous man, in OrDom; CCSG 23, p. 58.

[245] *Antirrhet.* 6. 9; FRANKENBERG, p. 522 f. and 6. 53–57; p. 530 f.

[246] 4; PG 79, 1144 BC.

[247] CSEL 13, p. 691.

[248] See Char 1. 52; CSC, p. 68.

[249] HAUSHERR, *op. cit.*, p. 80, seems slightly to underestimate the importance of Maximus' statements on *acedia*.

[250] Char 1. 49; CSC, p. 66.

soul, i.e. not only the irascible or the concupiscible element but also the rational faculty,[251] and that for this reason it is heavier than the other passions.

Maximus is thus very eager to stress the middle position of this vice. Though we have no reason to doubt that he agrees that it is, in its own nature, primarily attached to the irascible element of the soul, it is clear that the vice of *acedia* serves to underline *the aspect of unity,* in relation to the passions of the soul, more than the aspect of differentiation. It is thus another example of Maximus' conviction that, whatever differentiation may be made in this field, it cannot violate the basic unity of the human composite.

Vainglory (κενοδοξία)

We have seen that the position of vainglory, the first of the sins of pride, is not quite clear within the Evagrian tradition.[252] Logically it belongs more to the rational faculty than to the other elements of the soul, but as the third member of the Evagrian triad of basic vices it is at the same time closely attached to the body, and thus to concupiscence. This vice also therefore acquires a middle position in a 'trichotomist' perspective. It thus happens that Evagrius himself relates it closely both to gluttony and fornication,[253] and that he shows its possible connection with any of the three elements, concupiscence, anger or mind.[254]

Isolated, or regarded in immediate combination with pride, however vainglory can also here be seen *primarily in connection with the rational element.* For what is stressed in Evagrius and within the Evagrian tradition is its negative relation to knowledge (γνῶσις). Vainglory rules out true knowledge.[255] Evagrius also states explicitly that when the anger and concupiscence of the monk are not stirred during the night, the demons form dreams of vainglory.[256] Nilus too underlines that vainglory primarily concerns the mind, while *acedia* concerns the soul,[257] and in the *Tractatus ad eumdem Eulogium* we read that vainglory is the opposite of

---

[251] *Ibid.* 1. 67; p. 74.

[252] Cf. p. 254 above. —On the place and interpretation of κενοδοξία in general in ancient Christian writers, see further *art.* κενοδοξία, LAMPE, *A Patristic Greek Lexicon* 3, p. 741 f.

[253] See *De mal. cogitat.* 1; PG 79, 1201 A.

[254] See *Antirrhet.* 7. 33; FRANKENBERG, p. 534 f.

[255] See Evagrius, *Antirrhet.* 7. 24; FRANKENBERG, p. 534 f.; cf. 7. 42; p. 536 f.

[256] See *De mal. cogitat.* 28, in MUYLDERMANS, *À travers la tradition,* p. 51.

[257] *De octo spir. mal.* 16; PG 79, 1161 B.

truth.[258] In Cassian, finally, both *cenodoxia* and *superbia* are vices of the rational element.[259]

Concerning Maximus' understanding of vainglory, we have already seen that he establishes an interdependence between this vice and avarice.[260] This fact should, of course, be estimated in the light of his emphasis on the Evagrian triad of basic vices and their affinity to the body. It is, however, at the same time quite obvious in Maximus that its primary relationship is with the rational element in man. In accordance with the Evagrian tradition Maximus strongly underlines that vainglory —which is very difficult to overcome[261]—is a negation of true knowledge ($\gamma\nu\hat{\omega}\sigma\iota\varsigma$),[262] and that consequently, true knowledge excludes vainglory.[263] Since it is contrary to knowledge it blinds the rational element and destroys already established virtues.[264]

For this reason Maximus agrees with the Evagrian tradition that vainglory comes close to pride and appears, in the monk, when he has overcome his lower passions.[265] A monk's vainglory boasts about his virtues,[266] but a Christian ought to avoid all the vanities of the opposite evils of glory and shame,[267] for he awaits a higher kind of glory, which puts an end to all shame.[268]

Pride ($\dot{\upsilon}\pi\epsilon\rho\eta\phi\alpha\nu\acute{\iota}\alpha$)

The problems of the sin of pride cover a vast section of ancient Christian thinking, both in relation to religion in the strict sense and in relation to ethics. This is true also of Evagrius and the Evagrian tradition. This vast complex cannot, however, be treated within the context of this study. Here it may suffice to underline that, seen in a 'trichotomist' perspective the vice of pride belongs naturally to the field of the mind and of the rational faculty. The ambiguity of vainglory is more or less absent in the case of pride. Pride is the last and the most spiritual of the vices of the

---

[258] 4; PG 79, 1144 C.

[259] *Coll.* 24. 15; CSEL 13, p. 691.

[260] See Char 3. 83; CSC, p. 184.

[261] See *ibid.* 4. 43; p. 212.

[262] Cf. VON BALTHASAR, KL², p. 573 f. with references. However, von Balthasar's interpretation of Char 3. 84 seems to overstate the position of vainglory.

[263] See Char 1. 46; CSC p. 64.

[264] QuDub 91; CCSG 10, p. 70 f.

[265] In the man of the world vainglory has outward reasons. HAUSHERR, *Philautie*, p. 75, has correctly noticed that in this case vainglory tends to include the aspect of pride, which is further distinguished in regard to the monk.

[266] See e.g. Char 3. 84; CSC, p. 184.

[267] Ep 2; PG 91, 396 A.

[268] See Ep 35; PG 91, 629 B.

Evagrian hierarchy. Thus in a fragment from Evagrius pride is called an "immaterial" vice.[269]

As we have underlined above, pride is, in Evagrius' opinion, antithetically related to sensuality, and it appears in the monk, when other vices are overcome.[270] We should also notice that Nilus calls it a "swelling of the soul" (οἴδημα ψυχῆς),[271] and that Cassian underlines that both vainglory and pride may appear without the co-operation of the body.[272] It is further of particular importance that Cassian distinguishes very sharply between the six first vices of the hierarchy and the last two. The relationship between the vices of the first group is characterized by the fact that an earlier vice always gives rise to a later, when it is intensified. Between the first and the second group such a relationship does not exist. The latter type of vice is born when the vices of the first type are overcome. But within the second group, the same rule is again applicable, so that the vice of vainglory, in intensified form, gives rise to that of pride.[273] According to the *Tractatus ad eumdem Eulogium* also, pride seems to come from vainglory, though it shares this place with envy and all three are very closely knit together.[274]

Maximus' concept of pride is again clearly inspired by the Evagrian tradition.[275] It is the last of the vices, to which a life in self-love will in the end inevitably lead.[276] Maximus also stresses the fact that vainglory and pride belong together,[277] and that the former leads to the latter.[278] We learn further that pride—which Maximus, like ·Nilus, calls· a "swelling"[279]—arises, when the rest of the passions (of the monk) are rendered ineffective.[280] Once man has fallen for the temptation of pride, he is, however, again open also to the other temptations.

Further, in Maximus' opinion, pride has a double character. It establishes a wrong relationship both to God and to the neighbour. The monk boasting of his own virtues either deprives God of His glory or

---

[269] See *Par. Graec.* 913 (no. 44) and 3098 (no. 6); MUYLDERMANS, Mus 44 (1931), pp. 378 and 381, where the difference between pride and vainglory is so great that the latter is described as πολύυλος.

[270] See p. 241, nn. 62 and 63 above.

[271] *De octo spir. mal.* 17; PG 79, 1161 C.

[272] *Coll.* 5. 3; PICHÉRY, p. 190.

[273] *Coll.* 5. 10; PICHÉRY, p. 197 f.

[274] 4; PG 79, 1144 CD.

[275] VILLER, Aux sources de la spiritualité, RAM 11 (1930), p. 173, early noticed this dependence in relation to vainglory and pride.

[276] Char 3. 57; CSC, p. 170.

[277] *Ibid.* 3. 84; p. 184.

[278] *Ibid.* 3. 56; p. 170; 3. 59 and 61; p. 172.

[279] See Ep 2; PG 91, 396 A.

[280] Char 2. 40; CSC, p. 112.

scorns his brother because of his lack of the same degree of virtue.[281] In this context the relationship to God is, however, the most important factor. According to Maximus pride consists, first of all, of man's refusal to give the honour to God and to acknowledge the weakness of human nature.[282] It is a denial of the divine Cause both of virtues and nature.[283] But in the second place it also establishes a wrong relationship to one's neighbour.[284] Its remedy is, consequently, a true humility which excludes false boldness in relation to God and others,[285] and the ascription of one's right actions to God and not to oneself.[286] Pride is finally overcome by knowledge, a knowledge of one's own weakness and God's strength. It is thus primarily attached to *the rational element* of the soul, and for the same reason it threatens man even at the stage of 'contemplative' knowledge.[287]

We have thus seen that Maximus' treatment of the vices, here exemplified by those which belong to the Evagrian hierarchy, allows for an interpretation which regards them as types of misuse of the three faculties of the soul. In some cases this fact is clearly stated, in other cases not. It seems, however, as if Maximus developed this 'trichotomist' understanding of the Evagrian speculation on vices and passions, which he follows very closely, further than Evagrius did. But we have also noticed that this aspect of differentiation, applied to the vices, is balanced by the opposite aspect of the unity of the human composite. In relation to vices like avarice, *acedia* and vainglory Maximus uses the opportunity to stress their middle position and the inner relationship between all kinds of misuse of the powers and faculties of the human soul.

Finally, we have also been in the position to notice, in some cases, a corresponding stress on a good use of the same faculties which is related to those virtues which are regarded as a remedy for each passion. It is hardly possible to deny that Maximus, with all his attachment to the Evagrian tradition, has here made a personal contribution which is in harmony with his anthropology in general. This fact will be particularly apparent, when we now go on to demonstrate how his ability to keep the aspects of differentiation and unity together in this particular field is directly linked with his understanding of the double commandment of

---

[281] See *ibid.* 2. 38; p. 110.
[282] See *ibid.* 2. 38–39; p. 110 ff. and 3. 84; p. 184.
[283] Thal 64; CCSG 22, p. 221.
[284] See *ibid.* 54; CCSG 7, p. 449.
[285] See Char 3. 87; CSC, p. 186.
[286] *Ibid.* 3. 62; p. 172.
[287] See QuDub 35; CCSG 10, p. 151 f.

love, and the double character of self-love as related to the disastrous effect of the passions and vices in the human soul.

5. The double commandment of love and the disintegrating effect of the passions

We have seen that it is Maximus' conviction that the passions and vices may be differentiated according to the three faculties of the soul, and that the different vices thus imply a misuse of one or other of these faculties. We have also seen that some of the vices are contrary to others, and some exclude others, and that nevertheless they belong together, condition one another and are all expressions of a fundamental vice of self-love.

Against this background it seems obvious that a vicious life is, in Maximus' opinion, characterized by a process of disintegration. The different types of vicious misuse of man's faculties condition one another and are mutually dependent, but only to the destruction of the positive aspect of the unity of the human composite. No vice satisfies man, and for this reason it leads to other vices, and all vices, though particularly those of the concupiscible and rational faculties, separate man from God, who is the integrating goal of human life. But vices also separate man from his neighbour. The vices of the irascible faculty, with their descendents such as hate, slander, envy and resentfulness, which destroy human fellowship, are particularly relevant here.

This dissolution of the unity of man and of mankind is, however, contrary to the purpose which God has placed before man, and consequently contrary to the double commandment of love which expresses this purpose. The 'trichotomist' understanding of the passions and vices thus itself leads to an emphasis on self-love, the mother of all vices, seen as a refusal to accept this double commandment and the consequent relationships which constitute the true unity of man. This last conclusion is of primary importance to Maximus—a point where he has made a personal contribution to the wider Christian understanding of the psychology of the vices—and we shall therefore devote some space to a demonstration of his view of the disastrous effect of the vices and passions in relation to this basic denial of the double commandment of love, and try to relate it to his 'trichotomist' understanding.

Human passions and vices as the cause of a double separation

Our first view-point here is the disintegrating effect of the passions and vices, which Maximus emphasizes. We have underlined on several occasions that for Maximus the nature of sin and of the fall of man is expressed in the fact that man's natural capacity for spiritual pleasure is perverted into a search for sensual pleasure, as this is offered by the outward world of the senses in its manifold diversity.[288] In his self-love man has chosen to find his pleasure in the world and not in God. But this is contrary to his nature, and thus he has fallen a prey to a dialectic of pleasure and pain, which characterizes the life of fallen man in general.[289]

By following this pattern of sinful life, the individual sinner further establishes a sinful γνώμη, which gives a certain predisposition to his activities of will and aspiration.[290] And thus the following consequence is effected: involved in the dialectic of pleasure and pain, self-love gives rise to a whole host of passions, which may be differentiated accordingly, and thereby divide *the one human nature into thousands of parts.*[291] We must therefore conclude that in Maximus' opinion, there exists a certain relationship between a sinful attachment to the world of the senses in its diversity and the diversity of the vices and passions introduced into human life through sin. Furthermore the many and various passions and vices have serious effects on the unity of human nature. Not that they can destroy it entirely, since the principle of human nature (its λόγος φύσεως) is God's own pre-existent intention and purpose for man, but in so far as they destroy the outward manifestations of this unity.

Let us now see how Maximus describes this effect. First of all, he shows that it is linked with a false attention to the manifold character of the world around us, particularly as it is manifested in the individualities of other human beings.[292] Secondly, he underlines that it is the different opinions and imaginations, as well as the different methods of establishing sinful satisfaction, inspired by the Devil and resulting from this false attention, which divide the one human nature into fragments.[293] Thirdly, we notice that it is in relation to the individual γνώμη that this result becomes apparent.[294] Finally, Maximus emphasizes that the root of this split and division of human nature is to be found in self-love, which is also the root of all the passions.[295]

Here already, however, we can notice that the aspects of the individu-

---

[288] See e.g. Thal 61; CCSG 22, p. 85.
[289] See *loc. cit.* and e.g. Thal, *Prol.;* CCSG 7, p. 31 ff.
[290] See on γνώμη in ch. IV, B, pp. 213–218 above.
[291] See Thal, *Prol.;* CCSG 7, p. 33.
[292] See e.g. Ep 2; PG 91, 400 C and 401 A.
[293] See *ibid.;* 396 D–397 A.
[294] See e.g. OrDom; CCSG 23, p. 37 and p. 65 f.; cf. also Ep 2; PG 91, 396 D, 400 C–D and 401 A.
[295] See Thal, *Prol.;* CCSG 7, p. 31 ff.; Ep 2; PG 91, 396 D, 397 D and Ep 3; 408 D.

al human being and of the human race are mixed. An inner revolt of the passions within the individual coincides with the outward division which threatens mankind. It is rather characteristic of Maximus that, at least in one instance, he even establishes this identification explicitly, since, having enumerated a number of vices which obviously disintegrate humanity as well as the individual, he concludes by referring to *"the one man"* who is thus divided.[296] It is, therefore, not surprising that it is to the *inter-human* aspect of the unity of human nature that Maximus often refers, when he speaks of the divisive and disintegrating effect of the vices and passions. This fact must, however, not make us forget that even those vices which primarily concern the relationship between the individual and his neighbour have their root in a sin of sensible attachment, and a preference of worldly pleasures to God. The whole belongs together in Maximus' opinion. A good example of this coherence is a statement in Thal 65, where Maximus emphasizes that among the disastrous effects of gluttony, i.e. of the most bodily of all vices, is the fact that through self-love ($\phi\iota\lambda\alpha\upsilon\tau\iota\alpha$) it divides that which is otherwise kept together by love for men ($\phi\iota\lambda\alpha\nu\theta\rho\omega\pi\iota\alpha$).[297]

On this basis Maximus strongly emphasizes the disintegrating function of sins, passions and vices upon human nature as a whole. Thus he points out that there is a constant revolt and division in connection with fallen $\gamma\nu\omega\mu\eta$,[298] so that human nature is divided into many parts,[299] contrary to its own principle ($\lambda\delta\gamma\sigma\varsigma$) according to which it remains undivided.[300] A reconciliation must take place which prevents $\gamma\nu\omega\mu\eta$ from dividing human nature into pieces,[301] so that human willing is no more in revolt against God, since it is then united with the principle of its own human nature.[302]

The vices thus cause divisions, not only in the individual in relation to the principle and purpose of human nature, but also between the individual and his fellow human beings, simply because all men by God's providence are called to be united around this common human principle and purpose.[303] And consequently, the vices both separate brothers from one another,[304] and also separate the individual from *love,* since the

---

[296] Ep 2; PG 91, 397 D.
[297] CCSG 22, p. 297.
[298] Ep 2; PG 91, 400 C.
[299] *Ibid.;* 400 D.
[300] *Ibid.;* 401 A.
[301] OrDom; CCSG 23, p. 37 and p. 65.
[302] *Ibid.;* p. 65 f.
[303] See Char 4. 17; CSC, p. 200.
[304] *Ibid.* 4. 19; p. 200.

function of love coincides with the divine purpose set for man. Separation from love means, in fact, in this context, separation both from the divine end of man and from the unity of mankind. Particularly in *Cent. de char.* and Ep 2 Maximus underlines again and again this sinful separation from love, as well as the unifying function and purpose of love itself.[305]

According to Maximus, passions and vices thus cause *a double separation:* from God and the divine purpose for man, the principle of human nature, on the one hand, and from the neighbour and the whole of humanity on the other, and this separation is, as we have seen, sometimes also called a separation from love. This last fact, however, points inevitably in the direction of the *double* commandment of love. As the two aspects of human division and separation belong together, so also do the two elements of the commandment of love. We are, therefore, bound to ask whether Maximus himself carries through his own line of thinking in this direction and sees the sins, passions and vices as a transgression of *one or other* of the two elements of this commandment. And further, does his understanding of *self-love*, which is both the root of all passions and the negation of true love, consequently itself involve two different aspects, corresponding to the two elements of the commandment of love?

The double commandment of love as a principle of distinction between human passions and vices

In both these matters Maximus' own texts impel us to give an affirmative answer. He frequently refers, in connection with his treatment of virtues and vices, to the double commandment of love and strongly emphasizes that its two elements are deeply interrelated.[306] The double attitude of love is said to characterize the peace of the angels and all the saints from the beginning,[307] and love for God and for one's neighbour are both implied in the virtuous perfection of the individual mind.[308] Further the two aspects belong together, since love for one's neighbour makes firm one's love for God.[309] And more important, we can also notice that there are certain vices which primarily are transgressions of the commandment of love for one's neighbour, and others which primarily exclude love for God. Vices like hate, grief, wrath and resentfulness are easily

---

[305] See e.g. *ibid.* 4. 16–20; p. 200 ff.; Ep 2; PG 91, 401 B–D and Char 1. 71; p. 76.

[306] See e.g. in relation to love as the summit of all virtues, and indirectly as the destroyer of all vices, Ep 2; PG 91, 401 CD.

[307] Char 4. 36; CSC, p. 208.

[308] See *ibid.* 4. 40; p. 210.

[309] Asc 7; PG 90, 917 A.

referred to the first category,[310] and a vice like pride to the latter.[311] But what about the others? How far is this differentiation according to the two aspects of the commandment of love applicable to the list of vices in general? Maximus himself answers this question in Char 4. 75, where he refers the double character of love to the dichotomy of the passible part of the soul, saying that *love for God is opposed to concupiscence and love for one's neighbour to anger.*[312]

We see thus that the 'trichotomist' interpretation of the vices, with which this reference to concupiscence and anger is certainly connected, is used by Maximus not only to distinguish between different types of vices in general, but also for a distinction which is linked with the double commandment of love. Vices of the concupiscible part express a primary relationship to the world of the senses in search for their pleasures, which is a denial of man's call to love God above everything and to find his true pleasure and end in Him; and vices of the irascible part manifest a corresponding disobedience to the call to love one's neighbour as oneself. It goes without saying that the vices of the rational part can be expected to be regarded as a denial of both, though primarily of the love for God, since this represents the higher and wider aspect of true human life.

It should also be added that this idea is not confined to one particular passage. In the light of the passage quoted, Char 4. 75, other statements within the same context appear to make implicit references to the same idea. Thus we learn that concupiscence may be transformed into burning love for God and anger into divine charity,[313] or that those who abstain from pleasures, i.e. from that which is connected with the vices of the concupiscible element, should do so because of love for God.[314] And likewise Maximus stresses that the purpose of Christ's commandments is to set the mind free from incontinence and hate, and bring it to love for God and for its neighbour—where again we can see an implicit reference to the connection between the dichotomy of the passible part of the soul and the double commandment of love, since the term incontinence (ἀκρασία) is a good summary of the vices of the concupiscible, and the term hate of the vices of the irascible element.[315] It is thus difficult to avoid the feeling that Maximus' emphasis on the idea of the trichotomy

---

[310] See Char 1. 61; CSC, p. 72.

[311] See e.g. *ibid.* 3. 84 and 87; p. 184 ff. Secondarily vainglory and pride also disturb the right relationship to one's fellow human beings; cf. p. 276 f. above.

[312] CSC, p. 226. Maximus adds an interpretation of the two pence of Luke 10: 35 as referring to these two kinds of love as given for the restoration of sinful man.

[313] *Ibid.* 2. 48; p. 116.

[314] *Ibid.* 3. 65; p. 174.

[315] See *ibid.* 4. 56; p. 218.

of the soul, and particularly of the dichotomy of its passible part, in connection with his treatment of passions and vices, at least in a piece of writing such as his *Centuries on Charity,* is motivated to a greater or lesser degree by its capacity to express, not only the differentiations within the unity of the human soul, of which vices imply a misuse, but above all the fact that passions and vices mean a disobedience to the *two* aspects of the commandment of love.

The double perspective of self-love

This fact leads us, however, to our second conclusion. We asked earlier, whether Maximus also leaves room for an understanding of self-love which corresponds to this perspective of the vices. To this question too Maximus gives an answer. In Char 4. 37 we read that the monk should be no *self-pleaser,* in order not to hate his brother. Nor should he be a *self-lover,* for he ought to love God.[316] It is not difficult to see that this little chapter contains more than a reference to the double commandment of love. It also contains a statement about the two aspects of self-love. Self-love ($\phi\iota\lambda\alpha\upsilon\tau\iota\alpha$) in a first, and more basic sense, is a love for the body, a love of sensual lust, which implies a refusal of the true delight which is offered to man in God, and from this come all the vices. Self-love in a more restricted sense, on the horizontal level, is here called $\alpha\dot{\upsilon}\tau\alpha\rho\acute{\epsilon}\sigma\kappa\epsilon\iota\alpha$, and implies a sinful isolation from one's neighbour which is easily connected with the vices of the irascible element. It should also be remembered that in the *Liber asceticus* Maximus describes how Christ, who is free from all self-love, is first of all obedient to the commandment of love for God—by overcoming the temptations of the concupiscible element in the desert—, and secondly how—in the course of his passion—he shows his obedience also to the commandment of love for one's neighbour, in defeating the temptations related to the irascible faculty.[317]

The 'trichotomist' understanding of the vices is thus in Maximus closely linked with his stress on the double commandment of love, and this fact corresponds intimately with his emphasis on self-love as the root of all vices, and love as the summit of all virtues. Self-love leads to vices which disintegrate the human composite by disturbing its relationship to God and its fellow men. In this case differentiation becomes a negative factor, since it helps this process of disintegration. But love, on the other hand,

---

[316] CSC, p. 208.
[317] See Asc 10–15; PG 90, 920 A–924 C. Cf. p. 265 above.

implies virtues which manifest a right use of the differentiated faculties of man, and by doing so it unites him both with God and his neighbour. In this case differentiation underlines the aspect of unity. Man is not only an isolated individual with an isolated relationship to God. He is a member of the human species, and he shares with all human beings the same integrating principle of nature.

But finally, we have also seen that the disintegrating work of the passions and vices, rooted in self-love, starts with an attachment to the world in its manifoldness, an exterior world to which man is related by his own composite nature. We have earlier underlined that man as microcosm reflects this created world, the basic dichotomy of which he carries within himself, and the manifold character of which has its counterpart in his own differentiation.[318] Now we can see that this microcosmic character of man on the one hand leads to vicious destruction, when self-love rules in him, for self-love invites all the passions to perform their disintegrating function in accordance with the differentiated nature of man himself; but on the other that man's truly microcosmic character is fully established, when love in both its aspects rules in man, for love invites all the virtues to perform their task of transformation of the different human faculties, through their victory over the vices and their good use of these faculties.

In our next section we shall study, how this true establishment takes place in love, and how the virtues thus allow for an incarnation of the Logos in man as a result of this good use of the different faculties. There the aspect of differentiation is also, in a typically Maximian way, balanced by the aspect of unity, which the attachment to the λόγος of human nature *and* the relationship between this λόγος and the Logos-Christ together safeguard.

B.   Re-integration through the Virtues

We have seen how the vices, in Maximus' opinion, form a function of disintegration in relation both to the individual human being and to humanity as a whole. We have also tried to establish a certain connection between this aspect of disintegration and Maximus' stress on the idea of the trichotomy of the soul as applicable to the vices. In this context a 'trichotomist' principle of differentiation within the Evagrian hierarchy of vices—to which Maximus is attached—seemed to us to be of

---

[318] Cf. ch. III: A, 5; pp. 137–142 above.

particular interest, since the vices can be seen as forms of misuse of the different faculties of man.

When we now turn our attention to the field of virtues against the background of what has been said in the first section of this chapter, we must ask how far there is a correspondence between Maximus' understanding of the virtues and his understanding of the vices. Are the hierarchies of virtues in any sense counterparts to that of the vices? Do the individual virtues appear as counterparts to corresponding vices? And are these virtues also seen in a 'trichotomist' perspective, so that such virtues are to be understood as a good use of one of the three faculties of the soul? And we may finally continue with the following question: is there also a proper correspondence between self-love as the root of all the vices and true love as the summit of all the virtues? For only when all these questions are answered in the affirmative, will we be able to conclude that the aspects of differentiation and unity are fully balanced in Maximus' understanding of vices and virtues, and only in that case will we also be able to say that the idea of man as a mediating microcosm—a unified and unifying world in little—is worked out into the very details of his Christian anthropology.

1. Hierarchies of virtues compared with the hierarchies of vices

In his teaching on virtues Maximus depends on Evagrius and the Evagrian tradition to an even greater extent than in his teaching on vices. This is not least the case when he tries to establish a hierarchy of virtues. A direct comparison between Evagrius' letter to Anatolius, i.e. the prologue to his *Praktikos,* and the first chapters of Maximus' first century on charity is enough to prove his dependence. The only difference worth noticing is recognizable in relation to the concept of love, as we shall see later.

This fact however does not imply that there is in either of the writers a strict correspondence between their hierarchies of vices and their hierarchies of virtues. The reason is that the two types of hierarchy seem, at first sight, to be difficult to compare. First of all, there exists no fixed system of virtues comparable with Evagrius' hierarchy of eight vices. And secondly, the two types of hierarchy are constructed in very different ways. The hierarchy of virtues covers a larger field. It usually goes from the starting-point of human restoration, which is to be found in faith, to the end of Christian perfection in final blessedness. The space which, in the case of vices, is covered by the hierarchy of eight, thus corresponds to quite a small section of the hierarchies of virtues, and for this reason individual virtues corresponding to the vices of the Evagrian hierarchy are usually not enumerated in the hierarchies of virtues.

Maximus and the Evagrian hierarchy of virtues

This fact is best illustrated by Evagrius' hierarchy of virtues in the *Praktikos,* compared with that of Maximus in Char 1.[319] Evagrius' hierarchy consists of the following 'virtues': faith, fear of God, self-mastery, patience and hope, detachment, love, 'natural' knowledge, 'theology' and blessedness. Maximus' hierarchy contains the following elements: faith, fear of God, self-mastery, patience and long-suffering, hope in God, detachment and love. As we see, there are only few differences. One is that Evagrius joins patience and hope into a pair, while Maximus introduces long-suffering and combines it with patience, and establishes hope as a separate virtue. (In both cases, each virtue is supposed to lead on to the next.) Another, and more important difference is, as we have already indicated, that Evagrius attributes a relatively restricted position to love (ἀγάπη) as the end of *vita practica,* leading on to the higher virtue of γνῶσις, which unites with God, while Maximus ends his enumeration with love, though he adds in the next chapter a special passage on knowledge.[320]

This difference seems to indicate that Maximus does not wish to establish an order of superiority as between love and knowledge, since love in a wider sense not only involves a preference for the knowledge of God to anything else,[321] but also carries man in all his intellectual activity to full communion with God.[322] Thus in his hierarchy he accepts the Evagrian understanding of love in a more restricted sense, as the end of the *vita practica,* but believing as he also does in a wider concept of love, he prefers to leave the later virtues of Evagrius' hierarchy[323] out of his own.

It is also of interest in this context to notice that Evagrius' hierarchy probably goes back to a hierarchy of virtues established by Clement of Alexandria, consisting of faith, fear of God, hope, change of mind

---

[319] See *Pract., Prol.;* PG 40, 1221 BC and Char 1. 2–3; CSC, p. 50.

[320] Char 1. 4; CSC, p. 50.

[321] *Ibid.* 1. 1; p. 50. This definition of love is itself built on Evagrius, *Cent. gnost.* 1. 86; PO 28, p. 57.

[322] Cf. B, 4; p. 320 ff. below.

[323] See further about the problem of love as a whole and its relationship to knowledge, section 4 below; cf. also SHERWOOD, in ACW, pp. 92 and 235 f., n. 356.—On the general understanding of the life of virtues in Maximus, see VÖLKER, *op.cit.,* pp. 201–222.

($\mu\epsilon\tau\acute{\alpha}\nu o\iota\alpha$), self-mastery, patience, love and knowledge.[324] In Clement's version it seems as if love and knowledge were placed on a more equal level, and it is, therefore, not to be excluded that Maximus in his hierarchy, in fact, falls back upon Clement.[325]

But however important the differences between Maximus and Evagrius may be at this particular point, the similarity between the hierarchies remains the dominant fact. And in relation to the structure of the hierarchies, this similarity implies that, though Maximus, leaving the later Evagrian virtues out of the picture, concentrates his own hierarchy more on the field of the *vita practica,* both hierarchies contain only a very small section which corresponds exactly to that which is covered by the Evagrian system of eight vices. The so-called theological virtues in both writers are integrated into the hierarchy, and a virtue like fear of God in both cases occupies an important place, but none of all these virtues can be said to correspond exactly to any of the eight vices of the Evagrian system. The hierarchies are thus quite differently constructed.

The character of the correspondence between the hierarchies of vices and virtues

Must we then conclude that no correspondence exists, or better, that there is no possibility, in the way in which the hierarchies are constructed, of studying a correspondence which might be presupposed by the writers themselves? If we study those virtues, which are comparable to the vices of the hierarchy, we shall, in fact, find that this question may nevertheless receive a different answer from the one we might expect.

In Evagrius' system the virtues which may be compared are self-mastery, patience and detachment, and to some extent love; in Maximus' system they are self-mastery, patience and long-suffering, detachment, and also to some extent love. Now it is clear that a virtue like self-mastery is particularly opposed to those vices, which are most intimately connected with the body, i.e. at least gluttony and fornication. Likewise, patience, with or without long-suffering, must be primarily related to vices like wrath and grief, while detachment is a kind of positive counterpart to the vice of *acedia.* Love, finally, summarizes a virtuous obedience to the double commandment of love, which, at least in the case of Maximus, we have seen to be opposed to the vices of the different elements of the soul.

And seen in this perspective we are, thus, bound to conclude that

---

[324] See *Strom.* 2. 6; GCS Clem. 2, p. 129, 16 ff. Cf. Pegon, in SCH 9, p. 69 f., n. 3.

[325] On Maximus' understanding of the relationship between charity and knowledge, see further p. 320 ff. below.

there is at least a certain correspondence between the hierarchies of vices
and virtues, and that this correspondence is no less apparent in Maximus
than in Evagrius. The important difference is, however, that the hierarchies of virtues serve a different purpose from that of the hierarchy of
vices, and for this reason the correspondence between them is of a
general and summarizing character; it is not of a formal nature but rather
is related to their content. But even the degree of explicit correspondence
which exists allows for an understanding of certain of the virtues as
contrary to their corresponding vices, and as a *good* use of those faculties,
with which the vices are connected.

   In Maximus' case this restricted conclusion may also be illustrated by
some of the other classifications of virtues which he gives us. This is
particularly the case with a hierarchy of virtues, which Maximus
constructs in Ep 2 to demonstrate the variety of goods which love as the
summit of all virtues contains.[326] This list is much longer than that of
Char 1, and perhaps also more openly comparable with the hierarchy of
vices. It consists of the following virtues: faith, hope, humility, meekness, gentleness, mercy, self-mastery, patience, long-suffering, goodness,
peace and joy. If we leave out the theological virtues, we can easily make
the same sort of comparison here as in the case of the first hierarchy,
though the differentiation of this hierarchy allows for a more detailed
procedure.[327] Such a comparison is also facilitated by Maximus' own
indications about the vices or passions which the virtues enumerated are
supposed to conquer.

   Humility ($\tau\alpha\pi\epsilon\acute{\iota}\nu\omega\sigma\iota\varsigma$) and meekness ($\pi\rho\alpha\acute{o}\tau\eta\varsigma$) are thus, of course,
the corresponding virtues to the sins of pride, i.e. to the last two vices of
the Evagrian hierarchy. In fact, Maximus leaves us in no doubt about it,
for he says that humility, which is called the foundation of all virtue,[328]
helps men to know themselves and strikes down the "empty swelling of
pride", and that meekness leads them to escape from the opposite evils of
honour and shame ($\delta\acute{o}\xi\alpha$ and $\grave{\alpha}\delta o\xi\acute{\iota}\alpha$). In the last case we have no
difficulty in recognizing the vice of vainglory. About gentleness
($\pi\rho\alpha\ddot{\upsilon}\pi\acute{\alpha}\theta\epsilon\iota\alpha$), which obviously contains elements of both meekness
($\pi\rho\alpha\acute{o}\tau\eta\varsigma$) and detachment ($\grave{\alpha}\pi\acute{\alpha}\theta\epsilon\iota\alpha$), Maximus says that it "enables
us . . . to remain unchangeable in our attitude towards evil-doers, and
. . . to avoid becoming of a hostile disposition towards them"—a

---

[326] PG 91, 393 D–396 A.

[327] Cf. here also Gal. 5: 22–23.

[328] Notice here the similarity between this statement and the important position of
pride in the Evagrian tradition; but also remark that this hierarchy of virtues is constructed
in an order which is almost opposite to that of the hierarchy of vices.

statement which undoubtedly refers this virtue to the irascible element, and shows that it is contrary to wrath, and perhaps also to grief. Mercy (ἔλεος) is defined in such a way that it corresponds to grief, but perhaps also to avarice. The rest of the vices of this hierarchy are not defined or described, but Maximus at least gives us the important information about them—at the same time as making a reference to the dichotomy of the passible part of the soul—that they easily calm both anger and concupiscence. If we look at them, we might say that self-mastery refers to concupiscence, i.e. to gluttony and fornication, and the rest to different aspects of the vices of the irascible element, particularly to grief and *acedia*.[329] We may thus conclude that most of the elements of the Evagrian hierarchy of vices have their counterparts in this hierarchy of virtues.

Other enumerations of virtues and the problem of their correspondence to the vices

The rest of Maximus' enumerations are of less interest in our context. It should, however, be noticed that we find in all of them virtues which may be clearly referred to one or the other of the faculties of the soul, and also virtues which correspond to individual vices of the Evagrian hierarchy. The lists, however, are not constructed in any particular correspondence to the Evagrian hierarchy of vices, and one may always find reflections of other systems, e.g. the Platonic tetrad of prudence, courage, temperance and justice,[330] though this last principle of differentiation is, of course, in itself also a reminder of the 'trichotomist' perspective.

Thus in QuDub 1, 1 Maximus, dealing with virtues of the body and virtues of the soul, mentions among those of the soul e.g. humility, meekness, long-suffering, lack of resentfulness, lack of wrath, lack of envy, lack of vainglory, temperance and lack of avarice, which can all easily be provided with counterparts among the vices of the Evagrian hierarchy, or those closely connected with it.[331] In Ep 5, where vices and virtues are brought together, on the one hand we find all the elements of the *tetrad of capital virtues*, which we mentioned above, and on the other hand such virtues as humility, meekness, long-suffering, hospitality,

---

[329] That it is vices and virtues of the irascible element which predominate in this latter part of the list is probably due to the fact that Ep 2 deals particularly with aspects of neighbourly love.

[330] In Char 2. 79, CSC, p. 132 this tetrad is presented alone, together with its counterparts among the vices.

[331] CCSG 10, p. 137.

brotherly love, peace and charity.[332] And in Ep 45 Maximus mentions again e.g. mercy, long-suffering, humility, temperance, lack of resentfulness, hospitality, charity etc.[333] In the *Loci communes* finally, which reflect Maximus' understanding and where a great number of writers are quoted, particularly the virtues of the Platonic tetrad are exemplified.[334]

In all the last mentioned cases the principle of arrangement is different from that which is manifested in the Evagrian hierarchies of vices and virtues, and the 'trichotomist' view is only slightly reflected. But this does not exclude an interpretation of the virtues as counterparts to their vices. The lists of virtues, sometimes in the form of hierarchies, which Maximus in most cases constructs for a particular purpose in a specific context—a reason why they differ so much from one another— do not correspond in a strict sense to the hierarchy of vices. In different ways nevertheless they do correspond to other lists and enumerations of vices. Here we must not forget that Maximus often constructs lists of vices in the same way as he constructs his lists of virtues, i.e. for specific purposes, and these virtues are often presented as counterparts to vices. This tendency is most clearly demonstrated by the fact that many individual virtues are just defined as negations of vices. Finally, these lists always contain elements which have a reference to capital vices, either of the tetrad or of the Evagrian hierarchy, which often allow, in their turn, for a 'trichotomist' differentiation.

2. Correspondences between virtues and vices as seen in a 'trichotomist' perspective

Before we go on to the individual virtues and study their degree of correspondence to particular vices, we should devote some attention to some enumerations of virtues in Maximus, which are simply long lists of virtues, but which through their reference to the idea of the trichotomy of the soul, or of the dichotomy of its passible part, show to what extent Maximus understands virtues to be forms of good use of the same faculties of which vices are a misuse.

'Trichotomist' differentiations of virtues in Evagrius

Here again the Evagrian background must be emphasized. Evagrius himself in the *Praktikos* makes explicit 'trichotomist' differentiations of

[332] PG 91, 421 BC.
[333] PG 91, 649 A.
[334] Thus prudence in PG 91, 732 A–736 A; temperance 736 B–744 C; courage 744 D–749 B and justice 749 B–753 D.

virtues, though in one case only of outward and bodily practices. Thus in one place readings, vigils and prayers are referred to the mind, fasting, work and solitude to concupiscence and psalmody, long-suffering and mercy to anger.[335]

In another text Evagrius establishes a list of nine spiritual virtues, related to the three parts of the soul, but here the Platonic tetrad serves as the basis. Thus we learn that prudence, insight and wisdom belong to the rational part, temperance, charity and self-mastery to the concupiscible part, courage and patience to the irascible part, and finally justice to the whole.[336] It is however also of interest to notice, that this list contains the virtue of self-mastery and at the same time the virtue of charity as both related to the concupiscible element,[337] and further that the fruits of all these virtues are said to be knowledge and joy,[338] since this shows that the tetrad of virtues is here integrated into a wider spiritual understanding without losing its 'trichotomist' perspective. Immediately after this text Evagrius finally presents a third example of the same principle of differentiation. Here he obviously distinguishes between bodily virtues, related to concupiscence, and psychic virtues related to anger, and ends with a reference to the function of prayer in relation to the mind. Thus for concupiscence fasting, vigils and sleeping on the ground are prescribed, while long-suffering, freedom from resentfulness and mercy (or alms) are prescribed for anger.[339]

But in Evagrius there are also *other reflections* of a 'trichotomist' or 'dichotomist' understanding of virtues. Thus we learn that mercy (alms) and meekness are for anger,[340] that charity is "the bit of anger",[341] and that self-mastery is a remedy against the sins of the body and charity against those of the soul.[342] In other contexts Evagrius makes clear that meekness and long-suffering,[343] or charity supported by detachment and

---

[335] *Pract.* 1. 6; PG 40, 1224 A; cf. Maximus, Char 2. 47; CSC, p. 116, where in a similar statement the perspective is restricted to the dichotomy of the passible part. See also Evagrius, *De mal. cogitat.* 3; PG 79, 1204 C.

[336] *Pract.* 1. 61; PG 40, 1236 A–C.

[337] In the case of charity, this is motivated by the fact that man is created in the image of God, which shows that charity is here seen in a vertical perspective, as a relationship to God which is contrary to that relationship to the material world, which the vices of concupiscence imply.

[338] *Pract.* 1. 62; PG 40, 1236 C.

[339] *Ibid.* 1. 63; 1236 C–1237 B.

[340] *Ibid.* 1. 11; 1224 C.

[341] *Ibid.* 1. 26; 1228 D.

[342] *Ibid.* 1. 24; 1228 C.

[343] *De mal. cogitat.* 14; PG 79, 1216 CD and *Tract. ad Eul. monach.* 10; PG 79, 1105 CD.

long-suffering,[344] are directed against the vices of the irascible faculty, while self-mastery is directed against gluttony, i.e. concupiscence,[345] or against bodily passions, which to Evagrius are the same thing.[346] We also learn that fear of God is directed against vainglory[347] and humility against pride,[348] which may be an indirect reference to the rational element.

'Trichotomist' and 'dichotomist' differentiations of virtues in Maximus

In Maximus this 'trichotomist' or 'dichotomist' differentiation reappears, particularly in *Cent. de char.* As in Evagrius, a 'trichotomist' differentiation is, first of all, used in relation to outward means and practical exercises. Thus we learn that alms are good for the irascible part, and fasting for the concupiscible, while prayer purifies the mind and prepares it for contemplation.[349] In another passage, a number of these means, together with a number of psychic virtues, are differentiated according to the dichotomy of the passible part of the soul. Among these means there is also a further distinction between those belonging to a primary and those belonging to a secondary stage of development. Thus for instance Maximus teaches in relation to the irascible element that long-suffering, lack of resentfulness and meekness belong to the earlier stage, while charity, alms, kindness and benevolence belong to the later.[350]

But secondly—and more important in our context—there are also passages where virtues typical of the three parts are presented, and indeed shown to be counterparts to typical vices of the same elements, and thus interpreted as a proper use of them. In this sense we learn that knowledge and prudence are of the rational element, charity of the irascible and temperance of the concupiscible element,[351] or that self-mastery should characterize the concupiscible element and charity fill the irascible, while the mind should be occupied with prayer and spiritual contemplation.[352] It should be noted that another version of the same kind of differentiation even deals more clearly with the rational part as a separate element not wholly to be identified with the mind.[353]

---

[344] *Tract. ad Eul. monach.* 23; PG 79, 1124 C.
[345] *De mal. cogitat.* 25; PG 79, 1229 B.
[346] *Tract. ad Eul. monach.* 23; PG 79, 1124 BC.
[347] *Ibid.* 25; 1125 A.
[348] *Ibid.* 14; 1112 A.
[349] Char 1. 79; CSC, p. 80.
[350] See *ibid.* 2. 47; p. 116.
[351] *Ibid.* 3. 3; p. 144.
[352] *Ibid.* 4. 15; p. 200; cf. 4. 44; p. 212.
[353] *Ibid.* 4. 80; p. 230.

In a third kind of passages, finally, Maximus presents only a dual distinction. It may either be in the form of a differentiation between bodily methods and virtues of the soul, which can themselves again be easily divided into those for anger and those for concupiscence,[354] or in the form of a more general reference to charity and self-mastery as the capital virtues for anger and concupiscence respectively.[355]

Thus in this type of correspondence the 'trichotomist' perspective is far more strongly emphasized, both in Evagrius and in Maximus, than it is in the hierarchies and lists of virtues. It should, however, be added that this tendency seems to be even more apparent in Maximus than in Evagrius, while at the same time the rather formal character of some of Maximus' statements suggests that this view of things is self-evident in his case. We have also seen that he states explicitly that the capital virtues of each faculty should be regarded as the proper use of that faculty, being in this respect a counterpart to their vices. The aspect of differentiation is thus positively evaluated in relation to the virtues, in the same way as it was regarded as a means of discovering the disintegrating effect in relation to passions and vices.

The correspondence between individual vices and virtues in the Evagrian tradition

The degree of correspondence between virtues and vices is, however, equally obvious when we come to a study of definitions and descriptions of the individual virtues, which shows that the aspect of differentiation, though its psychological basis is primarily to be found in the trichotomy or dichotomy, is not restricted to this basis but is also to some extent elaborated into a distinction between different aspects of the good use and misuse of each faculty.

Here again Maximus builds on Evagrius and the Evagrian tradition. If we concentrate our attention on virtues related to the vices of the Evagrian hierarchy, we find that already in Evagrius himself there are clear counterparts to all the vices except avarice, which occupies, as we have seen, a somewhat ambiguous position. In some cases these counterparts differ, but in most cases the tradition seems to be fixed from the beginning. Thus self-mastery corresponds to gluttony[356] and temperance

---

[354] See *ibid.* 2. 57; p. 120.
[355] See *ibid.* 4. 57; p. 218 and 4. 72; p. 226.
[356] *De mal. cogitat.* 25; PG 79, 1229 B; cf. *Tract. ad Eul. monach.* 23; PG 79, 1124 BC.

to fornication.[357] Of the vices of the irascible faculty wrath has its counterpart in long-suffering[358] and grief in charity[359] or, together with *acedia*, in peace and joy.[360] Patience corresponds, however, more often to *acedia*.[361] And finally, vainglory and pride have their counterpart in humility.[362]

This differentiated correspondence is, however, more fixed and systematized in the later Evagrian tradition. Thus we find in Nilus that even avarice has its explicit counterpart, though vainglory, as in Evagrius, is presented as a very difficult and varying vice, which has no fixed counterpart.[363] The general scheme is almost identical with that of Evagrius. Thus we find the same correspondence between self-mastery and gluttony,[364] temperance and fornication,[365] long-suffering and wrath,[366] patience and *acedia*,[367] and humility and pride.[368] The virtues of poverty, which corresponds to avarice,[369] and "contempt", which corresponds to grief,[370] are added.

And in the *Tractatus ad eumdem Eulogium*—which should, for this and other reasons, not be regarded as written by Evagrius himself but rather as belonging to the later Evagrian tradition—the system of correspondence between virtues and vices in relation to the Evagrian hierarchy of vices with the addition of envy in this case, is entirely fixed, so that the systems of Evagrius and Nilus are here mingled into one. The final result is thus as follows: self-mastery—gluttony, temperance—fornication, poverty—avarice, joy—grief, long-suffering—wrath, patience—*acedia*, lack of vainglory—vainglory, lack of envy—envy, humility—pride.[371] In Cassian most elements of this Evagrian tradition

[357] *Pract.* 2. 58; PG 40, 1248 C; *De mal. cogitat.* 12; PG 79, 1213 C and *Tract. ad Eul. monach.* 22; PG 79, 1124 A.

[358] *Tract. ad Eul. monach.* 5; PG 79, 1100 D.

[359] *Loc. cit.*

[360] *Tract. ad Eul. monach.* 6; 1101 B.

[361] *Ibid.* 8; 1104 C and 12; 1109 AB.

[362] ταπεινοφροσύνη or ταπείνωσις, see *Pract.* 1. 22; PG 40, 1228 B and 2. 58; 1248 C, and *Tract. ad Eul. monach.* 14; PG 79, 1112 A.

[363] On vainglory, see *De octo spir. mal.* 15; PG 79, 1160 C–1161 A; cf. Evagrius' presentation of vainglory as the most difficult of all vices in *Tract. ad Eul. monach.* 14; PG 79, 1112 A.

[364] *De octo spir. mal.* 2; 1145 C.

[365] *Ibid.* 6; 1149 D–1152 A.

[366] *Ibid.* 9; 1153 D.

[367] *Ibid.* 13; 1157 D.

[368] *Ibid.* 18, 19; 1164 A, C.

[369] *Ibid.* 7; 1152 C and 8; 1153 AB.

[370] *Ibid.* 12; 1157 BC. —Even ἀπάθεια is emphasized, see *ibid.* 11; 1157 A and 12; 1157 B.

[371] *Tract. ad eumdem Eul.* 1; PG 79, 1141 A.

have been transferred to Latin ground, as may be seen from the following correspondences: *castitas—concupiscentia* and *fornicatio, patientia—furor, salutaris tristitia* (with the addition *plena gaudio*)—*tristitia, fortitudo—acedia* and *humilitas—superbia*.[372]

The correspondence between individual vices and virtues in Maximus

When we now come to Maximus' relationship to this particular tradition, two opposite observations can be made. Maximus on the one hand shows that he is acquainted with those correspondences between individual virtues and vices, which we know from the Evagrian tradition, at least in the form in which they appear in Evagrius' own writings, since Maximus' knowledge about the later and more fixed tradition at this point is more doubtful. But on the other hand it is obvious that his own interest in this type of correspondence is smaller than the interest which he manifests in relation to correspondences which are immediately linked with the 'trichotomist' idea, such as those we have demonstrated above. We must, therefore, try to give an explanation of this fact. But first let us see how Maximus manifests this third type of Evagrian correspondence between virtues and vices.

Self-mastery (ἐγκράτεια) is in Maximus also a clear counterpart to bodily passions.[373] It is understood as a remedy for the concupiscible faculty as a whole.[374] Sometimes it shares this general function with the virtue of temperance.[375] We may thus conclude that self-mastery is related as a positive counterpart to all the vices of the concupiscible element.[376] For this reason self-mastery however is, as in Evagrius, primarily related to gluttony, the first of the vices of concupiscence, but in the second place also to fornication and avarice.[377]

Temperance (σωφροσύνη) is used in a similar way in relation to the whole of the concupiscible element and its vices. This is not seldom the case in 'trichotomist' passages.[378] But on the other hand, Maximus is fully

---

[372] *Coll.* 5. 23; PICHÉRY, p. 214. Another form of the first correspondence is *continentia corporalis* as the counterpart of both gluttony and fornication, see *ibid.* 5. 4; p. 191.

[373] See Char 1. 64; CSC, p. 72. On the whole aspect of correspondence between vices and virtues, see my later study *Man and the Cosmos*, pp. 97–101.

[374] See *ibid.* 1. 65; p. 74; 4. 15; p. 200; 4. 57; p. 218 and 4. 79–80; p. 230.

[375] *Ibid.* 4. 44; p. 212.

[376] Cf. Asc 19 and 23; PG 90, 925 D and 929 AB.

[377] See Char 1. 84; CSC, p. 82 and 4. 49 and 68; pp. 214 and 224.

[378] See *ibid.* 3. 1; p. 144 (its counterpart is here ἀκολασία, summarizing all the vices of this element). Cf. also 3. 3; p. 144; 4. 44; p. 212 and 4. 96; p. 236.

aware of the fact that the primary counterpart to temperance is fornication.[379]

In the *Tractatus ad eumdem Eulogium* we found that *poverty* (ἀκτημοσύνη) is presented as the counterpart of the vice of avarice. In *Cent. de char.* Maximus mentions poverty as a term and a fact several times, but more in describing the positive conditions of the monks (together with their virtues) than as an explicit counterpart to the vice of avarice.[380] This fact is probably an indication that Maximus depends on Evagrius himself but not on the later Evagrian tradition at this point, though it does happen, on the other hand, that he mentions the vice of avarice in connection with an emphasis on monastic poverty.[381]

In relation to grief we can make a similar observation. In Evagrius we found that peace and joy, together with charity, are regarded as the counterparts to grief, while in the later Evagrian tradition charity is excluded from this position. Maximus now sees *charity* (ἀγάπη) as the regular counterpart to grief. Since grief belongs primarily to the irascible element of the human soul, we would expect him to refer here to charity in the sense of neighbourly love alone, but as a matter of fact he manifestly refers to love for God as well as love for one's neighbour, a fact which shows—in addition to his direct dependence on Evagrius— that he understands charity as always composed of its two aspects.[382] Thus Maximus may refer to charity in general,[383] or may contrast grief with love for God,[384] or—though more often—may oppose it to brotherly charity.[385] It goes without saying that the pair charity—grief in this context usually has a wide scope, and thus charity is to be understood as a remedy for all the vices of the irascible faculty.[386]

We have seen that *long-suffering* (μακροθυμία) corresponds to the vice of wrath in the whole of the Evagrian tradition. This correspondence also is reflected in Maximus, who sees long-suffering as one of the expressions of love for one's neighbour.[387] Here too however Maximus opens a wider perspective; in the *Liber asceticus* long-suffering is presented as a remedy for anger (θυμός) in an inclusive sense.[388]

---

[379] *Ibid.* 2. 18; p. 98.
[380] See *ibid.* 2. 88; p. 136; 3. 85; p. 184 and 4. 67; p. 222.
[381] See *ibid.* 3. 83; p. 184.
[382] See particularly *ibid.* 1. 41; p. 62, where love for God is explicitly made a prerequisite for absence of grief in relation to one's neighbour.
[383] *Ibid.* 1. 29; p. 58.
[384] See also *ibid.* 2. 58; p. 122.
[385] See *ibid.* 3. 15; p. 150 and 4. 27; p. 204.
[386] See *ibid.* 1. 61; p. 72.
[387] See *ibid.* 1. 38; p. 62 and 4. 55; p. 216.
[388] See Asc 20–22; PG 90, 928 A–929 A.

A similar tendency can be noticed in relation to vainglory which, as we have seen, has no fixed counterpart among the virtues in Evagrius or Nilus. The term ἀκενοδοξία which is introduced at this point in *Tractatus ad eumdem Eulogium,* is hardly found at all in Maximus. He seems, however, to some extent to emphasize vainglory's relationship to the rational faculty, but at the same time to point out that it threatens a good relationship with one's neighbour, and implies egocentric dangers. Consequently, he sees knowledge of God,[389] or humility,[390] or meekness[391] as its counterparts.

Humility (ταπείνωσις or ταπεινοφροσύνη) in Maximus however, as in the Evagrian and the Christian tradition in general, is the fixed counterpart of pride. This fact is sometimes indirectly[392] and sometimes directly expressed.[393] Thus Maximus presents humility as the opposite of different kinds of pride,[394] as a virtue able to destroy its "empty swelling".[395] Here its relation to true knowledge is of importance, a sign that it is both the culmination of the virtues and belongs to the rational element.[396] As such a culmination humility is also in the position to tame *all* the passions,[397] and may even be called the mother of all virtues.[398]

Maximus' critical attitude to a mere correspondence between vices and virtues

We have noticed how Maximus manifests his acquaintance with the Evagrian correspondence between individual virtues and individual vices—as it had been presented by Evagrius himself—but also that this acquaintance is not developed further into a more fixed system of correspondences, such as we have found in the later Evagrian tradition. At this last point Maximus is not only restrictive; rather he seems to be anxious to widen the perspective of many of the individual virtues, so that the aspect of *a positive use* of the faculties of the trichotomy themselves is more emphasized. But why is he less interested in a close correspondence between the individual virtues and vices, than in the

---

[389] Char 1. 46; CSC, p. 64.
[390] *Ibid.* 1. 80; p. 80.
[391] Ep 2; PG 91, 396 A.
[392] See e.g. Char 2. 38–39; CSC, p. 110 ff. and 3. 62; p. 172.
[393] See e.g. *ibid.* 3. 87; p. 186.
[394] Thal 52; CCSG 7, p. 427.
[395] Ep 2; PG 91, 396 A.
[396] See e.g. Thal 52; CCSG 7, p. 425 ff.; on knowledge and humility in Christ, cf. Ep 21; PG 91, 604 C.
[397] See Gnost 1. 15; PG 90, 1088 D.
[398] Ep 37; PG 91, 632 B.

correspondence which exists between virtues and vices in general as they are seen in a 'trichotomist' perspective?

One part of a possible answer to this question at least is directly related to what we have said about Maximus' 'trichotomist' understanding of the vices: that they are seen as sins against the two aspects of the divine commandment of love, or in other words, as two sides of the basic vice of self-love. Since the different vices can be understood as belonging to these two types of self-love, performing its disintegrating function in man, the corresponding virtues, as positive expressions of the two aspects of integrating love, must be more than mere counterparts to their vices. They must be seen as manifold expressions of one and the same love, in its double character. The aspect of differentiation must, consequently, not be allowed to overshadow the aspect of unity, i.e. the aspect of unifying love, for which rather it is able to provide an element of richness. And thus the aspect of love is primarily related to all the three faculties of the soul, and to the whole of man.

To support this answer however, we must provide evidence of three kinds. First of all we shall try to demonstrate at which points the aspect of unity is particularly safeguarded in Maximus' treatment of the virtues, and then we shall show that this emphasis on unity still leaves room for a stress on the aspect of differentiation. The latter kind of evidence will be given in the last section of this chapter, which deals with Maximus' understanding of the virtues as a multiform incarnation of the Logos. But before that, the first kind of evidence will be considered in relation to the concepts of both *detachment* and *love*.

The concept of detachment (ἀπάθεια) is of a particular interest, since it covers a virtuous state of the soul which well represents the aspect of unity in a more 'passive' sense. In the Christian tradition it is often understood as an equilibrium in the soul, a proper balance which opens the way to the true spiritual life of the mind. This at least is Evagrius' understanding of detachment. It seems as if the view of unity which is represented by this kind of detachment, is in harmony with a view of virtues and vices as related to one another in a fixed correspondence, since such a correspondence must lead to an equilibrium in the virtuous soul. But because we have found that Maximus is less interested than is the Evagrian tradition in a fixed correspondence of this kind, we must ask ourselves whether Maximus' concept of detachment differs in some way from that of Evagrius, and, more important, how far such an equilibrium as that of the Evagrian concept of detachment would be sufficient for him, particularly with regard to his understanding of love.

We must therefore, first of all, study Maximus' own concept of detachment in comparison with that of Evagrius, and then consider the way in which Maximus regards the virtues as expressions of love in its two aspects, and how love in his understanding of it is related both to detachment and to γνῶσις.

3. The state of detachment

Both Evagrius and Maximus regard ἀπάθεια as a middle stage in man's life of virtue, the consummation of the *vita practica*, leading evidently to a freedom, in love, which allows for proper knowledge and contemplation.[399] But is their understanding of detachment the same, and how do they conceive of it? We have already indicated that the answer to this question may throw some light upon their slightly different attitude to the correspondence between virtues and vices—and thus also on the problem of man's character as microcosm.

The concept of detachment in some of Maximus' predecessors

Both Evagrius' and Maximus' understanding of psychic detachment must be (evaluated) in comparison with that of a number of other Christian writers such as Clement of Alexandria, Origen and Gregory of Nyssa. It is a well-known fact that Clement may be regarded as the first writer to make the Stoic term ἀπάθεια, "impassibility", a key concept in the Christian theology of spiritual perfection. It is also a recognized fact that he was able to 'christianize' this concept by combining it with the Christian concept of love (ἀγάπη).[400] This combination obviously removed part of the purely negative character of the concept. ἀπάθεια is not only impassibility in the Stoic sense, but first of all a spiritual freedom which allows for a full human devotion to God in love, and in this sense, does not imply any indifference.

Thus already in Clement we find two characteristics of the Christian understanding of detachment: (1) it is *combined with love*, the object of which is God, and consequently it is regarded as a state of the soul which prepares for communion with God; (2) this relationship with God is reflected in ἀπάθεια itself, which is regarded as an *imitation of God*, who is himself ἀπαθής. The non-active character of the concept is however not entirely removed, since it is virtually understood as involving complete freedom from passions, and since the love with which it is

---

[399] Evagrius, *Pract., Prol.* PG 40, 1221 BC and Maximus, Char 1: 2–3; CSC, p. 50.
[400] Cf. e.g. CROUZEL, *Théologie de l'image de Dieu*, p. 69.

combined is regarded as an intimacy with God rather than a passionate desire for him. This fact leaves a certain ambiguity in the concept as we meet it on Christian ground, with which later Christian writers had to struggle to some extent.[401]

Clement sees detachment as the perfection of self-mastery (ἐγκράτεια),[402] a peace of the soul without desires. This peace is an image of God's own ἀπάθεια,[403] and of Christ's, whose ἀπάθεια is an image of God's.[404] Here, however, the particular 'christianization' of the concept enters into the picture, for Christ's perfection is obviously one of both detachment and love.[405] And thus, in this Christian combination of detachment *and* love, it seems unavoidable that the Stoic concept of detachment should colour the understanding of love, and the Christian image of love should colour the understanding of detachment. Love, in this sense, liberates man from both appetency (ὄρεξις) and passions, but prevents the true gnostic from becoming entirely indifferent and without compassion.[406] In fact, ἀγάπη replaces in the gnostic all "emotions", and this makes it possible for Clement really to speak indirectly even of emotions in this context, though only in so far as they are expressions of love.[407]

It should also be added that the state of perfection which is thus reached in the soul is called by Clement "the mark (χαρακτήρ) of justice"[408]—an expression which underlines the aspect of *equilibrium* in relation to detachment, since it reminds us of the fact that the four (Platonic) cardinal virtues, and particularly justice, were also certainly understood as a kind of equilibrium, excluding both positive and negative excesses.[409] It is this ancient ideal of a proper balance in the soul without exclusion of full devotion to the supreme aim of man's life, which the christianized concept of detachment also serves to express. Such a high vision of perfect peace and balance is, however, difficult to realize in practical life, and this may be one of the reasons why Origen attributed comparatively little importance to the concept of ἀπάθεια.[410]

---

[401] On the history of the concept of ἀπάθεια, see BARDY, *art.* Apatheia, DSp 1, coll. 727–746.

[402] Cf. RÜTHER, *Die sittliche Forderung der Apatheia,* p. 56 f.

[403] Cf. *ibid.,* p. 57 f. and 66 f.

[404] Cf. *ibid.,* p. 58 ff. and CROUZEL, *op. cit.,* p. 69.

[405] Cf. RÜTHER, *op. cit.,* p. 77.

[406] See *ibid.,* p. 73 f.

[407] Cf. *ibid.,* p. 95.

[408] Cf. CROUZEL, *op. cit.,* p. 69 with ref.

[409] Cf. at this point e.g. F. COPLESTON, *A History of Philosophy 1, Greece and Rome*[2], London 1961, p. 33 f.

[410] Cf. BARDY, *art. cit.,* col. 732 f.

Gregory of Nyssa, on the other hand, used it to a great extent. It plays an important part in Gregory's doctrine of spiritual freedom, and is as such closely connected with his concept of boldness (παρρησία)[411]—a fact which is linked with the same idea of intimacy with God which we found in Clement's understanding of a passionless love. Gregory's concept of detachment is further connected with such terms as virtue and purity,[412] but also with the concepts of justice (as in Clement) and blessedness, a triad of which the Kingdom of God is said to consist.[413] Like Clement Gregory also sees detachment as related first of all to the image of God in man.[414] This fact implies however, as Daniélou has pointed out, a non-Stoic attitude, since to Gregory detachment means the active participation of the soul in divine life[415] and imitation of the divine nature.[416] It is purity and ἀπάθεια which allow for the imprint (χαρακτήρ; cf. Clement) of the divine nature in the human soul.[417] The non-Stoic tendency however goes even further: Gregory is open to the idea of a kind of *pleasure* which is known in ἀπάθεια, and Daniélou again emphasizes the Christian character of Gregory's concept of detachment in his conclusion about its positive content: it is the life of Christ himself with his charity.[418]

A similar tendency is finally to be found also in Ps.-Denis, for whom likewise detachment is subordinated to love. Consequently, it has no purely negative function. It is a prerequisite for a true vision of God[419] and is not understood in a Stoic way.[420]

It is in comparison with this tradition that we shall now study Evagrius' concept of detachment and try to understand the difference which may exist between him and Maximus at this point. The similarities are obvious, but there are also interesting digressions from the general tradition.

[411] Cf. GAÏTH, *La conception de la liberté*, p. 53.
[412] Cf. DANIÉLOU, *Platonisme et théologie mystique*, p. 92.
[413] *In Eccles., hom.* 5; JAEGER, 5, p. 372, 1 ff.
[414] Cf. GAÏTH, *op. cit.*, p. 53 f.
[415] DANIÉLOU, *op. cit.*, p. 94.
[416] *Ibid.* p. 97.
[417] Cf. *ibid., op. cit.*, p. 101. Gregory's apophatic theology even includes human detachment as an important element, since detachment is said to allow man to know God, though he is inaccessible; cf. *ibid.*, p. 96.
[418] *Ibid.* pp. 93 and 103.
[419] Cf. VÖLKER, *Kontemplation und Ekstase bei Pseudo-Dionysius Areopagita*, p. 66 f.
[420] Cf. also ROQUES, Le primat du Transcendant dans la purification de l'intelligence selon de Pseudo-Denys, RAM 23 (1947), p. 162.

Evagrius' view of detachment

Evagrius' stress on detachment as the culmination of practical virtues is, in the first place, very strong. The *vita practica* consists of a keeping of the commandments, and the "flower" of this *vita practica* is detachment.[421] Evagrius, like Clement, regards it as the perfection of self-mastery, which it surpasses, since it implies a removal even of impassioned thoughts, while self-mastery means the abolition of active sin. For this reason detachment may be interpreted as the inward, spiritual circumcision, of which Paul speaks in Rom, 2: 29.[422] Detachment is thus restricted to the soul and its practices. The "practical" soul is its throne,[423] and it does not concern the mind but only the soul.[424]

Perfect detachment implies complete victory over the demons,[425] a certain stability of thought, regardless of outward impressions, and in this restricted sense therefore also a kind of blessedness,[426] since a detached soul is not only unmoved in relation to things, but also to the memories of things.[427] Thus Evagrius, like Gregory of Nyssa, can say that detachment together with true knowledge of things represents the Kingdom of God.[428] For this reason it may also be interpreted as the nuptial vestment, of which Christ speaks.[429]

Here, however, we touch a point, where a certain difference between Evagrius' understanding of detachment and that of the other Christian writers we have mentioned may perhaps be recognized. There are, in fact, certain statements on detachment in Evagrius which seem to express a more non-Christian, or at least more Origenist, understanding than may be found elsewhere. Evagrius' emphasis on the negative function at least is apparent. It is certainly true that detachment leads to positive knowledge as in Gregory, and that knowledge of God is, of course, understood as the goal of man, but it is characteristic of Evagrius that in

---

[421] See *Pract.* 1. 53; PG 40, 1233 B.
[422] *De mal. cogitat.* 25; PG 79, 1229 C.
[423] See *Mirror for Monks*, no. 31; GRESSMANN, p. 155.
[424] *Cent. gnost.* 1. 81; OCP 5, p. 230; cf. PO 28, p. 55. HAUSHERR, Une énigme d'Evagre le Pontique. *Centurie* II, 50, RSR 23 (1933), pp. 321–325, has shown that when in *Cent. gnost.* 2. 50 (PO 28, p. 81) Evagrius says that "the two heads will be crowned with rose and linen", he refers to ἀπάθεια as the crown of the soul and spiritual knowledge as the crown of the mind. He also calls attention to *Cent. gnost.* 3. 49 (PO 28, p. 117), where Evagrius states that the mind will not be crowned with "substantial knowledge" unless it has rejected its knowledge of the two battles, i.e. of anger and concupiscence (p. 325).
[425] See *Pract.* 2. 60; PG 40, 1248 D.
[426] *De mal. cogitat.* 22; PG 79, 1225 A.
[427] *Pract.* 1. 39; PG 40, 1232 B.
[428] *Ibid.* 1. 2; PG 40, 1221 D. Knowledge of the Holy Trinity is, of course, also the Kingdom of God, though here related to the mind (νοῦς), see 1. 3; *loc. cit.*
[429] See *ibid.*, 1. 64; 1237 D.

this context he has to emphasize, that a soul which, by the grace of God, is brought to such a knowledge "on the wings of detachment" has *departed from the body*.[430] Here the concept of detachment is therefore clearly connected with an Origenist dichotomy of man.

It is further certainly true that Evagrius sees love as the offspring of detachment,[431] and in this sense links the two concepts very closely, as do other representatives of a Christian understanding of detachment. But it is interesting to notice that it is only in its connection with this detachment, that love itself can be said to remove passions, to further long-suffering, to tame anger, to produce humility and to destroy pride, while love in itself is said to possess nothing but God, for it is God.[432] This statement seems, to some extent, to exclude even Clement's limited emphasis on emotional elements as expressions of love. As we shall see, it certainly excludes Maximus' understanding of charity as possessing all the virtues. As a matter of fact, Evagrius is even eager to underline this position at this point, since he states explicitly that he who is detached is really *free from the virtue* of patience, in the same way as he who is perfect is free from self-mastery. Both are obviously 'excluded', because they are regarded as unnecessary.[433] The *vita practica* is as a whole a stage to be passed and left behind.

We should perhaps also add a few other references in Evagrius to detachment as something purely 'negative', an emptiness of the soul which is established for the sake of the mind, the divine element in man. Evagrius differentiates very sharply between soul and mind at this point, restricting detachment to the sphere of the former. Another expression of this view is Evagrius' statement that it is a sign of detachment (i.e. from the soul) that the mind is so free that it begins to recognize its own splendour.[434] Likewise, Evagrius says that detachment belongs to a rational soul which denies worldly desires, a statement which in its context indicates that he would hardly accept the positive use of terms like desire and pleasure, which we found for instance in Gregory of Nyssa.[435]

We should notice finally that Evagrius states that it is not possible to love all the brethren equally, but that it is possible to live ἀπαθῶς with

[430] *Cent. gnost.* 2. 6; OCP 5, p. 230. This liberation from the body is very similar to what e.g. Plotinus understood by ἀπάθεια, but which a scholar like Daniélou denies to be the case in Gregory of Nyssa; see DANIÉLOU, *op. cit.*, p. 93 f.

[431] See *Pract.* 1. 53; PG 40, 1233 B.

[432] *Tract. ad Eul. monach.* 23; PG 79, 1124 C.

[433] See *Pract.* 1. 40; PG 40, 1232 B.

[434] *Ibid.* 1. 36; 1232 A.

[435] See *ibid.*, 1. 64; 1237 D.

them.[436] Here Evagrius clearly reveals a concept of ἀπάθεια which understands it as an equilibrium in a 'negative' sense, a kind of non-attachment, non-hostility, but not as an equilibrium in a positive sense, as equal love for one's neighbour. Detachment comes very close to Stoic indifference here, and its relationship with love is apparently seen as a relationship with love for God alone, while love for one's neighbour is restricted by circumstances that are overcome only through a 'passive' attitude of detachment. It is not difficult to see here that Evagrius' primary interest in relation to the virtues must be the fact that they overcome (and counter-balance) the vices, thus establishing an inner peace in the soul, which allows the mind to flee to God, and that these virtues imply a positive use of the faculties of the soul only in the sense that they bring these faculties to this inner peace.

Maximus' view of detachment and the Evagrian influence

In many respects Maximus shares the convictions of Evagrius, by whom he is strongly influenced at this point. Maximus agrees with Evagrius that detachment is closely connected with a virtuous keeping of the commandments, though it surpasses it.[437] He also agrees with him that detachment not only means freedom from an irrational influence by things but also from the thought of things, and that the ideas of things should be *mere* thoughts.[438] He also points out that concupiscence and anger ought to be detached in this way both from things and from imaginations caused by things.[439]

On the same line of thinking Maximus—in close association with Evagrius—develops in *Cent. gnost.* his mystical speculation on *the 6th day*, which symbolizes the natural development of "practical" virtues and is followed by the 7th day of natural knowledge and the 8th day which implies deification.[440] According to this speculation the 6th day may be celebrated either according to the law, the first stage, or according to the gospel, a second and more perfect stage. In the first case man flees from the tyranny of passions through the Red Sea into the desert of freedom from passions, i.e. negative ἀπάθεια, but arrives also at a final

---

[436] *Ibid.* 2. 100; 1252 B.

[437] See Char 1. 77; CSC, p. 78 and 2. 22; p. 100.

[438] *Ibid.* 1. 91 and 93; p. 84 ff. Things should be owned with detachment, see *ibid.* 2. 89; p. 138.

[439] *Ibid.* 3. 35; p. 160.

[440] See Gnost 1. 55; PG 90, 1104 B; cf. 1. 51; 1101 C. On the rôle and importance of this category of speculation in the ancient Church, see further the summary of von Balthasar, KL², p. 617 ff. with ref.

crossing of Jordan into the promised land of positive virtues;[441] in the second case even the very first movement of sin is killed in complete detachment, which leads to the fact that impassioned thoughts and even naked imaginations are effaced, a higher passage through the Red Sea into the desert of perfect ἀπάθεια, from which man is allowed by grace to enter the promised land of divine knowledge and to become himself a temple of the Holy Spirit.[442] In both cases detachment, the Sabbath of the desert, thus implies pure emptiness, but in both cases it also leads on to positive activities: in virtues and in higher contemplation. We should, however, notice with von Balthasar[443] that, though the scheme of thought is Evagrian, Evagrius' particular emphasis is laid on this negative emptiness of detachment, while Maximus allows also for a *natural* activity of virtues in close connection with detachment.[444] But this fact does, of course, not prevent him from speaking of the Sabbath as a perfect non-activity of passions.[445]

There is thus in Maximus on the one hand a clear stress on detachment as in itself an entirely 'negative' function, an emptiness from passions. At this point his dependence on Evagrius is apparent. We should even notice that when Maximus, following the Christian tradition in general, combines detachment very closely with love, this fact partly affects his presentation of love. Thus he points out e.g. that perfect love not only scorns the passions, but also this life itself as well as death—a good example of how the concept of detachment has to some extent coloured the concept of love.[446]

Detachment and love are, however, both integrated into a psychological development, which gives a perfectly clear explanation of how this character of love is understood. *Vita practica* thus implies a good use of human means, which leads to a purified condition of the soul, in which right discernment is made possible, and it is this discernment which results in a detachment, from which perfect love is begotten.[447] The crucial point is thus that detachment requires a calm and non-passionate

[441] Gnost 1. 52; 1101 C.
[442] 1. 53; 1101 D–1104 A.
[443] KL², p. 619 f.
[444] Cf. at this point Pyrrh; PG 91, 309 B.
[445] See also Thal 65; CCSG 22, p. 279. Cf. here the understanding of the Maximian concept of detachment as related to the crucial problem of life and death for man's mind, which is presented in UN MOINE DE L'ÉGLISE ORTHODOXE DE ROUMANIE (= A. SCRIMA), L'avènement philocalique dans l'Orthodoxie roumaine, *Istina* 3 (1958), p. 323. See also the analysis of the concept of ἀπάθεια in Maximus as presented by VÖLKER, *op.cit.*, pp. 410–423.
[446] See Char 1. 72; CSC, p. 76.
[447] See *ibid.* 4. 91; p. 234.

insight into God's creation, a rational discernment, and consequently this aspect defines its own character. Detachment is in Maximus no contempt for the created world, and the love that springs from detachment is a love for God as Creator, which never excludes its second aspect: love for one's neighbour.[448]

We should perhaps add here that it is in full accordance with this stress on discernment that Maximus also emphasizes the close relationship between detachment and humility. We have seen that humility, as the counterpart of pride, is primarily of the rational faculty,[449] and the combination of detachment and humility consequently emphasizes the fact that all the faculties of the soul must be involved. The psychological background of this combination is, of course, the fact that man in his partial knowledge, a knowledge which is always threatened by the passions of his passible faculties, must detach himself from passions and at the same time show humility, since his knowledge is limited.[450] Detachment is thus not only a preparation for knowledge, i.e. for a full and right use of the rational faculty as well as of the mind, but also a partner in the good use of the rational faculty, namely in humility. This good use is certainly conceived in negative terms in this context, but nevertheless it implies a true insight into one's own conditions.

An inner transformation of the concept of detachment

The Evagrian influence on Maximus' understanding of detachment thus seems to be partly modified on account of his integration of this concept into his general view of human restoration and perfection. But more important is the fact that we can also recognize another aspect of detachment in his writing, a more positive understanding of it. It seems, in fact, that if the traditional understanding of ἀπάθεια has to a certain extent coloured his understanding of love, to a much greater extent has this concept of love coloured his understanding of detachment. We can see this tendency first of all in Maximus' description of God's detachment of which, for Maximus too, man's is an imitation. God who is both good and detached, manifests thus these two attributes precisely in his equal love for all.[451] The aspect of balance and equilibrium which is so

---

[448] It is characteristic of Maximus that the chapter which follows his description of the psychological development, upon which we have now commented, deals with the neighbourly aspect of detachment and comes very close, in fact, to a description of neighbourly love; see 4. 92; *loc. cit.*

[449] Cf. p. 297 above.

[450] See Char 4. 57–58; CSC, p. 218.

[451] *Ibid.* 1. 25; p. 58.

intimately connected with the concept of ἀπάθεια is thus transferred to the plane of equality in the handling of others, and it is obviously the combination of goodness and detachment which allows for this change of accent. The result is, however, that the concept of detachment itself is provided with *an element of activity.*

This tendency is now also recognizable on the human level. A very close association between detachment and love is established first of all. We thus notice that Maximus several times describes the state of detachment in such a way that it becomes almost identical with love. To abstain entirely from vices and to show perfect love go together.[452] He who shows contempt for all passions, is also free from hate for his neighbour, i.e. he shows neighbourly love.[453] Consequently, an imperfect detachment implies imperfect charity.[454] He who is perfect in love has also attained the summit of detachment, both implying that the differences between "Jew and Greek", etc. of Gal. 3: 28 have disappeared. Detachment and equal love are almost the same thing, for men as well as for God.[455]

Consequently, Maximus is also quite unprepared to accept the Evagrian idea of detachment in relation to one's neighbour, which requires less than equal love for all,[456] though he is well aware of the difficulties involved in such a demand.[457] If we want a sharp distinction at this point it is certainly to love and not to detachment that this activity is attributed, but it seems equally clear that *the aspect of equilibrium in the concept of detachment has been transferred to the demand for equality in this activity of perfect love.*[458]

But we can advance further from here. We have already seen that Maximus is more eager than Evagrius to stress the close relationship between detachment and love, as well as the fact that for him detachment is integrated into a general view of human restoration and perfection, which involves all man's faculties. This last aspect we noticed as modifying the concept of detachment in its negative sense. But it can now be confirmed from a more positive side. For Maximus says explicitly that a perfect soul—and we remember that detachment is primarily related to the perfection of the soul—is one whose passible powers wholly tend

---

[452] See e.g. *ibid.* 4. 42; p. 210.
[453] *Ibid.* 4. 49; p. 214.
[454] *Ibid.* 4. 92; p. 234.
[455] See *ibid.* 2. 30; p. 106.
[456] See particularly *ibid.* 1. 61; p. 72 and 2. 10; p. 94.
[457] See 4. 82; CSC, p. 230.
[458] Cf. to this point also SHERWOOD's treatment of the difference between Evagrius and Maximus in relation to the demand for equal love, in ACW, p. 93.

towards God.[459] Now God is himself detached (ἀπαθής) and man's detachment should be an imitation of God's. But imitation is of a volitional disposition, of intention (διάθεσις), says Maximus, in the same sense as virtue is of γνώμη.[460]

It is thus the natural energy of man which is released and developed in imitation of God, though of course it works in co-operation with divine grace and in communication with Christ, who is God and man. And this natural energy must be of the whole of man, who is composed both of body and soul, both of sensible and intelligible elements, since this is in accordance with the principle of his nature. Thus detachment cannot be just a kind of emptiness. In its 'negative' aspect it is an emptiness from passions, but in its positive aspect it is related to a good use of all man's faculties with a view to his divine goal and in the service of love. Maximus says this explicitly in a passage of Thal 54 where he shows that the *habitus* of detachment is not only a negative condition for contemplation and true knowledge, a peaceful state as such, but also a state in which "the face" of man's psychic disposition (διάθεσις) is elevated in praise of God, a face which is *formed by many and varying virtues*.[461] It is thus not in emptiness that man has to praise God, but in the fulness of his virtues, which are of his nature, and these virtues are manifold, i.e. they vary according to the variety of man's own make-up, the differentiation of his natural faculties.

We may thus conclude that since Maximus' concept of detachment is so closely associated with the positive activities of love, we can now understand why he is less interested in establishing a naked equilibrium between virtues and vices, than in emphasizing the positive functions of the different faculties of the human soul, as they are developed in a manifold life of virtues. We have also seen that this attitude is hardly shared by Evagrius, and that Maximus, consequently, in spite of his dependence on Evagrius in his doctrine of virtues and vices, in this particular respect stands closer to other Christian writers who have used the concept of detachment in their theology.[462]

But then we should also be prepared to conclude that it is the idea of man as a created microcosm, clothed with a task of mediation, which serves best to describe Maximus' attitude to the positive function of virtues in relation to the different faculties of man. He is not, like

---

[459] Char 3. 98; CSC, p. 190.
[460] Ep 1; PG 91, 364 AB.
[461] CCSG 7, p. 445 ff.
[462] The basic aim is anti-Evagrian, says VON BALTHASAR, KL², p. 410, in a similar commentary on Maximus' use of the concept of ἀπάθεια. Cf. also KL², p. 557 f.

Evagrius, interested in a departure from the lower elements in man, but in a restoration and re-integration of man as a whole.

This re-integration however must take place in love, and in the next section we shall see how love as integrating factor is for this reason given the position of the summit of virtues—not as their abolition as we found in Evagrius. Further we shall also see how in its double character it is understood as the good use of the two possible faculties of the human soul, and finally how it is presented as the way to deification and spiritual fulfilment.

4. *Love—the integrating factor*

In this section we shall therefore pay attention to love from *three different angles:* a) love in relation to other virtues, as their summary and summit; b) love in its two aspects, love for God and love for one's neighbour, as applicable to the virtues of different faculties of the soul; and c) love in its general relationship to knowledge and deification.[463] Through this three-fold study we shall be in the position to see more clearly how Maximus maintains the idea of man as microcosm in his teaching on the 'natural' restoration of man through virtuous activity.

Charity as the inclusive summit of all the virtues

We have seen that Evagrius is of the opinion that perfect detachment makes the rest of the virtues unnecessary, and that love in itself possesses nothing but God.[464] These statements seem to manifest a primarily 'negative' understanding of virtues. Their sole function is to conquer the vices and establish an equilibrium in the soul, which makes it possible for the human mind to devote its whole intellectual attention in love to God. This view is, of course, also closely linked with Evagrius' sharp Origenist dichotomy between the lower and the higher parts of man. The composite character of the created human unity is only accidental, and this fact excludes a truly microcosmic understanding of man.

But what is Maximus' position in relation to this problem of love, detachment and the virtues in their differentiation? This is, in fact, a test question to discover how far Maximus is willing to draw the logical

---

[463] We shall return to point c. also in the context of ch. VI, where the aspect of human mediation will be studied. Here we shall concentrate our attention on the aspect of the restoration of man as microcosm. I have treated this theme in my later book *Man and the Cosmos*, pp. 101–108.

[464] Cf. p. 303 above.

consequences of his own understanding of man as a microcosm and of his refutation of Origenism.

Maximus, of course, frequently expresses the idea that ἀγάπη, which to him usually means both love and charity, is the most outstanding of all virtues, the summit and summary of them all.[465] Thus it is called the most cardinal or general of virtues.[466] We further learn that the virtues lead together to charity. They result or end in charity,[467] which is the supreme good of all goods.[468] This close connection with the virtues is also true of love in its aspect of desire (ἔρως), which is supported by all the virtues in its perfect attention to God.[469] But does this idea imply in Maximus, as it does in Evagrius, that charity as it were excludes the other virtues by making them unnecessary, or rather that charity includes the other virtues in that it fulfils their functions?

At first sight it might seem that the difference between Evagrius and Maximus is very small. In Char 1. 1 we learn that charity is a disposition in which no creature is to be preferred to "knowledge" of God,[470] a definition which comes very close to the Evagrian understanding of charity in its relationship to *gnosis*,[471] and which seems to put the whole stress on charity as the door to *gnosis* and to neglect the aspect of charity as the fulfilment of virtues. And likewise, Maximus stresses, explicitly or implicitly, the close connection between charity and *purification*,[472] and this fact may seem to make the 'negative' aspect of charity—charity as the final victory over all the passions—dominate over its positive aspect, its relationship to the virtues. However we must not forget that Maximus regards the virtues as natural to man, and for this reason he does not always have to point out the positive aspect of charity, or detachment, since restored man is to him always virtuous man.[473]

But more important, Maximus also makes it explicitly clear that he

---

[465] In the following pages, as in this thesis on the whole, we have chosen to render the term ἀγάπη, particularly in Maximus, "charity" as well as "love", since it includes both aspects, and since the word ἔρως requires a further attribute and should be translated "desirous love", etc.

[466] See Thal 40; CCSG 7, p. 269 and Amb 21; PG 91, 1249 B. ἀγάπη as the sum total of Christ's exemplary function is forcefully worked out by HEINZER, *op. cit.*, pp. 181–198. See also VÖLKER, *op. cit.*, pp. 423–445.

[467] Thal 54; CCSG 7, p. 451; cf. Ep 2; PG 91, 396 B.

[468] Ep 2; PG 91, 401 C.

[469] See Char 1. 11; CSC, p. 52.

[470] CSC, p. 50.

[471] See *Cent. gnost.* 1. 86; PO 28, p. 57, where the definition is almost identical with Maximus'.

[472] See Char 4. 72; CSC, p. 226; cf. 2. 6.; p. 92: ἔρως and purification. Cf. also e.g. PEGON, SCH 9, p. 69, n. 1.

[473] Cf. at this point HAUSHERR, *Philautie*, p. 134 f.

conceives of the relationship between charity and the other virtues in a way which is different from that which we have found in Evagrius. Thus in Ep 2 he points out—to the honour of charity—that it *possesses*, or includes, all the virtues, and he goes on to present a hierarchy of them, in which we have already found traces of both the Evagrian hierarchy and a 'trichotomist' understanding of the virtues.[474] No "form" of good is outside charity, he says, neither the other theological virtues, nor those which belong exclusively to the *vita practica*. And we can also notice that he emphasizes this character of charity despite the fact that these latter virtues are defined as counterparts to their vices.

Charity is thus not presented as a perfect substitute for the lower virtues, which 'excludes' them in principle since it makes them unnecessary, but as their fulfilment, which includes the other virtues in its higher unity and supports man with their strength.[475] A similar understanding of love seems to be manifested even elsewhere, where Maximus emphasizes that those who have acquired the perfection of love, having elevated the wings of the soul through the virtues, are those who are also "caught up in the clouds" (2 Thess. 4: 16) and will not come before judgment.[476]

We may ask for the reasons behind this difference of emphasis in Maximus, in comparison with Evagrius. His positive view of man, created as a composite unity, is, of course, the principle reason. If the virtues are functions of natural faculties in man, they cannot be excluded from man's higher activities. In one way or another, they must be integrated into them. But there are probably further reasons as well. One is that the virtues themselves, being a good use of natural faculties in man, are regarded as natural.[477] They are thus not accidental but necessary expressions of his nature.

Another is that Maximus makes a distinction in his general understanding of love between a natural desire (which is ἔρως) and a divine gift (which is ἀγάπη), as Sherwood has pointed out.[478] In love as a general function of man these two elements go together. They are intimately integrated and human charity will never lose its element of natural desire and aspiration—no more than man as a whole will ever lose the substantial difference which divides his nature from God's—but only in

---

[474] See Ep 2; PG 91, 393 C–396 B.

[475] Already PEGON, *òp. cit.*, p. 54 had noticed this inclusive character of love as it is conceived by Maximus, and also emphasized the difference between him and Evagrius at this point.

[476] See QuDub 1, 10; CCSG 10, p. 142.

[477] See Pyrrh; PG 91, 309 B, where this position is presented as a surprise to Pyrrhus, who cannot see how it is compatible with the qualitative differences among men.

[478] See SHERWOOD, in ACW, p. 83.

mystical union in charity will he be united with Him. And it is this integrated love, a natural desire carried by divine charity, which in fulfilment of the virtues is able to lead man on to his divine end, and only through it is it also possible for man the microcosm to perform his function of mediation.[479]

The double dimension of charity and the life of virtues

We noted above that there is in Maximus a certain connection between his interest in the trichotomy of the soul and his insistence on the *double* commandment of love, noticeable in his treatment of the vices.[480] Love for God is regarded as opposed to the passions and vices of the concupiscible faculty, and love for one's neighbour to those of the irascible faculty.[481] We said further that vices related to the rational faculty must be supposed to concern both aspects of the commandment of love, though particularly love for God since this is a higher form of love, which in principle includes love for one's neighbour. Finally, we noticed that to this differentiation of vices according to their relationship to one or the other aspect of the double commandment of love, i.e. as two kinds of disobedience to this commandment, corresponded a double kind of self-love, a "self-love" which is opposite to love for God and a "self-pleasing" which is contrary to love for one's neighbour.[482]

Now we must follow this line of thinking a little further. How far is this double differentiation also worked out by Maximus in relation to the *virtues* as positive manifestations? Are the virtues, in other words, presented as forms of love in both its aspects to the same extent as they are presented as virtues of one or the other of the elements of the soul? An affirmative answer to this question would be of importance, since it would imply that Maximus, in his presentation of love as integrating factor, at the same time upholds the aspect of differentiation, in relation to the soul and in relation to mankind, as well as in relation to the commandment of love itself, i.e. the microcosmic aspect of restored man and restored humanity.

As a matter of fact, it is not difficult to give such a positive answer, since the double character of love is emphasized throughout Maximus' treatment of the integrating power of love, and of the virtues as

---

[479] Even in relation to the work of charity human perfection is thus a matter of true *perichoresis*.

[480] See A, 4; pp. 281–284 above.

[481] See Char 4. 75; CSC, p. 226 ff.

[482] See *ibid*. 4. 37; p. 208, where they are presented as αὐταρέσκεια and φιλαυτία respectively.

manifestations of love. First of all, the concept of love itself contains a reference to this fact. We noticed above that love as desire (ἔρως), an expression of man's natural desirous capacity, is integrated with love as divine gift (ἀγάπη).[483] Now we can add that, from another point of view, these two aspects of love, love as desire and love as divine gift, are both reflected on the strictly *human* level in that concupiscence is transformed in love to ἔρως, and anger to ἀγάπη.[484] But these two kinds of love correspond again obviously to the two aspects of self-love which we mentioned above. Maximus emphasizes at least that love in its desirous sense (ἔρως τῆς ἀγάπης) excludes both a "feeling for oneself", and for other creatures.[485] This feeling for oneself can hardly be anything else than self-love in the sense of αὐταρέσκεια, and thus this statement concerns love in the sense of desire for God alone, i.e. as transformed concupiscence. Consequently, the commandment of love for God primarily relates to man's desirous attachment, which should be given to no creature at all, while the commandment of love for the neighbour demands a state of mind, which because of its fixed relationship to God includes a charitable affection (ἀγάπη in its restricted sense) for all human beings.

Maximus' emphasis on love for God is thus able to take the claim of neighbourly love into full account. Love for one's neighbour does not imply an attachment to men which is of the same character as the attachment which love for God implies. It is a state of the mind which

---

[483] See p. 311 above.
[484] See *ibid.* 2. 48; CSC, p. 116.—A. NYGREN, *Den kristna kärlekstanken genom tiderna. Eros och agape*[2], pp. 415-418, is obviously quite unaware of the complicated character of Maximus' concept of love. He thinks that Maximus uses the terms ἔρως and ἀγάπη without any distinction at all, and arrives, consequently, without any difficulty at the conclusion that it is the ἔρως-aspect, as he understands it, which dominates. It is true that Maximus affirms that God himself is both ἀγάπη and ἔρως (see Amb 23; PG 91, 1260 C) and does it with explicit reference to Ps.-Denis, who in *De div. nom.* 4, 11-12 (PG 3, 708 B-709 C) had defended the Christian use of the term ἔρως beside ἀγάπη (cf. VON BALTHASAR, KL[2], p. 416, n. 2)—and even regarded it as more divine—but also defined it in such a way that it means a unifying power which even includes the care of the higher for the lower (PG 3, 709 CD). How far Maximus agrees with Denis' higher evaluation of ἔρως is, however, not quite clear, since the scholion to which Nygren refers at this point may be written by John of Skythopolis and not by Maximus (see *In Div. nom.* 4, 12; PG 4, 265 A; cf. NYGREN, *op. cit.*, p. 415, n. 5). What remains a fact is that Maximus regards them as synonymous expressions *in relation to God*—as we can see in a scholion which it is most likely was written by Maximus himself (*In div. nom.* 4, 14; PG 4, 265 CD; on the authenticity of this scholion, cf. VON BALTHASAR, KL[2], p. 672). On the divine level ἔρως and ἀγάπη may thus be regarded as synonyms, since God is the Cause of all, but *on the level of human beings* they are separated into ἔρως as a natural desire and ἀγάπη as a divine state of mind. Nygren's failure to see this distinction has prevented him from understanding Maximus' expression ἔρως τῆς ἀγάπης (see NYGREN, *op. cit.*, p. 416, n. 3).
[485] Char 1. 10; CSC, p. 52.

shares in God's charity towards men. Love is thus able to include
positively the active functions of the human faculties of both concupiscence and anger. But of course, it also includes the power of the rational
faculty.

And consequently, Maximus is prepared to point out that the mind,
when it advances in the desire (ἔρως) of charity, is supported by *all* the
virtues and not least by pure prayer which is a virtue of the mind itself, or
of the rational faculty in service of the mind.[486]

This stress on the inclusion of all virtues in the work of love, the
supreme desire, implies, however, that neighbourly love also is regarded
as included in the love for God, an idea which Maximus expresses several
times.[487] It is expressed in a negative form when Maximus affirms that
love for God excludes hate towards one's neighbour,[488] and as a positive
claim when Maximus underlines that love for one's neighbour should be
caused by love for God.[489] With reference to 1 John 4: 20 Maximus even
goes as far as to say that benevolence towards one's neighbour is the
clearest proof that one loves God.[490]

As we pointed out above, the close connection between the concepts
of detachment and charity probably implies further that the aspect of
equilibrium, related to detachment, has been transferred to love as a
claim for *equal love* towards all. This claim is in fact very often repeated
by Maximus,[491] and he sees it clearly as an expression of perfect love. It is
most definitely, though paradoxically, formulated as a conviction that he
who loves nothing human, loves all men,[492] a statement which says that
he who devotes his loving desire entirely to God, is not affected by any
partial attachment to the world and is thus able to love all men equally in
imitation of God's own love for all. Resentfulness, on the other hand, is a
sign of worldliness and implies a worship of creatures instead of the
Creator.[493]

Thus it is obviously Maximus' conviction that love for God, the true
aim of man's life, in whom he is called to find his true pleasure, not only
eradicates all sins,[494] but also positively includes in itself all the virtues.

---

[486] See *ibid.* 1. 11; p. 52.
[487] *Ibid.* 1. 13; p. 54 and 1. 23; p. 56.
[488] *Ibid.* 1. 15–16; p. 54.
[489] *Ibid.* 2. 9; p. 92 ff.
[490] Ep 2; PG 91, 401 D–404 A.
[491] See e.g. Char 1. 61; CSC, p. 72; 1. 71; p. 76; 2. 30; p. 106; 4. 98; p. 238 and Ep 2; PG
91, 400 C.
[492] *Ibid.* 3. 37; p. 160.
[493] See *ibid.* 1. 20; p. 56.
[494] *Ibid.* 2. 7; p. 92.

Monastic activities and attitudes such as fasting, watching, singing, praying and thinking good of one's brethren are all expressions of love.[495] But how is this conviction also differentiated according to the trichotomy of the soul and to the dual character of the commandment of love? We shall try to answer this question in relation to each of the three psychic faculties.

The double commandment of love and Maximus' 'trichotomist' understanding of the virtues

The relationship between *love for God* and a good use of *the concupiscible faculty* is clearly stated by Maximus. Thus we learn that the holiness of temperance effects charity (i.e. for God),[496] or that he who keeps his body free from pleasure, may get even the support of the body itself in his service of higher, i.e. divine, aims.[497] Such activities as fasting and watching are also expressions of love for God.[498] Maximus even states that the faculty of concupiscence itself may be transformed into a holy desire for God, which moves man towards his aim.[499]

The relationship between *love for one's neighbour* and a good use of *the irascible faculty* is still more frequently indicated. Thus we learn that long-suffering and kindness belong to charity (for one's neighbour), though lack of them indirectly separates also from God,[500] or that doing good, long-suffering and patience are works of charity (for one's neighbour), and thus not only remedies for corresponding vices.[501] Charity is certainly regarded as a remedy against the passions of the irascible faculty;[502] but this is not enough, for nothing short of an active doing of good is in Maximus' opinion sufficient to express neighbourly love.[503]

Thus the aspect of equilibrium does not lead to a lack of activity. Long-suffering, which in the Evagrian tradition is the counterpart of wrath, certainly belongs to the fulness of love,[504] but love also includes a number of far more active neighbourly virtues, expressing a loving attitude to different categories of human beings.[505] As a matter of fact,

---

[495] See *ibid.* 1. 42; p. 64.
[496] *Ibid.* 1. 45; p. 64.
[497] *Ibid.* 1. 21; p. 56.
[498] *Ibid.* 1. 42; p. 64. Cf. above.
[499] See Ep 2; PG 91, 397 B.
[500] Char 1. 38; CSC, p. 62.
[501] See *ibid.* 1. 40; p. 62 and 4. 55; p. 216.
[502] See *ibid.* 1. 66; p. 74.
[503] *Ibid.* 2. 49–50; p. 116 ff.
[504] See *ibid.* 4. 26; p. 204.
[505] See the 17 virtues of this kind in Ep 2; PG 91, 405 A.

neighbourly love is far from being merely a substitute for the vices of the irascible element, or even for its differentiated virtues; it qualifies the irascible faculty itself.[506]

However, it should also be added that this intimate relationship between the two aspects of love and the dichotomy of the passible part of the soul, does not exclude an emphasis on the close connection which also exists between these two types of relationships themselves. Thus we learn that a flight from worldly desires, i.e. an expression of a loving attachment to God, places man above grief, which is primarily a vice of the irascible faculty.[507] The reason is, of course, that all virtues may be subsumed under love for God. But on the other hand, we also learn that not only love for God, but more directly love for one's neighbour, leads to a distribution of money, which certainly at the same time conquers the vice of avarice, usually connected with the concupiscible faculty.[508]

The rational faculty, and the mind, are also included in the work of love. In this case we are, of course, primarily concerned with *love for God.* Thus we learn that the fear of God, understood in a good sense, which presupposes the knowledge of God implied in faith, leads to reverence, i.e. a form of humility, a virtue of the rational faculty, which ought to be joined with love.[509] And it is a divine knowledge, which is united with charity, that leads man to illumination.[510] Knowledge should in fact be activated by charity.[511] The intellectual activity of pure prayer is likewise an expression of love for God.[512] Since the mind is the spiritual subject of man, this positive function of love in relation to the mind cannot, however, be restricted to love for God. In fact, Maximus points out explicitly that if love for God gives wings to the mind by which to communicate with God, love for the neighbour prepares it to think well of other human beings—two functions of the mind which are obviously of an interdependent importance.[513]

Thus we have seen that the supreme virtue of love, in Maximus' opinion, includes positively all the 'lower' virtues, which it does not replace but fulfils. We have also seen that this positive view of the virtues in relation to love is closely linked with Maximus' evaluation of love in

---

[506] See Char 4. 15; CSC, p. 200 and 4. 44; p. 212.
[507] *Ibid.* 1. 22; p. 56.
[508] See *ibid.* 1. 23; p. 56.
[509] *Ibid.* 1. 81–82; p. 80.
[510] *Ibid.* 1. 46; p. 64.
[511] See *ibid.* 1. 47; p. 66 and 1. 69; p. 74.
[512] See *ibid.* 2. 7; p. 92.
[513] See *ibid.* 4. 40; p. 162.

its two aspects as implying a right use of the three faculties of the human soul and a "winging" of the mind for the final communion with God.

But this also means that Maximus is not of the opinion that man leaves his passible functions behind him during the process of deification and Christian perfection. Through their good use they co-operate with the mind in the fulfilment of its true task. And it is through charity that this co-operation of the whole of man takes place. Charity implies in fact this restored and transformed passibility, which is to follow man through all his life as a human being. And for this reason Maximus is fully prepared to call *charity itself a blessed passion*.[514] There is indeed a blameworthy passion of love for the world, but in restored man this passion is replaced by the laudable passion of 'love for God, and neighbour.[515] Maximus' affirmation of human unity and differentiation as kept together could hardly be more clearly manifested than through his definition of charity. And thereby the positive view of man's microcosmic position is also expressed.

Charity in relation to faith and hope as agents of deification

Maximus thus ascribes to love an all-inclusive integrating function in relation to man as a differentiated being. But in that case what is the relationship between love and other agents of human perfection and deification? Evagrius tends to restrict the function of charity to the *vita practica*, of which however it is the end.[516] We have few reasons to suppose it, but we must ask: does Maximus limit its rôle in the same way? The answer to this question may here be restricted to two fields: the position of charity over against the other 'theological' virtues, faith and hope, and the relationship between love and higher knowledge (γνῶσις).

Maximus' reflection on *the three theological virtues*, like that of other Christian writers, is, of course, primarily based on 1 Cor. 13: 13, where the supremacy of charity is affirmed. For this reason it is of no particular interest for us simply to notice that Maximus accepts this supremacy. What interests us is his understanding of the virtues of faith and hope, since only this can help us to see the quality of his affirmation of the supremacy of charity. And the most interesting fact in this connection is that in the case both of faith and hope we can find traces of a criticism of the position of Evagrius and Origenism.

A striking fact in relation to Maximus' understanding of *faith* is his

---

[514] See *ibid.* 3. 67; p. 174 ff.
[515] See *ibid.* 3. 71; p. 176 ff.
[516] See *Pract.* 1. 56; PG 40, 1233 C.

high evaluation of this basic theological virtue. Both Evagrius and Maximus see faith as the foundation and starting-point of Christian life as a whole. Their comparative hierarchies of virtues present sufficient evidence at this point. Maximus also expresses the same idea elsewhere.[517] But Maximus goes further, and we have reason to believe that the high evaluation of faith as a whole, which we find in his writings, distinguishes him from Evagrius, for whom faith is only a kind of purified natural *gnosis*.[518]

To Maximus faith is, first of all, a gift of grace, given in baptism,[519] a power and a calling.[520] But further we learn that faith, understood in the light of Hebr. 11: 1, gives knowledge of God and divine things, a qualified knowledge in fact. This knowledge can be contrasted with sensual knowledge,[521] and is also regarded as an inward Kingdom of God.[522] We also learn that faith precedes hope and charity, which are both related to the truth which faith firmly establishes (ὑφιστῶσα).[523] Faith is a true knowledge from undemonstrable principles, an establishment (ὑπόστασις) of things which are above mind and reason.[524] It is thus in relation to this evaluation of faith that we have to understand Maximus' affirmation of the supremacy of love.

Also in regard to *hope* a difference from Evagrius may be noticed, at least indirectly. Evagrius sees the function of hope as one of assurance and confirmation, a parallel to faith as foundation and to charity as strength,[525] and so to some extent does Maximus as well.[526] But clearly he presents hope on a higher level, since he emphasizes that it is "the strength of the extremes, that is to say charity and faith".[527] It is related to the divine realities in a way which is similar to that of the other 'theological' virtues. Evagrius combines it very closely with patience in his hierarchy of virtues,[528] and it is a striking fact that the elimination of this close combination in Maximus' version of the hierarchy is one of the

---

[517] See e.g. Ep 2; PG 91, 393 C and 396 B.
[518] Cf. VON BALTHASAR, KL², p. 605 f.
[519] Cf. SHERWOOD, in ACW, p. 74.
[520] See Myst 1; PG 91, 668 A and 24; 705 B; cf. LOOSEN, *Logos und Pneuma*, p. 20.
[521] See Ep 2; PG 91, 393 CD.
[522] Thal 33; CCSG 7, p. 229.
[523] See Ep 2; PG 91, 396 B.
[524] See Gnost 1. 9; PG 90, 1085 D; cf. Hebr. 11:1.
[525] See *Tract. ad Eul. monach.* 11; PG 79, 1108 B.
[526] Maximus gives, however, very few statements on hope; cf. HEINTJES, Een onbekende leeraar, StC 11 (1935), p. 189 f.
[527] Ep 2; PG 91, 396 B.
[528] See *Pract., Prol.;* PG 40, 1221 BC.

very few differences between them.[529] Also in relation to hope Maximus underlines further that it is able to give an inner assertion, substance (ὑπόστασις), to the divine realities,[530] and as such it points itself to the object of both faith and charity.[531] As in the case of faith, so also in relation to hope we must measure the affirmation of the supremacy of charity with the high evaluation which Maximus gives of it.

But how does Maximus conceive of the relationship between the three theological virtues taken together? He seems to regard them as corresponding to a favourite triad of his: *beginning, middle* and *end* (ἀρχή—μεσότης—τέλος), which is characteristic of time and created beings.[532] For in Char 3. 100[533] Maximus emphasizes that time is divided into three parts, and that faith extends to all three, hope to one and charity to two, a statement by which he probably intends to say that faith, though being the beginning, is also related to middle and end, since for man there is no complete knowledge of God available, while hope is related to the middle (μεσότης) and charity both to the middle phase and to the end. Virtually, however, faith is attached to the beginning—it lays the foundation of Christian life—while hope performs a task of mediation,[534] since it indicates that which is believed and makes real that which is the object of love. And charity is above all related to the end, the consummation of all.[535]

The understanding of charity as connected with τέλος, end, may be confirmed in different ways. We learn, first of all, in Ep 2 that it "embraces altogether the supreme object of desire",[536] and this last expression is already in one of the Stoic fragments said to be a definition of τέλος.[537] Even Evagrius, in fact, regards the terms end (τέλος), the supreme object of desire (τὸ ἔσχατον ὀρεκτόν) and the final beatitude (ἡ

<hr/>

[529] See Char 1. 2–3; CSC, p. 50.
[530] See Ep 2; PG 91, 393 D.
[531] *Ibid.;* 395 B.
[532] For his general use of the triad, see Gnost 1. 5; PG 90, 1085 A; cf. VON BALTHASAR, KL[2], p. 603.
[533] CSC, p. 192.
[534] It is "the strength of the extremes" (ἄκρα). This last term indicates, in fact, that faith and charity are regarded as elements of a triad, and hope as μεσότης within this triad—a Neo-Platonic way of thinking reflected in Ps.-Denis. Cf. at this point VÖLKER, *Kontemplation und Ekstase*, p. 124.
[535] The sense of Char. 3.100 is obscure and our interpretation is not shared by the scholars who have commented upon it. VON BALTHASAR, KL[2], p. 465, n. 2 understands it almost in an Evagrian way; and so partly does PEGON, *op. cit.,* p. 151, n. 1. SHERWOOD, in ACW, p. 263, n. 189 comes closer to our interpretation, but thinks of a reference to the three laws of nature, Scripture and grace.
[536] PG 91, 396 C.
[537] See VON ARNIM, *Stoic. Vet. Fragm.* 3, p. 3 (no. 3).

ἐσχάτη μακαριότης) as synonymous expressions,[538] but he links them rather with knowledge than with charity. And secondly, Maximus presents charity as repose or fixity (στάσις), i.e. as the end of man's motion towards his divine goal, an end which is able to replace both faith and hope.[539] This term ('repose') (στάσις) is, however, at the same time part of Maximus' anti-Origenist triad of *becoming, motion,* repose (γένεσις—κίνησις—στάσις), and this triad is itself partly a parallel to the triad of beginning, middle and end.[540] Charity as both "end" and 'repose' is consequently integrated into a view of man's destiny, which is foreign to that of Evagrius. Maximus obviously sees the 'theological' virtues as instruments on man's way from beginning to end, from coming into being to repose, but at the same time this implies that his understanding of them is explicitly contrary to the Origenist—and Evagrian—teaching on man's creation, fall and restoration.[541]

That charity in its perfection implies to Maximus this attainment of the divine end of man's life is, finally, confirmed by the fact that he also underlines that charity alone gives full *enjoyment* (ἀπόλαυσις) of that which is believed and hoped for, and gives it by its very nature.[542] The term "enjoyment" had, in fact, since Gregory of Nyssa been used to express mystical communion with God,[543] an understanding which Maximus even explicitly shares, since he defines it himself as "participation in supernatural divine things".[544] It is in this sense that charity lasts for ever. It should indeed be noted that the terms "repose" and "enjoyment" are closely connected by Maximus. The mystical Maximian term ('ever-moving repose') (ἀεικίνητος στάσις) is explicitly identified with "enjoyment" (ἀπόλαυσις).[545] Thus it is made fully clear that charity alone, in Maximus' opinion, brings man to mystical union with God.

Charity and knowledge

Through this last conclusion we have in fact also answered the question about the relationship between charity and knowledge (γνῶσις). This

---

[538] See Ps.-Basil., *Ep.* 8; PG 32, 257 A–C.
[539] See Ep 2; PG 91, 396 C.
[540] See SHERWOOD, *The Earlier Ambigua*, p. 109.
[541] On Maximus' refutation of the Origenist conceptions at this point, see ch. II: 6; p. 81 ff. above.
[542] See Ep 2; PG 91, 393 D–396 A and 396 C.
[543] See Gregory of Nyssa, *In Cant. cant., hom.* 1; JAEGER, 6, p. 31 f.; *ibid., hom.* 14; p. 425; cf. a similar use of the word ἀπολαύειν in Ps.-Denis, *De div. nom.* 11, 2; PG 3, 952 A; 12, 2; 969 C and *Ep.* 8, 4; 1096 B.
[544] See Thal 59; CCSG 22, p. 53; cf. Amb 7; PG 91, 1077 AB.
[545] See Thal 59; CCSG 22, p. 53.

relationship is a problem which demands notice in the writers of the general tradition to which Maximus belongs, at least for scholars who aim at systematization. In the wider Alexandrian tradition where the mind (νοῦς) is superior to the soul (ψυχή), though often, as in the case of Evagrius, more or less identified with the rational element in man, and where charity (ἀγάπη) is linked with the *vita practica* and often understood only as purification, while knowledge means illumination, the following problem presents itself: is knowledge (γνῶσις) superior to love as the mind is superior to the soul? And if this is the case, how is this understanding of love compatible with the outstanding position it must be given on biblical grounds? In general terms, the answer to this question is, of course, that since knowledge and love condition each other, their relationship can hardly be understood as one of superiority and inferiority.[546]

In particular cases, however, this answer is not always quite convincing. Thus in Evagrius, where we have found that the mind usually represents the rational element in the psychological trichotomy of man,[547] one can hardly avoid the impression that γνῶσις is also superior to ἀγάπη, which seems to be exclusively conceived as purification of the soul and the door to knowledge. In the case of Maximus, however, we have already underlined that the mind, though it represents man as intelligible being, is usually distinguished from the rational element of the soul and serves as man's spiritual subject with a more direct relationship to *all* the parts of the soul, even though this distinction is not strictly upheld. And consequently, we might, even on this ground, expect that knowledge in Maximus' case is not presented as superior to charity. But recently we also noticed that Maximus attributes to charity the power of final union with God, a union which must be above γνῶσις, since man is unable fully to know God.[548] At this point Maximus' statement in Char 1. 100 is of the utmost importance, for there he underlines that the mind, even when "placed in God" and filled with desire (i.e. transformed concupiscence, or love as yearning), cannot penetrate into that which is proper to God, since this is forbidden to every creature, but finds encouragement in the divine attributes, i.e. in that which God reveals of himself.[549] Thus we see that, according to

---

[546] Cf. J. FARGES—M. VILLER, *art.* La charité chez les Pères, DSp 2 (1953), col. 553 f., where, however, no distinction at all is made between e.g. Evagrius and Maximus at this point.

[547] Cf. ch. IV: A, 3; p. 188 ff. above.

[548] See Ch. II: 1; p. 51 f. on the gulf which exists between God and all created beings.

[549] CSC, p. 88.

Maximus, even the illuminated mind seeks, in its desirous love, for something in God which it is not allowed to find, but in this very desire and love it is, nevertheless, allowed to be united with Him.

Thus if either love or knowledge has to be regarded as superior to the other, in the case of Maximus it is certainly love which is the superior. This position of Maximus in relation to the function of love in man's final union with God must also be kept in mind when we study statements by Maximus which concern 'lower' stages of human perfection. Otherwise we may misunderstand what he says. It is obvious that on its way to full illumination, the mind must be supported by love, and in this case it looks as if love as inferior serves the cause of knowledge as superior. But, as we have seen, this is only part of the total picture. It is always the context which explains each statement on love.[550] Divine charity is thus, on the one hand, a fruit of the purification from passions which "gladdens" the *soul*, and thus different from knowledge, which concerns the *mind*.[551] But, on the other hand, it is by means of love that the knowledge of God attracts the pure mind to itself.[552] One perspective dominates when Maximus says, in an Evagrian way, that love for God is to prefer the *knowledge* of God to everything else;[553] another, it seems, when he emphasizes that it is charity which leads to illumination, and that there is for this reason nothing greater than charity.[554] It is charity which prepares the mind for its advance in knowledge,[555] but knowledge is for this reason necessarily in need of charity.[556] Thus in general, Maximus stresses the 'gnostic' character of the human desire for God, but underlines at the same time both the fact that it is love which brings man to this knowledge and illumination, *and* the fact that human knowledge of God will never be complete. Only the desirous attachment to Him in perfect charity which ends in "ecstasy" unites man fully with God.[557]

---

[550] SHERWOOD, in ACW, pp. 92 and 237 f., n. 389 has noticed a similar difference of perspective, and emphasizes that Maximus gives charity an importance above knowledge.
[551] Cf. however Char 1. 27; CSC, p. 58, where charity as purification is distinguished from both *divine* charity and knowledge.
[552] Char 1. 32; CSC, p. 60.
[553] *Ibid.* 1. 1 and 4; p. 50.
[554] See *ibid.* 1. 9; p. 52.
[555] See *ibid.* 4. 60; p. 218.
[556] *Ibid.* 4. 62; p. 220.
[557] For a proper balance between the aspects of knowledge and love, see e.g. *ibid.* 1. 69; CSC, p. 74, and for the concept of 'ecstatic' love, see Amb 7; PG 91, 1073 C. From his study of the concept of "ecstasy" in Maximus, SHERWOOD, in ACW, p. 96, concludes: "The over-all sense is that of an outgoing of the volitive power, which effects the final gnomic harmony and unity in love"; cf. further ch. VI below.—Restricted to the inter-human level

Divine incarnation in the virtues

Maximus regards charity as the summit of all virtues and as the supreme power of human re-integration. Beyond all other means of restoration and sanctification, be they practical virtues or the two other 'theological' virtues, it serves incessantly and for ever to relate man and mankind to their end and purpose of unification. But in doing so, it does not extinguish the created differentiations of man; on the contrary, it uses the powers of the soul in their differentiation and is served by them in practical action. This last fact, however, means that though the aspect of unification naturally predominates in the case of love, it is nevertheless closely linked with an opposite aspect of differentiation. Love does not only effect a unified movement towards God as man's true end, but also a good use of the different human faculties and a right relationship between human beings. And this last effect is of no less importance than the first.

Through the whole of this thesis we have tried to demonstrate how Maximus is eager to keep these two aspects in proper balance, an eagerness which we understand to be of Chalcedonian inspiration. And consequently, we should not be surprised to find that this latter aspect is equally underlined in Maximus' treatment of the *vita practica* and a life of virtues. In fact, Maximus demonstrates the proper balance by establishing a clear correspondence between the integrating function of love as a unified movement towards God as man's true end and *Christ's own act of differentiation,* through which he as the Logos allows himself to be *incarnate in the manifold human virtues themselves.*

The work of integration through which man serves God, his true end, in a unified effort of all his faculties, is thus at the same time, in Maximus' view, an on-going incarnation of the Logos in mankind, which differentiates the divine presence according to the created diversity of human life. This latter idea is far from unique in itself, but Maximus has certainly used it more energetically, and in a more conscious correspondence with the opposite aspect of unification and deification, than most Christian writers before him. Let us then see how he expresses his conviction that there is a differentiated presence of Christ the Logos in the virtues of those who are being sanctified and deified in love.

---

charity is, however, as DALMAIS, RAM 29 (1953), p. 127, well expresses it: "... amour désintéressé de bienveillance, qui trouve son fondement dans l'unité de nature établie par le Créateur entre tous les hommes, indépendamment des sentiments d'affection ou d'animosité dont ils peuvent faire preuve les uns à l'égard des autres."

The idea of an incarnation of Christ in the virtues in Maximus' predecessors

It must, of course, be underlined first of all, that the idea of an incarnation or presence of Christ in the virtues was affirmed by Christian writers long before Maximus. This idea is in fact closely connected both with the earlier Christian theology of deification, to which we shall devote some attention in Chapter VI, and with the speculation on the birth and formation of Christ the Logos in the believers which is reflected in a great number of early Christian writers.[558] Here it may, however, be sufficient to mention a few influential expressions of this line of thought.

The idea of Christ's presence in the virtues of the believers presupposes the conviction that the Logos is the very substance of all virtues. This is e.g. made perfectly clear in Origen, who elaborates this speculation considerably. According to him Christ thus *is* the virtues, while man *has* virtues, and consequently Christian imitation of Christ means a kind of participation in Christ's own being.[559] Whether this participation is ontological or moral is, however, a problem which Origen hardly makes any effort to solve. As a matter of fact, it is interesting to notice that his understanding of Christ as subordinated to the Father seems to have helped him in his affirmation of Christ's presence. For he underlines explicitly that while the Father is simple, the Son is also multiple, and that for this reason Christ may be present in all virtues and men may participate in him to the extent to which they possess these virtues.[560] This last view-point, however, is particularly important in the context of our study, for it shows that it is the aspect of a *differentiated divine presence* which stands in the foreground already at an early stage of this tradition.

From these presuppositions Origen naturally advances to the affirmation that Christ is "born" in men through the virtues.[561] Or, from another angle, he emphasizes that there is a "formation" ($\mu\acute{o}\rho\phi\omega\sigma\iota\varsigma$) of Christ taking place in the Christians—a clear reflection of Paul's words in Gal. 4: 19. And this formation implies that Christ is formed in them according to those *virtues* which he is.[562]

Also in e.g. Methodius of Philippi virtue implies a formation of Christ in the heart of the believer, and again Gal. 4: 19 is the source of

---

[558] This whole stream of thinking was excellently treated already by H. RAHNER, Die Gottesgeburt. Die Lehre der Kirchenväter von der Geburt Christi im Herzen des Gläubigen, ZKTh 59 (1935), pp. 339–383.

[559] Cf. CROUZEL, *Théologie de l'image de Dieu*, p. 230. On this theme in Origen, cf. also M. HARL, *Origène et la fonction révélatrice du Verbe incarné*, Paris 1958, pp. 291 ff.

[560] Cf. CROUZEL, *op. cit.* p. 110.

[561] Cf. *ibid.*, p. 229.

[562] Cf. *ibid.*, p. 228.

inspiration. This idea is also closely linked with the conviction that both knowledge and virtue imply a birth of λόγοι in the heart.[563] The same speculation is further reflected in Gregory of Nyssa who sees all virtues as a participation in the virtue of the Logos.[564] Like Origen he affirms that Christ *is* virtue,[565] and he regards the virtues as radiations of the logos.[566] Gregory, however, is particularly interested in emphasizing the role of detachment (ἀπάθεια) in this context. Thus Christ is "the prince of detachment", whose purity is of nature, while that of Christians is, of course, only of participation. The aspect of differentiation is thus not particularly underlined by Gregory, but it is certainly implied in his understanding of Christ's presence in the virtues. An expression of this implication is the fact that Gregory regards the virtues as the *"colours"* of the image of God in man.[567]

Isolated reflections might even be found in Evagrius, though this idea is clearly not particularly Evagrian. It is characteristic of him that he uses it in combination with an emphasis on *detachment.* Thus we learn that the practical virtues are the "fleshes of Christ" (notice the plural form, which indicates an idea of differentiation), but also that he who eats of them will become detached.[568] It is obvious that the virtues are to Evagrius primarily expressions of the equilibrium of detachment, and only in this sense do they imply a communication with Christ.

Maximus' general understanding of Christ's inhabitation in the believer

When we turn to Maximus, this Evagrian perspective is quite absent. Maximus obviously emphasizes the idea of Christ's presence, birth and embodiment in the virtues in order to demonstrate that the work of human perfection has two sides. From one point of view it means restoration, integration, unification and deification; from another point of view it means divine inhabitation in human multiplicity. This double character is manifest almost everywhere when Maximus dwells on this theme, and the explanation can hardly be other than that Maximus' late Chalcedonian theology with its stress on *communicatio idiomatum* and *perichoresis* also brought him to the conviction that Incarnation and deification are two sides of the same mystery, as Dalmais has most

---

[563] Cf. RAHNER, *art. cit.*, p. 360.
[564] Cf. *ibid.*, p. 374, n. 30.
[565] See *Contra Eun.* 3, 7; JAEGER, 2, p. 236.
[566] See *In Cant. cant.*, hom. 3; JAEGER, 6, p. 90 f.
[567] Cf. DANIÉLOU, *Platonisme et théologie mystique*, p. 101.
[568] See *Mirror for Monks* 118–120; GRESSMAN, p. 163.

convincingly concluded.[569] Deification and Incarnation differ from each other in so far as deification is fulfilled only after death,[570] while Incarnation is established in a historical event, to which all other forms of incarnation have to be related, but it is Maximus' conviction that both are equally based on the fact that "God ever wills to become man in the worthy".[571]

Even in such an 'Evagrian' piece of writing as *Cent. gnost.* this double perspective, in combination with an emphasis on Christ's presence in the virtues, is clearly manifested. Thus Maximus affirms that the Logos "becomes thick" in the πρακτικός through the manners (τρόποι) of the virtues, and becomes flesh.[572] Obviously Maximus thinks not only of a human participation in divine virtues, but also of an active participation of Christ himself in the conditions of men, which allows for a close correspondence between the processes of divine incarnation and human deification.

Agents and forms of divine incarnation in the virtues of the believer

As a matter of fact, Maximus' doctrine about Christ's presence in the virtues of the believer is very detailed and goes very far. First of all, we learn that it is by the grace of *baptism* that Christ indwells in man, an element which belonged from the beginning to the Christian idea of a divine birth in man.[573] The idea of a birth is, secondly, related also to *faith*,[574] which, as we recall, is at the same time the basis of the hierarchy of virtues. Thus Maximus states that faith, which is originally born by the Logos, later itself becomes the mother of the Logos in man. The Logos is the son of faith in that He becomes incarnate out of faith by means of the virtues as they are practiced.[575] It is obviously as the source of virtues that faith is here presented as the mother of the Logos. But we notice at the same time that this presence of the Logos is regarded as an incarnation. We might add here that in another context Maximus emphasizes Christ's participation in human conditions still more by

---

[569] Cf. DALMAIS, *art.* Divinisation, II. Patristique grecque DSp 3 (1957), col. 1388.

[570] Cf. here DALMAIS, *loc. cit.* and SHERWOOD, *The Earlier Ambigua*, p. 135.

[571] Thal 22; CCSG 7, p. 143.

[572] Gnost 2. 37; PG 90, 1141 C.—A similar expression in Gregory Nazianzen, *Or.* 38, 2; PG 36, 313 B is commented upon by Maximus in Amb 33; PG 91, 1285 C–1288 A, though there the interpretation seems to be less fixed.

[573] Char 4. 73; CSC, p. 226. On the rôle of baptism at the beginning of this stream of thought, see RAHNER, *art. cit.*, pp. 339 ff. and 347 f.

[574] Cf. LOOSEN, *Logos und Pneuma*, p. 64.

[575] See Thal 40; CCSG 7, p. 273. See further my own later study *Man and the Cosmos*, pp. 108–112.

referring the symbolism of birth both to man and Christ: both Christians and the divine Logos are in this stage of life as in a mother's womb.[576]

We also learn however, that it is the *purification* from passions which prepares for the experience of an indwelling of Christ.[577] Here Maximus does not seem to advance much further than the position of Evagrius, and earlier in the same text Maximus says that purification by the commandments prepares for "the treasures of wisdom and knowledge" (he refers here to Eph. 3: 17 and Col. 2: 3), which are hidden in Christ who dwells in men's hearts by faith.[578] The reference is thus in the first place to an indwelling of Christ which belongs to the sphere of knowledge, since faith is to Maximus a knowledge about the existence of God as Cause which has to be perfected through the different stages of γνῶσις.[579] But the relationship between a keeping of the commandments and the indwelling of Christ is not only one of preparation to a 'gnostic' presence. The keeping of the commandments itself makes Christ to dwell in Christians.[580]

There is, in fact, according to Maximus a presence of the Logos in the believers through *both virtue and knowledge,*[581] and it would indeed be misleading to state that the former is of less importance than the latter. Maximus is always eager to stress the moral presence of God in a true believer, which he defines as a presence "according to well-being", i.e. a presence characteristic of man when he has used his free will to accept in obedience his relationship to God, the Cause of his being.[582]

Maximus in fact fully agrees with those of his predecessors who have affirmed a presence of Christ in the virtues, because the substance of all virtues is Christ.[583] And this is explicitly understood as *a divine incarnation in human virtuous living.*[584] There is, however, a clear link between this moral incarnation of Christ the Logos and the presence which is communicated through knowledge (γνῶσις) and contemplation by means of reason and intellect. For in the same sense as natural contemplation implies a communication, yes even a communion, with the Logos through the *logoi* of created things, which are all held together by the

---

[576] Amb 6; PG 91, 1068 A.
[577] Char 4. 76; CSC, p. 228.
[578] *Ibid.* 4. 70; p. 224.
[579] For this concept of faith, see Ep 2; PG 91, 393 C.
[580] See Asc 34; PG 90, 940 B.
[581] See Thal 62; CCSG 22, p. 135.
[582] See *ibid.* 61; CCSG 22, p. 105. cf. Amb 7; PG 91, 1084 B.
[583] See Amb 7; PG 91, 1081 D.
[584] See Amb, *Prol.;* PG 91, 1032 B; cf. Amb 10; 1145 B and the generalized systematic treatment of this topic in LOOSEN, *op. cit.,* pp. 65–74.

Logos, so also a keeping of the commandments means a communication with the Logos through the *logoi* of the commandments, i.e. through the differentiated presence of the divine Logos, who is in fact hidden in the commandments. It is thus this presence in the commandments which becomes an inhabitation of the Logos in those who are obedient and perform the works of the *vita practica*. In other words, those who keep the commandments communicate morally with the Logos, by developing virtues which are natural, since they imply a right relationship of these Christians to their own principle of nature (λόγος φύσεως).

This moral communication is closely linked with a knowledge of this principle. But the aspect of knowledge reaches still further, and therefore Maximus not only emphasizes the incarnation of Christ in the believer, but also at the same time stresses the elevation of the believer in γνῶσις to a final insight which is even higher than all commandments, an insight about the monadic source of the multiplicity of principles and rules, the One God himself.[585] As we can see, the moral aspect does not disappear at this higher stage of knowledge either, for it is God the Giver of the commandments who is contemplated.

At this point again we notice clearly the difference between Maximus and Evagrius. Moral perfection is for Maximus rather an aspect of human deification than merely a stage which has to be passed, before the mind may perform its higher contemplative functions. God is the source not only of being and ever-being but also of well-being, where the freedom of man's will plays such an important rôle.[586] And in this world, where the future state of blessedness is only fore-shadowed, not only the natural λόγοι but also the τρόποι of virtues serve as *types* of supernatural goods, through which God always freely becomes man in those who are worthy.[587]

And furthermore, on the other hand there is no Evagrian or Origenist confusion of moral and ontological orders involved, when Maximus speaks of a conformity with the divine object of contemplation which is established through γνῶσις.[588] The mind which in the end is joined with God in prayer and charity is said to contain all the divine attributes, but this statement obviously means that man reflects *morally* what God shows of himself. For according to Maximus God does not reveal even to

---

[585] See QuDub 142; CCSG 10, p. 101. Maximus understands this development as a movement from the different commandments to the affirmation of Deut. 6: 4: "The Lord our (Maximus: "thy") God is one Lord."

[586] See Amb 7; PG 91, 1084 BC.

[587] Thal 22; CCSG 7, p. 143; cf. SHERWOOD, *The Earlier Ambigua*, p. 134 f. and DALMAIS, *art. cit.,* col. 1388.

[588] Cf. SHERWOOD, in ACW, p. 261 f., n. 187.

the true "gnostic" what is really proper to him. The gnostic has to be content with His attributes.[589]

Deification implies in the end no ontological identification between God and man, but precisely a communication across the gulf which still separates creature and Creator, which on the part of God is an incarnation in human conditions, and on the part of man a development of natural capacities into a 'moral' reflection of the divine attributes, which is also a unification with God in virtue of divine charity and the desire of man's love.[590]

The aspect of reciprocity in relation to Christ's presence in human virtues

This view of the relationship between knowledge and virtue within the process of man's perfection and deification, leads, however, to a characteristic *reciprocity* which is noticeable everywhere in Maximus' writings; a reciprocity between the aspect of divine "economic" differentiation and Incarnation on the one hand, and human integration, unification and deification on the other. And this parallelism is of a particular interest in relation to the idea of Christ's incarnation in the virtues, for it shows how closely Christology and ascetic theology are integrated in Maximus' thinking.

We have seen that to Maximus Christ is present in the virtues of man's *vita practica*, and we have also seen that the human mind which is joined with God contains, in a moral sense, all the divine attributes. But in the light of the reciprocity which we have mentioned, we can go further and conclude that Maximus, consequently, regards *the divine attributes and the human virtues* (which we have found to be natural) *as corresponding to each other* in the same sense as Christ's Incarnation and man's deification correspond to each other. But this implies again that the relationship between the virtues, called forth by the divine commandments, and the revealed attributes of God in Maximus' thinking is patterned after the hypostatic relationship between divine and human in Christ.

And this is, finally, exactly what Maximus himself affirms in Ep 2, a piece of writing which is of a particular interest because it speaks much about human deification, even though it does not—probably because it is written for a man of the world—deal with 'gnostic' contemplation at all. There Maximus states explicitly that deifying love, which unites both God and man and individual human beings between themselves, allows

---

[589] See Char 2. 52; CSC, p. 118 as compared with 1. 100; p. 88.
[590] See further ch. VI: 10 and 11 below.

for a *reciprocal attribution* (ἀντίδοσις σχετική) between those who are united by it, i.e. a *communicatio* similar to that in Christ. And as in the case of Christ, this communication concerns precisely the individual attributes. Individual characteristics as well as their names, says Maximus, are thus made mutually useful. That is to say, that man acquires the divine attributes in relation to his own virtues (and, of course, also that gifts of grace and virtues are shared by Christians among themselves).

By this acquisition—which is of a moral character—man becomes god, and at the same time God, whose inner being is hidden for men, is called and appears as man. And Maximus goes on to quote Hosea 12: 10 (11),[591] which he interprets as meaning that *God in his great love conforms himself to everyone according to the amount of practical virtue which is found in everyone.* God is thus, as it were, differentiated according to human differentiations, which thereby gain their proper place and true meaning. God accepts likeness to men.[592] But this implies on the other hand, from the point of view of man, that man is at the same time deified, developing his *likeness* unto God, which is in Maximus always of a moral and volitional character.

The Christological convictions of Chalcedon and Constantinople about the character of the reciprocity which exists in Christ, are thus transferred to the level of virtues in such a way that human integration and unification, established through a right relationship to God as end, is maintained and confessed just in so far as human differentiation is also maintained, through an act of divine and human mutual appropriation.

It is not difficult to see, however, that it is this vision of the relationship between God and man in terms of the created world which is also expressed in Maximus' affirmation of man as microcosm. And only on this ground is it also possible for him to attribute to man a task of true mediation, as we shall see in our next and last chapter.

---

[591] In the *LXX* version the quotation reads: ἐν χερσὶν προφητῶν ὡμοιώθην.

[592] Ep 2; PG 91, 401 B.

CHAPTER SIX
Performing the Task of Mediation

In Chapter V we saw how Maximus' understanding of man as microcosm can easily be illustrated from the way in which he depicts the disintegrating work of the passions and vices as a misuse and the reintegrating work of the virtues as a corresponding good use of those psychic faculties which are a necessary part of the make-up of man as a composite being. We saw too how this view of man as microcosm is linked with an aspect of differentiation, which is negatively or positively evaluated according to the aim for which man uses his faculties. This differentiation in itself is a created quality which should be properly balanced in man by the opposite aspect of unity and unification, in the same way as the aspects of unity and differentiation in Christ are balanced against each other in the Christology of the councils of Chalcedon and Constantinople.

The microcosmic aspect, the aspect of differentiation, is, for this very reason, never isolated in Maximus' theology from the opposite aspect of mediation and unification. As microcosm man is called to be a mediator. His microcosmic character points towards a task of mediation which is the aim of his life, while his divine call to act as mediator presupposes his microcosmic differentiation. In this chapter we shall study Maximus' understanding of this task as it is related to the different stages of man's spiritual perfection, against the background of our insights from Chapter V.

Already in our short introductory section on man as "microcosm and mediator"[1] we indicated that this human task of mediation is nowhere else in Maximus' writings described so clearly and succinctly as in Amb 41, where Maximus speaks of a five-fold work of mediation which Christ has fulfilled on man's behalf, and which man now has to complete in imitation of him.[2] The five types of difference which are thus to be overcome, each in its appropriate way, are the following ones (here

---

[1] See ch. III: A, 5; pp. 133–143 above.
[2] See PG 91, 1304 D–1313 B.

presented in a chronological order): that between man and woman, Paradise and the inhabited world, heaven and earth, intelligible and sensible things and finally between created and uncreated nature. It seems clear even at first sight that these differences themselves are of differing character. Thus the first is caused by the fall and may be overcome on the strictly natural level through detachment, and the same is true of the second difference. The third is overcome through imitation of heavenly virtues and belongs to the sphere of "natural contempla- tion", while the fourth difference is likewise overcome through contem- plation, though this time of intelligible things. The fifth difference, finally, is overbridged only in mystical union with God. We can thus make a differentiation within this catalogue of dichotomies itself and this differentiation coincides to a great extent with the different stages of spiritual development. In performing his task of mediation man thus passes, in Maximus' opinion, from *vita practica* to *unio mystica*—an indication that Maximus regards *man's work of mediation as identical with his spiritual perfection.*

. We shall thus concentrate our attention in this chapter on the five types of mediation which Maximus presents in Amb 41 (and to some extent in Thal 48), and from there try to interpret the different aspects of his general understanding of man as mediator. But before we do this we shall study Maximus' systematic presentation of the different stages of spiritual development. And we shall conclude with a consideration of his concept of deification, which is so closely connected with all his thinking on the fulfilment of the purpose and true function of man as created in the image of God. In so doing we hope to be able to see how man's microcosmic character is an element of his differentiated created nature which is preserved to the end, even in the highest forms of communion with God.

1. A three-fold spiritual development

Maximus often divides Christian life into three stages or ways: what we should call *vita practica, vita contemplativa* and *vita mystica.* His terminology varies within this general scheme, but the three-fold pattern itself is fixed. It is obvious that he used this scheme primarily on account of the influence which Evagrius exerted on his understanding of the structure of spiritual life. There is a problem, however, as to how far this influence was decisive not only for Maximus' acceptance of the formal distinctions between the three stages, but also for his understanding of the stages themselves and their significance. Here again we should probably be right in seeing a modifying influence from other writers, particularly Gregory of Nyssa, since, as we shall find, there is in fact a considerable difference between Evagrius and Maximus at this latter point.

The three stages of spiritual life in Maximus' predecessors

A three-fold spiritual development—on the basis of a more general distinction between 'practical' and 'gnostic' activities—is in a very general sense presupposed among Christian writers as early as in Clement of Alexandria's reflections on man's spiritual functions:[3] first a life in struggle against the passions and for the acquisition of the virtues, then a contemplative life in *gnosis* and finally a true culmination of *gnosis* in a constant vision of God.[4] The first explicit Christian differentiation of this kind was, however, made by Origen, who differentiated between the three stages of *ethicum, physicum* and *enoptice* and differentiated between the books of Solomon accordingly, so that the *Book of Proverbs* was connected with the first stage, *Ecclesiastes* with the second and the *Song of Songs* with the third.[5]

Origen in his turn strongly influenced Gregory of Nyssa. Thus Gregory adopted Origen's interpretation of these three books of the Old Testament, and indeed his whole understanding of the development of Christian life may be subsumed under an analogous three-fold perspective.[6] This perspective includes three stages or aspects, named after the experience of Moses: the first is effected through *light* (διὰ φωτός), the second through the *cloud* (διὰ νεφέλης) and the third in *darkness* (ἐν γνόφῳ).[7] As in the case of the Alexandrian writers this three-fold differentiation is built on a more basic distinction between practical and

---

[3] On the general history of this differentiation in the ancient Church, cf. M. VILLER—K. RAHNER, *Askese und Mystik in der Väterzeit*, Freiburg i. Br. 1939, e.g. pp. 71, 76 f., 100 ff., 242, 271 and 276. For its background in Greek philosophy, cf. e.g. the clarifying article by G. PICHT, Der Sinn der Unterscheidung von Theorie und Praxis in der griechischen Philosophie, *Evangelische Ethik* 8 (1964), pp. 321–342, and also VON BALTHASAR, Die Hiera des Evagrius, ZkTh 63 (1939), p. 96.

[4] Cf. e.g. chapters 2–4 in VÖLKER, *Der wahre Gnostiker nach Clemens Alexandrinus*. Cf. also the important triad of παίδευσις, πρᾶξις and γνῶσις in Clement as applicable to the perfection of Christians; see VÖLKER, *op. cit.*, p. 220.

[5] See *Comm. in Cant. cant., Prol.*; GCS Orig. 8, p. 75, 6 ff.

[6] DANIÉLOU demonstrated this fact in his important monograph on Gregory, *Platonisme et théologie mystique*, Paris 1944.

[7] See *In Cant. cant., hom.* 1; JAEGER, 6, p. 18, and 11; p. 322 f.; cf. DANIÉLOU, *op. cit.*, the whole arrangement of which is made according to this three-fold differentiation.

contemplative life,[8] and the three stages refer to purification, contemplation and union respectively.

Thus for Gregory the first stage implies "separation", the contemplation of the second stage takes place "through the phenomena", while the final union of the third stage is a reality "outside of the phenomena".[9] However, Daniélou has noticed and strongly emphasized the fact that Gregory, being independent in his treatment of his Alexandrian predecessors, introduces an important change into the tradition, and substitutes for the chronological order of *vita practica* and *vita contemplativa* a *parallelism* of the three ways, each of which in fact includes a practical as well as a theoretical aspect. In this context Daniélou also underlines the striking fact that the third way, which implies union and is represented by charity (ἀγάπη), is defined in such a way that the practical aspect rather predominates in it.[10]

Among Maximus' predecessors the idea of the three stages is, however, most fully developed in Evagrius, whose systematization of the subject also had the greatest influence in relation to Maximus. Evagrius too builds on the foundation laid by Origen, but seems to have elaborated Origen's ideas considerably. He distinguishes between a stage of *vita practica* (πρακτική), a stage of natural contemplation (φυσική; cf. Origen) and, thirdly, a second form of higher contemplation (θεολογική).[11] The first stage consists of a keeping of the commandments,[12] and a development of practical virtues, symbolized by the flesh of Christ.[13] The second stage is sometimes simply called γνῶσις,[14] and consists of a contemplation and understanding of the nature of created things, symbolized by the blood of Christ.[15] The stage of "theology", finally, (simply called θεολογία)[16] consists of an understanding of the λόγοι concerning divine things and implies knowledge of God, symbolized by the heart of Christ.[17]

Maximus' use of the scheme of the three stages

Maximus starts from Evagrius—presupposing a more basic dual distinc-

---

[8] See *De vit. Moys.* 2.200; Daniélou, p. 96.
[9] Cf. Daniélou, *Platonisme*, p. 19 f.
[10] Cf. Daniélou, *op. cit.*, p. 22.
[11] See *Pract.* 1. 1; PG 40, 1221 D.
[12] See *Cent. gnost.* 1. 10; PO 28, p. 21.
[13] *Mirror for Monks* 118; Gressmann, p. 163.
[14] See *Pract., Prol.;* PG 40, 1221 C and *Pract.* 1. 56; 1233 C.
[15] See *Cent. gnost.* 1. 10; PO 28, p. 21 and *Mirror for Monks* 119; Gressmann, p. 163.
[16] See *Pract., Prol.;* PG 40, 1221 C and *Pract.* 1. 56; 1233 C.
[17] See *Cent. gnost.* 1. 10; *loc. cit.* and *Mirror for Monks* 120; *loc. cit.*

tion between "practical" and "theoretical" activity[18]—but elaborates the Evagrian systematization even further.[19] In the case of the third stage this elaboration seems, at least as far as the terminology is concerned, to be influenced by the language of Ps.-Denis.

Maximus, like Evagrius, calls the *first* stage πρακτική,[20] but more often πρᾶξις (*scil.* of the commandments or the virtues).[21] Most characteristic of him, however, is the fact that he uses more precise formulations. Thus he frequently calls the first stage πρακτική φιλοσοφία, an expression which indicates his high evaluation of the *vita practica*.[22] Its ethical implications and its connection with the development of virtues are also underlined in Maximus' systematic terminology itself. Thus it happens that sometimes he denotes it simply as ἀρετή,[23] or defines it as "ethical philosophy".[24]

Regarding *the second stage* we notice that Maximus follows Evagrius occasionally in calling it γνῶσις,[25] but usually he is more precise and defines it as "natural contemplation" (φυσική θεωρία)[26] or "natural philosophy" (φυσική φιλοσοφία),[27] or "gnostic contemplation" (θεωρία γνωστική)[28] or even—in its higher form—"spiritual contemplation", an indication that a true human contemplation even of the λόγοι of nature needs the aid of the Spirit.[29] However, we also meet the simple expression θεωρητική.[30]

In denoting *the third stage*, finally, Maximus shows the same tendency to be more precise than Evagrius, but seems to have been influenced by the terminology of Ps.-Denis, whose title μυστική θεολογία he uses as his favourite name for this stage. Thus we meet this last expression in

---

[18] Cf. LOOSEN, *Logos und Pneuma*, p. 9.

[19] For a systematic summary of Maximus' terminology, cf. LOOSEN, *op. cit.*, p. 8.

[20] See Char 2. 26; CSC, p. 102 and Gnost. 2. 96; PG 90, 1172 B.

[21] See Thal 25; CCSG 7, p. 159 and 55; CCSG 7, p. 509; cf. also Char 2. 90; CSC, p. 138 and Gnost 2. 51; PG 90, 1148 B.

[22] See Thal 3; CCSG 7, p. 55 and 10; CCSG 7, p. 83; Amb 20; PG 91, 1240 B; 37; 1293 B and 1296 B; 47; 1360 C and 50; 1369 C.

[23] See Thal 50; CCSG 7, p. 385 (in connection with the expression πρᾶξις τῶν ἀρετῶν and in contrast to γνῶσις) and Amb 10; PG 91, 1144 C (as a parallel to γνῶσις).

[24] See Amb 67; PG 91, 1401 D; cf. *ibid.;* 1397 C.

[25] See Thal 55; CCSG 7, p. 509.

[26] See Thal 25; CCSG 7, p. 161; Gnost 2. 96; PG 90, 1172 B; Amb 20; PG 91, 1240 B; 45; 1356 B; 47; 1360 C and 67; 1397 C.

[27] See Gnost 2. 96; PG 90, 1172 B; Amb 37; PG 91, 1293 B and 1296 B; 50; 1369 C and 67; 1401 D.

[28] *Scil.* τῆς φύσεως; see Amb 32; PG 91, 1285 A.

[29] See Char 3. 44; CSC, p. 164; Myst 2; PG 91, 669 C; Amb 10; PG 91, 1156 B and 51; 1372 B; cf. Amb 50, 1369 B.

[30] Char 2. 26; CSC, p. 102.

different contexts where Evagrius simply uses θεολογία.[31] We also find the parallel expression of θεολογικὴ μυσταγωγία,[32] and indeed other similar expressions such as θεολογικὴ φιλοσοφία[33] and θεολογικὴ σοφία.[34] Loosen finally adds at this point even expressions like θεολογικὴ χάρις[35] and "pure prayer" (καθαρὰ προσευχή), but in the last case we must notice that Maximus also reckons with a 'lower' form of pure prayer.[36]

Maximus thus follows Evagrius rather closely in his three-fold division of Christian life, though he elaborates his terminology, giving the names of the different elements a more precise form. But does he also follow him in regarding the elements as stages in a chronological order? Or does he rather understand them as parallel ways, where the "practical" and the "theoretical" aspects are kept together and are accorded a simultaneous importance, as we found, at least partly, to be the case in Gregory of Nyssa? From the conclusions which we have reached concerning Maximus' understanding of detachment and the relationship between love and the virtues, as well as the position of love as a whole,[37] we should be inclined to choose the latter alternative. In the scholarly discussion of this topic, however, different answers have been given. Thus Loosen regards the elements as "Stufen" in a chronological sense,[38] while Dalmais and Sherwood emphasize the fact that vita practica and vita contemplativa always go together.[39] A more precise answer can in fact be found, only if we study Maximus' own presentation of each element as well as their relationship to one another.

---

[31] See Thal 25; CCSG 7, p. 161 and 55; p. 509; Gnost 1. 39; PG 90, 1097 C; Myst 4; PG 91, 672 B; Amb 10; PG 91, 1149 B and 1168 A and 67; 1397 C. There are times, however, when Maximus also uses the Evagrian expression θεολογία, see Amb 71; PG 91, 1413 C.
[32] See Thal 40; CCSG 7, p. 269; Gnost 2. 96; PG 90, 1172 B; Amb 20; PG 91, 1241 C; 32; 1285 A and 50; 1369 B. However, notice also the expression θεωρητικὴ μυσταγωγία for all forms of contemplation, see Thal 3; CCSG 7, p. 55 and 52; p. 419.
[33] See Amb 37; PG 91, 1293 B and 1296 B and D; 50; 1369 C and 67; 1401 D.
[34] See Amb 20; PG 91, 1240 B.
[35] See Char 2. 26; CSC, p. 102.
[36] See Char 3. 44; CSC, p. 164; cf. LOOSEN, op. cit., p. 8 and n. 10, where he notices the two types of pure prayer.
[37] Cf. ch. V: B, 3–4; pp. 299–322 above.
[38] Cf. LOOSEN, op. cit., p. 7 ff.
[39] Cf. DALMAIS, La doctrine ascétique, Irénikon 26 (1953), p. 24, where the difference in relation to Evagrius is underlined, and SHERWOOD, in ACW, p. 87. At the 'stage' of θεολογία a corresponding problem reappears (cf. SHERWOOD, in ACW, p. 89): Evagrian introspection or Areopagite "ecstasy"? Here Evagrius represents a static aspect, while in the first case he represents a 'dynamic' aspect. In both cases however it is man's character of created unity which is at stake. We shall touch the second problem below in relation to our treatment of mystical union.

2. *Vita practica as the first element in the three-fold system*

For Evagrius this stage implies first of all purification from the passions which tyrannize over the soul, and the establishment of the equilibrium of detachment in it.[40] The beginning of the *vita practica* is faith and its end is love, which is at the same time the door to γνῶσις, the beginning of which is "natural contemplation".[41] This first stage is thus strictly distinguished from γνῶσις, which includes the *two* later stages of spiritual development. The reason for this is that the threefold distinction is based on a more fundamental dual distinction between practical and theoretical activities. The goal of the *vita practica* is thus to purify the mind from the passions, so that it may turn its attention to contemplation and to the divine realities.[42]

This, however, does not imply that only the passible parts of the soul are involved. Even in the *vita practica* man makes some use of his rational faculty. Thus he needs rational discernment in his fight against the passions,[43] and is already positively related to the very λόγοι of things, so that consequently his virtues should be combined with knowledge.[44] In principle, however, the Evagrian position seems clear: the *vita practica* is a stage of *preparation*, which is intended to set the mind free for its higher activities.[45]

In Maximus the preparatory character of this stage is also to some extent emphasized. As in Evagrius—but also as in the wider tradition to which he adheres—the *vita practica* is regarded as a prerequisite for true knowledge.[46] For Maximus too it means primarily a conquest of the passions.[47] It elevates man above them, just as in a similar sense true knowledge elevates him above all creatures.[48] It implies a purification

---

[40] See e.g. *Pract., Prol.;* PG 40, 1221 BC and *Mirror for Monks* 118; Gressmann, p. 163.

[41] *Pract.* 1. 56; PG 40; 1233 C and *ibid., Prol.;* 1221 C.

[42] See *Liber gnost.* 151; Frankenberg, p. 553.

[43] See *Cent. gnost.* 5. 65; PO 28, p. 205.

[44] See *Liber gnost.* 104; Frankenberg, p. 547 and 132; p. 551.

[45] In an isolated passage, known only in Latin, Evagrius says that action and contemplation, virtue and *gnosis* should be strongly kept together, see PG 40, 1278 A. But the authenticity of this text may be doubted; cf. von Balthasar, KL[2], p. 338 f., n. 2.

[46] See e.g. Gnost 1. 20; PG 90, 1092 A; cf. von Balthasar, KL[2], p. 574, who compares this text with Gregory Nazianzen's statement that πρᾶξις is a ladder to θεωρία, see *Or.* 4, 113; PG 35, 649 B–652 A and *Or.* 20, 12; 1080 B. Gregory regards the *vita practica* as of a lower spiritual stage than contemplation, but at the same time sees them as deeply interrelated. The similarity between Gregory and Maximus at this last point is emphasized in Plagnieux, *Saint Grégoire de Nazianze Théologien,* p. 362.

[47] Thal 51; CCSG 7, p. 403.

[48] *Ibid.;* p. 407.

from passions which corresponds to the purification from false notions which is effected by contemplation.[49]

But the *vita practica* in Maximus is never restricted to a fight against the passions, or to the establishment of an equilibrium in the soul.[50] It always implies an acquisition of positive virtues as well, virtues which actively express the two aspects of the commandment of love, and it is in this perspective that the multiform functions of the *vita practica* are regarded as an incarnation of Christ.[51] This last fact seems thus to preclude any exclusively low estimation of the first stage.[52] However, the problem is more complicated than it seems and the question of Maximus' relationship to Evagrius at this point is not to be solved simply by this affirmation.

Even Evagrius describes the "practical virtues" as the "fleshes of Christ", which shows that he uses at least the symbolism of incarnation in this context.[53] Maximus, for his part, sometimes presents the idea of an incarnation in the virtues in such a way as to show that it can include a negative perspective. For it is Maximus' conviction that human nature is purified—on the earthly level, as it were—through "practical philosophy", while the mind is elevated towards God through contemplative understanding.[54] He thus necessarily comes to the conclusion in *Cent. gnost.*, that he who lives in the *vita practica* certainly receives an incarnation of the Logos in his virtues, but that in this incarnation the Logos is, as it were, kept in the flesh, while the "gnostic" through his contemplation of divine things allows him to return to his Father.[55] Taken in isolation from the rest of Maximus' thinking, this view-point must be considered to be thoroughly Evagrian, and to show a rather negative evaluation of the *vita practica* as such[56]—particularly since it leads to an explicit warning against allowing the *vita practica* to continue too long, and in this way to become identified with legalism.[57] All these statements however need to be understood in a wider context of Maximian thinking.

---

[49] Thal 52; CCSG 7, p. 419; cf. 53; p. 435.
[50] Cf. ch. V: B, 3; pp. 304–309 above.
[51] Cf. ch. V: B, 4–5; pp. 309–330 above.
[52] Cf. however Loosen, *Logos und Pneuma*, p. 33, where the qualitative difference between the first and the second stages is clearly emphasized.
[53] Cf. pp. 325 and 334 above.
[54] See e.g. Thal 3; CCSG 7, p. 55.
[55] See Gnost 2. 47; PG 90, 1145 B and 2. 94; 1169 B.
[56] Cf. von Balthasar, KL[2], p. 553 f., who says that Maximus' view here resembles the Evagrian position "auf bedenkliche Weise", but stresses that it must be understood in the whole context of Maximus' thinking.
[57] Gnost 2. 41–42; PG 90, 1144 BC.

This wider orientation could easily start from Maximus' conviction —which certainly we found to some extent even in Evagrius—that the *vita practica* includes a good use of the rational faculty. In Maximus this conviction is not limited, in the way in which it seems to be in Evagrius. His very term "practical *philosophy*" indicates this fact, and in Chapter V we have already given examples to show that the virtues represent in Maximus' opinion a good use of all *three* faculties of the human soul.[58] On several occasions Maximus shows, in fact, that he regards the virtuous life of a Christian as a manifestation, not only of his victory over the passions and of the peace which reigns in the passible part of his soul, but also of his *reasonable* nature as such. The activities of the 'practical' soul are related to the function of the reasonable element (λόγος), while the 'contemplative' activity functions through the mind (νοῦς). The former leads to prudence (φρόνησις), the latter to wisdom (σοφία). The range of practical reason is thus according to Maximus rather wide, including not only reason itself but also prudence, "practice", virtue and faith, while the range of contemplative intelligence covers the fields of mind, wisdom, contemplation, knowledge and incorruptible knowledge. The end of the former is *goodness* and of the latter *truth,* and *both* these reveal God.[59] Thus *vita practica* and *vita contemplativa* are by necessity deeply interrelated and cannot be separated from each other, since both refer in the end to divine qualities, and both are related to the fact that man is a reasonable being.

Πρᾶξις and θεωρία—separated and yet united by one common purpose of human life

This idea of a deep and far-reaching relatedness between the "practical" and "theoretical" functions of Christian life is, in fact, predominant in Maximus' writings. And it is related to the whole process of Christian perfection, precisely because it is based both on the view of man as a created unity, and on the conviction that there is a correspondence between man's natural virtues and the qualities of God. Maximus thus affirms the "*syzygy*" (i.e. the synthesis without change or violation) of mind and reason, and consequently of wisdom and prudence, contemplation and "practice", knowledge and virtue, incorruptible knowledge and faith, in that he relates them all to that pair of divine qualities which are Truth and Goodness.[60] And this parallelism between truth and

---

[58] Cf. ch. V: B, 4; pp. 315–317 above.
[59] See Myst 5; PG 91, 673 C.
[60] *Ibid.;* 676 A.

goodness in man is linked not only with the interrelated activities of *vita practica* and *vita contemplativa,* but also with man as created according to both the *image* and the *likeness* of God, for the image of God in man is linked with the mind and is often related to God as Truth, and the likeness of God in man, which is developed by him in free acceptance of the will of God, is linked with the freedom of his reasonable nature and is related to God as Goodness.[61]

Thus the problem of 'higher' and 'lower' proves in the end to be irrelevant here. Again the principle of differentiation works well together with the principle of unity. The *vita practica* and the *vita contemplativa* are indeed kept apart, and yet deeply and indissolubly united, and this fact leads to a rather high estimate of the value of the former, and excludes the idea that it is *merely* a stage of preparation.

This principle of Maximus is perhaps nowhere so well illustrated as in his interpretation of *Luke 22: 8–12* in Thal 3. The text describes how Jesus sent Peter and John to prepare for the Last Supper, telling them that they were to meet a man carrying a pitcher of water, and should follow him into the house where they should ask the steward to show them a room for the meal. Maximus interprets this text in a very characteristic way. He says that Peter symbolizes the *vita practica* and John contemplation.[62] The man who carries the water is interpreted as those who carry the grace of God according to "practical philosophy" in the arms of their virtues.[63] The house is the *habitus* of true piety (εὐσέβεια), to which "the practical mind" thus comes with its virtues. The steward is the 'theoretical' mind which, having this virtue as its own by nature, is illuminated by the divine light of mystical knowledge.[64] The paschal lamb, finally, which is to be brought into this house and is to feed those who have gathered in it, is the Logos.[65]

Here we notice clearly that the two kinds of function go together, though the contemplative function is the higher, since it concerns the divine light of mystical knowledge, while the "practical mind" carries the virtues which are natural to man. It is further the mind—here depicted as the spiritual subject of man—which is said to be active in *both* cases, and it is clearly stated that it is only as far as it possesses its natural virtue that it is illuminated. We can also notice that the fact that the virtues are

---

[61] See ThPol 1; PG 91, 12 A; cf. Sherwood, in ACW, p. 98. Cf. however also ch. III: A, 4, "Additional note", p. 129 ff. above, where we noticed a number of variations on a similar theme: human reflections of the Holy Trinity.

[62] Thal 3; CCSG 7, p. 55. Cf. Blowers, *op.cit.,* p. 134 f. and p. 174, n. 173.

[63] *Loc. cit.*

[64] *Ibid.;* p. 57.

[65] *Ibid.;* p. 59.

regarded as natural, does not exclude a stress on the function of divine grace in relation to them. Finally, the presence of the Logos—to be consumed—is granted only in a house which has thus been prepared by both. Consequently, Maximus concludes that the one who carries the pitcher and the steward of the house are both two different persons and also one and the same. As πρακτικός and γνωστικός they are separate, but in view of their common nature they are one.[66] Thus the functions of both *vita practica* and *vita contemplativa* are rooted in human nature, and both are rewarded with the presence of the Logos.

This dual element could also be illustrated from a number of other texts, which all have in common the fact that they stress the mutual relationship between practice and contemplation, virtue and knowledge. Dalmais has called attention to three such passages.[67] In the first of them Maximus emphasizes that he who seeks the Lord through contemplation, seeks him "in the fear of the Lord", which is to say that he seeks him in practising the commandments. Otherwise he will not find Him.[68] And in the third text he demonstrates how πρᾶξις and contemplation ought always to be united.[69] It is in the second passage, however, that Maximus gives the most explicit formulation of the interrelation of the two functions. There he says that in a true Christian life the *vita practica* should be made into a *contemplation in action*, and contemplation into *mystagogical practice*, and thus that virtue should be the revelation of γνῶσις, and γνῶσις be the power which maintains virtue.[70] The aspects of knowledge and virtuous activity are thus according to Maximus intimately connected in the life of a Christian.[71] This connection not only implies that they are both important, and that one cannot be isolated from the other, or substituted for the other. It also implies that they support each other in their own functions, and thus condition the perfection of each other, though this perfection— as in the Alexandrian tradition—is considered to start on the basis of faith with the *vita practica*, and to continue through contemplation which is related to the wisdom of God and which leads us into a union with Him, which is beyond all knowledge and all merely human effort.

It is in full harmony with this view that Maximus underlines the reciprocity of *vita practica* and contemplation, of virtue and knowledge,

---

[66] *Ibid.;* p. 57.
[67] Cf. DALMAIS, *art. cit.,* p. 24 f.
[68] Thal 48; CCSG 7, p. 339.
[69] Amb 10; PG 91, 1108 AB.
[70] Thal 63; CCSG 22, p. 171.
[71] Cf. Thal, *Prol.;* CCSG 7, p. 23.

with regard to its bad effects as well as to its good. The attacks of the evil powers are directed against both,[72] and when the mind is stained for some reason, this fact effects both practice and contemplation.[73] Thus victory and wisdom, virtue and knowledge, and goodness and truth are interrelated in the same way as practice and contemplation.[74] It is true that particularly in *Cent. gnost.* Maximus affirms a difference between them, in a way which is very similar to that of Evagrius. We have already seen examples of this affirmation, and we may here add another one, which is also basically Evagrian: the man of *vita practica* glorifies God in his virtues, but he who has reached the state of detachment and lives in contemplation, is himself glorified by God's grace.[75] But this differentiating idea—which has its root in Philo and was developed by Origen before being taken over by Evagrius[76]—does not exclude the intimate relationship between the two functions which Maximus affirms elsewhere, since Maximus speaks of a *mutual glorification* of God and man, and thus in his own way modifies the tradition which he has received from Origen and Evagrius.[77]

To Maximus it is obviously the *interplay* between the two aspects which is of a particular importance, since the grace of God is in his opinion necessary even for "natural contemplation"[78]—and most important, also for a life of virtue.[79] The 'synergistic' aspect predominates in his view of the whole of Christian perfection over the Evagrian interest in sharp categories of differentiation. Maximus is therefore prepared to call the relationship between virtue and knowledge one of "identity" ($\tau\alpha\upsilon\tau\acuteo\tau\eta\varsigma$)—a term which denotes an intimate unity without violation of its parts, a 'synthetic' unity.[80]

Thus however strong Maximus' expressions of a differentiation between the stages of *vita practica* and *vita contemplativa* are in a piece of writing such as *Cent. gnost.*, in the end they only confirm the fact that the general Maximian principle of differentiation and unity as mutually dependent, is also applicable to the relationship between the different 'stages' of Christian life. And this gives the *vita practica* a far more

---

[72] Thal 50; CCSG 7, p. 387.
[73] See Thal 52; CCSG 7, p. 423 ff.
[74] See Thal 54; CCSG 7, p. 447.
[75] See Gnost 2. 72; PG 90, 1157 A; cf. the same idea of detached $\gamma\nu\tilde{\omega}\sigma\iota\varsigma$ as a reward for the efforts of a virtuous life, in 1. 17; 1089 AB.
[76] Cf. von Balthasar, KL², p. 517.
[77] Cf. von Balthasar, KL², p. 569.
[78] Cf. *op. cit.*, p. 517.
[79] Cf. Loosen, *op. cit.*, p. 22 with n. 20.
[80] Cf. von Balthasar, KL², p. 231 and ch. I: A; p. 36 above.

important rôle in Maximus' thinking than it ever had in Evagrius. As the first element in the three-fold system it is decisive also for the rest of them.

3. *The second element—contemplation of the nature of things*

Man's capacity for contemplation plays an important rôle in all early Christian theology, though the dangers and difficulties of some forms of contemplation are not ignored. The importance attributed to contemplation (θεωρία) is primarily of a Platonic inspiration. Plato saw the world of ideas as the object of contemplation and the νοῦς as its human organ.[81] Exclusively related to that which is intelligible, to him it implied a union between the soul and the idea,[82] giving the ultimate explanation of the world[83] and a view of Being.[84] In later Platonism this understanding was converted into a slightly less intellectual concept, with a greater stress on purification as a necessary preparation, and on its own particular character as supreme "vision".[85] In Philo and a number of Christian writers both these views seem to be represented. The second element in our three-fold system of spiritual perfection, however, with which we are dealing here, only concerns the lower part of contemplation, that is to say that kind of contemplation which is related to the created world, contemplated in its λόγοι, and which is thus usually called "natural contemplation" (θεωρία φυσική).[86]

The idea of "natural contemplation" in this sense, i.e. a (lower) contemplation of the very nature of things through their λόγοι, goes back among Christian thinkers to Clement of Alexandria, who uses the expression θεωρία φυσική.[87] It was further developed by Origen, who

---

[81] Cf. ARNOU, *art.* La Contemplation chez les anciens philosophes du monde gréco-romain, DSp 2, col. 1721.

[82] Cf. FESTUGIÈRE, *Contemplation et vie contemplative selon Platon*, pp. 85 and 89 ff.

[83] Cf. FESTUGIÈRE, *op. cit.*, p. 93 ff.

[84] *Ibid.*, p. 88.

[85] This type of understanding is most elaborated in Plotinus, cf. ARNOU, *art. cit.*, coll. 1728–31.

[86] It should be noted here that Evagrius draws a distinction not only between *vita practica* on the one hand and *all* forms of contemplation on the other, but also between a higher and a lower form of contemplation, the first type being concerned with the Holy Trinity and the second (which is itself further differentiated) identical with θεωρία φυσική; see *Cent. gnost.* 3. 41; PO 28, p. 115 and *Ep.* 58; FRANKENBERG, p. 607; cf. *Cent. gnost.* 2. 16; PO 28, p. 67.

[87] See *Strom.* 1.1; GCS Clem. 2, p. 11, 16 f. and 2.2; p. 115, 13; cf. VÖLKER, *Der wahre Gnostiker*, pp. 316–320.—Miss Hilda GRAEF, Oxford, kindly provided me with valuable references related to the concept of θεωρία from her notes for the Oxford Patristic Greek Lexicon. See now F. L. CROSS, *A Patristic Greek Lexicon*, p. 648 f.

uses the terms φυσική, θεωρία τῶν νοητῶν and κατανόησις τῶν νοητῶν as equivalents,[88] and still more by Gregory of Nyssa, for whom the reality which in later writers like Evagrius and Maximus is expressed by the term θεωρία φυσική is a most important element in Christian life, though he himself does not use the actual expression.[89]

Gregory speaks about a θεωρία τῶν ὄντων in general, i.e. a contemplation of the world from above,[90] and a θεωρία τῶν νοητῶν, i.e. a contemplation of the intelligible world in a Platonic sense which takes place when man through purification accepts the "night of the senses".[91] Starting from the nature around us and arriving at a higher knowledge of divine things, it depends all the time on the Holy Spirit.[92] This contemplation and the knowledge to which it leads are 'natural', since they are concerned with the real nature of things, and are at the same time a part of θεολογία since this nature points to the divine purpose for the things.[93] Contemplation even leads to a knowledge of God himself, though it is inferior to the mystical experience of the third stage.[94] It is against this background that Evagrius' reflections on contemplation in general and "natural contemplation" in particular are also to be understood.[95]

The concept of contemplation in Evagrius

Evagrius distinguishes not only between a lower and a higher type of contemplation (the latter of the Holy Trinity); within the former he

---

[88] See *Comm. in Cant. cant., Prol.;* GCS Orig. 8, p. 75, 8; *Contr. Cels.* 3. 56; 1, p. 251, 14 and *Comm. in Io.* 10, 40; 4, p. 218, 8. Cf. the more general term γνῶσις τῶν ὄντων, *Comm. in Matth.* 12, 15; 10, p. 104, 29 f. On the expression ἡ τῶν ὄντων θεωρία, cf. VÖLKER, *Das Vollkommenheitsideal des Origenes* (BHTh 7), Tübingen 1931, p. 93.

[89] Cf. VÖLKER, *Gregor von Nyssa*, p. 147.

[90] Cf. DANIÉLOU, *Platonisme et théologie mystique*, p. 149.

[91] See e.g. *De vit. Moys.* 2. 154–157; DANIÉLOU, p. 78 f. Cf. DANIÉLOU, *Platonisme et théologie mystique*, p. 135.

[92] Cf. VÖLKER, *Gregor von Nyssa*, p. 175 ff.

[93] Cf. DANIÉLOU, *op. cit.*, pp. 136 and 149.

[94] The θεωρία of the second 'stage' is contrary both to the senses and to the world of the divine nature itself, see *In Cant. cant., hom.* 6; JAEGER, 6, p. 177 f.; cf. ARNOU, *art. cit.*, col. 1773 f.

[95] It should be noted here that a speculation similar to that of Gregory of Nyssa is also found in the other Cappadocian Fathers, though in a far more restricted form. Thus Gregory Nazianzen differentiates between *vita practica* including purification and a θεωρία which leads in the end to θεολογία (see e.g. *Or.* 39, 8; PG 36, 344 A and *Carm.* 1. 2, 33; PG 37, 928; cf. PLAGNIEUX, *op. cit.*, pp. 108 ff. and 289), and Basil likewise probably reckons with a contemplative function exerted on the basis of an active life of purification (cf. Ps.-Basil [?], *Const. asc.* 2, 2; PG 31, 1341 A and 1, 1; 1328 B), though the form of natural contemplation which he develops on Scriptural grounds in his commentary on the divine act of creation, deals first of all with the richness and manifoldness of the visible world to the glory of God the Creator and marvels at its beauty (cf. TH. ŠPIDLÍK, *Sophiologie de Saint Basile*, p. 225 ff.).

also differentiates between four degrees or forms of it. Together they form the well-known Evagrian concept of *the five θεωρίαι* or five types of knowledge. Of these types of contemplation however two are concerned with the history of the world (linked directly with the Origenist myth of creation and fall), i.e. those which are related to God's providence and judgment,[96] and only two of them can normally be called "natural contemplation" in a more strict sense. These two are distinguished in that one is related to visible and corporeal beings and one to invisible and incorporeal beings,[97] and the gnostic is supposed to climb from the lower to the higher of these forms.

Thus Evagrius makes clear that there is a scale of contemplations, and that the mind has to advance from the lower to the higher. During this process it becomes itself more and more purified and in the end leaves behind all its bodily and sensual connections, not only its imaginations but also its concepts and notions. Men and other rational beings should indeed feed on contemplation of the sensible world,[98] but the mind should continue its ascent further through the different forms of contemplation.

The stage of θεωρία in general occupies a middle position between *vita practica* and θεολογία, but includes itself a considerable development from lower to higher. Material knowledge may become immaterial, Evagrius affirms.[99] Consequently, the mind has to advance from contemplation of *corporeal* or sensible beings, in which it is still assisted by the body and which is multiform, to contemplation of *incorporeal* beings, which is of a material character but requires a naked mind—in order that it may finally arrive at a *knowledge of the Holy Trinity,* which not only requires a naked mind but is also immaterial.[100] Only this highest form of knowledge, however, is quite undifferentiated. Therefore, though the contemplation of intelligible beings is higher than that of corporeal

---

[96] Cf. ch. II, 3; pp. 66–72 above.

[97] See e.g. *Cent. gnost.* 1. 27; PO 28, p. 29; *Mirror for Monks* 135–136; GRESSMANN, p. 165 and *Ep.* 7; FRANKENBERG, p. 571; cf. *Cent. gnost.* 1. 75; PO 28, p. 53 and *Mirror for Monks* 110; GRESSMANN, p. 162. Cf., however, also *Cent. gnost.* 1. 70; BNJ 5 (1926/27), p. 413, where Evagrius draws a three-fold distinction between a contemplation of intelligible and incorporeal beings and of aeons.—The idea of five θεωρίαι is found even in *Sel. in Psalm.*, attributed to Origen, and was for this reason supposed by Bousset to be an expression of Origen's influence on Evagrius (see BOUSSET, *Apophthegmata*, p. 311 f.; cf. also VILLER, RAM 11, 1930, p. 244, n. 130), but VON BALTHASAR, ZkTh 63 (1939) proved later these passages to be by Evagrius himself.

[98] See *Cent. gnost.* 2. 88; PO 28, p. 95.

[99] *Cent. gnost.* 2. 63; PO 28, p. 85.

[100] See *Cent. gnost.* 3. 19 and 21; PO 28, p. 105.

nature,[101] both of which take place in the second stage of spiritual development, even the former is lower than the supreme knowledge of the third stage, since both are still manifold.[102] All forms of human contemplation are in fact differentiated, though supernatural things are not differentiated like the contemplation of them.[103]

This process of ascent implies to Evagrius—who sees it in the perspective of his Origenist understanding of creation and fall—a return of the mind to its original state of being. Therefore, the supreme knowledge of the Holy Trinity is not called the last or the ultimate, but the *first* type of knowledge, while "natural contemplation" is the *second* form—or the *third* form, in as far as it concerns corporeal beings.[104] The 'gnostic' thus passes from "the second contemplation" to "the first contemplation", in order to arrive at a knowledge of the Godhead.[105] Consequently, the order of the different stages of spiritual development in the life of a Christian is clearly marked as the reverse of the order of man's original fall and degradation.[106] Stripped of all sensual impulses, the mind returns stage by stage to its original existence. And for this reason, it is also quite clear that it is *a real assimilation of the mind* which gradually takes place.

Contemplation of corporeal and incorporeal beings is, in Evagrius' interpretation, "the Book of God", in which the mind is inscribed through its knowledge.[107] This statement need not necessarily be interpreted with a view to the Origenist myth, but when taken together with other statements of a similar kind, it would seem to suggest that in the end the Evagrian concept of contemplation can in itself hardly be distinguished from the context of Origenist thinking—and in this sense it has been widely influential.[108] The mind, which is divine, returns through the process of contemplation to its home, origin and original function, and thereby the circular movement from fall and second

---

[101] See e.g. *Cent. gnost.* 1. 74; PO 28, p. 53.

[102] *De orat.* 57; PG 79, 1180 A.

[103] See *Cap. cognosc.* in *Par. Gr.* 913; Mus 44 (1931), p. 375 f., no. 18.

[104] See *Cent. gnost.* 1. 27; PO 28, p. 29; 1. 74; p. 53 and 3. 19 and 21; p. 105; cf. LEMAÎTRE, Contemplation. Theoria physikè, DSp 2, col. 1824 f.

[105] See *Cent. gnost.* 3. 61; PO 28, p. 123.

[106] See e.g. *Cent. gnost.* 2. 4; PO 28, p. 63. Notice in this context also Evagrius' statement that light bodies are *before* heavy bodies (*Cent. gnost.* 2. 72; PO 28, p. 89).

[107] *Sel. in Ps.* 138. 16; PG 12, 1661 C.

[108] The term *teōria*, which is frequently found in Syriac mystical literature as a technical term for mystical seeing, seems thus to have been borrowed from Evagrius, as we are reminded in G. WIDENGREN, Researches in Syrian mysticism. Mystical experiences and spiritual exercises, *Numen* 8 (1961), p. 172 ff., where the author also gives many examples from Syrian writers of a later time of the Origenist idea of a complete assimilation of the mind into its object (see p. 191 ff.).

creation and through purification to perfect knowledge of the divine unity is completed.[109]

Maximus and the Evagrian understanding of contemplation

Maximus' understanding of this second "stage" of spiritual development is certainly influenced by Evagrius' presentation of man's contemplative capacities, not only in the terminological field but also with regard to the definitions and descriptions themselves. But how deep is this influence? Since we have found that Evagrius' concept of contemplation is closely linked with his Origenist standpoint, we should expect that after all it is limited; unless we assume that here is a point where Maximus, in fact, went through an Origenist crisis of the kind which von Balthasar at one time suggested.[110]

The points of similarity between Evagrius and Maximus are obvious. Viller emphasized strongly the almost identical expressions and ways of thinking which he noticed in this field, and he particularly underlined the fact that Maximus shares the Evagrian concept of *the five contemplations* (though he thought of the latter as originated by Origen).[111] This point of dependence is indeed striking, and not less so since we now know that this concept is of Evagrian origin. In *Cent. de char.* it is presupposed in several instances and in 1.78 it is explicitly stated. A comparison between that passage and Evagrius' *Cent. gnost.* 1.27 leaves no doubt about the dependence of the one on the other.[112] So far we are thus still at the position of Viller, who could see no differences at all between the two writers. But from there we must go further, and we can do so precisely at this text where the dependence is least debatable, since there are differences even here.

A closer comparison between Char 1.78 and Evagrius' *Cent. gnost.* 1. 27 shows that there are at least three differences which seem to be of interest in our context. First of all, Evagrius speaks of five "knowledges", but Maximus of five δόγματα. This change might imply an escape from

---

[109] Cf. LEMAÎTRE, *art. cit.,* col. 1824 f.

[110] Cf. our Introduction above, p. 11.—It should be noted in this context that as far as the θεωρία φυσική is concerned, Maximus is less than usually subject to a balancing influence from Ps.-Denis, since the term θεωρία in the writings of the Areopagite usually concerns either sacraments and rites or biblical symbolism, but does not refer to "natural contemplation" in the Evagrian sense. His general understanding of the objects of θεωρία as symbols (see below) is, however, of Dionysian inspiration. On Ps.-Denis' use of the term θεωρία cf. J. LEMAÎTRE—R. ROQUES—M. VILLER, Contemplation chez les Grecs, 1. Étude de vocabulaire, DSp 2, col. 1785.

[111] VILLER, Aux sources de la spiritualité de Saint Maxime, RAM 11 (1930), p. 243 ff.

[112] See Char 1. 78; CSC, p. 80 and Evagrius, *Cent. gnost.* 1. 27; PO 28, p. 29; cf. VILLER, *art. cit.,* p. 244.

the idea that human contemplation lies altogether in the field of ontological relationships. Secondly, there is an inversion of order between those contemplations which Evagrius calls the second and the third. Evagrius mentions incorporeal beings before corporeal beings—in accordance with his idea of a pre-existent fall—while Maximus speaks of "visible and invisible beings". It seems at least likely that Maximus made this change of order because he wanted to avoid the Evagrian connections with the Origenist myth. Thirdly, a corresponding change of order is found in relation to the fourth and fifth contemplations in the Evagrian system, i.e. between those related to judgment and providence. At this point we know that the Evagrian order is directly linked with an Origenist view of judgment as referring to the second creation, and providence to the restitution of an original spiritual unity; this is a view which Maximus explicitly rejects in other texts.[113] Thus all these differences point towards the conclusion that the influence of Evagrius has been considerably modified—at exactly those points where Evagrius' assertion of the five contemplations is undistinguishable from his Origenism. It is only where this connection is not immediately in evidence that Maximus preserves the Evagrian teaching.

This is particularly true in the case of "natural contemplation" in a stricter sense. Here also Maximus prefers in fact to work with triads.[114] Thus he sometimes mentions only one type of contemplation, that of created beings, and in order to form a triad combines this with purification as its preparation and knowledge of the Trinity as its finality.[115] Or else he leaves out the aspects of providence and judgment —which present him with peculiar problems—and forms a triad which includes two kinds of "natural contemplations", i.e. contemplation of visible creation and knowledge of invisible creation, to which is added the highest form of knowledge, that of the Holy Trinity.[116] In both these cases the elements of spiritual development are clearly presented as successive stages.

· This fact, however, does not imply that all Christians have to pass through the same stages. There is in Maximus' opinion a deification which takes place through love also on the pure basis of the *vita*

---

[113] Cf. ch. II, 3; pp. 66–72 above.

[114] Cf., however, a five-fold scheme of natural contemplations, different from the Evagrian concept, though related to it, in Amb 10; PG 91, 1133 A–1137 C (cf. reference to it in Amb 67; PG 91, 1397 C): of substance, motion, difference, mixture and position. On the interpretation of this text and the refutation of Evagrian Origenism which it contains, cf. SHERWOOD, *The Earlier Ambigua*, p. 36 f. and 144 ff.

[115] See e.g. Char 1. 86; CSC, p. 82; cf. Evagrius, *Cent. gnost.* 1. 74; PO 28, p. 53.

[116] See Char. 1. 94; CSC, p. 86; cf. 1. 97; *loc. cit.*

practica.[117] Ep 2, which since it is written to a layman hardly ever deals with "natural contemplation", but which contains many statements both about deification and union with God, proves this position, as also does *Liber asceticus.* Only that kind of contemplation which is pure prayer is necessary for both the "gnostic" and the πρακτικός.[118] But "pure prayer" is one of the terms by which Maximus denotes the *third* element in this three-fold system of spiritual development.[119] Thus there seems, in fact, to be a way of *two stages* for the man of the world and of *three stages* for contemplative monks, for the former, as well as some non-contemplative monks, may arrive at pure prayer and union with God without contemplation, while the 'gnostic' cannot do away with the *vita practica,* since this is a necessary preparation for his contemplation.

This division between two types of ways to perfection is probably made possible by two factors: on the one hand by Maximus' stress on the part played by the rational functions within the *vita practica,* and by his conviction that the keeping of the commandments involves a communication with the Logos through the λόγοι of these commandments, and the incarnation of Christ in the virtues, on the one hand, and on the other by his very sharp distinction between contemplation in general and the stage of θεολογία.[120] At these points however, Maximus is rather far from Evagrius. Evagrius would hardly accept a union with God without natural contemplation, since his main stress lies on this point of contemplation, for which the *vita practica* is merely a preparation and of which union with God is a natural outcome. Consequently, Maximus disagrees with Evagrius with regard to the evaluation of the *vita practica* in connection with the life of contemplation, and yet is free to agree with him in his description of "natural contemplation", provided that the latter is a limited experience.

The purpose and function of "natural contemplation"

What then for Maximus is the purpose of "natural contemplation" and how does it work? First of all, it is given as a gift of grace to fallen man, and is inseparable from Scriptural interpretation. In fact, contemplation of the meaning of Scripture is, in the whole tradition to which Maximus

---

[117] Cf. ch. V: B, 5; pp. 325–329 above.
[118] Cf. also SHERWOOD, in ACW, p. 87 f., who emphasizes this fact very strongly.
[119] Cf. LOOSEN, *Logos und Pneuma,* p. 8.
[120] On this last distinction, see further below. Cf. SHERWOOD, in ACW, p. 88 ff., who underlines this distinction with great emphasis. LOOSEN, *op cit.,* p. 8 with n. 10, seems here to think of a more general chronological order, and consequently he regards the two types of pure prayer (see at this point Char 2.6; CSC, p. 92) as belonging to two quite different *stages* of perfection.

adheres, a part of "natural contemplation".[121] Thus Maximus maintains that there is a parallel between the contemplation of things and of the Law and the Prophets on the one hand, and between the higher contemplation of the Logos which holds all the λόγοι together and the Gospel on the other.[122] Likewise he makes clear that the whole process of contemplation takes place in the Spirit.[123] Secondly, it is equally obvious that "natural contemplation" aims at a knowledge of God as Cause of all that exists, but—and this is important—no more than that.[124]

But how does the mind function in contemplation, and how does Maximus conceive of this process? Maximus obviously elaborates his ideas about "natural contemplation" on the basis of a concept of a hierarchy of being, which is probably inspired by the hierarchies of the Areopagite. Thus he teaches that in its lower form, the contemplation of visible things, it may consist not only of an examination of the natural λόγοι of these things, but also of those which are "signified" by them, or even of their cause itself. And when he goes on to contemplation of invisible things, i.e. the angels, he says that it seeks not only their natural λόγοι and the cause of their existence, but also reflects on that which is related to them, and that providence and judgment which concerns them.[125] These statements seem to imply that it is the task of "natural contemplation", not only to see the λόγοι of created beings both in their differentiation according to natures—as indications of the purpose of God for each nature—and in their relationship to their common Cause the Logos, who keeps them together, but also to see them in their symbolical relationship, a hierarchical relationship of a prophetic character which points in the direction of the attributes of God and is closely linked with His providence and judgment.[126]

But since there is a question here of the Maximian understanding of providence and judgment, which is different from Evagrius' Origenist view which mingles moral and ontological viewpoints together,[127] an indirect criticism of Evagrius is probably also to be found here. This criticism seems to be indicated by Maximus himself, when he applies the categories of providence and judgment to the contemplation of *invisible*

---

[121] Cf. LEMAÎTRE, *art.* Contemplation ou "Science véritable", DSp 2, coll. 1801–1872. On knowledge as grace in Evagrius and his predecessors, cf. VON BALTHASAR, KL², p. 516 f.
[122] See Myst 23; PG 91, 697 D–700 B.
[123] Cf. LOOSEN, *op. cit.,* p. 94 with references.
[124] See Amb 20; PG 91, 1241 C.
[125] Char 1. 98–99; CSC, p. 88.
[126] Cf. ch. II, 3; pp. 66–72 above.
[127] Cf. SHERWOOD, in ACW, p. 39.

beings,[128] for we ought to recall that contemplation of providence and judgment are the two *lower* forms of "natural contemplation" in Evagrius' system, while here they are referred to the highest form, the contemplation of the angels. Maximus' concept of the hierarchy of created being seems thus to imply at all levels a divinely willed differentiation and unity in proper balance in a way which is foreign to Evagrius.

Thus, according to Maximus, it is through this very differentiation that the mind works its way to a unified knowledge of the divine Cause. Integrated with the mind which devotes itself to "natural contemplation in the Spirit" is a sensibility which helps it to investigate the nature of sensible things and their more divine λόγοι. Maximus also underlines that it is the Logos Creator who is revealed through this kind of contemplation, though the head of the Logos is the divine Νοῦς to whom the Logos finally brings the mind through its contemplation of beings (θεωρία τῶν ὄντων), by supplying it with the intelligible representations of divine things.[129] Thus through its contemplation of the principles of created things (οἱ λόγοι τῶν γεγονότων), and through the simple ideas to which these principles lead, the mind advances to a simple knowledge (γνῶσις) which is according to the primal Logos—in order, however, later to be united with God *above* all notion.[130] The aim of contemplation is indeed to arrive at a knowledge, which is neither formed by sensibility, nor contains a notion which needs a pronounced word to be understood, as Maximus says with reference to the experience of Adam, who lived naked in the simplicity of knowledge before he fell from this state of blessed existence.[131] But this position of Maximus does not imply any contempt for the sensible world as such. In the highest state of communion with God man is not indifferent to that world but sees it as God sees it.

Maximus therefore seeks to keep the different aspects together. It is true that he agrees with Evagrius that the 'gnostic' should leave behind not only "concupiscent thoughts of things", but also the contemplation of visible things in general.[132] But this does not necessarily mean what it

---

[128] See Char 1.99; CSC, p. 88.

[129] Thal 25; CCSG 7, p. 161. In this way the Logos is revealed as κτίστης, ποιητής and τεχνίτης through contemplation of creation, see Amb 10; PG 91, 1128 C; cf. LOOSEN, *op. cit.*, pp. 45 and 75. To this whole problem of Maximus' understanding of the "natural" contemplation of the λόγοι, cf. also above all DALMAIS, La théorie des "Logoi", RSPT 36 (1952), pp. 244–249.

[130] See Thal, *Prol.*, CCSG 7, p. 27.

[131] See Amb 45; PG 91, 1356 B.

[132] See Char 1.94; CSC, p. 86.

means to Evagrius. In fact, there are instances to show a considerable difference. One is the understanding of both virtue and knowledge as part of *a communion with the incarnate Christ*. Already Evagrius calls the virtues "fleshes of Christ", and "natural contemplation" "blood of Christ", and finally knowledge of God the "breast", i.e. the heart, of Christ.[133] Now Maximus follows him in this tradition, but, as it seems, with some significant changes. To him also the virtue is the flesh of Christ, but the blood of Christ is "knowledge" without further specification, and finally θεολογία is called "the bones of Christ", which keep all together. Already here the differences are interesting. By choosing the word γνῶσις instead of Evagrius' expression θεωρία τῶν γεγονότων, and the word θεολογία where Evagrius speaks of knowledge of God, Maximus obviously emphasizes the relativity of *all* human knowledge and the non-rational character of the last stage. By choosing the expression "the bones of Christ" he further refers more clearly than Evagrius to the whole of Christ and gives his symbolism a less spiritualistic tone.[134]

But even more interesting are the reasons which he indicates for using this eucharistic symbolism. He thus says that the flesh of the Logos is the λόγοι of sensible things, and the blood of the Logos the λόγοι of intelligible things, while the bones are the λόγοι of the Deity, which are above any notion.[135] By these explanations Maximus establishes a relationship between virtue and lower contemplation as both related to the divine rationality of things, and by referring both virtue and knowledge in this way to degrees of λόγοι, he clearly makes the *vita practica* and the *vita contemplativa* into parallel phenomena, particularly since he relates them to a "theology" which is above both, and yet is said to keep all together.[136] Thus our earlier impressions are confirmed: his high evaluation of a flight through contemplation away from all 'lower' connections with the sensible world, does not at all exclude a positive evaluation of the sensible world itself, or of the *vita practica* as the right way to live in accordance with the principles of that world.

A perpetual death and resurrection with Christ

Another instance which is of a similar character and is equally interesting is connected with the idea of a suffering of Christ and a death with Christ in man's spiritual endeavour. Here we recall that Maximus is in line with

---

[133] See *Mirror for Monks* 118–120; GRESSMANN, p. 163.
[134] See Thal 35; CCSG 7, p. 239. Cf. BLOWERS, *op. cit.*, p. 75 f., n. 44.
[135] *Loc. cit.*
[136] *Ibid.*; p. 241.

Evagrius, when he emphasizes that the purification or the *vita practica* implies a death, and progress through contemplation a resurrection with Christ,[137] or states that the Christian who remains in the *vita practica* prevents Christ's ascension to his Father.[138] But for this reason it is all the more important to point out that he also regards the *vita contemplativa* in its different forms and stages as a crucifixion of Christ and with Christ, for here he is not in full accordance with Evagrius.[139] Thus he describes in Amb 47 how such a crucifixion with Christ takes place through the *whole* of man's spiritual development. The 'gnostic' is not above this crucifixion.[140] On the contrary, he experiences his own particular form of it.

. . Thus we learn that there are *three kinds* of spiritual crucifixion.[141] The first of these takes place in ("practical philosophy") through *detachment*, which implies a death to the temptations of the sensible world. This is a participation in, or imitation of, the crucifixion of *the flesh of Christ*, and through it the Christian advances to "natural contemplation", i.e. to *the soul of Christ*. The second kind of crucifixion takes place within this "natural contemplation" through an eventual abandonment of the mind's *symbolical contemplation* concerning things. This corresponds to the crucifixion of *the soul of Christ*, and through it man advances to the uniform and simple "mystagogia" of theological understanding, that is to say from the soul to *the mind of Christ*. The third crucifixion goes even further than that, and takes place through the final denial of all explicit *qualities of God* in relation to what He is in Himself. This implies what we might call the crucifixion of *the mind of Christ*, and through it the Christian advances, as it were, from the mind of Christ to his very *divinity*. Thus Maximus balances the more or less Evagrian idea of a continuing resurrection with Christ with the corresponding idea of a crucifixion, which does not stop short even of the last stage of spiritual development. By doing so, he excludes the Evagrian idea of a simple

---

[137] See e.g. Gnost 2.95; PG 90, 1169 CD; QuDub 142; CCSG 10, p. 101 and Amb 48; PG 91, 1364 A; cf. Evagrius, *Cent. gnost.* 4. 89, PO 28, p. 175 and 5. 35; p. 191.

[138] See Gnost 2. 47; PG 90, 1145 BC; cf. von Balthasar, KL[2], p. 553.

[139] The difference between Evagrius and Maximus at this point is mainly one of accent, and for this reason it seems very subtle. Cf. von Ivánka, Der Philosophische Ertrag, JOBG 7 (1958), p. 31, where Maximus' expressions in this particular context are understood as "bedenkenlose Übernahme euagrianischen Denkens" (!).

[140] In Evagrius a 'spiritualistic' understanding at this point is obvious. It should, however, be noted that he nevertheless regards "natural contemplation" as "the body of that which is" (*Cent. gnost.* 2. 5; PO 28, p. 63) and as a last piece of clothing (*ibid.* 3. 8; PO 28, p. 101), though this expresses a position which is not at all identical with that of Maximus.

[141] See Amb 47; PG 91, 1360 CD.

return of the mind from an existence which has been only accidentally bodily and limited.

We should also notice here Maximus' stress on the *symbolical* character of "natural contemplation". For Evagrius the final union with God is granted to the naked mind for ontological reasons, and consequently, what "natural contemplation" still lacks is this complete original nakedness of the mind, which allows it to return to the Monad. Therefore, he can regard it—with its differentiating categories of being —as a last veil taken from the world of sensibility into which the mind had fallen, and simply as a weakness from which the mind should escape. To Maximus on the other hand, this very limitation of "natural contemplation" has a symbolical function which leads the mind on to the divine realities, in the knowledge of which man has again to experience his weakness, not only on account of the fall but also because of the fact that his human nature depends on God and is distinguished from God. This understanding of "natural contemplation" as an experience of a merely symbolical reflection of the divine realities—and thereby as a communion through the incarnate soul of Christ—which leads on to an apophatic understanding of man's capacity for knowing God, is clearly of Ps.-Dionysian inspiration, and seems to imply—indirectly already in the field of the *vita contemplativa*—another refutation of Evagrian Origenism.

This general position of Maximus, which might be summarized as involving on the one hand a more positive evaluation of the *vita practica* on the basis of its own rational character, and on the other a more restricted appreciation of the *vita contemplativa,* than we have found in Evagrius, leads in the end to a balancing of the first two elements of the three-fold system of spiritual development, which gives to each of them its proper place and value without absolutizing either of them—and makes of the highest stage, that of true knowledge of God and finally of union with Him, an element which holds the whole together.

This vision of Maximus—which is very characteristic of him—is perhaps best expressed in his exegesis of Psalm 22 (23): 5. There he interprets the "table" which God prepares before the enemies as the *vita practica* in which the passions are overcome by active virtue, and the "oil" with which God anoints the head as *the contemplation of created things* which anoints the mind, while it is the "chalice" which overflows which is seen as the true knowledge of God.[142] The knowledge of the last

---

[142] Char 3.2; CSC, p. 144. It should be noted that at least in other details this interpretation probably goes back to an earlier Alexandrian tradition (cf. VILLER, RAM 11, 1930, p. 261), but this fact does not remove its personal tone.

stage, it seems, "overflows", in Maximus' opinion, precisely because it is entirely the gift of grace, the gift of divine love, and is not the result of an ontological coherence. The two earlier stages are *both* restricted and of a somewhat parallel value.

4. *The final state of union—no question of continuity. Differences between Evagrius and Maximus*

Evagrius draws a sharp distinction between the *vita practica* and contemplation, but a much less strong distinction between the stages of "natural contemplation" and θεολογία. The reason for this position is the fact that Evagrius regards man's "contemplative" function as his principal spiritual activity. The *vita practica* is merely a preparation for it, and the stage of θεολογία is a natural fruit of it, the last—or better, the first—of the five forms of contemplation. The position of Evagrius here marks, of course, a considerable difference between him and Maximus with regard to the understanding and content of θεολογία as a whole. Let us for a moment analyse this difference.[143]

Example one: the problem of "substantial knowledge"

There are three specific examples which deserve our particular attention in this context, since they illustrate rather clearly what we want to emphasize. The first of them is connected with Evagrius' concept of "substantial knowledge" (γνῶσις οὐσιώδης), which should be regarded as one of the most important expressions of his idea of an ontological relationship between the divine mind and the divine object of its contemplation, and which is based in his case, it seems, on the Origenist conception of a primitive henad of rational beings. It is true that this idea works with two presuppositions, which would be shared by a number of Greek Fathers: the general conviction that one who gains knowledge is always patterned after this knowledge,[144] and a faith in God as himself being the "substantial knowledge".[145] For this reason Evagrius' position is less exclusively his own than it might at first look. But a study

---

[143] A wider analysis of Maximus' understanding of spiritual perfection and mystical union with God, against the background of his different predecessors, will be given under 6. below.

[144] This view is however closely connected with the Platonic conviction that the knowing subject must be equal to the object of its knowledge. On Evagrius at this point, cf. Refoulé, *Immortalité de l'âme*, RHR 163 (1963), p. 22: "Ce principe commande la mystique d'Évagre"; cf. also Idem, *La christologie d'Évagre*, OCP 28 (1961), pp. 256 ff.

[145] For this second conviction in Maximus, see Thal 56; CCSG 22, p. 11

of Evagrius' use of the concept of γνῶσις οὐσιώδης shows that he understands it not merely in the relative sense which these two presuppositions might imply. Indeed he underlines very strongly that it is God who *is* knowledge by substance,[146] or that the Trinity alone *is* it.[147] He further emphasizes that Christ possesses it.[148] But he also points out very clearly that such a "substantial knowledge" is the highest form of knowledge which may be open to the *mind,*[149] or that it is a sign of the perfect mind.[150] The detached mind will be crowned with it.[151]

If we now compare Evagrius at this point with other Christian writers, he holds a rather distinctive position. Of his predecessors Origen certainly attributes such a knowledge to God, but knows of no *definition* of God as "substantial knowledge".[152] J. Lemaître has to some extent tried to harmonize Evagrius' understanding with the rest of the Greek Christian tradition on this point, but he has hardly succeeded in doing so. He refers to the obvious fact that Evagrius regards this kind of γνῶσις as higher than all other kinds of knowledge, and sees it as open only to experience by grace. It is thus a mystical knowledge—and not merely a rational one—and an experience of the divine presence in the mind. But he must nevertheless agree to the objection that since Evagrius' terminology at this point left very few traces in later literature, it must be seen as rather peculiar to himself, and not simply as a minor variation of a common theme.[153] It is thus difficult to avoid the conclusion that Evagrius' term expresses his own Origenist position.

In relation to Maximus the efforts of Viller to present parallel expressions to the Evagrian concept, are an evident failure. Beside

---

[146] See *Cent. gnost.* 1. 89; PO 28, p. 59.

[147] *Cent. gnost.* 2. 47; PO 28, p. 79; 4. 77; p. 171 and 5. 56; p. 201; cf. *Ep.* 28; FRANKENBERG, p. 586 f.

[148] See *Cent. gnost.* 3. 3; PO 28, p. 99; 6. 16; p. 223 and *Cap. cognosc.* 1; Mus 44 (1931), p. 374 (*Par. gr.* 913, no. 1).

[149] See *De orat.* 73; PG 79, 1184 A.

[150] *Cent. gnost.* 3. 12; PO 28, p. 103.

[151] *Cent. gnost.* 3. 49; PO 28, p. 117. For the interpretation of this passage, cf. HAUSHERR, Une énigme d'Évagre le Pontique, RSR 23 (1933), p. 325.—The naked mind, in Evagrius' opinion, will easily be able to receive "substantial knowledge", though not because it is incorporeal but because it is *made* susceptible of God. Thus Evagrius never identifies God and mind, and yet God as "substantial knowledge" is received precisely by the mind in its "nakedness"; cf. REFOULÉ, RHR 163 (1963), pp. 22–27. The Origenist presuppositions are obvious.

[152] Cf. VON BALTHASAR's presentation of the examples of this concept to be found in the Evagrian material of *Sel. in Psalm.,* which contains this concept, Die Hiera des Evagrius, ZkTh 63 (1939) p. 184 f.

[153] Cf. LEMAÎTRE, La contemplation, DSp 2, col. 1838 ff.

Maximus' affirmation that God alone is γνῶσις by nature, which we have quoted above[154]—a passage which even related this quality of God explicitly to his function *as Creator* and thus does not pretend to express the very essence of God—he has only a scholion on this particular text to refer to, and even this scholion points out that God is above *all* knowledge, *as he is above the mind.*[155]

To Maximus θεολογία is not only the supreme form of knowledge, as it is to Evagrius; it is a relationship, above *all* knowledge that human beings can imagine, with a God who is himself above knowledge.[156] To stress this understanding of the highest stage of spiritual perfection Maximus frequently uses the apophatic extravagances of the literary style of Ps.-Denis. Viller was of the opinion that this fact did not change the content of Maximus' mysticism, and that it was only a sign that he understood Evagrius as being in perfect harmony with the Areopagite; an Evagrian idea is simply expressed in Dionysian style.[157] But this cannot possibly be the right solution, since Maximus shows in other instances that he rejects "the Origenist errors".[158] It seems far more acceptable to presume that Maximus, here as elsewhere, uses as much as he can of Evagrius, but in order to make his own position clear he balances the Evagrian expressions which he employs by the use of a Dionysian terminology which he regards as orthodox.[159] However, the fact that he corrects Evagrius and in doing so refers to the apophatic terminology of the Areopagite, does not necessarily imply that in the case of Maximus we must suppose a simple choice between the positions of Evagrius and Ps.-Denis. Maximus is an eclectic, and his personal position ought not to be fully identified with that of any of his authorities.[160]

Whatever arguments may be brought forward to support this last conclusion, the difference between Maximus and Evagrius with regard to the mystical relationship to God in θεολογία cannot be denied. A most striking indication of this fact was produced by Viller himself. In his effort to prove Maximus' almost complete dependence in relation to

---

[154] See p. 355, n. 145.

[155] Thal 56, *schol.* 14; CCSG 22, p. 21; cf. the Maximian compilation *Quinquies cent.* 3. 74; PG 90, 1292 D–1293 A.

[156] A γνῶσις οὐσιώδης in any intellectual sense is also excluded in the case of Maximus because he regards God as above οὐσία (see Amb 1; PG 91, 1036 B; 7; 1081 B and 17; 1224 B).

[157] Cf. VILLER, *art. cit.,* p. 248 f., n. 141.

[158] Cf. SHERWOOD, in ACW, p. 90; cf. p. 261 f., n. 187 and VON BALTHASAR, KL², p. 465, n. 1.

[159] Cf. SHERWOOD, *The Earlier Ambigua,* p. 141.

[160] Cf. SHERWOOD, in ACW, pp. 90 and 96; see also his extensive note in *The Earlier Ambigua,* pp. 124–128, n. 1.

Evagrius, he also presents two parallel texts to illustrate their common understanding of the supreme knowledge of God.[161] Evagrius' *Cent. gnost.* 3. 15[162] and Maximus' *Char* 3. 99.[163] Now it is obvious, however, that a comparison between these passages—which are indeed comparable in many ways—shows rather the reverse of what Viller intended, i.e. their differences rather than their complete similarity.

It is true that both writers agree that the perfection of the human mind consists in its supreme knowledge of God, but from then onwards at a number of other points Maximus' formulations make the difference plain. Thus, in a Ps.-Dionysian manner, he characterizes this highest knowledge as a super-knowledge ($\dot{v}\pi\epsilon\rho\epsilon\gamma\nu\omega\kappa\omega\varsigma$), while Evagrius explicitly states that "the immaterial knowledge", which is thus the perfection of the mind, *is* the Trinity alone (thus referring to the debatable concept of $\gamma\nu\tilde{\omega}\sigma\iota\varsigma$ $ο\dot{v}\sigma\iota\dot{\omega}\delta\eta\varsigma$).[164] And Maximus goes on to call this super-knowledge *a supreme ignorance* through which God the *Unknowable* is made known, while Evagrius merely points out that such a knowledge is free from all matter. Finally Maximus, having stated this quite different character of the knowledge of the perfect mind, refers back to the "natural contemplation" of God's creation, and to the knowledge of the divine *providence and judgment* (a concept in relation to which we know that Maximus corrects the Evagrian position) which it has given, and closes by another warning against misunderstanding the mystery with which he is dealing: he speaks in a human way. Thus, the lower knowledge of natural contemplation has not lost its importance at the highest stage of perfection, precisely because the highest form of knowledge is of such a different character from all other knowledge that man still needs the support of other insights.

A parallel to this passage in this particular respect is to be found in *Char* 1. 100, where Maximus says that the mind which is placed in God can find no encouragement in what is proper to God (i.e. in its search for positive knowledge) but is consoled by the divine attributes.[165] Among these attributes goodness and wisdom are included, and we know from

---

[161] VILLER, *art. cit.,* p. 247 f.

[162] See PO 28, p. 103. Viller knew it only in the version presented by FRANKENBERG, *op. cit.,* p. 199.

[163] CSC, p. 190.

[164] Here it ought to be noted that Viller was unaware of this last element, since it is lacking in the text he knew. It is only due to Guillaumont's presentation of the more reliable version called S₂ of the Syriac text, that we now are in the position to see that the contrast between Evagrius and Maximus at this point is even sharper than e.g. Sherwood still presumed.

[165] CSC, p. 88.

other texts that Maximus regards the incarnation of Christ in the virtues and in "natural contemplation" respectively as positively informative here.[166] It thus seems as if Maximus precisely in *Char* 3. 99 indicates two of the characteristics of his own position: the 'otherness' of the supreme knowledge of God (it has to be expressed in negative terms), and the support which the mind receives at this highest stage from the experiences of the *vita practica* and the *vita contemplativa*. But what is the corresponding close of Evagrius' sentence? In the more reliable version its end is most illuminating: the naked mind will be able to *see* the Trinity.[167]

Viller's position, that the differences between Maximus and Evagrius on this point are of no particular importance, and that the harmony between Evagrius and Denis was never doubted by Maximus,[168] thus seems to be untenable. Another comparison, e.g. between Maximus' *Char* 3. 45[169] and Evagrius' *Cent. gnost.* 1. 87,[170] confirms this impression.[171] Evagrius states simply that all (rational) creatures are created for knowledge of God, and gives, as the reason for affirming that the knowledge of God is superior to everything else, this, that all which is created for something else is inferior to that for which it is created. Maximus agrees that "the knower" is ordered to "Him who is known", but he states that God is known *in ignorance* and is Himself beyond all knowledge, and he presents again, it seems, the idea that man is supported in this kind of knowledge by the *vita practica* and the *vita contemplativa* (though here the former is more clearly subordinated to the latter, since it is the aspect of knowledge which is being stressed). This repeated emphasis on these two points cannot possibly be accidental. On the contrary, it shows that Maximus rejects the position of Evagrius both in its denial of empirical man as in principle a unity, and in its tendency to believe in a positive knowledge of God as He is in Himself.

Example two: the problem of "infinite ignorance"

Our second illustrative example is closely linked with the problem of "substantial knowledge", namely the concept of "infinite ignorance" and

---

[166] Cf. pp. 328 and 350 f. above.

[167] S₁ is less provocative at this point than S₂. It says only that one who is deprived of the supreme knowledge is far from perfection, see PO 28, p. 102 f.

[168] VILLER, *art. cit.*, p. 248 f., n. 141.

[169] CSC, p. 164.

[170] PO 28, p. 56 f.; cf. MUYLDERMANS, *Evagriana*, p. 58.

[171] Such a comparison was suggested by SHERWOOD, *The Earlier Ambigua*, p. 141.

Evagrius' relationship to it. This discussion was started by Viller who put forward his own idea, that in Maximus' opinion the Evagrian and Ps.-Dionysian positions as regards the character of the supreme knowledge of God open to the human mind were in harmony with each other. He referred to Evagrius' *Cent. gnost.* 3. 88 where the term "infinite ignorance" seemed to be used to denote mystical knowledge of God, and not—as one would have expected in Evagrius—the extreme degree of the principal vice of the rational faculty.[172] Here, he argued, Maximus had an apophatic term which corresponded rather well with many of the expressions of the negative theology of the Areopagite. It must have made it easier for him to make use of the Evagrian ideas in combination with Ps.-Dionysian expressions.

Later Hausherr studied the concept of "infinite ignorance" in relation to Viller's discussion.[173] Though he made it perfectly clear that the difference between the two positions is great, he seemed to agree with Viller in assuming that Maximus had found no problem in harmonizing them.[174] On the other hand, however, he admitted that since "ignorance" is so frequently used by Evagrius to designate a vice, it is very surprising to find it in a positive context.[175] But he quoted *Pract.* 1. 59[176] where Evagrius at least refers to others who affirm that there are two kinds of "ignorance", one which has a limit and one which has not, and offered three alternative interpretations of such an unlimited "ignorance".[177] Having argued, finally, that the writers to whom Evagrius refers here are Origen and Gregory Nazianzen, he came to the conclusion that such an "ignorance" in the case of Evagrius should be understood as pertaining to other creatures than the νοῦς, and its "infinity" understood with regard to God as related to the proper substance of the mind. Thus after all Hausherr was convinced that this "ignorance" is very different from the darkness (γνόφος) of both Gregory of Nyssa and Ps.-Denis (which

---

[172] See PO 28, p. 134 f. Here again it must be noted that VILLER, *art. cit.*, p. 248, n. 141, only knew the version called S₁ in the presentation of FRANKENBERG, *op. cit.*, p. 257. See further below.

[173] HAUSHERR, "Ignorance infinie", OCP 2 (1936), pp. 351–362.

[174] HAUSHERR, *art. cit.*, p. 352, also noticed that the Armenian translation of the text, based on a Syriac version, presents a positive expression, "knowledge" instead of "ignorance", which eliminates the object of discussion entirely, but he judged that this version was not reliable.

[175] For this reason he discussed the possibility of there being an original Greek term other than ἀγνωσία, and on the basis of a similar text in Thalassius (*Cent.* 1. 56; PG 91, 1433 A) he suggested ἀπειρία, "infinity", without however restricting himself to this possibility.

[176] PG 40, 1236 A.

[177] HAUSHERR, *art. cit.*, p. 355 ff.

Evagrius excludes in the same sense as he excludes the Areopagite "ecstasy"), and that it is in the end compatible with Evagrius' general understanding of the mind's vision of the Holy Trinity.[178]

The passage from the *Praktikos* is nevertheless still extremely difficult to interpret. The most attractive solution in relation to the rest of Evagrius' thinking is, of course, the one which Hausherr underlines: that "ignorance" without end relates to creatures other than the mind. But if this is the case, this text has no particular relevance for the interpretation of the "infinite ignorance" of *Cent. gnost.* 3. 88, which is presented as a blessed quality. The riddle of this latter text may however now be solved in quite a different way. Unfortunately, the original Greek text has not yet been found,[179] but something similar has happened. Guillaumont has presented a more reliable Syriac text of *Cent. gnost.*, and has also investigated the manuscripts of the version which was used by Frankenberg. And the result of his investigations is in both cases most illuminating, so far as our particular problem is concerned.

He has shown in the first place that it is quite probable that the reading "infinite knowledge" instead of "infinite ignorance" is not a misrepresentation on the part of the Armenian translation but probably the original reading of S_1, i.e. the version which was known to Frankenberg and on which both Viller and Hausherr built their discussion.[180] And secondly, it has become clear, that the most reliable Syriac text (that which Guillaumont names S_2) reads "infinite knowledge" and not "infinite ignorance".[181] For this reason we are almost bound to conclude that Evagrius never knew an "ignorance" in a sense which would have made it easy for his teaching on the highest form of human contemplation and knowledge to be interpreted in the light of Ps.-Denis. If this is what Maximus did, or better, if he balanced the Evagrian statements with the aid of the Areopagite, we must conclude that he did so rather to correct the underlying Evagrian doctrine than to affirm it.[182]

---

[178] *Ibid.*, p. 359 f.

[179] HAUSHERR, *art. cit.*, p. 354, expressed the wish that Muyldermans might be successful in this as in so many other cases.

[180] See PO 28, p. 134 with n. 88.

[181] See PO 28, p. 135.

[182] HAUSHERR, *Ignorance infinie ou science infinie*, OCP 25 (1959), pp. 44–52, even after Guillaumont's publication of S_2, again tried to defend his original position, though without any convincing success. His grounds for doing so are mainly the following: 1) The text S_2 is of a later time than S_1, and the only Syrian writer who pronounced any opinion on it, Joseph Ḥazzâyâ, regarded it as a falsification. 2) If Guillaumont is right in assuming a *lapsus calami* as the possible explanation of the change from "knowledge" to "ignorance", a similar calamity might as well have changed "ignorance" into "knowledge". 3) The idea of "infinite ignorance" is not incompatible with Evagrius' theology, since knowledge of the

Example three: the problem of "pure prayer"

Our third example is provided by the concept of pure prayer (καθαρὰ προσευχή). This time the term as such is frequently used both by Evagrius and Maximus. Their understanding of it, however, differs in a characteristic way. To Evagrius pure prayer means *purified prayer,* i.e. a prayer which is freed from passionate desires and, sometimes, from intellectual representations and notions. In the last case it is free from all attachment to the sensible world. In both cases however, the attribute "pure" is used in a negative sense: this prayer is pure *from* something.

Now it is striking that if we look at those texts where Evagrius uses the term "pure prayer", we find that most of them concern the *vita practica.* Thus we learn that freedom from impassioned thoughts is a prerequisite for it.[183] It is pure in so far as man is purified from his passions. The possibility of a pure prayer depends on the detachment of the passible part of the soul. Consequently, Evagrius points out that wrath and fornication—i.e. outstanding vices of the irascible and the concupiscible elements—prevent man from keeping his prayer (εὐχή) pure, and when they interfere with his prayer, they easily lead him to *acedia.*[184] Anger and wrath are particularly dangerous here, since they prevent or destroy pure prayer.[185] Therefore, pure prayer should be desired, in the same way that anger should be banished and moderation—the main virtue of the concupiscible element—should be loved.[186] But prayer in Evagrius' opinion is also itself a means by which to purify the mind, and as such it is parallel to alms which heal anger and fasting which overcomes concupiscence.[187] This understanding of the relationship between purity

---

Trinity as the supreme state of knowledge need not imply that the Trinity is the *object* of knowledge, but rather the *subject,* i.e. a strictly mystical knowledge by which God, as "substantial knowledge", illuminates man. Against these arguments a number of objections may be raised: 1) The date of S₂ is not decisive, since Guillaumont builds his preference on the fact that the Greek fragments of *Cent. gnost.* which we possess correspond with it. The testimony of Joseph Ḥazzāya is not particularly important. As an Origenist (cf. WIDENGREN, *Numen* 8 (1961), p. 165) he might even have wanted to minimize the importance of the more shocking version S₂. We should also notice that Babai as an anti-Origenist (cf. WIDENGREN, *art. cit.,* p. 163) wrote his commentary to S₁. 2) We need hardly to assume a *lapsus calami* in Hausherr's direction, unless we are convinced that the idea of "infinite ignorance" *is* compatible with Evagrius' thinking. 3) As in the case of "substantial knowledge", there are too many instances to show that Evagrius imagined Divinity as the object of human knowledge, to accept Hausherr's argument.

[183] *Mirror for Nuns* 38; GRESSMANN, p. 149.
[184] *Pract.* 1. 14; PG 40, 1225 A.
[185] See *ibid.* 1. 30; PG 40, 1229 B; *De mal. cogitat.* 5; PG 79, 1205 CD, and 16; 1220 AB.
[186] *De mal. cogitat.* 24; PG 79, 1228 B.
[187] *De mal. cogitat.* 3; PG 79, 1204 C.

and prayer is maintained also in the later Evagrian tradition. Thus Nilus regards pure prayer as excluded by a vice like grief.[188]

Only in a few cases is pure prayer considered as more than a virtue of the rational faculty. In these it is closely linked with "natural contemplation". It is characteristic, however, that it is not free from temptations. It is a state of mind where the 'gnostic' both looks for God as Creator and offers pure prayer to Him, but which the Evil One wishes to destroy.[189] On the other hand, it is in such a prayer that "natural contemplation" culminates, for it is defined as "removal of thoughts",[190] and in it the mind proceeds beyond thoughts and forms.[191] In such a contemplative pure prayer one may however still be tempted by the vice of vainglory.[192]

On the other hand, Evagrius sometimes presents it as a sudden gift of grace. Thus we learn that it can happen that a man fails to keep his prayer pure, even though he makes efforts to do so, while in other instances his soul comes close to pure prayer without his efforts. Here human weakness and grace from above are together called upon to assist us in making our prayer pure, says Evagrius, and through both we are taught not to attend to ourselves but to know the Giver of all gifts.[193] Pure prayer is here clearly depicted as a very high form of spiritual activity, given by God's grace, but we should notice that it is still understood as almost identical with a pure soul. Therefore, one is not surprised to find that—even in this high estimation of it—it is not only seen as a supreme gift of grace, but also as a human means to call for mercy, the gift of grace.[194]

We may thus conclude that pure prayer for Evagrius is closely connected with all the functions of the mind as man's intellectual faculty, not least with its purification from worldly things, and as such is hardly higher than "natural contemplation". At least it is not of a different character from other functions of the mind, though it is a gift of God.

In the case of Maximus the picture is far more complicated. One or two things however are clear from the beginning. First there are very few texts where pure prayer is as intimately connected with the *vita practica* as it is in most cases in Evagrius. Secondly the higher evaluation of the concept which is found explicitly in Evagrius in only a few cases,

---

[188] See Nilus, *De octo spir. mal.* 11; PG 79, 1156 C.
[189] *Ep.* 1; FRANKENBERG, p. 567.
[190] *De orat.* 70; PG 79, 1181 C.
[191] *Cap. cognosc.* 23; FRANKENBERG, p. 443; Latin text (*Barb. lat.* 3024), see Mus 44 (1931), p. 60 f.
[192] *De orat.* 72; PG 79, 1181 D.
[193] *Tract. ad Eul. monach.* 30; PG 79, 1133 A.
[194] *Sel. in Psalm.* 65; PG 12, 1504 A.

predominates in Maximus. For him it is always a state above the immediate struggle of the *vita practica*, though it may be soiled, as Evagrius also points out, by thoughts of concupiscence and anger, which in that case lead the mind to *acedia.*[195]

Further Maximus sometimes connects it with contemplation of the second "stage", but more usually presents it as forming *the summit of the third 'stage'*, θεολογία. When it is connected with lower contemplation, however, it is presented as the true virtue of the mind as intellectual faculty, since it separates it even from the thoughts of things.[196] Here the term *pure* prayer is obviously used to design a prayer which is *purified* from other notions than those of God, but this 'negative' understanding of the concept is used only in relation to the highest form of contemplation. Pure prayer means to Evagrius purified prayer, to Maximus usually supreme prayer, prayer formed by God alone.

Maximus' double concept of pure prayer

This last point becomes more clear when we notice that Maximus works, in fact, with a double concept of pure prayer.[197] In Char 2. 6 Maximus says explicitly that there is one form of pure prayer for the Christians of the *vita practica* and one for those of the *vita contemplativa*. Neither of them is included within these 'stages', but both are above them, and neither of them seems as such to be subordinated to the other, though the form which is open to the 'gnostic' seems to be the more excellent.

The *first* kind is an *undistracted prayer* on the basis of true fear and hope and *in the presence of God*, which is free from the thoughts (νοήματα) of the world.[198] It is thus the fruit of a *vita practica* into which—as is usual in Maximus—some spiritual contemplation is integrated.[199] The *second* kind, however, seems to be an *ecstatic prayer* (which even leads the mind outside itself), based on desirous love (ἔρως) and a maximum of purification. It is conscious only of God and concerned with His properties alone, thus receiving pure impressions of Him.[200] It is thus above all forms of contemplation and characterized by a blessed rapture. Undistracted prayer and pure prayer in the second sense are thus not synonyms—though both are called pure prayer—nor is the first one

---

[195] Char 1. 49; CSC, p. 66.
[196] Asc 19; PG 90, 925 D–928 A.
[197] Cf. SHERWOOD, in ACW, p. 87 f., where this fact is strongly emphasized.
[198] CSC, p. 92.
[199] See Char 2. 5; CSC, p. 90.
[200] Char 2. 6; CSC, p. 92.

greatly inferior to the second one, since both experience the presence of God in some way.[201]

Concerning *undistracted prayer* Maximus emphasizes that it is both a sign and a fruit of love (ἀγάπη) for God.[202] The *vita practica*, and that spiritual contemplation which ought to be integrated with it, together help the mind to arrive at undistracted prayer.[203] Therefore, he can also say that it is only when the mind is without matter and form (ἄϋλος and ἀνείδεος) that it is open to undistracted prayer,[204] and the mind is, in Maximus' view, without matter thanks to practical exercises, and without form thanks to contemplation.[205] Furthermore, as we saw in Char 2. 6, this is a state of mind which is without thoughts (νοήματα), but we are warned that it is not outside the boundaries of detachment.[206] In this way Maximus elevates pure prayer above practical virtues and yet at the same time shows how these virtues have to support the mind, and how man is a single whole. Thus pure prayer is open even to the man of *vita practica*, and even for him it clearly means that the mind is as it were outside the flesh and the world, and is entirely free from matter and form in its prayer. This prayer is thus 'informed' only by the presence of God himself.[207]

We should notice that even in the *Liber asceticus*, where Maximus never mentions "natural contemplation", he is eager to stress this supreme function and character of pure prayer. It is built directly on the virtues of *vita practica* and is a gift of God. Thus we learn that the grace of prayer joins the mind to God and thereby also withdraws it from the thoughts. Then the mind becomes God-like and can pray without ceasing (1 Thess. 5: 17).[208] This fact does not imply, however, that the mind is liberated from then on from the attacks of the demons. On the contrary, even at the summit of prayer they try to instigate evil desires instead of simple thoughts about sensible things.[209] To Maximus such a high evaluation of the pure prayer of the πρακτικός is, of course, not irreconcilable with a realistic view of the continuing spiritual struggle. The state of pure prayer is to him a pure grace, but man is a composite

---

[201] In both these cases PEGON, SCH 9, pp. 92, n. 2 and 95, n. 1 seems to be mistaken.
[202] Char 2. 1; p. 90.
[203] *Ibid.* 2. 5; p. 90.
[204] *Ibid.* 2. 4; p. 90.
[205] See Amb 30; PG 91, 1273 C. This could, of course, be also said of pure prayer of the second type.
[206] Char 1. 88; CSC, p. 84.
[207] *Ibid.* 2. 61; p. 122.
[208] Asc 24; PG 90, 929 C.
[209] Char 2. 90; CSC, p. 138.

whole, who will always need the support of his acquired virtues and his human desire for God.

There is, however, as we have seen, also *a more excellent form of pure prayer*. It is intimately linked with contemplation, and therefore is sometimes not easily distinguished from the highest forms of contemplation. But there are always some features which are characteristic of it. First of all, it is linked with desirous love (ἔρως), i.e. the love which finally aims at mystical union with God. The mind is in this way winged with pure prayer and rises above all things.[210] Secondly it is presented as itself the supreme state of spiritual communion with God. Therefore, the one who loves God is concerned for pure prayer from the beginning, and throws aside every passion which hinders his way towards it.[211] Thirdly, pure prayer of this kind is not primarily understood as a purified prayer. It is rather its absolute concentration on God alone which makes it pure. This fact becomes particularly clear in Char 3. 44, where Maximus refers to the three-fold pattern of spiritual development, saying of the *virtues* that they *separate* the mind from passions (thus here he mentions the virtues in their 'negative' function alone), and of the *contemplations* that they *separate* it from simple thoughts, but of pure prayer that *it places the mind before God himself*.[212] He might have said that it "separates" the mind from itself, but his main interest at this point is to stress the positive function of pure prayer in relation to God. By doing so he makes his difference with Evagrius clear, for for him the aspect of separation dominates the concept of *pure* prayer.

Pure prayer more than purified prayer

From what we have said it is obvious that Maximus regards pure prayer as very difficult to attain.[213] Its characteristics in relation to the created world are those of the state of θεολογία. Therefore, it implies that the mind contemplates God alone and is simple because God as the object of its contemplation is simple (μονοειδής), and thus receiving its 'information' from God alone it is transfused with the divine light.[214] In this stage of perfection the mind has passed beyond both prudence (the quality which summarizes the *vita practica*) and knowledge (the fruit of the *vita contemplativa*), though these reflect divine qualities on the level of creation, and it examines the λόγος "about" God Himself as far as it

---

[210] See also *ibid.* 1. 11; p. 52.
[211] *Ibid.* 2. 7; p. 92.
[212] CSC, p. 164.
[213] See e.g. Char 4. 51; CSC, p. 214.
[214] *Ibid.* 3. 97; p. 190.

can.[215] This is still an intellectual function of the mind, and we must assume that pure prayer goes even farther, into the impenetrable mystery of the divine essence, where no concepts are sufficient. But since man is a composite unity of body, soul and mind, this going forth into the Divinity itself—which is not ontological or moral but mystical—must still be supported by the virtues and insights of the rest of man.

Therefore undistracted prayer, which is one form of pure prayer, in the sense of a prayer without matter and form, is in itself also a sign of detachment and love—i.e. the fruits of the *vita practica.* Thus even at the highest stage of prayer the mind cannot progress without these qualities, by which it is strengthened.[216] Concerning the second form of pure prayer, Maximus likewise makes clear that it has to be supported positively both by detachment, as a fruit of the *vita practica,* and by the knowledge gained through "natural contemplation".[217] Through such freedom from passions and such illumination it becomes fit to pray as it ought, i.e. in pure concentration upon God, and receives from Him alone the divine qualities as objects of "theological" contemplation.

Thus we must conclude that for Maximus pure prayer is no longer just a purified prayer, but *a prayer in pure concentration upon God* which reaches out in love to God, certainly as He manifests Himself to the naked mind, but probably also as He is in Himself, i.e. in the very mystery of His being. It is true that the term "ecstasy" is more proper here,[218] but Maximus draws no very sharp distinction between ecstasy and pure prayer. Evagrius has a far more intellectual approach at this point. For him pure prayer is purified prayer, and as such it is the prayer of a mind which is made pure. But a pure mind is in Evagrius' opinion a mind restored to full divine communion, able to contemplate God in itself. For Maximus on the contrary, the mind as created must reach outside itself to find God as He is, and pure prayer is thus for him a formless contemplation of God in the qualities which He shows by grace. And it aims beyond these to the communion with God as He is in Himself. At this point Maximus is assisted by Ps.-Dionysian apophatic theology, and not by Evagrian thinking, though he agrees with Evagrius that the mind may be fully illumined by God in prayer alone, and though he seems to be less interested in divine darkness than Ps.-Denis.[219]

Maximus accepts that there is a gulf between God and *all* created

---

[215] *Ibid.* 2. 26; p. 102.
[216] See *ibid.* 4. 42; p. 210.
[217] *Ibid.* 2. 100; p. 142.
[218] On this concept in Maximus, see further pp. 422–425 below.
[219] Cf. SHERWOOD's discussion of these problems, in ACW, pp. 88 f. and 95 f.

things, including the human mind, but he is more interested in the interplay between divine condescension and human desirous ascension —all in an inter-change of love—than in an analysis of the mystery of the darkness of God in relation to all concepts. Pure prayer for Maximus is an expression of the love for God which never ends, and as such it is part of his apophatic theology, but it is at the same time characterized by that illumination which God gives freely by grace to a human mind which is pure in concentration on Him alone.

Another triad of spiritual development

Before we begin our analysis of the five types of mediation which according to Amb 41 and Thal 48 man is called to perform in imitation of Christ there is a parallel three-fold pattern of spiritual development which ought to be shortly treated. We refer to the doctrinal and chronological triad of *being—well-being—ever-being* (εἶναι—εὖ εἶναι—ἀεὶ εἶναι). The importance and function of this triad has been sufficiently analysed by von Balthasar and Sherwood, and for this reason we shall restrict our own account to a short presentation of its most relevant aspects.

It should be noted, first of all, that the background of this triad is not at all Evagrian. Its roots are probably to be found in the distinction between "living" and "well-living" (ζῆν and εὖ ζῆν) which is to be found in Aristotle and on Christian ground in Clement of Alexandria.[220] Maximus' nearest predecessor at this point, however, is probably Ps.-Denis, who distinguishes, in relation to spiritual beings, between εἶναι and εὖ εἶναι and links the latter state with the idea of an imitation of God, so as to come to His likeness.[221] The background of this terminology in Ps.-Denis, in its turn, is probably Neo-Platonist, and the possibility cannot be excluded that the whole triad has its origin in Proclus.[222] At the same time, however, one should notice that Maximus also provides it with a biblical basis. The triad of being, motion and life in God, which may be deduced from Acts 17:28, is thus explicitly referred to the principles of being, well-being and ever-being.[223]

This biblical triad is, in fact, not the only one which is supposed to correspond more or less to that of being, well-being and ever-being. Another for example is the well-known anti-Origenist Maximian

---

[220] Cf. von Balthasar, KL², p. 623.
[221] See *De div. nom.* 4, 1; PG 3, 696 A; cf. von Balthasar, KL², p. 537.
[222] Cf. Sherwood, *The Earlier Ambigua*, p. 67 f., n. 27.
[223] See Amb 7; PG 91, 1084 B.

triad of *becoming, motion* and *rest.*[224] We can also refer to the parallel triad of *beginning, medium* and *end,* which Maximus himself relates explicitly to our triad.[225] A certain relationship exists also to the triad of *faculty, energy* and *quiescence* (δύναμις, ἐνέργεια, ἀργία), as well as to that of *substance, intentional relationship* and *grace* (οὐσία, σχέσις, χάρις).[226]

Furthermore it is of interest here that our triad is related to the idea of *three human births.* Thus man's double birth in body and soul (which is simultaneous)[227] is parallel to the category of being, while his birth in baptism corresponds to that of well-being, and his third and final birth in resurrection to that of ever-being.[228] This three-fold scheme of births is prepared and prefigured, however, by Christ, who for men's sake himself suffered the corresponding three births. Consequently, man's passage through the stages of our triad is also connected with these *three redemptive births of Christ.* Thus Christ's Incarnation in the flesh (his first birth as man) corresponds to the human principle of being (λόγος τοῦ εἶναι), and his own baptism corresponds to the principle of well-being (λόγος τοῦ εὖ εἶναι), while his resurrection implies that true believers will be allowed to follow him into eternal life according to the principle of ever-being (λόγος τοῦ ἀεὶ εἶναι).[229] And finally, we should also notice that Maximus relates our triad to his concepts of *the three days* (the 6th, 7th and 8th day of creation)[230] and *the three laws* (natural law, written law and law of grace).[231]

But what is the sense of our triad and how is it related to the three-fold system of spiritual development? A number of texts are illuminating here, and Maximus' systems of corresponding triads help us to understand further the content of the triad of being, well-being and ever-being. From these texts it becomes clear that the state of ever-being was, in Maximus' opinion, at the very beginning open to man, not in virtue of

---

[224] Cf. p. 81 f.; notes 216–217, above and SHERWOOD, *op. cit.,* p. 172, n. 63. On the relationship between this triad and its equivalents within the context of Maximus' complicated refutation of Origenism, cf. also IDEM, Maximus and Origenism, *Berichte zum XI. Internationalen Byzantinisten-Kongress, München 1958,* and VON IVÁNKA, Der philosophische Ertrag, JOBG (1958), p. 27 ff. with n. 2.

[225] See Amb 7; PG 91, 1073 C.

[226] See Amb 20; PG 91, 1237 A and 65; 1392 A; cf. VON BALTHASAR, KL², p. 140.

[227] Cf. ch. III: A, 1; p. 95 ff. above.

[228] See Amb 42; PG 91, 1325 BC.

[229] Amb 42; PG 91, 1348 D.

[230] On the symbolism of the 8th day in general in the early Church, cf. DANIÉLOU, *Bible et liturgie,* Paris 1951, pp. 355–387.

[231] See Gnost 1. 56; PG 90, 1104 C (cf. Amb 65; PG 91, 1392 B–D) and Thal 64; CCSG 22, p. 237 (cf. *schol.* 50; *ibid.,* p. 243). To this complex in Maximus, see also BLOWERS, *op. cit.,* p. 166 f., n. 108.

his nature, but on account of God's grace which was freely offered to
him.[232] In his fall, however, he turned away from God and failed to
acquire this grace. Now the way to it is open only through Christ, who has
accepted the human mode of being for man's sake, has established in his
own life the perfect state of well-being, and finally granted his followers
the way to eternal life through his resurrection. Man has to follow him,
on the basis of his own nature which God has created for communion
with Himself, that nature which Christ shares. This is the general outline
from which the triad is to be understood, and its different elements are to
be analysed in the light of it.

Thus *being* simply means the participation of all creatures in God as
Being, since He gives of His own when He creates. The principle of this
being thus differs according to different natures, and man's principle of
being (λόγος τοῦ εἶναι) coincides with his principle of nature (λόγος τῆς
φύσεως), though his life of course is part of being in general. Being is
given by God the Creator,[233] and to individual man at his—first—birth
in body and soul.[234] Rational natures thus participate in God (as Being)
by their very being, and individuals by their existence.[235] Now in the case
of men this participation implies that they bear the image of God, and
for this reason they are also moved towards him as their end, for God is
their beginning in so far as he is the ground of their being.[236] Their being
thus includes *naturally* the power and the faculty by which to move to the
second state of well-being.[237]

This second state, of *well-being*, is of a particular interest for several
reasons. It is connected with the will and freedom of man, and it offers at
the same time the first link with Maximus' three-fold scheme of spiritual
development. Thus it represents *both* the *vita practica* and the *vita
contemplativa*. The state of being implies mere existence, but the state of
well-being is formed by man's *use* of his natural capacities for communion with God. It is an *intermediate phase*, which includes man's use of
his faculty of *motion*.[238] Thus the state of well-being is due to man's

---

[232] On the problem of divine grace and human freedom in Maximus, see further the
discussion report in DÖLGER-BECK, *Diskussionsbeiträge zum XI. Internationalen Byzantinistenkongress*, pp. 37–40.

[233] See Thal 60; CCSG 22, p. 79.

[234] See Amb 42; PG 91, 1325 B.

[235] Char 3. 24; CSC, p. 154.

[236] Amb 7; PG 91, 1073 C.

[237] See Amb 65; PG 91, 1392 AB.

[238] The concept of motion in God of Acts 17: 28 is related to the principle of well-being,
see Amb 7; PG 91, 1084 B. That Maximus here uses the word principle (λόγος) implies,
however, at the same time the idea that this motion corresponds to some sort of divine
predestination in the sense of a willed aim of human life (σκοπός); cf. SHERWOOD, *The*

motion as well as to his γνώμη.[239] But since it here concerns fallen man, it depends on his second birth in baptism,[240] and is received through victory over the passions, as well as through positive virtue.[241] It further implies, "gnomically", the actualization of the faculty of motion in free energy.[242] Man moves according to his γνώμη through well-being towards his divine end. Maximus can also say that it depends on the choice (προαίρεσις) of self-moving creatures.[243]

So far well-being is thus seen to be a fruit of the *vita practica*. But it is also connected with "natural contemplation", as we have pointed out, for well-being implies a participation not only in God's goodness but also in His wisdom. Such a two-fold participation—a share in goodness and wisdom which depends on the will and judgment of rational beings[244]— is due to men's "gnomic" aptitude for well-being, i.e. their worthiness of it.[245] Finally, such a participation means that man not only bears the image of God by virtue of his nature, but in well-being also develops his *divine likeness*, and this in Maximus is always on account of man's free decision.[246]

The last fact, however, implies that man can also choose evil instead of good. And such a choice has repercussions for his *ever-being*, for "ever-being" in Maximus' opinion is usually identical with *ever-well-being*. The state of true ever-being is certainly a gift of divine grace, but there is no way to it except through moral well-being. Therefore, man may alternatively cause *ill-being* for himself, because of his vice and a wrongly directed use of his natural capacity for motion.[247] Those who by choice use their being in accord with nature are finally granted ever-well-being, but those who use it contrary to their nature are given "ever-ill-being", which is a negation of true ever-being.[248] Thus there is a privation of goodness and knowledge open to man in his freedom, and his well-being therefore always depends on his own will and judgment.[249]

Earlier Ambigua, p. 174 and particularly IDEM, Maximus and Origenism, in *Berichte zum XI. Intern. Byz.-Kongr.*, pp. 16–23.

[239] See Amb 10; PG 91, 1116 B.
[240] Amb 42; PG 91, 1325 B.
[241] Amb 42; PG 91, 1329 A.
[242] Amb 65; PG 91, 1392 AB.
[243] Amb 65; PG 91, 1392 AB; cf. SHERWOOD, *The Earlier Ambigua*, p. 202.
[244] See Char 3. 27; CSC, p. 156.
[245] See Char 3. 24; CSC, p. 154. On the relationship between the term "aptitude" and the concept of γνώμη, cf. SHERWOOD, in ACW, p. 259, n. 153.
[246] See Char 3. 25; CSC, p. 154; cf. ch. III: A, 4: p. 128 f. above.
[247] Amb 42; PG 91, 1329 A.
[248] Amb 65; PG 91, 1392 D.
[249] See also Char 3. 29; CSC, p. 156 ff.

This fact does not prevent Maximus, however, from stating with great emphasis that man's true ever-being is due to God's will and counsel alone,[250] for it is also his conviction that it is granted by sovereign divine grace to those who have proved to be worthy of it through their well-being.

In itself true ever-being thus corresponds to the third stage of Maximus' three-fold system, and is of an eschatological and mystical character. It is through the resurrection of Christ that it is open to man, and it is finally received by man in his own resurrection.[251] It is the rest and quiescence and end of rational beings.[252] It is also a "limit" (ὅρος), and as such it is mystically called the Sabbath.[253] It is therefore the law of grace alone which provides this persistence of ever-well-being.[254] And consequently, if the 6th day symbolizes the principle of being and the 7th day the *mode* of well-being (τρόπος τοῦ εὖ εἶναι),[255] then the 8th day manifests "the mystery of ever-well-being".[256] Here we are thus at the fulfilment of spiritual perfection, and as in the case of the stage of θεολογία or μυσταγωγία, it is entirely above natural human capacities and human efforts to attain. Both are freely given by God, and are received from him in burning love.

But it is Maximus' conviction that man has not brought his divine task of mediation to its proper end, until he has arrived here. For he is

---

[250] See *ibid.* 4. 13; p. 198; 3. 28; p. 156 and Thal 60; CCSG 22, p. 79.

[251] See Amb 42; PG 91, 1325 BC and 1348 D.

[252] On well-being as end, see Amb 7; PG 91, 1073 C.

[253] See Amb 65; PG 91, 1392 BC.

[254] Thal 64; CCSG 22, p. 237. Notice Maximus' careful avoidance of all Origenism in relation to this stage.

[255] The word τρόπος is generally used by Maximus in relation to man's natural freedom and will.

[256] Gnost 1. 56; PG 90, 1104 C.—We are obviously very close to the idea of *apocatastasis* in some of Maximus' statements on spiritual development. This problem has been widely discussed by the scholars. E. MICHAUD, Saint Maxime le Confesseur et l'Apocatastase, *Rev. Intern. de Théologie* 10 (1902), pp. 257–272, argued that Maximus in fact teaches *apocatastasis*. When Maximus writes about "ages" and "eternities" after judgment, he always teaches the *apocatastasis*, he concluded (p. 271). He was later followed by GRUMEL, *art.* Maxime le Confesseur, DTC 10 (1928), col. 457, and by VON BALTHASAR (who regarded the doctrine as honoured in silence by Maximus), KL¹, pp. 367–372 and *Die Gnost. Centurien*, p. 7. Finally SHERWOOD, *The Earlier Ambigua*, pp. 205–221, devoted considerable attention to the problem and came to a different conclusion: Maximus does not teach the *apocatastasis*, nor does he honour it in silence, but the tension between universal salvation and eternal damnation is preserved in its integrity (p. 222). VON BALTHASAR, however, has not changed his opinion later, see KL², pp. 355–359.—The concept of *ever ill-being* of Amb 65 (PG 91, 1392 D)—in combination with the stress on the divine grace alone as active in deification—seems anyhow to be sufficient to show that Maximus does not teach *apocatastasis*, and that he rather keeps the tension than even honours it in silence.

called to hold together *all* that is distinguished and separated—even God and his creation.

6. First mediation: between the sexes

When man is restored in Christ he is called to perform a five-fold work of mediation. This is Maximus' teaching in Amb 41, and also in Thal 48[257] where 2 Chron. 26: 9–10 is interpreted accordingly. If we follow this work in its chronological order, the first kind of mediation is that between male and female.

Maximus regards procreation through sexual intercourse as providentially introduced into man's life after his fall, and concludes that another way of procreation must have been open to man before the fall.[258] Sexual differentiation, as we now know it, is thus itself due to the fall, and therefore this first kind of human mediation takes place in relation to elements of created life which have been separated through sin and against the original creative will of God. The reconciliation of male and female into a higher human unity is thus part of man's purification from sin, and involves the use of that new freedom in Christ, into which he has been baptized.

Male and female in some of Maximus' predecessors

However, before we consider how Maximus develops this idea of a sexual synthesis, we must try to indicate the extent to which he may have been inspired by earlier Christian tradition.[259] Certainly, in the first place we must refer back to Gregory of Nyssa, who believed in a primitive absence of sexuality and saw the latter as a result of sin. But apart from him there is obviously also some material in the Alexandrian tradition and elsewhere to which particular attention ought to be called in this context. In relation both to Maximus himself and to his predecessors it is apparent that a Scriptural testimony such as that of *Gal. 3: 28* is of a particular importance here, with its specific reference to the restoration

---

[257] For this last reference, see CCSG 7, p. 333 f. Cf. BLOWERS, *op. cit.*, p. 175, n. 184 and *ibid.*, p. 153, n. 19. See also my own study *Man and the Cosmos*, pp. 80–91.

[258] See e.g. Amb 42; PG 91, 1317 A and 1309 A; cf. SHERWOOD, Maximus and Origenism, in *Berichte zum XI. Intern. Byz.-Kongr.*, pp. 8–16, and ch. III: B, 1 and 3; pp. 151 ff., and 169 f. above.

[259] The subject which we touch upon here is, of course, very vast and varied, if we think of the understanding of male—female in general in the early Church. Here we must concentrate our attention to those points which are of particular interest in relation to Maximus' interpretation of the first mediation. For a more general survey, cf. however D. S. BAILEY, *The Man—Woman Relation in Christian Thought*, London 1959, pp. 19–102.

in Christ of man as created in the image of God. For this reason we propose to make our own analysis of the problem of sexual mediation and synthesis in relation to the exegesis of this text presented by these writers.

We noticed earlier that Philo—using Plato's image of the chariot and the two horses—interpreted *anger* and *concupiscence* as male and female impulses.[260] On Christian ground he is here immediately followed by Clement of Alexandria, who alters the perspective however, and says that the expression "male and female" in Gal. 3: 28 denotes anger and concupiscence. But what is of interest in our context is that he then goes on to say that when the soul is detached from that which divides it in this way—i.e. from the diversive tendencies to impassioned affection and aggressivity—it is brought to unity. And such a unity implies that there is "neither male nor female".[261] Clement is eager to avoid a literal understanding of the Pauline words, but it seems that he does not exclude a certain spiritual relationship between the categories of male and female and the passible faculties of the human soul.

And therefore, it is not surprising to find that he also allows for a concrete result of this new unity in Christ. Thus he points out that a "gnostic" woman, after having given birth to her children, is regarded by her husband as a *sister*, and she for her part forgets her husband, except when she looks at her children. Man and wife regard themselves as brother and sister, since they have the same Father.[262] And Clement continues: Souls are in themselves not male or female but only souls, and thus it may be that woman will in the end be transformed into man, and become "non-female, manly and perfect".[263] This double line of interpretation—a spiritualized understanding of "male and female" as referring to anger and concupiscence, and an ascetic reflection on the concrete consequences of the new union in Christ—can be followed later in both its aspects.[264]

We must however concentrate our attention on those writers who have certainly influenced Maximus. In Evagrius we find the *first* type of interpretation. He makes it quite clear that he understands "male and

---

[260] See ch. IV: A, 3; p. 185 f. with n. 86. Notice particularly that he also presents them as *brother* and *sister*.

[261] *Strom.* 3, 13; GCS Clem. 2, p. 238 f.

[262] On the relationship between this understanding of the spiritual requirements of matrimony and early Christian *syneisaktism*, cf. BAILEY, *op. cit.*, p. 33 f.

[263] *Strom.* 6. 12; *ibid.*, p. 482.

[264] On Clement's understanding of matrimony and man—woman relationship in general, see further e.g. F. QUATEMBER, *Die christliche Lebenshaltung des Klemens von Alexandrien nach seinem Paedagogus*, Vienna 1946, pp. 137–140.

female" as referring to anger and concupiscence, and consequently he affirms that detachment—as representing the final victory over the passions of both these faculties—leads to the result that in Christ there is "neither male nor female".[265] Here it is clear that "male and female" refers to that sensibility which the mind, as the true image of God, leaves behind when it becomes united with Christ the Logos. It thus goes without saying that even the bodily distinctions have to be neglected and their desires entirely overcome in this process.

In Gregory Nazianzen's writings we have found no reference to anger and concupiscence in this context, but he makes it quite evident that all the distinctions of Gal. 3: 28 are "signs of the flesh". When Christ becomes all in all, they are therefore overcome, and there is then neither male nor female. Thus the true image of God is restored in man, and he bears the divine stamp alone.[266]

In Gregory of Nyssa, however, the same idea is elaborated into a whole theology. To him the ideal primitive state of man contained no sexuality.[267] Thus the latter is seen as a result of sin,[268] and it is the cause of all apostasy.[269] The distinction between male and female is, in Gregory's opinion, superadded to the original (or better: ideal) creation of man "in the image", for in Christ—who is the Image—there is "neither male nor female".[270] Consequently, marriage did not exist in Paradise.[271]

As in the case of Clement these theological reflections, however, also lead to practical consequences for those who are in Christ. It is Gregory's conviction that Matt. 22: 30 shows that men are called to live without marriage, as the angels, for thus it must have been "in the beginning".[272] But angels are many, and thus, Gregory concludes, sexual intercourse is no necessary prerequisite for multiplicity.[273] This primitive and eschatological way of living must now be prefigured among Christians in an ascetic life, and here holy virginity is of the greatest importance to Gregory. A true Christian, he says, must choose between two forms of marriage, one "bodily" and one "spiritual", and his choice can be but

---

[265] See *Pract.* 1. 63; PG 40, 1237 B and *De mal. cogitat.* 3; PG 79, 1204 C.
[266] *Or.* 7, *In laud. Caes. fratr.* 23; PG 35, 785 C.
[267] Cf. VON BALTHASAR, *Présence et pensée,* e.g. p. 52, n. 5 and DANIÉLOU, *Platonisme et théologie mystique,* p. 51.
[268] Cf. DANIÉLOU, *op. cit.,* p. 167 and CAMELOT, La théologie de l'image de Dieu, RSPT 40 (1956), p. 458: cf. also GAÏTH, *La conception de la liberté,* p. 55 ff.
[269] Cf. GAÏTH, *op. cit.,* p. 56.
[270] See *De hom. opif.* 16; PG 44, 181 A.
[271] *Ibid.* 17; 188 AB.
[272] *Ibid.;* 188 C.
[273] *Ibid.;* 189 AB.

one.[274] These two ways are mutually exclusive, for no man can serve two masters. Spiritual marriage, however, is now open and common for both men and women, precisely on the ground that in Christ there is "neither male nor female". Thus in this spiritual marriage man does not desire an earthly woman but true Wisdom as the divine goal of his ἐπιθυμία, and the soul (notice the implicit reference to the soul as female) is attached to the incorruptible Bridegroom and has her love (ἔρως) related to true Wisdom, which is God.[275]

Thus the practical asceticism of virginity in the case of Gregory is linked with a spiritualization which resembles that of Clement and Evagrius: from a spiritual point of view male and female are regarded as primary forces of passibility,[276] and the practical results of the affirmation of Gal. 3: 28 are combined with this spiritual understanding. But at the same time there is a considerable difference between Gregory on the one hand and Clement and Evagrius on the other: in Gregory these forces are not eliminated but transferred to a higher spiritual life, where they may perform their true functions within man's communion with God.[277]

Maximus on male and female

The same two aspects which we have now noticed in some of Maximus' predecessors are both to be found in his own writings, and are even intimately interwoven. In his commentary on the Lord's Prayer, on the one hand, he gives an extensive interpretation of Gal. 3: 28, in which the expression "male and female" is explicitly said to denote *anger and concupiscence*.[278] On the other hand, in his descriptions of man's mediating functions he seems—on the basis of his convictions about the primitive state of man—to reckon with a spiritual endeavour on the part of man through which even the concrete sexual differences are transformed and transferred to a common human unity. How are these two aspects interrelated? This question coincides more or less with another: how is human mediation between the sexes effected in this world?

To answer this last question we must to some extent recapitulate what we have found earlier about Maximus' general teaching on man's fall and

---

[274] See *De virg.* 20; JAEGER 8, 1, p. 325.

[275] *Ibid.;* p. 328.

[276] Cf. the terms ἐπιθυμία and ἔρως.

[277] This corresponds very well with the positive use of the passible faculties which we have seen that Maximus allows for. A non-sexual state of man in Paradise was also affirmed by Augustine; see *De bono coni.* 2; CSEL 41, pp. 188–190 and *De Gen. ad litt.* 9, 5–11; CSEL 28, 1, pp. 273–281.

[278] Cf. the explanations to this text given by DALMAIS, Un traité de théologie contemplative, RAM 29 (1953), pp. 132 f., 135 f., 137, 139 and 159 with ref.

restoration, so as to integrate it into our particular context of media-tion.[279] Man's fall was due to bodily desire and search for sensual lust. That is Maximus' basic conviction, and it is confirmed through his definition of self-love as love for the body, which he considers to be the root of all sins and passions and the primitive sin which caused the fall. But thanks to a providential arrangement by God lust is always united with a subsequent pain. Thus sensual lust leads to its own destruction, and man who seeks for such a lust is always punished by the pain which follows it. This is a providential arrangement, since it constitutes a sign that man's desire should be directed towards God, who alone is its true object and alone is able to satisfy him with true pleasure. But there is also another providential arrangement, which is closely linked with this. Man's fall led to his corruption; having failed to obtain immortality, he suffers death from then onwards. In this way man was doomed to destruction, though destined to live on. Instead of granting him immor-tality, God then safeguarded the continuing life of mankind through a secondary law of procreation—another than the original way of multi-plying himself which Maximus assumes that man had at his disposal in his unfallen state—a new law which did not violate the dialectic between pleasure and pain, but used it for its purpose. According to this arrangement man was to gain his life through an act of bodily desire and sensual pleasure, but this pleasure was to be immediately combined with pain and corruption: destruction of virginity, birth through pain and finally death. In this way, man was at the same time to become more and more enslaved by the law of sin which led to death, since he was always bound to find his own life through sensual pleasure, a pleasure which can never satisfy him but always leads to pain.[280]

Here, however, Maximus' general view of sexuality and of the distinction between male and female naturally comes into its right perspective. Sexual intercourse in fallen man is a sign of the disastrous dialectic between pleasure and pain, to which man is enslaved. The very term *birth* (γέννησις) is coloured by this fact, and for this reason is often put into sharp contrast with the more neutral term of "coming into existence" (γένεσις). Through his very birth fallen man is bound to destruction on account of Adam's sin.[281] Only through Christ is man rescued from this prison, and his mode of life is renewed by being

---

[279] Cf. ch. III: B above.

[280] This divine pedagogical arrangement was intended to lead to freedom from any desirous attachment to the body, Maximus suggests in Amb 8; PG 91, 1104 B; cf. SHERWOOD, in *Berichte zum XI. Intern. Byz.-Kongr.*, p. 16 ff.

[281] See e.g. Amb 31; PG 91, 1276 BC.

restored to its original purpose.[282] This liberation took place through an
act, in which Christ was *born* as a man and yet broke the sinful law of
procreation. He was born by a woman like any child, but was conceived
without seed (σπορά, which here represents the aspect of sensual
pleasure) and also without destruction of the virginity of his mother
(without φθορά, which represents the aspect of consequent pain); and
thus he was free to take upon himself a voluntary death which was in his
case no longer a judgment upon fallen human nature but had become a
judgment upon sin itself.[283] Christ's coming into existence (γένεσις) was a
voluntary birth (γέννησις) implying a free acceptance of fallen nature,
through which man could be saved from his slavery and was made free to
enter a true relationship with God.[284] Through his own birth without
sexual intercourse Christ also liberated mankind from the sinful distinction, which existed between man and woman—a distinction which
involves a relationship of sensual desire, which yet creates no lasting
unity.[285]

Here we are thus able to see what Maximus means by his assertion
that in Christ there is "neither male nor female". The relationship
between these two forms of mankind which we now know is one marked
by sin. But in Christ it is overcome through a birth—a sinless way of
coming into existence—which has destroyed man's slavery both to lust
and death.[286] Consequently, there is no longer a necessary σπορά and
φθορά. The way is open once again for man to receive eternal life from
God. That eternal life will be given to man after his resurrection, but it
may certainly be anticipated already here on earth. To such an anticipation man is now called through his *second birth,* that *of baptism,*[287]
through which he may pass from *being* to *well-being.* The being which
fallen man possesses in this world is stained by the fall, and will not be
finally changed until it is transformed after death into ever-being. In the

---

[282] The second part of Evagrius' *Letter to Melania* (which was unknown to Frankenberg
but is now known in its Syriac version through the ms. Br. Mus. Add. 17192) shows that this
view found explicit support in Evagrius; see the important edition of the text by G.
VITESTAM, p. 23 f.

[283] See Thal 61; CCSG 22, pp. 91–95; Amb 41; PG 91, 1313 CD and 42; 1341
C.—Evagrius, *ibid.,* p. 23 presents man as enslaved by "conception and birth". The
difference between him and Maximus is, however, quite clear. Maximus stresses strongly
the provisional character of this law of birth, through which life is preserved in spite
of man's fall, while Evagrius even goes so far as to say that Christ is the divine leaven
hidden in the dough "without any leaven of humanity" (*ibid.;* p. 24).

[284] See Amb 42; PG 91, 1316 D–1317 A.

[285] Amb 41; PG 91, 1309 A.

[286] See Thal 61; CCSG 22, p. 93.

[287] Cf. p. 369 above.

meantime in Christ however man has the freedom to pass from mere being to well-being, i.e. to pass through baptism into the *vita practica* with all its virtues, and the *vita contemplativa* with its spiritual contemplations.[288]

This middle stage of well-being is the place in which we should therefore introduce the idea of *an anticipating mediation between male and female*. Maximus does not deny the value of marriage. It is the way in which man is born in this fallen world, and to reject it would be to reject the Creator, who has introduced it, and it would be Manichaeism.[289] It remains a fact however that a generic sin is at work in the passible element itself.[290] But in the *vita practica* man is called to transform the passions of this element into virtues, supporting the spiritual communion of the mind with God. Thus it is obviously *in the practical exercise* of these virtues that we are to find the true mediation between male and female.

The result of the first mediation

This last conclusion in fact is already evident with regard to Christ, whom Christians are called to follow and to imitate. For according to Maximus Christ himself in a mystical manner, through the Spirit removed the difference between male and female by freeing the common principle of nature (λόγος φύσεως) of both male and female from the singularities which lead to passions.[291] Through his obedience and his *lack of misuse of the faculties*, he thus liberated man from the difference between male and female.[292] We ought, however, to notice the way in which this was done. Christ carried out this mediation by subsuming the singularities of male and female under their common λόγος, and also that he did it by avoiding the misuse of his (passible) faculties. The mediation is not effected by the elimination of anything which is human and which therefore pertains to man or woman, nor by the elimination of the passible faculties themselves. In both cases all is ordered under the common principle of human nature. And this ordering is clearly the result of mediation.

Such an ordering under the direction of the principle of nature is in fact the aim of the *vita practica*, as well as of the *vita contemplativa*. And

---

[288] See e.g. Amb 42; PG 91, 1325 BC.

[289] See Amb 42; PG 91, 1340 BC; cf. von Balthasar, KL², p. 197. Misogynia is likewise unacceptable, cf. Hausherr, *Philautie*, p. 72.

[290] See Thal 21; CCSG 7, p. 131.

[291] Thal 48; CCSG 7, 333 ff.

[292] Amb 41; PG 91, 1309 A.

in both cases we have seen that such a subordination does not imply the elimination of any element, but their right use, in support of the higher functions.[293] And this fact leads us back to the spiritualized interpretation of "male and female". For what are anger and concupiscence but those passible faculties, which ought to be ordered and subordinated under reason and mind, in order to support man in his higher efforts?

Thus this interpretation of "male and female" proves to be closely linked with the more literal interpretation. Male and female in passionate action are the main expressions of a sinful misuse of anger and concupiscence. Therefore, it is not surprising that in his commentary to the Lord's Prayer Maximus says, that anger and concupiscence are the signs and passions of a nature which is subject to corruption ($\varphi\theta o\rho\hat{a}$) and coming into being ($\gamma\acute{e}\nu\epsilon\sigma\iota\varsigma$).[294] The relationship between the sinful law of procreation and a sinful use of the passible faculties of the soul is so close, that it is natural for Maximus to combine them in this way. But in Christ there are no such "signs", for in him the laws of sinful birth and corruption are broken.[295] Thus Maximus is able to maintain that man's overcoming of the passions of these elements which brings them into a whole, directed by the $\lambda\acute{o}\gamma o\varsigma$ in its relationship to Christ the Logos, is at the same time also a transcendence of the differentiation between male and female. For to describe such a transcendence in Christ is the aim of his exegesis of the Lord's Prayer.[296]

Thus we see that Christ the Mediator who by his good use of all his faculties and by the ordering of the elements of his human make-up obeyed the divine principle of human nature, not only broke the sinful law of procreation, which was operative through misuse of the passible faculties and a maintenance of the distinction between male and female. He also paved the way for man's task of mediation which, in anticipation of the final union of male and female, is to be worked out as an ordering of the passible faculties under Christ the Logos. Here as in Gregory of Nyssa the two aspects are, therefore, combined and interwoven in the perspective of a human life, where the passible faculties are used in their proper way: to direct and strengthen the mind and the whole of man in his relationship to God. Through the 'spiritualized' interpretation of "male and female" as anger and concupiscence such an anticipation in imitation of Christ is made possible here on earth.[297]

---

[293] Cf. pp. 339–343 above.
[294] OrDom.; CCSG 23, p. 51.
[295] Cf. *ibid.;* p. 54 f.
[296] Cf. the conclusions reached by DALMAIS, *art. cit.,* e.g. p. 139.
[297] VON BALTHASAR, KL², p. 194 f., has underlined, in relation to his treatment of the

Again we have found that an overcoming of differences, as presented by Maximus, does not imply an elimination of them as such, but rather their proper use. Though sexual intercourse will not remain, Maximus shows clearly that the human faculties which it manifests, those of anger and concupiscence, will remain, in that they support man in his relation to God in Christ. And it is precisely this transformation of them into *a positive support* which is clearly the aim of man's work as mediator, for even this work is to be understood in terms of the Chalcedonian formula.

That this Maximian idea of a good use and support from below as the aim of mediation is really relevant also for the differentiation between male and female, is finally demonstrated most clearly by Maximus himself in Amb 48, a section where he describes *a cosmic communion* with Christ the Logos. In this communion man is said to communicate through the different parts of Christ's body—and no parts are excluded. Among all these forms of communion there is one which is related to *Christ's belly*—a symbolism which obviously denotes a relationship to a true kind of passibility—and in describing this, Maximus makes clear that this kind of communion denotes a spiritual and *positive use of man's generative power* (τὸ γόνιμον). This use is further said to imply—and notice here the concrete sensual and sexual imagery—that the soul becomes *"pregnant"* with spiritual contemplations, and carries within itself an ever-burning flame of *desirous love* (ἔρως), i.e. for God.[298]

Thus in the end even sexual experience represents to Maximus an aspect of man's relationship to God, which has its proper place in his communion with Christ. In performing the first type of mediation man, therefore, may be said to restore this male-female aspect of human life to its proper place and use. Its transformation means its realization.

7. *Second mediation: between Paradise and the inhabited earth*

The second type and stage of mediation is related to Paradise and the inhabited earth. We are here again concerned with a difference caused by the fall of man. As regards the difference between male and female we noticed that mediation was effected through a renewed attention to, and a realization of their common principle of human nature. A similar reference to the common human λόγος is relevant also in this second

"sexual synthesis", that anger and concupiscence in Maximus' thinking are representative of all passions, and thus also of those which pertain to sexual relationship. Though he does not arrive explicitly at our conclusions concerning the realization of the sexual synthesis by men, he, therefore, seems to point in the same direction.

[298] PG 91, 1364 B, D.

mediation, and it is again effected through the *vita practica*. The only difference is that while in the first case it was the transformation of the basic passible faculties through the *vita practica* which dominated the picture, here it is rather the aspect of *mortification* which comes into the foreground; but the positive virtues particularly as they are summarized in equal love for one's neighbour also have a place.

Some particular elements of Maximus' understanding of the second mediation are to be found, if we study his own short descriptions of it in Thal 48 and Amb 41. In the first text Maximus says about Christ that he has established the unity of the earth by removing the difference between the Paradise and the inhabited earth (οἰκουμένη).[299] Thus here Paradise is of an earthly character.[300] And in Amb 41 we likewise learn that it is *the earth* which is divided in this way.[301] And of Christ Maximus says here that he sanctified the inhabited world (οἰκουμένη) *through his human behaviour,* and entered Paradise after his death *as he had promised one of the robbers* (see Luke 23: 43), for to Christ there was no longer any difference between Paradise and the inhabited world. And when he appeared again in the latter after his resurrection and was together with his disciples, he manifested *the restored unity of the earth* and showed that it was again in accordance with its original λόγος.[302] Finally we also learn that man, having revealed the *one* man and the *one* λόγος of human nature by way of his first mediation, is now called to unite Paradise and the inhabited world *through his own conduct* and so to *make the earth one,* so that it is no more divided on account of its different parts, but rather held together in relation to him, since he is no more attracted to any particular one of these parts.[303]

Thus we may conclude that in relation to the second mediation Maximus refers to differentiations of the created earth which have caused this basic distinction between Paradise and the rest of this world, and consequently to the fall of man which implied that he preferred the different sensual sensations of the created world to God as Creator. In Maximus' opinion, this fall, in its turn, implied a deeper and sinful differentiation according to the individual desires and γνῶμαι of men, a differentiation which is overcome only through the virtues as expressions of love for God and one's neighbour. Thus the second mediation

---

[299] CCSG 7, p. 333 ff.
[300] On the idea of an earthly and sensible Paradise in Origen, cf. M. RAUER, Origenes über das Paradies, in *Studien zum Neuen Testament und zur Patristik* (TU 77), pp. 253–259.
[301] PG 91, 1305 A.
[302] PG 91, 1309 B.
[303] PG 91, 1305 D.

concerns life on earth and divisions among men, which are to be overcome through a new moral behaviour in imitation of Christ, who made the earth one through his own conduct.

It seems possible to discover two specific ideas in the background here: the idea of an earthly Paradise of moral conduct and virtues, and an interpretation of Luke 23: 43 in relation to this, which refers to an imitation of Christ in relation to the world and in particular to other human beings. Let us briefly study each of these ideas.

A Paradise of virtues

The idea of a Paradise of virtues—which is (not explicitly) stated by Maximus but only possibly presupposed as already known and so hinted at—in fact goes back to early Alexandrian theology. Already in Philo we find an allegorical interpretation of the Genesis story, which contains this idea, and an interpretation of the Paradise itself as a symbol of virtue.[304] Daniélou has shown that this line of interpretation continues—along with the typological exegesis of the text—first of all in Origen, Ambrose and Gregory of Nyssa.[305] Particularly in the writings of the latter two fathers there are clear examples of an allegorical exegesis which expresses the idea of a paradise of virtues. The trees of Paradise are the virtues, or the four rivers of Paradise are the four cardinal virtues, etc.[306] In these cases it is obvious that this kind of exegesis represents an immanentism, which is contrary to the literal and the Christological-typological interpretations, though these two types of understanding are sometimes found side by side. Even in the case of Origen the allegorical interpretations of Paradise seem not to have excluded the idea of an original *earthly* Paradise.[307]

Against this background Maximus' contribution is particularly interesting, since it succeeds in combining an understanding of Paradise as an earthly reality with an idea which resembles that of a human paradise of virtues. The heavy attacks of an Epiphanius against Origen for spiritualizing the concept of Paradise[308] would thus fail of their purpose in the case of Maximus. He presupposes an earthly Paradise, and he starts from the life of Christ, and yet he affirms a realization of the unity between Paradise and the rest of the earth which is effected through a virtuous

---

[304] Cf. DANIÉLOU, *Sacramentum futuri*, p. 45 ff.
[305] DANIÉLOU, *op. cit.*, pp. 48 and 50 f.
[306] DANIÉLOU, *op. cit.*, pp. 50 f.
[307] For a revised understanding of Origen at this point, see RAUER, *art. cit.*
[308] See *Panarion* 64, 47; GCS Epiph. 2, p. 472 f.; cf. *Ancoratus* 54–55, 58 etc.; 1, pp. 63 ff. and 67 ff.

life. The way to Paradise has been re-opened by Christ through his death, and in virtue of his truly human conduct. This fact may now be manifested by men through their own obedience to the divine commandments in imitation of Christ, who shows "a godlike way to life". This combination of the two types of interpretation is characteristic of Maximus, as we can see for example in the beginning of the *Liber asceticus*.[309]

But how is it possible for him to make such a combination? The only adequate answer is, of course, that he sees this moral realization of the unity between Paradise and the inhabited earth as an anticipation of that human state of life which will be granted to true believers after their resurrection. The paradise of virtues is not for him an immanent substitute for the visible Paradise, but a manifestation in moral (and 'gnostic') terms of the coherence in the Logos of the whole created world, a manifestation which is not least effective in man's outward relationships to other created beings.

Luke 23: 43 and the re-establishment of Paradise

For this reason this first idea is, further, easily combined with a corresponding interpretation of Luke 23: 43, for there Christ's death and resurrection safeguard the literal and historical relevance, while his promise to the penitent thief on the cross seems to imply immediate spiritual consequences related to this age. The explicit reference which Maximus makes to this text in Amb 41[310] shows, in fact, that it plays a central rôle in relation to his understanding of the second mediation. According to this interpretation, through his death and resurrection Christ reveals that there is no real difference between the different parts of the earth, and opens a free entry into Paradise. Consequently, his promise to the thief is an invitation to follow him in this realization of the unity of the created earth. Thus we are more or less bound to think that the thief represents *all* who follow Christ, and who thus effect the second type of mediation.

In the older Christian interpretation of this text there are, in fact, at least two characteristics which point in the same direction. First of all, there is a certain stress on the close relationship between Christ's promise about Paradise and his *descent into Hades*.[311] And secondly,

---

[309] Asc 1; PG 90, 912 AB.
[310] See PG 91, 1309 B.
[311] On the close relationship between the motifs of *ascension* and *descensus* in early Christian reflection, see e.g. BESKOW, *Rex Gloriae*, pp. 103–106 and 141–147 with ref.; cf.

there is also a conviction that Christ's words are directed to all Christians, and that this fact has some relevance for Christian *mortification*, and spiritual exercises. Thus Origen closely links the promise of Luke 23: 43 with the sign of Jonah which Christ promises in Matt. 16: 4, and concludes that His descent into Hades is this sign.[312] And he says that Christ's words to the thief are for all those, for whom Christ descended into Hades.[313] Thus Christ's promise concerning Paradise is intimately related to his victorious suffering and death, and Origen concludes that Christ will lead Christians to Paradise, but at the same time at once refers to the remaining sufferings of the Christians, as they are presented in Col. 1: 24.[314]

Gregory of Nyssa also combines Luke 23: 43 with Matt. 16: 4, but is eager to deny that Paradise itself is found in Hades (ἐν ὑποχθονίοις), or, of course, that Hades is found in Paradise.[315] Thus we see that the Christ-like way through suffering and death, as well as through human mortification, is stressed by the Christian writers with regard to this text, and also that Christ paved the way to Paradise for all true followers of him and gave them the same promise as he gave to the thief.

The same general understanding of the way back to Paradise is expressed by Maximus, when he says that Christ through his death led back to life him (i.e. man) who had been made dead through sin and in sin.[316] But in one place (in Amb 53) he also gives a more detailed interpretation of the position of the two thieves. There he starts from one of the "difficulties" in Gregory Nazianzen's *In sanctum Pascha*, which says: "If you are crucified together (i.e. with Christ) as a robber, get acquainted with God as a wise one",[317] and gives four parallel interpretations of this sentence. According to the first of these—which together with the third is of particular interest in our context—the wise thief is every man who suffers for his sins as one who is responsible, and who thus shares in himself the sufferings of the λόγος who suffers innocently for his sake, and so gets to know the Logos who is simultaneously present.[318]

also J. KROLL, *Gott und Hölle. Der Mythus vom Descensus-kampfe* (StBW 20), Berlin 1932, p. 58 ff.
[312] *Comm. in Matth.* 12, 3: GCS Orig. 10, p. 73, 1 ff.
[313] *In Gen., hom.* 15, 5; GCS Orig. 6, p. 134, 12 ff.; cf. *In Lev., hom.* 9, 5; GCS Orig. 6, p. 425, 14 ff.
[314] See *Exhort.* 36; GCS Orig. 1, p. 33, 19 ff.
[315] *In Christi resurr., or.* 1; PG 46, 616 A.
[316] Char 2. 93; CSC, p. 140.
[317] *Or.* 45, 24; PG 36, 656 C.
[318] Amb 53; PG 91, 1372 D.

The thief is here understood as the man who is enslaved by his sensuality, but who accepts the consequent verdict of pain. For in so doing he becomes acquainted with Christ the Logos, who is present in the λόγοι of the world and suffers through his Incarnation. Such a man accepts his pain as a mortification—we can add: by transforming it into an active *vita practica*—and consequently he enters justly with his λόγος into the land of true knowledge, *"the paradise"*, that is to say a knowledge through which he becomes acquainted with the reason of his own suffering.[319] The imprudent thief, on the other hand, is the one who because of his sinful γνώμη does not get to know the λόγος of righteousness, which suffers with him out of love for men (φιλανθρωπία).[320] Symbolically the thieves are thus understood as types of the individual man who is enslaved by sin, but reference is also made to the cosmic incarnation and suffering of Christ after the pattern of his suffering on Golgotha. And the prudence of the penitent thief is interpreted as his acceptance of pain as *a voluntary mortification, by which he is prepared to enter into the paradise of higher knowledge.*

The second interpretation of the same text is less interesting to us here, though it deals with man when he is approaching the end of his life.[321] The third interpretation, however, is of a special interest. There we learn that everybody is by nature, since he consists of soul and body, *a double thief* who, according to the double law which belongs to his two constituent elements, is *mystically crucified together with the Logos for virtue's sake.* For on the one hand the law of his flesh conflicts with the λόγος of virtue like an imprudent thief, and on the other hand the law of the spirit is received like a wise thief, together with the saving Logos through the modes (τρόποι) of the *vita practica,* which even though they are toilsome, prepare a way of entrance into the place of the festival (i.e. the paradise) of complete knowledge.[322] Here again it is thus the voluntary mortification which is put into the foreground, and the suffering and repentent thief is its symbol. And since this way of life, manifested in the *vita practica,* expresses those modes which are in accordance with the λόγος of humanity, it also contains the incarnate Logos himself, who by being allowed to be present in the virtues of men opens the way to the paradise of full communion with God. Again the idea of a continuing incarnation of Christ builds the bridge between a literal and an allegorical understanding of the text.

---

319 See *ibid.,* 1373 A.
320 *Loc. cit.*
321 *Ibid.;* 1373 BC.
322 *Ibid.;* 1373 CD.

The fourth interpretation adds very little to the others seen from our point of view. Nevertheless it repeats the idea that the wise thief is a man who mortifies his passions, and is thus deemed worthy to be crucified with Christ, yes even *on his right side*, which implies that he performs his virtuous acts with reason and knowledge and is no stumbling block to any human being.[323] Maximus then goes on to show that there is thus a crucifixion with Christ the Logos which takes place even at the higher stages of spiritual perfection, and that through it man is made fit to enter a paradise, both in this world and in the world to come where there is no longer any need for a forgiveness of sins.[324]

A new relationship to other human beings

We have thus noticed that Luke 23: 43 is interpreted by Maximus in such a way as to unite a more historical and literal understanding of Christ's crucifixion with an allegorical application of it to the individual sinner in his sanctification, and that the mediating link is the idea of a cosmic and moral incarnation of Christ the Logos in the λόγοι. But this implies, in its turn, that the way to Paradise which this interpretation presents, passes through a practice of mortification, which is voluntary but contains a pain which is in itself a result of sin. And therefore, we can also conclude that Christ's mediation between Paradise and the inhabited earth of sinners leads to a continuing suffering and crucifixion in the sinners themselves, in which they are allowed to share actively in order that thereby they may arrive at a true knowledge and full communion with God. It is that human conduct which implies a virtuous acceptance of mortification which effects this mediation.

But it leads us further on, even to a new relationship with other human beings. The repentant thief arrives at an insight into the cause of his pain, and thus accepts it. And therefore he is no stumbling block to other human beings. This latter aspect of the interpretation of the penitent thief is more clearly emphasized in another text, Ep 11. There Maximus underlines the attitude of God in Christ (his φιλανθρωπία) which transforms harlots and publicans and thieves, and thus brings them with Him into Paradise. Thereby we are to learn what love for men (φιλανθρωπία) and gentleness is, and neither to sin any more, nor to be unfriendly and hostile towards sinners.[325] Thus the divine φιλανθρωπία

---

[323] *Ibid.*; 1373 D–1376 A.—The ancient symbolism of "the right hand side" denotes that which is good and valuable. Cf. e.g. the rôle of the angels on the right hand of God in Origen, see S. T. BETTENCOURT, *Doctrina ascetica Origenis* (SA 16), Rome 1945, p. 9 ff.

[324] See *ibid.*; 1376 B.

[325] PG 91, 456 BC.

is to be imitated by repentant sinners and thieves, whose attitude to others should be the same as God's towards them.

Now we know that for instance in *Cent. de char.* Maximus is always very eager to point out that love for one's neighbour should imply tolerance and gentleness towards the insults, injustice and hostility of others, and therefore we can easily see that this imitation of the divine φιλανθρωπία itself forms part of the sufferings of virtuous mortification.[326] But already in relation to the first type of mediation a conscious consideration of the common principle of human nature alone, without false regard for its diversities, was involved. In the case of this second mediation the situation is the same. The process of mortification on account of one's own sin, which liberates the λόγος from its slavery, allows no place for any consideration of the moral differences, or other distinctions, among men. The modes of the *vita practica* contain all the positive uses of individual characteristics in the service of the common principle. Here Maximus speaks of a mutual communication between men,[327] a communication by which Christ is again said to be present. But for this very reason the common human λόγος alone should be considered, since it integrates all that is human.

In relation to the first mediation we referred to Gal. 3: 28. Here we may refer e.g. to the parallel text of Col. 3: 11; the corresponding distinction between Barbarian and Scythian in that text is interpreted by Maximus precisely in accordance with what we have just said. Maximus says that this distinction, now removed in Christ, signifies the separation within one and the same human nature, which results from the sinful revolt of men according to their own particular γνώμη.[328] This revolt expresses the very nature of sin, since it is marked by the fundamental sinful search for pleasure which leads inescapably to pain.

The transformation of earthly pain

In relation to the first mediation we noticed that though the difference between male and female is removed through their integration into the higher unity of human nature, this fact nevertheless implies that the basic powers and faculties which are at work in the fallen relationship between man and woman are not eliminated but transformed into a spiritual and positive use of man's generative power. Is there also in the second type of mediation a corresponding positive function left to those parts which

---

[326] Cf. our presentation of detachment in ch. V: B, 3; pp. 306–309 above.
[327] See Ep 2; PG 91, 401 B.
[328] OrDom; CCSG 23, p. 55. On the rôle and function of γνώμη, see pp. 213–218 above.

constituted the division, so that a proper place is granted to what is natural in the differentiation itself? It is Maximus' opinion that individual desires which cut human nature asunder are transformed in Christ into *individual virtues*, between which there is a mutual communication in the service of the whole life of Christ as it is present in human virtues as a whole. A reference to this opinion is, of course, one of the possible answers to our question. Even in the case of sinful differentiation the mediation in Christ is a true mediation, in that it does not entirely eliminate but transforms the original causes of separation.

But a further answer is also possible. We have seen that the mediation between Paradise and the inhabited earth is effected by man in imitation of Christ through a voluntary mortification which implies an acceptance of the painful results of sin as positive suffering. Thus even the sinful conditions themselves which now divide mankind may be granted a spiritual use which leads to true communion with God. And is not this fact a further sign that mediation in Maximus' view is no simple elimination of distinctions, but allows for a combination of an element of differentiation, positively evaluated, and a corresponding element of unification?

This stress on *a positive acceptance of the pains* which are inherent in fallen human conditions, is in fact not confined to Maximus' discussion of the second mediation, or of the crucifixion of the thief together with Christ. Virtuous life in general, in Maximus' opinion, is inescapably connected with labours (πόνοι).[329] They are an obvious consequence of the dialectic between pleasure and pain which the fall has inaugurated.[330] The chain of this dialectic is broken in Christ, and thanks to baptism Christians share in this work of liberation, but it is to be fully realized through a voluntary acceptance of a kind of pain.[331] As in Christ's death the judgment on human nature changed into a judgment on sin, so in the life of Christians this judgment is taken over, and its weapon is used for the annihilation of personal sin, in imitation of Jesus.[332]

---

[329] See e.g. Char, 2. 34; CSC, p. 108 and Ep 2; PG 91, 400 B. A similar idea is frequently found in Christian ascetic literature. It may be in the form of a doctrine of the *flagella Dei* as in Gregory the Great (cf. R. GILLET, Spiritualité et place du moine dans l'Eglise selon Saint Grégoire le Grand, in *Théologie de la vie monastique*, p. 337 and n. 60), or simply in the form of the conviction that monastic life is κόπος and πόνος as later in Theodore Studites (cf. J. LEROY, Saint Théodore Studite, *op. cit.*, p. 431). For Theodoret of Cyrus, for example, the term πόνος simply denotes ascetic practice (cf. P. CANIVET, Théodoret et le monachisme Syrien avant le concile de Chalcédoine, *op. cit.*, pp. 274 and 277, n. 221).

[330] See from a negative aspect Char 2. 58; CSC, p. 122.

[331] See the interpretations of the penitent thief above, and further e.g. Thal 61; CCSG 22, p. 99 and Char 2. 66; CSC, p. 124.

[332] See Thal 61; *ibid.*, p. 99. The New Testament (Pauline) background of this

Such a voluntary suffering leads to a blessed knowledge of the cause of pain, i.e. to an insight into the conditions of fallen life, and the guilt and responsibility of man over against God the Creator. Such a painful truth is in fact necessary, if man is to be fully restored. Only through these labours does he arrive at a true detachment, and this is one of their positive results.[333] But Maximus goes even further and affirms that also "natural contemplation" contains labour ($\pi\acute{o}\nu o\varsigma$), through which man arrives at a knowledge of truth.[334]

Labours often also appear in inter-human relations. There they take the form of insults, etc.,[335] and they ought to be endured as a penance, necessarily combined with humility.[336] They are overcome, however, through an equal love for all which borrows some of its characteristics from detachment.[337] But these labours are never merely a blind result of the fallen state of mankind. Seen from another aspect afflictions of all kinds—even in the form of demons—are among the things permitted by God, and in one place Maximus, referring to others, enumerates five reasons for this. Of these reasons the second is of a particular interest in our context, since it states that, by acquiring virtue in combat and labour ($\pi\acute{o}\nu\dot{\omega}$), men should be helped to hold it fixed and steadfast.[338] And in Ep 2 Maximus emphasizes in the same manner that virtues and labours together purify the $\lambda\acute{o}\gamma o\varsigma$ of man.[339]

Thus even the labours, which are the differentiated forms of pain due to man's fall, are given a positive function within the spiritual development of man in Christ. Through development of his virtues, in free acceptance of these labours, man thus follows Christ on his victorious way through death to Paradise. And in so doing, man also manifests the

---

conviction is clear. On this topic, see e.g. E. LARSSON, *Christus als Vorbild,* Uppsala 1962, particularly p. 287 ff.

[333] See e.g. Thal 51; CCSG 7, p. 405. For an analysis of Thal 51, see BLOWERS, *op. cit.,* p. 245, n. 168.

[334] See Thal 50; CCSG 7, p. 383.

[335] See Char 1. 28; CSC, p. 58 and 4. 88; p. 232.

[336] See *ibid.,* 3. 87; p. 186.

[337] Cf. ch. V: B, 3; pp. 306–309 above.

[338] See Char 2. 67; CSC p. 124 ff.

[339] PG 91, 400 B.—Other similar terms should also be mentioned in this context. There is, first of all, an affliction ($\theta\lambda\tilde{\imath}\psi\iota\varsigma$) which characterizes this world, see *Expos. in Ps. 59;* CCSG 23, p. 21 and Ep 35; PG 91, 629 B. Maximus distinguishes here between a $\theta\lambda\tilde{\imath}\psi\iota\varsigma$ $\sigma\omega\tau\acute{\eta}\rho\iota o\varsigma$ and a $\theta\lambda\tilde{\imath}\psi\iota\varsigma$ $\dot{o}\lambda\acute{e}\theta\rho\iota o\varsigma$, see Gnost 2.95 (PG 90, 1172 A); cf. VON BALTHASAR, KL², p. 540. Man is further called to a grief ($\lambda\acute{\upsilon}\pi\eta$) which is in accordance with God's mind, and which is sometimes identified with $\pi\acute{o}\nu o\varsigma$ (see Ep 4; PG 91, 413 A–420 B and Thal 58; CCSG 22, p. 35 ff.). This grief for sin is, finally, even called $\pi\acute{e}\nu\theta o\varsigma$, see Thal 56; CCSG 22, p. 3 ff. (On the concept of $\pi\acute{e}\nu\theta o\varsigma$ in general in the Eastern Christian tradition, see HAUSHERR, *Penthos. La doctrine de la componction dans l'Orient chrétien,* Orientalia Christiana Analecta 132, Rome 1944.)

fact that in God's purpose for creation there is only one earth. In obedience to God's commandments this may be effected even in this world in virtue of Christ's Incarnation.

We ended our analysis of the first mediation with a reference to Amb 48, with its description of a spiritual manducation, which at the same time is a kind of cosmic communion through the different members of Christ's body as it is incarnate in the world. Here too such a reference is proper. And since we are again dealing with an aspect of the *vita practica,* it is perhaps Maximus' description of the spiritual eating of *"the hands of Christ"* which is particularly relevant. For here we learn that those are to eat of his hands who direct the entire *practical* energy of their soul to the fulfilment of God's commandments,[340] and as we have seen, it is through Christ's presence in the laborious development of the virtues—in response to these commandments—that Christians are allowed to enter the paradise of higher spiritual communion, which makes the world one.

8. Third mediation: between heaven and earth

If the first two forms of mediation are to be referred to the *vita practica,* it is equally obvious that the next two mediations are intimately connected with the *vita contemplativa,* and that the third mediation represents its lower form, i.e. the contemplation of sensible creatures. This third type of mediation is defined as a unification of heaven and earth through man in Christ, and, according to Maximus' presentations in Thal 48 and Amb 41, contains the following characteristics.

It has been effected by Christ in that he *ascended into heaven* with his earthly body, consubstantial with ours, and thereby demonstrating *the unity of sensible nature* through the elimination of the particularity of its separating division.[341] This demonstration shows that in the end there is only one nature of sensible things, which is thus inclined (νεύουσα) towards itself.[342] This realization in Christ also implies a restoration of man to his original vocation which is to effect this mediation in his own life. This he does, by allowing his life to resemble—as far as is possible for man—*the virtuous perfection of the angels.* Through the lightness of the spirit he gains victory over bodily heaviness by means of a continuing *spiritual ascent towards heaven* in desire for God.[343] Thus Maximus describes it as a kind of angelic life of contemplation of the sensible

---

[340] PG 91, 1364 D.
[341] Amb 41; PG 91, 1309 BC.
[342] Thal 48; CCSG 7, p. 235.
[343] Amb 41; PG 91, 1305 D–1308 A.

creation in its oneness in the Logos, which at the same time involves an ascent into heaven with Christ while already here on earth. But how more specifically does he conceive of this process? We shall try to analyse the different elements of his description in their proper context.

Likeness to the angels

First of all, Maximus stresses the likeness to the angels which is contained in the third mediation. He does indeed underline this likeness in other instances as well, but here he mostly follows his predecessors. He says for instance that he who loves God necessarily leads an "angelic life" on earth,[344] a statement which probably reflects the general ancient Christian idea that monastic life is in a special sense an angelic life.[345] As to the rôle of angels in general and the content of an angelic life, Maximus also agrees with his predecessors. To Origen for instance angels and demons played a very great rôle, and the good angels were to him of immense importance for man's spiritual perfection.[346] Gregory of Nyssa for his part emphasized the angelic character of the original state of man, and human spiritual perfection as a participation in angelic joy.[347] The idea of likeness to the angels as a perfection of man, and a similar stress on participation in their joy is also found in Ps.-Denis,[348] who is particularly well-known for his extensive meditation upon the mysteries of the world of angelic powers.[349] Evagrius closely follows Origen and the Egyptian monastic tradition and stresses both the pedagogical function of the angels and the ascetic state of likeness to them.[350]

Likewise Maximus himself insists that the angelic good powers assist us in the good and exhort us to pursue it.[351] He further mentions a virtuous likeness to the angels as forming part of man's spiritual development, and within the ascetic context he particularly emphasizes that such

---

[344] Char 1. 42; CSC, p. 64.

[345] Cf. SHERWOOD, in ACW, p. 250, n. 32. On this monastic concept of "angelic life" in the Christian tradition in general against its New Testament background, see further E. VON SEVERUS, Bios angelikos. Zum Verständnis des Mönchleben als "Engelsleben" in der christlichen Überlieferung, *Maria Laach* (1960), pp. 73–88 and my own art. Änglalivet i munkgestalt, *Kyrkohistorisk årsskrift* 1972, pp. 59–83 (with a summary in English).

[346] Cf. e.g. DANIÉLOU, *Origène*, Paris 1948, pp. 235–243. See also BETTENCOURT, *Doctrina ascetica Origenis*, pp. 24–28 and 33 f.

[347] Cf. DANIÉLOU, *Platonisme et théologie mystique*, p. 165 (see further also p. 95) and VÖLKER, *Kontemplation und Ekstase*, p. 72.

[348] Cf. VÖLKER, *loc. cit.*

[349] Cf. VÖLKER, *op. cit.*, pp. 120–141 with ref.

[350] See e.g. *De orat.* 80–81; PG 79, 1184 D–1185 A; 113; 1192 D and *Cent. gnost.* 3. 65; PO 28, p. 125.

[351] See Char 2. 32; CSC, p. 108 and 3. 93–94; p. 188.

a likeness implies *an angelic peace* which consists of love for God and love for one another.[352] Maximus also analyses the knowledge of God and of his creation which is possessed by the angels, the likeness to which man is called to acquire himself.

This last analysis obviously is of a particular interest in relation to the third and fourth mediation. The angels know God's creation in an immediate way (i.e. they know its λόγοι directly) but according to Maximus not without restriction, since they do not know it from within the divine Wisdom as God does.[353] They likewise know God through participation and not as He knows Himself.[354] But what is most important here, however, is that the angels are not ignorant of anything which in the created world is divided into parts, since all that they know, they know from the side of the λόγοι themselves and thus understand all the differentiations of creation.[355] It is to such a knowledge that man, too, is called by the grace of God, and this means that the differentiation of things, which to the fallen mind is a continual cause of confusion, since man's desire is directed towards the world in its diversity and not towards the divine aim of human life, becomes in itself no longer a hindrance to a true knowledge, once the Logos in the λόγοι has been grasped. But in order to arrive at this point man has to leave his affective relationship to this world and ascend to spiritual contemplation.

If we now look again at the other characteristics of the third mediation, it immediately becomes clear that it is precisely this kind of ascent which is involved, and this is the reason why reference is made to the likeness to the angels. The third mediation is thus that which is effected at the very border line between the *vita practica* and the *vita contemplativa*. Likeness to the angels implies not only that inner peace which is at the culmination of the *vita practica*[356] and which true contemplation presupposes, but also a participation in the immediate character of angelic knowledge.

Now it is clear, that the *third mediation* refers to this earlier stage of peace and preparation for higher contemplation which thus unites heaven and earth, while the *fourth mediation* refers to the second stage which also implies an angelic form of knowledge.[357] The form of mediation with which we are now concerned is thus to be understood as

---

[352] *Ibid.* 4. 36; p. 208.
[353] See *ibid.* 3. 21; p. 152; cf. PEGON, SCH 9, p. 130, n. 1.
[354] See also Char 3. 22; CSC p. 152.
[355] See *ibid.* 3. 34; p. 160.
[356] Cf. Ep 2; PG 91, 396 AB.
[357] See the two references to angels related to the third and the fourth mediation respectively in Amb 41; PG 91, 1305 D and 1308 A.

one which is realized in man's breaking away from his subservience to this world, in search for knowledge about God as Creator as seen through the principles of His creation. Therefore, it is also understood as an ascension with Christ and an imitation of him.[358]

Ascension with Christ the Incarnate

The idea of an ascension with Christ, however, is not only connected with faith in his historical ascension in human form to the right hand of his Father. As in the case of the *vita practica* and the first two mediations, it is also intimately linked with Maximus' dominant idea of a universal incarnation of Christ the Logos in the world.[359] This incarnation takes place in words and letters in the Scripture, but also in created things through the λόγοι which are held together by the universal Logos. Thus Maximus says that the Logos who nourished the angels (notice the reference to angelic contemplation) "became thick" in this manifold incarnation among us.[360] He is also said to "become thick" in the virtues of the *vita practica*.

But from there Maximus goes on to say that in the same way he may be said to "become thin" in the man of contemplation.[361] There is thus *a spiritual ascent in contemplation* which, as it were, follows Christ on his way back to his Father. The divine condescension of Christ to man thus leads man on to the corresponding human ascension to God. Therefore, Maximus also says that for him who seeks the λόγος concerning God only according to the flesh, the Lord does not ascend to his Father, but for those who seek it through high contemplations he does ascend.[362] Or in another formulation: Those who having conquered their passions in the *vita practica*, turn to "gnostic philosophy" (i.e. "natural contemplation"), "allow" the Logos to return to his Father.[363] Or to choose the imagery of the transfiguration of Christ: The disciples are prepared

---

[358] On Christ's ascension as prototype for the fulfilment of the life of Christians already in Pauline theology, see LARSSON, *op. cit.,* p. 260 ff.

[359] Cf. ch. II: 4; pp. 75–79 above.

[360] See Amb 33; PG 91, 1285 C.

[361] Gnost 2. 37; PG 90, 1141 C.

[362] *Ibid.* 2. 47; 1145 B.

[363] *Ibid.* 2. 94; 1169 B.—Isolated from other Maximian texts these last statements might seem to imply that man leaves the *vita practica* and is in no further need of it, when he starts his progress to contemplation, but such an interpretation is entirely contrary to Maximus' intentions. Especially in *Cent. gnost.*, where he deals primarily with different forms of contemplation and mystical knowledge, he underlines strongly the necessity to advance further than just to the *vita practica*, but he does not regard "natural contemplation" as a necessary prerequisite for deification (cf. pp. 341 f. and 348 f. above).

through virtue to ascend to the mount with Christ, where he is revealed to them through contemplation.[364]

This ascension itself implies a kind of spiritual assimilation to the life of the angels. This becomes particularly clear in Maximus' commentary on the Lord's Prayer, where the third petition gives him an occasion to underline that unity between men and angels which consists in a common individual obedience to the divine will. When this obedience is realized, a similar inner peace is also established, which implies that the tendencies of the concupiscible and irascible faculties to revolt have been destroyed and that the rational faculty alone is ruling in man.[365]

This unity of will and God-ward movement between men and angels, which is manifested in man's ascent to contemplation on the basis of Christ's condescension towards man, may also be put into a wider cosmic perspective. To the corresponding movements of divine condescension and human ascension in Christ, which are immediately related to the salvation of man, corresponds in its turn a cosmic interaction of expansion and contraction (διαστολή and συστολή).[366] This reciprocal movement—towards unity in one λόγος and towards individualized realization of this λόγος in the created particularities—is always understood from a Christological presupposition and in anthropological terms. In this its other aspect, however, human ascension is, consequently, also to be interpreted as *a participation in the cosmic motion of contraction.* In contemplation man follows this contraction: indeed by following it he also realizes it through himself, because contemplation of the λόγοι of things in their unity keeps these things together, since it implies their proper use and obedience to the purpose of Christ's reconciling incarnate presence in them. Thus there is a cosmic movement of the individual elements, which makes them more and more like the general principle of the reasonable substance as such, and which man follows in his act of contemplation. In the things themselves there is a desire for *well-being,* a tendency away from what is merely individual and differentiated, which man shares with them. And thus is revealed to man a Logos which is one and the same for all.[367]

---

[364] See Amb 10; PG 91, 1125 D.

[365] See OrDom; CCSG 23, p. 57 f.; cf. DALMAIS, RAM 29 (1953), p. 141 f.

[366] Cf. ch. II: 1 and 6; pp. 60 f. and 81 ff. above.

[367] See Thal 2; CCSG 7, p. 51. VON IVÁNKA, Der philosophische Ertrag, JOBG 7 (1958), pp. 23–49, sees this dynamism of unification of the Cosmos in the Logos as the decisive argument in Maximus' refutation of Origenism—even to such an extent that he sometimes seems to neglect the aspect of differentiation, as it is preserved in Maximus even in his theology of unification.

In this way a mediation takes place when man breaks away from his dependence on earthly impulses. He is allowed to know the λόγοι of things, first of all of sensible things, without being sensually attracted to them, and to know all these λόγοι as one Logos. At the same time however he also feels the opposite movement of expansion, which allows the one Logos to be known as many λόγοι in the "natural contemplation" of the difference and manifoldness of creation.[368] The angels share this knowledge, but what is significant here is that this theology of the λόγοι, which corresponds rather well to the mystical contemplation of the angels in Ps.-Denis, is always centred on Christ, the Logos, and this means that the stress on the importance of angels in Maximus is never allowed to minimize the cosmic importance of Christ and his Incarnation—as is to some extent the case in Ps.-Denis.[369] For Maximus it is more valuable than anything else in relation to God's creation to be able to underline that the many λόγοι are the one Logos.[370] All things are defined by their own λόγοι and by those of the things around them, and are circumscribed by them,[371] and yet all are parts of the cosmic Logos, who is Christ incarnate in things.

This last fact now leads us to an important consequence. The ascent in the *vita contemplativa* from what is merely a "practical" use of sensible things themselves in the virtues of the *vita practica,* an ascent through which the Logos becomes "thin", for Maximus never signifies that man passes outside the realm of the Incarnation of the Son of God. As a person in the Godhead, Christ is above all λόγοι, and therefore even the presence which is open to the contemplative mind of man is due entirely to the divine condescension, and is an aspect of this incarnation. Thus there is a *spiritual communion with the body of Christ* taking place at the stage of contemplation, which is not different in principle from the communion through the virtues of the *vita practica.*

The mind which is engaged in "natural contemplation" certainly has as its head the Logos of faith himself who is here revealed as the Creator of all that is, but the "woman" of this mind (see 1 Cor. 11: 3) is still the sensibility with which this contemplation is necessarily united.[372] On the one hand, man is always a composite unity of body and soul. The Godhead, on the other, is always above all created elements, however subtle they may be. And for this double reason there is no other

---

[368] See Amb 7; PG 91, 1077 C.
[369] Cf. DALMAIS, *art. cit.,* p. 141.
[370] Amb 7; PG 91, 1081 BC.
[371] *Ibid.;* 1081 B.
[372] See Thal 25; CCSG 7, p. 162.

communion with God available to man, but that which is due to divine grace and condescension.

Thus Maximus points out that the λόγοι of sensible things are the flesh of the Logos which is being revealed, in the same sense as the λόγοι of intelligible things are his blood. And thus it is made clear that the Logos himself is "the teacher"—i.e. the revealer—of both kinds of λόγοι, the understanding of which constitutes a spiritual communion with the Logos.[373] And the body of Christ which, according to the Gospel, was besought by Joseph of Arimathea,[374] seen in the same perspective, not only symbolizes the different elements of man, or the commandments, or the virtues—in all of which the Logos is present—but also the very λόγοι of things themselves.[375]

The "cosmic liturgy"

Through Christ, the Creator Logos who is in the λόγοι which are contemplated in the stages of "natural contemplation"—those of sensible things and of intelligible things—the whole creation is one. And that is why the ascent of man to contemplation also involves the revelation of this basic unity—and a mediation, which is first of all between heaven and earth. When the contemplative mind follows the λόγοι of sensible things to their common source, it finds that there is, in the end, *only one nature*—active of course in a differentiated existence in the lower natures of the different species—*which inclines towards itself.*[376] That is not to say, that there are no differences, nor that those differences which we can see are mere fancies, but that all the λόγοι are reducible to a common λόγος which unites them all in a common purpose established by God in His creation. And thus, says Maximus, the whole creation is in fact one— *"like another man"*—completely perfected through the mutual interaction of its parts, and inclined (νεύουσα) towards itself according to one and the same idea.[377] Already in this third type of mediation man is on his way to this final insight, and to its realization through man himself as contemplative mind.

The ascension and mediation which we have now described is, to conclude, understood by Maximus as a "cosmic liturgy", to use the characteristic title of von Balthasar's study. Maximus himself makes this very clear in his interpretation of the Liturgy, in which also the whole

---

[373] See Thal 35; CCSG 7, p. 239.
[374] Luke 23: 52.
[375] See Amb 54; PG 91, 1376 C.
[376] See Thal 48; CCSG 7, p. 335.
[377] Amb 41; PG 91, 1312 AB.

cosmic work of mediation is in fact described. Thus in relation to the third mediation we read in chapter 23 of the *Mystagogia*, that the first entrance during the Synaxis symbolizes the human exodus out of this world, as seen in its mutually contradictory diversity, through a "natural contemplation"—of things but also of divine providence—which, *by the assistance of the angels*, leads on to its ('logical') culmination in the Gospel (i.e. the revelation of the Logos himself). And this liturgical—and cosmic—process taken altogether is understood to be a symbol of the 'psychic' virtues (i.e. not the virtues of the flesh) nor yet the spiritual virtues).[378] Thus we are indirectly brought back here to that consideration of the role of the angels and of man's likeness unto them in virtues, which Maximus presented to us in his basic description of the third mediation itself.[379] Supported from beneath by all the virtues, man performs his mediating function between heaven and earth, in that he finds in Christ the creative principle of all that part of creation which he can recognize with his senses, and through the grace of God he contemplates Him in it as one. He sees the multitude of things, but through them he knows the one Logos. The world is held together in its differentiation, and what he experiences with his senses he thus knows with his reasonable mind.

But since this knowledge is strictly consequent upon the Incarnation of Christ, the process of this third mediation is, from another point of view, to be seen as another form of man's spiritual manducation of the body of Christ, as it is presented in Amb 48. But this time what we find is rather a communion with *"the eyes of Christ"*, for this form of manducation is described in the following way: He who should eat of "the eyes of Christ" is the one who is able to understand the visible creation in a spiritual way, and thus is capable of bringing together the λόγοι of the things which he has grasped through his senses and his mind into one single glorification of God.[380] Such a glorification is involved in the contemplation of God as the Creator in Christ, who holds all together in a providential whole, differentiated and yet one.

9. Fourth mediation: between intelligible and sensible creation

We noticed earlier that Maximus accepts the Evagrian distinction between five types of contemplation which are open to the human mind.[381] Within the field of "natural contemplation" in the strictest sense

---

[378] Myst 23; PG 91, 697 C–700 B.
[379] See Amb 41; PG 91, 1305 D.
[380] PG 91, 1364 C.
[381] See p. 347 f. above.

this system includes a distinction between contemplation of visible and invisible, i.e. between sensible and intelligible, creatures.[382] This last differentiation, however, also forms the basis of the distinction between the third and the fourth mediation. There are thus two types of mediation within the *vita contemplativa*, as there are within the *vita practica*. Against this background it becomes obvious that our analysis of the third mediation is to a very large extent relevant for the fourth. We shall then simply point out certain characteristics which are particularly related to the latter.

Maximus' descriptions of the fourth type of mediation as found in Amb 41 and Thal 48 may be summarized in the following five points.

a) It is a mediation which unites the sensible and intelligible things of God's creation.[383] The elements between which man is here called to mediate thus both belong to the created order. Their difference is, therefore, ontological[384] but it is not 'theological'. The created status of intelligible beings is not, according to Maximus' theology, essentially different from the created status of sensible things, as tends to be the case within Origenist speculation with its idea of a primitive henad of intelligible beings and of two acts of creation.

b) The fourth mediation was effected by Christ in his continuing ascension through the divine and intelligible orders of angelic powers *with soul and body*, i.e. with the whole human nature.[385] This is a crucial point which Maximus is evidently very eager to stress, for it is precisely this ascension of human nature as a whole, in its composite character, into the heavenly world which manifests the unity of the whole creation. In other words it is the Incarnation of Christ the Logos in human nature which makes this manifestation possible, and as a divine revelation it remains itself an incarnation. Human nature is carried by Christ through the angelic hierarchies on to the Father.

c) Furthermore this fact implies that Christ has revealed in himself the common inclination (σύννευσις) of all creation into one undivided and 'non-disintegrating' whole in accordance with one universal λόγος— which is in Christ.[386] The ascending movement of Christ returning to his Father, enclothed in his humanity, through all the different orders of created being (the third and fourth mediation) thus corresponds to an

---

[382] See Char 1. 78; CSC, p. 80.
[383] Amb 41; PG 91, 1305 A.
[384] Cf. our analysis of the importance of the basic ontological dichotomy in Maximus, ch. IV: A. 1; pp. 170–173 above.
[385] Amb 41; PG 91, 1309 C.
[386] *Loc. cit.*

inclination in creation itself towards its unity in the Logos. And this inclination is manifested by Christ on man's behalf.

d) But in doing this he has also shown that there is, in fact, one common λόγος for the whole of creation—regardless of the basic dichotomy which differentiates the intelligible and sensible—a common principle which holds it all together, but is itself hidden in God's good counsel.[387]

e) Finally, man is called, as in the beginning, to perform this mediation in Christ *through a likeness—in knowledge—to the angels,* which implies, according to Maximus, that there is no longer any difference between positive knowledge and supreme ignorance. Man through his acquisition of the same knowledge as that possessed by the angels, may also be granted in the end an immediate knowledge of God, which is itself an impenetrable and inexpressible insight.[388] The higher form of "natural contemplation" which is involved in this type of mediation brings man to the limit of his possible knowledge and to the very border-line between revelation and apophatic theology.

Thus the fourth mediation effects a reduction of all the λόγοι of things—without their annihilation, of course—to *one single principle,* the very principle of creation itself, which keeps it all together before God. No further reduction is possible; only the mystery of God himself is left for man to desire and to try to penetrate into. Intelligible realities and revealed divine attributes—understood through an analogical process which depends on created things—properly belong to the mind.[389] But beyond this point man cannot reach on account of his composite nature and microcosmic constitution. If in the fifth mediation he does nonetheless reach beyond this point, it is only thanks to mystical illumination.[390] Here, however, what is important is to notice this border line, for it is the fact that it is placed exactly at this point which is decisive for Maximus' understanding of the common principle of created beings.

A common λόγος of all creation

There remain, however, two particular questions which ought to be asked in relation to this fourth mediation, since the answers given to them reveal very clearly how Maximus conceives of human mediation in general. The first question relates to the character and possible definition

---

[387] See Thal 48; CCSG 7, p. 333 ff.
[388] Amb 41; PG 91, 1308 AB.
[389] See Char 3. 71; CSC, p. 176 ff.
[390] Cf. p. 423 ff. below.

of the common principle of all creation, and the second question concerns the way in which the last type of 'natural' mediation is performed.

What, first of all, is this common principle, which unites all created beings, regardless of what we have called the basic dichotomy? In Amb 48 Maximus calls it a secret. It is regarded as hidden in God's own counsel.[391] In itself this answer is not surprising, for a principle common to the whole creation—and we must recall that the λόγοι of things are understood by Maximus, in an Areopagitic way, as "wills" of God[392]— must be the basic motive for which God acted as Creator in the beginning. To ask for this principle is thus in a way to ask why God created at all. God's own reason for creating the world—which we have described as an act by which he overbridges the gulf between him and all that may be created[393]—is hidden in God himself. To understand it man would have to be immanent in God and know his "thoughts" from within. But such a knowledge is excluded in principle in Maximus' theology on account of his rejection of Origenism.

And yet, this negative answer is not wholly satisfying, for the λόγοι by God's grace are nevertheless open to man's understanding in virtue of his own microcosmic character. He communicates with them through his own reason. Consequently, as the world in little he should be able to communicate also with the universal λόγος of the world in large. If it is a λόγος which keeps the world together, it should be accessible to him as a reasonable being. How does Maximus solve this dilemma?

He solves it in a very characteristic way. He gives a definition which is open to man as reasonable being, but which at the same time maintains the divine secret as such: *the divine principle which holds the entire creation together is that it should have non-being as the ground of its being.*[394] The principle of creation thus itself points outside creation to a Creator who is able to create out of nothing.[395] We can add that for this reason the only principle which is able to circumscribe the whole of God's creation is one which marks the very limit dividing creation from non-being. Thus all pantheism and all simple emanationist ideas are excluded at one and the same time, in spite of the fact that even this supreme λόγος of creation implies an incarnate presence of the divine Logos-Christ in the world.

[391] Cf. p. 400 above.
[392] Cf. ch. II: 2; p. 69 ff. above.
[393] Cf. ch. II: 1; p. 51 above.
[394] Amb 41; PG 91, 1312 B.
[395] On this idea in Maximus, cf. ch. II: 1; pp. 50–64 above.

The character of 'natural' human mediation

Therefore, at its highest stage, in "natural contemplation" the mind arrives at an absolute frontier line, and the fourth mediation, consequently, itself signifies that this border line is reached. This last fact, however, immediately brings us to our second question: how does Maximus conceive of human mediation up to this point? The basic dichotomy in creation is of great importance to Maximus, implying as it does a distinction between a sensible and an intelligible world. These are partly combined, but in principle they are different from each other. Maximus sometimes refers to this as a difference between outward appearance and inward λόγος. In any case, man has a central position in relation to this dichotomy, since he is himself of a composite nature, and consists of both mind and sense.[396] But how is his work of mediation effected in relation to it?

Man's microcosmic position implies that his senses are naturally related to sensible and bodily natures, while his mind is in communication with intelligible and incorporeal things, which it is likewise able to know by substance.[397] It is this dual character of the human composite which constitutes man as a microcosm, able to mediate between those two types of being with which he is consubstantial. But man's dual character never threatens or violates his unity, for there is also a common principle of man, which holds his elements together: the very principle that he should consist of a sensible body and a rational and intelligible soul.[398] Man the microcosm is thus reducible to one principle of nature, which holds his constituent elements together. But we have also seen that the macrocosm too is reducible to one principle of being: that it should have its being from non-being. Consequently, man's mediating function, based on the fact that he is a microcosm, must lead precisely to a realization of this basic unity of the world in its common principle. And since his own principle implies that his elements are not violated or separated—a Chalcedonian principle—the same must be true of the world as macrocosm. The realization of its common principle cannot violate its constitutive elements; they have in fact their own λόγοι, which have all pre-existed in God.

Thus we are prepared to see how Maximus conceives of this work of human mediation in the world in its totality, a work which leads to the very border line of creation itself. He describes it explicitly in Amb 10.

---

[396] See Thal 32; CCSG 7, p. 225.
[397] Thal 58; CCSG 22, p. 33.
[398] See ch. III: 1, p. 97 f. above.

The whole created nature, he says, is divided into intelligible and sensible beings. The former are eternal, the latter temporal; the former are open to the intelligence of the mind, the latter to sense. Manifold is the relationship which exists between the thinking subjects and the objects of their thought, and between sensible things and those who sense them. And thus man, who consists of both soul and body, and has a natural relationship to both worlds, is both grasped and circumscribed and himself grasps and circumscribes. Through his natural substance he is circumscribed and defined, and through his spiritual power he himself circumscribes.[399] He is thus an active subject as well as a limited object of noetic activity. And by his own natural differentiation he is both circumscribed through the intelligible and sensible creatures, and circumscribes himself as a sensible and intelligible being.[400] In other words, through his activities of perception he is able to hold the world together as a subject which is itself part of the world.

This, however, would seem as such to be an immanent function. And yet it cannot be, for man is more than the centre of the created world. He is this microcosm precisely because he is created in the image of God.[401] What man does in his mediating activity is that he grasps and perceives the created world in all its orders through his senses as well as through his mind—including himself as object of perception—and holds it together in its pure relationship to the Logos Creator in virtue of his pure mind and his purified sense, which excludes any misuse of the created things. Thus he is free to perform his mediation as *a liturgical function in the world before God who has created it out of nothing,* and now he is also in the position to receive by grace God's own communication concerning Himself, i.e. knowledge of the Holy Trinity in θεολογία, since he has come to the border of natural knowledge (the principle of creation itself) and is no more sinfully attached to the world in its manifoldness. His mind is naked and open to mystical illumination.

In the 23rd chapter of his *Mystagogia* Maximus describes this stage of human mediation in the following way. It is symbolized by the closing of the doors of the Church, which is followed by the Great Entrance with the holy mysteries of divine illumination, of which man is now allowed to

---

[399] PG 91, 1153 AB.

[400] *Loc. cit.*

[401] Man is in fact more than microcosm. Not only Maximus but also other representatives of the Eastern tradition regard his position in this way. For this reason SCRIMA, *L'avènement philocalique, Istina* (1958), p. 462, feels free to express the common Eastern Christian conviction at this point in the following paradoxical way: man is in fact not defined as a microcosm but as a *macrocosm.* This is to overstate the case, but it points out an important aspect of this whole stream of thinking.

partake. This he greets with the kiss of peace and with the confession of his faith. All the ideas of the world are gathered together in one single unity, but this unity itself signifies the limit, beyond which man can go only through the grace of God who created him in the image of Himself.[402]

However, this nakedness of man in front of the Absolute does not destroy the composite character of man's nature, which is the very basis of his microcosmic function. Man does not "depart from the body", as Evagrius conceived,[403] but remains in it. His mediating function leads to Maximus' affirmation that this process must mean that *even the flesh should be acquainted with God* and adorned with divine reflections.[404] Even at the stage of the fourth division man, therefore, communicates with Christ through His *eyes,* for even this highest form of "natural contemplation", that of intelligible beings in their λόγοι and of the whole creation in its common principle as a communion with the Logos, is only open to man on account of God's condescension in Christ, who in his Incarnation in the world of things crossed the gulf between God and creation and became incarnate to fulfil man's joy.[405] And therefore, the general principles of Maximus' cosmology and Christology are maintained to the very end of man's natural work of mediation.

10. *Fifth mediation: between God and His creation*

The last and highest form of mediation which man is called to fulfil according to Maximus' systematization is different from all the others. It belongs to the third 'stage' of spiritual development, θεολογία, and implies mystical union. It is effected when man 'leaves' the sphere of creation—and even the last kind of differentiation: that which separates man and all created beings from God the Uncreated—and is united with God beyond his own nature. It is a paradoxical mediation, beyond all the τρόποι and λόγοι relevant to the first four. But this fact nevertheless does not exclude the dialectic of differentiation—unification and plurality—unity which we have found to be characteristic of all that Maximus has to say about man and his relationships. On the contrary, it is rather confirmed by the fact that it is established as a mystery to man in the being of God himself.

Let us therefore see how Maximus describes the fifth mediation, and

---

[402] Cf. PG 91, 700 BC.
[403] Cf. p. 303 above.
[404] See Amb 10; PG 91, 1112 CD.
[405] See Amb 48; PG 91, 1364 C.

on the basis of this description analyse a few points which are of a particular relevance to the problem which we have now indicated. Again we can summarize his presentation of the matter in five statements.

a) The fifth mediation is related to a difference which separates all that is created from "uncreated nature", i.e. from God as He is in Himself.[406] When Maximus uses the expression "uncreated nature" here, he does not imply by it that there is any comprehensible parallel as such between divine nature and created nature, so that they would simply be two different natures which would be supposed to obey the same logical laws. In view of Maximus' apophatic theology in general, such a simple parallelism is obviously excluded. Therefore, man cannot come to any conclusions about the divine uncreated "nature" from what he knows about created natures in general or about creation as such. Consequently, Maximus stresses that God is not knowable from his creation in such a way that we may know his essence or his very qualities—even though we can understand that he has created it out of His goodness. In relation to His essence and proper qualities there is complete ignorance, for there is no unity of substance between God and his creation, and consequently no common λόγος or principle of understanding which might be used for both.[407]

b) The principle (λόγος) and mode (τρόπος) through which nonetheless they are united by God is thus above nature.[408] This statement is interesting because it shows that Maximus' negation of any positive understanding of this unity between God and creation does not prevent him from presupposing that there is nevertheless a supernatural, or better 'super-logical', principle which God possesses with a view to this unification. Man can understand in faith that it is a kind of λόγος, but what it is, is incomprehensible.

c) What is further revealed to faith is that on man's behalf Christ has effected even this mediation, in virtue of his hypostatic union of created and uncreated nature. And it was effected when Christ attained to God through his ascension, i.e. attained to Him from the point of view of Christ's humanity. He thus appeared before God as man, when he had fulfilled all that God had decreed on our account, and thereby performed his fifth and final mediation.[409] Christ's ascension as man to the right hand of the Father is the ground of this mediation, but no outward manifestation of it is possible as in the four other cases.

---

[406] See Amb 41; PG 91, 1304 D.
[407] See *ibid.;* 1305 A.
[408] Thal 48; CCSG 7, p. 335.
[409] See Amb 41; PG 91, 1309 CD.

d) Nevertheless man has still to effect it in his own life in Christ. It is not a matter of human rationality or inter-human ethics as such, and yet it has to be demonstrated in man's life. How is this to be? Here Maximus shares Gregory of Nyssa's conviction: only through love (ἀγάπη). The unity between God and creation is demonstrated by grace in love, a love which is incessantly directed towards God, and is at the same time a continuing participation in divine love.[410] The mystical union is one of love—the summit of all virtues and the perfection of all knowledge.

e) Through this mediation in Christ man should *penetrate* (περιχωρεῖν) *entirely into God*—and become all that God possibly is, though *without ontological identity*—and receive Him instead of himself and be awarded God alone as the reward for his ascension.[411] We should notice here that the fifth mediation thus implies a full realization of the human consequences of the hypostatic union in Christ. God and man are not only no longer separated and divided but are united without confusion or change, and their union also implies a true communication and inter-penetration, so that Christ brings man into heaven, and man enters entirely into God. The Chalcedonian theology, such as Maximus understood it, thus remains the core even of his presentation of the fifth mediation, which results in mystical union.

The supernatural character of the fifth mediation, entirely realized through divine grace, is thus firmly established. There are, however, *three* specific problems which need to be further discussed in relation to Maximus' theology in general, since they may serve to throw more light upon the relationship between this particular point of doctrine and his general theological principles, as we have tried to analyse them in this thesis. They may also illuminate his relationship to some of his predecessors in mystical theology, particularly Evagrius and Ps.-Denis. These problems are: Maximus' rigid apophatic theology; his affirmation, in spite of this, of a λόγος and τρόπος by which this union is effected; and his understanding of ecstasy in love.

The tradition of apophatic theology

The expressions of a negative or apophatic theology concerning God which we have found in Maximus are numerous and often striking. However, his personal contribution is only understandable against a general Christian background. For this reason we shall indicate a few characteristics of this background.

---

[410] See *ibid.;* 1308 B.
[411] *Loc. cit.*

The incomprehensibility of God was affirmed by all orthodox theologians before Maximus, and this affirmation is the basis of all apophatic Christian theology. In this sense it has been truly said to have its root in Clement of Alexandria, who said e.g. that God is known, not from what He is, but from what He is not.[412] Later Origen similarly claimed that God the Father is in the darkness of incomprehensibility,[413] and in relation to Evagrius von Balthasar has called attention to his statement that God cannot be grasped by the mind, for if he were, he would not be God.[414] The last expression must, of course, be understood in Evagrius' own context, but even so it is a clear expression of a general agreement.

A more elaborated apophatic theology, however, is to be found in Gregory of Nyssa. In regard to him the problem is far more complicated than in the earlier Fathers. It has been argued that certain distinctions must be made within the general field of apophatic theology, and that these are of a particular relevance with regard to Gregory of Nyssa. Thus Lossky distinguishes between the idea (represented by Clement) that God is inaccessible by nature, and the idea (represented by Origen—and we may add, Evagrius) that God is inaccessible because of the weakness of human reason as obscured by the flesh, and argues that Gregory clearly chooses the first of these alternatives.[415] This distinction seems, however, to be made too sharply, as Daniélou has pointed out, particularly in relation to Gregory. One should, therefore, perhaps rather make a distinction with Puech between an ignorance based on the inadequacy of our knowledge of God in comparison with that of other objects of understanding, and an ignorance based on the naked inadequacy of the mind as such in relation to God as the supreme object of its desire, a distinction which coincides with Gregory's own differentiation between a night of the senses and a night of the mind.[416]

In any case it remains a fact that it was Gregory who first developed a theology of the *divine darkness* (γνόφος)—a concept which as such was to

[412] See *Strom.* 5. 11; GCS Clem. 2. p. 374, 14 f. On Clement as the originator of apophatic Christian theology, see LOT-BORODINE, La doctrine de la déification dans l'Église grecque, RHR 105 (1932), p. 9.—Clement was inspired, however, not only by a Greek philosophical outlook in general, but also by Philo, for whom the affirmation of the incomprehensibility of God is the basis of his theology of revelation; cf. e.g. DANIÉLOU, *Sacramentum futuri*, p. 188 f.

[413] Cf. CROUZEL, Origène, précurseur du monachisme, in *Théologic de la vie monastique*, p. 35 f.

[414] *De octo vit. cogitat.* 9; PG 40, 1275 C; cf. VON BALTHASAR, KL², p. 84.

[415] LOSSKY, La théologie négative dans la doctrine de Denys l'Aréopagite, RSPhTh 28 (1936), p. 204 ff.

[416] See H.-CH. PUECH, La ténèbre mystique chez le Pseudo-Denys, *Ét. Carm.* 23: 2 (1938), p. 42 and DANIÉLOU, *Platonisme et théologic mystique*, p. 198.

be found already in Philo—and related his speculation on mystical union to it. In this sense he is the decisive predecessor not only of Ps.-Denis but also of a mystic like John of the Cross.[417] Gregory can also be said to prepare the position of Maximus, even though the concept of γνόφος does not play a dominant role in the writings of the latter.[418] Their basic understanding of human ignorance is the same. They both affirm that God's οὐσία is impenetrable.[419] Further, they share the same view of the relationship between mystical knowledge in darkness and the supreme function of love.[420]

In Gregory Nazianzen we also find a considerable degree of negative theology. His writings are full of negative predications of God. His apophatic position, however, is perhaps less absolute than that of Gregory of Nyssa. There is for him a certain relativity in both ignorance and knowledge. Advancement in the knowledge of God requires, of course, a gradual purification, and the divine light is clearly supposed to blind the mind to a greater and greater extent. But the material world also is a mystery to Gregory, into which man cannot fully penetrate.[421] It has indeed been argued that he is no pessimist in relation to knowledge of God and that he accounts for a limited knowledge, not only of the fact *that* He is, but also of *what* He is, but this remains to be qualified.[422]

Apophatic theology in Ps.-Denis and Evagrius

In Ps.-Denis the apophatic attitude is absolute. His *Mystical Theology* deals entirely with God in His incomprehensibility, and his concept of θεολογία—which is for him a complex term covering not only negative and mystical theology, but also symbolical and affirmative theology—is at least sharply distinguished from φυσιολογία, and also in principle from the 'economy of salvation'.[423] The nature of God is hidden to man, and he is not able to arrive at a knowledge of God outside the *via negativa*. Here Denis relies on Neo-Platonic inspiration but also on Gregory of Nyssa.[424]

---

[417] Cf. DANIÉLOU, *op. cit.,* p. 191.

[418] The term is known to him, however, even in the sense in which it was used by Philo, see Gnost 1. 84; PG 90, 1117 C; cf. VON BALTHASAR, KL², p. 587 f.

[419] On Gregory at this point, cf. VÖLKER, *Kontemplation und Ekstase,* p. 144 f.

[420] Cf. DANIÉLOU, *op. cit.,* p. 232.

[421] Cf. PLAGNIEUX, *Grégoire de Nazianze,* p. 262 ff. The understanding and implications of apophatic theology in Gregory Nazianzen is further worked out in a forthcoming dissertation by S. BERGMANN, Lund.

[422] See PLAGNIEUX, *op. cit.,* pp. 278–287.

[423] See ROQUES, Note sur la notion de 'Theologia' chez le Pseudo-Denys l'Aréopagite, RAM 25 (1949), p. 203 ff. On the four types of θεολογία, cf. *ibid.,* pp. 207–211.

[424] Cf. VÖLKER, *op. cit.,* p. 143.

In the case of Denis however, this absoluteness of the apophatic attitude leads to interesting consequences, and here he may in the end be profitably compared with a writer like Evagrius. Negative theology to Denis implies an ascending movement towards higher and higher attributes. Thus the negative form of these attributes does not mean that they are privations. They ought rather to be understood as a gradual transcendence.[425] They are not a non-affirmation, but a *super-affirmation*.[426] This attitude leads to the result that mystical theology is also a real knowledge and a contemplation. The *via negativa* is a means by which we really grasp what God is not, and in a superaffirmative sense, that is to say that the negative predications reflect in a way *what* God is.[427]

In fact he establishes here a special dialectic through a combination of positive expressions (θέσεις) about God in virtue of participation and analogy, with negative predications (ἀρνήσεις) in virtue of God's impenetrable nature, a combination which leads to *antithetical affirmations*—such as "unintelligible intellect", "super-divine divinity", etc.—which are obviously to be understood as in a sense positive confessions, which are certainly not nonsense and above pure negation.[428] This paradoxical attitude is an expression of the fact that in the end this is not a matter of subject and object in the mode of rational thinking, but a matter of mystical union.[429]

In the case of Ps.-Denis the absolute apophatic attitude thus leads finally to something which is more or less its opposite. The way of negation is the way of supreme affirmation. The antithetical arrangement of positive and negative predications is highly affirmative. And in another context, his emphasis on the absolute transcendence of God, also leads paradoxically to an affirmation of the whole world and of a divine immanence in it.[430]

If we now compare this position with that of Evagrius, we arrive at an interesting result. We mentioned above the distinction observed by Lossky between a human ignorance due to the fact that God's own nature

---

[425] On the concept of transcendence in Ps.-Denis, see further ROQUES, Le primat du transcendant dans la purification de l'intelligence selon le Pseudo-Denys, RAM 23 (1947), pp. 142–170.

[426] Cf. ROQUES, RAM 25 (1949), p. 209.

[427] Cf. VÖLKER, *op. cit.*, p. 144.

[428] Cf. VÖLKER, *op. cit.*, p. 146 with n. 2. See further on the idea of a three-fold movement of the soul towards God, VÖLKER, *op. cit.*, p. 191 f.

[429] Cf. LOSSKY, *The Mystical Theology*, p. 28. See, however, VÖLKER's criticism of Lossky's identification of negative theology and ecstasy, *op. cit.*, p. 188, n. 4.

[430] Cf. VON BALTHASAR, KL², p. 87 f.

is incomprehensible, and an ignorance which is due to the weakness of embodied human reason. Now it is clear that, if this distinction holds good, in spite of the fact that it may be too sharply formulated, the first alternative is relevant not only in the case of Gregory of Nyssa but also in that of Ps.-Denis. To him the negative predications are, as we have seen, primarily caused by his conviction that God is beyond and transcendent in relation to all else, and thus that He is by nature impenetrable. Nevertheless, this position leads to a kind of divine cosmic immanence —primarily in virtue of the λογοι and the hierarchies.

In the case of Evagrius it is equally clear that the second alternative is relevant. From his Origenist presuppositions he regards the mind (which is more or less identified with man's rational faculty) as fallen from an original contemplative relationship with God and embodied for purification in the flesh. Consequently, in Evagrius' opinion, it has through its practical ascetic exercises to break away from this sinful dependence and "depart from the body"[431] in order to return to its perfect communion with God. Now it is obvious, that probably Evagrius is also a man who has had some mystical experiences. It would at least be wrong to understand his position as purely intellectualistic. He states clearly that the mind cannot grasp God.[432] By this he means that its knowledge of God is different from all other kinds of knowledge. It is the naked mind which contemplates God and the Trinity, and this nakedness implies that nothing is left in the mind but the divine reflection itself.[433] But if this is true we are at the opposite pole from Ps.-Denis; the divine reality is revealed within the very self of man. But at the same time we have reached another form of immanentism, that of the divine presence in the mind. Both types of apophatic theology—that of extreme purification and that of extreme negation—thus result in an immanentism which, in a way, eliminates the proper concern of negative theology: to stress the difference between empirical man and God himself.

Maximus and the tradition of apophatic theology

In relation to Maximus we must now ask the question: does he follow one or the other of these paths, or does he find a new alternative? The question has been asked both by von Balthasar and Sherwood, and both have arrived at a conclusion which suggests that Maximus' position is not to be identified with that of either Evagrius or Denis, though he had

---

[431] Cf. p. 303 above.

[432] Cf. p. 407 above.

[433] VON BALTHASAR emphasizes that in this context the idea of the divine spark of the soul is not far from Evagrius, see KL², p. 87.

learned much from both of them.[434] We are in agreement with this conclusion—for reasons which will be shown later—and further we agree that the right solution is to be found in Maximus' concept of love and will (Sherwood) and his Chalcedonian convictions (von Balthasar). We hope, however, to be able to take the argument a little further than either von Balthasar or Sherwood has done, with the aid of the particular insights which we have worked out in this thesis.

In the first place Maximus is influenced by both Evagrius and Ps.-Denis. We have seen how his whole scheme of spiritual development, his understanding of vices and virtues, his demand for the purification and nakedness of the mind, etc. are elements which are presented in a way which is strikingly similar to that of Evagrius—and to such an extent, that we have had to show in details the points at which this similarity is qualified so as to exclude identification of theological content. A similar dependence is equally demonstrable in relation to Ps.-Denis and his apophatic teaching and terminology. Thus Maximus uses the super-affirmative style of the Areopagite, which again serves to distinguish him from Evagrius.[435] The same similarity can easily be shown in relation to negative predications of the divine. God is described as "unrelated" and "incomparable",[436] or Divinity is defined as indivisible, non-quantitative, non-qualitative, simple, without distance, infinite, motionless, without beginning, unbegotten, one and alone, unrelated, ineffable and unknowable, etc.[437]

Maximus' profession of ignorance in relation to God is furthermore no formality. He makes his position perfectly clear. Again and again he underlines that what we can understand from "natural contemplation", and through the manifestations of God's creation, is merely the fact *that* God is, not what He is, since He is above all that we know.[438] Thanks to the λόγοι of creation contemplated by man, God is thus believed to exist, but not more than that.[439] This knowledge about the plain fact that God *is*, is mediated through the λόγοι of creation in that they proclaim the meaning of the existence of these things themselves, and thus provide only an indirect knowledge of God.[440] Maximus thus seems to be less 'optimistic' at this point than Gregory Nazianzen. Now, it is clear, however, that this indirect knowledge of God is in some sense qualified:

---

[434] See VON BALTHASAR, KL², pp. 84–90 and SHERWOOD, in ACW, pp. 89–91, 94–99.
[435] See Char 3. 99; CSC, p. 190.
[436] Amb 9; PG 91, 1105 D.
[437] See Amb 17; PG 91, 1232 BC.
[438] See Amb 10; PG 91, 1133 C.
[439] Gnost 1. 9; PG 90, 1085 CD.
[440] See Thal 13; CCSG 7, p. 95.

creation itself testifies to a Goodness, Wisdom and Power, which is a kind of reflection, or adumbration, of the Holy Trinity here on earth.[441] But how is this fact compatible with the restrictive attitude which he shows elsewhere, and with his affirmation that no other knowledge of God is available through creation except simply *that* He is?

This is a very pertinent question, for there can be no doubt that Goodness, Wisdom and Power—or other combinations of the same kind—are understood by Maximus as being some kind of divine qualities. The answer which should be given however, is a double one. They are, first of all, only understood as Trinitarian reflections by the believer who has been illuminated by God himself as to His qualities— and again these qualities are only revealed facts about God, not His very being. Secondly, it seems obvious that Maximus includes this triad, theologically, under the idea *that* God is, rather than under any affirmation of *what* He is. This becomes clear when we read that even those λόγοι of providence and judgment, which are known through "natural contemplation", are only manifestations of the fact *that* God is,[442] for it is obvious from other instances that providence and judgment, in an ontological sense, refer precisely to such divine qualities as Wisdom and Goodness as being active in creation. Wisdom and Judgment refer to the natural differentiation of the world, and Goodness and Providence to its unification through motion and will.[443] Thus it becomes apparent that from the strict point of view of "natural contemplation" these qualities, which are adumbrations of the Trinity, are nevertheless only expressions of the fact *that* God is. They are expressions of Him as active in the world, but do not express what He is in himself. Nor are they understood as Trinitarian reflections until man has gained some knowledge of the Trinity at the highest stage of spiritual development.

Elsewhere in fact, Maximus affirms that precisely at this point man does not gain intellectual information about the nature of God—which he seeks—for only above reason is he united with Him. But his intellect is "encouraged" by the divine attributes, such as e.g. by His *goodness* and *wisdom* and *power* that *makes, governs* and *judges* His creatures.[444] Maximus is thus capable of affirming *both* an ignorance about the qualities of God, and a Trinitarian reflection in creation which encourages the believer.

---

[441] See e.g. Char 1. 96; CSC, p. 86; cf. SHERWOOD, in ACW, pp. 37–41, and ch. III: A, 4: p. 129 ff. above.
[442] See Amb 34; PG 91, 1288 BC.
[443] Cf. SHERWOOD, *The Earlier Ambigua*, pp. 36 f. and 144 ff.
[444] Char 1. 100; CSC, p. 88.

This last example however, also shows, that what interests Maximus particularly is not so much the apophatic expressions as such, or even the *via negativa* as the right way to God as such, but rather the maintenance of a strict transcendence and a gulf between God and all that is created.[445] At this point he appears to be even stricter than Ps.-Denis, whom he criticizes indirectly by his own attitude. He says for instance that the method of negation does not arrive at its goal, for nothing can be defined through negation.[446] The negative way is thus not more effective than the affirmative way, since the οὐσία of God remains ineffable. Here Denis' position is simpler, since he obviously has a certain confidence in his negative predications. Maximus expresses the same idea even more clearly, when he states elsewhere that God is above both cataphatic and apophatic characterization. God is not close to anything else which is or which is expressible, nor is he close to anything else which is not or is not expressible.[447]

Finally we may say that Maximus professes a certain dialectic of affirmation and negation which in a formal sense is similar to the antithetical affirmations of Ps.-Denis, but which is quite different as regards its motivation and intention. Again Maximus is more restrictive and more 'pessimistic'. He says that affirmation and negation are opposite to each other and yet go well together. But how? Maximus answers: the negations show *what* God is not, while the affirmations tell us what it means to say that the being thus negated *is*. And on the other hand, the affirmations simply tell us *that* this being is—or what it might be,—while the negations tell us what it means to say that the being thus affirmed *is not*. Maximus thus keeps the two methods in perfect balance, a balance which preserves at the same time the limited character of human knowledge of God—and not widens it, as is the case in Denis. But Maximus goes even further and says explicitly, that compared with each other these two methods manifest their *antithetical* opposition, but in relation to God, they show their kinship by effecting an encounter of the extremes.[448] It is difficult not to draw the conclusion here that what in Denis' view is positive—that they are entirely opposite to each other and thereby paradoxically express something about God—is negative in Maximus' view: in their opposition they do not express anything about God, but they mark the limit of human knowledge. And conversely, what

---

[445] Cf. von Balthasar, KL², p. 88.
[446] Amb 16; PG 91, 1221 D–1224 A.
[447] Myst, *Prol.;* PG 91, 664 C. Sherwood, in ACW, p. 31 underlines the importance of this statement.
[448] See Amb 34; PG 91, 1288 C.

in Denis' view is negative—that the knowledge they give is only a paradoxical knowledge and an affirmation through mystical super-expression—is positive in Maximus' view: they affirm God in their mutual and integrated *limitation*. They encounter each other and thereby show their relatedness to each other and to God.

Apophatic and Trinitarian theology in Maximus

Maximus thus follows neither Evagrius nor Ps.-Denis into their opposite forms of divine immanence. He maintains the absolute transcendence itself as a revelation of God. But is this also true with regard to the Holy Trinity? We should expect his doctrine of the Trinity to belong to positive theology. This, however, is not the case.[449] Trinitarian theology to Maximus is an integral part of negative theology, and is different from the divine "economy". Here his position to some extent resembles Ps.-Denis' distinction between "economy" and θεολογία—even in so far as it is sometimes difficult to uphold, since it is always difficult to study God outside of his manifestations.[450] But at the same time, Maximus' standpoint here shows more clearly than elsewhere how he conceives his middle position between the Evagrian and Dionysian alternatives.

Maximus' theology of the Trinity seems to be related to the apophatic principle in two ways: a) in that it is entirely the result of revelation; b) in that it is presented as itself part of negative theology. He is thus in the position to quote Denis who says that God is known to us neither as Unity nor as Trinity.[451] This statement obviously serves to exclude any other understanding of the Trinity than that provided by negative theology. Within this right context, however, the same truth can be expressed in positive terms: man cannot understand how *God is both Unity and Trinity* at the same time.[452] Or still more positively expressed: *the mystery of the Trinity is its super-logical relationship to Unity.* Trinity is thus in the first place not an "economic" and revelatory, but a mystical concept, which testifies to the mystical relationship between unity and diversity in God.

But it is this double quality of unity and diversity, which is *also* characteristic of creation. Diversification and unification, manifoldness and unity condition each other in it and keep each other in proper balance. At this point Christological insights go well together with

---

[449] Cf. VON BALTHASAR, KL², p. 93.
[450] Cf. ROQUES, RAM 25 (1949), p. 203 ff.
[451] Amb 10; PG 91, 1188 A; cf. SHERWOOD, in ACW, p. 35.
[452] See Amb 10; 1168 AB.

cosmological analyses. The same is true of Trinitarian insights. These express a similar balance between differentiation and unity, or better: of unity in differentiation and differentiation in unity. This fact therefore already characterizes the knowledge of God which we may obtain from creation: He is revealed as the one Creator and the one Logos, and yet as active in diversification.

Thal 13, which is indirectly related to Trinitarian speculations, shows this point clearly.[453] The triad of Being, Wisdom and Life which Maximus mentions there is certainly, as Sherwood says, another adumbration of the Trinity in creation,[454] but he seems not to have noticed *how* this Trinitarian 'revelation' functions. What is it in creation which reflects the mystery of the Trinity? The answer seems to be this: Being as it is analysed in 'natural contemplation' leads in the end to *unity* (the one Logos); Wisdom analysed in the same way leads to *multiplicity* (the many λόγοι), and Life, finally, analysed as movement from multiplicity to unity without annihilation, *combines them* in a perfect triad.

Seen in the perspective of faith, this is, however, a true reflection of the mystery of the Holy Trinity, though precisely of such a kind as merely to "encourage" the mind to seek for knowledge about God as He is in Himself. And it *is* such a reflection, because the Trinitarian concept itself keeps the aspect of unity and the aspect of multiplicity together in God. Here again, at the very summit of mystical theology, a dialectic between unity and diversity is the final dynamism of Maximus' thought, a fact which at the same time explains why his Trinitarian theology has to be negative theology.

Multiplicity and unity are integrated in creation, in such a way as to evoke our wonder, as a kind of divine reflection (when the elements of the triad are regarded as attributes of God). Through *faith* we also know that they are not mutually exclusive in God, but are one and the same, and that this is the very mystery of God, which man can experience in mystical union alone. There it becomes also man's own unification with God in absolute distinction, i.e. in ontological separation from God.

The λόγος and τρόπος of mystical union

This last conclusion now properly leads us to our *second* question: How can Maximus, in spite of his apophatic theology, affirm a λόγος and τρόπος through which the fifth union is effected?[455] Is it not above all such

---

[453] CCSG 7, p. 95.

[454] Cf. Sherwood, in ACW, p. 38. Cf. also Blowers, *op. cit.*, p. 177, n. 188.

[455] See Thal 48; CCSG 7, p. 335.—On the λόγος and τρόπος duality as relevant for Maximus' understanding of deification, see also Larchet, *op. cit.*, pp. 77–82.

concepts? Does not the very idea of a λόγος related to man which directs his relationship to something beyond his own nature, threaten the coherence of his own principle (λόγος) of nature? There seem to be two possible answers to our question as far as the term λόγος is concerned. One is that Maximus uses the term here in a figurative, i.e. mystical sense. This solution may look plausible in itself, since we are here in the field of mystical theology and above logical rules. If we study Maximus' formulation, however, it immediately appears less plausible, for he says explicitly that Christ has united created and uncreated nature according to "*the* supernatural principle (λόγος) and mode (τρόπος)", while earlier he had characterized the principle of unification of sensible and intelligible creation as "some mystical λόγος". He seems thus here to refer to a particular principle and mode, and not to anything which is merely understood in a figurative sense.

But on the other hand, it is equally obvious that he does not refer to a λόγος of the same kind as those which we know through creation, since those λόγοι define the very nature of created beings, it may be either their differentiated substances or creation as a whole. A λόγος which concerns man, but is above nature and creation, would thus necessarily violate or eliminate human nature as such. It would constitute a super-nature, in which human nature would be swallowed up. This fact is clear in relation to Maximus' Christology.[456] Maximus is, in fact, very firm at this point. It is quite impossible, he says, that there should be a created nature which is not from the beginning and always one and the same in relation to its λόγος, or that it should be susceptible to increase or decrease in itself, for its metaphysical λόγος is always perfect in that it exists.[457] The innovation which is brought about by Christ with regard to fallen man does, therefore, not pertain to the λόγος of human nature, but to its mode (τρόπος). The perfection of humanity which is effected by Christ does not add anything to human nature, but merely fulfils what is in accordance with its λόγος, since otherwise this innovation would destroy human nature. Such is Maximus' understanding of Chalcedonian theology.[458]

The possibility is thus excluded, it would seem, that Maximus in our text refers to a kind of super-human λόγος which would regulate man's final perfection in mystical union. We must try the other possible answer. The easiest way to approach it is perhaps through the other term of our text: τρόπος. This term—which is not related to being but to existence—

---

[456] Cf. ch. I: A above.
[457] See Amb 42; PG 91, 1345 BC.
[458] See *ibid.*; 1341 D.

is open to innovation. It is man's mode of existence which is changed in Christ and not his λόγος of nature. When in Amb 41 Maximus thus speaks of a "supernatural τρόπος", he uses an expression which is in full accordance with his theological principles, for, in his view, in the Incarnation the natural λόγοι, which always remain the same, and the τρόποι which are "beyond nature" are combined without interfering with each other's spheres.[459] And the result is a "synthetic hypostasis" which unites the two modes of existence into one unity without any violation of the two natures and their λόγοι.[460] This unity of modes in relation to the union of natures—as Maximus understands it within his own elabora- tion of the theology of Chalcedon and Constantinople—is also that which allows for a true *communicatio idiomatum* which even involves *perichoresis,* as Maximus shows in an important passage of Amb 5.[461] Thus Christ's human sufferings take place in a divine mode and his divine acts in a human mode. We are, therefore, almost impelled to draw the conclusion that when Maximus mentions a supernatural mode in which man is mystically united with God beyond the boundaries of creation in his fifth mediation, this statement refers to *the divine mode of human existence.*

But what about the supernatural λόγος in this context? Even this expression is now understandable. Not that there is a higher common λόγος for the two natures in Christ. There is no analogy *here* between the unity of body and soul in man, for which there is a common λόγος, and the unity of divine and human natures in Christ.[462] The analogy between these two unities is entirely restricted to the fact that both may be called synthetic unities.[463] And since the "synthetic hypostasis" which is established in Christ and which includes two inseparable natures is and has to be *quite unique,* there is no analogy between it and the "synthetic nature" of man on the ontological level.[464] Maximus says this explicitly himself: there is no (common) λόγος which effects an analogous relation in Christ between the natures, as there is in "synthetic natures".[465] It is impossible that the λόγος of our text should refer to something which Maximus here denies. But there is still another possibility, for it is precisely this ontological non-relativity of the natures in Christ which enables man to have his hypostatic—i.e. existential—sharing in Divini-

---

[459] See Amb 5; PG 91, 1056 A.
[460] Cf. p. 47 f. above and VON BALTHASAR, KL², p. 242.
[461] See PG 91, 1056 AB; cf. p. 30 above.
[462] Cf. ch. III: A, 1; pp. 101–104 above.
[463] Cf. p. 102 above.
[464] Cf. VON BALTHASAR, KL², p. 243, who refers to Ep. 13; PG 91, 532 B.
[465] *Ibid.;* 532 B.

ty. The way is open to the affirmation that man has his hypostasis in the Logos.[466] But is it not precisely this hypostatic relationship to which this text refers as one which is being perfected in mystical union without violation of the natures? And what other λόγος could Maximus then think of than *the personal Logos himself,* who is the hypostasis of man. The τρόπος mentioned in our text is thus the divine mode of human existence, and the λόγος also mentioned there is the divine hypostasis of the Logos, in which man finds his existential fulfilment.

The concept of ecstasy in Maximus' predecessors

Our *third* and final question is of a corresponding importance: What is the character of the ecstatic penetration into God which Maximus seems to affirm with regard to the fifth mediation? The word for this "penetration" is *perichoresis,* which shows that at this point too we are within the Christological context, since *perichoresis* is a key term in Maximus' Christology.[467] But since this penetration takes place on behalf of the whole creation, and yet beyond the whole creation, it nevertheless seems appropriate to call it an *ecstasy.* We shall, therefore, try to answer our question through an analysis of Maximus' concept of human ecstasy.

Here again the position of some of Maximus' predecessors should be examined first of all. There are three writers who need to be particularly considered at this point: Gregory of Nyssa, Evagrius and Ps.-Denis.[468]

Gregory of Nyssa is the first Christian writer to have elaborated any theological theory about ecstasy. Through the investigations by Daniélou we are comparatively well informed about the position of this writer. Thus it is clear that his concept of ecstasy in its widest sense—which includes even other terms than ἔκστασις—expresses *an ever continuing going forth* from the obstacles and limitations of this world towards God the Impenetrable.

Four types or degrees of such a going forth may be recognized: 1) from sin through asceticism and mortification, 2) out of the sensible world in contemplation, 3) out of the intelligible world through higher contemplation and 4) mystical ecstasy characterized as a blessed (and sober) drunkenness.[469] This wider context of a movement of gradual departure

---

[466] Cf. VON BALTHASAR, KL², p. 243.

[467] Cf. ch. 1: A; pp. 23–36 above.

[468] A common relationship to the Neo-Platonist evaluation of ecstasy should, of course, be presupposed in those writers who like Gregory and Ps.-Denis use the concept more widely.

[469] Cf. DANIÉLOU, *Platonisme et théologie mystique,* p. 260.—On the concept of "sober

thus includes both the idea of an ascetic and contemplative purification and a final ecstasy in the strict sense of the word. These two forms are of course different, but not of an entirely different character, for even though Gregory allows for an ecstasy of the present moment as well as a final beatitude, the idea of a continuing going forth is so dominant in his thought, that he can even speak of a progress and tension with regard to man and God which continues in eternity (cf. his famous idea of "*epectasis*").[470]

Of ecstasy in the strict sense Gregory thinks that it is possible for a man as it were to go forth from his nature even before he departs from the body—as in the case of Stephen.[471] In view of his idea of spiritual life as a process he further calls it an "ecstasy towards the divine", etc.[472] As such it is characterized as a blessedness—a point where he disagrees with Origen who distrusted ecstasy[473]—and is understood as a mystical state.[474] Finally it is understood as a departure from oneself (ἔκστασις ἑαυτοῦ), applicable to the mystic as prepared for the highest mysteries having returned to Paradise through detachment.[475]

Gregory's doctrine of ecstasy is thus a rich and varying one, but what is most interesting in it is the fact that it involves an idea of a continuing going forth, even in eternal life, which marks out the specific context in which it has to be understood. It should also perhaps be added that the idea of Christian life as a continuing 'emigration' of the mind towards God—though without the additional concept of *epectasis*—is also found in Diadochus of Photice.[476] Thus we learn that he who loves God goes forth incessantly towards God in love,[477] and hope is defined accordingly as an 'emigration' (ἐκδημία) of the mind in love towards that which is hoped for.[478] In Gregory Nazianzen the idea of an 'emigration' (ἐκδημία) of the mind towards God is likewise found.[479]

Evagrius' position to a large extent is contrary to that of Gregory of

---

drunkenness" in Gregory and its background in earlier thinking, see H. Lewy, *Sobria ebrietas* (Beihefte zu ZNW 9), Giessen 1929.

[470] On this concept—for which Daniélou coined the Gregorian term "epectase"—see P. Deseille, *art.* Epectase, DSp 4, coll. 785–788.

[471] See *Or. in S. Steph.*; PG 46, 713 BC; cf. Daniélou, *op. cit.*, p. 267.

[472] Cf. Daniélou, *op. cit.*, p. 273.

[473] Cf., however, Völker, *Gregor von Nyssa*, p. 204 with n. 5, who sees no real difference.

[474] Cf. Daniélou, *op. cit.*, pp. 261 and 265.

[475] See *In Cant. cant., hom.* 1; Jaeger, 6, p. 25; cf. Daniélou, *op. cit.*, p. 182.

[476] He also speaks of an 'emigration' away from God, see *Cap. gnost.* 36; des Places, p. 105, 18.

[477] *Cap. gnost.* 14; des Places, p. 91, 15 f.

[478] *Cap. gnost., Prol.;* des Places, p. 84, 4 f.

[479] See *Or.* 6, 2; PG 35, 724 A.

Nyssa. He clearly shares Origen's scepticism about emotional ecstasy. In this sense he seems to identify it with an inclination towards evil or with vices and a weakness like μανία.[480] In the sense of a going forth, an 'emigration', however, he seems to have accepted a position which is similar to that which we have found in Gregory and Diadochus. The term which Diadochus uses for the process, ἐκδημία, was in fact an Evagrian word.[481] Evagrius understands it as a progressive departure from the world of the senses and imaginations towards the perfect communion with God of the naked mind.[482] What it excludes therefore, is *not* ecstasy in the sense of a standing outside of created things—for the nakedness of pure prayer implies precisely this kind of rapture—but ecstasy in the sense of a standing outside of oneself.[483] If we can thus talk of a concept of ecstasy in Evagrius, in spite of the fact that he is sceptical about all kinds of popular ecstatic experiences, it is nevertheless an ecstasy in a restricted sense, which perfects and does not transcend the function of the pure mind.[484]

In the case of Ps.-Denis, however, ecstasy means precisely this departure from oneself, and for this reason the positions of Denis and Evagrius have been described as being in extreme contradiction to each other.[485] Both Sherwood and von Balthasar, however, have tried to show that such a sharp distinction between the two positions is to some extent unjust, and above all leads to an unjust evaluation of the position of Maximus as influenced by them both.[486] However there seems to be little doubt of Denis' favourite attitude to ecstasy in its stricter sense, even though the term ἔκστασις as such is rare in Denis and has not yet become a *terminus technicus*.[487]

His position here, of course, does not exclude the aspect of 'emigration' out of the world, which he stresses for the same reasons as both

---

[480] See *Cap.* 33. 9; PG 40, 1265 B and *De octo vit. cogitat.* 9; PG 40, 1276 A.

[481] See e.g. *De orat.* 46; PG 79, 1176 D; cf. HAUSHERR, "Ignorance infinie", OCP 1936, p. 351, n. 62.

[482] Cf. e.g. J. KIRCHMAYER, *art.* Extase chez les Pères de l'Église, DSp 4, col. 2100.

[483] See the penetrating study of ecstasy in Maximus in relation to Evagrius and Ps.-Denis in SHERWOOD, *The Earlier Ambigua*, p. 139; cf. VON BALTHASAR, KL², p. 350.

[484] Cf. also B. KRIVOCHEINE, The Holy Trinity in Greek patristic mystical Theology, *Sobornost* (1957), p. 468.

[485] See HAUSHERR, *art. cit.,* pp. 351–362, who nevertheless agreed with VILLER, RAM 11 (1930), p. 248, n. 141 that Maximus regarded these two writers as in complete harmony with each other, and even tried to show how he was able to unify their teachings.

[486] See SHERWOOD, *The Earlier Ambigua*, pp. 124–128, n. 1 and VON BALTHASAR, KL², p. 88.

[487] Cf. ROQUES, *art.* Contemplation, extase et ténèbre chez le Pseudo-Denys, DSp 2, Paris 1953, col. 1896 and VÖLKER, *Kontemplation und Ekstase*, p. 201.

Gregory of Nyssa and Evagrius: no union with God is possible without complete purification.[488] Seen in this perspective, ecstasy as rapture is simply the end of a progressive departure from the world, and a culmination of the *via negativa*.[489] This first aspect is expressed in different ways,[490] and its importance is shown by the fact that the terms "emigration" and "ecstasy" are even used as synonyms.[491] This departure is even described in Gregory's terms of sober drunkenness, and is then identical with ecstasy in the proper sense.[492] The second aspect implies, however, that ecstasy is understood as a *union beyond the intellect* and an immediate vision of God.[493] This proper aspect of ecstasy is further characterized by Denis' stress on its passive character—the famous concept of a *"suffering of the Divine"*[494]—and at the same time by his affirmation that it takes place *in love* (both ἔρως and ἀγάπη), in both cases probably on the inspiration of Gregory of Nyssa.[495] Finally, we may note that it is Völker's opinion that the Ps.-Dionysian ecstasy is not only the natural and logical summit of his negative theology but something more: the expression of a personal positive experience.[496]

Among the predecessors of Maximus we find three types of ecstasy represented: the Evagrian 'emigration' which ends in the naked mind receptive of knowledge of the holy Trinity, the Gregorian type of an ever on-going 'emigration' into blessed and sober drunkenness and finally the Ps.-Dionysian type of ecstasy in the proper sense, that is to say outside of oneself, as a "suffering" of the Divine. It is characteristic of the first type that it does not reach beyond the natural capacity of the mind, and of the second that it reaches beyond everything and yet finds no rest. It is characteristic of the third type, finally, that it seems to receive in its ecstasy some sort of superintellectual information about the Divinity itself. What is Maximus' position in relation to these types?

---

[488] Cf. ROQUES, *art. cit.,* col. 1898, who underlines the difference between Ps.-Denis and Gregory Nazianzen in that he accounts for the ἐκδημία aspect only in Gregory (together with Origen and Evagrius), but recognizes an ἔκστασις aspect too, and a predominant one, in Denis. But VÖLKER has, *op. cit.,* pp. 201 f., 204, 208 ff., demonstrated the far-reaching similarity between Gregory of Nyssa and Denis with regard to the concept of ecstasy, though he also emphasizes Gregory's more explicit stress on ascetic preparation (p. 217).

[489] Cf. ROQUES, *art. cit.,* col. 1897.

[490] See e.g. ἐκβαίνειν about Christ in *De div. nom.* 1, 4; PG 3, 592 AB.

[491] See *De div. nom.* 3, 2; PG 3, 681 D.

[492] Cf. VÖLKER, *op. cit.,* p. 202.

[493] Cf. ROQUES, *art. cit.,* col. 1898 and VÖLKER, *op. cit.,* p. 205.

[494] Cf. VÖLKER, *op. cit.,* p. 206.

[495] Cf. ROQUES, *art. cit.,* col. 1900 f. and VÖLKER, *op. cit.,* p. 206.

[496] See VÖLKER, *op. cit.,* p. 215 ff.

Maximus and the different types of ecstasy

It can immediately be said that both the 'emigration' aspect and the aspect of ecstasy proper are represented in Maximus, but he is not to be identified with either of the two positions. With regard to Gregory of Nyssa's idea of *epectasis* it seems evident that he rejects it on the grounds of its philosophical consequences, since he does not identify the eternal rest with movement.[497] But he shows his appreciation of the Gregorian paradox of mystical divine presence and human distance by using an expression like "fixed ever-motion", safely balancing it against his own paradox "ever-moving rest".[498] With regard to Maximus' combination of Evagrian and Ps.-Dionysian elements, Sherwood has made a thorough-going analysis of the problem of Maximus' understanding of ecstasy, and our conclusions below will rely on his to a great extent.[499]

When Maximus uses the idea of ecstasy in its 'emigration' aspect, he is naturally inspired by Evagrius, since this aspect is so closely linked with his general idea of spiritual development—the rôle of detachment in the *vita practica,* the importance of departure from imaginations and even from notions in the *vita contemplativa,* etc.—which is also inspired by Evagrius, though modified by Maximus' own anti-Origenist corrections. In this context he speaks both of an "emigration" and of a "rapture". Thus in pure prayer the mind passes outside all things,[500] or passes outside the flesh and the world.[501] The virtuous man "emigrates" towards God, and an ἐκδημία takes place in prayer.[502]

It is characteristic, however, that Maximus stresses some elements in this picture, which allow him to be more radical than Evagrius. He thus underlines that the rapture of the mind takes place *in love,*[503] particularly through love in its aspect of desire (ἔρως τῆς ἀγάπης), and likewise that the mind in this 'emigration' finds a divine treasure which leaves it unconscious even of itself. Even Evagrius conceives of the naked mind in a similar way, and he also regards knowledge of the Holy Trinity as a mystical knowledge which is supernatural in relation to the mind as such, but he nevertheless underlines the capacity of the mind to such an extent that he still leaves the impression of an intellectualist attitude. And it is this impression which is avoided by Maximus, who combines his

---

[497] See Gnost 2. 88; PG 90, 1165 D–1168 A; cf. DESEILLE, *art. cit.,* col. 786.
[498] See Thal 65; CCSG 22, p. 285; cf. VON BALTHASAR, KL², p. 564.
[499] See SHERWOOD, *The Earlier Ambigua,* pp. 124–154.
[500] Char 1. 10; CSC, p. 52; cf. 1. 19; p. 56.
[501] *Ibid.* 2. 61; p. 122.
[502] *Ibid.* 2. 28; p. 104 and 3. 20; p. 152.
[503] *Ibid.* 1. 12; p. 54.

emphasis on the mind's unconsciousness of itself, which characterizes the mind in its final 'emigration', with references to *other* creatures, which also underline its limited character.[504]

We must therefore agree with Sherwood in his conclusion that Maximus never follows Evagrius so far as to affirm a natural capacity for Trinitarian knowledge in the mind.[505]

A similar attitude is noticeable in Maximus with regard to the aspect of ecstasy proper, as it was developed by Ps.-Denis. The Dionysian idea of a *"suffering of the Divine"* is accepted by Maximus to some extent, though in a modified form.[506] Such a modification was obviously due to the fact that Monenergistic and Monothelite circles used the Dionysian concept in their favour.[507] It is characteristic of Maximus that he interprets the Dionysian expression "to suffer the unqualified" to imply a *suffering to be moved.*[508] And he adds further that he who loves something surely *suffers ecstasy* towards it as loved.[509]

Maximus thus accepts the Dionysian idea in such a way that human activity is maintained and the possibility of a Monothelite understanding excluded. Suffering is transferred to the realm of movement and will, and excites an activity instead of eliminating it. When Maximus later had to explain his first interpretation he made this standpoint still more clear.[510] The idea of ecstatic passivity signifies to Maximus a self-evident dominance of grace in deification.[511] The deified man thus suffers an ecstasy which brings him *outside himself,* i.e. beyond his natural capacity, in pure grace.[512] He accepts that in this sense the supreme stage of spiritual perfection, which he is willing to call "assumption", is called a $\pi \acute{a} \theta o \varsigma$, which thus unites man with God on the ground of God's own grace.[513]

Maximus gives a very clear summary of his position in relation to ecstasy and passion in Thal 22, where he describes how man passes from the contemplation of the $\lambda \acute{o} \gamma o \iota$ of things, which are created out of

---

[504] See *ibid.* 1. 10; p. 52 and 2. 6; p. 92.

[505] SHERWOOD, *The Earlier Ambigua*, p. 141: "... nowhere does Maximus take over Evagrian thought to such an extent that the pure or perfect mind may seem to have a power receptive of knowledge of the Holy Trinity ...; much less is there any hint of the soul seeing itself in prayer."

[506] On this acceptance, cf. VÖLKER, Der Einfluss Pseudo-Dionysius Areopagita auf Maximus Confessor, in STOHR, *Universitas* I, p. 249.

[507] Cf. SHERWOOD, *op. cit.,* p. 128, n. 5.

[508] Amb 7; PG 91, 1073 B.

[509] *Ibid.;* 1073 C.

[510] See ThPol 1; PG 91, 33 C–36 A; cf. SHERWOOD, *op. cit.,* p. 130, 135.

[511] Cf. also Amb 7; PG 91, 1088 C–1089 A.

[512] See Amb 20; PG 91, 1237 AB.

[513] *Ibid.;* 1237 D.

nothing, to the divine Cause *in ignorance,* and then is correctly said to *suffer,* for he is not effective beyond his natural limits—though he is active within them—but is *illuminated by grace.*[514] Thus for Maximus ecstasy implies a real departure from oneself in the Ps.-Dionysian sense into the ineffable sphere of Divinity,[515] and this is understood as a suffering of the Divine, in that it is not due to human activity but to divine grace. But on the other hand, this is not a doing away with free will, but rather its affirmation in a "voluntary outpassing" (ἐκχώρησις γνωμική)—to use Sherwood's translation—i.e. an 'emigration' of the will to that which alone satisfies man's natural desire and brings all his motion to its rest: God Himself.[516]

Sherwood has correctly emphasized the great importance of this Maximian dialectical solution to the intricate problem of human will and human passivity in deification. It implies a use of the Ps.-Dionysian idea of ecstasy, which strictly maintains the gulf between created and uncreated and avoids all Monothelite consequences of the idea of a suffering of the Divine, without diminishing the supreme rôle of grace. We are again bound to agree with Sherwood that the influence of Denis is evident, but that Denis never achieved such clarity.[517]

Both in relation to Evagrius and to Ps.-Denis Maximus thus both accepts and modifies the positions of his predecessors. But is there anything further to be said about his own? How is the dialectic which we have noticed worked out? There are in fact a number of further remarks to be made which may throw some more light on the problem. Von Balthasar and Sherwood have both pointed to the solution, but neither of them seems to have drawn all the conclusions possible.

In Chapter II we started our presentation of Maximus' cosmology with a reference to the idea of a gulf (χάσμα) between God and the whole of creation. Now we have seen that this gulf is preserved by Maximus even in his mystical theology, in spite of the fact that the fifth mediation implies a unification of created and uncreated nature. It takes place in a "voluntary outpassing" on the part of man, and in illuminating grace on the part of God. On the basis of his natural desire for God as his true end man finally suffers the Divine by grace and is thus deified. A unification takes place without confusion or change of either created or uncreated nature, which yet brings them into inseparable oneness. But that is to say,

---

[514] CCSG 7, p. 141.

[515] See Gnost 1. 81; PG 90, 1116 B; cf. von Balthasar, KL², p. 636.

[516] See Amb 7; PG 91, 1076 BC; cf. Sherwood, in ACW, pp. 49 and 95. That man's natural energy is not suppressed in deification is also strongly stressed by Larchet, *op. cit.,* p. 293 f. See also his thoughtful discussion of ecstasy in Maximus, *ibid.,* pp. 282–288.

[517] Cf. Sherwood, *The Earlier Ambigua,* p. 137.

in fact, that it takes place according to the principles which govern the unification of the two natures in Christ according to Maximus' Chalcedonian convictions, principles which we have also found to play an equally decisive rôle in Maximus' cosmology and anthropology.

Christology and mystical union

This fact leads us, however, to ask whether there are any further indications that mystical union is consciously understood by Maximus in Christological terms. In fact there are. Let us first refer to the fact that Ps.-Denis once presented the somewhat audacious idea of an *ecstasy of God*. This ecstasy implies God's 'emigration' out of Himself in love in the case of the divine Incarnation in Jesus, and is understood as an example of the ecstatic character of all love.[518] This idea is interesting in that it introduces a certain correspondence between God and man as loving subjects. An ecstatic 'emigration' of God Himself into the created world takes place. But even more interesting is the fact that Maximus uses this kind of thinking—though in a restricted way—and shows that the Divine, which is in itself unmovable, as ἔρως and ἀγάπη is moved, while at the same time as an object of love it moves towards itself those which are capable of receiving this activity.[519] There is thus a kind of *reciprocal movement of God and man* taking place towards each other, though without any confusion.

And Maximus goes on to explain the character of this divine motion. Thus the Divinity as cause of the enquiry *concerning the mode of its existence* is said to be moved.[520] This last statement ought now to be compared with what Maximus says in Char 1. 100. There we learn that when the mind—which is "placed in God", i.e. at its highest stage of perfection in mystical union—enquires about the λόγοι which concern God Himself, i.e. the principles of God's own nature, it receives no encouragement, but is nevertheless encouraged by the divine attributes.[521] If now we recall the Maximian distinction between "principle of nature" and "mode of existence", we can more easily understand what Maximus wishes to say. In relation to man it is the "mode of existence" but not the "principle of nature" which is innovated, and the different virtues which man acquires in the *vita practica* likewise belong to his transformed "mode of existence". When now Maximus says that Divini-

---

[518] *De div. nom.* 4, 13; PG 3, 712 AB; cf. VÖLKER, *Kontemplation und Ekstase*, p. 202.

[519] Amb 23; PG 91, 1260 C.

[520] *Ibid.;* 1260 D. P. BLOWERS has analysed this concept in his article Maximus the Confessor, Gregory of Nyssa and the concept of 'perpetual progress', *Vigiliae Christianae* 46 (1992), pp. 151–171.

[521] CSC, p. 88.

ty is moved as cause of "the enquiry concerning the mode of its existence", this must be a reference to the "encouragement" which he mentions in Char 1. 100. The enquiry about God's principle of being is not satisfied, but the enquiry about His "mode of existence"—which is unseparable from his relationship to His creation—is satisfied through an illumination about His attributes. Now these attributes are to some extent identical with the reflections of the Trinity which "natural contemplation" may find in creation, and also in man's virtues as places of a divine incarnation. Thus we must conclude that Maximus' idea is that God with regard to the manifold incarnation of the divine Logos in the world is moved *towards man,* and this motion is an answer to the quest for the divine mode of existence.

Here however we must add, that this is precisely Maximus' position in his Christology: that it is in his mode of existence that man has received a deifying renewal in Christ, and also that in the field of "mode of existence" the *communicatio idiomatum* takes place as a *perichoresis.* The interpenetration of divine and human in Christ, is thus reflected in man's mystical union with God. And this fact has further repercussions. In a passage in Amb 10 Maximus says, not only that man and God are exemplars one of the other, but also that God becomes man, insofar as man has in charity deified himself, and that *"man is as much rapt by God to the unknown, as he has himself manifested God, invisible by nature, through his virtues".*[522] Here several details are of great interest. First of all, Maximus uses here the *tantum—quantum* formula, which is intimately linked with his Christology in general, and with his use of the *perichoresis* idea in particular.[523] Secondly, man's charity is seen to be active in his deification; it is love which reaches beyond the borders of human nature. Thirdly, and this is most important, there is a correspondence between man's ecstasy to God and his own manifestation of the virtues. Since this manifestation is understood as an incarnation, and since these virtues are reflections of the divine attributes, and as such manifestations of God's 'ecstasy' towards man—if we are allowed to use Denis' terminology—they obviously represent the "encouragement" which man is promised in mystical union.

Thus we see that *the natural desire of man, seeking for God, finds its rest in Him through a process of interpenetration, which maintains the gulf and the fixity of the natures but communicates the modes of existence as human virtues and divine attributes.* And this attitude—which is Chalce-

---

[522] See Amb. 10; PG 91, 1113 BC. Sherwood, in ACW, p. 90, draws attention to this passage, but he does not make quite so much use of it as he might have done.
[523] Cf. p. 31 above.

donian in the Maximian sense and nothing else—explains why Maximus stops short of some of the expressions of Ps.-Dionysian ecstasy and Evagrian 'emigration'. The mind is illuminated by God on its own ground, and only in love and "gnomic emigration" does man reach outside himself. Thus deification coincides, it seems, with man's own illumination—the perfection of his intellectual faculty—but this illumination, in its turn, depends on the virtues—the perfection of man's passible faculties.

Thus Maximus is able to preserve his double emphasis on distinction and differentiation on the one hand, and natural unity and supernatural unification in love on the other. It is true to say with von Balthasar, that the supreme union with God is fulfilled not only in spite of, but rather in and through the preserved distinction.[524] The leading principle of this thesis is most clearly confirmed.

11. Deification—the purpose of human life

We must close our presentation of Maximus' theological anthropology with a short description of his idea of deification. It is appropriate for many reasons. One is that in Maximus' view human mediation is fulfilled in deification. Another is that deification, as Maximus sees it, is the perfect expression of the principle of unity in differentiation, which we have found to be the working idea of his thought.

The Christian concept of deification has a long history before Maximus, and his own position has to be understood against this background. However, no more elaborate presentation of this history is necessary for our purpose. The general trend is coherent, and the idea of deification in the Greek Fathers in general has been rather well treated in a number of monographs.[525]

The concept of deification in the Christian tradition before Maximus

The earlier Greek Fathers such as Irenaeus, Clement of Alexandria and Origen certainly had a concept of deification, particularly linked with the idea of the divine image in man and of man's sonship with God in

---

[524] Cf. VON BALTHASAR, KL², p. 90.

[525] Classical studies are LOT-BORODINE, La doctrine de la déification dans l'Église grecque jusqu'au XIe siècle, RHR 105–106 (1932), pp. 5–43, 525–574 and 107 (1933), pp. 8–35 and J. GROSS, La divinisation du chrétien d'après les Pères grecs, Paris 1938. A valuable later summary is DALMAIS, art. Divinisation: II. Patristique greeque, DSp 3, coll. 1376–1389. A recent survey, in many ways magnificent, is given in LARCHET, op. cit. with a special reference to Maximus.

Christ,[526] but it is not until Athanasius that a real theology of deification was developed. This theology can be said to have its starting-point in the famous dictum: "The Logos became man in order that we should become gods . . ."[527] This statement—which we certainly ought to notice because it contains that aspect of reciprocity in Christ, which is the root of e.g. the *tantum—quantum* formula as we find it in Maximus—was worked out in two integrated ideas, both based on the Incarnation in Christ: 1) communication of knowledge about God through Christ's revelation and 2) Christ's suffering to obtain immortality for men. The adoption of men into the divine sonship is further identified with deification in Athanasius, as it had been in the earlier tradition, though it is at the same time made clear that this kind of assimilation to God is never to be understood as identification.[528] This divine filiation was the very purpose of the Incarnation.[529] There is finally, of course, a strong stress on Baptism and on the Holy Spirit as the supreme agent of deification.[530]

The Cappadocian Fathers in general follow Athanasius. Both Basil and Gregory Nazianzen give explicit expression to the idea of deification, though their attitude is restrictive because of possible misunderstandings.[531] Some new perspectives were added by Gregory of Nyssa, who however was also rather restrictive. Thus he stressed strongly the distinction (διάστημα) which exists between man and God and also the difference between God's immutability and man's ever-moving character. By freely accepting this mutability Christ liberated man from death—an important aspect of deification from the very beginning. To the importance of Baptism, received by faith, he adds an understanding of the Eucharist as a unification of the deified flesh of Christ with ours.[532] Thus deification is explicitly understood on the basis of the union of the Logos with the whole of man, through which human nature is deified in Him.[533]

This last mentioned elaboration of the idea shows that in its further

---

[526] For the importance of this idea in Irenaeus see e.g. A. GILG, *Weg und Bedeutung der altkirchlichen Christologie*, Munich 1955, p. 38 f.; for the different aspects of the idea in Origen, see CROUZEL, *Théologie de l'image de Dieu*, pp. 164 (the rôle of grace), 230 ff. (participation in Christ through the virtues), 233 (deification of the mind) and 240 (the rôle of love).

[527] *De incarn. Verbi* 54; PG 25, 192 B.

[528] Cf. DALMAIS, *art. cit.,* col. 1381 and GILG, *op. cit.,* p. 84 ff.

[529] Cf. BURGHARDT, *The Image of God,* p. 124 f.

[530] Cf. GILG, *op. cit.,* p. 86.

[531] Cf. DALMAIS, *art. cit.,* col. 1382 f.; on Gregory Nazianzen, cf. also PLAGNIEUX, *Grégoire de Nazianze,* pp. 186 and 427.

[532] Cf. DALMAIS, *art. cit.,* col. 1383.

[533] Cf. e.g. GAÏTH, *La conception de la liberté,* p. 150 f.

development it is deeply rooted in Christology. As a matter of fact, the later development of Christology favoured the acceptance of deification as a permanent element in Christian doctrine. This may be seen e.g. in the case of Cyril of Alexandria, for whom deification is made certain through the double consubstantiality of Christ. Cyril also emphasizes that human nature is thus deified in principle in Christ by virtue of the Incarnation, and this deification is worked out in the case of the individual through the gift of the Spirit.[534] Cyril also sees resemblance to the divine primarily as a matter of sanctification on the basis of man's call to realize the divine likeness in himself, which leads to an evaluation of the virtues in combination with a concept of ontological holiness, which characterizes his understanding of deification.[535]

A new element was to some extent introduced by Ps.-Denis, in whose writings the word θέωσις finally replaced θεοποίησις as the technical term.[536] Here we notice the influence of later Neo-Platonism. Otherwise Denis hardly goes beyond his predecessors. He stresses that deification is the aim of creation and sees it as realized in likeness and union with God.[537] It is a pure gift of divine grace,[538] and is effected by means of Baptism and the Eucharist.[539] Through the hierarchies man ascends to divine virtue.[540] Ps.-Denis is thus in many ways as careful to avoid misunderstandings as are the Cappadocians.[541]

Maximus' doctrine of deification—a summary of his theological anthropology

Maximus' understanding of deification depends to a great extent on that of Ps.-Denis, as his use of the term θέωσις clearly shows, but he is also

---

[534] Cf. DALMAIS, *art. cit.*, col. 1384.

[535] Cf. BURGHARDT, *op. cit.*, p. 83.

[536] The term θέωσις had been used earlier, though not as *the* technical term. Thus there are a number of examples of its use within the common speculation on divinization in Gregory Nazianzen, e.g. the following passages: *Or.* 25, 16; PG 35, 1221 B (on Christ's deification as not progressive); *Or.* 39, 16; PG 36, 353 B (on the divinization of Christ's body at his baptism; *Or.* 21, 2; PG 35, 1084 C (relationship to contemplation); *Or.* 25, 2; PG 35, 1200 B (effected through the Eucharist) and *Poem. mor.;* PG 37, 957 A (effected through charity). In later writers the term is frequently used. Such is the case with Maximus, but we find it also e.g. in Ps.-Leontius of Byzantium, *Adv. Nestor.* 1, 18; PG 86, 1468 D (deification of human nature through the Incarnation) and Procopius of Gaza, *Comm. in Prov.* 18; PG 87, 1408 A (defication of creatures by grace) and 9; 1301 D (through the Eucharist). Reference can also be given to a late writer like Anastasius Sinaita, *Viae dux* 2; PG 89, 77 B (deification is not a change of nature but an elevation to what is better) and 14; 244 C (effected through union with divine nature).

[537] See *De eccles. hier.* 1, 3; PG 3, 376 A.

[538] See *ibid.* 1, 4; 376 B.

[539] *Ibid.* 2. 2, 1; 393 A and 6. 3, 5.; 536 C.

[540] *Ibid.* 1, 2; 373 A.

[541] Cf. VÖLKER, *Kontemplation und Ekstase,* p. 76 f. and DALMAIS, *art. cit.,* col. 1385 ff.

indebted to his other predecessors and to the general tradition which we have outlined. He strongly emphasizes that deification is effected entirely by the agency of divine grace, and that its means are the Church, the sacraments, etc.[542] But his main personal contribution lies in the way in which he combines the doctrines of Incarnation and deification by means of the *tantum—quantum* formula linked with the concepts of *communicatio idiomatum* and *perichoresis.*[543] And it is this fact which at the same time makes it possible to present *his doctrine of deification as a summary of his whole theological anthropology.*[544]

Thus for Maximus the doctrinal basis of man's deification is clearly to be found in the hypostatic unity between the divine and human nature in Christ. But this effect of the Incarnation—that human nature is deified in its hypostatic union with the divine in Christ—is in its turn based upon the purpose of God's creation, for He created man to become partaker of divine nature.[545] This participation of the divine nature however, is not effected on account of human nature. Consequently, it must be effected on account of the hypostatic union between human nature and the divine Logos. Thus Maximus points out very sharply, that if deification were according to human nature, then it would be nature which effected it, but now it is not so, since it is due to God's purpose and grace alone.[546] Thus it is characteristic of deification, as Maximus understands it, that it is effected precisely under the conditions which are those of the hypostatic union in Christ, i.e. in perfect coherence and yet without any change or violation of the natures.

We analysed above, in connection with our statement of Maximus' view of ecstasy, a passage in Amb 10 which we found to be of particular interest.[547] It is of equal interest for his doctrine of deification, for it shows clearly how closely his thinking on deification is linked with his understanding of Chalcedonian Christology. It is Maximus' conviction, that deification is not by human nature, although man is created in the image of God. Man's relationship to his archetype, consequently, does

---

[542] Cf. SHERWOOD, in ACW, pp. 72–81.

[543] SHERWOOD, in ACW, p. 72, likewise notices the importance of the "anti-strophic arrangement" at this point.

[544] DALMAIS, *art. cit.,* col. 1387, calls Maximus' position the definite synthesis. For a later treatment of Maximus' understanding of deification, see GARRIGUES, *op. cit.,* pp. 83–199. See also VÖLKER, *Maximus Confessor,* pp. 471–489 and particularly LARCHET, *op. cit.,* who confirms the central position of the doctrine of deification in the whole universe of Maximian theology.

[545] See Ep 24; PG 91, 609 C with ref. to 2 Peter 1: 4 (an important Scripture passage in the Christian development of the idea of deification).

[546] See Amb 20; PG 91, 1237 AB.

[547] Cf. p. 426 above.

not imply such a participation as would presuppose an ontological unity. God and man are exemplars one of another, says Maximus. Their relationship thus lies in the field of imitation, of capacity for mutual adaptation of the modes of existence.

This position makes it possible for Maximus to say, on the one hand, that there is no power inherent in human nature which is able to deify man,[548] and yet, on the other, that God becomes man *insofar as* man has deified himself—obviously on the basis that man has a natural desire to find his pleasure in God alone.[549] Using the *tantum—quantum* formula he expresses that mutual penetration and communication which is possible within a hypostatic union.

Now it is clear, that this last statement is to be understood both in a general sense, and in relation to the individual. In the *first* case, he refers to the divine Incarnation in Jesus, where the formula simply indicates that divine embodiment and human deification necessarily take place at the same time. For as we recall, there is not even a γνώμη in Christ, at least according to Maximus' later understanding,[550] and thus in Christ human nature is in principle united with the Logos—and finding its hypostasis there—and related to this nature there is also a natural will, which wills to find its rest in God alone. But since there is no hesitation in the case of Christ, no weighing of alternatives, Maximus can say that God is incarnate *insofar as* man has deified himself. In the *second* case—when the text is applied to the individual Christian—it must be understood in analogy with what we have just said. Man has no natural power to deify himself, but in Baptism he has been liberated so as to choose freely what is good for him. And therefore, another incarnation takes place in the believer, an incarnation in his virtues—though they are still natural—which is realized as a revelatory movement of God towards man.[551] Man exerts his virtuous activity and receives by grace reflections of the divine attributes in himself, since God and man are exemplars. Again the two movements are thought of as taking place at the same time. Man has deified himself through the gift of charity, while at the same time God's divine attributes are made effective in him.

But now we can also see immediately that what Maximus calls deification is not restricted to the highest 'stage' of spiritual perfection. Or better: since deification is being worked out already in the *vita practica*, and deification should be considered the highest form of

---

[548] See ThPol 1; PG 91, 33 B. Cf. LARCHET, *op. cit.*, p. 298 ff.

[549] See Amb 10; PG 91, 1113 BC. Here one should notice the "analogical character of deification", as this is pointed out by LARCHET, *op. cit.*, pp. 342–345.

[550] Cf. ch. IV: B, 2; pp. 214 ff. above.

[551] Cf. ch. V: B, 5; p. 329 above.

perfection, there is obviously no fixed chronological order between the different elements in Maximus' scheme of spiritual perfection. Deification is as it were simply the other side of Incarnation—i.e. incarnation both in Jesus and in the individual—and thus it takes place wherever this incarnation takes place, i.e. whenever the Divine can be said to 'penetrate' into the human in virtue of the exchange of attributes which comes about through the hypostatic union.

This position of Maximus is most clearly expressed in one of his early writings, when he says, using a somewhat daring formulation: "In fact, the most perfect work of charity and the end of its activity is to allow, through a reciprocal attribution (i.e. *communicatio*), the individual characteristics (*idiomata*) of those who are bound together by it, as well as their names, to become mutually useful, so that man is made god and God is called and appears as man . . .".[552] In the whole context of Maximus' writings it is obvious that this "communication" is strictly to be understood, not as a mixture of the natures, nor of their wills, but as a co-ordination of human and divine activities, which preserves the characteristics of each of them, but allows for a revelation of God in human categories (through the reflection of His attributes), and for man's relationship to God in future "ever-being" thanks to the same qualities, to be summed up in the divine gift of love.

We could say the same about "natural contemplation". It is effected through a process in which the mind is brought to a nakedness and a unified understanding which reflects the divine simplicity.[553] There again by grace man is given identity and simplicity from God. Together with the immortality of the body and the immutability of the soul, this simplicity is the final gift which deification implies. That this is granted to man, however, will be finally revealed and realized only after death— in the life hereafter which is given to man through Christ as an "ever-well-being".[554]

---

[552] Ep 2; PG 91, 401 B.

[553] See Myst 5; PG 91, 680 AB.

[554] Cf. SHERWOOD, in ACW, p. 72 and DALMAIS, *art. cit.,* col. 1388. For a recent treatment of the concept of "ever-moving rest", see FARRELL, *op. cit.,* p. 148 ff. (where the author criticizes my contention in *Man and the Cosmos*, p. 145).

Conclusions

We are at the end of our presentation of Maximus' understanding of the position and function of man. And the circle is closed. We started with Maximus' Christology as the basis of all his theology, and we have returned to it in our last section, to find that his doctrine of deification almost coincides with his doctrine of Christ. Christ the Creator Logos and Christ the Mediator is the centre of his vision of man the microcosm in his relationship to God and the whole created world.

This fact is, of course, of outstanding importance for the historical evaluation of Maximus' own contribution to the development of Christian thinking. It is not his philosophical presuppositions, nor his positive or controversial relationship to any of his predecessors or to other streams of Christian thinking as such, which constitutes the most relevant element of his theology. It is rather his visionary understanding of the Person of Christ which is most important, not only for himself but also for the evaluation of his rôle. The hypostatic relationship between human and divine in Christ, as he understands it in his personal faithfulness to both Chalcedon and Constantinople, is alone able to manifest and safeguard the purpose for which man was created, deification, while preserving man himself unchanged in his natural make-up. It alone establishes man in an unchangeable union with God forever, if only he is willing, by divine grace, to receive the deifying powers as effective within himself.

From this point of view, however, it would be entirely misleading to ask the question, which of these elements is most important to Maximus. He is not more interested in the aspect of unification, in the fact that in Christ the whole creation is held together in one immutable Logos and man is led to union with God forever, than in the fact that the differentiated purposes of the created species and natures are thereby fulfilled, or that the different elements of man's make-up are preserved and restored to their right function. Both are of equal importance, since they are merely two aspects of the same fact, and these aspects condition each other. Nature and grace are not in opposition to each other, for when human nature is truly developed, it is open to divine grace which establishes that relation to God, for which human nature was created.

Sherwood once presented an analysis of the history and contemporary state of research on Maximus.[1] He distinguished between three different approaches to Maximus: one from the point of view of his spirituality, as seen in the wider context of a common tradition (Viller and Hausherr), one from the point of view of Maximus as a *locus classicus* of Byzantine tradition, being both different from, and positively related to, the Latin Western tradition (Sherwood himself), and one from the point of view of Maximus' general theological attitude as a pattern for modern theology in its relationship to the general thinking of our time (von Balthasar).[2] With all its generalizations this presentation is still very stimulating. But it leads its author to a further question, which is almost identical with that which we have constantly discussed: what is the real centre of Maximus' theology?

Here Sherwood notices an important difference between von Balthasar on the one hand and von Ivánka, and possibly Sherwood himself, on the other. For von Balthasar the Christological formula of Chalcedon is the key to Maximus' synthesis, even to his understanding of the world structure. For von Ivánka the context is wider than the dogmatic problem or the controversies with the Monophysites and Monothelites.[3] The key idea of Maximus is the idea of "ultimate union of all creatures in the Incarnate Word". For this reason both von Ivánka and Sherwood himself regard Maximus' relationship to Origenism as of primary importance. However, von Balthasar's view fits into the wider context of von Ivánka.[4]

Our thesis has to a great extent treated precisely the same problems as are indicated in relation to the above-mentioned scholars. Are we then in the position to throw any light on the question which Sherwood presents in his searching article? The answer cannot but be affirmative. We took our point of departure in Maximus' faithfulness to the councils of Chalcedon and Constantinople, and throughout our study we have found that the Christological insights of these two councils are relevant to

---

[1] SHERWOOD, Survey of Recent Work on St. Maximus the Confessor, *Traditio* 20 (1964), pp. 428–437. Cf. my own extended introduction above.

[2] SHERWOOD, *art. cit.*, pp. 432–435.

[3] See VON IVÁNKA, Der philosophische Ertrag der Auseinandersetzung Maximos des Bekenners mit dem Origenismus, JOBG 7 (1958), pp. 23–32. Cf. also IDEM, Einleitung, in MAXIMOS DER BEKENNER, *All-eins in Christus*, p. 6 f. It would seem unfair, however, to suggest that von Balthasar restricts his interest to those points of dogma, which Sherwood mentions here.

[4] SHERWOOD, *art. cit.*, p. 434.

Maximus, not only in his cosmology but also in all his anthropological considerations. At this point we agree with von Balthasar that the basic vision of Maximus is formed by these insights. But we have gone a little further and tried to establish the conclusion, that Maximus' Christology implies that the Chalcedonian juxtaposition of the two principles of unity and distinction is finally overcome in the conviction, held by Maximus, that each of them is fully relized only when the other is equally realized. And this conviction allows for Maximus' understanding of *perichoresis.*

This fact, however, leads us to the further conclusion that the idea of von Balthasar—which is virtually an idea of unity in diversity—does not necessarily fit into the wider context of von Ivánka—the idea that Maximus accepts diversification in creation as something good only with a view to its full realization in a final unity. For these two aspects are reciprocal and condition each other. Diversified created natures, and human 'synthetic' nature, find their fulfilment in unity with God through Christ, not in spite of their diversity, but as the true manifestation of it. And this unity implies at the same time a continuing incarnation of the Logos in diversified creation. The movements of contraction and expansion go together. Von Balthasar has seen this most clearly. He has demonstrated it mostly in the field of cosmology. We have tried to do the same in the field of Maximus' general anthropology, psychology and doctrine of sanctification and deification. Von Ivánka and Sherwood are right in regarding the union of human and divine natures in the incarnate Logos as the key to Maximus' vision, and as the divine intent which he claims to have discovered through the mystery of Christ,[5] but precisely for this reason von Balthasar is also right in stressing the proper balance of unity and diversity. Later research has not altered that basic insight.

Finally, we have seen in this study that such a balance is relevant even in relation to the highest forms of spiritual development. Maximus' doctrine of the Trinity preserves it within the realm of negative theology, and his understanding of ecstasy and mystical union maintains it through its insistence on the gulf which remains between God and the whole creation on the ontological level, as well as its reference to the co-operation between natural desire and divine love in the field of moral and mystical communion with God. Sherwood refers at the end of his article to a key problem, which had not been sufficiently treated so far: the concept of "participation" in Maximus and his predecessors.[6] On the

---

[5] Cf. *ibid.,* p. 435.

[6] See *ibid.,* p. 435 f.—This requirement was hardly sufficiently met in the conclusive

basis of what we have now said, we are indeed prepared to agree with him about the importance of this problem and the need for further studies related to it. The closest effort to meet this requirement is probably attempted in Larchet's recent study on deification, but still a lot is to be done.

monograph on Maximus by VÖLKER, *Maximus Confessor als Meister des Geistlichen Lebens*, Wiesbaden 1965, which appeared during the printing process of the first edition of this book (cf. p. 16 above).

BIBLIOGRAPHY

A. Texts and Translations

1. Maximus

The complete works in Greek are to be found in J. P. MIGNE, *Patrologia Graeca,* vols. 90–91, Paris 1865.

Quaestiones ad Thalassium I–LV are edited in C. LAGA-C. STEEL, *Maximi Confessoris Quaestiones ad Thalassium I, Quaestiones I–LV, una cum latina interpretatione Ioannis Scotae Eriugenae iuxta posita,* Leuven University Press, Turnhout-Brepols, 1980 (=CCSG 7). Other critical editions are:

Maximi Confessoris Quaestiones ad Thalassium II, Quaestiones LVI–LXV, una cum latina interpretatione Ioannis Scotae Eriugenae iuxta posita, Leuven University Press, Turnhout-Brepols 1990 (=CCSG 22).

Maximi Confessoris Quaestiones et Dubia, ed. JOSÉ H. DECLERCK, Leuven University Press, Turnhout-Brepols, 1982 (=CCSG 10).

Maximi Confessoris Opuscula exegetica duo, ed. PETER VAN DEUN, Leuven University Press, Turnhout-Brepols, 1991 (=CCSG 23).

Capituli sulla carità, editi criticamente con introduzione, versione e note (Verba Seniorum, N.S. 3), ed. A. CERESA-GASTALDO, Rome 1963 (=CSC).

Translations into English

SAINT MAXIMUS THE CONFESSOR, *The Ascetic Life. The Four Centuries on Charity.* Translated and Annotated by POLYCARP SHERWOOD, O.S.B., S.T.D., The Newman Press, Westminster, Maryland, and Longmans, Green and Co., London, 1955 (=ACW).

The Philokalia: The Complete Text Compiled by St. Nikodimos of the Holy Mountain and St. Makarios of Corinth, vol. 2, pp. 48–305. Edited and translated by G.E.H. PALMER, P. SHERRARD, and K. WARE. London, 1981.

The Church, the Liturgy and the Soul of Man: The Mystagogia of St. Maximus the Confessor, translated with historical note and commentaries by J. STEAD, Still River, Massachusetts 1982.

Maximus Confessor: Selected Writings. Translations and Notes by GEORGE C. BERTHOLD. Introduction by JAROSLAV PELIKAN. Preface by IRÉNÉE-HENRI DALMAIS, O.P., SPCK, London 1985.

The Disputation with Pyrrhus of Our Father among the Saints Maximus the Confessor. Translated from the Greek by JOSEPH P. FARRELL, South Canaan, Pennsylvania, 1990.

Translations into French

MAXIME LE CONFESSEUR, *Centuries sur la charité.* Introduction et traduction de JOSEPH PEGON, S.J., Éditions du Cerf, Paris-Editions de Labeille, Lyon, 1943.

MAXIME LE CONFESSEUR, *Lettre à Jean le Cubiculaire sur la charité,* in *La Vie Spirituelle* 79 (1948), pp. 296–303.

SAINT MAXIME LE CONFESSEUR, *Le Mystère du salut.* Textes traduits et présentés par ASTERIOS ARGYRIOU. Avec une introduction de I.-H. DALMAIS, O.P., Les Éditions du soleil levant, Namur 1964.

MAXIME LE CONFESSEUR, *Livre ascétique,* translated by P. DESEILLE, in *L'Évangile au désert. Des premiers moines à saint Bernard,* "Chrétiens de tous les temps", Paris 1965, pp. 161–191.

Saint Maxime, moine et confesseur, Brève interprétation de la Prière de Notre Père (Mt 6/9–13) pour un ami du Christ, in ALAIN RIOU, *Le monde et l'Église selon Maxime le Confesseur,* Beauchesne, Paris 1973, pp. 214–239 and *Cent chapîtres sur la théologie et l'économie dans la chair du Fils de Dieu I,* in *ibid.,* pp. 240–261.

MAXIME LE CONFESSEUR, *Trois grand textes de Maxime sur l'agonie écrits entre 642 et 646,* in FRANÇOIS-MARIE LÉTHEL, *Théologie de l'agonie du Christ. La liberté humaine du Fils de Dieu et son importance sotériologique mises en lumière par saint Maxime le Confesseur,* Éditions Beauchesne, Paris 1979, pp. 123–126.

Philocalie des Pères neptiques: Maxime le Confesseur, publiée pour la première fois par saint NICODÈME L'HAGIORITE à Venise, en 1782, Abbaye de Bellefontaine 1985.

The 45 letters by Maximus are translated by E. PONSOYE in SAINT MAXIME LE CONFESSEUR, *Correspondence,* Nîmes 1988 (mimeographed).

SAINT MAXIME LE CONFESSEUR, *Questions à Thalassios.* Introduction by J.-C. LARCHET et translation and notes by E. PONSOYE, Les Éditions de l'Ancre, Suresnes 1992.

SAINT MAXIME LE CONFESSEUR, *Ambigua*. Introduction by J.-C. LARCHET, preface, translation and notes by E. PONSOYE, comments by D. STANILOAE, Les Éditions de l'Ancre, Paris-Suresnes 1994.

Translations into German

Maximus der Bekenner, All-eins in Christus. Auswahl, Uebertragung, Einleitung von ENDRE VON IVÁNKA, Johannes Verlag, Einsiedeln 1961.

MAXIMUS DER BEKENNER, *Die Mystagogie*, in HANS URS VON BALTHASAR, *Kosmische Liturgie. Das Weltbild Maximus des Bekenners.* Zweite völlig veränderte Auflage, Johannes Verlag, Einsiedeln 1961, pp. 409–481.

MAXIMUS DER BEKENNER, *Viermal hundert Sprüche über die Liebe*, and *Die gnostischen Centurien* (with comments), in *ibid.*, pp. 482–643.

Translations into Italian

MASSIMO IL CONFESSORE, *Umanità e divinità di Cristo*, translation, introduction and notes by A. CERESA-GASTALDO (Collana di testi patristici, no. 19), Rome 1979.

MASSIMO IL CONFESSORE, *Il Dio-uomo. Duencento pensieri sulla cognoscenza di Dio e sull' incarnazione di Cristo*, introduction, translation and notes by A. CERESA-GASTALDO (Già e non ancora, no. 66), Milan 1980.

MASSIMO IL CONFESSORE, *Meditazioni sull' agonia de Gesù*, translation, introduction and notes by A. CERESA-GASTALDO (Collana di testi patristici no. 50), Rome 1985.

2. *Classical and Patristic Figures*
(Only editions available in 1965 are listed here.)

ALEXANDER OF ALEXANDRIA
Epistola 1, PG 18, 547–572.

AMBROSE
Expositio evangelii Lucae, CSEL 32:4, 1902. (C. SCHENKL.)

ANASTASIUS SINAITA
Viae dux, PG 89, 35–310.

ARISTOTLE
De anima, BT, 1911.[2] (G. BIEHL, O. APELT.)
Ethica Eudemia, BT, 1884. (F. SUSEMIHL.)
Ethica Nicomachea, BT, 1912.[3] (F. SUSEMIHL, O. APELT.)
Magna Moralia, BT, 1883. (F. SUSEMIHL.)

Metaphysica, BT, 1913. (W. Christ.)
The Physics 1–2, LCL, 1929–1935. (P. H. Wicksteed, F. M. Cornford.)
Ps.-Aristotle, *On Virtues and Vices,* in *The Athenian Constitution, The Eudemian Ethics, On Virtues and Vices,* LCL, 1952³, pp. 483–503. (H. Rackham.)

Athanasius
Contra gentes, PG 25, 3–96.
De incarnatione Verbi, PG 25, 95–198.
Fragmenta varia, PG 26, 1217–1262.
G. Mueller, *Lexicon Athanasianum.* Berlin 1952.

Augustine
Confessiones, CSEL 33, 1896. (P. Knöll.)
De bono coniugali, CSEL 41, 1900, pp. 185–231. (J. Zycha.)
De civitate Dei, CSEL 40:1–2, 1899–1900. (E. Hoffmann.)
De diversis quaestionibus, PL 40, 11–148.
De doctrina Christiana, PL 34, 15–122.
De Genesi ad Litteram, CSEL 28:1, 1894, pp. 1–435. (J. Zycha.)
De Genesi, adversus Manichaeos, PL 34, 173–220.
De musica, Bibliothèque Augustinienne 7, Paris 1947. (G. Finaert, F. J. Thonnard.)
Epistola 155, CSEL 44, 1904, pp. 430–447. (Al. Goldbacher.)
In Ioannem, PL 35, 1379–1976.
Quaestiones in Heptateuchum, CSEL 28:2, 1895, pp. 1–506. (J. Zycha.)

Barsanuphius
Doctrina, PG 86:1, 891–902.

Basil of Caesarea
Opera, PG 29–32.
Ps.-Basil(?), *Constitutiones asceticae,* PG 31, 1321–1428.
Ps.-Basil, *De hominis structura,* PG 30, 9–62.

Basil of Seleucia
Oratio 4, PG 85, 61–76.

Cassian
Collationes, CSEL 13, 1886. (M. Petschenig.)
Conférences 1–8. Introduction, texte latin, traduction et notes. (SCH 42.) Paris 1955. (E. Pichéry.)
De Coenobiorum institutis, PL 49, 53–476.
Ps.-Nilus, *De octo vitiosis cogitationibus,* PG 79, 1435–1472.

Cicero
De natura deorum, BT Cic. 14, fasc. 45, 1933.² (O. Plasberg, W. Ax.)

CLEMENT OF ALEXANDRIA
Opera, GCS Clem. 1, 1905 (O. STÄHLIN); 2³, Berlin 1960 (O. STÄHLIN, L. FRUECHTEL); 3-4, 1909-1936 (O. STÄHLIN).

CYRIL OF ALEXANDRIA
Opera, PG 68-77.
Ps.-Cyril, *De sacrosancta Trinitate*, PG 77, 1119-1174.

CYRIL OF JERUSALEM
Catechesis 4, PG 33, 453-504.
    q((16))
DENIS OF ALEXANDRIA
Interpretatio in Lucam, PG 10, 1589-1596.

DIADOCHUS OF PHOTICE
Œuvres spirituelles. Introduction, texte critique, traduction et notes.² (SCH 5 bis.) Paris 1955. (É. DES PLACES).

DIDYMUS OF ALEXANDRIA
De Trinitate, PG 39, 269-992.

DOROTHEUS
Doctrina 1, PG 88, 1617-1640.

ELIAS ECDICUS
Ps.-Maximus, *Capita alia*, PG 90, 1401-1462.

ENNAEUS OF GAZA
Theophrastus, PG 85, 871-904.

EPIPHANIUS OF SALAMIS
Opera, GCS Epiph. 1-2, 1915-1922. (K. HOLL).

EUSEBIUS OF CAESAREA
Contra Marcellum, GCS Eus. 4, 1906, pp. 1-58. (E. KLOSTERMANN.)
Demonstratio evangelica, PG 22, 13-794.

EVAGRIUS PONTICUS
Opera, PG 40, 1213-1286.
W. FRANKENBERG, *Euagrius Ponticus.* (AGWG, N.F. 13:2.) Berlin 1912. (Syriac texts with retranslation into Greek.)
Seconde partie du traité, qui passe sous le nom de "La grande lettre d'Évagre le Pontique à Mélanie l'Ancienne". Publiée et traduite d'après le manuscrit du British Museum Add. 17 192. (Scripta minora Regiae Societatis Humaniorum Litterarum Lundensis 1963-1964:3.) Lund 1964. (G. VITESTAM.)

Les six Centuries des "Kephalaia Gnostica" d'Évagre le Pontique. Édition critique de la version syriaque commune et édition d'une nouvelle version syriaque, intégrale, avec une double traduction française. (PO 28:1.) Paris 1958. (A. GUILLAUMONT.)

H. GRESSMANN, *Nonnenspiegel und Mönchsspiegel des Euagrios Pontikos* zum ersten Male in der Urschrift herausgegeben. (TU 39:4b, pp. 146–165.) Leipzig 1913.

Ps.-Basil, *Epistola 8,* PG 32, 245–263.

Ps.-Nilus, *De malignis cogitationibus,* PG 79, 1199–1234.

Ps.-Nilus, *De oratione,* PG 79, 1165–1200.

Ps.-Nilus, *Tractatus ad Eulogium monachum,* PG 79, 1093–1140.

Greek Fragments

J. MUYLDERMANS, Evagriana, Mus 44 (1931), pp. 37–68.

IDEM, Note additionnelle à: Evagriana, Mus 44 (1931), pp. 369–383.

IDEM, *Evagriana.* Paris 1931.

IDEM, *À travers la tradition manuscrite d'Évagre le Pontique.* Essai sur les manuscrits grecs conservés à la Bibliothèque Nationale de Paris. (Bibl. du Mus. 3.) Louvain 1932.

E. PETERSON, Noch einmal Euagrios Pontikos, BNJ 5 (1926/27), pp. 412–418.

I. HAUSHERR, Nouveaux fragments d'Évagre le Pontique, OCP 5 (1939), pp. 229–233.

Ps.-Nilus (Evagrius?), *Tractatus ad eumdem Eulogium,* PG 79, 1139–1144.

GREGORY THE GREAT
Homiliae in Evangelia, PL 76, 1075–1314.

GREGORY NAZIANZEN
Opera, PG 35–38.
The Five Theological Orations. (Cambridge Patristic Texts.) Cambridge 1899. (A. J. MASON.)
Library of the Nicene and Post-Nicene Fathers, translated into English with prolegomena and explanatory notes. Second series 7 (Ann Arbor, Michigan 1955), pp. 185–498. (C. G. BROWNE, J. E. SWALLOW.)

GREGORY OF NYSSA
Opera, PG 44–46.
Gregorii Nysseni opera auxilio aliorum virorum doctorum edenda curavit W. JAEGER, 1–3:1, 5, 6, 8:1. Berlin-Leiden 1921–1962.
Adversus Apollinarem, JAEGER 3:1, 1958, pp. 129–233. (F. MUELLER.)
Contra Eunomium, JAEGER 1–2, 1960.² (W. JAEGER.)
De virginitate, JAEGER 8:1, 1952, pp. 215–343. (J. P. CAVARNOS.)
In Canticum canticorum, JAEGER 6, 1960. (H. LANGERBECK.)
In Ecclesiasten homiliae, JAEGER 5, 1962, pp. 195–422. (P. ALEXANDER.)
La vie de Moïse ou traité de la perfection en matière de vertu. Introduction et traduction.² (SCH 1 bis.) Paris 1955. (J. DANIÉLOU.)

Library of the Nicene and Post-Nicene Fathers. Second series 5. Ann Arbor, Michigan 1954. (W. MOORE, H. A. WILSON.)
Ps.-Gregory, *In Scripturae verba: Faciamus hominem ad imaginem et similitudinem nostram,* PG 44, 257–298.
Ps.-Gregory, *Quid sit, ad imaginem Dei et ad similitudinem,* PG 44, 1327–1346.

IRENAEUS
Adversus haereses, PG 7, 433–1224.

JEROME
Contra Ioannem Hierosolymitanum, PL 23, 355–396.
De nominibus Hebraicis, PL 23, 771–858.

JOHN CHRYSOSTOM
In epistolam primam ad Corinthios homiliae, PG 61, 9–382.
In Genesin homiliae, PG 53.
In Matthaeum homiliae, PG 58.

JOHN OF DAMASCUS
De fide orthodoxa, PG 94, 789–1228.
De octo spiritibus nequitiae, PG 95, 79–98.
Sacra parallela, PG 96, 9–442.

JOHN OF THE LADDER
Scala Paradisi, PG 88, 631–1164.

LACTANTIUS
De ira Dei, CSEL 27:1, 1893, pp. 65–132. (S. BRANDT.)

LEONTIUS OF BYZANTIUM
Opera, PG 86:1–2.
Ps.-Leontius, *Adversus Nestorianos,* PG 86:1, 1399–1768.

(Ps.-) MACARIUS MAGNUS
Homiliae in Genesin (excerpts), PG 10, 1375–1406.

MELETIUS
De natura hominis, PG 64, 1075–1310.

METHODIUS
De resurrectione, GCS Method., 1917, pp. 217–424. (N. BONWETSCH.)

NEMESIUS OF EMESA
De natura hominis, PG 40, 503–818.

Cyril of Jerusalem and Nemesius of Emesa (LCC 4, 1955), pp. 201–466. (W. TELFER.)

NILUS OF ANCYRA
De monachorum praestantia, PG 79, 1061–1094.
De octo spiritibus malitiae, PG 79, 1145–1164.

ORIGEN
Opera, GCS Orig. 1–2, 1899 (P. KOETSCHAU); 4, 1903 (E. PREUSCHEN); 5, 1913 (P. KOETSCHAU); 6–8, 1920–1925 (W. A. BAEHRENS); 9², 1959 (M. RAUER); 10–12, 1935–1955 (E. KLOSTERMANN).
Selecta in Genesin, PG 12, 91–146.
(Ps.-) Origen (Evagrius?), *Selecta in Psalmos,* in Origenis opera, Berlin 1831–1848 (C. H. E. LOMMATZSCH), 12–14; and PG 12, 1053–1686.

PHILO
Opera quae supersunt 1–7. Berlin 1896–1930. (L. COHN, P. WENDLAND.)

PLATO
Opera 1–5, BO, new impression 1946–1950. (J. BURNET.)

PLOTINUS
Enneades, BT, 1–2, 1883–1884. (R. VOLKMANN.)

PORPHYRY
Opuscula selecta, BT, 1886. (A. NAUCK.)

PROCOPIUS OF GAZA
Commentarii in Proverbia, PG 87:1, 1221–1544.

PS.-DENIS THE AREOPAGITE
Opera, PG 3.
Die Hierarchien der Engel und der Kirche. München-Planegg 1955. (W. TRITSCH.)
Mystische Theologie und andere Schriften mit einer Probe aus der Theologie des Proklus. München-Planegg 1956. (W. TRITSCH.)
Von den Namen zum Unnennbaren. Auswahl und Einleitung. Einsiedeln 1956. (E. VON IVÁNKA.)
A. VAN DEN DAELE, *Indices Pseudo-Dionysiani.* (Université de Louvain: Recueil de Travaux 3:3.) Louvain 1941.

SEXTUS(?)
H. CHADWICK, *The Sentences of Sextus.* A Contribution to the History of early Christian Ethics. (TSt, N.S. 5.) Cambridge 1959.

SOCRATES
Historia ecclesiastica, PG 67, 29–842.

THALASSIUS
Centuriae, PG 91, 1427–1470.

THEODORE SPOUDAEUS
Le texte grec de l'Hypomnesticum de Théodore Spoudée, AB 53 (1935), pp. 49–80. (R. DEVREESSE.)

THEODORET OF CYRUS
In Zachariam, PG 81, 1873–1960.
Interpretatio Epistolae ad Romanos, PG 82, 43–226.

THEOPHILUS OF ANTIOCH
Ad Autolycum, PG 6, 1023–1168.
Bibliothek der Kirchenväter. Eine Auswahl patristischer Werke in deutscher Übersetzung.² Kempten-Munich 1911–1928. (O. BARDENHEWER, TH. SCHERMANN, K. WEYMANN)—2. Reihe, Munich 1932–1938. (O. BARDENHEWER, J. ZELLINGER.)

3. Miscellaneous

ACHELIS, H., *Die ältesten Quellen des orientalischen Kirchenrechts.* 1. *Die Canones Hippolyti.* (TU 6:4.) Leipzig 1891.
Sacrorum conciliorum nova, et amplissima collectio, ed. by MANSI, J. D., 9–11, Florence 1763–1765.
Acta conciliorum oecumenicorum, ed. by SCHWARTZ, E., 3, Strassburg 1940.
Conciliorum Oecumenicorum Decreta, ed. by ALBERIGO, J.-JOUANNOU, P.P.-LEONARDI, C.-PRODI, P., Freiburg i. Br. 1962.
MALVY, A.-VILLER, M., *La Confession Orthodoxe de Pierre Moghila,* métropolite de Kiev 1633–1646, approuvée par les patriarches grecs du 17:e siècle. (Orientalia Christiana 39.) Rome-Paris 1927.
DIELS, H., *Doxographi Graeci.*² Berlin-Leipzig 1929.
Philocalia 1–2, ed. by Macarius of Corinth and Nicodemus Hagiorites. Venice 1782.
Early Fathers from the Philocalia. Selected and translated from the Russian text by KADLOUBOVSKY, E. and PALMER, G. E. H., London 1953.
Stoicorum veterum fragmenta 1–4, ed. by VON ARNIM, H., Leipzig 1903–1924.
*Die Fragmente der Vorsokratiker*⁷ 2, ed. by DIELS, H., Berlin 1954.

B.   Literature

ALLERS, R., Microcosmus, from Anaximandros to Paracelsus, *Traditio* 2 (1944), pp. 319–407.

ALONSO, J.-M., En torno al 'neocalcedonismo', *XV Semana Española de teología* 1956 (= *Verdad y Vida* 14, 1956), pp. 393–424.

ALTANER, B., *Patrologie.* Leben, Schriften und Lehre der Kirchenväter.[5] Freiburg i. Br. 1958.

AMAND, E., Les états de texte des homélies pseudo-basiliennes sur la création de l'homme, RB (1949), pp. 3–54.

AMANN, E., art. Théopaschite, DTC 15, coll. 505–512. (1946.)

ARNOU, R., art. Platonisme des Pères, DTC 12, coll. 2258–2392. (1935.)

—— art. La contemplation chez les anciens philosophes du monde gréco-romain, DSp 2, coll. 1716–1762. (1953.)

BAILEY, D. S., *The Man-Woman Relation in Christian Thought.* London 1959.

BALTHASAR, H. URS VON, Die Hiera des Evagrius, ZkTh 63 (1939), pp. 86–106, 181–206.

—— Das Scholienwerk des Johannes von Skythopolis, Schol 15 (1940), pp. 16–38. (Reprinted in KL[2], pp. 644–672.)

—— *Die 'Gnostischen Centurien' des Maximus Confessor.* Freiburg i. Br. 1941. (Revised and reprinted in KL[2], pp. 482–643.)

—— *Présence et pensée.* Essai sur la philosophie religieuse de Grégoire de Nysse. Paris 1942.

—— *Liturgie Cosmique.* Maxime le Confesseur. French translation of KL[1] by L'HAUMET, L. and PRENTOUT, H.-A. Paris 1947.

—— *Kosmische Liturgie.* Das Weltbild Maximus des Bekenners. Zweite, völlig veränderte Auflage. Einsiedeln 1961. (= KL[2].)

BARDENHEWER, O., *Geschichte der altkirchlichen Literatur* 5. Freiburg i.Br. 1932.

BARDY, G., art. Acédia, DSp 1, coll. 166–169. (1937.)

—— art. Apatheia, DSp 1, coll. 727–746. (1937.)

BAUSENHART, G., *In allem uns gleich ausser der Sünde: Studien zum Beitrag Maximos' des Bekenners zur altkirchlichen Christologie,* Tübinger Studien zur Theologie and Philosophie, vol. 5. Mainz, 1992.

BECK, H.-G., art. Maximus, RGG[3] 1, col. 814. (1960.)

BELLINI, E., Maxime interprète du Pseudo-Denys l'Aréopagite, in *Maximus Confessor: Actes du Symposium sur Maxime le Confesseur, Fribourg, 2–5 septembre 1980,* pp. 37–49. Edited by F. HEINZER and C. VON SCHÖNBORN. Paradosis, no. 27. Fribourg 1982.

BERNARD, R., *L'image de Dieu d'après saint Athanase.* Paris 1952.

BERTHOLD, G., The Cappadocian Roots of Maximus the Confessor, in *Maximus Confessor: Actes du Symposium sur Maxime le Confesseur, Fribourg, 2–5* septembre 1980, pp. 51–59. Edited by F. HEINZER and C. VON SCHÖNBORN. Paradosis, no. 27. Fribourg 1982.

—— Did Maximus the Confessor Know Augustine? *Studia patristica,* vol. 17, 14–17. Edited by Elizabeth Livingstone. Oxford and New York 1982.

—— History and Exegesis in Evagrius and Maximus, in *Origeniana Quarta: Die Referate des 4. internationalen Origeneskongresses (Innsbruck, 2–6. September 1985)*, pp. 390–404. Edited by L. LIES. Innsbrucker theologische Studien, vol. 19. Innsbruck and Vienna 1987.

—— The Church as Mysterion: Diversity and Unity according to Maximus Confessor, *Patristic Byzantine Review* 6(1987), pp. 20–29.

—— Levels of Scriptural Meaning in Maximus the Confessor, SP XXVII, 1993, pp. 129–144.

BESKOW, P., *Rex Gloriae. The Kingship of Christ in the Early Church.* Uppsala 1962.

BETTENCOURT, S. T., *Doctrina ascetica Origenis.* (SA 16.) Rome 1945.

BIHLMEYER, K.-TÜCHLE, H., *Kirchengeschichte 1.* Paderborn 1958.

BLOWERS, P. M., *Exegesis and Spiritual Pedagogy in Maximus the Confessor.* An Investigation of the *Quaestiones ad Thalassium,* Notre Dame, Indiana 1991.

—— Gregory of Nyssa, Maximus the Confessor, and the Concept of 'Perpetual Progress', VC 46 (1992): 151–171.

—— The Logology of Maximus the Confessor in His Criticism of Origenism, in *Origeniana Quinta,* pp. 570–576. Edited by R. J. DALY. Bibliotheca Ephemeridum Theologicarum Lovaniensium, vol. 105. Leuven, 1992.

—— The Analogy of Scripture and Cosmos in Maximus the Confessor, SP XXVII, 1993, pp. 145–149.

—— Theology as Integrative, Visionary, Pastoral: The Legacy of Maximus the Confessor, *Pro Ecclesia* 2 (1993), pp. 216–230.

BOOJAMRA, J., Original sin according to St. Maximus the Confessor, *Saint Vladimir's Theological Quarterly* 20(1976), pp. 19–30.

BORNERT, R., *Les commentaires byzantins de la divine liturgie, du VIIe au XVe siècle.* Archives de l'Orient chrétien, no. 9. Paris 1966.

—— Explication de la liturgie et interprétation de l'écriture chez Maxime le Confesseur, in SP 10, Berlin 1976, pp. 323–327.

BOUSSET, W., *Apophthegmata. Studien zur Geschichte des ältesten Mönchtums.* Tübingen 1923.

BOUYER, L., *Le sens de la vie monastique.* Paris 1950.

BRATSIOTIS, P., *Die Lehre der orthodoxen Kirche über die Theosis des Menschen,* Brussels 1961.

BRIA, I., The knowledge of God according to Saint Maximus the Confessor, *Studii Theologice* 9(1957), pp. 310–325 (in Rumanian).

BROCK, S., An Early Syriac Life of Maximus the Confessor, AB 91 (1973), pp. 299–346.

BRUNE, F., La rédemption chez saint Maxime le Confesseur, *Contacts* 30 (1978), pp. 141–171.

BURGHARDT, W. J., Cyril of Alexandria on "Wool and Linen", *Traditio* 2 (1944), pp. 484–486.

―――― *The Image of God in Man according to Cyril of Alexandria.* (SCA 14.) Washington 1957.

CAMELOT, TH., La théologie de l'image de Dieu, RSPT 40 (1956), pp. 443–471.

CANART, P., La deuxiéme lettre à Thomas de S. Maxime le Confesseur, *Byzantion* 34 (1964), pp. 415–449.

CANIVET, P., Théordoret et le monachisme Syrien avant le Concile de Chalcédoine, in *Théologie de la vie monastique,* Paris 1961, pp. 241–282.

CASPAR, E., Die Lateransynode von 649, ZKG 51 (1932), pp. 75–137.

―――― *Geschichte des Papsttums* 2. Tübingen 1933.

CAYRÉ, F., *Handleiding der Patrologie* I. Paris-Doornik-Rome 1948.

CERESA-GASTALDO, A., art. Maximos Confessor, LThK² 7, coll. 208–210. (1962.)

―――― Tradition et innovation linguistique chez Maxime le Confesseur, in *Maximus Confessor: Actes du Symposium sur Maxime le Confesseur, Fribourg, 2–5 septembre 1980,* pp. 123–137. Edited by F. HEINZER and C. VON SCHÖNBORN. Paradosis, no. 27. Fribourg 1982.

CHADWICK, H., The Identity and Date of Mark the Monk, *Eastern Churches Review* 4 (1972): 125–130.

―――― John Moschus and His Friend Sophronius the Sophist, *Journal of Theological Studies* N.S. 25 (1974): 49–74.

CHITTY, D. J., *The Desert a City: An Introduction to the Study of Egyptian and Palestinian Monasticism under the Christian Empire.* Oxford 1966.

CHRISTOU, P., The Infinity of Man in Maximus the Confessor, in *Maximus Confessor: Actes du Symposium sur Maxime le Confesseur, Fribourg, 2–5 septembre 1980,* pp. 261–271. Edited by F. HEINZER and C. VON SCHÖNBORN. Paradosis, no. 27. Fribourg, 1982.

COLOMBÁS, G., La biblia en la espiritualidad del monacato primitivo, *Yermo* 2 (1964): 113–129.

CONGAR, M.-J., La déification dans la tradition spirituelle de l'Orient, *Supplément à la* VS 43 (1935), pp. 91–107.

CROCE, V., *Tradizione e ricerca: Il metodo teologico di san Massimo il Confessore.* Studia patristica mediolanensia, no. 2. Milan 1974.

CROUZEL, H., *Théologie de l'image de Dieu chez Origène.* Paris 1956.

―――― L'image de Dieu dans la théologie d'Origène, SP 2 (TU 64), 1957, pp. 194–201.

―――― Origène, précurseur du monachisme, in *Théologie de la vie monastique,* Paris 1961, pp. 15–38.

DALEY, B., Apokatastasis and 'Honorable Silence' in the Eschatology of Maximus the Confessor, in *Maximus Confessor: Actes du Symposium sur Maxime le*

Confesseur, Fribourg, 2–5 septembre 1980, pp. 309–339. Edited by F. HEINZER and C. VON SCHÖNBORN. Paradosis, no. 27. Fribourg 1982.

DALMAIS, I.-H., S. Maxime le Confesseur, Docteur de la charité, VS 79 (1948), pp. 296–303.

——— La théorie des 'logoi' des créatures chez saint Maxime le Confesseur, RSPT 36 (1952): pp. 244–249.

——— L'oeuvre spirituelle de S. Maxime le Confesseur. Notes sur son développement et sa signification, *Supplément de la* VS 21 (1952), pp. 216–226.

——— La doctrine ascétique de saint Maxime le Confesseur d'après le *Liber Asceticus, Irénikon* 26 (1953): pp. 17–39.

——— Un traité de théologie contemplative: Le commentaire du Pater Noster de saint Maxime le Confesseur, RAM 29 (1953): pp. 123–159.

——— Divinisation. II. Patristique grecque, *Dictionnaire de spiritualité* III, 1957, col. 1376–1389.

——— L'anthropologie spirituelle de S. Maxime le Confesseur, *Recherches et débats du Centre catholique des intellectuels français* 36 (1961), pp. 202–211.

——— Saint Maxime le Confesseur et la crise de l'origénisme monastique, in *Théologie de la vie monastique: Études sur la tradition patristique*, pp. 411–421. Théologie, no. 49. Paris 1961.

——— L'anthropologie spirituelle de saint Maxime le Confesseur, *Recherches et débats* 36 (1961): pp. 202–211.

——— La fonction unificatrice du Verbe Incarné dans les œuvres spirituelles de saint Maxime le Confesseur, *Sciences ecclésiastiques* 14 (1962): pp. 445–459.

——— Place de Mystagogie de saint Maxime le Confesseur dans la liturgie byzantine, SP, V, Berlin 1962, pp. 277–283.

——— St Maxime le Confesseur. Une synthèse théologique, VS 107 (1962), pp. 316 ff.

——— L'héritage évagrien dans la synthèse de saint Maxime le Confesseur, SP, VIII, Berlin 1966, pp. 356–363.

——— Le vocabulaire des activités intellectuelles, volontaires et spirituelles dans l'anthropologie de S. Maxime le Confesseur, in *Mélanges offerts au P. M.-D. Chenu* (Bibliothèque thomiste no. 37), Paris 1967, pp. 189–202.

——— Mystère liturgique et divinsation dans la Mystagogie de S. Maxime le Confesseur, in *Epektasis. Mélanges patristiques offerts au Cardinal Daniélou*, Paris 1972, pp. 55–62.

——— Théologie de l'Eglise et mystère ligurgique dans la Mystagogie de S. Maxime le Confesseur, SP, XIII, Berlin 1975, pp. 145–153.

——— Maxime le Confesseur, *Dictionnaire de spiritualité*, X, 1980 col. 836–847.

——— La manifestation du Logos dans l'homme et dans l'Église: Typologie anthropologique et typologie ecclésiale d'après Qu. Thal. 60 et la Mystagogie, in *Maximus Confessor: Actes du Symposium sur Maxime le Confesseur, Fribourg, 2-5 septembre 1980,* pp. 13-25. Edited by F. Heinzer and C. von Schönborn. Paradosis, no. 27. Fribourg 1982.

——— La vie de Saint Maxime le Confesseur reconsidérée?, SP XVIII/1, 1982, pp. 26-30.

——— L'innovation des natures d'après S. Maxime le Confesseur (à propos de l'Ambiguum 42), SP, XV, 1984, pp. 285-290.

Danielou, J., *Origène.* Paris 1948.

——— *Sacramentum Futuri.* Paris 1950.

——— *Platonisme et théologie mystique.* Essai sur la doctrine spirituelle de Grégoire de Nysse.² Paris 1954.

——— *Bible et liturgie.* La théologie biblique des Sacrements et des fêtes d'après les Pères de l'Église.² (Lex Orandi 11.) Paris 1958.

——— *Philon d'Alexandrie.* Paris 1958.

Deseille, P., art. Épectase, DSp 4, coll. 785-788. (1959.)

Devreesse, R., La vie de S. Maxime le Confesseur et ses recensions, AB 46 (1928), pp. 5-49.

——— Le texte grec de l'Hypomnesticum de Théodore Spoudée, AB 53 (1935), pp. 49-80.

——— La fin inédite d'une lettre de Saint Maxime, RSRUS 17 (1937), pp. 23-35.

——— La lettre d'Anastase l'apocrisiaire sur la mort de saint Maxime, AB 73 (1955), pp. 5-16.

Diepen, H. M., *Les Trois Chapîtres au Concile de Chalcédoine.* Oosterhaut 1953.

Disdier, M.-Th., Les fondaments dogmatiques de la spiritualité de S. Maxime le Confesseur, EO 29 (1930), pp. 296-313.

——— Élie l'Ecdicos et les hetera kephalaia attribués à S. Maxime le Confesseur et à Jean de Carpathos, EO 31 (1932), pp. 17-43.

Dölger, F.-Beck, H.-G., *Diskussionsbeiträge zum XI. Internationalen Byzantinistenkongress, München 1958.* Munich 1961.

Domanski, B., *Die Psychologie des Nemesius.* Münster 1900.

Doucet, M., Vues récentes sur le "métamorphoses" de la pensée de S. Maxime le Confesseur, *Science et Esprit* 31 (1979), pp. 269-302.

——— Est-ce que le monothélisme a fait autant d'illustres victimes? Réflexions sur un ouvrage de F.-M. Léthel, *Science et Esprit* 35 (1983), pp. 53-83.

——— La volonté humaine du Christ, spécialement en son agonie. Maxime le Confesseur interprète de l'Ecriture, *Science et Esprit* 37 (1985), pp. 123-159.

Draeseke, J., Maximus Confessor und Johannes Scotus Erigena, ThStKr 84 (1911), pp. 20-60, 204-229.

Dupont, V. L., Le dynamisme de l'action liturgique. Une étude de la *Mystagogie* de saint Maxime le Confesseur, RSR 65 (1991), pp. 363-387.

Edsman, C.-M., Arbor inversa, *Religion och Bibel* 3 (1944), pp. 5-33.

ELERT, W., *Der Ausgang der altkirchlichen Christologie.* Eine Untersuchung über Theodor von Pharan und seine Zeit als Einführung in die alte Dogmengeschichte. Berlin 1957.

EPIFANOVITCH, S. L., *Prepodobnyj Maksim Ispovendnik i visantijskoje bogoslovie,* Kiev 1915.

FARGES, J.-VILLER, M., art. La Charité chez les Pères, DSp 2, coll. 523–569. (1953.)

FARRELL, J. P., *Free Choice in St. Maximus the Confessor,* South Canaan, Pennsylvania 1989.

FESTUGIÈRE, A.-J., *Contemplation et vie contemplative selon Platon.* Paris 1936.

FLICHE, A.-MARTIN, V., *Histoire de l'Église* 5, Paris 1938.

FLOROVSKY, G., The Anthropomorphites in the Egyptian Desert, in *Creation and Redemption,* pp. 89–96. The Collected Works of Georges Florovsky, vol. 4. Belmont, Mass. 1975.

—————— *The Byzantine Ascetic and Spiritual Fathers.* The Collected Works of Georges Florovsky, vol. 10. Translated by R. MILLER, A.-M. DÖLLINGER-LABRIOLLE, and H. SCHMIEDEL. Vaduz 1987.

—————— *The Byzantine Fathers of the Sixth to Eighth Century.* The Collected Works of Georges Florovsky, vol. 9. Translated by R. MILLER, A.-M. DÖLLINGER-LABRIOLLE, and H. SCHMIEDEL. Vaduz 1987.

FRANKENBERG, W., *Euagrius Ponticus.* (AGWG N.F. 13:2.) Berlin 1912.

FRIZ, K., art. Maximus Confessor, EvKL 2, col. 1275. (1958.)

GAÏTH, J., *La conception de la liberté chez Grégoire de Nysse.* (Études de Philosophie Médiévale 43.) Paris 1953.

GALTIER, P., L'Occident et le néo-chalcédonisme, Greg 40 (1959), pp. 54–74.

GARRIGUES, J.-M., Le Christ dans la théologie byzantine. Réflexions sur un ouvrage du P. Meuendoorff, *Istina* 15 (1970), pp. 351–361.

—————— Théologie et Monarchie. L'entrée dans le mystère du "sein du Père" (Jn 1.18) comme ligne directrice de la théologie apophatique dans la tradition orientale, *Istina* 15 (1970), pp. 435–465.

—————— L'énergie divine et la grâce chez Maxime le Confesseur, *Istina* 19 (1974), pp. 272–296.

—————— La Personne composée du Christ d'après Maxime le Confesseur. *Revue thomiste* 74 (1974): pp. 181–204.

—————— *Maxime le Confesseur: La Charité, avenir divin de l'homme.* Théologie historique, no. 38. Paris 1976.

—————— Le dessein d'adoption du Créateur dans son rapport au Fils d'aprés s. Maxime le Confesseur, in *Maximus Confessor: Actes du Symposium sur Maxime le Confesseur. Fribourg, 2–5 septembre 1980,* pp. 173–192. Edited by F. HEINZER and C. VON SCHÖNBORN. Paradosis, no. 27. Fribourg 1982.

GATTI, M. L., *Massimo il Confessore. Saggio di bibliografia generale ragionata e contributi per una ricostruzione scientifica del suo pensiero metafisico e religioso,* Milan 1987.

GAUTHIER, R.-A., S. Maxime le Confesseur et la psychologie de l'acte humain, RTAM 21 (1954), pp. 51–100.

GENEAKOPLOS, D.-J., Some Aspects of the Influence of the Byzantine Maximos the Confessor on the Theology of East and West, *Church History* 38 (1969), pp. 150–163.

GERSH, S., *From Iamblichus to Eriugena: An Investigation of the Pre-History and Evolution of the Pseudo-Dionysian Tradition.* Studien zur Problemsgeschichte der antiken und mittelalterlichen Philosophie, vol. 8. Leiden, 1978.

GILG, A., *Weg und Bedeutung der altkirchlichen Christologie.*[2] (Theologische Bücherei 4.) Munich 1955.

GILLET, R., Spiritualité et place du moine dans l'Église selon saint Grégoire le Grand, in *Théologie de la vie monastique,* Paris 1961, pp. 323–351.

GOUILLARD, P., Supercheries et méprises littéraires: L'œuvre de saint Théodore d'Édesse, REB 5 (1957), pp. 137–158.

GREEN, W. M., Initium Omnis Peccati Superbia. Augustine on pride as the first sin, *University of California Publications in Classical Philology* 13:13 (1949), pp. 407–432.

GRILLMEIER, A., Die theologische und sprachliche Vorbereitung der christologischen Formel von Chalkedon, Chalk I, pp. 5–202. (1951.)

——— Der Neu-Chalkedonismus. Um die Berechtigung eines neuen Kapitels in der Dogmengeschichte, HJG 77 (1958), pp. 151–166.

GRILLMEIER, A.-BACHT, H., *Das Konzil von Chalkedon.* Geschichte und Gegenwart. 3 vols. Würzburg 1951–1954. (= Chalk)

GROSS, J., *La divinisation du chrétien d'après les Pères grecs.* Paris 1938.

GRUMEL, V., La comparaison de l'âme et du corps et l'union hypostatique chez Léonce de Byzance et S. Maxime le Confesseur, EO 25 (1926), pp. 393–406.

——— Notes d'histoire et de chronologie sur la vie de Saint Maxime le Confesseur, EO 26 (1927), pp. 24–32.

——— art. Maxime le Confesseur, DTC 10, coll. 448–459. (1928.)

——— Recherches sur l'histoire du monothélisme, EO 27 (1928), pp. 6–16, 257–277; 28 (1929), pp. 19–34, 272–282; 29 (1930), pp. 16–28.

GUILLAUMONT, A., *Les "Kephalaia gnostica" d'Évagre le Pontique et l'histoire de l'Origénisme chez les Grecs et chez les Syriens.* (Patristica Sorbonensia.) Paris 1962.

GUILLAUMONT, A. and C., Le texte véritable des Gnostica d'Évagre le Pontique, RHR 142 (1952), pp. 156–205.

——— art. Évagre le Pontique, DSp 4, coll. 1731–1744. (1961.)

HALDON, J. F., *Byzantium in the Seventh Century: The Transformation of a Culture.* Cambridge, 1990.

HALLEUX, A. DE, Palamisme et Scolastique. Exclusivisme dogmatique ou pluriformité théologique?, *Revue théologique de Louvain* 4 (1973), pp. 409–442.

HANSON, R. P. C., Interpretation of Hebrew names in Origen, VC 10 (1956), pp. 103–123.

HARL, M., *Origène et la fonction révélatrice du Verbe incarné.* Diss. Paris 1958.

HARNACK, A., *Dogmengeschichte* 2⁴, Tübingen 1909.

HARRISON, V., *Grace and Human Freedom according to St. Gregory of Nyssa.* Lewiston, Maine, 1992.

HAUSHERR, I., L'origine de la théorie orientale des huit péchés capitaux, OCh 86 (1933), pp. 164–175.

―――― Une énigme d'Évagre le Pontique. *Centurie* II, 50, RSR 23 (1933), pp. 321–325.

―――― "Ignorance infinie", OCP 2 (1936), pp. 351–362.

―――― Nouveaux fragments d'Évagre le Pontique, OCP 5 (1939), pp. 229–233.

―――― *Penthos.* La doctrine de la componction dans l'Orient chrétien. (Orientalia Christiana Analecta 132.) Rome 1944.

―――― *Philautie.* De la tendresse pour soi à la charité, selon Saint Maxime le Confesseur. (Orientalia Christiana Analecta 137.) Rome 1952.

―――― Korreferat zu P. Sherwood, Maximus and Origenism, in *Berichte zum XI. Internationalen Byzantinisten-Kongress, München 1958,* Munich 1958. (2 pp.)

―――― Ignorance infinie ou science infinie, OCP 25 (1959), pp. 44–52.

―――― *Les leçons d'un contemplatif.* Le 'Traité de l'oraison' d'Évagre le Pontique. Paris 1960.

HEFELE, C. J., *Conciliengeschichte* 3. Freiburg i.Br. 1858.

HEINTJES, J., Een onbekende leeraar van ascese en mystiek: Sint Maximus Confessor, StC 11 (1935), pp. 175–200.

―――― De opgang van den menschelijken geest tot God volgens Sint Maximus Confessor, BiNJ 5 (1942), pp. 260–302; 6 (1943), pp. 64–123.

HEINZER, F., *Gottes Sohn als Mensch. Die Struktur des Menschseins Christi* bei Maximus Confessor (Paradosis No. 26), Fribourg 1980.

―――― Anmerkungen zum Willensbegriff Maximus Confessors, *Freiburger Zeitschrift für Philosophie und Theologie* 28 (1981), pp. 372–392.

―――― L'explication trinitaire de l'économie chez Maxime le Confesseur, in *Maximus Confessor: Actes du Symposium sur Maxime le Confesseur, Fribourg, 2–5 septembre 1980,* pp. 159–172. Paradosis, no. 27. Edited by F. HEINZER and C. VON SCHÖNBORN. Fribourg 1982.

HEINZER, F.-VON SCHÖNBORN, C., eds. *Maximus Confessor: Actes du Symposium sur Maxime le Confesseur, Fribourg, 2–5 septembre, 1980.* Paradosis, no. 27. Fribourg 1982.

HELMER, S., *Der Neuchalkedonismus.* Bonn 1962.

HOECK, J. M., art. Johannes v. Damaskus, LThK² 5, coll. 1023–1026.

HOFMANN, F., Der Kampf der Päpste um Konzil und Dogma von Chalkedon von Leo dem Grossen bis Hormisdas, Chalk 2, pp. 13–94. (1953.)

HOLL, K., *Amphilochius von Ikonium in seinem Verhältnis zu den grossen Kappadoziern.* Tübingen 1904.

HOLTE, R., *Béatitude et sagesse.* Saint Augustin et le problème de la fin de l'homme dans la philosophie ancienne. (Études Augustiniennes.) Paris 1962.

HOMMEL, H., Mikrokosmos, RhM 92 (1943), pp. 56–89.

HULTGREN, G., *Le commandement d'amour chez Augustin.* Interprétation philosophique et théologique d'après les écrits de la période 386–400. Paris 1939.

IVÁNKA, E. VON, Κεφάλαια: Eine byzantinische Literaturform und ihre antiken Wurzeln, *Byzantinische Zeitschrift* 47 (1954): pp. 285–291.

—— Der Philosophische Ertrag der Auseinandersetzung Maximos des Bekenners mit dem Origenismus, JOBG 7 (1958): pp. 23–49.

—— Korreferat zu P. Sherwood, Maximus and Origenism, in *Berichte zum XI. Internationalen Byzantinisten-Kongress, München 1958,* Munich 1958. (2 pp.)

JUGIE, M., art. Monothélisme, DTC 10:2, coll. 2307–2323. (1929.)

JUNGLAS, P., *Leontius von Byzanz.* Studien zu seinen Schriften, Quellen und Anschauungen. (FLDG 8:3.) Paderborn 1908.

KARAYIANNIS, V. *Maxime le Confesseur. Essence et énergies de Dieu.* Paris 1993.

KIRCHMEYER, J., art. Extase chez les Pères de l'Église, DSp 4, coll. 2087–2113. (1959.)

KÖPPEN, K.-P., *Die Auslegung der Versuchungsgeschichte unter besonderer Berücksichtigung der Alten Kirche.* (BGBE 4.) Tübingen 1961.

KRANZ, W., Kosmos und Mensch in der Vorstellung des frühen Griechentums, NGWG, N.F., Fachgr. 1, vol. 2 (1936–38), pp. 121–161.

—— *Kosmos* 1–2. (Archiv f. Begriffsgeschichte 2:1–2.) Bonn 1955–57.

KRIVOCHEINE, B., The Holy Trinity in Greek Patristic Mystical Theology, *Sobornost* (1957–58), pp. 462–469, 529–537.

KROLL, J., *Gott und Hölle.* Der Mythus vom Descensuskampfe. (StBW 20.) Berlin 1932.

LACKNER, W., *Studien zur philosophischen Schultradition und zu den Nemesi-oszitaten bei Maximos dem Bekenner,* Graz 1962.

—— Zu Quellen und Datierung der Maksimosvita, AB 85 (1967), pp. 253–316.

—— Der Amtstitel Maximos des Bekenners, JOBG 20 (1971), pp. 63 ff.

LADNER, G. B., The Philosophical Anthropology of Saint Gregory of Nyssa, DOP 12 (1958), pp. 58–94.

LAGA, C., Maximi Confessoris ad Thalassium Quaestio 64, in *After Chalcedon: Studies in Theology and Church History Offered to Professor Albert Van Roey for His Seventieth Birthday*, pp. 203–215. Edited by C. LAGA, J. A. MUNITZ, and L. VAN ROMPAY. Orientalia lovaniensia analecta, no. 18. Leuven 1985.

——— Maximus as a Stylist in *Quaestiones ad Thalassium*, in *Maximus Confessor: Actes du Symposium sur Maxime le Confesseur, Fribourg, 2–5 septembre 1980*, pp. 139–146. Edited by F. HEINZER and C. VON SCHÖNBORN. Paradosis, no. 27. Fribourg 1982.

LAGA, C.-MUNITZ, J. A.-VAN ROMPAY, L., eds. *After Chalcedon: Studies in Theology and Church History Offered to Professor Albert Van Roey for His Seventieth Birthday*. Orientalia lovaniensia analecta, no. 18. Leuven 1985.

LAMPE, G. W. H., ed., *A Patristic Greek Lexicon* 1–3. Oxford 1961–64.

LAMPEN, W., De Eucharistie-leer van S. Maximus Confessor, StC 2 (1926), pp. 35–54.

LANCZKOWSKI, G., art. Makrokosmos und Mikrokosmos, RGG³ 4. coll. 624–625. (1960.)

LARCHET, J.-C., Nature et fonction de la théologie négative selon Denys l'Aréopagite, *Le Messager Orthodoxe* 160 (1990), pp. 3–41.

——— Le baptême selon saint Maxime le Confesseur, RSR 65 (1991), pp. 51–70.

——— La pensée de saint Maxime le Confesseur dans les Questions à Thalassios, *Le Messager Orthodoxe* 161 (1991), pp. 3–34.

——— *La divinisation de l'homme selon saint Maxime le Confesseur.* Thèse de doctorat en théologie, Université de Strasbourg II, Strasbourg 1994.

LARSSON, E., *Christus als Vorbild.* Eine Untersuchung zu den paulinischen Tauf- und Eikon-texten. Diss. (Acta Seminarii Neotestamentici Upsaliensis 23.) Uppsala 1962.

LEBON, J., *Le monophysisme sévérien.* Diss. Louvain 1909.

——— Ephrem d'Amid, pàtriarche d'Antioche (526–44), *Mélanges d'Histoire offerts à Charles Moeller* 1 (1914), pp. 197–214.

——— Restitutions à Théodoret de Cyr, RHE 26 (1930), pp. 523–550.

——— La christologie du monophysisme sévérien, Chalk I, pp. 425–580. (1951.)

LEFÈVRE, Y., *L'Elucidarium et les Lucidaires.* Contribution, par l'histoire d'un texte, à l'histoire des croyances religieuses en France au moyen âge. (Bibl. des Écoles Françaises d'Athènes et de Rome 180.) Paris 1954.

LE GUILLOU, M.-J., The forewords to the dissertations by A.RIOU, J.-M. GARRIGUES, F.-M. LÉTHEL and P. PIRET (see these items).

——— Lumière et charité dans la doctrine palamite de la divinisation, *Istina* 19 (1974), pp. 329–338.

——— Quelques réflexions sur Constantinople III et la sotériologie de Maxime, in *Maximus Confessor: Actes du Symposium sur Maxime le Confesseur, Fribourg, 2–5 septembre 1980*, pp. 235–237. Edited by F. HEINZER and C. VON SCHÖNBORN. Paradosis, no. 27 Fribourg 1982.

LEISSNER, A., *Die Platonische Lehre von den Seelenteilen nach Entwicklung, Wesen und Stellung innerhalb der Platonischen Philosophie.* Diss. Nördlingen 1909.

LEMAÎTRE, J., Contemplation (Contemplation chez les grecs et autres orientaux chrétiens [II. La Θεωρία φυσική), DSp 2, part 2.

────── art. Contemplation ou "Science véritable", DSp 2, coll. 1801–1872. (1953.)

LEMAÎTRE, J.-ROQUES, R.-VILLER, M., art. Contemplation chez les Grecs, 1. Étude de vocabulaire, DSp 2, coll. 1762–1787. (1953.)

LEROY, J., Saint Théodore Studite, in *Théologie de la vie monastique*, Paris 1961, pp. 423–436.

LECLERCQ, J., *The Love of Learning and the Desire for God: A Study of Monastic Culture.* 3rd ed. Translated by C. MISRAHI. New York 1982.

LÉTHEL, F.-M., *Théologie de l'agonie du Christ: La liberté humaine du Fils de Dieu et son importance sotériologique mises en lumière par saint Maxime le Confesseur.* Théologie historique, no. 52. Paris 1979.

────── La prière de Jésus à Gethsémani dans la controverse monothélite, in *Maximus Confessor: Actes du Symposium sur Maxime le Confesseur, Fribourg, 2–5 septembre 1980*, pp. 207–214. Edited by F. HEINZER and C. VON SCHÖNBORN. Paradosis, no. 27. Fribourg 1982.

LEWY, H., *Sobria ebrietas.* Untersuchungen zur Geschichte der antiken Mystik. (Beihefte zur ZNW 9.) Giessen 1929.

LEYS, R., *L'Image de Dieu chez Saint Grégoire de Nysse.* Brussels and Paris 1951.

LIDDELL, H. G.-SCOTT, R., *A Greek-English Lexicon.* A New Edition by JONES, H. S. Oxford 1925–1940.

LOOSEN, J., *Logos und Pneuma im begnadeten Menschen bei Maximus Confessor.* (MBTh 24.) Münster (Westf.) 1941.

LOSSKY, V., La théologie négative dans la doctrine de Denys l'Aréopagite, RSPT 28 (1936), pp. 204–221.

────── *The Mystical Theology of the Eastern Church.* London 1957. (Transl. of *Essai sur la Théologie mystique de l'Église d'Orient*, Paris 1944.)

LOT-BORODINE, M., La doctrine de la déification dans l'Église grecque jusqu'au XIᵉ siècle, RHR 105–106 (1932), pp. 5–43, 525–574, and 107 (1933), pp. 8–35.

────── *La déification de l'homme selon la doctrine des Pères grecs*, Paris 1970.

LOUTH, A., *Discerning the Mystery: An Essay on the Nature of Theology.* Oxford 1983.

────── St. Denys the Areopagite and St. Maximus the Confessor: A Question of Influence, SP XXVII, 1993, pp. 166–174.

LUBAC, H. DE, *Histoire et esprit: L'intelligence de l'Écriture d' après Origène.* Paris 1950.

—— *Exégèse médiévale: Les quatre sens de l'Écriture.* 2 parts, 4 vols. Théologie, nos. 41, 42, 59. Paris 1959, 1961, and 1964.

MADDEN, N., The *Commentary on the Pater Noster:* An Example of the Structural Methodology of Maximus the Confessor, in *Maximus Confessor: Actes du Symposium sur Maxime le Confesseur, Fribourg, 2–5 septembre 1980,* pp. 147–155. Edited by F. HEINZER and C. VON SCHÖNBORN. Paradosis, no. 27. Fribourg 1982.

—— Composite Hypostasis in Maximus Confessor, SP XXVII, 1993, pp. 175–197.

MATSOUKAS, N., *Kosmos, Anthropos, Koinonia kata ton Maximo Homologete.* Athens 1980.

MAYER, A., *Das Gottesbild im Menschen nach Clemens von Alexandrien.* (SA 15.) Rome 1942.

McGINN, B.-MEYENDORFF, J.-LECLERCQ, J., eds. *Christian Spirituality (I): Origins to the Twelfth Century.* World Spirituality: An Encyclopedic History of the Religious Quest, vol. 16. New York 1985.

MERKI, H., ΟΜΟΙΩΣΙΣ ΘΕΩΙ: *Von der platonischen Angleichung zur Gottähnlichkeit bei Gregor von Nyssa.* (Paradosis 7.) Fribourg 1952.

MEYENDORFF, J., *Christ in Eastern Christian Thought.* Crestwood, N.Y. 1975.

—— *Byzantine Theology.* 2nd ed. New York 1979.

MICHARD, E., Saint Maxime le Confesseur et l'apocatastase, *Revue Internationale de Théologie* 10 (1902), pp. 257–272.

MICHAUD, E., Saint Maxime le Confesseur et l'apocatastase, *Rev. Intern. de Théologie* 10 (1902), pp. 257–272.

MICHEL, A., art. Idiomes (Communication de:) DTC 7:1, coll. 595–602. (1922.)

MIGUEL, P., Peira. Contribution à l'étude du vocabulaire de l'expérience religieuse dans l'oeuvre de Maxime le Confesseur, in SP VII, 1966, pp. 355–361.

MOELLER, CH., Un représentant de la christologie néo-chalcédonienne au début du VIᵉ siècle en Orient, Nephalius d'Alexandrie, RHE 40 (1944–45), pp. 73–140.

—— Le chalcédonisme et le néo-chalcédonisme en Orient de 451 à la fin du VIᵉ siècle, Chalk I, pp. 637–720. (1951.)

—— Textes 'monophysites' de Léonce de Jérusalem, ETL 27 (1951), pp. 467–482.

MOINE DE L'ÉGLISE ORTHODOXE DE ROUMANIE, UN (= SCRIMA, A.), L'Avènement Philocalique dans l'orthodoxie Roumaine, *Istina* (1958), pp. 295–328 and 443–474.

MONTMASSON, E., La chronologie de la vie de Saint Maxime le Confesseur, EO 13 (1910), pp. 149–154.

—— La doctrine de l'apatheia d'après s. Maxime, EO 14 (1911), pp. 36–41.

MUCKLE, J. T., The Doctrine of St. Gregory of Nyssa on Man as the Image of God, MS 7 (1945), pp. 55–84.

MÜHLENBERG, E., Synergism in Gregory of Nyssa, *Zeitschrift für die neutestamentliche Wissenschaft* 68 (1977), pp. 93–122.

MUYLDERMANS, J., Evagriana, Mus 44 (1931), pp. 37–68.

——— Note additionelle à: Evagriana, Mus 44 (1931), pp. 369–383.

——— *Evagriana*. Paris 1931.

——— *À travers la tradition manuscrite d'Évagre le Pontique.* Essai sur les manuscrits grecs conservés à la Bibliothèque Nationale de Paris. (Bibl. du Mus. 3.) Louvain 1932.

——— Une nouvelle recension du *De octo spiritibus malitiae* de s. Nil, Mus 52 (1932), pp. 235–274.

NELLAS, P., *Deification in Christ: Orthodox Perspectives on the Nature of the Human Person.* Crestwood, N.Y., 1987.

NICHOLS, A., *Byzantine Gospel: Maximus the Confessor in Modern Scholarship.* Edinburgh: T. & T. Clark, 1993.

NUYENS, F., *L'Évolution de la psychologie d'Aristote.* The Hague/Paris 1948.

NYGREN, A., *Den kristna kärlekstanken genom tiderna. Eros och agape 2.²* Stockholm 1947.

OLERUD, A., *L'Idée de macrocosmos et de microcosmos dans le Timée de Platon.* Uppsala 1951.

OSBORN, E. F., *The Philosophy of Clement of Alexandria.* (TSt 3.) Cambridge 1957.

PEGON, J., *Maxime le Confesseur, Centuries sur la charité.* Introduction et traduction. (SCH 9.) Paris-Lyon 1945.

PEITZ, M. W., Martin I. und Maximus Confessor, HJG 38 (1917), pp. 213–236, 429–458.

PELIKAN, J., Council or Father or Scripture: The Concept of Authority in the Theology of Maximus the Confessor, in *The Heritage of the Early Church: Essays in Honor of Georges Florovsky,* pp. 277–288. Edited by D. NEIMAN and M. SCHATKIN. Orientalia christiana analecta, no. 195. Rome 1973.

——— *The Christian Tradition. A History of the Development of Doctrine, 2: The Spirit of Eastern Christendom (600–1700).* Chicago 1974.

——— The Place of Maximus Confessor in the History of Christian Thought, in *Maximus Confessor: Actes du Symposium sur Maxime le Confesseur, Fribourg, 2–5 septembre 1980,* pp. 387–402. Edited by F. HEINZER and C. VON SCHÖNBORN. Paradosis, no. 27. Fribourg 1982.

PELLEGRINO, M., Il Platonismo di San Grigorio Nisseno nel Dialogo intorno all' anima e alla risurrezione, RFN 30 (1938), pp. 437–474.

PETERSON, E., L'Immagine di Dio in S. Ireneo, SC 19 (1911), pp. 3–11.

——— Noch einmal Euagrios Pontikos, BNJ 5 (1926/27), pp. 412–418.

PICHT, G., Der Sinn der Unterscheidung von Theorie und Praxis in der griechischen Philosophie, *Evangelische Ethik* 8 (1964), pp. 321–342.

PIRET, P., Christologie et théologie trinitaire chez Maxime le Confesseur, d'après sa formule des natures "desquelles, en lesquelles et lesquelles est le Christ", in *Maximus Confessor: Actes du Symposium sur Maxime le Confesseur, Fribourg, 2–5 septembre 1980*, pp. 215–222. Edited by F. HEINZER and C. VON SCHÖNBORN. Paradosis, no. 27. Fribourg 1982.

—— *Le Christ et la Trinité selon Maxime le Confesseur*. Théologie historique, no. 69. Paris 1983.

PLAGNIEUX, J., *Saint Grégoire de Nazianze Théologien*. Paris 1952.

PLASS, P., Transcendant Time in Maximus the Confessor, *The Thomist*, 44 (1980), pp. 259–277.

—— 'Moving Rest' in Maximus the Confessor, *Classica et mediaevalia* 35 (1984): pp. 177–190.

POHLENZ, M., Poseidonios' Affektenlehre und Psychologie, NGWG (1921), pp. 163–194.

—— *Die Stoa*. Geschichte einer geistigen Bewegung 1–2. Göttingen 1948–49.

PRADO, J. J., *Voluntad y naturaleza: La antropología filosófica de Maximo el Confesor*. Rio Cuarto, Argentina 1974.

PRESTIGE, G. L., *God in Patristic Thought*.[2] London 1952.

PREUSCHEN, E.-KRÜGER, O., *Handbuch der Dogmengeschichte* 1.[2] Tübingen 1923.

PUECH, H.-CH., La ténèbre mystique chez le Pseudo-Denys, *Études Carmélitaines* 23:2 (1938), pp. 33–53.

QUASTEN, J., A Pythagorean Idea in Jerome, AJPh 63 (1942), pp. 207–215.

—— *Patrology* 1–3, Utrecht/Brussels/Antwerp-Westminster, Maryland 1949–1960.

QUATEMBER, F., *Die christliche Lebenshaltung des Klemens von Alexandrien nach seinem Paedagogus*. Vienna 1946.

RAHNER, H., Die Gottesgeburt. Die Lehre der Kirchenväter von der Geburt Christi im Herzen des Gläubigen, ZKTh 59 (1935), pp. 333–418.

RAUER, M., Origenes über das Paradies, in KLOSTERMANN, E., *Studien zum Neuen Testament und zur Patristik* (TU 77), Berlin 1961, pp. 253–259.

REFOULÉ, F., La christologie d'Évagre et l'origénisme, OCP (1961), pp. 221–266.

—— Immortalité de l'âme et résurrection de la chair, RHR 163 (1963), pp. 11–52.

REYPENS, L., art. Ame, DSp 1, coll. 433–469. (1937.)

RICHARD, M., Le Néo-chalcédonisme, MSR 3 (1946), pp. 156–161.

—— Léonce de Byzance, était-il origéniste?, REB 5 (1947), pp. 31–66.

RIESENFELD, H., Le caractère Messianique de la tentation au désert, in MASSAUX,

E., etc., *La venue du Messie*. (Recherches Bibliques 6.) Louvain 1962, pp. 51–63.

RIOU, A., *Le monde et l'église selon Maxime le Confesseur*. Théologie historique, no. 22. Paris 1973.

—— Index scripturaire des oeuvres de S. Maxime le Confesseur, in *Maximus Confessor: Actes du Symposium sur Maxime le Confesseur, Fribourg, 2–5 septembre 1980*, pp. 404–421. Edited by F. HEINZER and C. VON SCHÖNBORN. Paradosis, no. 27. Fribourg 1982.

RONDEAU, M.-J., Le Commentaire sur les Psaumes d'Évagre le Pontique, OCP 26 (1960), pp. 307–348.

ROQUES, R., Le primat du Transcendant dans la purification de l'intelligence selon le Pseudo-Denys, RAM 23 (1947), pp. 142–170.

—— Note sur la notion de 'Theologia' chez le Pseudo-Denys l'Aréopagite, RAM 25 (1949), pp. 200–212.

—— *L'Univers Dionysien*. Structure hiérarchique du monde selon le Pseudo-Denys. Paris 1954.

—— art. Contemplation, extase et ténèbre chez le Pseudo-Denys, DSp 2, coll. 1885–1911. (1953.)

ROREM, P., *Biblical and Liturgical Symbols within the Pseudo-Dionysian Synthesis*. Studies and Texts, vol. 71. Toronto 1984.

RÜTHER, TH., *Die sittliche Forderung der Apatheia in den beiden ersten christlichen Jahrhunderten und bei Klemens von Alexandrien*. Ein Beitrag zur Geschichte des christlichen Vollkommenheitsbegriffes. (FThSt 63.) Freiburg i.Br. 1949.

SCHIWIETZ, S., *Das morgenländische Mönchtum* 1–2. Mayence 1904 and 1913.

SCHÖNBORN, C. VON, *Sophrone de Jérusalem: Vie monastique et confession dogmatique*. Théologie historique, no. 20. Paris 1972.

—— Plaisir et douleur dans l'analyse de saint Maximus d'après les *Quaestiones ad Thalassium*, in *Maximus Confessor: Actes du Symposium sur Maxime le Confesseur, Fribourg, 2–5 septembre 1980*, pp. 273–284. Edited by F. HEINZER and C. VON SCHÖNBORN. Paradosis, no. 27. Fribourg 1982.

SCHÖNFELD, G., *Die Psychologie des Maximus Confessor*. Diss. Breslau 1918. (Unprinted, not available to the author.)

SCHOORS, A.-VAN DEUN, P., eds. *Philohistôr: Miscellanea in homorem Caroli Laga septuagenarii*. Leuven, 1994.

SCHWAGER, R., Das Mysterium der übernatürlichen Naturlehre. Zur Erlösungslehre des Maximus Confessor, ZkTh 105 (1983), pp. 32–57.

SEEBERG, R., *Dogmengeschichte 2*. Erlangen-Leipzig 1923.

SELLERS, R. V., *The Council of Chalcedon*. A Historical and Doctrinal Survey. London 1953.

SEVERUS, E. VON, Bios angelikos. Zum Verständnis des Mönchsleben als "Engelsleben" in der christlichen Überlieferung, *Maria Laach* (1960), pp. 73–88.

SFAMENI GASPARO, G., Aspetti di "doppia creazione" nell' antropologia di Massimo il Confessore, SP XVIII/1, 1985, pp. 127-134.

SHERWOOD, P., Notes on Maximus the Confessor, *Amer. Benedictine Review* 1 (1950), pp. 347-356.

―――― *An Annotated Date-list of the Works of Maximus the Confessor.* (SA 30.) Rome 1952.

―――― *The Earlier Ambigua of St. Maximus the Confessor.* (SA 36.) Rome 1955.

―――― *St. Maximus the Confessor: The Ascetic Life. The Four Centuries on Charity.* Translated and annotated. (ACW 21.) London 1955.

―――― Maximus and Origenism. APXH KAI TEΛOΣ, in *Berichte zum XI. Internationalen Byzantinisten-Kongress, München 1958,* Munich 1958 (27 pp.).

―――― Exposition and Use of Scripture in St. Maximus, as Manifest in the *Quaestiones ad Thalassium,* OCP 24 (1958): pp. 202-207.

―――― Survey of Recent Work on St. Maximus the Confessor, *Traditio* 20 (1964), pp. 428-437.

SOPPA, W., *Die Diversa capita unter den Schriften des hl. Maximus Confessor in deutscher Bearbeitung und quellenkritischer Beleuchtung.* Dresden 1922.

SPANNEUT, M., *Le stoïcisme des Pères de l'Église de Clément de Rome à Clément d'Alexandrie.* (Patristica Sorbonensia I.) Paris 1957.

ŠPIDLÍK, TH., *La Sophiologie de S. Basile.* (Orientalia Christiana Analecta 162.) Rome 1961.

SQUIRE, A. K., The Idea of the Soul as Virgin and Mother in Maximus the Confessor, SP VIII, pp. 456-461. Texte und Untersuchungen, vol. 93. 1966.

STÄHLIN, O., art. ἡδονή, φιλήδονος, in KITTEL, K., *Wörterbuch zum Neuen Testament* 2, pp. 911-928. (1933-35.)

STANILOAE, D., La christologie de saint Maxime le Confesseur, *Contacts* 142 (1988), pp. 112-120.

―――― Commentaire des *Ambigua,* SAIN MAXIME LE CONFESSEUR, *Ambigua.* Paris-Suresnes 1994.

STARR, J., St. Maximos and the Forced Baptism at Carthage in 632, BNJ 16 (1940): pp. 192-196.

STEAD, J., The Image of Man, *The Downside Review* 92 (1974), pp. 233-238.

STEIN, L., *Die Psychologie der Stoa* 1-2. (Berliner Studien f. dess. Philologie und Archäologie 3:11, 7:1.) Berlin 1886-1888.

STEINER, M., *La tentation de Jésus dans l'interprétation patristique de saint Justin à Origène.* Paris 1962.

STEITZ, C. G., Die Abendmahlslehre des Maximus Confessor, *Jahrbuch für deutsche Theologie* 11 (1886), pp. 229-238.

STELZENBERGER, J., *Die Beziehungen der frühchristlichen Sittenlehre zur Ethik der Stoa.* Munich 1933.

STÉPHANOU, E., La coexistence initiale du corps et de l'âme d'après saint Grégoire de Nysse et saint Maxime l'Homologète, EO 31 (1932), pp. 304–315.

STIGLMAYR, J., Maximus Confessor und die beiden Anastasius, *Katholik* 88 (1908), pp. 39–45.

STRAUBINGER, H., *Die Christologie des hl. Maximus Confessor.* Bonn 1906.

STRUKER, A., *Die Gottebenbildlichkeit des Menschen in der christlichen Literatur der ersten zwei Jahrhunderte.* Münster i.W. 1913.

STUDER, B., Zur Soteriologie des Maximus Confessor, in *Maximus Confessor. Actes du Symposium sur Maxime le Confesseur, Fribourg, 2–5 september 1980,* pp. 239–246. Edited by F. HEINZER and C. VON SCHÖNBORN. Paradosis, no. 27. Fribourg 1982.

TELEPNEFF, G.-BISHOP CHRYSOSTOMOS, The Person, Pathe, Asceticism, and Spiritual Restoration in Saint Maximus," *Greek Orthodox Theological Review* 34 (1989), pp. 249–261.

TELFER, W., *Cyril of Jerusalem and Nemesius of Emesa.* (LCC 4.) London and Philadelphia 1955.

TERNUS, J., Das Seelen- und Bewusstseinsleben Jesu. Problemgeschichtlich-systematische Untersuchung, Chalk 3, pp. 81–237. (1954.)

THEODOROU, A., Ἡ περὶ θεώσεως τον ἀνθρώπου διδασκάλια τῶν Ἑλλήνων Πατέρων τῆς Ἐκκλησίας μέχρις Ἰωάννου τον Δαμασκηνοῦ, Athens, 1956.

―――― Die Lehre von der Vergottung des Menschen bei den griechischen Kirchenvätern, *Kerygma und Dogma,* 7 (1961), pp. 283–310.

―――― Cur Deus Homo? Ἀπρούπόθετος ἤ ἐμπρούπόθετος ἐνανθρώπησις τοῦ Θεοῦ Λόγου (Σχόλιον εἰς τὴν θεολογίαν τον ἀγίου Μαξίμου): Ἐπιστημονικη Ἐπετηρὶς τῆς Θεολογικῆς Σχολῆς τοῦ Πανεπιστημίου Ἀθηνῶν, 19 (1972), pp. 295–340.

Théologie de la vie monastique. Paris 1961.

THUNBERG, L., *Microcosm and Mediator: The Theological Anthropology of Maximus the Confessor* (First edition). Lund 1965.

―――― Early Christian Interpretations of the Three Angels in Genesis 18, SP VII, pp. 560–570. Texte und Untersuchungen, vol. 92. Berlin 1966.

―――― Änglalivet i munkgestalt. Randanmärkningar till ett motiv i fornkyrkans monastiska tradition, *Kyrkohistorisk årsskrift* 1972, pp. 59–83.

―――― The Human Person as Image of God. I. Eastern Christianity, in McGINN, B.-MEYENDORFF, J.-LECLERCQ, J., eds., *Christian Spirituality (I): Origins to the Twelfth Century.* World Spirituality: An Encyclopedic History of the Religious Quest, vol. 16. New York 1985, pp. 291–312.

―――― *Man and the Cosmos: The Vision of St. Maximus the Confessor.* Crestwood, N.Y. 1985.

UEBERWEG, FR., *Grundriss der Geschichte der Philosophie,* I: PRAECHTER, K., *Die Philosophie des Altertums.* Berlin 1926.

UNGER, D. J., Christ Jesus, Center and Final Scope of all Creation according to Maximus Confessor, *Franciscan Studies* 9 (1949), pp. 50–62.

UTHEMANN, K.-H., Das anthropologische Modell der hypostatischen Union bei Maximus Confessor, in *Maximus Confessor. Actes du Symposium sur Maxime le Confesseur, Fribourg, 2–5 september 1980,* pp. 223–233. Edited by F. HEINZER and C. VON SCHÖNBORN, Paradosis, no. 27, Fribourg 1982.

VILLER, M., Aux sources de la spiritualité de saint Maxime. Les œuvres d'Évagre le Pontique, RAM 11 (1930), pp. 156–184, 239–268.

VILLER, M.-RAHNER, H., *Askese und Mystik in der Väter-Zeit.* Freiburg i.Br. 1939.

VÖGTLE, A., Woher stammt das Schema der Hauptsünden?, ThQ 122 (1941), pp. 217–237.

—— art. Achtlasterlehre, RACh 1, coll. 74–79. (1950.)

VÖLKER, W., *Das Vollkommenheitsideal des Origenes.* (BHTh 7.) Tübingen 1931.

—— *Fortschritt und Vollendung bei Philo von Alexandrien.* Leipzig 1938.

—— *Der wahre Gnostiker nach Clemens Alexandrinus.* (TU 57.) Leipzig 1952.

—— *Gregor von Nyssa als Mystiker.* Wiesbaden 1955.

—— *Kontemplation und Ekstase bei Pseudo-Dionysius Areopagita.* Wiesbaden 1958.

—— Der philosophische Ertrag der Auseinandersetzung Maximos des Bekenners mit dem Origenismus, *Jahrbuch der österreichischen byzantinischen Gesellschaft* 7 (1958), pp. 23–49.

—— Der Einfluss Pseudo-Dionysius Areopagita auf Maximus Confessor, in STOHR, A., *Universitas* I, Mayence 1960, pp. 243–254.

—— Der Einfluss des Pseudo-Dionysius Areopagita auf Maximus Confessor, in KLOSTERMANN, E., *Studien zum Neuen Testament und zur Patristik* (TU 77), Berlin 1961, pp. 331–350.

—— Zur Ontologie des Maximus Confessor, in *. . . und fragten nach Jesus. Beiträge aus Theologie, Kirche und Geschichte. Festschrift für E. Barnikol zum 70. Geburtstag,* Berlin 1964, pp. 57–79.

—— *Maximus Confessor als Meister des geistlichen Lebens,* Wiesbaden 1965.

VRIES, W. DE, Die syrisch-nestorianische Haltung zu Chalkedon, Chalk I, pp. 602–635. (1951.)

WAGENMANN, J. A., art. Maximus Konfessor, RE 12, pp. 457–470. (1903.)

WALLACE, M., *Affirmation and Negation in the Theology of St. Maximus the Confessor.* (In typescript.) Pontificium Institutum S. Anselmi, Rome 1960.

WESER, H., *S. Maximi Confessoris praecepta de incarnatione Dei et deificatione hominis exponuntur et examinantur.* Halle-Berlin 1869.

WIDENGREN, G., Researches in Syrian mysticism. Mystical experiences and spiritual exercises, *Numen* 8 (1961), pp. 161–198.

WILD, J., *Plato's Theory of Man.* Cambridge, Mass. 1946.

WILPERT, P., art. Begierde, RACh 2, coll. 62–78. (1954.)

WINGREN, G., *Man and the Incarnation.* A Study in the Biblical Theology of Irenaeus. Edinburgh and London 1959.

WOLFSON, H. A., *Philo.* Foundations of Religious Philosophy in Judaism, Christianity and Islam 1–2.² Cambridge, Mass. 1948.

—— *The Philosophy of the Church Fathers.* Cambridge, Mass. 1956.

WUTZ, F., *Onamastica sacra* 1–2. (TU 41:1–2.) Leipzig 1914–15.

WYTZES, J., The twofold way. II. Platonic influences in the work of Clement of Alexandria, VC 14 (1960), pp. 129–153.

YOUNG, R. D., Gregory of Nyssa's Use of Theology and Science in Constructing Theological Anthropology, *Pro Ecclesia* 2 (1993), pp. 345–363.

ZELLER, E., *Die Philosophie der Griechen,* vols. 2:1⁴ and 3:2.⁴ Leipzig 1889 and 1903.

ZÖCKLER, O., *Das Lehrstück von den sieben Hauptsünden.* Beitrag zur Dogmen- und zur Sittengeschichte insbesondere der vorreformatorischen Zeit. Munich 1893.

List of Abbreviations

1. Abbreviations related to Maximian texts and studies

Works of Maximus:

Thal	Quaestiones ad Thalassium
QuDub	Quaestiones et dubia
OrDom	Orationis Dominicae expositio
Asc	Liber asceticus
Gnost	Capita 200 theologica et oeconomica
ThPol	Opuscula theologica et polemica
Pyrrh	Disputatio cum Pyrrho
Ep	Epistulae
Myst	Mystagogia
Amb	Ambiguorum liber de variis difficilibus locis Sanctorum Dionysii Areopagitae et Gregorii Theologi
Char	4 Centuriae de charitate

Scholarly works:

CSC	Massimo Confessore: Capituli sulla carità. Critical edition, with Italian translation, introduction and notes by A. Ceresa-Gastaldo, Rome 1963.
CCSG	Corpus Christianorum, Series Graeca
in ACW	Sherwood, P., St. Maximus the Confessor: The Ascetic Life, The Four Centuries on Charity. (ACW 21.) London 1955.

KL¹   Balthasar, H. Urs von, Kosmische Liturgie (first edition), Freiburg
        i.Br. 1941.
KL²   Von Balthasar, Kosmische Liturgie (second edition), Einsiedeln 1961.

2. General abbreviations

AB   Analecta Bollandiana. Brussels, 1882 ff.
ACO   Acta Conciliorum œcumenicorum, ed. by E. Schwartz. Berlin, 1914 ff.
ACW   Ancient Christian Writers, ed. by J. Quasten and J. C. Plumpe.
        Westminster (Md.) and London, 1946 ff.
AGWG   Abhandlungen der Gesellschaft der Wissenschaften zu Göttingen.
AJPh   American Journal of Philology. Baltimore, 1880 ff.
BGBE   Beiträge zur Geschichte der Biblischen Exegese, ed. by O. Cullman,
        etc. Tübingen, 1955 ff.
BHTh   Beiträge zur historischen Theologie. Tübingen, 1929 ff.
BiNJ   Bijdragen van de Philosophische en Theologische Faculteiten der
        Nederlandsche Jezuïeten. Roermond and Maastricht, 1938 ff.
BNJ   Byzantinisch-neugriechische Jahrbücher. Athens, 1920 ff.
BO   Scriptorum Classicorum Bibliotheca Oxoniensis. Oxford.
BT   Bibliotheca Scriptorum Graecorum et Romanorum Teubneriana,
        Leipzig.
CE   The Catholic Encyclopedia. New York, 1907–1914; Suppl. 1922.
Chalk   Das Konzil von Chalkedon. Geschichte und Gegenwart. Ed.: A.
        Grillmeier and H. Bacht. Würzburg, 1 (1951), 2 (1953), 3 (1954).
CSEL   Corpus Scriptorum Ecclesiasticorum Latinorum. Vienna, 1866 ff.
DOP   Dumbarton Oaks Papers. Cambridge (Mass.), 1941 ff.
DSP   Dictionnaire de spiritualité, ed. M. Viller, Paris 1932 ff.
DTC   Dictionnaire de Théologie Catholique, ed. A. Vacant, E. Mangenot,
        and E. Amann. Paris, 1903–1950.
EO   Échos d'Orient. Paris, 1897–1942.
ETL   Ephemerides Theologicae Lovanienses. Louvain, 1924 ff.
EvKL   Evangelisches Kirchenlexikon, ed. by H. Brunotte and O. Weber.
        Göttingen 1955 ff.
FLDG   Forschungen zur christlichen Literatur- und Dogmengeschichte.
        Mayence, 1900 ff.; Paderborn, 1906 ff.
FThSt   Freiburger Theologische Studien. Freiburg i.Br., 1910 ff.
GCS   Die griechischen christlichen Schriftsteller. Leipzig, 1897 ff.
Greg   Gregorianum. Rome, 1920 ff.
HJG   Historisches Jahrbuch der Görresgesellschaft. Cologne, 1880 ff.; Mu-
        nich, 1950 ff.
JOBG   Jahrbuch der Österreichischen Byzantinischen Gesellschaft. Vienna,
        1951 ff.
LCC   Library of Christian Classics, ed. J. Baillie, J. T. McNeill, H. P. van
        Dusen. Philadelphia and London, 1953 ff.

LCL	Loeb Classical Library. London and Cambridge (Mass.), 1912 ff.
LThK²	Lexikon für Theologie und Kirche. 2nd ed. Freiburg i.Br., 1957 ff.
Mansi	J. D. Mansi, Sacrorum Conciliorum Nova et Amplissima Collectio. Florence, 1759–1798. Reprint and continuation: Paris and Leipzig, 1901–1927.
MBTh	Münsterische Beiträge zur Theologie. Münster, 1923 ff.
MS	Mediaeval Studies. Toronto, 1939 ff.
MSR	Mélanges de Science Religieuse. Lille, 1944 ff.
Mus	Le Muséon. Revue d'études orientales. Louvain, 1881 ff.
N.F.	Neue Folge.
NGWG	Nachrichten der Gesellschaft der Wissenschaften zu Göttingen. Phil.-hist. Klasse. Göttingen, 1865 ff.
N.S.	New Series.
OCh	Orientalia Christiana. Rome, 1923–1934.
OCP	Orientalia Christiana Periodica. Rome, 1935 ff.
PG	Migne, Patrologia Graeca.
PL	Migne, Patrologia Latina.
RACh	Reallexikon für Antike und Christentum, ed. by T. Klauser. Leipzig, 1941 ff. Stuttgart, 1950 ff.
RAM	Revue d'Ascétique et de Mystique. Toulouse, 1920 ff.
RB	Revue Bénédictine. Maredsous, 1884 ff.
RE	Realencyklopädie für protestantische Theologie und Kirche, founded by J. J. Herzog, 3rd ed. by A. Hauck. Leipzig, 1896–1913.
REB	Revue des Études Byzantines. Paris, 1946 ff.
RFN	Rivista di Filosofia Neoscolastica. Milan, 1909 ff.
RGG³	Religion in Geschichte und Gegenwart. 3rd ed. by K. Galling. Tübingen, 1957 ff.
RHE	Revue d'Histoire Ecclésiastique. Louvain, 1900.
RhM	Rheinisches Museum für Philologie. Bonn, 1833 ff.
RSPT	Revue des Sciences Philosophiques et Théologiques. Paris, 1907 ff.
RSR	Recherches de Science Religieuse. Paris, 1910 ff.
RSRUS	Revue des Sciences Religieuses. Strasbourg and Paris, 1921 ff.
RTAM	Recherches de Théologie Ancienne et Médiévale. Louvain, 1929 ff.
SA	Studia Anselmiana. Rome, 1933 ff.
SC	Scuola Cattolica. Milan, 1873 ff.
SCA	Studies in Christian Antiquity, ed. by J. Quasten. Washington, 1941 ff.
SCH	Sources Chrétiennes, ed. by H. de Lubac and J. Daniélou. Paris, 1941 ff.
Schol	Scholastik. Freiburg i.Br., 1926 ff.
SP	Studia Patristica. Papers Presented to the Second International Conference on Patristic Studies Held at Christ Church Oxford 1955 (TU 63/64). Berlin, 1957. 2 vols.
StBW	Studien der Bibliothek Warburg. Leipzig and Berlin, 1924 ff.
ThQ	Theologische Quartalschrift. Tübingen, 1819 ff.; Stuttgart, 1946 ff.

TSt	Texts and Studies, ed. by J. A. Robinson and C. H. Dodd. Cambridge, 1891 ff.
TU	Texte und Untersuchungen. Leipzig and Berlin, 1882 ff.
VC	Vigiliae Christianae. Amsterdam, 1947 ff.
VS	La Vie Spirituelle. Paris, 1909 ff.
ZKG	Zeitschrift für Kirchengeschichte (Gotha). Stuttgart, 1876 ff.
ZkTh	Zeitschrift für katholische Theologie. Innsbruck, 1877 ff.
ZNW	Zeitschrift für die neutestamentliche Wissenschaft und die Kunde der älteren Kirche. Giessen, 1900 ff.

INDEX OF PASSAGES

Classical and Patristic Figures

INDEX OF NAMES

incarnate
↳

CPSIA information can be obtained
at www.ICGtesting.com
Printed in the USA
LVHW091454101120
671290LV00023B/75